A HISTORY OF THE
ATHENIAN CONSTITUTION

A HISTORY OF THE
ATHENIAN CONSTITUTION

TO THE END OF
THE FIFTH CENTURY B.C.

BY

C. HIGNETT

FELLOW OF HERTFORD COLLEGE
OXFORD

OXFORD
AT THE CLARENDON PRESS
1952

Oxford University Press, Amen House, London E.C. 4

GLASGOW NEW YORK TORONTO MELBOURNE WELLINGTON
BOMBAY CALCUTTA MADRAS KARACHI CAPE TOWN IBADAN

Geoffrey Cumberlege, Publisher to the University

PRINTED IN GREAT BRITAIN

PREFACE

THE history of the Athenian constitution has normally been the subject of disconnected chapters in a history of Greece, or of an excursus in a work on Greek constitutional antiquities. Even the *Atthis* of de Sanctis, which first suggested the idea of this book, deals with the whole history of Athens to the year 445 B.C. I have here tried to confine my theme to the development of the constitution, and to include only so much of the political and general history of Athens as seemed necessary to make that development intelligible. This limitation, by reducing the length of the book, has enabled me to extend my survey from 445 to the end of the fifth century B.C., and thereby to exhibit the flaws which appeared in the radical democracy before and after Perikles' death and to trace the vicissitudes to which it was exposed by the reactionary movements in the closing years of the fifth century. Some friendly critics have suggested that I ought to have carried the story down to the death of Demosthenes, but the year 401 B.C., as the author of the *Athenaion Politeia* realized, provides a more appropriate terminus for an historical treatment of the Athenian constitution. By then the radical democracy, assisted by the generosity of some of its Spartan conquerors, had finally triumphed, and nothing remained but to introduce minor modifications of detail and adjustments to changing conditions.

In his *Atthis* de Sanctis, following the example of certain continental scholars, notably Beloch, subjected the ancient authorities, including the *Athenaion Politeia*, to a severely critical examination. English and French scholars (Macan was a prominent exception) have on the whole been too conservative to give their approval to this sceptical treatment of the ancient sources, and some of them have adopted, either openly or tacitly, the convenient hypothesis that the accounts of the constitutions of Solon and Kleisthenes given by the Atthidographers were derived from original documents. I have considered this hypothesis in my first chapter and have tried to demonstrate that it is untenable. Beloch and others certainly carried their scepticism too far in some directions, but in some, as I shall attempt to show, they failed to carry it far enough, for they were still unconsciously dominated by misconceptions which had become

firmly established. As the works of Beloch and de Sanctis have
never been translated into English, I hope that this book will
serve to introduce some of their ideas to readers who are unable
to consult them in the original.

In general I have been less concerned to cite the latest publication than to rescue meritorious works of the past from unde-
served oblivion (a Roman historian recently told me that in
his opinion the most illuminating treatment of a question under
discussion was a paper written by Zumpt before 1860). For my
chapters on the fifth century I have made extensive use of the
works of Edouard Meyer. Although on many topics, for example
the revolutions of 411 and 404 B.C., Meyer elucidated the problems and provided convincing solutions, his conclusions seem
often to be less well known than more recent but less probable
hypotheses. I have therefore made it one of my aims to revive
suggestions put forward by Meyer and other able scholars of his
time and to give them a wider currency. Like all others who
have worked in this field, I owe a great debt to the *Aristoteles
und Athen* of Wilamowitz.

Naturally I do not imply that there is nothing of value to be
found in more recent writings. I have obtained much help from
Ferguson, Kahrstedt, and other contemporaries cited in the
Bibliography, especially from the *Atthis* of Jacoby, to which I
have repeatedly referred in my earlier chapters. I have read it
more than once, and always with renewed admiration for the
wide range of its author's erudition and the soundness of his
judgements. Although Jacoby's commentary on his text of the
Atthidographers has not appeared in time to be used by me, I
was privileged some years ago to attend a seminar held by him
on this subject. But the modern scholar to whom I am most
deeply indebted is Professor Wade-Gery. In the following pages
I have sometimes dissented from his views, but I have never
done so without careful consideration and many misgivings, and
even when I have been unable to agree with his conclusions I
have never failed to profit from his examination of a problem.
His numerous papers have been a constant source of enlighten-
ment and inspiration, and he has generously discussed several
questions with me both orally and in writing. I have also learnt
much from two classes held by him, on Athenian Families and
on the Strategoi.

I take this opportunity to acknowledge my great obligations

to two of my Oxford friends, R. Meiggs and J. P. D. V. Balsdon, who have taken a keen interest in this book throughout its progress and encouraged me to complete it. Mr. Meiggs read it when it was in manuscript and suggested several corrections and additions (some of which appear in the form of appendixes or supplementary notes) ; Mr. Balsdon read the proofs and detected many errors and obscurities. The book has been greatly improved by their criticisms ; for all blemishes that may remain I myself must be held responsible.

Finally I wish to express my grateful thanks to the Delegates of the Oxford University Press for the compliment they have paid me in undertaking the publication of this book, and to all the members of the Press who have been concerned in any way with its appearance in print ; in this connexion I would add that the comparatively frequent appearances in its pages of the last letter of the English alphabet reflect the practice of the Press, not my own.

C. H.

CONTENTS

SPECIAL ABBREVIATIONS xi

I. THE SOURCES 1

II. FROM MONARCHY TO ARISTOCRACY 33

III. THE ARISTOCRATIC STATE 47

IV. SOLON 86

V. FROM SOLON TO KLEISTHENES 108

VI. KLEISTHENES 124

VII. FROM KLEISTHENES TO EPHIALTES 159

VIII. THE REVOLUTION OF 462 193

IX. RADICAL DEMOCRACY 214

X. THE DECLINE AND FALL OF THE ATHE-
NIAN EMPIRE 252

XI. THE OLIGARCHIC REVOLUTION OF 404 AND
THE SECOND RESTORATION 285

APPENDIXES

I. THE REVISION OF THE LAWS 299

II. PROBLEMS OF THE PRE-SOLONIAN STATE AND OF ITS
ORGANIZATION 305

III. THE DATE OF SOLON'S LEGISLATION 316

IV. THE METHOD OF APPOINTMENT IN THE SIXTH CEN-
TURY TO THE ARCHONSHIP AND OTHER MAGISTRA-
CIES 321

V. PEISISTRATOS AND THE PHILAÏDAI 326

VI. THE DATE OF KLEISTHENES' REFORMS 331

VII. CHRONOLOGICAL PROBLEMS IN THE HISTORY OF THE
YEARS 506–480 336

VIII. THE DATE OF THE EPHIALTIC REVOLUTION 337

IX. THE INSTITUTION OF ΔΙΚΑΣΤΙΚΟΣ ΜΙΣΘΟΣ 342

CONTENTS

X. THE CITIZENSHIP LAW OF 451/450   343

XI. THE STRATEGIA: SOME PROBLEMS   347

XII. THE REVOLUTIONS OF 411   356

XIII. THE INSTALLATION OF THE THIRTY   378

XIV. THE ORDER OF EVENTS DURING THE RULE OF THE
THIRTY   384

SUPPLEMENTARY NOTES   390

SELECT BIBLIOGRAPHY   398

INDEX   403

SPECIAL ABBREVIATIONS

In addition to the customary abbreviations the following have been used, mainly in the footnotes, to save space. For the same reason a book is normally cited by the author's name alone if it is the only work by him listed in the Bibliography, and in references to books published in more than one volume (e.g. Bonner and Smith) the first volume is intended unless a later volume is expressly quoted. The author regrets that his references to Busolt–Swoboda constitute an exception to this general rule, but references to the *Staatskunde* are usually (except in Chapter III) to the *second* volume. The *Politics* of Aristotle is cited throughout by the pages of the Berlin edition, and by the lines as given in the Teubner text of Immisch (1909).

And. (or Andok.)	= Andokides.
A.P.	= The *Athenaion Politeia* attributed to Aristotle.
A.T.L.	= Meritt, Wade-Gery, and McGregor, *The Athenian Tribute Lists*.
Beloch	= Beloch, *Griechische Geschichte²*.
BS	= Busolt–Swoboda, *Griechische Staatskunde*.
C.A.H.	= *The Cambridge Ancient History*.
De Sanctis	= De Sanctis, *Atthis²*.
F.G.H.	= Jacoby, *Die Fragmente der griechischen Historiker*.
F.H.G.	= C. and T. Müller, *Fragmenta Historicorum Graecorum*.
Jac.	= Jacoby, *Atthis*.
Kahr.	= Kahrstedt, *Studien zum öffentlichen Recht Athens*, i, ii.
Ledl	= Ledl, *Studien zur älteren athenischen Verfassungsgeschichte*.
Lys.	= Lysias.
R.-E.	= Pauly–Wissowa–Kroll, *Real-Encyclopädie*.
S.I.G.	= Dittenberger, *Sylloge Inscriptionum Graecarum* (unless otherwise stated, the reference is to the 3rd edition, Leipzig, 1915–24).
Tod	= Tod, *A Selection of Greek Historical Inscriptions*, i, ii.
Wil.	= Wilamowitz, *Aristoteles und Athen* (sometimes cited as *A.A.*).
X.A.P.	= The *Athenaion Politeia* printed among the works of Xenophon, e.g. in vol. v of the Oxford Classical Text of Xenophon, and edited by Kalinka (Leipzig and Berlin, 1913).

I. THE SOURCES

Introduction

THE democratic constitution in force at Athens during the fourth century until 322[1] is better known to us than any other in ancient Greece. Its component parts and their working are illuminated by the numerous decrees inscribed on stone which have been preserved and by copious references in the great orators; moreover, the second part of the *Constitution of Athens* ascribed to Aristotle contains a valuable survey of the principal organs of the constitution and their functions at the time when the account was written, between 329 and 322.[2] This mass of material supplies most of the evidence used in those modern accounts of the Athenian democracy which deal with its parts statically and consider it in the period of its fullest development. The discovery of the *Athenaion Politeia* has enabled us to correct some details in the account previously current, and the labours of scholars have elucidated others, and there is so little scope for controversy that any good modern handbook can be used as a trustworthy guide to the details of the Athenian democracy in its maturity, the democracy of the Demosthenic Age.

For these reasons no attempt will be made here to give a static account of the Athenian constitution in the fourth century. The object of this book is to examine once more the stages through which that constitution evolved to its maturity; its justification is the controversial character of the subject, which is due to two main causes, the inadequacy of our evidence and the disagreements between scholars in their valuations of the various parts of that evidence. The dispute turns essentially on the extent to which fourth-century writers may be presumed to have had access for the period before 462 to contemporary documentary evidence, but before we can examine that problem we must first survey the literary tradition down to 330, with special reference to the antecedents and the technique of the writers who composed local chronicles of Athens, the Atthidographers.

---

[1] *All dates given are* B.C.
[2] On the date cf. Sandys' edition (1912), introd. xlix, and see below, Note B.

The literary tradition to Androtion

The literary tradition started with the epic poets, whose works contain some allusions to the early organization of Attica.[1] Next came the poems of Solon. These might have been expected to be a source of great value, but though they throw much light on Solon's personality and some on his economic reforms, they are almost silent about his constitutional innovations. His poems have indeed been preserved to us only in fragments,[2] though some of these are of considerable length. Yet it is a fair assumption that a complete text would tell us no more; if it had contained any clearer references to Solon's constitution, they would have been used by the fourth-century historians who delved into the poems for information, and would have been transmitted to us either in the *Athenaion Politeia* or in Plutarch's *Life of Solon*. The skolia of the late sixth and early fifth century are interesting survivals and occasionally of some importance for political history.[3]

In Greece the writing of history did not begin until the fifth century. The first literary account of the earlier history of Athens was given by Herodotus, who in a number of digressions provides the materials for a more or less continuous survey of events in Athens during the eighty years (561–481) from the first seizure of power by Peisistratos to the Persian Wars.[4] This survey seems to have been based mainly on the oral traditions preserved by the λόγιμοι ἄνδρες, probably members of the aristocratic families to which Herodotus had access during his residence in Athens;[5] these oral traditions received their first literary fixation in the pages of Herodotus, and were further utilized by Thucydides. It was almost certainly the aristocratic tradition that preserved the details of Kylon's attempt to make himself tyrant, for the slaughter of Kylon's followers had started a controversy which still raged in the fifth century.[6] But with this solitary exception the tradition had little to record from the period before Peisistratos. Solon appears in Herodotus[7] as a sage and a poet and the author of an Athenian code of laws,

---

[1] See below, p. 35.
[2] These are conveniently collected (with translation and notes) in Linforth, 129 ff.
[3] C. M. Bowra, *Greek Lyric Poetry*, 402 ff.; Jac. 160 and 339, n. 53.
[4] Jac. 221.   [5] Jac. 216.   [6] Jac. 186–8 and notes.
[7] i. 30. 2 (sage), i. 29, ii. 177. 2 (lawgiver), v. 113. 2 (poet); cf. also Jac. 332, n. 12.

but not as a constitutional reformer; Herodotus regards Kleisthenes, not Solon, as the founder of Athenian democracy.[1]

Towards the end of the fifth century another immigrant to Athens from the other side of the Aegean, Hellanikos of Lesbos, wrote the first local history[2] of Athens; Thucydides[3] calls it ἡ Ἀττικὴ ξυγγραφή, but it is more convenient to describe it as the first Atthis, the name invented later for this type of historical writing.[4] Hellanikos set out to chronicle the history of Athens from its earliest beginnings in the time of the kings right down to the last years of the Peloponnesian War.[5] We are not here concerned with his reconstruction of the regal period. For the 'historical period' he certainly used Herodotus and possibly ventured to correct him on some points;[6] he may well have obtained from the aristocratic tradition further details which Herodotus had not troubled to record. But if the evidence of the fragments may be taken as typical, he had little more than Herodotus to tell of Solon.[7] In the popular tradition represented by Aristophanes Solon, though he receives the epithet φιλόδημος,[8] is still essentially the author of the Athenian code.

Herodotus had referred only incidentally to events of the Pentekontaetia, but for this period and for that of the Peloponnesian War the evidence available to Hellanikos was fuller and more varied than for the period before the Persian War.[9] After 462 the publication of official documents on stone became commoner. Writers, not primarily historical, had dealt with recent events. For Kimon's career there were the recollections of Ion of Chios,[10] for Themistokles and Perikles the attacks of Stesimbrotos of Thasos.[11] In the last two decades of the fifth century speeches made in the courts began to be published; a notable

[1] vi. 131. 1.
[2] Local history was a type probably invented by Charon of Lampsakos; on his date cf. F. Jacoby in *Studi Ital. di filologia classica*, xv, 1938, 207 ff. On Hellanikos cf. Jacoby (*Atthis*), *passim*, and L. Pearson, *The Local Historians of Attica*, 1–26.   [3] i. 97. 2.
[4] For a suggestion on the origin of the name cf. Jac. 84–85.
[5] Cf. frr. 171–2 in Jacoby, *F.G.H.* i. 147–8 (= frr. 25–26 in iii B, 49–50; cf. Müller, *F.H.G.* i, p. 56, fr. 80, and iv. 632), also Pearson, op. cit. 24.
[6] Jac. 223–4 and 397, n. 48, also p. 159 (for the argument that Thucydides in vi. 54. 1 meant Hellanikos by τοὺς ἄλλους).
[7] Jac. 387, ll. 10–12.
[8] In *Clouds* 1187; cf. also *Birds* 1660 ff. for another reference to Solon.
[9] See below, p. 13.
[10] Cf. Jacoby in *C.Q.* xli, 1947, 1–17 and his *F.G.H.* iii B, no. 392, frr. 12–16.
[11] On Stesimbrotos cf. Jacoby in *F.G.H.* ii D, pp. 343–4.

instance was the great speech, read and highly praised by
Thucydides,[1] which Antiphon had made in his own defence
when tried for his part in the revolution of 411.

The framework used by Hellanikos in his account of the
historical period was probably an official list of the eponymous
archons[2] which had been published about 425,[3] after the appearance of Herodotus' work. It is reasonably certain that the list
went back as far as the archonship of Solon, and quite feasible
that it should have started with that of Kreon,[4] the earliest of
the annual archons known to us (682/681). Androtion and Philochoros are known to have arranged their material for the historical period annalistically, grouping the events of each Athenian
year under the appropriate archon,[5] and it is a reasonable
conjecture that this practice was initiated by the first Atthidographer, Hellanikos. The method of dating events by archon-
years was in common use at Athens, and thereby the chroniclers
were enabled to fill out their chronological framework with a
fair amount of detail, at least for the fifth century. Thucydides[6]
censured Hellanikos' chronology of the Pentekontaetia on the
ground that it was lacking in ἀκρίβεια, but this does not exclude
the use of archon-years by Hellanikos; Thucydides disparaged
such a system of dating as less scientific than his own practice
of arranging his materials under the 'summers' and 'winters' of
war-years.[7]

Did the official list provide more than a mere framework?
It is reasonable to suppose that it also contained information
on important events closely connected with the archonship,
such as the notices of years in which the election of the archons
was regarded as illegal or irregular (ἀναρχίαι) and the reference
to the substitution of partial sortition for election as the method
of appointment, but it is very unlikely that the list included
references to other constitutional changes which were not connected with the archonship.[8] There may have been lists of other
officials and priests which, with the notes included in them,
might have furnished further historical material, but we have

[1] viii. 68. 2. On the *Pro Polystrato* (= [Lys.] xx) delivered probably in 410
see below, Appendix XII, pp. 364 ff.   [2] Jac. 173 ff., cf. 89.
[3] On the date cf. *Hesperia*, viii, 1939, 60.
[4] Jac. 172–3. Plato (*Hippias Maior* 285 E) indicates the possibility of learning
by heart the names of all the Athenian archons since Solon. On Kreon's date
see below, p. 40, n. 3.   [5] Jac. 90.   [6] i. 97. 2.
[7] Jac. 397, n. 49.   [8] Jac. 175–6. Cf. also BS 38 and n. 2.

no evidence for the existence at Athens of such lists in early times, apart from that of the eponymous archons.[1]

Jacoby[2] doubts whether Hellanikos made much more use of documentary sources, including inscriptions, than Herodotus and Thucydides had done, apart from the archon-list. If his Athenian history consisted of only two books,[3] Hellanikos' narrative must obviously have been more jejune than that of his Athenian successors, who were able to supplement the first Atthis with details drawn from fuller knowledge or a keener interest in local institutions. Yet to Hellanikos must belong the credit for creating the Atthis as an account of the history, institutions (religious as well as secular), and monuments of Athens.[4] The new type of record which he introduced to Athens was destined to attract many imitators, but it was not until the middle of the fourth century that a native Athenian chronicler arose to write a new and expanded Atthis.

In the interval the wells of historical truth had been fouled by the activities of political propagandists. During the closing years of the fifth century some Athenian oligarchs hit upon the ingenious idea of representing their reactionary programme as a return to the constitution enjoyed by Athens in the days of their ancestors, the πάτριος πολιτεία. Possibly a few of them ransacked the past in the genuine expectation that they would find there the object of their search, but others went to work with less scruple and simply projected their ideals backwards into a time of which little was known. It is now generally agreed that the constitution ascribed to Drakon in the *Athenaion Politeia* must be rejected on internal grounds as the invention of some oligarchical pamphleteer who wrote in the last quarter of the fifth century.[5] An oligarchic writer of this period, perhaps the same man, produced a political history of Athens rewritten from the standpoint of his own party, in which he meted out unsparing condemnation to all the great statesmen of the past,

[1] Jac. 91–94.
[2] Jac. 224. He says that 'that time did not yet care about reading inscriptions', but the only justification offered for this remark is the description of *I.G.* i². 761 (Tod, 8) in Thuc. vi. 54. 7, on which see the explanation of Tod, p. 11.
[3] This is the view expressed in Jac. 111 (cf. 313, n. 91), though on p. 113 he says that Hellanikos did not divide his work into books himself (see also his remarks in *R.-E.*, s.v. 'Hellanikos', col. 142). Cf. also βραχέως in Thuc. i. 97. 2.
[4] Jac. 224.
[5] Cf. J. W. Headlam in *C.R.* v, 1891, 166–8 and Sandys' note on *A.P.* 4. For a full discussion see Ledl, 18–76.

moderate conservatives like Kimon as well as radicals like
Kleophon.[1] Solon's Seisachtheia was correctly represented as a
general cancellation of all existing debts, but his memory was
blackened by the allegation that he and his friends had made
money out of the cancellation;[2] it is noteworthy that the friends
of Solon named in this libel were the ancestors of three men
prominent towards the end of the Peloponnesian War, Kallias,
Konon, and Alkibiades.[3]

It was an unlucky accident that the history of the Athenian
constitution was falsified at this early stage in the tradition to
provide the oligarchs with a justification in the past for their
political programme. Naturally the matter was not allowed to
rest here by their opponents, who in due course produced their
own interpretation of the *patrios politeia*. This counter-propa-
ganda of the democrats proved more disastrous in its effects
than the propaganda of the oligarchs, for it was more successful
in imposing its version on posterity. It rested on the simple
assumption that Solon in the early sixth century had established
most of the institutions in force in the late fifth century; the
Athenian democracy had suddenly emerged fully grown from
the old aristocratic government, a birth as miraculous as that
of Athena herself. Obviously this view left little room for any
process of gradual development, and it necessitated the following construction:[4]

'Solon's constitution failed because it was too far in advance
of its time, and it was reduced to an empty form under the
tyrants. After their expulsion Kleisthenes re-established the
democracy with slight modifications. During and after the Persian Wars the Areopagus greatly increased its prestige and
succeeded in acquiring powers inconsistent with the constitution,
so that a fresh reform by Ephialtes was needed to deprive the
Areopagus of these usurped powers and restore the constitution
of Kleisthenes and Solon.'

This interpretation of Athenian constitutional history may

[1] Wil. i. 62–64 and 161 ff., where he gives a reconstruction of the tract. On
p. 165 he argues that its author was Theramenes; F. Dümmler in *Hermes*, xxvii,
1892, 260–86 had suggested Kritias.

[2] *A.P.* 6. 1–2.

[3] The names are supplied by Plutarch (*Solon* 15. 7); on their significance cf.
Wil. i. 62–63.

[4] The 'democratic' version can be reconstructed from such passages as
Isokrates vii. 16 and *A.P.* 23. 1 and 25. 2. The author of the *A.P.* is inconsistent
in his attitude to Kleisthenes (22. 1 and 29. 3); for the reason cf. Jac. 384, n. 30.

seem to us very artificial, but it triumphed over the propaganda of the oligarchs. The majority of the Athenians were democrats and willing to be convinced, and were already accustomed to regard and speak of Solon as the author of their laws. Moreover, the oligarchic account of the matter was almost as unreal and artificial as that of the democrats. The oligarchs and their programme were dominated by the ideas of their own age, ideas reflected in the bogus constitution which they fathered on Drakon.[1] They might talk of the restoration of the *patrios politeia*, but their real aims would not have been satisfied by a mere return to the constitution of Kleisthenes or even to that of Solon. Their leaders, trained in the new sophistic culture, fully realized that the kind of reaction for which they were striving could not be justified by genuine precedents; the history to which they appealed was a sham.

Traces of both versions, the oligarchic and the democratic, can be most clearly seen in the *Athenaion Politeia*. The former version manifestly belongs to the end of the fifth century, but the development of the latter is something of a mystery. If the publication of the first Atthis written by an Athenian, Kleidemos, is correctly dated after 354,[2] the genesis of the democratic version cannot be ascribed to him,[3] for Isokrates in a well-known passage of his *Areopagitikos*, written not later than 355,[4] refers to that democracy which Solon ὁ δημοτικώτατος γενόμενος established by law and which Kleisthenes, after he had expelled the tyrants and restored the rule of the people, proceeded to reconstitute as it had been in the beginning. Kleidemos did indeed challenge the oligarchs on some points, notably on Solon's complicity in the alleged trickery connected with his Seisachtheia, for it seems probable that statements in the *Athenaion Politeia* attributed to οἱ δημοτικοί are really taken from Kleidemos.[5] Hence the absence, in surviving fragments of Kleidemos,[6] of any mention of Solon is less significant than the similar silence in our fragments of Hellanikos, for in the interval the democratic version of Solon's political achievement

---

[1] Cf. BS 55.

[2] Jac. 74; presumably he infers the date from Kleidemos, fr. 8.

[3] As is apparently done by Jac. 74.

[4] § 16. On the date of Isokrates vii, cf. W. Jaeger in *Harvard Stud.* suppl. vol. i, 1940, 409–50.   [5] *A.P.* 6. 2 and 18. 5; cf. Jac. 75 (also 294, n. 25).

[6] Jac. 75 (modified in 294, n. 26) makes too much of it. On Hellanikos cf. Jac. 77 and 387, ll. 10–12.

had taken shape, and it must surely have been reproduced at some length by Kleidemos, whose democratic sympathies are well attested. Kleidemos was obviously not its creator, and if our presentation of it is correct, Isokrates cannot have created it either, for its account could not be reconciled with his own views on the ancient power of the Areopagus.[1]

So far we have spoken of the democratic version without qualification, but the opposition to the oligarchs actually consisted of two sections, the radical democrats and the moderate democrats,[2] and signs of the differences between these two sections can be clearly detected in our tradition. Kleidemos probably belonged to the radical democratic section, for on the publication of his work he received the rare distinction of a reward conferred by the state.[3] Moreover, although he challenged the oligarchic slanders against Solon he did not deny the fact that Solon's Seisachtheia was indeed a cancellation of outstanding debts.[4] This fact was a rock of offence to the moderates, for cancellation of debts and redistribution of land were the two nightmares that haunted the Athenian bourgeoisie in the fourth century.[5] So Androtion, a moderate and a pupil of Isokrates, explained in his Atthis, which he wrote soon after Kleidemos, that the Seisachtheia was in reality a scaling-down of debts by 27 per cent. effected by a change-over of the state currency from the Aiginetan to the Euboic system.[6] It was probably Androtion who first introduced into the Atthis Isokrates' ideas about the Areopagus.[7] On many questions the opinions of the moderates must have been nearer to the truth than those of the radicals, for there can be no doubt that the constitution of Athens in Solon's day was, as Aristotle said in the *Politics*,[8] decidedly less democratic than that of the fourth century, but it is evident from the *Athenaion Politeia* that Androtion in his account of the Areopagus was still unduly influenced by the radical view and had failed to work out his standpoint afresh.

[1] The 'radical' view in *A.P.* 25. 2 is clearly incompatible with that of Isokrates.
[2] These terms are indispensable; Jacoby's refusal to use them (293, n. 22) seems to me to reintroduce unnecessary confusion.
[3] Jac. 7, citing Tertullian, *de anima* 52 (cf. *F.G.H.* iii B, p. 51).
[4] I assume that he was the author of the apologia in *A.P.* 6. 2.
[5] Cf. the terms of the heliastic oath in Dem. xxiv. 149.
[6] Plut. *Solon* 15. 3-4. Cf. Jac. 74 and Kahr. i. 133, n. 3, and on Androtion's relations with Isokrates Jacoby, *F.G.H.*, no. 324, testimonia 1 and 2.
[7] Jac. 74.   [8] 1274[a]11 ff.

It is strange that half a century elapsed before the example set by Hellanikos was copied, and that the work of Kleidemos should then have been followed by several other Atthides. Whatever may be the explanation of these facts,[1] the only Atthides relevant to this inquiry are those of Kleidemos and Androtion, for theirs seem to have been the only fourth-century chronicles consulted by the author of the *Athenaion Politeia*, and the later Atthides survive merely in fragments which contribute little or nothing of importance. Kleidemos and Androtion (and likewise their successors) began at the beginning and continued the historical survey until they reached contemporary events, as Hellanikos had done.[2] Thus they covered not only the period already dealt with by Hellanikos but also the events which had occurred between the publication of his work and their own time. For the first half of the fourth century they must have had copious evidence, and for the closing years of the fifth century they could draw on the first two books of the *Hellenika* written by Xenophon, whose account of the oligarchical governments at Athens in 404–403 was certainly used by them.[3] Thucydides was now available for the detailed history of the years 432–411 and contained three interesting digressions into earlier Athenian history: on the unification of Attica, on the conspiracy of Kylon, on the tyranny of Peisistratos' sons and its overthrow.[4] These digressions seem to have been based partly on the aristocratic tradition,[5] partly on Thucydides' own critical reconstructions. They were of great value to the Atthidographers, for although materials were fairly abundant for the history of Athens from the middle of the fifth century onwards, the literary evidence at least must have been scanty for the period before 462, and it was precisely this period that was most important for the development of the constitution. Hence conservative scholars in modern times have tended to argue that the fourth-century Atthidographers must have had sources no longer extant, either documentary sources which Hellanikos did not trouble to consult or a literary source which was not available in his time.

The second hypothesis was started by Wilamowitz, perhaps

---

[1] For a suggestion see Jac. 73–74.   [2] Jac. 105–7.
[3] Cf. Sandys, introd. lxvi. The suggestion of Wilamowitz (i. 166) that Xen. *Hell*. ii. 3. 19 and *A.P.* 36. 2 were both derived from a lost work by Theramenes is unnecessary and improbable.
[4] i. 126, ii. 15, vi. 54–59.   [5] Cf. Jac. 342, n. 69.

because he realized more clearly than some of his critics the difficulties of the alternative. Kleidemos is known to have written an ἐξηγητικόν[1] as well as his Atthis, and from this it is a natural inference that he was one of the exegetai, the professional expounders of sacred law and the repositories of the sacred traditions. The family of the Eumolpidai were the official expounders of the traditions of the temple of Eleusis; the unwritten laws laid down by them were binding and no other family was allowed to usurp their functions.[2] There must have been exegetai in the old aristocratic state of Athens (before its union with Eleusis) whose later representatives are to be found in the ἐξηγηταὶ ἐξ εὐπατριδῶν.[3] Jacoby distinguishes from these the ἐξηγηταὶ πυθόχρηστοι, whom he regards as officials of the Athenian state first instituted by Solon.[4] He thinks that Kleidemos must have belonged to the latter,[5] but Kleidemos' political views are not sufficient to prove this. The example of Lykourgos shows that in the Demosthenic period anti-Macedonian aristocrats were prepared to co-operate with democrats in politics and to use a revival of the old religion as a means to the regeneration of the state.

That the various boards of exegetai should have committed their sacred lore to written records jealously guarded from the knowledge of the vulgar is credible enough, and also that the publication of some of this lore by Kleidemos should have provided antiquarians with new and valuable material for the study of Athenian religious institutions. It is, however, most unlikely that the records of the exegetai should have thrown any valuable light on the constitutional history of Athens. From this difficulty Wilamowitz sought a way out by his famous assumption that the aristocratic exegetai had at an early date begun to keep a brief chronicle of important events which was continued by their successors;[6] he also supposed that this priestly chronicle had been edited and published by an unknown writer about 380. This supposition is refuted by the plain statement of

---

[1] Athenaios 409 F = Kleidemos, fr. 20 (14 in Jacoby, *F.G.H.*, no. 323).

[2] *I.G.* i². 76 (Tod, 74), ll. 36–37, Tod, p. 183, also Andok. i. 115–16 (on which cf. Jac. 26).

[3] Jac. 34.

[4] Op. cit. 28 ff. On 37 ff. he ascribes their creation to the time of Solon.

[5] Op. cit. 75–76, cf. 280, n. 34. His argument (254, n. 78) that the Εὐπατριδῶν πάτρια were not published till Roman times seems inconclusive.

[6] *A.A.* i. 280 ff.; the anonymous exegetes of 380 appears on p. 286.

Pausanias[1] that Kleidemos was the first Athenian to publish an Atthis, and is moreover superfluous; if the priestly chronicle had existed, why should not Kleidemos, probably himself one of the exegetai, have been the first historian to use it as a source and make its contents accessible to the general public?[2] The main part of the Wilamowitz hypothesis, the assumption of a priestly chronicle, was never supported by valid evidence, and its falsity has now been conclusively demonstrated by Jacoby.[3]

Jacoby has proved that the literary form of the local chronicle and probably the chronological framework as well were taken over from Hellanikos by the later Atthidographers, and that like Hellanikos they dealt with all the antiquities of Athens, of which the constitution formed only a part.[4] Naturally they expanded and modified the materials they found in Hellanikos, and they differed from him and from one another in details. There has been a tendency to overstress the elements in the tradition which the Atthidographers had in common and to label this uniform tradition as 'the Atthis'. But it is difficult to isolate this unchanging core in the tradition, and to write of the Atthis without qualification may suggest to the unwary reader a primary Atthis like Wilamowitz's priestly chronicle.[5] The term is a convenient one, but in the following pages it will be strictly limited to its only legitimate use, to describe the evidence of one or more Atthidographers on points where we have no evidence of their disagreement; passages in the *Athenaion Politeia* which obviously came from an Atthidographic source will also be ascribed to 'the Atthis'.

There was certainly a difference of emphasis in the different Atthidographers. Curiosity about the religious institutions of Athens was probably more marked in the native Athenian writers than in Hellanikos.[6] Even within the purely political history there seems to have been a shifting of interest. Hellanikos had perhaps said little of Solon,[7] whereas in the fourth-century chroniclers Solon displaces Kleisthenes as the founder of the democracy. Greater prominence may have been given to the history of the constitution in the Atthis of Androtion,

---

[1] x. 15. 5; cf. Jac. 7.   [2] This point is well made by Jac. 7.
[3] See his *Atthis* (especially pp. 52–60).
[4] Op. cit. 119–23 and 223–5.   [5] Cf. Jacoby's protest (op. cit. 2).
[6] Cf. Jac. 138 on the special interests of Kleidemos and Demon.
[7] See above, p. 3 and cf. Jac. 77.

written after 343.[1] Androtion had been an active politician,
whose father Andron had been a member of the 400 in 411.[2] He
may therefore be assumed to have had a special interest in
constitutional history. Among the methods which he employed
in his investigation of the past was the examination of obsolete
laws;[3] he may also have attempted to trace survivals from an
earlier time in laws that were still valid.

The argument from the present to the past could be applied
to institutions as well as laws and had already been so used by
Thucydides.[4] In dealing with periods for which there is no
direct evidence historians have always resorted to this method
of reconstruction, and it was largely used by the Atthidographers for the early period of Athens, as can be seen from the
Athenaion Politeia.[5] The application of the method to Athens
was sound, for the Athenians often allowed old institutions to
survive after they had been deprived of their political importance, and though the fourth-century historians made some
mistaken inferences from their materials, they have preserved
in this way many curious survivals on which modern scholars
can base a more probable reconstruction.

The Atthidographers and the documentary evidence

There are two problems presented by the attitude of the
earlier Atthidographers towards the documentary evidence:
how much of this evidence was available to them for the period
before 462, and to what extent did they use such documents as
there were? Of the Athenian public inscriptions still preserved
extremely few can be dated before 462. This is not an accident,
as the practice of inscribing important documents on stone
seems to have grown up slowly; the laws of Solon were apparently written originally on tablets of wood.[6] The earliest decrees
of the people to be inscribed on stone were probably set up
in the last decade of the sixth century, after the expulsion of
the tyrants, but there was no great increase in the number of

---

[1] When he was in exile (Plut. *Moralia* 605 c). He was in Athens certainly till
346 (Tod, ii. 167 and pp. 156–7) and probably till 343 (if Didymos, *De Demosthene*
viii. 15 is correctly restored): see F. R. Wüst, *Philipp II* (Munich, 1938), 66–67
and Bloch, 341 ff.

[2] On Andron cf. Busolt, iii. 1466, no. 4 and Kirchner, *P.A.*, no. 921.

[3] Cf. fr. 4 (36 in Jacoby, *F.G.H.*). Androtion was probably the source of the
citation from 'the old laws of Solon' in *A.P.* 8. 3; cf. Wil. i. 51 f.

[4] e.g. in ii. 15.   [5] Especially in *A.P.* 3.
[6] See below, Note A.

official records on stone until after 462, when radical democracy was established by the laws of Ephialtes. It has been suggested[1] that the increase was the logical consequence of Ephialtes' revolution and that popular governments favoured publication of state transactions. Jacoby has pointed out[2] that when Krateros made the first collection of Athenian decrees for publication, the decrees down to the middle of the fifth century required only two books, whereas those from the next forty years took six books.

It is also noteworthy that the comparatively numerous inscriptions from the period 462–404 which are still extant are almost exclusively administrative decrees; they show the organs of the radical democracy at work but throw little light on their origins. The two chief exceptions are significant, for they belong to a time soon after the restoration of the radical democracy in 410. Probably the recent oligarchic revolution had called the attention of the radical leaders to the need for an official publication on stone, accessible to the general public, of all the laws, including the old laws which still remained in force. The Athenians had continued to observe the old laws on homicide, and an inscription of 409/408[3] professes to be an exact copy of Drakon's legislation dealing with cases of involuntary homicide. A fragmentary law regulating the powers of the βουλή which still survives also belongs to the last decade of the fifth century, but the opinion that it was a verbatim copy of a Kleisthenic original is untenable.[4] Anyhow this inscription indicates that the constitutional laws as well as the other laws were under review after 410, and presumably those still in force would be copied on stone (like the rest of the laws), but the copies would not include any laws which had been superseded by the revolution of 462 or by subsequent legislation.

In 404 the triumphant oligarchs took down from the Areopagus the laws of Ephialtes and Archestratos which had limited and defined the powers of the Areopagus council;[5] these laws had presumably been continued at the radical restoration of 410, but the words of our authority do not reveal whether the laws removed by the oligarchs were inscribed on wood or stone,

---

[1] Cf. B. D. Meritt, *Epigraphica Attica* (1940), 89 ff.
[2] Article on Krateros in *R.-E.* xi. 2. 1617–21; cf. his *Atthis*, 207.
[3] *I.G.* i². 115 (Tod, 87).
[4] *I.G.* i². 114; see below, pp. 153 f.   [5] *A.P.* 35. 2.

nor is it clear that this copy on the Areopagus was the only official publication of these particular laws. As they had transferred to other bodies (notably the Council of Five Hundred) powers previously vested in the Areopagus,[1] it is natural to suppose that the laws relating to the 500 must have been remodelled in 462 or soon after as a result of Ephialtes''reforms.

The obvious question raised by the recodification which began in 410 is: were the Athenians of the fifth century in the habit of preserving obsolete laws? And if so, where did they preserve them? Kahrstedt has shown[2] that the use of the Metroön as the repository of the state archives is probably not earlier than 403, the year of the second restoration. Thompson had dated the institution of the Metroön archives to the first democratic restoration in 410, but his grounds for this dating and for his belief that the archives had been kept earlier in the council building, the Bouleuterion, are inadequate.[3] Kahrstedt maintained that, whereas after 403 the documents in the Metroön archives were the official originals and the publications on stone merely copies (so that less trouble was taken to guarantee their scrupulous accuracy), before 403 the official documents were simply the publications on wood and stone, and no replicas of these were preserved in archives.[4] Naturally Kahrstedt would not deny that officials, notably the secretary of the council, must have kept during the fifth century some records of their activities, but so far as these records were the raw material of history they would be of the same type as the decrees collected by Krateros; as Jacoby puts it,[5] the archives of the various officials would contain 'not the regulations concerning their office (these occurred in the laws from which they were collected later) but the individual pieces of business and the cases with which they were concerned'. Even if we admit that each official took over and preserved in his archives the materials handed down by his predecessor, as Jacoby seems to assume, these would hardly have included constitutional laws such as those enacted by Kleisthenes and possibly by Solon. There is the further difficulty that Athens was sacked by the Persians in 480, and we cannot be sure that the various archives,

[1] *A.P.* 25. 2.   [2] *Klio*, xxxi, 1938, 29.
[3] *Hesperia*, vi, 1937, 215 f. and 216, n. 1. He relies mainly on the anecdote from Chamaileon in Athenaios 407 B–C, on which cf. Wil. *Aus Kydathen*, 205, n. 10; cf. also Kahrstedt, op. cit. 32, n. 1 and the valuable discussion in Jac. 383, n. 27.
[4] *Klio*, xxxi. 25–32.   [5] *Atthis*, 384, n. 27.

if they existed then, were all taken to a place of safety in time.[1]

If the constitutional laws of Kleisthenes and of Solon before him were not preserved in the archives of the various officials, they might conceivably have been preserved in some public building, the Prytaneion for example. This would imply that the Athenians set a value on the careful conservation of such epoch-making documents even when they had become politically obsolete, but this attitude of mind, however natural it may seem to us, was surely alien to the realism of the fifth-century Athenians. The two upheavals which had as their result the supersession of the constitutions created by the laws of Solon and those of Kleisthenes were inspired by a new principle; why should the victors have been anxious to treasure the laws in which were enshrined the ideals of their vanquished opponents? The survival of Kleisthenes' laws in the late fifth century seems at first sight to be proved by the motion proposed and carried by Kleitophon on the eve of the oligarchic revolution in 411,[2] that the committee instructed to draft a new constitution 'should also investigate the ancient laws enacted by Kleisthenes when he created the democracy', but who shall say whether Kleitophon was sincere in his proposal or the committee successful in its search?[3]

Jacoby, accepting as self-evident the belief that 'records of the council' from the time of Solon did not exist, says[4] that 'they began to exist, in whatever form, when the constitution of Kleisthenes made the Council instead of the archon the supreme executive in Athens'. On the next page he accepts Wade-Gery's attractive hypothesis[5] that Kleisthenes 'carried through his reforms on the basis of psephisms which were passed in an Assembly still in a revolutionary condition' and adds that 'if he did it is possible that these psephisms were to be found in the records of the Council if one looked for them'. But how can Jacoby entertain such a possibility without inconsistency? The question whether Solon did or did not create a popular council is here irrelevant. If the council which first began to keep

---

[1] Linforth, 279 f. Jacoby (357, n. 25) is quite sure that the archives were saved in 480.

[2] *A.P.* 29. 3. I assume that the last eleven words in this section are *not* part of Kleitophon's motion; Jacoby (384, n. 30) thinks that they were probably added by Androtion.   [3] Cf. the doubts expressed by Ledl, 24.

[4] Jac. 206.   [5] *C.Q.* xxvii, 1933, 17–29; Jac. 207.

records was the Kleisthenic Five Hundred, how could its records
include the psephisms which first created it, psephisms passed
in the time of its supposed predecessor, the Solonian Four
Hundred, who according to Jacoby did not keep records of their
proceedings? There are other grounds, which must be examined
later, for doubting the existence of Kleisthenes' constitutional
laws in the fourth century. We may, however, note here that the
dispute about the ostracism law is significant.[1] Why did not
the defenders of its attribution to Kleisthenes settle the question once for all by reference to the actual text of his laws if
they still existed? The same difficulty is raised by the disputes
of the Atthidographers about the constitution of Solon;[2] why
did they not decide them by consultation of the original laws?

Faced with this difficulty, Wilamowitz[3] drew the obvious
inference that the constitutional laws of Solon were no longer
extant in the fourth century. But he also maintained, in view
of the general character of the Atthidographic tradition, that
the early chroniclers did not undertake any systematic research
into such documents as there were;[4] on his view this was unnecessary because from Kleidemos onwards they had at their
disposal the authentic tradition preserved in the priestly
chronicle. Jacoby, while rightly rejecting the supposed chronicle,
agrees with Wilamowitz that the early Atthidographers did not
make much use of documentary evidence.[5] When dealing with
times earlier than their own they wrote, in Jacoby's words, 'on
the basis of predecessors' narratives, and where such a narrative
does not exist, on the basis of the general conception accepted
in their circles about the development of the Attic State'.[6]
Jacoby admits that the Atthidographers never attempted to
correct this general conception from non-literary sources, but
from this fact concludes that 'they evidently did not believe
that the picture as it had been handed down would be changed
in essential features if they consulted documents other than
those readily accessible to all'; presumably by these last words
are meant documents engraved on stone in public places.
Jacoby's premisses are sound, but the natural conclusion from
them is that the Atthidographers did not consult documents
other than those published on stone because there were none
of any importance still extant.

[1] See below, pp. 159 f.   [2] See below, p. 25.   [3] i. 55.
[4] i. 285–6; cf. Jac. 388, n. 66.   [5] Jac. 209 and 204–5.   [6] Jac. 205.

Jacoby, however, holds that actual research into documents was inaugurated by Aristotle and his pupils,[1] but though he asserts that historically important documents could as late as the fourth century 'be found in the various archives and on the stones'[2] he never defines what these documents were. One may admit the possibility that interesting information could be collected from the sources mentioned by Jacoby, but it would concern matters of detail and would illuminate the working of the constitution rather than its history. We may cite Jacoby's example of the complete list of generals for the year 441/440,[3] but we owe this to an Atthidographer, Androtion, who is also credited with research into obsolete laws. Some modern scholars seem to hold that the account given by the *Athenaion Politeia* of Solon's constitution, and especially of his new method of appointment to the archonship, was derived by the author from an official copy of Solon's laws which previous writers had not troubled to consult,[4] but this is to rate the industry of the earlier Atthidographers very low. Jacoby has stated[5] (but refused to discuss) the three important questions raised by such a view: (1) Were the old axones of Solon still preserved in the fourth century? (2) What was the relation between the fourth-century code and the legislation of Solon? (3) What use was made of both by Aristotle and his followers? To these questions we must now turn.

The fourth-century code and the laws of Solon

The Athenian code in the fourth century was the product of a revision of the laws undertaken in 403 after the second restoration of the radical democracy. An inscribed stone discovered on the site of the Athenian agora by the American excavators[6] indicates that this revision merely carried to its end the revision begun in 410; the inscriptions on two sides of the stone, one in the Attic, the other in the Ionic alphabet, point to the conclusion that an official copy on stone of the revised code was started in the Attic alphabet after 410 and completed in 403–401 in the

---

[1] Jac. 209.   [2] Jac. 209, section (*d*).   [3] Jac. 91.
[4] This is implied rather than clearly stated, but seems to follow from the assumption that the account in *A.P.* 8. 1 was derived from a documentary source and from the fact that it differs from the source followed by Aristotle in the *Politics* 1273^{b}41–1274^{a}2.
[5] Jac. 388, n. 64.
[6] Published with full discussion by J. H. Oliver in *Hesperia*, iv, 1935, 5 ff.

Ionic alphabet, which was adopted in 403 for official use.[1] Andokides gives the decree of Teisamenos carried on the occasion of the revision of 403;[2] the text is uncertain in places, but provision is clearly made for the inclusion of new laws in the revised code. Later we find in existence a regular procedure, probably instituted now, for the introduction of any further modification of the new code that might be found desirable in the course of time;[3] the people were to consider the code at the beginning of every year and refer proposed alterations to a panel of 500 nomothetai chosen from those who served as jurors in the law-courts. New rules of law which merely supplemented the code of 401 were embodied in decrees (psephismata) each of which was known and quoted by the name of the man who had proposed it; inversely it would seem that a decree quoted in the fourth century in a legal context by the name of its author is subsequent to the last codification of the laws.[4]

Laws cited from the code of 403 are often described by the orators as laws of Solon,[5] and it has sometimes been maintained that all the laws included in the fourth-century code were in fact Solonian in origin, though altered in details.[6] Lysias in his tenth speech quotes certain laws for the archaic expressions contained in them; this shows that some archaic laws were included in the later code and that the archaisms in their phraseology were not removed at the revision of 403. Other laws still valid in the fourth century are proved to derive from the sixth century by the principles they embody,[7] and there is no difficulty in admitting that laws obviously archaic may be attributed in substance to Solon's own code, though they were probably altered in detail and amplified later. But the view that all the laws in the code of 401 were of this type is demonstrably false, and even the orators occasionally admit that some of the laws in the code were not the work of Solon.[8] A speech in the Demosthenic corpus asserts the Solonian authorship of a

---

[1] Cf. 'Suidas', s.v. Σαμίων ὁ δῆμος: τοὺς δ' Ἀθηναίους ἔπεισε χρῆσθαι τοῖς τῶν Ἰώνων γράμμασιν Ἀρχῖνος ἐπὶ ἄρχοντος Εὐκλείδου.

[2] Andok. i. 83–84; see below, Appendix I.   [3] Cf. Appendix I, p. 299.

[4] Cf. J. Schreiner, de corpore iuris Atheniensium, 62 ff.

[5] Cf. Schreiner, 30 ff.

[6] e.g. by C. Sondhaus, de legibus Solonis (Jena, 1909) cited by Schreiner, 36.

[7] Schreiner, 33.

[8] Cf. Schreiner, 30 ff.; he pointed out that the attribution of a law to Solon by an orator usually has a rhetorical value, and that it is never employed by Isaios.

law on inheritance which refers to the archonship of Eukleides, the Athenian year 403/402.[1] The procedure which provided for the regular revision of the laws was probably introduced in 403 and almost certainly not much earlier, but it is ascribed by Demosthenes to a law of Solon.[2]

This practice of referring to any law in the extant code as Solon's law can be traced back to the fifth century. So Aristophanes in the *Birds*[3] cites as Solon's a law of inheritance which clearly cannot belong to Solon's code. Andokides even ascribes to Solon a decree which, as quoted in our texts of Andokides, can be dated by its preamble to the beginning of the Athenian year 410/409.[4] Relying on these and other pieces of evidence, Schreiner argued that in the orators 'the laws of Solon' simply means all the laws included in the code, whether archaic or not,[5] and he seems to have proved his case.

In the decree of Teisamenos the unrevised code still in force is described as 'the laws of Solon and the ordinances of Drakon'. This implies that until 410 there had been no official revision of the Athenian laws since their codification by Solon. The same implication underlies the distinction drawn in the *Athenaion Politeia*[6] between 'the laws of Solon still in force' and 'the laws of Solon no longer in use'. But is the implication valid? Schreiner held[7] that a fresh revision of the laws had been necessitated by every fundamental change in the constitution. This view is too extreme to be accepted, but it is equally difficult to believe that there had been no revision of the Athenian code between the date of Solon's legislation and 410.

The silence of our authorities is not sufficient to prove that there had been no such revision. Athens in the sixth century passed through a period of rapid internal development. Herodotus[8] says that Peisistratos did not alter the existing magistracies or change the laws, but if he retained the Solonian code he must have supplemented it with fresh statutes such as that providing pensions for men disabled in war,[9] and possibly he made some attempt to adapt the provisions of the old code to

---

[1] [Dem.] xliii. 51 (but possibly the orator did not mean Solon by ὁ νομοθέτης in 50).

[2] xx. 89–90; see Appendix I.   [3] ll. 1660 ff.

[4] i. 96. Schreiner (op. cit. 71) suggested that the insertion here of the decree of Demophantos was due to the error of an editor.

[5] Op. cit. 49 ff.   [6] 8. 1 and 8. 3.

[7] Op. cit. 40–41 and 47–48.   [8] i. 59. 6.   [9] Plut. *Solon* 31. 3.

changed economic conditions. The author of the *Athenaion Politeia* believed that after the expulsion of the tyrants Kleisthenes found it necessary to overhaul the legal system, as some of the Solonian laws had lapsed under the tyranny and new laws were required.[1] Although he seems to have been thinking mainly of constitutional laws, it is intrinsically probable that the Kleisthenic reorganization included a revision of the Solonian code, a revision in which he may have retained much of the old material.

Linforth has suggested[2] that the Athenian code was destroyed during the Persian occupations of Athens in 480 and 479, and that when the Athenians returned to their city they had to reconstruct their code. If he is right, the reconstructed code presumably incorporated any additions that had been made to the code since the time of Kleisthenes. The reforms of Ephialtes in 462 included the transference to other bodies of judicial powers formerly possessed by the Areopagus,[3] and must therefore have involved alterations in some provisions of the code, but this need not have extended to a general revision. Perikles' law concerning the citizenship in 451/450 carried with it certain changes in the law of inheritance; this later form of the law is quoted by Aristophanes as 'Solon's law'.[4] It is natural to infer from this that a part of the existing code affected by recent legislation was redrafted to meet the changed conditions; possibly the thesmothetai were empowered to remove such anomalies in the code as owed their origin to recent legislation. If a new statute dealt with subjects not included in the code at its last revision, it was presumably cited by the name of its author; if it dealt with an old subject in a new way, it is probable that it replaced the previous statute on the subject and itself became at the next revision the relevant νόμος Σόλωνος.[5]

The conclusion of this long discussion would seem to be that in the fourth century 'the laws of Solon still in use' must be identical with the code of 401. Some of the statutes in this code certainly contained a nucleus which went back to the sixth century.[6] We may perhaps credit the Athenian antiquarians of the fourth century with the capacity to distinguish such archaic survivals in the contemporary code of Athens, though

---

[1] 22. 1.   [2] *Solon the Athenian*, 279–80.
[3] See below, c. viii.   [4] *A.P.* 26. 4 and Ar. *Birds* 1660 ff.; cf. Schreiner, 50.
[5] Schreiner, 60–65 and 36.   [6] Schreiner, 55–56.

we may doubt their ability to separate the original Solonian nucleus in a particular statute from the later accretions. Schreiner showed[1] that the archaic statute on theft quoted by Lysias is given in a fuller version by Demosthenes, and that the additional provisions in Demosthenes seem to belong to a later age than Solon's. This question is not of very great importance, as few scholars would maintain that many of the constitutional arrangements of Solon survived unchanged in the code of 401. The law regulating the appointment of the treasurers of Athena was assumed to be the Solonian law on the subject by the Atthidographers[2] probably because the qualifications prescribed in it for eligibility to the office were an anachronism in the fourth century.

By parity of reasoning 'the laws of Solon no longer in use' ought to mean those parts of the code in force before 410 which had been excluded from the new code at the revision begun in 410 and completed in 401. We have seen that the code in use immediately before this revision need not have been the original code drafted by Solon. There is, however, one serious difficulty in Linforth's view which must now be faced. The author of the *Athenaion Politeia* asserts[3] that there were many references to the ναύκραροι and the monies for which they were responsible to be found in 'the laws of Solon no longer in use'; it is not known whether this erudition was the fruit of his own researches or borrowed from Androtion, who certainly mentioned expenditure by the Kolakretai, the former superintendents of the state treasury, ἐκ τῶν ναυκραρικῶν.[4] Many scholars accept the assertion in the *Athenaion Politeia*[5] that Kleisthenes replaced the naukraroi by the demarchoi; from this it would follow that the statute or statutes consulted by Androtion were pre-Kleisthenic originals which had survived until the fourth century.

This conclusion would be momentous if it could be securely established, but the evidence on which it rests is very shaky. We may clear the ground by admitting that the naukraroi may well have existed in some form at the time of Kylon's conspiracy[6] and therefore before Solon's legislation, and also that in this connexion it makes no difference whether the law (or laws) assigning financial duties to them were the work of Solon

---

[1] Op. cit. 37.   [2] *A.P.* 8. 1 and 47. 1.   [3] 8. 3.
[4] Fr. 4 (36 in Jacoby, *F.G.H.*, no. 324).   [5] 21. 5.
[6] So the story repeated by Hdt. v. 71, on which cf. Jac. 368, n. 84.

or, as some think, Peisistratos. The essential fact is that the Atthidographers do not agree on the date of their abolition. Kleidemos, our earliest extant authority, plainly asserts[1] that they survived the reforms of Kleisthenes, and this view seems more probable than the statement in the *Athenaion Politeia*, perhaps derived from Androtion, that Kleisthenes abolished them. The naukraroi may well have continued until the great transformation of the Athenian navy after 483 made some new system necessary;[2] even so it may not have been till after the Persian War was over that the Athenians, driven by the course of events to maintain a large navy after the emergency, at last realized the inadequacy of the old machinery and created a new organization in which the former functions of the naukraroi were transferred to the demarchs.

If this supposition is tenable, a pre-410 code in which the naukraroi were mentioned might have been no earlier than 479 or 478. Alternatively we might discard Linforth's view and assume that the last revision of the whole code before 410 was a revision by Kleisthenes, in which, if we accept Kleidemos' testimony, the references to the naukraroi would naturally have been retained. But though some statutes in the pre-410 code might have survived unchanged from the time of Kleisthenes it is probable, for reasons already given, that the same could not be said of all parts of the code. Thus we get the criterion that 'the laws of Solon no longer in use' is equivalent to the code in force before 410, which may represent a revision of Solon's code by Kleisthenes, emended in parts by post-Kleisthenic alterations. There were certainly Solonian elements in the code as revised by Kleisthenes,[3] but it may well be doubted whether the Atthidographers were competent to distinguish between the parts derived from Solon's original code and the additions made by Kleisthenes.

The whole of the preceding discussion would presumably be dismissed as entirely irrelevant by those who believe that a large part of Solon's original code survived as an antiquarian

---

[1] Fr. 8. I cannot understand Jacoby's statement (*Atthis*, 317) that Kleidemos dealt with the naukraries 'in speaking of the constitution of Kleisthenes in which, according to the conception of the *Atthis*, the demes replaced them'. Surely Kleidemos differed on this point from the Atthidographer followed by the *A.P.* in 21. 5, and one of them must be mistaken. Cf. Busolt, ii². 417–18, n. 7.

[2] So Wil. ii. 165 and n. 52, in which he defends the account given by Kleidemos.

[3] See above, p. 20.

curiosity to the fourth century and was accessible to Athenian investigators.[1] What are the grounds for this belief? The Alexandrian scholar Didymos is said to have written a book about the tables of Solon,[2] and Plutarch professes to give an account of these tables or 'axones' and of the rotating stands on which they were mounted, though he adds that in his own time only a few small fragments still survived, which were preserved in the Prytaneion at Athens.[3] He quotes three laws from the axones, an amnesty-law, a law fixing the price of victims to be offered at sacrifices, and a law forbidding the export from Attica of all natural produce except olive-oil, and for each law he cites the number of the axon on which it appeared.[4] But the evidence adduced by Plutarch cannot be accepted without question at its face value. The text of the amnesty-law in the form in which he gives it is hardly compatible with a date in the first half of the sixth century,[5] and there are other difficulties about its attribution to Solon. Plutarch himself notes the discrepancy between the prices prescribed for victims in the sixteenth axon and the value of animals in Solon's time, and his comment, that the victims to be supplied under the provisions of this law had to be of superior quality,[6] may only be some scholar's hypothesis to explain away the discrepancy.

These difficulties point to the solution that the ultimate authority for Plutarch's citations, who may have been Demetrios of Phaleron,[7] obtained them from a code which, though earlier than the revision of 410, was not the code promulgated by Solon. As we have already seen, the assumption that a large part of the original code had survived to the fourth century, though certainly convenient, is exposed to serious objections. However conservative the Athenians of the fifth century may have been in religion or even in the reconstruction of their legal code, in politics they had no sentimental interest in the past and no practical use for it until late in the century, when its possibilities as a source of propaganda became manifest.

---

[1] So, for example, Gilbert, introd. xxxvi ff.   [2] Plut. *Solon* 1. 1.
[3] *Solon* 25. 1. Does καθ' ἡμᾶς there refer to the time of Polemon? Cf. Polemon, fr. 48 in *F.H.G.* iii. 130 and cf. Sandys, introd. xxxiii.
[4] *Solon* 19. 4, 23. 4, 24. 1–2.   [5] See Appendix II, p. 313.   [6] *Solon* 23. 4.
[7] De Sanctis, 201–2, n. 2 suggested that Plutarch's source, Didymos, used the five books of Demetrios περὶ τῆς Ἀθήνησι νομοθεσίας (Diog. Laert. v. 80), on which cf. Jac. 333, n. 20 and *F.G.H.* ii B, p. 961 (with reff. given there).

Lysias in his attack on Nikomachos, one of the legal experts who drew up the code of 401, contrasts the rules for sacrifices in the new code to their disadvantage with those prescribed in the κύρβεις and στῆλαι, which must be the tablets or stones on which was inscribed the code in force before 410.[1] The context indicates that the kyrbeis belonged to an earlier period than the stelai; probably they represented the original code as contrasted with later religious innovations decreed by the people and recorded on stone. What then were the kyrbeis? Plutarch says that Solon inscribed his laws on wooden tablets (axones) which were also called kyrbeis; in support of this view he quotes 'Aristotle' (apparently the *Athenaion Politeia*) and two lines of Kratinos,[2] who in describing the contempt shown by his generation for the old ways says that they use the kyrbeis of Solon and Drakon as firewood. Another explanation mentioned by Plutarch, that on the kyrbeis were inscribed the rules for religious rites and sacrifices and on the axones the rest of the code, is probably no more than a deduction from Lysias.[3]

Oliver suggests[4] that during most of the fifth century the word kyrbeis could be applied either to the contents of the code or to the objects on which it was written, the wooden axones; in the fourth century the term came to be applied to the revised code of 401, and in time also to the stones on which the new code was inscribed. Hence the kyrbeis came to be distinguished from the wooden axones which contained the earlier code although originally they were identical, and this distinction led later commentators astray. Oliver refers[5] to the pre-410 code as 'the body of ancient law', which he presumably ascribes to Solon, but as he maintains that the copy of the revised code made in 410–401 was the first publication on stone of the code,[6] the wooden axones (also called kyrbeis) which contained the code in force before 410 may on his own showing belong to any date earlier than 410. If Oliver is right, any code prior to that

[1] xxx. 17 ff.; the greater antiquity of the κύρβεις is implied in § 18.
[2] *Solon* 25. 1–2; see the collection of the ancient evidence in the paper by L. B. Holland cited in Note A.
[3] It is taken seriously by Holland (op. cit. 349–50).
[4] *Hesperia*, iv, 1935, 9–10.
[5] Op. cit. 9 (near the foot of the page).
[6] Op. cit. 10. He thinks that the stelai of Lys. xxx. 17, were later (pre-410) additions to the earlier code.

of 410 would have been inscribed on wood. There is no difficulty in the assumption that an earlier code was extant and was consulted by inquirers in the fourth century; as it was certainly earlier than the fourth-century code and was attributed, like all Athenian codes, to Solon, the antiquarians who used it naturally concluded that it was Solon's original code.

It is therefore a tenable hypothesis that the 'axones of Solon' cited by later writers were those parts of the code in force before 410 which were preserved in the fourth century, probably in the Prytaneion;[1] they may have been removed thither from the Stoa Basileios when the revised code was set up there. The wooden axones may have been consulted by the Atthido-graphers and were presumably utilized by the Peripatetics who wrote on the laws of Athens. Theophrastos collected the laws of the Greek states in twenty-four books, in which the Athenian code must have bulked largely,[2] and Demetrios of Phaleron wrote five books περὶ τῆς Ἀθήνησι νομοθεσίας;[3] Aristotle himself is credited in the *Vita Menagiana* with the authorship of a work περὶ τῶν Σόλωνος ἀξόνων in five books,[4] but we have no citations from it and possibly there is confusion with the work of Demetrios. Bloch, referring to these collections of 'laws which Aristotle and his pupils had brought together', remarks[5] that 'nobody disputes that in this collection the code of 410/401 was the most important item', but Demetrios at least must have allotted some space to the pre-410 code. Demetrios may have been the source used by Hellenistic scholars such as Didymos for their accounts of the axones; Polemon, however, probably consulted the originals.[6]

The code preserved on the axones in the fourth century seems to have contained no laws directly concerned with the constitu-tion.[7] It is noteworthy that the Atthidographers, when dis-cussing problems raised by the constitution of Solon, deal with them not by reference to the text of his laws[8] but by the use of arguments from probability. Thus the argument in the *Athenaion*

---

[1] Cf. Polemon, fr. 48 in *F.H.G.* iii. 130. The κύρβεις in the Stoa Basileios (*A.P.* 7. 1) are presumably the code of 410–401.

[2] Cf. Bloch, p. 357 and n. 4.   [3] See above, p. 23, n. 7.

[4] Accepted by Jac. 385, n. 51; cf. Gilbert, introd. xxxvi, n. 3.

[5] Op. cit. 371, n. 3.

[6] See p. 23, n. 3, and n. 1 above.

[7] So Wil. i. 55.

[8] Apart from the law referring to the naukraroi cited by Androtion; see above, p. 21.

Politeia about the nature of the four property-classes, which
were supposed to have been instituted by Solon, was evidently
derived from the Atthis, as an abbreviated version of it is
found in Plutarch's *Life of Solon*.[1] Moreover, of the laws ascribed
to Solon by ancient writers which have the strongest claim to
authenticity, as being quoted verbally or cited with reference
to a particular axon, none, with the possible exception of the
law mentioning the naukraroi, can be regarded as a constitutional statute.[2]

Various explanations of these facts have been propounded.
The view that Solon merely codified the customary rules of law
previously observed and did not introduce any constitutional
changes is too extreme to be accepted; it is, however, possible
that he was not the author of a written constitution.[3] Another
suggestion is that as the constitutional laws of Solon became
obsolete more rapidly than his other laws they disappeared
early, while the rest of his code was preserved.[4] Gilbert, who
seems to have approved this hypothesis, maintained[5] that the
fourth-century chroniclers used a compilation of early laws,
from which, though it did not include specifically constitutional
laws, they were able to glean information about the early
history of the Athenian constitution, in the same way as
Plutarch used the amnesty-law ascribed to Solon to prove the
existence of the Areopagus in pre-Solonian times. It cannot be
denied that some information about the history of the constitution could have been gleaned in this way, but the validity of
the results obtained would obviously depend on whether the
laws employed for the purpose could be accurately dated.
Moreover, it is unsafe to assume, in default of any indication
in the context, that a particular statement in an ancient writer
was based on the application of this method of reasoning.
Gilbert, writing just after the discovery of the *Athenaion
Politeia*, rashly claimed that this type of reconstruction had
been used by the author for his constitution of Drakon, which
is now generally agreed to be unhistorical.

The dangers of accepting a law as Solonian on the evidence
of a fourth-century historian may be illustrated from the
ascription to Solon of a law to penalize those citizens who held

---

[1] *A.P.* 7. 4; Plut. *Solon* 18. 1.   [2] Cf. Beloch, i². 1. 365, 2. 318 ff.
[3] Cf. the valuable discussion in Jac. 333–4, n. 21.
[4] So apparently Wil. i. 55.   [5] Op. cit., introd. xxxiii ff.

aloof from the strife of political parties; this law is mentioned in the *Athenaion Politeia* and in Plutarch.[1] Both say that Solon, to ensure the stability of the state, passed a law threatening with deprivation of citizenship all those who, when the state was divided by the struggle of parties, refused to support either side. This might be regarded as an archaic equivalent to the law in some modern states imposing penalties on those who refrain from voting at elections. But when the offence was actually committed at Athens, nothing is heard of Solon's alleged law. During the civil war in 404/403 a citizen called Philon retired from Attica and settled over the border at Oropos. This unpatriotic conduct was brought up against him when later, after his return to Athens, he tried to secure admission to the council, as we learn from the orator Lysias, who spoke for his opponents. Philon argued in his defence that if it had been a crime to absent himself from the state at such a time, there would have been a law against it, as there was against any acknowledged crime. To this Lysias replied[2] that Philon's misconduct was so heinous that no politician had ever contemplated it and no lawgiver had ever dreamt that any citizen could be guilty of it. The arguments of Philon and Lysias are only intelligible on the assumption that the neutrality law ascribed to Solon is unhistorical,[3] and as Lysias' speech seems to have been delivered some time after 403[4] it is practically certain that no such law can have appeared in the code of 401. Whether the writer who first gave currency to the law simply invented it or drew an over-hasty inference from some passage in Solon's poems on the dangers of neutrality in party strife, the fact remains that he had no documentary evidence for his assumed law, and had not the speech of Lysias against Philon been preserved the invention might have passed unchallenged.

The 'Αθηναίων πολιτεία

We are now in a position to conclude that the fourth-century evidence for the constitution of Solon is much less satisfactory

[1] *A.P.* 8. 5; Plut. *Solon* 20. 1.   [2] xxxi. 27–28.

[3] I had already reached this conclusion before I read Gilliard, 292, or the review (of an article by E. Graf) in *B.P.W.* 1936, coll. 473–4. The tradition is accepted without criticism by B. Lavagnani in his paper in *Riv. Fil.* xxv, 1947, 81–93.

[4] Blass dated it to 398, but a date soon after 403 is proposed by L. Gernet in the Budé edition of Lysias (Gernet and Bizos), ii. 173.

than it claims to be. If the arguments used above are valid, many of the modern accounts of Solon's constitutional reforms rest on unsound foundations. It is probable that scholars who have written since the discovery of the *Athenaion Politeia* have been led astray by the supposed authority of a work ascribed to Aristotle; it was naturally valued above its merits in the period just after its discovery, but it ought to be possible now to assess it at its true worth. The most valuable part of it is the account of the Athenian constitution as it was in the author's own time; here he was writing as a contemporary on facts within his own knowledge. But in his description of the history of the constitution down to 401 he was dealing with a period on which he had no first-hand information. Perhaps he might have found out something fresh about his subject by independent research, though the absence of trustworthy early records would have made his task difficult. But all the internal evidence tends to show that in his historical survey he was content to utilize the writing of his predecessors;[1] thus the value of any statement in chapters 1–41 of the *Athenaion Politeia* is entirely dependent on the value of its source. Evidently the writer drew largely on the Atthides already published, and it is possible to distinguish with fair precision those parts of his account in which he is reproducing an Atthis.[2] He also used, directly or indirectly, an oligarchic pamphlet of the late fifth century which gave a survey from the oligarchic standpoint of Athenian political history from Solon to Theramenes; its author was obviously an ardent partisan, and his judgements of Athenian statesmen were so warped by party bias that they are not worthy of serious consideration.[3]

These facts about the composition of the *Athenaion Politeia* are now generally accepted. All the discussions about its authorship are therefore from an historical point of view strictly irrelevant; if we know the source of a particular sentence we can estimate its worth. But although the ascription of the work to Aristotle, accepted by eminent modern authorities,[4] ought not to affect our judgement of its value, it actually produces an inclination, which perhaps in some scholars is merely sub-

---

[1] This has always been obvious since the *A.P.* was discovered; see now Jac. 207–8.   [2] Cf. Wil. i, c. 8.

[3] See above, p. 5.

[4] e.g. E. M. Walker (see bibliography); cf. Sandys[2], introd. xlix ff.

conscious, to treat its statements with greater respect than they deserve on their intrinsic merits.

The arguments used in defence of the attribution to Aristotle are logically sound, but the conclusion is only obtained from them *per saltum*. It may be admitted that the book was certainly written during the lifetime of Aristotle and by someone familiar with his ideas; moreover, the evidence of quotations in ancient writers proves that our *Ἀθηναίων πολιτεία* is identical with that familiar to them and ascribed by them to Aristotle. Some objections, such as the difference in style between this and the works of Aristotle hitherto known, are easily answered, and the discrepancies in details between the *Athenaion Politeia* and the *Politics* might be explained by the simple assumption that Aristotle had changed his mind since he wrote the *Politics*, though it is remarkable that in every instance the change seems to have been for the worse.[1]

Such arguments are pointless because they do not touch the supreme difficulty, the immeasurable superiority of the *Politics* to the *Athenaion Politeia* in breadth of treatment and soundness of judgement.[2] The data used by Aristotle in the *Politics* may not always be correct, but the way in which he handles them is masterly, and the value of his generalizations is not affected by the faulty character of some of his instances. In his long reference to Solon[3] he displays a caution which is in marked contrast with the credulity on the same subject shown in the *Athenaion Politeia*. The historical survey in the *Athenaion Politeia* resembles a careful essay written by a modern research student who brings to his task much industry but no judgement.[4] Anyone who disregards the ancient attribution to Aristotle and decides for himself on the internal evidence of the treatise is bound to conclude that it was written by one of Aristotle's pupils. Presumably the ancients ascribed it to Aristotle because it was one of the *Politeiai*, constitutional histories of particular states, issued by his school.

---

[1] See Note B.

[2] This difficulty was first brought to my notice when I was an undergraduate at Corpus Christi by the President of my College, Thomas Case, whose knowledge of the Aristotelian writings was unsurpassed.

[3] *Politics* 1273^b35–1274^a21. The suggestion of H. Diels (cf. Sandys, introd. lxiv) that the *A.P.* is more genuinely Aristotelian than the *Politics* need not be taken seriously.

[4] Cf. Kahr. ii. 49, n. 6.

Modern scholars have often assumed[1] that Aristotle must have reserved for himself a subject so important as the constitution of Athens, but perhaps the subject was less important to him than to us; as the material contained in the historians and Atthidographers was abundant and accessible he may well have thought that the task of writing a connected account of the history of the Athenian constitution was one which might safely be left to a pupil. It is doubtful whether Aristotle ever saw the result; it seems unlikely that if he had he would have allowed it to be given to the world as a product of his school until it had been subjected to drastic revision.

Although the *Athenaion Politeia* is not the account which Aristotle himself would have written, its discovery was not unworthy of the enthusiasm which it evoked. Its later chapters are a precious contemporary record of the fourth-century constitution, and even the historical survey in the earlier chapters has at least transmitted to us some parts of the sources on which it was based. From it can be reconstructed the oligarchic interpretation of Athenian history current in Athens at the end of the fifth century, and that interpretation, though of little historical merit, has great historical interest. More important are the large borrowings made by the author from the Atthides, especially Androtion's. Seventy years ago the work of the early Atthidographers was known only from scanty fragments; now we can reconstruct more fully their account of political and constitutional history.

Other sources: conclusion

Of the fourth-century historians Theopompos was the most important for our purpose; he devoted the tenth book of his *Philippika* to a digression on the political leaders of Athens,[2] which seems to have been used by Plutarch. The collection of laws by Theophrastos and the five books on Athenian legislation by Demetrios of Phaleron have already been mentioned;[3] their work was supplemented by the collection of decrees made by Krateros the Macedonian.[4] In the first half of the third century Philochoros wrote an Atthis of which some valuable fragments

[1] e.g. Walker, 136, also his *Greek History* (Oxford, 1921), 145.
[2] Cf. the collection of fragments in Jacoby, *F.G.H.* ii B, pp. 555–7 or in Grenfell and Hunt's Oxford Text of the *Hellenica Oxyrhynchia*.
[3] See above, p. 25, n. 2, and p. 23, n. 7.
[4] On Krateros cf. Jacoby in *R.-E.* xi. 2. 1617 ff. and *Atthis*, 208–9.

remain.[1] It is unlikely that Philochoros or the subsequent anti-quarian writers had access to sources other than those which we have described. Alexandrian researchers worked through the materials at their disposal, and the importance to us of Plutarch's *Lives*, notably those of Solon, Kimon, and Perikles, is that he has preserved for us extracts from the mass of historical writing and research available in his time. Occasional references to our subject are also to be found in late antiquarians and lexicographers, though their importance has been diminished by the discovery of the *Athenaion Politeia*.[2]

From this review of the evidence it is clear that the ancient writers on the constitutional history of Athens who have been preserved to us are defective, either because, like the great historians, they were not primarily interested in the subject, or because, like the Atthidographers, they employed in their reconstructions materials which were less trustworthy than they believed them to be. We have seen that the epigraphic evidence is of limited assistance, since the relevant inscriptions are with few exceptions later than 450. In the face of these difficulties, how can a modern researcher hope to produce an account truer than that of the Atthis? If he rejects this ancient evidence, on what can he rely, and how can the truth of his results be tested?

This statement of the problem is misleading. The history of the Athenian constitution given by the Atthis has to be rejected not only on internal grounds, because it is incredible in itself and contrary to all probability, but also because the conditions of political life which it presupposes at Athens in and after the time of Kleisthenes are contradicted by the account of Herodotus. Herodotus may have been careless of strict accuracy in constitutional details, but his general picture of political life in the Greek states and particularly in Athens during the period 510–480 is clear and vivid, and has every claim to be considered a faithful representation. He was here describing the events of the generation before his own birth, events which could be remembered by many still living when he was a young man. The conditions which he describes may clash with our preconceived ideas of Athenian political development in this period, but, as Berve has contended,[3] we must use Herodotus' narrative to

---

[1] Jacoby, *F.G.H.* iii B, no. 328 (Müller, *F.H.G.* i. 384–410).
[2] For a survey of some late writers and their citations from the *Politeiai* (including the *A.P.*) cf. Sandys, introd. xxxiv ff.   [3] *Die Antike*, xii, 1936, 1–28.

correct our own ideas on the subject, and not presume to interpret it by the evidence of fourth-century writers who uncritically
transferred to the Athens of Kleisthenes the political conditions
of their own day.

Herodotus may therefore be used to supply the background
for the age of Kleisthenes, and provides a criterion by which
we can judge our reconstructions of Athenian political history
in the period 510–480. We have a detailed knowledge of the
constitution of Athens in the fourth century, and have sufficient
literary and epigraphic evidence from the second half of the
fifth century to reconstruct the constitutional history of Athens
in the period from 462 to 401. The evidence of Herodotus and
some valuable dated notices from the Atthis enable us to work
back to the reforms of Kleisthenes. As we have already seen, it is
possible to establish the main outlines of the pre-Solonian aristocratic state. Any changes which may be assumed to have taken
place between this form of government and that of Kleisthenes
would then be left for attribution to Solon or to the tyrants.

There would be manifest advantages in an exposition of the
Athenian constitution that reversed the chronological order,
that started with the period of which our knowledge is greatest
and traced the history of the constitution back to Kleisthenes.
But though professional historians may analyse the development of the Athenian constitution in this way, a connected
account of the subject must treat it chronologically, avoiding
as far as possible the drawbacks of this method by explaining
at each stage the evidence or arguments on which the conclusions are based. It has been the purpose of this chapter to
explain the peculiar difficulties presented by the evidence for
part of the early period, but the errors of the Atthidographers
need not drive us to scepticism. Historical technique has made
great progress since their time; we can fairly hope to make a
better use than they of the facts which they have transmitted
to us,[1] and we can draw on evidence available to them which
they either ignored or misunderstood. There is no dispute about
the main stages in the development of the Athenian constitution, and a sound critical method has only to define more carefully the limits of our knowledge and to fill the lacunae when
possible with a reconstruction which is most in accord with fact
and probability.

[1] Cf. Gilliard, 61.

II. FROM MONARCHY TO ARISTOCRACY

THE direct evidence for the constitution of Athens in the pre-Solonian period is limited to two documents, an inscription of 409/408[1] which purports to be a transcript of Drakon's law on homicide, and a copy of an amnesty-law quoted by Plutarch[2] and ascribed by him to Solon. But these documents cannot be accepted without question at their face value, for both laws were re-enacted more than once, and the version which has been preserved may represent in both cases a later revision of the original text.[3]

Although the contemporary records are so scanty, it is possible to reconstruct the main features of the development at Athens from monarchy to aristocracy and the principal institutions of the aristocratic state. One method of reconstruction is provided by the argument from survivals, from the institutions of a later age to their presumed antecedents in the past. This method was used for the early period by Thucydides and the Atthidographers and the subject certainly offers a good field for its application; it may be difficult to say whether a particular institution goes back to Solon or to Kleisthenes, but the traces of the aristocratic state which were preserved like fossils in the later democracy are so distinctive that their origin is unmistakable.

The results obtained by this method may be supplemented by a cautious use of analogy; the Homeric poems reveal the beginnings of the development from monarchy to aristocracy, and the institutions characteristic of Greek aristocracies can be studied in Greek states which developed more slowly than Athens and preserved all or some of these institutions into the fifth and fourth centuries.

An account of the early political history of Athens based on the application of these methods of inquiry must be to some extent hypothetical, but though many of the details must remain obscure or uncertain, the origins and results of the constitutional development in this period can be reconstructed in outline with a fair degree of certainty.

[1] *I.G.* i². 115 (Tod, 87).   [2] *Solon* 19. 4.
[3] See below, Appendix II, pp. 306 ff.

The beginning of the *Athenaion Politeia* is lost, but its contents can be recovered in part from the summary in the forty-first chapter, the epitome of Herakleides,[1] and the extant fragments. From these and other sources it is clear that the Atthis dealt with four main subjects in the pre-Solonian period, the origin of the four tribes and of other subdivisions of the citizen-body, the unification of Attica, the Athenian kingship and the transition from kingship to aristocracy, and the character of the aristocratic government before Solon. I propose to deal with the same subjects but in a different order; though the four tribes are probably anterior to the unification, the problems connected with the early organization of Attica can be discussed more conveniently in conjunction with the aristocratic state.

The unification of Attica

Thucydides gives the following account:[2] Attica before the union was divided into several independent states, whose rulers occasionally co-operated with the king of Athens in an emergency, but at other times disregarded him and even waged war on him. Theseus, who combined ability with adequate power, abolished the local governments and made Athens the political centre for the whole country, though he allowed the inhabitants of the states thus absorbed to live on their own lands as before. The Athenians still commemorate the unification in a public festival called ξυνοίκια.[3]

Thucydides' choice of the term ξυνοικίζειν was perhaps influenced by the name of the festival,[4] but it was misleading. In his day it meant something quite different, a concentration of population from scattered villages into a town which then formed the political centre of the state, as at Elis in 471[5] or at Megalopolis in 368/367.[6] The type of unification ascribed by Thucydides to Theseus is political and does not necessarily involve any transference of population to the political centre; in fact his account is a digression to explain why the majority of Athenian citizens still lived outside the city in 431. συμπολιτεία, not συνοικισμός, is the more precise term for a political

[1] *F.H.G.* (Müller) ii. 208 ff; the epitome is printed in most texts and editions of the *A.P.* Cf. *R.-E.* viii. 1, s.v. Herakleides (no. 51), 490 f.

[2] ii. 15. 1–2.　　　　[3] Plut. *Theseus* 24. 4 calls it μετοίκια; cf. BS 777, n. 1.

[4] Cf. de Sanctis, 21 and 24.　　　　[5] Diod. xi. 54. 1.

[6] Pausanias viii. 27. For the date cf. Diod. xv. 72. 4 and Beloch, iii². 2. 170; Meyer and others (cf. BS 1402, n. 1) date the foundation to the summer of 369.

unification of formerly independent states, such as that contained in the convention between Stiris and Medeon.[1] Later writers[2] fell into the error of assuming that the political unification was accompanied by a great influx of population into Athens from the smaller towns. This is disproved by Thucydides, but we may assume that the local chiefs now admitted to the king's council would henceforth reside in Athens, the centre of government.[3]

An early date for the unification of Attica is implied in its ascription to Theseus, which was the view current at Athens in the fifth century; this would make it earlier than the Trojan War and a fortiori earlier than the colonization of Ionia. Meyer and others who accept the early date suggest that Attica was the only region in Greece where the large state, characteristic of the 'Mycenaean' period, had survived the centrifugal tendencies of the post-Mycenaean age into historic times.[4] This contention derives some support from the Homeric poems; the catalogue in the *Iliad* seems to regard Attica as unified under the control of the King of Athens,[5] and a passage in the *Odyssey*[6] describes Sounion as the 'headland of Athens'. If the evidence of the poems is not anachronistic it proves that most of Attica was included in a single state in early times.

Those who accept this conclusion admit that Eleusis and the Marathonian tetrapolis were not included in this early unification. Eleusis is not mentioned in the *Iliad* or in the *Odyssey*, and the solitary reference to Marathon[7] proves nothing, but there are special reasons for believing that they were not included in the Athenian state till comparatively late. The incorporation of Eleusis cannot have taken place much before 700, for it appears as still independent in the Homeric hymn to Demeter, which was probably composed early in the seventh century.[8] The late inclusion of the Marathonian tetrapolis, which in historic times is a purely religious association, is

---

[1] *S.I.G.* 647 (2nd cent.); cf. de Sanctis, 22.

[2] e.g. Isokrates x. 35; cf. Busolt, ii². 92, n. 2.

[3] Cf. Plut. *Theseus* 32. 1. Wade-Gery (*C.Q.* xxv, 1931, 6 ff.) sees in this and in the ἐν βουλευτήριον of Thuc. ii. 15. 2 references to the origin of the Areopagus. Note that in Solon's time the ἄστυ is the residence of the nobles, who in his poems are the ἀστοί and as such contrasted with the πενιχροί; cf. Meyer, *Forsch.* i. 307. [4] *Forsch.* ii. 516; cf. *G.A.* iii². 311–12.

[5] ii. 546–58.   [6] iii. 278.   [7] *Odyssey* vii. 80.

[8] Cf. T. W. Allen and W. R. Halliday, *The Homeric Hymns* (1936), 111–14 and de Sanctis, 34–35.

inferred partly from its geographical position and partly from the fact that it had special representatives in Athenian embassies to Delphi.[1]

Even if we exclude Eleusis and Marathon from the first unification of Attica, the view that the rest of Attica had been united in a single state continuously from the Mycenaean period is open to serious objections. If the union had taken place so early, why was the tradition of the original disunion still so clear in the fifth century, reflected in the persistent stories of the early wars between Athens and other communities in Attica? Plutarch's statement[2] that there was no intermarriage in the classical period between the demes of Pallene and Hagnous seems to indicate that the time was not far distant when Attica had been divided into a number of little states, each quarrelling with its neighbours. If most of Attica was really united in a single state in the Mycenaean Age, we must assume that the union was dissolved by the centrifugal tendencies prevalent throughout Greece in the subsequent period of confusion, and that the work of unification had to be repeated in the eighth century, the age of unitary movements elsewhere in Greece.

Thucydides[3] believed that even before Theseus the King of Athens held a vague suzerainty over the whole of Attica, and that in times of danger the local chiefs would meet in council with him; Theseus substituted for this loose union a centralized government and a permanent council with their seat in Athens. Plutarch asserts[4] that Theseus created a new order in the state, the Eupatridai, in addition to the orders of the farmers and craftsmen which already existed, and that he reserved to this new order the control of government and religion.

Both Plutarch and Thucydides connect with Theseus' achievement the establishment of the festival called *Synoikia*, and it has been suggested[5] that their accounts were derived from the ritual of this festival and the traditional explanations of it preserved by the ἐξηγηταί; if the event commemorated in the festival was not the actual unification, it was probably its complement, the meeting of the noble families from the different

---

[1] Cf. A. Boëthius *Die Pythaïs* (Upsala, 1918), c. 3, especially 43 ff., also *S.I.G.* ii. 541, n. 1.   [2] *Theseus* 13. 4.   [3] ii. 15. 1.

[4] *Theseus* 25. 2; Jac. 247, n. 49 ascribes this to an author whose description was 'obviously under the influence of the Platonic State' and suggests Theophrastos. Wade-Gery (in *C.Q.* xxv. 5–6) tentatively attributed this section of Plutarch to Aristotle.   [5] By Wade-Gery, op. cit. 9–10.

parts of Attica who formed the aristocracy of the new state.[1] There are, however, some elements in the ancient accounts which are clearly mythical, such as the tradition that Theseus abdicated his monarchical powers after he had completed his task.[2] The festival was almost certainly connected with the unification, but probably preserved the memory of the central fact only, not of the details. It is difficult to believe that the final unification was effected as early as 'Theseus' or that it was carried through at a single stroke; it is more likely that it was the result of a gradual process during the eighth century ending with the incorporation of the Marathonian tetrapolis and Eleusis.[3]

The successive inclusion of the small communities of Attica in the Athenian state seems to have been accomplished in the main by peaceful methods. None of them was reduced to an inferior position; there were no perioikoi or helots in Attica. Though the cult of the temple at Eleusis became part of the official religion of Athens, the noble Eleusinian families[4] retained the religious privileges in connexion with it which they had previously possessed. Athens itself gained in prestige from the union, for its king was now ruler of a united Attica, and the city had become the political centre of the whole country.

The political unification of Attica must have strengthened its resistance to the aggression of foreign powers and prevented open warfare for the future between the communities included in the new state. Even before the union the King of Athens must have had a council of the nobles who lived near the citadel; henceforth it included the princely and noble families from all the regions of Attica. It is impossible to decide what measure of authority was possessed by the government of Athens after the unification, or to know whether its writ ran in the remoter parts of the country, but the degree of centralization assumed by many modern writers seems improbable. The effectiveness of the central authority was presumably proportionate to the solidarity of its members; it was also limited by their private ambitions. They were not prepared to surrender the great local powers and influence on which their prestige

[1] Cf. de Sanctis, 24 and n. 1.
[2] Cf. de Sanctis, 88 and n. 4, also Plut. *Theseus* 25. 3 and *A.P.* 41. 2 (with Sandys' note).   [3] BS 777; cf. Bonner and Smith, 59.
[4] The Eumolpidai and the Kerykes; cf. de Sanctis, 61–62 and 137.

depended, and the anarchy of the early sixth century showed
how far they could push their defiance of the government at
Athens when it was paralysed by internal feuds. But in the
period just after the union the local magnates had a common
interest in the struggle to undermine the powers of the king
and to establish their own supremacy in the state.

The Transition from Monarchy to Aristocracy[1]

A chronological tradition represented by the Parian Marble
states that Athens was governed by kings from Kekrops I to
Hippomenes. These kings all held their power for life and belonged, apart from Kekrops I, to two dynasties. The first consisted of fourteen rulers, from Erichthonios to Thymoites; in
the list of this dynasty given by the Parian Marble Theseus
comes ninth, but the tradition known to Herodotus gave only
Erechtheus, Pandion, and Aigeus between Kekrops and Theseus,
and the same tradition is presupposed in the names given by
Kleisthenes to his new tribes.[2] It is unnecessary for our purpose
to examine the stages by which this original list was expanded,
for all the names included in both the earlier and the later lists
of the first dynasty are those of Athenian gods or local heroes
and have no historical reality.

The list of the second dynasty contains nineteen names, the
first four being Melanthos, Kodros, Medon, and Akastos.
Melanthos and Kodros are certainly legendary; Melanthos is
connected with the Apatouria,[3] the festival of the dead, which
was celebrated both in Ionia and in Athens, and Kodros was
worshipped at Athens in a shrine which he shared with Neleus
and Basile,[4] apparently Chthonian deities. Akastos is proved
to be historical by the occurrence of his name in the oath taken
by the nine archons, that they would observe the oaths taken
'in the time of Akastos'.[5] The family to which Akastos and his
descendants belonged was that of the Medontidai,[6] whose name
seems to be derived from their kingly power. It is therefore

---

[1] Cf. Jacoby, *Atthis*, 121; for a fuller discussion cf. his article in *Klio*, ii, 1902,
406–39 and Ledl, *Studien*, 107–272. On the list of kings cf. also de Sanctis, 99–116.

[2] Cf. BS 784, n. 1.

[3] On Melanthos cf. Ledl, 225–6 and W. Kroll in *R.-E.* xv. 1. 434 f.; see also
Hellanikos, fr. 80 (125 in Jacoby, *F.G.H.* i [23 in iii B]) and H. W. Parke, *History
of the Delphic Oracle*, 337.

[4] *I.G.* i². 94 (date 418/417); cf. Ledl, 232 ff.

[5] *A.P.* 3. 3.   [6] Pausanias iv. 5. 10.

probable that Medon, the father of Akastos, is really mythical, the fictitious ancestor of the Medontidai, and that Akastos is the first historical figure in the Medontid family tree.[1]

Why were the Medontidai connected through Medon with the legendary Melanthos and Kodros? The connexion may have been made by genealogists in order to link by a common ancestry the royal house at Athens and the ruling families of Ionia,[2] who claimed descent from Kodros or his supposed ancestor Neleus. Herodotus[3] says that the family of Peisistratos claimed to be descended from the Neleidai of Pylos like the royal family at Athens, and this proves that the connexion between the Medontidai and the leading Ionian families had been established as early as the first half of the sixth century. The ramifications of these genealogical constructions need not be followed out here. It is sufficient to note that the connexion of the Medontidai with Melanthos and Kodros is secondary, and that they were the only family in Athens whose claim to have exercised regal power can be accepted as historically valid ;[4] the Kodridai are simply the Medontidai under another name, due to their assumed connexion with Kodros.

The Athenian state was never without a king; as Plato says,[5] βασιλεῖς μὲν γὰρ ἀεὶ ἡμῖν εἰσιν· οὗτοι δὲ τότε μὲν ἐκ γένους τότε δὲ αἱρετοί. In classical times he was one of the annual magistrates called 'the nine archons'.[6] His functions are described in the *Athenaion Politeia*,[7] which states that he is responsible for the conduct of all πάτριοι θυσίαι, and that he presides over all courts dealing with cases of homicide. He has lost all the old powers of the kingship except those connected directly or indirectly with religion; his office has ceased to be hereditary, and is no longer tenable for life.

Through the discovery of the *Athenaion Politeia* we have recovered the account given by the Atthidographers of the decline of the kingship and the transference of power to the aristocracy. According to this account,[8] the magistrates of the aristocratic state had at one time held office for life, but their term had later been limited to ten years. The earliest and most important magistracies were those held by the βασιλεύς, πολέμαρχος,

---

[1] Ledl, 236–7.   [2] Cf. Ledl, 229.   [3] v. 65. 3; cf. Ledl, 230 ff.
[4] On the claim of the Metionidai (Pausanias vii. 4. 5) cf. Ledl, 240–1.
[5] *Menexenos* 238 D.
[6] But he is always called βασιλεύς simply, *not* ἄρχων βασιλεύς.
[7] c. 57.   [8] *A.P.* 3. 1–4.

and ἄρχων; of these the kingship naturally existed from the beginning, the office of polemarch being a later creation and that of archon later still. When the archonship was instituted (there was a dispute whether this occurred in the reign of Medon or of his son Akastos) it was taken over by the royal family, the Kodridai, who surrendered the kingship in return for the privileges conferred on the archon. The thesmothetai were appointed much later, when the other magistracies had been further limited in duration from ten years to one year.

In the later chronological scheme for this period, which in its final form goes back to the Alexandrian scholar Eratosthenes,[1] the last two kings are Melanthos and Kodros; they are followed by thirteen archons who retain the archonship for life, starting with Medon and Akastos. In 752/751[2] begins a list of seven archons, each holding office for ten years. The annual archonship begins in 682/681 with Kreon, the first archon to give his name to the Athenian year.[3]

There are obvious affinities between these two accounts. The author of the *Athenaion Politeia*[4] is less precise; he is not sure whether Medon or Akastos was the first life-archon, and he does not give the number of decennial archons. In both accounts the members of the royal family after Kodros or his son Medon are life-archons, not kings, and this is the version which is usually followed by Pausanias.[5]

The author of the *Athenaion Politeia* implies that this was the view generally accepted by historians, and that disagreement was confined to the question of the date at which the life-archonship was instituted. Plato, however, believed[6] that the descendants of Kodros inherited his kingship, and the notices in the Parian Marble speak of the Medontidai down to Hippomenes not as life-archons but as kings.[7] Pausanias also adopts this version in one passage,[8] and in another definitely asserts

---

[1] This scheme has been traced through Kastor to Eratosthenes; cf. Jacoby's article in *Klio*, ii, 1902, 430, also BS 784, n. 1 and the work by E. Schwartz cited there.

[2] Dionysios, *A.R.* i. 71. 5 equates the first year of Charops (the first decennial archon) with Olympiad 7. 1 = 752/751.

[3] The date of Kreon follows from that of Charops. 682/681 is defended by de Sanctis, 81, n. 1; cf. also Cadoux, 88–89.

[4] 3. 3; note that already οἱ πλείους made Medon the first.

[5] iv. 5. 10 and 13. 7. For the version followed in the *A.P.* cf. also the epitome of Herakleides, § 3 (c. 1, l. 21 in Kenyon's Oxford Text).

[6] *Symposion* 208 D.   [7] §§ 27–31.   [8] i. 3. 3.

that Hippomenes (who comes fourth in the list of decennial archons) belonged to the family of the Medontidai.[1] A legend ascribed the fall of Hippomenes to his gruesome punishment of his daughter's adultery.[2] This part of the evidence presupposes the existence of an ancient authority which knew nothing of the life-archonship and made the Medontidai rule Athens as kings until the reign of Hippomenes, when the life-kingship was abolished.[3]

We have seen already that the Medontidai were the only family in Athens which could truthfully claim to have held the life-kingship, and that their recognition as the *genos basilikon* can be traced back to the first half of the sixth century. In an inscription of the fifth century[4] the Medontidai are found owning land close to the Acropolis, the ancient residence of the kings. These facts are sufficient to discredit the hypothesis of Wilamowitz[5] that the Medontidai were a new family, distinct from the Kodridai, who took away the substance of power from the Kodridai by the creation of the life-archonship; this supplanted the kingship as the supreme authority in the state and was made hereditary in the Medontid family. Though this supposition explains some of the difficulties, the assumption that the Medontidai were a family distinct from the Kodridai is flatly contradicted by the ancient evidence, and there is no warrant for the existence of a family of Kodridai, apart from the Medontidai themselves and certain Ionian families which might be so called as all claiming descent from Kodros.[6]

The explanation given in the *Athenaion Politeia* for the decline of the kingship is improbable in itself.[7] Obviously the archonship was instituted by the nobles to limit the power of the king. Yet they allow him to exchange the old office for the new, to retain the substance of his powers in return for the shadow, to hold these powers for life, and to hand them on to his descendants. The same argument is fatal to the credibility of the life-archonship in any form; it is unlikely that a jealous

---

[1] iv. 13. 7.

[2] Herakleides, § 3, 'Suidas', s.vv. Ἱππομένης and παρ' ἵππον καὶ κόρην. Cf. BS 786, n. 2 and Jac. 145.

[3] The legend could be and was adapted to fit the theory of the life-archonship; cf. Ephoros in Diod. viii. 22 and in Nikolaos of Damascus, fr. 51 (49 in Jacoby, *F.G.H.* ii A, no. 90).   [4] *I.G.* i². 871.

[5] *Hermes*, xxxiii, 1898, 119 ff.

[6] Meyer, *Forsch.* ii. 534; cf. Ledl, 227 ff.   [7] Cf. Ledl, 258.

aristocracy would consent to confer on one of their members
for life the powers which they had just wrested from the king.
As the account of the *Athenaion Politeia* is untenable, it cannot
be a genuine tradition but must reproduce the unfounded
speculations of an Atthidographer, and preference should be
given to the other version, in which the Medontidai are regarded
as kings.

On linguistic grounds the office of polemarch must have been
subsequent in origin to the archonship.[1] Other Greek states may
have had polemarchs without archons to precede or follow them,
but if the polemarch had come first at Athens the archon would
surely have been given a title less vague than that of ἄρχων.
The priority of the πολεμαρχία may have been inferred from
the tradition which made Ion polemarch;[2] it is defended in the
Athenaion Politeia on the ground that the archon, unlike the
king and the polemarch, possessed no functions which could be
traced back to an early date. But the tradition about Ion does
not prove the existence of an annual polemarch, and the argument in the *Athenaion Politeia* is defective, as the later functions
of the archonship, when it had been stripped of some of its
original powers, do not adequately represent its position in the
aristocratic state.

De Sanctis falls into the same error when he argues[3] that the
creation of the archon was not intended to limit the power of
the king, but to deal with disputes about property and inheritance which were now for the first time being brought under the
control of the state. As Ledl remarked,[4] this is equivalent to
saying that the archon was so called ἀπὸ τοῦ μὴ ἄρχειν. It is
clear from the story of the Kylonian conspiracy that the nine
archons, headed by ὁ ἄρχων, were the supreme executive in
pre-Solonian Athens.[5] The translation 'regent'[6] expresses most
accurately the archon's original position; he must have been
instituted by the nobility to take over the executive powers
of the king in internal affairs.

If we combine the conclusions reached in the preceding discussion we obtain the following reconstruction. The kingship

[1] De Sanctis, 124.   [2] *A.P.* 3. 2, Pausanias i. 31. 3; cf. Hdt. viii. 44. 2.
[3] Op. cit. 119 ff., especially 123 (followed in *C.A.H.* iii. 592).
[4] *Studien*, 256.
[5] Thuc. i. 126. 8; on this passage note the comments made by Jac. 187–8 and
369, n. 86.
[6] So Wilamowitz in *Hermes*, xxxiii. 128; cf. Ledl, 256.

at Athens was at one time hereditary in the Medontid family.
Later the nobles secured the appointment of an official called
ἄρχων, who took over most of the king's powers; the archonship was from the first an annual office.[1] This settlement was
guaranteed by an oath sworn by the archon,[2] which recalls the
oaths exchanged every month at Sparta by the kings and
ephors. Ledl[3] believed that the king surrendered to the archon
at the same time the command of the army, and that the institution of the polemarch was due to a later subdivision of the
powers previously conferred on the archon, but the analogy of
Sparta, where the hereditary kings retained the command of
the army after they had lost most of their other powers,[4] makes
it probable that the powers given to the polemarch were taken
directly from the king. Thus the institution of an annual official
called πολέμαρχος was a later development than the creation of
the archonship and marks the second stage in the limitation of
the royal authority.[5] Finally, the life-kingship was abolished;
on the death or deposition of the last Medontid king the kingship was made an annual office and thrown open to all the nobles.

The decennial archons interposed in our sources between the
life-archons (or kings) and the annual archons have no historical
reality. Similar fictions are found in the annals of other Greek
states between the life-kings and the beginning of official and
authentic lists of magistrates.[6] The δεκαετεῖς were firmly established in the Athenian tradition when the *Athenaion Politeia*
was written, and their invention may go back to Hellanikos.[7]
It does not follow that he also invented the ἄρχοντες διὰ βίου,
and the mutation of the last four of these (who are identical
with the last four kings) into the first four decennial archons
seems to have been the work of a later chronographer, probably
Eratosthenes.[8] The list of decennial archons in its final form
contains seven names, ending with Leokrates, Apsandros, and
Eryxias. Ledl maintained that in the official archon-list published about 425 and consulted by Hellanikos these were the
first three names, that they were annual archons, and that the

---

[1] See below, p. 44.
[2] *A.P.* 3. 3; cf. Xen. *Lac. Pol.* 15. 7 and Plut. *Pyrrhos* 5. 5.
[3] Op. cit. 256.   [4] Hdt. vi. 56.   [5] So Glotz and Cohen, i. 397.
[6] Jacoby in *Klio*, ii, 1902, 437; cf. his *Atthis*, 347, n. 23 and Ledl, 208.
[7] Jac. 348, n. 28.
[8] Jacoby in *Klio*, ii, 1902, 438 suggested this as a possible explanation; cf.
Ledl, 202.

list must therefore have begun in 686/685, not 683/682.[1] He assumed that some writer later than Hellanikos transformed the first three annual archons into decennial archons. It is, however, incredible that any Atthidographer should have taken such liberties with the official list.[2] We may therefore conclude that the list began with the archonship of Kreon, which was probably the year 682/681.

Has this date any other significance? The obvious hypothesis is that the official list of archons began to be kept from their first appointment. So Jacoby, rightly rejecting as fictitious the decennial archons, says[3] that he considers 'the institution of an annually changing ἄρχων beside the βασιλεύς (who need by no means have simultaneously became an annual official) to be a single and revolutionary act of the nobility'. This revolutionary act he seems to date just before the year of Kreon in the following words:[4] 'I believe the aristocrats capable of having recognized at once the necessity of entering in a list the annually changing archons because a designation of the years was even more needed in daily life than in politics.' This reasoning is not convincing. If the life-kings continued, their reigns were available for dating purposes as before. If, on the other hand, the need for some more precise or less cumbrous dating was being felt, why should not the list have been instituted to meet a growing need at some date subsequent to the introduction of the archonship?

De Sanctis, who accepts (as I do) the priority of the archon to the polemarch,[5] agrees that in or about 682 the Athenians began to record regularly the names of their eponymous archons, but refuses to regard this as a proof that anything began or ended in 682.[6] Yet he dates the institution of the archonship later than the incorporation of Eleusis in Athens (which he dates to the second half of the eighth century). He argues[7] that though the superintendence of the rites of the Mysteries remained in the hands of the Eleusinian families, the official direction was transferred to the Athenian king, who must therefore at this time have been the head of the state, whereas this position was held by the archon when Athens began, probably

---

[1] Ledl, 208-9.   [2] Jac. 172 and 348, n. 28.   [3] Jac. 347, n. 23.
[4] Loc. cit.   [5] *Atthis*, 124.   [6] Op. cit. 154.
[7] Ibid. (the facts to which he refers are in *A.P.* 57. 1 and the last sentence of 56. 3).

in the first half of the seventh century, to send a delegation to
the great Ionian festival of Apollo at Delos. The argument is
not decisive, for the Athenian kings may have retained their
religious headship of the state as long as they held office for life.

If the institution of the archonship constituted the first stage
in a process in which the abolition of the life-kingship was the
last, it is difficult to believe that it took place as late as 682.
The transition from monarchy to aristocracy in Ithaka is fore-
shadowed in the *Odyssey*,[1] and its beginning in Athens should
belong to the second half of the eighth century. The history of
the isthmus states, where aristocracy was succeeded by tyranny
not later than 625 (and probably some thirty years earlier)[2]
seems to show that the triumph of the aristocracy in those
states was complete before the end of the eighth century. It
may, however, be argued that the political development of the
isthmus states had been accelerated and that of Athens re-
tarded by local conditions.

The alternative, for those who persist in attaching significance
to the date 682, is to suppose that it was the year in which the
hereditary life-kingship was replaced by an annual kingship
open to all the nobles.[3] This seems plausible, but it cannot be
more than a guess, and the story which connects the end of the
life-kingship with the name of the Medontid Hippomenes is
obviously an aetiological myth.[4]

A further problem is raised by the mention of the King
Akastos in the oath taken by the archons 'to execute their
oaths as in the days of Akastos',[5] which seems to date the origin
of the archonship to his reign. The genealogy of the Medontidai
given by the chronographers contains sixteen names inclusive
from Akastos to Hippomenes. Ledl tried to defend the substantial accuracy of the list, but he had to admit the interpolation of three obviously Alkmaionid names,[6] and some at least

---

[1] Book xxiv; cf. W. Warde Fowler, *City-State*, 88 ff. (especially the ref. in
89, n. 3 to *Odyssey* xxiv. 483 ff. and 546).

[2] For a defence of the earlier date (*c.* 655) cf. Wade-Gery in *C.A.H.* iii. 764–5
and the remarks of C. M. Bowra, *Greek Lyric Poets*, 435–7. The later date, based
on evidence in Herodotus and defended by A. R. Burn in *J.H.S.* lv, 1935, 130–46,
appears to me less probable.

[3] I do not know whether anyone has maintained this view but it seems tenable,
in spite of Ledl, 265. Jac. 347, n. 23 clearly dates the end of the life-kingship
later; Ledl, 266 puts it as late as 650.

[4] Jac. 145; see above, p. 41.

[5] *A.P.* 3. 3; cf. BS 789 and de Sanctis, 97.   [6] Op. cit. 237–9.

of the others are not free from suspicion.[1] On Ledl's view, that
the deposition of Hippomenes was about 650 and later than the
earliest annual archons,[2] the latest possible date for Akastos
was 900, but a date in the tenth century for the institution of
the archonship is inconceivable. We must assume either that
the reign of Akastos falls within the eighth century[3] or that the
inference drawn by the Atthidographers from the archontic
oath was erroneous. If the first alternative is correct, the family
tree of the Medontidai can no longer be regarded as a trustworthy source, and the place of Akastos at the head of it (after
Medon) must be due to conjecture.[3] On the second alternative
the oath could be later in origin than Akastos' reign. Nothing
can safely be inferred from the fact that the oath was taken
by all the nine archons in historic times, as the formula may
easily be earlier than the institution of the polemarch and
thesmothetai, but the occurrence of the name Akastos in the
oath need not be taken as proof that the oath was contemporary
with him. If it was later, the reference in it to Akastos might
be explained as a device to provide the usurpation of authority
by the nobles with a respectable antiquity.

The Athenian kings were apparently too weak to resist by
force the successive encroachments on their position, and the
appropriation of their powers by the aristocracy seems to have
been effected without much trouble;[4] the word βασιλεύς has
none of the bitter associations of the Roman *regnum*. By the
abolition of the life-kingship and the transference of its religious
functions to an annual official the development was carried to
its logical conclusion, and the triumph of the aristocrats was
complete.

[1] Cf. de Sanctis, 96 ff.
[2] He dates the end of the Medontid line of life-kings *c.* 650 (op. cit. 266) and
regards Hippomenes as the last of them (200 f.).
[3] Cf. de Sanctis, 97 and BS 789.
[4] So de Sanctis, 137.

III. THE ARISTOCRATIC STATE

THE citizens of Athens in the pre-Solonian state were sub-divided into four tribes (φυλαί) and smaller groups called φρατρίαι; every full citizen was a member of a tribe and of a phratry, and membership in both was hereditary.[1] According to the Atthis the phratries were originally subdivided into γένη, in which all the citizens were included.[2] But by the fourth century there were many Athenian citizens who were not members of a genos; these formed groups within the phratries which were probably known as θίασοι.[3] Membership in the genē and the thiasoi was hereditary, as in the tribes and phratries.

Socially the Athenians in the early period were divided into three classes, εὐπατρίδαι, γεωργοί, and δημιουργοί[4]—nobles, farmers, and craftsmen; in the aristocratic state the functions of government and the priesthoods of the state religion belonged exclusively to the Eupatridai.[5]

The Atthis also ascribes to the period before Solon a sub-division of each of the four tribes into three τριττύες and twelve ναυκραρίαι.[6] Some of the ancient references to the naukraries suggest that they were territorial divisions[7] and they have usually been regarded by modern scholars as administrative districts. If this view is correct, the naukrary to which an Athenian citizen belonged would be determined by the place in which he lived. Yet how can this conclusion be reconciled with the Atthis? How can the naukrary, based on the principle of locality, have been a subdivision of the tribe, in which membership was hereditary? Either the statement of the Atthis is false, and the naukraries were purely local divisions independent of the tribal organization, or we must assume that the birth-tribes were in some sense local. This assumption plays an important part in some modern theories about the origin of the four tribes.

The beginnings of this political and social organization must have been described in the early part of the *Athenaion Politeia*;

---

[1] Membership of both presumably descended in the male line only. This was proved for the γένη by W. Dittenberger in *Hermes*, xx, 1885, 6.

[2] *A.P.* fr. 3 (5 in Thalheim's text).

[3] Cf. *I.G.* ii². 1237 (*S.I.G.* iii. 921) and Wade-Gery in *C.Q.* xxv, 1931, 1.

[4] *A.P.* fr. 3 (though the εὐπατρίδαι are not mentioned there) and 13. 2.

[5] As in Plut. *Theseus* 25. 2 and Diod. i. 28. 5.

[6] *A.P.* 8. 3.   [7] See below, p. 68.

it has now been lost, but a fragment of it preserved in citations[1]
shows that it gave the following account of the political organization, probably derived from the Atthis. The whole
citizen-body was divided into 4 tribes, and each of these into
3 subdivisions called τριττύες or φρατρίαι. Each of the 12 phratries
contained 30 γένη, and every γένος contained exactly 30 men;
thus there were 360 γένη in all and 10,800 citizens. This account
implies that the whole organization was instituted at the same
time, and the period to which it was ascribed by the Atthis was
certainly that of Ion,[2] with whom the institution of the 4 tribes
is connected in the *Athenaion Politeia*.

It is also stated by the writers who quote this fragment that
the citizen-body (πλῆθος) of Athens at this time was composed
of γεωργοί and δημιουργοί; the εὐπατρίδαι are not mentioned in
this context. Francotte suggested[3] that the πλῆθος of farmers
and craftsmen was to be identified with the commons as distinct from the nobles, and that only the nobles belonged to the
tribes, phratries, and genē. But even if the second part of
Francotte's picture was true for pre-Solonian Athens,[4] it is
incredible that 'Aristotle' should have thought so, unless the
lexicographers have grossly misrepresented his views.[5] Against
the first part it has been urged[6] that the account of the lexicographers is in harmony with that of Plutarch, who ascribes
the creation of the order of Eupatridai to Theseus at the time
of the unification of Attica. But there can be no certainty that
this statement was taken by Plutarch from 'Aristotle'; Jacoby
has adduced strong arguments to prove that it was not, and
that Plutarch's source here was an author who was influenced
by Plato's ideal state in his description of the Athens of
Theseus.[7]

Historically the fixation of the order of Eupatridai may be
dated to the final unification of Attica,[8] but the creation by
Theseus of a class of nobles with special privileges seems incompatible with the popular account, which was apparently
accepted by the Atthidographers, that he was the founder of

[1] Fr. 3.
[2] As Wade-Gery proved (op. cit. 3); cf. *A.P.* 41. 2.
[3] *La Polis grecque*, 10 ff.
[4] Jacoby (*Atthis*, middle of p. 318) remarks that the organization was 'probably limited to the aristocracy'.
[5] Cf. Wade-Gery, op. cit., p. 3, n. 1.
[6] By Wade-Gery, op. cit. 3.   [7] Jac. 247, n. 49.
[8] As it apparently was by Thucydides (ii. 15. 2); cf. Wade-Gery, op. cit. 6–8.

democracy.[1] The solution of this problem, if it could be found, would be relevant only to the beliefs of the Atthidographers. We cannot accept, as they did, the historical reality of Ion and Theseus, but their belief in it was not an essential part of their reconstruction; the distinction between Ion and Theseus may be regarded as a convenient shorthand distinction between the Athenian state prior to the unification and the form which it assumed at the unification.

The origins of the tribes, phratries, and genē may well go back to a time prior to the final unification of Attica in the eighth century. But the Atthis went farther than this; it ascribed them to an artificial creation imposed on the citizen-body by a single act. The arbitrariness of this account is shown by the fact that the numbers of the tribes, phratries, and genē correspond with those of the seasons, months, and days of the year; it is clearly inconsistent with any view which sees in the emergence of these groupings the result of a natural and gradual development. Francotte[2] tried to maintain that these subdivisions were both natural and artificial; they had existed from early times, and the legislator who used them as the foundation of his reorganization merely remodelled them in such a way as to satisfy his love of symmetry.

Most scholars, however, have attributed this love of symmetry not to a legislator but to the Atthidographers,[3] and have seen in it the proof that we have before us an imaginary construction. Even Francotte could not accept the 10,800 citizens, though he went so far as to suggest[4] that they represented the number of land-allotments into which the soil of Attica was divided, each genos receiving thirty of them. The figure 360 given for the genē is almost equally incredible, and the assertion that there were twelve phratries is at least doubtful.

A further difficulty is raised by the dating of this reorganization to a period anterior to the unification of Attica. As Ion was traditionally the creator of the four tribes, it was natural that the Atthidographers should credit him with the creation of the subdivisions of the four tribes since on their view it was part of the same reform. But if this organization belonged to a time before the unification of Attica, it must surely have been re-modelled at the unification, when the number of citizens was

[1] See above, p. 37, n. 2. [2] Op. cit. 37–38.
[3] e.g. de Sanctis, 58; see below, p. 59 and n. 7. [4] Op. cit. 33.

greatly increased. The new citizens could not have been simply incorporated in the existing divisions; they might have been allowed to enter the phratries, but the genē were narrow family associations to which strangers could not be admitted. Francotte evaded the difficulty by making the reorganization contemporary with the unification, but since he wrote it has been proved[1] that this solution is inconsistent with the Atthis; this contradiction is fatal to his reconstruction, which was professedly based on a close adherence to the statements of the Atthis.

These problems are insoluble because they are unreal. They vanish when we recognize that the account produced by the Atthidographers cannot be accepted as a whole. Their task here required an historical imagination and a critical insight which they lacked; the best that they could achieve was an arbitrary simplification which ignored many of the difficulties. Such a solution has no claim to authority and must not be allowed to bias the course of our inquiry into the same questions.

The four tribes

The names of the four tribes were Geleontes, Hopletes, Argadeis, and Aigikoreis.[2] These suggested to some ancient writers[3] the theory that they were the names of occupations; the last three were explained as warriors, artisans, and shepherds, and the Geleontes were regarded as either farmers or priests. This explanation found favour with Gilbert, who was inclined to see in these divisions the traces of some primitive caste-system,[4] but it is obviously only a guess prompted by the character of the tribe-names. It seems to have been unknown to the writers of the fifth century, for both Herodotus[5] and Euripides[6] explain the names as formed from those of Ion's sons. When the tribes are enumerated in inscriptions the Geleontes always come first, but the Hopletes, who, if originally warriors, ought to come second, are usually found in the last place.[7] Moreover, the Athenian aristocracy, the Eupatridai,

---

[1] By Wade-Gery's demonstration (*C.Q.* xxv. 3) that in the Atthis this organization is ascribed to Ion. Francotte, 7–8, had admitted that he found a difficulty in the role ascribed by the *A.P.* to Ion.

[2] Cf. the note of How and Wells on Hdt. v. 66. 2.

[3] Cf. Plut. *Solon* 23. 5 and Strabo, 383.   [4] *G.C.A.* 103 and n. 3.

[5] v. 66. 2.   [6] *Ion*, 1575 ff.

[7] Cf. Busolt, i². 279, n. 3 (also ii². 102, n. 7) on the inscriptions from Kyzikos

must have been found in all four tribes, as each tribe was headed by a φυλοβασιλεύς who was always a Eupatrid.[1] It is possible that the names of the tribes were really derived from those of ancient deities; Γελέων appears as a title of Zeus in a late inscription, and a Ζεὺς Ὁπλόσμιος was worshipped in Arcadia.[2]

These tribes are usually described as the four Ionic tribes; the description is convenient but has given rise to serious errors, and it is safer to refer to them as the four 'Attic' tribes. It is true that all or some of them existed in the Ionian states of the Aegean islands and Asia Minor and in the colonies of those states. Thus all four are found at Kyzikos and two of them at Perinthos, colonies of Miletos and Samos respectively.[3] But in Kyzikos we also find side by side with the four tribes two non-Attic tribes, the Βωρεῖς and the Οἴνωπες, and the Οἴνωπες are found at Tomoi, which like Kyzikos was a colony of Miletos.[4] Moreover, an inscription from Miletos itself[5] mentions the Οἴνωπες, Βωρεῖς, and Ὁπληθες, presumably a local variant of Ὁπλῆτες. It has reasonably been supposed[6] that half of the Milesian tribes are here represented, and that the other three were the Geleontes, Argadeis, and Aigikoreis, as in the Milesian colony Kyzikos.

The above facts are in agreement with what Herodotus relates about the colonization of the Ionian towns in Asia Minor. He says[7] that though Athens was responsible for the foundation of these towns and supplied a large proportion of the colonists, the original settlers included elements drawn from various peoples in Greece. This account may be open to criticism in details, but it is now generally agreed[8] that it is substantially correct, and that a considerable percentage of the Ionians of Asia Minor were of the same stock as the Athenians. Thus the four Attic tribes in Miletos would be the descendants of the colonists supplied by Athens, while the alien elements were included in the Boreis and Oinopes. Possibly these two tribes

which give as the official order Geleontes Argadeis Aigikoreis and Hopletes; the Hopletes also came last in Hdt., loc. cit. Cf. K. Latte in R.-E. xx. 1. 994 ff.

[1] Busolt, ii². 103 and n. 1, quoting Pollux, viii. 111 (with Wecklein's emendation of τέσσαρες for δέ; cf. A.P. 8. 3 and Sandys' note).
[2] Evidence in Busolt, ii². 103, n. 2; cf. How and Wells on Hdt. v. 66. 2.
[3] Cf. Szanto, 46 ff. and BS 118–20 and 132, also Busolt, i². 279, n. 3 and 280, n. 1.
[4] Cf. Busolt, i². 280 and Szanto, 57.
[5] S.I.G. i. 57.   [6] n. 3 on S.I.G. i. 57.   [7] i. 146.
[8] Cf. Busolt, i². 282, n. 1 and J. Wells, Studies in Herodotus, c. 1.

were artificial divisions created for these alien settlers; it is curious that the same two tribes should have been used for the purpose at both Miletos and Samos.[1]

This explanation postulates that the four 'Ionic' tribes existed in Athens as sections of the citizen-body at a date earlier than the Greek colonization of Ionia. It is not known how or where the name 'Ionians' (an earlier form of which, Iavones, is attested by Homer[2]) first arose. Bury's view[3] that it was borrowed by the colonists from an aboriginal non-Greek people is unconvincing, but the name must certainly have come into use later than the colonization of Asia Minor by the Greeks, and probably on the east side of the Aegean. The adoption of the common name 'Ionian' was naturally followed by the invention of an eponymous ancestor Ion, but he is clearly out of place in the Athenian genealogies; he is not one of the Kings of Athens and has to be introduced as στρατάρχης or πολέμαρχος.[4] But if the Ionian name arose beyond the Aegean, the Athenians were not slow to adopt it. In the sixth century they were eager to claim relationship with their kinsmen in Asia, and Solon proudly called Attica 'the oldest of Ionian states'.[5]

When the Ionians had invented Ion they proceeded to connect with his name the tribal divisions which they had brought with them from Greece. As Ion was assigned to a generation long before the colonization of Ionia, the Ionians must have believed that the tribal divisions ascribed to Ion had originated in Greece. The application of the name 'Ionic' to these divisions is in part responsible for a modern theory which holds that they came into existence, like the Ionian name, in Asia Minor,[6] but this is contrary to probability and to ancient tradition.

On the other hand, those who believe that history can be extracted from myths, taking the myth of Ion at its face value, have concluded that the four tribes were somehow alien to Attica, imposed by foreign 'Ionian' conquerors on a primitive

[1] Their existence in Samos has been inferred from their appearance in its colony Perinthos, but the inference is denied by Szanto, 53.

[2] *Iliad* xiii. 685 (where it is used of the Athenians); cf. the *hymn to Apollo*, l. 147.   [3] *E.H.R.* xv, 1900, 288–91; cf. Wells, op. cit. 11.

[4] Hdt. viii. 44 (with note in How and Wells) and *A.P.* 3. 2. On the legends of Ion cf. Meyer, *Forsch.* i. 142 ff.

[5] Fr. 4 (Diehl), l. 2; translation by Linforth, 133. Their attitude probably changed later, but note the remarks of Lenschau in *R.-E.* ix. 2. 1870.

[6] Wil. ii. 140–1, followed by Latte in *R.-E.* xx. 1. 1001.

'Pelasgian' population.[1] This conquest was connected by
Greenidge[2] with the unification of Attica, but the mythological
tradition places Ion some generations before Theseus. The in-
trusion of Ion into Athenian mythology may be interpreted by
those who care to do so as a folk-memory of foreign conquest;
it is simpler to explain it as a later addition clumsily grafted
on the original legend.

It is now admitted by most scholars that, though the name
'Ionian' probably arose in Asia Minor, the four tribes must
have existed in Attica before the colonization of Ionia, but the
origins of the organization are still disputed. Meyer, accepting
the statement of the Atthis that the naukraries were subdivisions of the tribes, concluded that the tribes were territorial
divisions into which Attica was divided for administrative purposes after its unification;[3] all citizens resident in a particular
division would thus be members of the same tribe. This explanation presupposes that the unification of Attica preceded
the colonization of Ionia; we have already seen[4] that the
assumption of such an early date for the unification is difficult
but not impossible. If the four tribes were territorial, it may
seem strange that they should all recur in Miletos. Meyer did
not notice this difficulty, but it may be evaded by the assumption that the colonists of Miletos were drawn equally from the
four divisions of Attica.

The obvious objection to Meyer's theory is that it postulates
a remarkable degree of evolution in the Athenian state by the
twelfth century;[5] not only is the unification of Attica complete,
but the centralization of its government has been carried so far
that the rulers can impose on the country a division into four
administrative areas. This picture of primeval Attica cannot be
disproved; it is certainly different from the picture of political
conditions in Greece contained in the Homeric poems, but the
Homeric state may represent a relapse from a higher development into something more primitive. On the other hand,
Meyer's account is a hypothetical construction, and there is no
guarantee that it corresponds with the reality.

The question can only be settled by a consideration of analogous organizations found in other Greek states at the beginning

[1] This view seems to be tacitly presupposed in Francotte, 36–38.
[2] *Handbook*, 128.   [3] *Forsch.* ii. 529–30.   [4] See above, p. 36.
[5] Cf. the objections raised by H. Bolkestein in *Klio*, xiii, 1913, 424–50.

of their history. In some of the states of the Dorian group, such
as Argos, Sikyon, and Sparta, there existed in the seventh
century a division into three 'Dorian' tribes called Hylleis,
Pamphyloi, and Dymanes,[1] and it is probable that the same
tribes existed at Corinth before the rule of the tyrants. At
Sparta all the citizens were included in these three tribes, but
at Sikyon and Argos, possibly at Corinth also, there was a fourth
tribe ;[2] the history of Sikyon suggests that this fourth tribe may
have been created there and elsewhere for the pre-Dorian element in the population, which was thereby admitted to a share
in the organization of the state by its conquerors. This evidence
indicates that the three Dorian tribes formed part of the
common heritage of all the Dorians, dating back to a time before
they had split up into independent states. If they originated
in the second millennium before Christ they must have been
a 'natural' division, perhaps reflecting the combination of
groups originally separate, not divisions consciously created by
human agency in a previously existing whole.

This analogy points to the conclusion that the four Attic
tribes were also natural in origin, of very early date, and owing
nothing to any deliberate human organization.[3] They must be
earlier than the colonization of Ionia; they cannot have been
borrowed later by the Athenians from Ionia, as the Boreis and
Oinopes, which presumably existed in Miletos at the time when
it planted a colony in Kyzikos[4] and probably from its own
foundation, are not found in Attica, and on the same ground
we must rule out the suggestion that the four tribes might have
been borrowed from Athens by the Ionian states at a date later
than their foundation.

It is impossible to say whether the four Attic tribes originated
in Attica or elsewhere. The Athenians claimed that they were
autochthonous, that their ancestors had always lived in Attica.
Herodotus accepts this claim, but sometimes maintains that the
Ionians originally dwelt in the north of the Peloponnese; this

[1] For Argos and Sikyon cf. Hdt. v. 68. 1, for Sparta Tyrtaios, fr. 1 (Diehl),
l. 12. Δωριέες τριχάικες occur in *Odyssey* xix. 177 (ll. 175–7 may be a later interpolation). Cf. *Iliad* ii. 668 and see BS 130.

[2] BS 131 and Wells, op. cit. 29; cf. Hdt. v. 68. 1 on Sikyon and Busolt, i². 215,
n. 3 on Corinth.

[3] The validity of the analogy is denied by Szanto, 46.

[4] Szanto, 56, rejects the inference, but his assumption that the tribal divisions
of Kyzikos were not introduced till a time considerably later than its foundation
seems arbitrary.

contention is merely an inference from unsound premises and must be rejected.[1] If the ancestors of the Athenians were invaders who conquered Attica, and if they were already organized in four tribes when the conquest took place, it is possible that they divided the conquered territory into four parts, assigning one to each of the four tribes; this hypothesis is based on the belief that the four tribes were in some sense territorial, but provides a more plausible explanation for the alleged fact than that advanced by Meyer. The main objection to it is that the evidence for the supposed conquest is unsatisfactory; moreover, the occurrence of the three Dorian tribes in various parts of the Argolid, which may have formed a single state at first after the Dorian conquest,[2] throws doubt on the territorial character ascribed by implication in the Atthis to the Attic tribes.

The phratries

The phratry is mentioned in Homer as a subdivision of the tribe; Nestor advises Agamemnon to marshal the army in groups consisting of men from the same tribe and the same phratry.[3] Homer also uses the adjective ἀφρήτωρ[4] in conjunction with ἀθέμιστος and ἀνέστιος to describe a man who is cut off from the normal relationships of civil life. In the homicide law of 409/408 ascribed to Drakon there is a provision which allows an exile banished for involuntary homicide to return to Attica if the relatives of the murdered man give their consent; if there are no near relatives of the murdered man still living, the question is to be decided by ten men of his phratry chosen ἀριστίνδην, that is, from the aristocratic members of the phratry.[5] This clause in the law is clearly archaic in character and may safely be regarded as pre-Solonian; it shows that the phratry had a place in the civil law of the aristocratic state, and also that the phratry included among its members plebeians as well as nobles.

Membership of a phratry retained some importance in the fifth and fourth centuries as it was still limited to citizens. Although after the reforms of Kleisthenes the official criterion

---

[1] Hdt. i. 145; cf. Wells, *Studies*, 12.

[2] On the share (λῆξις) of Temenos cf. Ephoros in Strabo, 358, also P. N. Ure, *The Origin of Tyranny* (1922), 179–80. Cf. Busolt, i². 214–16.

[3] *Iliad* ii. 362–3. [4] *Iliad* ix. 63–64. [5] *I.G.* i². 115 (Tod, 87), ll. 13 ff.

of citizenship was membership of a deme, the list kept by each deme only included male citizens who had attained their eighteenth year.[1] Thus the phratry-lists, which may be regarded as ecclesiastical registers independent of the civil registers kept on behalf of the state by the demes,[2] provided the only record of the citizen-rights of women and minors; moreover, an adult male, if his right to appear on the list of his deme was questioned, could plead his membership of a phratry as proof of his status. It is to be noted that in accordance with Athenian legal practice the list of the phratry or the deme was not admissible as evidence in such cases; the defendant had to cite witnesses in order to prove that he was duly admitted to the phratry or deme.

In the fourth century the phratries were composed of smaller groups; these were of two types, the γένη and the θίασοι.[3] The term used for members of a thiasos was ὀργεῶνες; members of a genos were called γεννῆται or ὁμογάλακτες.[4] Every phratry probably contained one or more thiasoi, but it is doubtful whether the γένη appeared in all the phratries. An inscription of the phratry of Demotionidai, dated 396/395,[5] ordains that in this particular phratry (which seems to be composed exclusively of thiasoi)[6] the thiasos is to decide first on the claims of candidates for admission, but anyone rejected by the thiasos has a right of appeal to the whole phratry. Every phratry, genos, and thiasos was empowered to make its own statutes, which were valid provided that they did not conflict in any way with the laws of the state.[7]

The deities worshipped by the phratries were Zeus Phratrios, Athenaia Phratria, and Dionysos Melanaigis,[8] who were all

---

[1] A.P. 42. 1. The deme register was called ληξιαρχικὸν γραμματεῖον; cf. I.G. i². 79, l. 6 and [Dem.] xliv. 35.

[2] Toepffer, A.G. 17. On the enrolment of girls in the phratry cf. Isaios iii. 73–79 and Kahr. i. 240.

[3] These terms are usually assumed to be exclusive, but Wade-Gery in C.Q. xxv, 1931, 1 says 'a Genos is a Thiasos'. Some lexicographers (cf. Gilbert, 149, n. 2) identify ὀργεῶνες (for which cf. Isaios, ii. 14) and γεννῆται.

[4] The two terms seem between them to include the whole citizen-body in the law quoted by Philochoros, fr. 94 (35 a in Jacoby); see below, p. 61, also BS 253 and n. 2.

[5] I.G. ii². 1237 (S.I.G. iii. 921). See also Appendix II, pp. 313 ff.

[6] Wade-Gery (loc. cit.) says that some of the θίασοι in this phratry may have been γένη, but many scholars have denied this (e.g. BS 253).

[7] Cf. Gilbert, 191 and n. 4, also BS 192–3, n. 4 and 254.

[8] Cf. S.I.G. iii. 921 for Zeus Phratrios and 922 (from Kos) for Athenaia Phratria; on Dionysos Melanaigis cf. R.-E. i. 2677–8.

connected with the Apatouria. This festival, 'the gathering of the fathers', was the great annual occasion on which the members of each phratry met together to offer solemn worship to their protecting deities and to vote on the admission of members' children.[1] The cults of Zeus Herkeios and Apollo Patroös were also among those celebrated by the phratries;[2] the right to share in them was in the classical period common to all Athenian citizens and was actually used officially as a criterion of citizenship.[3]

Each phratry had its own priest and its own head ($\phi\rho\alpha\tau\rho\acute{\iota}$-$\alpha\rho\chi\sigma$), both apparently annual, also its own place of meeting.[4] The phratry of the Dyaleis, which may have been formed by the fusion of two other phratries,[5] is mentioned in an inscription of 300/299 recording a lease of a plot of land belonging to the phratry; as the lessee and the two phratriarchs all belong to the deme of Myrrhinous, it has been suggested that most of the members belonged to the same deme, just as the majority of the Demotionidai seem to belong to the deme of Dekeleia.[6] As each phratry had its own shrine in a particular locality, and as in most cases this was probably the place in which the majority of its members resided, the phratry, though based on birth, may be said to have had a territorial character.

The origins of the phratry and of its component parts, the genē and the thiasoi, are no less disputed than the origin of the four tribes. It was once the fashionable view that the ancient state developed from the family through the village, that it was due to a fusion of originally independent atoms,[7] but it is more probable that the phratry and its subdivisions arose within a previously existing whole which provided the conditions necessary for their development.[8]

---

[1] Wil. ii. 274. Cf. Xen. *Hell.* i. 7. 8 and *I.G.* ii². 1237, also Toepffer, s.v. in *R.-E.* i. 2672 ff. The true explanation of the name is given by the scholion on Ar. *Acharnians* 146. For admissions at other times cf. Gilbert, 196–7 and 197, n. 1, citing Isaios vii. 15.

[2] Cf. passages cited by Sandys on *A.P.* 55. 3 (p. 217).

[3] *A.P.* 55. 3; cf. the younger Kratinos in Athenaios 460 F. Plato, *Euthydemos* 302 D says that Zeus was not worshipped as $\pi\alpha\tau\rho\tilde{\omega}os$ either in Athens or in any of the Ionian states, but cf. *S.I.G.* iii. 987, l. 35 (Chios). For his worship in a phratry of a non-Ionian state cf. *S.I.G.*² 438 (the Labyadai at Delphi). See also de Sanctis, 46.   [4] BS 255; Gilbert, 210.

[5] *I.G.* ii². 1241; cf. de Sanctis, 47 and Wade-Gery in *C.Q.* xxv, 1931, 139, n. 3.

[6] Cf. Gilbert, 149, n. 1.

[7] e.g. W. Warde Fowler, *City-State*, 28 ff. (especially 40).

[8] Cf. de Sanctis, c. 2, and on the $\gamma\acute{\epsilon}\nu\eta$ Meyer, *Forsch.* ii. 512–28.

A clue to the origin of the phratry has been found in the famous fifth-century inscription which records the legal code at Gortyn in Crete.[1] The provisions regulating adoptions ordain that anyone intending to adopt a son should announce his intention formally in the ἀγορά to the assembly of citizens from the stone from which speakers must address the people, and should also give to his ἑταιρεία a sacrificial victim and a πρόχοος of wine.[2] As the formalities observed in adoptions at Athens included the offering of a victim on the altar of the phratry, we may conclude that the Cretan ἑταιρεία was an institution analogous to the Athenian phratria, and the Zeus Hetaireios recorded as Cretan by Hesychios may have corresponded to the Zeus Phratrios of the Athenian phratries.[3] We also find at Gortyn a class of ἀφέταιροι, free men but not full citizens, who were probably so called because they were not qualified for admission to a ἑταιρεία and were therefore excluded from citizenship;[4] with this may be compared Homer's use of the word ἀφρήτωρ.

In Homer the ἑταῖροι are closely connected with the ἔται; these terms have been carefully analysed by Glotz,[5] who proved that they are not to be identified either with the κασίγνητοι (not brothers but near relations comparable with the Athenian ἀγχιστεῖς) or the πηοί (kinsmen by marriage). As the ἑταῖροι and the ἔται are not identical, Glotz suggested that the ἑταῖροι were the men of military age in the association whose members were called ἔται, and that the collective name for this association was φρήτρη.

Probably the ἑταῖροι fought together in war because they were accustomed to co-operate in peace, and a passage in the *Odyssey*[6] shows that the ἔται of a murdered man were expected to aid his κασίγνητοι in avenging his death; this explains the place assigned to the phratry in Drakon's homicide law. The origin of the groups of ἔται is to be found in voluntary associations of neighbours for self-help in a period when the primitive state

---

[1] *I.J.G.* i. 352 ff. (for other reff. cf. Tod, p. 69).
[2] Gortyn code x. 34 ff.
[3] Cf. de Sanctis, 43. The method of objection to an adoption in an Athenian phratry was to remove the victim from the altar of Zeus Phratrios; cf. [Dem.] xliii. 14.   [4] De Sanctis, 42.
[5] *La Solidarité de la famille dans le droit criminel en Grèce* (1904) 85 ff.; cf. BS 250–1 and n. 1. Glotz showed that the meaning of κασίγνητοι was proved by *Iliad* xv. 545 ff. and *Odyssey* xvi. 115 ff.
[6] xv. 272–6; cf. the first sentence of the old law in [Dem.] xliii. 57.

left to its individual members the task of protecting their lives and property.[1] These groups may have been fluid and impermanent at first, but gradually became more rigid with the development of settled conditions, so that membership in them was finally made hereditary. When the group had acquired continuity and its traditions and cults were differentiated from those of the other groups, the transformation of its members from ἔται into φράτορες was complete.[2]

If the phratries originated in voluntary associations, it is unlikely that there would have been precisely three of them in each of the four tribes. Those modern scholars who believe that this was true in the classical period rely on the statement of the Atthis that each of the four tribes was subdivided into three phratries in the time of Ion.[3] But the reorganization of the citizen-body ascribed to Ion by the Atthis is too symmetrical to be credible; the twelve phratries may be as real as the four tribes or as artificial as the 360 genē. It is now admitted that Kleisthenes did not increase the number of phratries which he found in existence,[4] but there is no ground for fathering on the Atthis the assumption that the number of phratries had remained unchanged from the time of Ion to the eve of Kleisthenes' reforms. Speaking of the period just before Solon, the Atthis asserts that each tribe was subdivided into three parts, but its identification of these trittyes with the phratries is questionable.[5] Some have maintained that the organization of the citizen-body attributed to Ion was simply a transcript of that actually existing in some historic period, such as the end of the sixth century,[6] but it is incredible that there ever were at Athens 360 genē each containing thirty citizens. Probably the details of the early organization given by the Atthis, apart from the four tribes, had no claim to historical reality.[7]

What we know of the phratries in the fifth and fourth centuries can hardly be reconciled with the view that they were only twelve in number.[8] To meet this difficulty the suggestion

[1] Cf. de Sanctis, 45.   [2] De Sanctis, 43.   [3] *A.P.*, fr. 3.
[4] Cf. de Sanctis, 345 and n. 4, also Wade-Gery in *C.Q.* xxvii, 1933, 26–28.
[5] *A.P.*, fr. 3 (also 8. 3). Cf. W. S. Ferguson in *Classical studies presented to Edward Capps* (1936), pp. 152 and 157.
[6] Cf. A. Zimmern, *Greek Commonwealth*[4] (1924), 147 and J. A. R. Munro in *C.Q.* xxxiii, 1939, 87 ff.   [7] Cf. de Sanctis, 58 ff. and K. Latte in *R.-E.* xx. 752.
[8] This was pointed out by H. Sauppe in his first *commentatio de phratriis atticis* (in the *index scholarum*, Göttingen, 1886), pp. 4–5; cf. A. Körte in *Hermes*, xxxvii, 1902, 587.

has been made[1] that in the fifth century, when membership of a deme was the official criterion of citizenship, poorer citizens ceased to enrol their children in a phratry on account of the outlay necessary at the two ceremonies of the Meion and the Koureion,[2] and that in consequence less than half of the population was now included in the phratries. The references to the phratry in decrees conferring Athenian citizenship, which empower the new citizen to choose his own tribe, deme, and phratry,[3] have then to be explained away as due to the incurable conservatism of the Athenians, who carefully preserved the old formulae long after they had outlived their meaning![4]

This hypothesis is untenable. Even if Thetes had ceased to be members, there must have been at least 18,000 adult male members of the phratries in the Periklean Age, about 1,500 in each phratry, if there were no more than twelve phratries. It is difficult to believe that so many met together in each phratry at the Apatouria to decide on the qualifications of the children whose parents were trying to secure their admission, and some of the accounts of these gatherings which we possess suggest that the members were more intimate than would have been possible in a society of 1,500 members.[5] In view of these difficulties, and in default of positive evidence to the contrary, we must conclude that the number of phratries at Athens was far greater than twelve in the fifth and fourth centuries, and also in the aristocratic state of the pre-Solonian period.[6]

[1] By Ferguson in *C.P.* v, 1910, 264. But in his article cited above he expresses the view (p. 157) that 'the chances are against their having been as few as twelve'.

[2] On these cf. *R.-E.* xx. 751–2 and Wade-Gery in *C.Q.* xxv, 1931, 131, n. 3. Latte in *R.-E.* argues that these ceremonies were for boys only, not girls, who instead were admitted on marriage to the phratry of their husband with the offering of the γαμηλία (cf. Pollux, viii. 107 cited in *S.I.G.* iii. 921, n. 6). That a daughter was introduced, presumably within a year of her birth, by her father to his phratry is proved by Isaios iii. 73.

[3] e.g. *I.G.* i². 110 (Tod, 86) 14 ff. and ii². 237 (Tod, ii. 178) 21 f.

[4] Cf. Wil. ii. 276.

[5] Cf. Sauppe, loc. cit. (with citation of Plato, *Timaios* 21 B), and J. H. Lipsius in *Leipziger Studien*, xvi, 1894, 170 f. A phratry-list from the early fourth century (*I.G.* ii². 2344) contains only twenty names (text and discussion by A. Körte in *Hermes*, xxxvii, 1902, 582–9) but it has been doubted whether this represented the full membership of the phratry; A. von Premerstein (*Ath. Mitt.* xxxv, 1910, 113) maintained that the twenty constituted a thiasos.

[6] Sauppe thought that Kleisthenes had been responsible for the increase in the number of the phratries. The alternative (for those who do not believe that there were only twelve phratries in the fifth century) is to suppose that there never were twelve, and that on this point the Atthidographers were wrong. Cf. de Sanctis, 58 and *R.-E.* xx. 748.

The γένη and the θίασοι

According to the Atthis[1] the γένη were created in the time
of Ion as subdivisions of the phratry, thirty to each of the
twelve phratries; there is no reference to the thiasoi, and it is
assumed that every citizen is a member of a genos. Genē which
number 360 and each of which contains exactly thirty members
cannot be units based on real kinship. Artificial genē created
by a radical reorganization of the citizen-body are found later
in Samos,[2] but their appearance in primitive Attica must be
due to the Atthidographers' passion for symmetry. The account
given by the Atthis shows that its authors regarded the genos
as a subdivision of the phratry, and as such earlier than the
thiasos.

Philochoros[3] quotes a law which ordained that the phratry
must admit καὶ τοὺς ὀργεῶνας καὶ τοὺς ὁμογάλακτας οὓς γεννήτας
καλοῦμεν. The view of Wilamowitz[4] that Philochoros was merely
quoting a by-law of a particular phratry has been generally
rejected, but though this law must be a law of the state its
date is uncertain. It has been attributed by some scholars to
Kleisthenes, by others to Solon;[5] the word ὀργεῶνες certainly
occurred in laws attributed by ancient antiquarians to Solon,[6]
but even if these laws were demonstrably Solonian the thiasoi
of orgeones to which they referred might be different from those
recognized in a later period by the state as subdivisions of the
phratries. Further, the significance of the law quoted by Philochoros is not clear; does it lay down a new rule or reaffirm an
old one? Had the orgeones previously enjoyed membership of
the phratries, or were they now being admitted for the first
time? In any case no one doubts that the law of Philochoros
must be Kleisthenic at latest, and that after Kleisthenes' reforms, if not before, citizenship was not confined to members of
the genē.

The social prestige of the gennetai was certainly higher in
later times than that of the orgeones. Aischines[7] boasts that the

---

[1] A.P., fr. 3.
[2] C.A.H. v. 315–16 and the article by Swoboda cited on p. 517; cf. BS 260 f.
and Busolt, iii, 1428, n. 3.   [3] Fr. 94 (35 in Jacoby, F.G.H. iii B).
[4] ii. 269–70; cf. Latte in R.-E. xx. 751.   [5] See below, Note C.
[6] e.g. Seleukos cited in F.H.G. iii. 500 (fr. 1 in Jacoby, F.G.H. iii B, no. 341);
cf. de Sanctis, 65, n. 1 and 67, n. 1.
[7] ii. 147; Kahr. i. 233 seems to infer from εἶναι δ' ἐκ φατρίας τὸ γένος that
Atrometos also belonged to a genos.

phratry of his father Atrometos shares the same altars as the genos of the Eteoboutadai, which supplies the priestess of the state cult of Athena Polias; Atrometos clearly belonged to a thiasos, not a genos, but the members of this thiasos prided themselves on their inclusion in the same phratry as the Eteoboutadai. Probably they looked down on phratries which were composed entirely of thiasoi, like that of the Demotionidai, and considered it a distinction to be connected in any way with the Eteoboutadai, one of the most important genē. A parallel to this inclusion of two different types of groups in a phratry is provided by an inscription from Chios[1] which shows a phratry composed of two genē and various other groups (οἱ Ἕρμιος, οἱ Τηλάγρου, &c.).

These facts might be explained by the assumption that in the phratries the members of the genē, both at Athens and at Chios, were the descendants of the original inhabitants, whereas the orgeones were descended from aliens later admitted to citizenship. We might compare the contrast at Syracuse in the early fifth century between the demos and the aristocracy of γαμόροι, who seem to have been the descendants of the original colonists.[2] This explanation would agree with the early date given by the Atthis for the origin of the genē and with its silence about the thiasoi.

There are, however, formidable objections to the view that the genē were contemporaneous with the phratries. Homer mentions the phratry and the ἔται but knows nothing of the genos; his κασίγνητοι are to be identified not with the gennetai but with the ἀγχιστεῖς.[3] The genos has no place in the civil or criminal law of archaic Athens. It is the phratry, not the genos, to which certain functions are assigned in the homicide laws of Drakon;[4] the members of a murdered man's phratry are associated with his near relatives in the prosecution of his murderer, and in cases of involuntary homicide, when there are no near relatives of the victim still living, the ten men who are to decide whether the murderer may be allowed to return are chosen from the victim's phratry. If an Athenian died without a will, an old law ordained that preference should be given to

---

[1] Michel, *Recueil*, no. 1114; cf. *S.I.G.* iii. 987, n. 1 and BS 254, n. 1.
[2] Cf. Hdt. vii. 155. 2, with the note in How and Wells.
[3] See above, p. 58 and n. 5. On what follows cf. de Sanctis, 56 ff.
[4] [Dem.] xliii. 57 and *I.G.* i². 115 (Tod, 87).

his ἀγχιστεῖς, but if he had no near relatives on his father's side the property passed not to his genos but to his mother's relatives.[1] These facts cannot easily be reconciled with a belief in the early origin of the genos. But before we examine the modern theories on this question we must first consider what is known about the genē of the classical period.

The genos in the fifth and fourth centuries was a group of families which believed themselves to be descended from a single ancestor, who was always a hero or a god.[2] It must be distinguished from a family group such as the Peisistratidai, who were the direct descendants of a prominent member of the family and called themselves by a name formed patronymically from his.[3] The Bouselidai mentioned in the speech against Makartatos were the descendants to the fourth generation in the male line of Bouselos of Oion and shared the same family tomb. Such a group seems to have been called an οἶκος,[4] and might form part of a genos.

Every Athenian claimed to be descended from a god, Apollo Patroös,[5] but only the members of the genē professed to be able to trace their descent in an unbroken line to the mythical ancestor who was always the founder of a particular genos. It is to be noted that such descent was traced in the male line only[6]—a member of a genos belongs to the genos of his father. But though membership of a genos was governed by this rule, a member of one genos might boast of his descent in the female line from an ancestor of another and more distinguished genos; this seems to be the explanation of Alkibiades' claim to descent from Eurysakes.[7] As the ancestor of the genos was always a mythical figure, we cannot be sure whether the members of a genos in the fifth century were actually descended from an original group of interrelated families or not; Toepffer and others believe that the connexion between the families composing a genos was artificial from the beginning.

[1] Isaios xi. 1–2 and [Dem.] xliii. 51. The law of Gortyn states (vii. 47 ff.) that an heiress who is not sought in marriage by her near relatives may take a husband from the same *tribe*.   [2] BS 249; cf. Wade-Gery in *C.Q.* xxv, 1931, 1.

[3] Cf. Wade-Gery in *C.Q.* xxv, 82. On the Bouselidai cf. [Dem.] xliii. 79 ff.

[4] Hdt. v. 66. 1 (οἰκίη) and Plut. *Per.* 3. 1. Wade-Gery (op. cit. 82 ff.) thinks that the Alkmaionidai were an οἰκίη in this sense as being the direct descendants of the Alkmaion who was a contemporary of Solon, but they are usually regarded as a γένος on the evidence of Pausanias ii. 18. 9.

[5] Plato, *Euthydemos* 302 C.   [6] See above, p. 47, n. 1.

[7] Plato, *Alkibiades* i. 121 A; see, however, Meyer, *Forsch*, ii, n. 3 on pp. 532–3.

Most of the names of genē which have been preserved[1] are patronymic in form; seven are geographical. A few genē, such as the Αἰγειροτόμοι, were called by names which are names of occupations; these were apparently fancy names, perhaps comparable with the devices of canting heraldry,[2] and cannot be regarded as evidence for the origins of the genē which bore them.

As some of the demes or parishes of Attica have a name which is identical with that of a genos,[3] it is probable that each genos had originally been connected with a particular district. This local connexion had certainly been impaired before the end of the sixth century, when Kleisthenes made membership of a deme the condition of citizenship. Kleisthenes assigned citizens to demes according to their place of residence, but for the future made membership of a deme hereditary in the male line like membership of a genos. As seven members of the genos Brytidai in the fourth century belonged to six different demes,[4] the ancestors of these gennetai must have been living in six different demes at the time of Kleisthenes' reforms.

The names of about fifty of the Athenian genē are known to us.[5] Their social importance in the classical period is attested by the fact that the priesthoods of some important state cults were hereditary in particular genē.[6] Thus the priestess of Athena Polias[7] and the priest of Poseidon Erechtheus were always chosen from the genos of the Eteoboutadai, and the Bouzygai held the priesthoods of Ζεὺς ἐν Παλλαδίῳ and Ζεὺς Τέλειος;[8] the Eleusinian genē of the Eumolpidai and the Kerykes were the heads of the Eleusinian mystery-cult, and the chief priests of the cult were chosen from these two families, the hierophant from the Eumolpidai, the other three (including the δᾳδοῦχος) from the Kerykes.[9]

---

[1] Cf. de Sanctis, 63 f. and n. 3.

[2] Cary in C.A.H. iii. 585; cf. Sir Walter Scott, Waverley, c. 14.

[3] Cf. de Sanctis, 62, n. 3.   [4] [Dem.] lix. 61.

[5] Cf. de Sanctis, 63, n. 3. On the Salaminioi see below, Note D.

[6] De Sanctis, 62.

[7] Aischines ii. 147. The evidence for the priesthood of Poseidon Erechtheus in [Plut.] vitae x oratorum (Moralia 843) seems dubious, though Toepffer held that if the male line died out a priesthood could descend in the female line. Cf. also Apollodoros, Bibliotheca iii. 15. 1 and the evidence cited ad loc. by Frazer (Loeb edition, vol. ii).

[8] I.G. ii². 5055 and 5075 (also 3177); cf. Toepffer, A.G. 145–7 and S. Wide in Ausonia, vii, 1912, 192–3.

[9] For the evidence cf. Dittenberger in Hermes, xx, 1885, 1–40.

Some of these cults may originally have been cults of the
genē which had later been taken over by the state, others seem
to have been from the first state cults. Each genos had its own
cult independent of the state cults; thus the Eteoboutadai worshipped their founder Boutes,[1] the gennetai of Isagoras sacrificed
to Karian Zeus,[2] and the cult of Demeter Achaia is said by
Herodotus[3] to be limited to the Gephyraioi, the genos to which
Harmodios and Aristogeiton belonged.

The succession to the priesthoods of the state cults can be
shown in some cases to be a perquisite not of the genos but of
a particular branch of it; the office of δᾳδοῦχος at Eleusis was
held in unbroken succession for several generations by a particular family within the genos of the Kerykes, the descendants
of Phainippos,[4] and the priesthood of Poseidon Erechtheus
seems to have been hereditary in the family of the orator
Lykourgos.[5]

This fact complicates still further the question about the
origin of the genē. It is likely that the aristocrats in the period
of their ascendancy had secured control of the chief priesthoods
and retained their monopoly of their priestly functions after the
loss of their political powers. Kallias, who held the priestly
office of δᾳδοῦχος, is known to have been a Eupatrid.[6] But if the
priesthood belongs in each case to the particular family and
not to the whole genos,[7] it is unsafe to infer the character of the
whole from that of the part. Some gennetai were Eupatridai;
probably all Eupatridai were gennetai.[8] But were all gennetai
members of the Eupatrid order?

The author of the *Athenaion Politeia* seems to have believed
that the genē still included plebeian members after the creation
of the Eupatrid order by Theseus, but it is unsafe to assume
that his statement was based on the composition of the genē
in his own time. Equally inconclusive is the recent attempt to
prove from a fragment of Polemon that the genē always contained members who were not Eupatrids.[9] But though this view

[1] Toepffer, *A.G.* 16 and 20. On Boutes cf. Frazer's Apollodorus, ii. 101, n. 2.
[2] Hdt. v. 66. 1, where συγγενέες = γεννῆται; cf. Wade-Gery in *C.Q.* xxv. 82, n. 1.
[3] v. 61. 2.　　　　　　　　　　[4] Dittenberger, op. cit. 10 and 22.
[5] Cf. Toepffer, *A.G.* 127.　　　　　　[6] Xen. *Symposion* 8. 40.
[7] P. Roussel in *Mélanges Bidez* (1934), ii. 831 suggests the possibility that if
the sons of a dead δᾳδοῦχος were not old enough to undertake the duties the
priesthood passed to another branch of the family.
[8] It is unlikely that any Eupatrid was not a member of a genos, in spite of
Wade-Gery's remarks in *C.Q.* xxv. 130.　　　　[9] See Appendix II, pp. 315 f.

cannot be proved beyond a doubt, it remains a tenable hypothesis, and has recently been revived by Kahrstedt, who has
put forward the following version of it:[1]

'Originally all citizens who owned land, including non-nobles,
were members of the genē. In the economic crisis which preceded Solon's reforms, many small freeholders lost their land
and were in consequence excluded from the genē, which in this
way lost their original character and came to be almost wholly
composed of aristocratic members. Solon restored the citizenship to the dispossessed farmers and extended it to those who
had previously been excluded from full citizen-rights. In order
to facilitate their entry into the phratries he organized them in
thiasoi, and imposed on the phratries by law the obligation to
admit them to membership along with the gennetai.'

This reconstruction is certainly in harmony with the Atthis.
But it is arguable that the expropriation of the small freeholders
of Attica in the generation before Solon has been exaggerated
by the author of the *Athenaion Politeia*,[2] and after all the account of the Atthis is itself probably a reconstruction with no
special claim on our acceptance. It may have been excogitated
by an Athenian aristocrat who regarded the gennetai as the
only representatives of the original Athenian stock and looked
down on the rest as the descendants of serfs, freedmen, and
alien intruders. Or it may be the work of a writer[3] who was
familiar with a state in which the genē had successfully usurped
all political privileges and had excluded the rest of the population from citizenship; so in Samos, when the democracy
triumphed, the aristocratic genē were drastically reorganized
and thrown open to the commons.

The Atthis evades the difficulty about the origin of the
Eupatrid order by making it the creation of Theseus at the
unification.[4] This is almost certainly pure fiction, as there must
have been local aristocracies before the unification. It is not
a fatal weakness in the hypothesis which we have been con-
sidering that it does not provide a simple criterion of Eupatrid
birth such as the identification of Eupatrids and gennetai

[1] i. 231 ff.
[2] Cf. W. J. Woodhouse, *Solon*, c. 3 (especially pp. 19–20).
[3] De Sanctis, 59 suggested Hellanikos; on Samos see above, p. 61, n. 2.
[4] So Wade-Gery in *C.Q.* xxv. 4 ff., but it is not certain that the crucial passage
of Plut. *Theseus* (25. 2) is from an Atthis or even from 'Aristotle'; cf. Jac. 247,
n. 49.

postulated by the rival theory; the aristocrats themselves may have decided whether a new family was of sufficient age and importance to be admitted to the circle of the governing class. The fundamental objection to the account of the Atthis and to the modern views based on it is that they fail to meet the arguments for the late origin of the genē.

These arguments are the chief support of the rival theory, which maintains that the genē were aristocratic corporations and that all gennetai were Eupatridai. Meyer, the principal advocate of this theory,[1] suggested that the genos was originally an association of families (which may or may not have been interrelated) who had acquired landed possessions in the more settled conditions which followed the great migrations, and combined to promote their interests at the expense of their poorer neighbours. As they claimed to trace their descent in unbroken line from a heroic or divine ancestor, they called themselves εὐπατρίδαι, and on the overthrow of the monarchy established a monopoly of political and religious functions which lasted until the reforms of Solon. But owing to the lateness of their origin the genē as such had no place in the civil or criminal law of Athens. Moreover, the non-nobles had formed associations of their own within the phratries called thiasoi, and the gennetai were never powerful enough to expel the non-nobles from the phratries and thereby deprive them of citizenship; the presence of non-nobles in the phratries is attested by Drakon's law of homicide, if the relevant clause of the law[2] is really pre-Solonian. Finally, the question was settled by the law, due either to Solon or to Kleisthenes,[3] which guaranteed for the future the right of members of the thiasoi to inclusion in the phratries and in the citizen-body.

In what follows I accept the theory of Meyer, and assume that every Eupatrid was a member of a genos and every gennetēs was a Eupatrid.

The naukrariai and the trittyes

Herodotus introduces the ναύκραροι in connexion with the conspiracy of Kylon, which he dates vaguely 'before the age of Peisistratos'; he declares that their presidents (πρυτάνεις)

---

[1] *G.A.* iii². 278 ff. and *Forsch.* ii. 517 ff.
[2] *I.G.* i². 115 (Tod, 87), ll. 18–19.
[3] See above, p. 61, n. 3.

were at that time the supreme executive of Athens.[1] The ναυκραρίαι are first mentioned by the Atthidographers. A fragment of Kleidemos[2] states that when Kleisthenes altered the organization of the tribes the naukraries were affected by the change, and henceforth were fifty in number. The author of the *Athenaion Politeia* asserts[3] that each of the four old tribes was divided into three trittyes and twelve naukraries, and that this division already existed before the reforms of Solon. In his account the naukraroi are officials at the head of the naukraries, responsible for taxation and expenditure; as he compares them later[4] with the demarchs, he must mean that there was one naukraros at the head of each naukrary, or forty-eight in all. He adds that Kleisthenes created the demes to replace the naukraries, and that the demarchs had the same functions as those previously exercised by the naukraroi.

As evidence of the financial duties of the naukraroi he cites passages from 'the old laws of Solon which they no longer use'[3] which frequently mention that 'the naukraroi shall collect the money' or that 'they shall pay out the money from the ναυκραρικὸν ἀργύριον'. These citations from the law seem to have been taken from Androtion, who is quoted by a scholiast for the statement that the κωλακρέται were to supply envoys to Delphi with a travelling allowance from the ναυκραρικὰ ἀργύρια.[5] Possibly Androtion was also the source for two other quotations from the law given by Photios[6] (a) ἐάν τις ναυκραρίας ἀμφισβητῇ and (b) τοὺς ναυκράρους τοὺς κατὰ τὴν ναυκραρίαν; the second of these seems to imply that there was more than one naukraros in a naukraria.[7]

Elsewhere[8] the naukraroi are defined as 'those who provided the ships and acted as trierarchs and were subordinate to the polemarch'. Pollux says[9] that each naukrary supplied a ship and two horsemen. Hesychios defines the ναύκλαροι (*sic*) as 'those who collected the levies of taxation from each district and who were later called demarchs'. This suggestion that the naukraries were local divisions is supported by a lexicographer's comment on the word Κωλιάς: 'a region of Attica . . . also a naukraria'.[10]

---

[1] v. 71. 2.　　　　[2] Fr. 8 (cited from Bk. III).　　　　[3] 8. 3.
[4] 21. 5.　　　　　　　　　　　　　　　　　[5] Fr. 4 (36 in Jacoby).
[6] Cited by Sandys, 33, Gilbert, 133, n. 1.
[7] The plural is explained otherwise by de Sanctis, 142, n. 2.
[8] In Bekker, *Anecd*. i. 283. 20.　　　　　　[9] viii. 108.
[10] Bekker, *Anecd*. i. 275. 20. But Beloch, i². 2. 323–4 points out that there was a

No definite date is given by the ancient writers for the institution of the naukraroi or of the naukrariai. The view of the Atthidographers that they were pre-Solonian seems to be merely a deduction from the mention of the naukraroi in Herodotus; as they dated Kylon's unsuccessful coup before the legislation of Drakon they naturally concluded that the naukraroi existed in the aristocratic state. But though we must reject the ingenious modern attempt[1] to bring the Kylonian conspiracy down to the interval between Peisistratos' second loss of power and his final tyranny, the solution of the problem is not so simple. Thucydides pointed out that the nine archons were the chief executive at Athens in the time of Kylon, and the position assigned in Herodotus to the presidents of the naukraroi must be derived from a source which was trying to shift the responsibility for the execution of the Kylonians from the chief archon, the Alkmaionid Megakles.[2] Naturally the presidents of the naukraroi must have been important enough to make the invention plausible, but this condition is valid not for the generation of Kylon but for that in which the apologia for the Alkmaionidai was first put forward; the authors of the apologia transferred the blame for the murder of the Kylonians to the presidents of the naukraroi because they had been sufficiently important within living memory to give colour to the assertion of their guilt. But if the apologia was invented during the political strife between Isagoras and the Alkmaionid Kleisthenes, it would merely show that the naukraroi and their presidents had existed under the tyranny.[3]

If the obsolete laws cited by Androtion were genuine laws of Solon, they would prove that the naukrariai either existed before Solon or were created by him, but it is impossible to feel any confidence in Androtion's attribution of these laws to Solon. As the naukrariai were finally abolished on the occasion of the reorganization of the Athenian navy by Themistokles, any law which mentioned them as still existing would be prior to 483 and

genos called Κωλιεῖς and maintains that the name of the naukrary must have been derived from it.

[1] De Sanctis, 280 ff., Beloch, i². 2. 302 ff.; against their view cf. F. E. Adcock in *C.A.H.* iv. 661–2 and Ledl, 77–104, also Jac. 366, n. 77 and 367, n. 81.

[2] Cf. Jac. 187 and 368, n. 84; he points out that Thucydides also was trying to exculpate the Alkmaionidai and criticizes the accuracy of his statement in i. 126. 8.

[3] This argument is implicit in the remarks of Ledl, 98 (cf. 397). It is possible that the apologia belongs to a date in the second half of the fifth century.

therefore sufficiently archaic to be ascribed to Solon without question by a fourth-century antiquarian.[1]

Thus the creation of the naukraries, though almost certainly pre-Kleisthenic, need not be earlier than the rule of Peisistratos. Those who make Peisistratos the author of the naukraric system urge that the functions of the naukraries as described by the Atthidographers presuppose a degree of centralization in administration which is inconceivable before the tyranny. So de Sanctis[2] stresses the statements in the *Athenaion Politeia* that the naukraroi were concerned with the εἰσφοραὶ and controlled a permanent naukraric treasury as proof that the naukraries must have been instituted under the tyranny, when direct taxation was first introduced. The primary object of their institution was to revive and develop the naval power of Athens, but as the taxes collected by the naukraroi were not used exclusively for naval purposes, the choice of the name naukrariai may have been partly intended to disguise the real nature of the new fiscal organization and to justify it to the taxpayers by the needs of maritime defence.

This explanation of the name is not entirely convincing, and de Sanctis has not considered the possibility that Peisistratos may have remodelled and adapted to new purposes a pre-existing system, which previously had only been used for the organization of the navy. Naukraros seems to mean a ship-captain;[3] possibly in early times the captain and the owner of the ship were identical. Kahrstedt[4] maintains that Athens did not possess any state-owned warships before 483, and in time of war had to levy ships from private shipowners. These, the naukraroi, were organized in groups called naukrariai, and each group supplied one of its ships when a fleet was required. As the naukrary was not a division of the citizen-body but a group of rich individuals, it was rightly compared by Kleidemos to the symmoriai of taxpayers in his own day.

Kahrstedt[5] argues that though every shipowner was a naukraros, the term must be used in a more restricted sense in references to the naukraros as an official, to denote the leading man in a naukrary; he suggests that these heads or presidents of

---

[1] See above, pp. 21 f. Beloch, i[2]. 2. 327 dates the law to the time of Peisistratos. Possibly the new laws enacted by Peisistratos would be inscribed on wood and added to the pre-existing ἄξονες.

[2] 306 f.   [3] Cf. H. Hommel in *R.-E.* xvi. 2. 1938 ff. and Kahr. i. 246–7.

[4] Op. cit. 246 ff.   [5] Op. cit. 248 and top of 247.

the naukraric groups were called 'prytaneis', and that they were the prytaneis of the naukraroi mentioned by Herodotus. Possibly ἀμφισβητεῖν ναυκραρίας may indicate a dispute between rival claimants to the position of prytanis.[1]

This hypothesis provides a plausible account of the origins of the system, and English history affords a parallel for the imposition of the costs of naval defence on the inhabitants of the coastal districts. But when the naukraries were compelled, perhaps by Peisistratos, to undertake other administrative functions,[2] the organization must have been extended to cover the whole of Attica, or alternatively all the wealthier citizens who were liable to taxation.

The presidents of the naukraroi may at this stage have become responsible for the mustering of the hoplites, and it has been suggested[3] that this may be the reason for their prominence in Herodotus' account of the Kylonian affair, as the Kylonians are said by Thucydides[4] to have been besieged in the Acropolis by the whole citizen levy. But it is unsafe to conflate in this manner the narratives of Herodotus and Thucydides; Herodotus gives a very peculiar version of the conspiracy which is quite different from that of Thucydides and implies that the conspirators were detected before they were able to seize the Acropolis.[5]

We have seen that according to the account given in the *Athenaion Politeia*[6] each tribe was divided into three trittyes, and there were twelve naukraries to each tribe. The form of statement employed indicates that the trittyes and the naukraries represent two different systems of subdivision, and the assertion in Pollux[7] that there were four naukraries to each trittys may well be no more than a hasty inference from this passage; thus the trittyes probably had no connexion with the naukraries.

Till recently little was known of these pre-Solonian trittyes, and they were sometimes dismissed as an anachronistic anticipation of the Kleisthenic trittyes.[8] This view has now been refuted

---

[1] Hommel, op. cit. 1947 (cf. Kahr. 248, n. 2) thinks that the phrase may indicate an attempt to evade the obligations of a naukraros, and compares the ἀντίδοσις.

[2] Hommel assumes an evolution in the functions of the naukraries but regards their financial functions as pre-Solonian.

[3] By Busolt, ii². 190, n. 2.   [4] i. 126. 7.

[5] Cf. Ledl, 398–402.   [6] 8. 3.   [7] viii. 108.

[8] e.g. by R. W. Macan in his edition of Hdt. iv–vi, vol. ii, p. 136, and by de Sanctis, 59 and 308, n. 3.

by the discovery of an Athenian inscription which refers to the trittys of the Leukotainioi as a subdivision of the old Attic tribe of the Geleontes.[1] The inscription, which contains regulations for state sacrifices, belongs to the end of the fifth century, and shows that the four old tribes and their subdivisions retained religious privileges long after they had been deprived of all political importance; presumably the Geleontes, who always come first of the four tribes on inscriptions, offered the sacrifice on behalf of all the four tribes.[2]

It is unlikely that the twelve trittyes originated in the same period as the four tribes, and they were probably an artificial creation. The date and purpose of these subdivisions cannot be determined; probably nothing was known of them in the fourth century except their survival within the four old tribes, and their ascription to the pre-Solonian period must have been merely a reasonable conjecture. Religious functions are clearly implied for the original trittyes by the name Leukotainioi;[3] they can hardly have been created merely to offer sacrifices, but their other functions are unknown.

The twelve trittyes are identified with the twelve phratries by some of the lexicographers, who claim for the identification the authority of the *Athenaion Politeia*.[4] This identification cannot be accepted by those who maintain that the phratries must have numbered more than twelve, but it may have been made by the author of the *Athenaion Politeia*, who certainly held that there were twelve phratries in the time of Ion,[5] and it is not sufficient disproof of the identity to point to the existence of the two names.[6] Busolt, however, suggested that the lexicographers misinterpreted their source;[7] the real meaning of the passage which they garbled was that each tribe was divided in three ways, into ἔθνη (the social classes), into phratries, and into trittyes. But whatever may have been the view of the Atthis, the trittyes had no more connexion with the phratries than they had with the naukraries.

What was the relation between the naukraries and the tribal organization? They were almost certainly not subdivisions of

[1] Cf. J. H. Oliver in *Hesperia*, iv, 1935, 5 ff. (also Ferguson's article cited above, p. 59, n. 5). The relevant passage is lines 30 ff. of Oliver's second inscription.
[2] Cf. Ferguson, op. cit. 154.
[3] Ibid., 157.
[4] Cf. *A.P.*, fr. 3 in Kenyon's text.
[5] See above, p. 48.
[6] As Ferguson does (op. cit. 157).
[7] ii². 107, n. 3.

the trittyes or of the phratries; with the trittyes they are connected only in the untrustworthy statement of Pollux, and the
same statement, interpreted on the erroneous assumption that
phratry and trittys were identical, is the sole warrant for any
connexion between the naukraries and the phratries. That they
were subdivisions of the four tribes, twelve to each tribe, is
explicitly stated by the author of the *Athenaion Politeia*.[1] But
how, if they were administrative districts, could they have been
related to an organization based on the principle of birth?
Meyer's solution,[2] that the tribal divisions were originally local,
is improbable. Others[3] have assumed that the connexion between the naukraries and the tribes is a figment of the Atthidographers, whose failure to realize the difficulties involved in the
alleged connexion is said to be characteristic of their superficial
approach to the problems of the aristocratic state.[4]

De Sanctis[5] maintains that not only the connexion but even
the number forty-eight was invented by the Atthidographers.
Accepting from Kleidemos the statement that in the time of
Kleisthenes there were fifty naukraries and from the *Athenaion
Politeia* the view that they were abolished by Kleisthenes, he
concludes that there were always fifty naukraries as long as they
existed, and that therefore they cannot have been subdivisions
of the four tribes.

This argument is unsound; it is just as likely that the fifty
naukraries in Kleidemos may be a fiction due to his assumption
that the naukraries must have been reorganized by Kleisthenes
to form subdivisions of his ten new tribes. In any case the assertion in the *Athenaion Politeia* that the naukraries were abolished
by Kleisthenes and replaced by the demes is improbable; Macan[6]
has shown that the author's parallel between the naukrary and
the deme is in many respects unsatisfactory.

Some of the difficulties are removed if the connexion between
the naukraries and the phratries is rejected, and if a naukrary is
regarded as a group of taxpayers rather than a subdivision of
the whole citizen-body.[7] A naukrary might in that case have
been composed of the tax-payers living in a certain region who
belonged to a particular tribe. But if members of each of the

---

[1] 8. 3. [2] *Forsch*. ii. 529. [3] e.g. de Sanctis, 308.
[4] Wil. ii. 147–8.
[5] Loc. cit. [6] Op. cit. 139.
[7] Cf. Beloch, i². 2. 325 and Hasebroek, 55–58.

four tribes were to be found in various parts of Attica,[1] we should have to assume a division of Attica into twelve regions, each containing four naukraries. The ancient authorities, however,[2] seem to imply a closer connexion between a naukrary and a particular locality than is provided by this explanation. Our evidence is conflicting and insufficient for a final solution of the problems which it raises; if we stress the passages which describe the naukraries as local divisions we must conclude that they cannot have been subdivisions of the four tribes.

The magistrates and the council

The development of the magistracy at Athens was due partly to the devolution of powers originally held by the king, partly to the growing complexity of judicial business.[3] Even the basileus, archon, and polemarch, who shared the powers originally united in the kingship, acquired a jurisdiction which seems to have been in the main a later accretion to their original functions, and the duties of the six thesmothetai were apparently from the first purely judicial. This evolution reflects the gradual assumption by the state of the responsibility for the maintenance of public order and of the right to regulate disputes between its members.[4] In the developed democracy the judicial functions of these magistrates were limited to the holding of the preliminary inquiry and to the presidency over the court of jurors which tried the case,[5] but in the aristocratic state each magistrate must have been competent to decide without assistance or interference the cases brought before him,[6] though there may have been a right of appeal to the council against unjust decisions.[7]

Of these magistrates the archon was clearly the most important. He had displaced the king as the supreme executive in civil affairs, and as such probably presided over the meetings of the council and the popular assembly.[8] As head of the govern-

---

[1] De Sanctis, 308. [2] Cf. Bekker, *Anecd*. i. 275. 20.
[3] De Sanctis, 119. [4] Ibid. 118.
[5] See below, pp. 221 ff. [6] Kahr. i. 162–3 and 163, n. 1.

[7] The right is mentioned only in the bogus 'constitution of Drakon' (*A.P.* 4. 4) but may well be authentic; cf. Bonner and Smith, 95 f.

[8] Greenidge, *Handbook*, 136. See below, pp. 83 and 92. The archon presumably presided over the council except when it sat as a homicide court (BS 791 suppose that the basileus continued to preside over the Areopagus even after he became an annual official; this view seems improbable).

ment he had his official residence in the Prytaneion,[1] the centre
of the polis, which contained the sacred hearth of the state. In
the proclamation made by the archon at the beginning of his
year of office he guaranteed the security of private property,[2]
and he had jurisdiction in all cases arising out of the rights of
parents, orphans, and heiresses;[3] thus he was concerned to
maintain the interests and the permanence of the family. His
religious functions were naturally connected with those ceremonies which were later in origin than the archonship; the
earliest of them appears to be the appointment of the chief
Athenian representative sent to the Ionian festival of Delos.[4]
The concentration of such wide powers in a single magistrate is
characteristic of this stage of political development in Greece
according to Aristotle,[5] who sees in it one of the main causes of
the rise of the early tyrannies. It is not surprising that at Athens
the archonship was the magistracy which was the chief object
of political ambition and of party strife in this period, as it
continued to be until early in the fifth century.[6]

The polemarch had taken over from the king the command of
the army, and seems to have been responsible in the last resort
for the mustering of the fleet.[7] In the field he presumably had
full power to punish military offences, including the right to
inflict sentence of death.[8] His civil jurisdiction was limited to
cases affecting the position or interests of aliens resident in
Attica.[9] As leader of the army he offered the state sacrifices to
Enyalios.[10]

Although the basileus had lost most of the powers of the old
kingship he retained its religious privileges;[11] he supervised the
state religion and controlled the sacrifices of the oldest cults.
His jurisdiction was connected with his official functions; thus
he tried all offences against religion and settled disputes about
the succession to the hereditary priesthoods. When the state
suppressed blood-feuds, the presidency in all the courts created
for the various types of homicide cases was reserved for the king.
His wife, who bore the title basilinna or basilissa, also presided

---

[1] A.P. 3. 5.   [2] A.P. 56. 2.
[3] A.P. 56. 6; cf. Glotz and Cohen, i. 398–9.
[4] A.P. 56. 3 (end); cf. de Sanctis, 122–3.
[5] Politics 1305ª15; cf. BS 787.   [6] A.P. 13. 2.
[7] See above, p. 68, n. 8.   [8] De Sanctis, 126; Kahr. ii. 245.
[9] A.P. 58. 2–3; cf. de Sanctis, 126 ff.
[10] A.P. 58. 1.   [11] Details in A.P. 57.

over some of the ceremonies of the state religion, and in the
annual rite which celebrated the mystical marriage of Dionysos
she represented the bride of the god. This rite took place in the
Boukoleion, which on this ground was assumed by the Atthis
to have been originally the official residence of the basileus.[1]
But the inference may be unfounded, and perhaps the basileus
continued to live on the Acropolis in the palace of his predecessors, the Medontid kings, until the occupation of the Acropolis
by Peisistratos compelled him to remove to the Stoa Basileios.[2]

Little is known of the four phylobasileis, who even in later
times were chosen from the Eupatridai.[3] In the fourth century
they were associated with the basileus in the homicide court
which sat at the Prytaneion. The jurisdiction of this court was
a curious survival which preserved the ideas of a more primitive
age.[4] It tried cases of homicide in which the murderer was
unknown, passing sentence in such cases on the instrument with
which the murder had been committed; it also tried and convicted animals or inanimate objects which had caused the death
of a human being. Possibly the court of the basileus and the
phylobasileis had once possessed a wider and more important
jurisdiction, but the view that it retained extensive judicial
powers in the seventh century must be rejected.[5] Apart from
their participation in this court we have no clue to the original
functions of the phylobasileis. Whatever these may have been,
it is probable that they declined in importance with the decline
in the powers of the hereditary kingship.

The author of the *Athenaion Politeia* ascribes the origin of the
thesmothetai to a time later than the abolition of the decennial
magistrates, therefore later than 682/681, and declares[6] that they
were appointed in order to record judicial decisions and to preserve the record for the guidance of judges in similar cases.
Neither the date nor the motive here alleged for their institution
inspires any confidence. The date seems to be based on the
absence of any tradition that the office had ever been more
than annual, but despite the Atthis the magistracies held by
the archon and the polemarch must also have been annual from
the beginning; thus the conclusion is unsound. It is, however,

---

[1] *A.P.* 3. 5 and [Dem.] lix. 72–79.   [2] Cf. de Sanctis, 155–6.
[3] Cf. K. Latte in *R.-E.* xx. 1027–8 and Sandys on *A.P.* 8. 3.
[4] Cf. *A.P.* 57. 4 (end) and the authorities cited by Sandys in his note.
[5] Cf. de Sanctis, 188 ff. and see below, Appendix II, pp. 311 f.
[6] 3. 4. Cf. Ledl, 268 ff. and Bonner and Smith, 85 ff.

a priori probable that the thesmothetai were later in origin than the archon and the polemarch; that they were at least pre-Solonian is shown by Thucydides' reference[1] to the nine archons as the chief executive of Athens at the time of the Kylonian conspiracy. The motive given in the *Athenaion Politeia* for their creation is obviously no more than an inference from their name.[2] It ignores the fact that the name was sometimes applied to all the nine archons,[3] and does not account for the independent jurisdiction later exercised by the thesmothetai.

Probably the thesmothetai were so called, as Thirlwall suggested,[4] 'because, in the absence of a written code, those who declare and interpret the laws may properly be said to make them'. Hence the name could be used of all the archons, but was usually restricted to the six junior archons. The six thesmothetai appear to have been the first magistrates in Athens whose duties were exclusively judicial. It is possible that there were not six at first, and that the number gradually increased with the growth of the state's jurisdiction;[5] this view would imply that they tried cases independently, not as a board.

Though the archon, polemarch, basileus, and thesmothetai are often grouped together as 'the nine archons' they did not form a college.[6] Each of the three senior magistrates had his own official residence and his own sphere of jurisdiction, though later they occasionally dined together with the six junior magistrates in the Thesmotheteion.[7] Thucydides refers to 'the nine archons' as the chief executive in the age of Kylon, but it was the archon Megakles who had to bear the responsibility for the murder of the Kylonians.[8]

These magistrates had few helpers in the business of administration. The polemarch was perhaps assisted by four strategoi,[9] each responsible for mustering and leading the citizen levy of a single tribe, and the naukraric organization may have existed in a primitive form for the organization of the fleet. Probably the financial system was first elaborated by the tyrants,

---

[1] i. 126. 8 (but note the criticism of this passage in Jac. 187–8).

[2] Bonner and Smith, 85, following de Sanctis, 133.

[3] Dem. lvii. 66 (cf. 70); cf. also passages cited by BS 801, n. 5.

[4] *History of Greece*, ii. 17 (cited by Sandys on *A.P.* 3. 4) = ii. 20 in the edition of 1846. [5] De Sanctis, 137. But cf. Busolt, ii². 179, n. 1.

[6] Cf. de Sanctis, 154–5 and Ledl, 271–2.

[7] *A.P.* 3. 5. [8] Cf. Jac. 187–8.

[9] W. Schwahn in *R.-E.*, Supplbd. vi, 1935, 1071 f. De Sanctis, 311, less probably, attributes their creation to Peisistratos.

but the κωλακρέται[1] may have supervised a central treasury of which the principal revenues must have been supplied by fines and confiscations, and the treasurers of the temple of Athena may have been already, as they were later,[2] officials appointed by the state.

The nine archons and the other officials must have been subject to some control in the exercise of their duties. Special powers had to be conferred on them, apparently by the popular assembly, to deal with the Kylonians,[3] which shows that in normal times they were responsible for their actions; perhaps there was a right of appeal to the council against illegal acts of a magistrate.[4] De Sanctis maintains that the control of the council over the executive was indirect and therefore ineffective, and also that the independence enjoyed by each of the magistrates must have fostered rivalry and anarchy.[5] But each magistrate had his own sphere of duties, and the control over the executive possessed by the council was adequate so long as its members were sufficiently united to enforce their will.

Tenure of the magistracies must have been reserved in the aristocratic state for members of the Eupatrid order.[6] The author of the *Athenaion Politeia* says[7] that wealth was a necessary qualification as well as birth; this may have been a condition not legally prescribed but observed in practice, as impoverished aristocrats would be unable to maintain their position among the richer members of their class.[8]

It is not certain how the magistrates were appointed at this time. In the *Athenaion Politeia*[9] we read that the Areopagus summoned before it the candidates for office, examined them, and then appointed the best man to each post. This statement echoes a passage in the *Areopagitikos* of Isokrates,[10] and may safely be dismissed as one of Isokrates' inventions to glorify the

---

[1] On the κωλακρέται cf. BS 599 and Gilbert, 114, n. 1, also *A.P.* 7. 3 and Androtion, fr. 4 (36 in Jacoby). See above, p. 21. The existence of debts owed to the state is presupposed in *A.P.* 6. 1.   [2] *A.P.* 8. 1.

[3] Thuc. i. 126. 8, on which cf. Wade-Gery in *C.Q.* xxvii, 1933, 22–23. Kahrstedt's view (ii. 278 and 203, n. 1) is affected by his acceptance of a post-Solonian date for the conspiracy of Kylon.

[4] See above, p. 74, n. 7.   [5] De Sanctis, 157.

[6] Ar. *Politics* 1293ᵇ7–11 stresses birth as the qualification for office in an aristocracy. So in Drakon's law (*I.G.* i². 115, l. 19) the committee of ten phratry members is chosen ἀριστίνδην by the Ephetai.

[7] 3. 1.   [8] Cf. Ledl, 380 f.

[9] 8. 2.   [10] vii. 22; cf. Ledl, 384, n. 1.

Areopagus. It is too good to be true that in all appointments to office in this period the most suitable man was invariably selected.

Aristotle in the *Politics*[1] seems to think that Solon in this respect made no change; if he is right, the magistrates before Solon must have been elected by the people. Election by the assembly of the people seems to be presupposed in our accounts of the appointment of Solon.[2] The balance of probability is in favour of popular election, though the minor magistrates may have been appointed by the Areopagus. It has been conjectured that when the transition took place from monarchy to aristocracy the assembly of the armed men secured the right to elect the archon as the price of its acquiescence in the change.[3] But in fact, if the nobles could agree among themselves on the choice of magistrates they could limit the nominations to the number of posts to be filled, and so reduce the part played by the assembly to a merely formal approval of the names submitted to it.[4]

Full citizenship, and with it membership of the popular assembly (ἐκκλησία or ἀγορά) was probably limited to those who owned their own land.[5] Legislation was almost unknown in pre-Solonian Athens,[6] administration and jurisdiction were in the hands of the executive and under the control of the council, and the assembly counted for little more than it did in the Homeric poems, except on the rare occasions when the dissensions of its rulers made its right of election to office something more than an empty formality.

So far it has been assumed that Athens in this period had a council of nobles which held the supreme power in the state, and in fact no one now doubts that there was such a council, the lineal descendant of the Homeric Council of Elders. Controversy is confined to the question whether there was any continuity between this council and the later Areopagus. In antiquity the terms in which the problem was stated were different: was the Areopagus created by Solon or had it existed before his reforms?

Plutarch in his *Life of Solon*[7] gives a summary of the contro-

---

[1] 1273[b]41–1274[a]2.   [2] *A.P.* 5. 2 and Plut. *Solon* 14.
[3] Cf. Ledl, 388–9.   [4] Ledl, 389.
[5] This supposition is accepted by those who believe that Solon admitted the Thetes to the ekklesia, e.g. Busolt, ii². 273, n. 1, Kahr. i. 59.
[6] On the legislation of Drakon see below, pp. 307 ff.
[7] 19. 3–5. Cf. J. W. Headlam in *C.R.* vi, 1892, 293–5, also Bonner and Smith, 88 ff. and Ledl, 286 ff.

versy. He begins with a statement of the popular view that the Areopagus owed its origin to Solon, and then cites the arguments put forward on either side. On one side it was urged that the homicide laws of Drakon never referred to the Areopagites but always spoke of the Ephetai, on the other that the Areopagus was mentioned in the amnesty-law of Solon in such a way as to prove its existence before his archonship.

Though Plutarch and later inquirers have taken these contentions seriously, they are both irrelevant to the question, and the problems raised by the evidence on which they rely may be relegated to an appendix.[1] Even if Plutarch or his authority had before him a complete copy of the homicide laws of Drakon, their silence about the Areopagus would not disprove its existence; it would merely show that, like the Roman senate, it had no judicial functions as a body. On the other side the amnesty-law, if genuinely Solonian, proves that there was a law-court[2] which tried cases of murder on the hill of Areopagus,[3] but not that its members also acted as a council; the Areopagus in the fourth century when it met as a council sat in the Stoa Basileios.[4] The popular Athenian belief that the Areopagus was instituted by Solon has been thought to represent an authentic ancient tradition,[5] but more probably it is merely an illustration of the fourth-century tendency to ascribe everything to Solon.

Though Isokrates shared the popular opinion,[6] his pupil Androtion seems to have maintained that the Areopagus was pre-Solonian,[7] and Aristotle in the *Politics*[8] decides that Solon did not abolish the council which he found in existence. The author of the *Athenaion Politeia* has no doubts, and describes[9] with an air of certitude the composition and powers of the Areopagus in the aristocratic state. But these powers are the same, and described by the author in almost the same words, as

---

[1] Appendix II, pp. 308 ff.
[2] Cf. Ledl, 296–7. On the date of the amnesty-law see below, Appendix II, p. 313.
[3] The existence of such a court is implied in our accounts of the legendary homicide trials; cf. Jac. 121.
[4] [Dem.] xxv. 23; cf. BS 794–5.   [5] Plut. *Solon* 19. 3; cf. Ledl, 320.
[6] This seems to follow from vii. 16 and 37; cf. Keil, 100–1. G. Mathieu, *Les idées politiques d'Isocrate* (Paris, 1925), 146–7, gives no ground for his belief that Isokrates in vii regarded the Areopagus as pre-Solonian. The views of Isokrates, xii, are peculiar; cf. Keil, 86 ff.
[7] This is denied by Jac. 74, but cf. Busolt, ii². 34, n. 3.
[8] 1273^{b}41–1274^{a}2.   [9] 3. 6.

those which he later attributes to the Areopagus under the constitution of Solon,[1] with the exception of one function which he believed to be demonstrably due to Solon himself. This shows that the author's account of the pre-Solonian Areopagus is no more than a bold reconstruction (perhaps due to Androtion) based on the assumption that its powers were substantially the same after Solon as before. His statement that it was composed of ex-archons before Solon must also be an inference from its composition in the post-Solonian period and has no claim to authority.[2]

Some modern scholars have concluded that the problem was wrongly stated by the ancient writers, and that the aristocratic council of pre-Solonian times was a body different in composition from the later Areopagus. It has been suggested[3] that the council was composed of the fifty-one Ephetai and the nine archons, but this is pure speculation, as there is no evidence that the Ephetai had any functions outside the homicide-courts presided over by the basileus.

Meyer[4] argued from Herodotus' reference to the presidents of the naukraroi that the naukraroi formed a council, and that this was the real counterpart in pre-Solonian Athens of the Homeric gerousia. As he had to find some alternative explanation for the existence of the Areopagus, he assumed that it was instituted later than the naukraric council, though before the time of Solon, and that it developed out of the consultation by magistrates of their predecessors in office.

This explanation of the origin of the Areopagus is unconvincing. After rejecting the main items in the account of the pre-Solonian Areopagus given in the *Athenaion Politeia*, how could Meyer legitimately accept as a fact its statement that the pre-Solonian Areopagus was recruited from ex-archons, a statement which is as hypothetical as the rest? The passage in Herodotus[5] adduced by Meyer does not necessarily mean that the naukraroi formed a council; this is not proved by the mention of prytaneis.

---

[1] 8. 4. Cf. Busolt, ii². 144, n. 1, Greenidge, 145, and Ledl, 298–9.

[2] The practice of recruiting the Areopagus from ex-archons is ascribed to the pre-Solonian period by several scholars; so de Sanctis, 145, who compares (irrelevantly) the practice in Rome and in Crete (Ar. *Politics* 1272ᵃ33).

[3] e.g. by L. Lange, on whose theories cf. Busolt, ii². 138–9, n. 6 and de Sanctis, 145, n. 1. For Kahrstedt's version of this theory see below, p. 309.

[4] *G.A.* ii (first edition), 354–5; cf. iii². 324–5.

[5] v. 71. 2. On prytaneis cf. Ledl, 397.

It is indeed doubtful whether the later Athenian use of the term prytanis for the president of a deliberative body can be admitted for the seventh century. These two arguments really exhaust Meyer's case, for that which he bases on the amnesty-law ascribed to Solon is irrelevant. Even if this law proved, as Meyer asserted, the existence of a court presided over by the basileus and phylobasileis which sat in the Prytaneion and judged those who were accused of insurrection or of trying to set up a tyranny, there is nothing in the law to show that the jurors in this court were the naukraroi, or that the court also functioned as a council.

Thus the modern attempts to find traces of an aristocratic council other than the Areopagus in the pre-Solonian period are no more successful than the ancient attempts to demonstrate the pre-Solonian existence of the Areopagus, and for the same reason; since the controversy began the evidence available has never been sufficient to decide the question. But if we start from the conviction that the aristocratic state must have had a council of nobles the problem is simplified. Even if Solon created a fresh council with a new basis of membership, he presumably included in it at the start those who had already held the archonship; these ex-archons would be for the most part prominent members of the Eupatrid order who had already sat in the old aristocratic council, and to this extent there would be continuity in personnel between the old council and the new. It is, however, more likely that Solon retained the old council and merely ordained that for the future it should be recruited from ex-archons. The jurisdiction retained by the later Areopagus in the most important cases of homicide and the fact that its membership was tenable for life are further indications of its continuity with the pre-Solonian council, as both are characteristic of the Spartan gerousia.[1] Probably the council of the aristocratic state was simply called ἡ βουλή, and the title ἡ ἐξ Ἀρείου πάγου βουλή was adopted later when a second council was created.[2]

At Sparta the members of the gerousia were chosen by the people; this may have been a later innovation. Only those over sixty years of age were eligible,[3] and so the Spartan gerousia

---

[1] Busolt, ii². 138–40 and 138, n. 6.
[2] So Busolt, ii². 140, n. 2 (following Grote).
[3] Plut. Lykourgos 26. 1; cf. Ledl, 405 f. and Gilbert, 48.

was a genuine Council of Elders. Nothing can be affirmed with certainty about the character or composition of the pre-Solonian council at Athens, except that it must have been confined to the Eupatridai. It may have been composed of the heads of all the genē, or it may have been restricted to a comparatively small number of families.[1]

The powers of the Athenian council were probably not defined until the legislation of Solon, but definition may imply limitation, and the vagueness of its powers facilitated their extension.[2] It must have enjoyed a prestige far greater than that of the annual magistrates, for its members, drawn from the leading families of the aristocracy, held their seats for life. As the repositories of the ancient traditions, they could direct and if necessary punish the magistrates, thus controlling administration and policy; as the guardians of public order they probably exercised now, as later, the right of summoning before their tribunal offenders against religion and morality.[3] The amnesty-law attributed to Solon may indicate that they also had the right to try those who had attempted to subvert the constitution,[4] and that in such cases, as in trials for deliberate homicide and for offences against the state religion, they were presided over by the basileus; when the Areopagus met as a council his place as president must have been taken by the archon.[5]

This outline of the position held by the pre-Solonian council is a reconstruction resting, like that in the *Athenaion Politeia*, on the assumption that its powers were not substantially diminished by Solon. A council invested with such powers was potentially supreme, and the Athenian council in its prime presumably had the authority requisite for the effective enforcement of its privileges. Through this council the Eupatrid aristocracy maintained its supremacy in the government and watched jealously over its executive officials. Aristocratic predominance was favoured by the conditions governing warfare on land at this time; in the eighth century the cavalry, drawn from the horse-owning aristocrats, was the chief arm in war, and the pikemen, not yet organized in the phalanx, counted for little.[6] The right

[1] Busolt, ii². 141 and Ledl, 408 ff.
[2] Cf. the analysis of their powers by Headlam in *C.R.* vi, 1892, 296 ff.
[3] *A.P.* 3. 6 and Isokrates vii. 46.
[4] See below, p. 90.
[5] See above, p. 74, n. 8.   [6] Cf. Ar. *Politics* 1297^{b}16 ff.

to elect the magistrates retained by the ekklesia was useless so long as loyalty to the aristocracy overruled the rivalries of individual nobles.[1]

Under this government the aristocratic members of the genē could exploit their political and military dominance in their own interests. It has been doubted whether the law as a whole was codified until the time of Solon;[2] even if there was an earlier codification due either to Drakon or to the thesmothetai, magistrates drawn from the Eupatrid order might be expected to wrest the law in favour of their own class. As Solon says in his poems,[3] the verdicts in cases of debt by which Athenians were condemned to be sold abroad as slaves were sometimes just, sometimes unjust; the law of debt was harsh, but its application by Eupatrid judges was harsher still.

The position of the landless poor (Thetes) before Solon is obscure; they were certainly excluded from the ekklesia,[4] probably from the phratries also,[5] and if their private rights approximated to those of a full citizen rather than to those of a resident alien, the practical efficacy of these rights may have depended on their placing themselves under the protection of a powerful noble. They are sometimes referred to as πελάται, a word used by Plutarch as the equivalent of the Roman *clientes*.[6]

Those plebeians who had freeholds must have been less unprotected than the Thetes, for even if their membership of the ekklesia was valuable potentially rather than actually, they were strong enough to maintain their membership of the phratries. Though citizenship in itself was little more than an empty privilege to a plebeian in an aristocratic state, the brotherhood of phratores to which citizenship gave admission must have done something to protect its individual members against illegal violence. But the phratry was powerless to defend its members against an oppression exercised under legal forms. The wealthy Eupatrids could not resist the temptation to exploit their control of jurisdiction to the detriment of their

[1] So Ledl, 389.
[2] See below, p. 308.
[3] Fr. 24 (Diehl), ll. 9–10; cf. Linforth, 136–7.
[4] See above, p. 79, n. 5.
[5] This is merely a conjecture but it seems a reasonable one.
[6] I am speaking of those Thetes who had not sunk to the position of ἐκτήμοροι. *A.P.* 2. 2 identifies them, but the confusion of thought in this chapter is notorious; cf. Woodhouse, *Solon*, c. 3. For the equation of πελάται and *clientes* cf. Plut. *Romulus* 13. 7.

poorer neighbours,[1] and strove to reduce them to a position of economic as well as of political inferiority. In the end their selfishness overreached itself; the despised masses, persecuted to the limits of their endurance, found a champion who made a breach beyond repair in the structure of the aristocratic state.

[1] Cf. the passage of Solon, fr. 24, cited above.

IV. SOLON

THE seventh century in Greece was a period of transition and change. As more settled conditions were established and the numerous Greek colonies planted in this period round the shores of the central Mediterranean created new markets, a great development of commerce and industry ensued which was bound to react on the political life of the Greek states. In the words of Thucydides,[1] when Greece became more powerful and devoted herself even more than before to the acquisition of wealth, tyrannies were set up in many of the cities. The impact of the economic revolution shook the predominance of the horse-owning aristocracies, based on their ownership of land, and in many places the oppressed commons were organized by a popular leader who overthrew the rule of the nobles and revived the monarchy in his own person.[2] These monarchs, whose position was not inherited like that of the old limited monarchs but resembled a dictatorship resting on the support of the masses, came to be known by the name of $\tau\acute{v}\rho\alpha\nu\nu o\iota$, tyrants, a term which may have been borrowed from Lydia.[3]

Athens was not at first directly affected, for her economic development was more gradual than that of the Isthmus states; she had taken no part in the colonization movements of the eighth and seventh centuries, and her commerce and industries were apparently still on a small scale. The first armed rising against the aristocratic government of Athens was a consequence of the establishment of tyranny in the neighbouring state of Megara. Kylon, a rich noble who had married the daughter of Theagenes, the new tyrant of Megara, tried to make himself tyrant of Athens.[4] With the support of his own followers and a force supplied by Theagenes he was able to seize the Acropolis, but the nobles and commons soon besieged him there; Kylon escaped but his followers were compelled to surrender, and though they had been promised that their lives would be spared they were promptly executed by the order of the chief archon, the Alkmaionid Megakles.[5]

[1] i. 13. 1.
[2] Sometimes he even assumed the old title of $\beta\alpha\sigma\iota\lambda\epsilon\acute{v}s$; cf. Hdt. v. 44. 1 and 92 ε 2 and BS 382, n. 1.   [3] Cf. Archilochus, fr. 22 (Diehl).   [4] Thuc. i. 126. 2 ff.
[5] Thuc., loc. cit., and Hdt. v. 71 do not mention Megakles; his part in the

This fiasco may have been partly due to Kylon's reliance on foreign aid;[1] the presence of Megarian troops in his following may have helped to rally the masses against him. But it also suggests that if the people already had grievances against the nobles they had not yet become acute, since they were prepared to defend the government of the aristocracy against a usurper.[1] Yet, though Kylon's coup ended in failure, it had important results. The unity of the Athenian aristocracy, like that of the Roman senate, had probably always been more apparent than real, as the ambitions of individual families clashed with loyalty to their order, but the bitter enmities provoked by the Kylonian conspiracy and the blood-bath in which it ended aggravated the previous discords within the aristocratic state and revealed them to all the world. Many of the nobles may have been connected by ties of marriage or interest with the Kylonians. Whatever may have been the cause, it is certain that the ruthless action taken by Megakles provoked a reaction which in the end was strong enough to drive him into banishment and with him those members of his clan who shared his responsibility for the massacre.[2] It has even been suggested that the homicide legislation of Drakon was intended to put an end to blood-feuds among the nobles which had been started by the Kylonian affair.[3]

These dissensions impaired the prestige of the government and paralysed its energies. Moreover, at this juncture it alienated its former supporters, the small freehold farmers, by refusing to redress their just grievances. The nature of these grievances is to some extent explained by the poems of Solon.[4] It is clear that many of the farmers, compelled by circumstances to borrow from the rich nobles, had been unable to repay their loans and had in consequence forfeited their freeholds; some had even been sold into slavery abroad. Those who had lost their farms either left Attica to seek a livelihood elsewhere or stayed where they were and accepted a position of semi-serfdom as tenants of the rich landowners.[5]

Kylonian affair and the fact that he was chief archon at the time are supplied by Plut. *Solon* 12. 1. On the date cf. Jac. 366, no. 77 and Ledl, 77 ff.
   [1] Cf. BS 800.
   [2] Plut. *Solon* 12. 2–4 and *A.P.* 1; cf. Jac. 366–7, nn. 77 and 81.
   [3] So F. Cauer cited in BS 816, n. 3.
   [4] Especially the poem quoted in *A.P.* 12. 4 (= Diehl, fr. 24); cf. Linforth, 182 ff.
   [5] The above seems to me the most satisfactory explanation of the poem; cf. Glotz and Cohen, i. 411–12 and BS 826, n. 1.

The causes of this economic crisis are not revealed by Solon, and the modern attempts at an explanation are far from satisfactory. It is tempting to connect it with the economic development elsewhere in Greece already mentioned, and to suggest as many have done that it was due to the introduction of money into a society unfamiliar with it as a medium of exchange.[1] But it is very doubtful whether money was in common use in Attica before the middle of the sixth century. Probably the real causes of the distress which drove the farmers to borrow from their rich neighbours were simpler, such as plundering raids of Megarians and other enemies, and a succession of bad harvests.[2]

Whatever may have been the causes, the consequence was the expropriation of a number of farmers and the acquisition of their farms by the rich. Hence the dispossessed demanded a redistribution of land both before and after the reforms of Solon.[3] But it is improbable that all the farmers had lost their freeholds; the statement in the *Athenaion Politeia* that the whole land was in the hands of a few is bound up with a fundamentally false view of the situation which Solon had to face.[4] There must have been many freeholders left whose determination to resist expropriation constrained the nobles to accept the appointment of Solon;[5] these farmers formed the mass of Solon's supporters and benefited from his cancellation of debts.

Their agitation against the nobles was mainly economic, but though their primary object was the redress of their immediate grievances, they might be induced to see in the composition of the government the cause of their sufferings and to support a programme of political reform. It is generally agreed that Solon's supporters included not only the farmers but some of the rich and influential citizens as well. Naturally these people joined forces with the farmers on political, not on economic grounds; they saw in this agrarian agitation an excuse for wresting political power from its present holders. Solon claims that he 'brought the people together',[6] but the sequel indicates

[1] So F. E. Adcock in *C.A.H.* iv. 32–33.

[2] Cf. de Sanctis, 193. The view expressed in the text has been challenged and should perhaps be regarded as merely a personal view. Experts appear to disagree in the interpretation of the numismatic evidence.

[3] Plut. *Solon* 13. 6 and 16. 1.   [4] *A.P.* 2; cf. the analysis in Woodhouse, c. 3.

[5] Presumably Solon was helped by powerful friends (cf. Jac. 272, n. 225), and the reactionary nobles could no longer count on the support of the demos which had rallied round them against Kylon.

[6] Fr. 24 (Diehl), ll. 1–2, cited in *A.P.* 12. 4.

that in his organization of the people he was aided by powerful men whose motives were not disinterested. To what class did these men belong, and what were the sources of their power? These questions must be deferred until a detailed examination of the scope of Solon's reforms has made it possible to attempt an answer to them.

In the past the true significance of Solon's reforms has been obscured by the erroneous fourth-century view which made him the founder of Athenian democracy and resulted in the ascription to Solon of institutions and changes for which he was not responsible.[1] Even Aristotle in the *Politics*, while reacting against the current account,[2] hardly realized to what extent the truth had been distorted by a false historical tradition. Solon retained the political organs of the aristocratic state, and in the following discussion I shall try to prove that their functions and powers, though carefully defined and limited by Solon in his code, remained substantially the same as before.

The powers of the Areopagus were apparently defined by Solon and to that extent limited, but the author of the *Athenaion Politeia* seems to be justified in his assumption that they remained essentially unaltered.[3] He gives a summary of them, but this is incomplete, and the ancient authorities who describe the transference in 462 of most of the old powers of the Areopagus to the Council of Five Hundred and the dikasteria fail to give a clear account of the change. As the Areopagus continued to hold an important position in the state until the revolution of 462 it is essential to reconstruct as far as possible the functions which it exercised in the sixth century.[4]

(1) It retained its previous jurisdiction under the presidency of the basileus in trials for deliberate homicide.[5] (2) In later times, trials for impiety were held in the dikasteria but were always presided over by the basileus.[6] Before 462 the Areopagus had probably tried such cases, and all others connected with the state religion. After 462 they still tried those who were charged

---

[1] Cf. B. Niese in *Historische Zeitschrift*, lxix, 1892, 38–68, especially 56 ff.

[2] *Politics* 1274^{a}11 ff.

[3] The assumption follows from a comparison of *A.P.* 3. 6 and 8. 4; see above, pp. 80 ff.

[4] For attempts at reconstruction cf. Wil. ii, c. 8 and de Sanctis, 145 ff.; see also Bonner and Smith, 94–97 and 257–68.

[5] *A.P.* 57. 2–3.

[6] *A.P.* 57. 2; cf. Bonner and Smith, 260.

with the destruction of any of the sacred olive trees.[1] (3) The
Areopagus as the council of the basileus must have exercised
a general supervision over the temporalities of the official cults.
In the fourth century the basileus brought before the Council of
Five Hundred the question of the leases of temple-lands;[2] presumably the Areopagus had dealt with this before 462. (4) It is
stated in the *Athenaion Politeia*[3] that Solon allowed it to retain
the right to hear complaints against wrongdoers and to punish
those who were convicted; it could impose fines and was not
bound to give reasons for its decision in such cases. Its power of
arrest is implied in a story which is apparently unhistorical,[4] but
the Council of Five Hundred possessed this power later,[5] and it
is safe to assume that it was enjoyed by the Areopagus also
before 462. (5) In the fourth century those who were accused
of plotting to subvert the constitution were impeached before
the people, and the law under which they were prosecuted was
the νόμος εἰσαγγελτικός.[6] The author of the *Athenaion Politeia*[3]
ascribes to Solon the first law on this subject, and says that
cases under it were tried by the Areopagus. He implies that this
was an addition made by Solon to the previous powers of the
Areopagus. His authority for the ascription of this law to Solon
is unknown,[7] and he does not explain its relation to the old law
(which he quotes later)[8] against those who attempted to set up
a tyranny. Anyhow the amnesty-law suggests that the Areopagus had even before Solon been the court which tried conspirators against the constitution,[9] and if Solon passed a law on
this subject his purpose can only have been to give more precise
definition to the previous powers of the Areopagus in this
sphere. (6) Magistrates accused of illegal conduct could be
denounced to the council in the fourth century by private
citizens.[10] In the *Athenaion Politeia* the Areopagus is said to have
had this power of hearing complaints in the time of Drakon,[11]
and it may be assumed that it continued to exercise this power
until it was transferred by Ephialtes to the Council of Five

---

[1] *A.P.* 60. 2 and Lys. vii; cf. Bonner and Smith, 258.
[2] *A.P.* 47. 4; cf. Wil. ii. 190.   [3] 8. 4.
[4] *A.P.* 25. 3 and Wil. ii. 194–5; cf. de Sanctis, 408–10 for a criticism of the story.
[5] The exercise of the power was limited to specific offences; cf. Dem. xxiv.
144 ff. and Bonner and Smith, 343–4.
[6] The evidence is given and discussed by Bonner and Smith, c. 10.
[7] Objections are raised by Gilliard, 57, n. 2, and 281.   [8] 16. 10.
[9] Plut. *Solon* 19. 4; cf. de Sanctis, 149.   [10] *A.P.* 45. 2.   [11] 4. 4.

Hundred. The right to ensure that the magistrates kept their oath to obey the laws[1] presumably belonged to the Areopagus, and these powers, combined with its function of prosecuting conspirators against the constitution, may be held to constitute the 'guardianship of the laws' ascribed to it by ancient writers.[2]

Under the later democracy every magistrate had to pass a scrutiny (δοκιμασία) before entering an office. The Council of Five Hundred was responsible for the scrutiny of its successors; other officials were examined in a law-court.[3] The nine archons alone had to submit to a double scrutiny, first before the council, then in a law-court.[3] Some have maintained that the δοκιμασία of the magistrates was entrusted to the Areopagus by Solon,[4] but it is more probable that it was first instituted by Kleisthenes and belonged from its inception to the Council of Five Hundred.[5]

The powers ascribed to the Areopagus in the above reconstruction are mainly religious and judicial. It has also been credited with financial functions, especially the control of the state treasury,[6] but the evidence is weak. The story that in 480 it made a payment of eight drachmas to each of the citizens and thereby persuaded them to man the ships which fought at Salamis[7] finds no support in Herodotus and seems to be an invention of the fourth century.[8] In the *Athenaion Politeia*[9] it is stated that the fines imposed by the Areopagus were deposited by it on the Acropolis. These fines may have been given to the treasury of Athena, but it is more probable that they were paid into the state treasury. There must have been a state treasury,[10] administered by the kolakretai, but the items of state expenditure and revenue in this period were apparently small, and the control of finance could therefore in normal circumstances be left to a board of minor magistrates; presumably they had to give an account of their administration to the Areopagus at the end of their year of office.

Our authorities throw no light on the relations between the Areopagus and the magistrates in the sixth century, and it is

---

[1] *A.P.* 7. 1.

[2] *A.P.* 3. 6, 4. 4, 8. 4, also Isokrates vii. 37 and 46. Plut. *Solon* 19. 2 ascribes to Solon the conferment of this function on the Areopagus, but cf. BS 797 and n. 1.   [3] *A.P.* 45. 3 and 55. 2.

[4] e.g. de Sanctis, 150 and Wil. ii. 189.   [5] See below, pp. 205 ff.

[6] Wil. ii. 190–1; de Sanctis, 152, is more cautious.   [7] *A.P.* 23. 1.

[8] So de Sanctis 152 and n. 3; cf. E. M. Walker in *C.A.H.* v. 473.   [9] 8. 4.

[10] *A.P.* 6. 1 includes 'public debts' among those cancelled by Solon, but the value of this testimony is doubtful.

not known whether the archon was required by constitutional custom to consult the Areopagus before he submitted any important proposal to the people. It is reasonable to suppose that he safeguarded himself in this way when the Areopagus was still supreme, and that it acted at one time, like the Roman senate, as the *consilium* of the magistrates.[1] But by the time of Solon its authority had been so undermined by the dissensions between its members that magistrates with a strong backing could probably defy it with impunity. The right to convene and preside over the popular assembly belonged to the archon,[2] and he could now safely disregard the claim of the Areopagus to be consulted first.

A council which prepared the agenda for a popular assembly was described by the Greeks as probouleutic, but the description is inapplicable to the part played by the Areopagus in this respect. And even if the archon always took its opinion on questions which he proposed to bring before the ekklesia, it must be remembered that apart from the annual assembly for the election of magistrates the ekklesia had no regular meetings in the pre-Solonian period; it was the policy of the aristocrats to restrict the number of its meetings and the extent of its competence to a minimum. The presence in a state of a probouleutic council implies the existence of an ekklesia with extensive and important powers. Hence the statement of Plutarch that Solon created a new probouleutic council of 400 members, if correct, would be a decisive proof that he intended the ekklesia to develop into the effective sovereign of the state. The crucial importance of this question to our understanding of Solon's constitutional reforms demands a detailed examination of the arguments which have been urged for and against the truth of Plutarch's account.

In the *Athenaion Politeia* there is only a curt reference to the creation of the new council:[3] 'Solon made a Council of Four Hundred, 100 from each tribe'. Aristotle in the *Politics* ignores it altogether. Plutarch says[4] that Solon, apprehensive of the revolutionary temper of the people, created the new council and ordained that no business could come before the assembly without the previous sanction of this council; he also implies that the original 400 were chosen by Solon himself.

---

[1] This seems to be the view of Bonner and Smith 94.
[2] See above, p. 74.   [3] 8. 4.   [4] *Solon* 19. 1.

The first reference to the existence in the sixth century of a Council of Four Hundred is found in the constitution promulgated by the oligarchs in 411, which ordains that there shall be a council of 400 members κατὰ τὰ πάτρια,[1] and a council of 401 members appears in the so-called constitution of Drakon,[2] which is a fabrication of oligarchic propaganda. It might be suggested that the oligarchs genuinely proposed to revive a Solonian institution, and that they chose the number 400 for their own council because Solon's had contained the same number. But it is far more probable that the number was one chosen by them to suit their own requirements, the minimum necessary to ensure the success of their experiment, and that they then proceeded to invent a precedent for it, fathering their invention on either Drakon or Solon. The invention was later accepted by the radicals, who found in it a Solonian anticipation of the Council of Five Hundred, the citadel of the developed democracy.

Though the Atthidographers accepted the Solonian Council of Four Hundred as historical, they had nothing more to record of it than the bare mention of its creation by Solon, repeated by the author of the *Athenaion Politeia*. The brevity of his reference to it is only intelligible on the assumption that his sources contained no details, and the fuller version in Plutarch looks like the conjecture of a later scholar who assumed that the functions of this council were the same as those of the later Council of Five Hundred. It has been suggested[3] that Plutarch's comparison of the two councils (the new boulē and the Areopagus) to two anchors steadying the ship of state was derived from an actual poem by Solon, but if this had been the case surely he would have quoted the original poem, and the comparison may easily have been due to Plutarch himself.[4]

There is no certain evidence of the existence in Athens of a council other than the Areopagus in the period between the legislation of Solon and the introduction of Kleisthenes' reforms. We read in Herodotus[5] that soon after the expulsion of the

---

[1] *A.P.* 31. 1.   [2] *A.P.* 4. 3.

[3] By Miss K. Freeman, *The Work and Life of Solon*, 79, n. 1; cf. Wade-Gery in *C.Q.* xxvii, 1933, 24, n. 1 and F. Stähelin in *Hermes*, lxviii, 1933, 345.

[4] The verb σαλεύειν occurs in Plut. *Moralia* 1123 F (also, in a different sense, 493 D). The metaphorical use of σάλος with reference to the ship of state is an obvious one, found e.g. in Sophokles (*O.T.* 22–24 and *Antigone* 162–3).

[5] v. 72. 2.

tyrants the βουλή offered vigorous opposition to Kleomenes of
Sparta when he tried to dissolve it. Herodotus seems to date this
incident after the acceptance of Kleisthenes' reforms;[1] thus the
boulē in question might be Kleisthenes' new Council of Five
Hundred.[2] It has been objected to this that Herodotus had
telescoped the events, that according to the more precise account
in the *Athenaion Politeia* the reforms had been introduced by
Kleisthenes but not yet accepted by the people,[3] that even if
they had been accepted there had been no time to carry them
into effect,[4] and that therefore the council in question was not
the Council of Five Hundred; the possibility that it may have
been the Areopagus is brushed aside in a footnote,[5] and so the
required conclusion is obtained that it must have been another
council, which can have been none other than the shadowy
Solonian Council of Four Hundred.

Every link in this chain of proof is weak. Wade-Gery has
shown[6] that the order of events in the account of the *Athenaion
Politeia* is really the same as in Herodotus, but that for convenience the author delays his description of Kleisthenes' reforms until he has finished his narrative of the party struggles
in Athens which followed their introduction. It is true that the
new council was to be based on an elaborate reorganization of
Attica which could not be carried out in a moment, but Kleisthenes may have secured the appointment of a provisional
Council of Five Hundred to hold office until the necessary
preparations for his new consitution were completed.[7] But
though the boulē which opposed Kleomenes may have been
a new Council of Five Hundred, it is more probable that it was
the Areopagus, which possessed the prestige and personnel
required for vigorous and effective action in this crisis. Since the
time of Solon it had been recruited from ex-archons, and during
the years 546–510 the tyrants had secured the appointment of
their relations and friends to the chief annual magistracies;[8]
thus the Areopagus in 507 would be mainly composed of the
supporters of the tyrants, and the Athenian oligarchs headed by

---

[1] On the chronology see below, Appendix VI.
[2] As suggested by Bonner and Smith 189.
[3] So Walker in *C.A.H.* iv. 139.
[4] This is the main argument adduced by Ledl, 278 ff.
[5] By Walker in *C.A.H.* iv. 140, n. 1. Ledl, 285, says the possibility is 'excluded'
but gives no reasons.   [6] *C.Q.* xxvii, 1933, 18–22.
[7] Cf. Bonner and Smith, 189.   [8] Thuc. vi. 54. 6.

Isagoras, relying on the presence of their ally Kleomenes with a small Spartan force, would naturally attempt its dissolution.

The evidence of epigraphy has been called in to prove directly and indirectly the existence and probability of a Solonian Council of Four Hundred. Fragments of a stelē found on the Acropolis contain a mutilated sixth-century inscription[1] recording a decree of the people. When this inscription was first known, the last letters preserved on the stone were ι τ ε σ β; some scholars explained the last letter as the first of a proper name, that of the archon for the year, but others assumed that it was the first letter of the word βουλῆς (in the form β ο λ ε σ). The latter view has received some additional support from the discovery of a new fragment,[2] which joins the other and gives the reading ι τ ε σ β . λ ε. Yet a reference at the end of the inscription to the βουλή, which is not mentioned in the preamble, raises difficulties, as is shown by the variety of the restorations proposed, and even now the restoration of an archon-name remains a possible solution.[3]

At one time the inscription was dated before 560 and regarded as proof of the early existence of a probouleutic council which could only be the Council of Four Hundred attributed by tradition to Solon. Recent writers prefer to assign the inscription to a date soon after the adoption of Kleisthenes' reforms,[4] so that even if βολεσ is read in the last line it cannot prove the existence of a popular council before those reforms.

Another inscription, found in Chios and ascribed to a date about 600,[5] refers to the existence in Chios of a βουλὴ δημοσίη, apparently side by side with an aristocratic council. But the precision of the date suggested for this inscription seems illusory, and the argument that because Chios had two councils in 600 Athens must have been provided with a second council by Solon is manifestly inconclusive. In the early sixth century the Ionians of Asia Minor had far outstripped their Athenian kinsmen in all the arts of civilization,[6] and were politically mature enough to experiment with constitutional novelties which would have been incongruous in a community just emerging from aristocratic control.

---

[1] *I.G.* i². 1 (Tod, 11).   [2] Cf. E. Schweigert in *Hesperia*, vii, 1938, 264.
[3] P. Roussel in *Rev. arch.* xviii, 1941, 214.
[4] Bibliography in Cadoux, 119, n. 265.
[5] Wilamowitz in *Berl. Abh.* 1909, 64 ff.; cf. Tod, pp. 1–3.
[6] For a different (unconvincing) view cf. R. M. Cook in *J.H.S.* lxvi, 1946, 67 ff.

This incongruity provides the principal argument against the existence of a second council in Solonian Athens.[1] Though we have refuted the attempts to find positive proofs of its existence in the ancient sources earlier than the propagandists of 411, it must be admitted that their silence is not decisive. But unless we can accept the fourth-century account of Solon as a statesman who with uncanny prescience foresaw and provided for all the requirements of radical democracy, we are entitled to ask what was the function contemplated by Solon for his second council. Even if Solon, like the author of the Spartan rhetra, made provision for regular monthly meetings of the ekklesia,[2] the business of preparing the agenda for these meetings was surely not so exacting as to require the creation of a new council for the purpose. According to one modern explanation,[3] which recalls that suggested by Plutarch, it was 'needed to prevent hasty decisions in times of excitement'. But if the second council existed for this purpose, what was it doing when Aristion was able to propose and the ekklesia to approve the grant of a body-guard to Peisistratos,[4] who was thereby assisted to make himself tyrant? If Solon created a new council, it must have been one of the most futile constitutional experiments recorded in history. As the evidence and the arguments for its existence are unconvincing,[5] we can dismiss it as an invention and conclude that after Solon's reforms, as before, there was only one council at Athens, the Areopagus.

The powers and composition of the ekklesia were probably not much altered by Solon's legislation. Aristotle[6] asserts that Solon gave to the people the bare minimum of political power, but this is apparently no more than an inference from Solon's own words:[7] 'to the demos I have given such a measure of privilege as is sufficient, neither robbing them of their former rights nor holding out the hope of greater.' This passage implies that the political privileges possessed by the people were the

---

[1] Cf. Niese in *H.Z.* lxix, 1892, 65–66 and de Sanctis, 251. N. L. Ingle (in *C.R.* xxv, 1911, 236–8) tried to solve the difficulty by providing the supposed council with judicial functions on the Chian model.

[2] Plut. *Lykourgos* 6. 2; the interpretation of the passage is disputed. Cf. N. G. L. Hammond in *J.H.S.* lxx, 1950, 43 and n. 8.

[3] F. E. Adcock in *C.A.H.* iv. 54.

[4] *A.P.* 14. 1; for an attempt (unconvincing) to meet this objection cf. BS 846–7, n. 2.

[5] On the 'archaeological' argument cf. Note E.　　　　[6] *Politics* 1274a15.

[7] Fr. 5 (Diehl), ll. 1–2; cf. *A.P.* 12. 1 and Linforth, 134–5.

same after Solon's reforms as before, but that its full exercise of
them was now guaranteed by the reign of law which he had
established. They included the election of the chief magistrates[1]
and presumably the final voice in the declaration of war and the
conclusion of peace;[2] these prerogatives may have belonged
de iure to the assembly in the pre-Solonian state, but must often
have been reduced *de facto* to an empty formality by aristocratic
management. It may also be assumed that after Solon the
assembly alone was competent to make or modify laws, though
Solon's code was guaranteed against any alteration for a period
of ten years,[3] and it certainly had the right to confer on individuals privileges contrary to the laws.[4]

Aristotle[5] says that Solon empowered the demos to demand
from the magistrates an account of their administration
(εὐθύνειν). This statement is apparently an anticipation of the
later functions of the popular courts, the Dikasteria, which are
usually regarded by fourth-century writers as one of Solon's
innovations. So the author of the *Athenaion Politeia* declares
that Solon's most democratic reform was the institution of
appeal from the magistrates to the Dikasterion.[6] An archaic law,
possibly Solonian, which is quoted by Lysias and Demosthenes,
indicates that the popular court was called ἡ ἡλιαία;[7] this court
is authorized in the law to impose a punishment of five days in
the stocks as an additional penalty in convictions for theft.

As ἡλιαία seems to be connected with a word for assembly
found in inscriptions of some Peloponnesian states,[8] it is reasonable to suppose that the Heliaia was the ekklesia sitting in a
judicial capacity. Probably it was the only popular court established by Solon; the references to dikasteria in some ancient
accounts of his reforms must be anachronistic.[9] The most plausible
explanation of the function assigned to the Heliaia by Solon is
that of Wilamowitz.[10] He conjectured that each of the Solonian
laws regulating the competence of the magistrates defined the
penalties which the magistrate could inflict on his own authority,
and that if he wished to exceed them he had to secure the

---

[1] Ar. *Politics* 1274ᵃ16.   [2] Cf. BS 847.
[3] So Hdt. i. 29. 2; *A.P.* 7. 2 makes the period 100 years!
[4] *A.P.* 14. 1.   [5] *Politics* 1274ᵃ17 and 1281ᵇ32–34.
[6] 9. 1; cf. Bonner and Smith, 153 and n. 3.
[7] Lys. x. 16, Dem. xxiv. 105.
[8] Cf. the comments of Buck in Bonner and Smith, 157, n. 5.
[9] Cf. Bonner and Smith, 153 and n. 3.   [10] *A.A.* i. 60, n. 29.

approval of a jury of citizens. With this view may be combined
the suggestion put forward by Adcock,[1] that the magistrates
may have tried cases on market days and that their courts were
attended by such citizens as had the leisure. This innovation
may be looked upon as the seed which was to develop into the
popular courts of the Periklean Age, when the judicial powers of
the magistrate had been limited to the preliminary investigation
(*anakrisis*), but no such development can have been contemplated by its author, who apparently intended the Heliaia to
act merely as a safeguard against the infliction of excessive
penalties by magistrates.

Was the composition of the assembly altered by Solon? In
the Atthis he is credited with the admission of the thetes to the
ekklesia and to the popular court(s),[2] and this evidence has
usually been accepted as decisive. But it is impossible to regard
all the statements of the Atthis about Solon as based on the text
of his laws, and this one may well be no more than a plausible
conjecture. Confirmation of it might be found in the rise of
Peisistratos to power, as the ekklesia which voted him his body-
guard must have contained a large number of his supporters,
and many of these were landless men who looked to him for the
redistribution of land which they desired. Yet the admission of
landless citizens to the ekklesia would have been a bold expedient which seems alien to the cautious conservative tempera-
ment of Solon and would have played straight into the hands of
the revolutionaries. The true explanation may be that Solon
made no alteration in the qualification for membership of the
ekklesia, but that in the troubled years which followed his
legislation there was a difference between *de iure* and *de facto*
membership. Possibly the farmers who had once owned land
and had lost it to their creditors continued to attend the
assembly; it is even conceivable that, as the tide of popular
agitation rose, poor citizens were present at its meetings without
any justification, and that the authorities were either unable or
unwilling to enforce their exclusion.

The powers previously possessed by the magistrates were
limited, like those of the Areopagus, by the fact that they were
carefully defined in Solon's code and that safeguards were provided against their arbitrary extension, but in substance they
seem to have been the same as before. The chief archon con-

---

[1] *C.A.H.* iv. 56.   [2] *A.P.* 7. 3, Plut. *Solon* 18. 2.

tinued to be the supreme executive in the state and to preside over the meetings of the ekklesia,[1] perhaps even to convene them. He also presided over the sessions of the Areopagus with the exception of those for judicial and religious business in which the presidency was still reserved for the basileus.[2] Election of the magistrates by the people had existed in form before Solon, and though the author of the *Athenaion Politeia* asserts that he changed the method of appointment, it is more probable that he allowed the ekklesia to retain its prerogative,[3] which was henceforth made more effective by the disunion of the nobility and the competition of ambitious politicians for popular favour.

From the point now reached in this survey of Solon's reforms it might appear that with reference to the three principal organs of the state, the council, the assembly, and the magistracy, he had merely given legal confirmation to their existing functions. But though their functions remained the same, their composition was transformed, that of the ekklesia apparently *de facto* only and in defiance of Solon's intention, whereas the innovations introduced by him into the composition of the magistracy and of the Areopagus represent a deliberate attempt to wrest the monopoly of effective political power from its former holders. The means adopted by Solon to this end were extremely simple. It is unnecessary to assume, as some scholars have done, that he drew up an elaborate written constitution; he merely inserted into those parts of his code which dealt with the magistrates and the Areopagus provisions on the conditions of eligibility which automatically ensured the achievement of his main political objective.[4]

These provisions substituted wealth for birth as the qualification for election to office and thereby for admission to the Areopagus, which was henceforth to be recruited from ex-archons.[5] The basis of the new qualification was supplied by the four property-classes ($\tau\epsilon\lambda\eta$), the creation of which was attributed by the Atthis[6] to Solon; the assumption in the *Athenaion Politeia*[7]

[1] See above, pp. 74 and 92; cf. BS 846 and Rosenberg in *Hermes*, liii, 1918, 308 f., also de Sanctis, 251.

[2] For an approximation to this view cf. Bonner and Smith, 94.

[3] See below, pp. 321 ff.   [4] Cf. Gilliard, 269–71.

[5] This view, expressed by Plut. *Solon* 19. 1, is to be preferred to that followed in *A.P.* 3. 6 and accepted by many scholars (e.g. de Sanctis, 145) that the recruiting of the Areopagus from ex-archons goes back to the seventh century.

[6] Plut. *Solon* 18. 1.   [7] 7. 3; cf. the note in Sandys.

that they had existed before is due to the author's acceptance of
the bogus 'Constitution of Drakon'. In the fourth century there
was a discussion about the definition of the second class, the
ἱππάδα τελοῦντες;[1] as this was argued on grounds of probability
and without reference to Solon's laws, Busolt maintained that
the laws could not have defined the telē and that therefore they
must have been presupposed by Solon as an already existing
institution.[2] It is more probable that in the fourth century the
Solonian law defining the telē was no longer in existence. If
the telē had existed before Solon, what could have been their
function?[3] The old view that they were used by Solon or later to
provide a sliding scale for taxation has long been exploded,[4] and
in any case the existence of direct taxation before the tyranny
is unlikely.[5]

Membership of a telos depended on the receipt of an annual
income of a certain number of measures of natural produce,
which could be either corn, oil, or wine.[6] Those who had an
income of over 500 measures belonged to the first class, the
Pentakosiomedimnoi; the second class, the Hippeis, had over
300 measures, the third, the Zeugitai, had over 200. All whose
annual income fell below 200 measures were included in the
fourth class, the Thetes. The names of the last three classes had
previously possessed a social significance,[7] but Solon gave them
a more rigid meaning in his new scheme, and within the Hippeis
marked off the richest men by a name as artificial as his classification.[8] There is no reason for doubting the statement in the
Athenaion Politeia[9] that the produce by which a man's telos was
determined had to come from his own property, with its consequence that the possession of land was an essential qualification
for membership of the first three classes. It has been calculated[10]
that a Zeugite in Solon's day need not have possessed more than

---

[1] *A.P.* 7. 4 (summarized in Plut., loc. cit.).   [2] Cf. BS 821 and n. 1.

[3] Cf. BS 821 for the desperate solution that their institution was connected
with the naukraric organization.

[4] Cf. Beloch in *Hermes*, xx, 1885, 245 and BS 838, n. 1.

[5] De Sanctis, 232–3, inferred the early existence of the εἰσφορά (in an extraordinary form) from *Odyssey* xiii. 14, xix. 197, xxii. 55.

[6] *A.P.* 7. 4, Plut. *Solon* 18. 1. On the serious problems raised by our evidence
for the τέλη cf. the important article by Miss Chrimes cited in the Bibliography.

[7] Cf. de Sanctis, 230–1.

[8] Cf. ibid. 232–3, and for a different view BS 822.

[9] 7. 4 ἐκ τῆς οἰκείας; cf. BS 836, n. 4.

[10] De Sanctis calculated that a Zeugite must have had a minimum of 17·4
hectares (about 43 acres) of cultivable land; cf. Beloch, i². 1. 302–3.

43 acres of cultivable land, a Pentakosiomedimnos not more than
110. But large tracts of Attica are not cultivable, and later
statistics suggest that at this time the two highest telē did not
include more than one-fifteenth of the whole citizen-body.

It is possible that after they had been created the property-
classes came to be used to decide the incidence of military obligations, members of the first two classes serving in the cavalry and
the Zeugitai in the infantry, while the Thetes rowed in the fleet.
But the main purpose of their institution seems to have been to
provide a basis and a justification for Solon's redistribution of
political privileges.[1] Perhaps the fourth class was to enjoy
merely the private rights of citizenship (which may or may not
have comprised admission to the phratries) and membership of
the ekklesia was to be confined to the first three classes. Or the
ekklesia may have been open as before to all freeholders, even
those who counted under the new classification as Thetes, and
the special privilege open to the third class consisted in eligibility
to the minor offices of state. The chief magistrates were chosen
only from the first two classes, and Pentakosiomedimnoi alone
could be elected to the board of treasurers of Athena.[2]

Demetrios of Phaleron believed that under Solon's laws
the archonship was reserved for members of the first class.[3] The
same conclusion has been drawn from a passage in the *Athenaion
Politeia*;[4] the author, after stating that Solon restricted office to
the first three classes, gives a list of magistrates in which the
archons come first and before the treasurers of Athena, and as
he adds the comment that the offices open to each class were
proportionate to its place in the scale of wealth, the conclusion
seems inevitable that the archons cannot have been selected
from a wider circle than Athena's treasurers and must therefore
have been chosen exclusively from the first class. But the
acceptance of this conclusion as a fact by Demetrios may be no
more than an inference from this passage in the interests of his
argument; he is trying to refute the legend of Aristeides' poverty,
and contends that his election to the archonship proves him to
have been a Pentakosiomedimnos.[5] The inference is not cogent,

---

[1] BS 840. The view that the classes had a military origin is to be rejected;
cf. de Sanctis, 231, n. 1 and BS 823, n. 1.

[2] *A.P.* 8. 1.   [3] Plut. *Arist.* 1. 2.

[4] 7. 3. Probably the author really believed that Solon had limited the office
to the highest class; cf. de Sanctis, 246.

[5] His testimony is accepted in BS 841 and n. 4.

as the political importance of the archons may be the reason for their appearance at the head of the list in the *Athenaion Politeia*.

Moreover, the contention of Demetrios depends for its validity on the assumption that the conditions postulated for Solon's time were still in force during the first decade of the fifth century; this assumption implies that the archonship was thrown open to the Hippeis somewhere between 489 and 457/456 (when the Zeugitai became eligible),[1] the most plausible occasion being that of the change in the method of election adopted in 487/486. Yet the author of the *Athenaion Politeia*, though he obviously has a special interest in the history of the archonship and records the admission of the Zeugitai to the office, says nothing of any such change in his account[2] of the reform of 487/486. From this we are entitled to infer that there had been no change in the conditions of eligibility for the archonship between Solon's reform and the law of 457/456 admitting the Zeugitai, and that therefore the Hippeis must have been eligible for the office as well as the Pentakosiomedimnoi under the new rules introduced by Solon.[3]

Who were the beneficiaries of this innovation, which was the essence and almost the sum total of Solon's political reforms? If landed property was indispensable for membership of the two highest classes, they must have been landowners in possession of seventy acres and upwards of cultivable land who had hitherto been excluded from office under the rules governing eligibility before the reform. Some of those who see the motive force of the reform in the rise of a class of rich merchants resentful of their exclusion from political power have assumed that Solon must have accepted for his property-classes the equation found later between a drachma and a measure of natural produce.[4] Others, who rightly reject this as contrary to the only piece of positive evidence on the subject, suggest that Solon wished the *nouveaux riches* to qualify themselves for office by the purchase of land, which would give them a stake in the country and an interest in maintaining the stability of the new order.[5] But the true significance of the reform is lost in this explanation. There must surely have been already in existence a number of landed

[1] *A.P.* 26. 2.   [2] 22. 5.

[3] So de Sanctis, 247, Ledl, 344–7; and Wade-Gery in *C.Q.* xxv, 1931, 78 and n. 1.

[4] e.g. A. Boeckh and C. F. Lehmann-Haupt (cf. the latter's *Solon of Athens*, Liverpool, 1912) criticized by BS 820, n. 2.

[5] Cf. BS 836 and n. 4, also Wade-Gery in *C.Q.* xxv, 78.

proprietors who helped to provide Solon with the backing needed
to secure his appointment as *nomothetes*, and were ready to
derive immediate personal advantage from his destruction of
the Eupatrid monopoly of office. Further, there is no evidence
for the presence in Attica at this time of a body of rich merchants and manufacturers; the development of Athenian trade
and industry in the sixth century belongs to the post-Solonian
period and especially to the rule of the tyrants.[1]

Yet the existence of influential landowners who were not
Eupatrids seems at first sight as difficult to accept as the other
hypothesis. Perhaps after all there were Eupatrids who were
excluded from office until Solon's reforms. It is conceivable that
the government was not open to all Eupatrids, but was restricted
to the members of a small number of noble families,[2] and was
therefore what the Greeks called a δυναστεία. We know so little
of pre-Solonian Athens that this explanation is at least entitled
to consideration. It has also been conjectured that admission to
the order had formerly been in the gift of the king,[3] and that
the abolition of the life-kingship destroyed the possibility of en-
nobling new families; hence those which had risen to prominence
in the century before Solon found themselves excluded from
membership of the Eupatrid order and from the political
privileges which it conferred. But the order of Eupatridai seems
to have come into existence independently, not by creation of
the kings, though it is likely enough that it became steadily
more exclusive.

Another possibility is suggested by a consideration of the
families which played a leading part in Athenian politics during
the generation after Solon. Two of them, the Philaïdai and the
family of Peisistratos, had their homes at Brauron in east
Attica[4] and seem to have been political allies.[5] The party led by
Peisistratos was called 'the men from beyond the hills'[6] and was
strong in east Attica and the region of Marathon in the north-
east.[7] Hence it is possible that when these regions were incorporated in the Athenian state the local dynasts were not yet

---

[1] Cf. BS 760 and n. 2.
[2] As in Crete and Elis (Ar. *Politics* 1272ᵃ33 f. and 1306ᵃ15 ff.); cf. Ledl, 407.
[3] Cf. Wade-Gery in *C.Q.* xxv, 1931, 1 ff. (especially 8).
[4] Plut. *Solon* 10. 3; [Plato], *Hipparchos* 228 B.
[5] See below, Appendix V.
[6] Ὑπεράκριοι in Hdt. i. 59. 3; see below, p. 110 and n. 9.
[7] So Peisistratos landed there on his final return in 546 (Hdt. i. 62. 1).

powerful enough to insist on their inclusion in the circle of ruling families.

Little is known of the antecedents of Peisistratos; his father Hippokrates appears in Herodotus as a man of some distinction, and is said to have claimed descent from the same stock as the royal family of Athens.[1] This claim, however, may have been a fiction invented later, when Peisistratos became tyrant, to place his family on an equality with that of the Medontidai;[2] the name of his genos, if he belonged to one, is not known,[3] and his descendants are simply called Peisistratidai.

The Philaïdai present a more complex problem. Toepffer in his study of the legends relating to the family[4] argued that their connexion with Salamis was secondary and probably a product of the Athenian claim to Salamis in the sixth century, and that in Herodotus[5] they trace their descent from Aiakos and Aigina. Pherekydes gave a genealogy of the Philaïdai, preserved in Markellinos' life of Thucydides,[6] which begins with Philaios son of Aias, though in another account[7] Philaios is the grandson of Aias. This genealogy indicates that the family had no connexion with the indigenous heroes of Attica; the Aiginetan origin which it postulates for the Philaïdai may be real or fictitious. As the name Miltiades, borne by some members of the family, is not uncommon outside it, Toepffer[8] rightly refused to infer anything from the occurrence of an archon Miltiades in the second quarter of the seventh century. Possibly Hippokleides, archon in 566/565,[9] was the first Philaïd to hold the archonship; the earlier archonship of his father or ancestor Teisandros occurs in a passage of Markellinos' quotation from Pherekydes which is now regarded as an interpolation.[10] Hence it is a tenable hypothesis that the Philaïdai, though influential in their own district and eminent enough to secure a marriage alliance with the Kypselid

---

[1] i. 59. 1 and v. 65. 3.

[2] Cf. Ledl, 230 ff. But the name Peisistratos seems to indicate that the family claimed Pylian origin at the time of his birth, as it is the name of Nestor's son in Homer, *Odyssey* iii. 36.

[3] The suggestion of Wilamowitz (*Hermes*, xxxiv, 1899, 225) that it may have been the Philaïdai seems impossible; cf. de Sanctis, 268, n. 2.

[4] *A.G.* 269 ff.   [5] vi. 35. 1, where Philaios is son of Aias.

[6] § 3 = Pherekydes, fr. 20 (2 in Jacoby, *F.G.H.* i, pp. 59–60).

[7] Pausanias i. 35. 2. Jacoby, i, p. 388 (in his note on Pherekydes, fr. 2) rejects this account as an error or a later invention.

[8] *A.G.* 280, n. 1; cf. Cadoux, 90 and n. 85.

[9] Cf. Cadoux, 104 and n. 173.

[10] It is bracketed by Jacoby in *F.G.H.* i, p. 60; cf. Berve, *Miltiades*, 2, n. 1.

rulers of Corinth,[1] were not one of the ruling families of Attica in the pre-Solonian period.

The theory suggested above that the families of Peisistratos and Hippokleides were 'new families' excluded from the government before Solon is not directly supported by any ancient authority, but is a speculation based on the following facts: they both have their homes in a remote part of Attica, they are both connected with the tyranny, and their leaders attain to prominence in the years between Solon's reform and the beginning of the tyranny. It is natural to see in their rise to power a consequence of Solon's innovations, and to assume that they had supported his appointment, presumably in order to destroy the monopoly which excluded them from office. But the claim of Hippokleides and Miltiades to trace their descent from a mythical ancestor shows that their family possessed one of the characteristic marks of an aristocratic genos,[2] and it was certainly recognized as such later.[3] Plutarch says that the deme Philaïdai in the Brauron area got its name from the descendants of Philaios,[4] and the genos was presumably called by the same name.[5]

Even if this attempt to identify some of the 'new families' is perhaps too speculative to be accepted, we must still assume that the more influential men among Solon's adherents were in the main landowners who were excluded from office. They seem, however, to have been supported in their claims by some of those Eupatrid houses which had hitherto monopolized the government, in particular by the Alkmaionidai. Although the expulsion of the Alkmaionidai after the Kylonian affair probably affected only those who had actually taken part in the massacre and not their descendants,[6] the family had remained under a cloud and at variance with the rest of the great nobles. Hence an alliance with the new families against the old nobility opened up to the Alkmaionidai an attractive prospect of restoring their old prestige and influence.

[1] The father of Miltiades the oikist was called Kypselos (Hdt. vi. 35. 1); the natural inference that he was descended from the Corinthian Kypselos is supported by Hdt. vi. 128. 2, since the Hippokleides there mentioned probably belonged to the same family (Cadoux, n. 173; cf. Berve, op. cit. 2 ff.). See below, Appendix V.   [2] Cf. W. Dittenberger in *Hermes*, xx, 1885, 4.

[3] So Metrodoros in his περὶ εὐγενείας (Diog. Laert. x. 1).

[4] Plut. *Solon* 10. 3; for a member of the deme cf. *I.G.* i². 220 (Tod, 71), l. 3.

[5] So Berve, op. cit. 1–2, rightly argues against the doubts of Beloch, ii². 2. 37.

[6] Cf. Ledl, 102–4. See also Jac. 272, n. 225.

Clearly the principal aim of the new alliance must have been to destroy the political monopoly of the ruling families, and the economic agitation started by the farmers merely provided the opportunity. The divergent aims of the leaders and the masses could be reconciled in the claim that the security of the people demanded for its maintenance a radical transformation in the personnel of the magistracy and the council, and doubtless Solon realized that the exclusion from the government of men influential in their own districts constituted a menace to the unity of the state. But the reforms which resulted from this attack on the existing conditions not unnaturally bore the stamp of their origin. The Eupatrid monopoly of power was shattered, but the economic reforms were half-hearted and inadequate.[1] Solon's codification of the law, possibly the first complete codification,[2] was an important achievement, and did something to protect the masses from oppression. Yet their main grievances were economic, and to satisfy these Solon, who was apparently a typical conservative reformer, did no more than the bare minimum necessary to stave off an imminent revolution. The farmers threatened with expropriation were determined not to submit tamely to their fate, so Solon cancelled their debts. He probably abolished the serfdom of the Hektemoroi,[3] but did nothing to provide with a livelihood either the ex-serfs or the other farmers who had already been expropriated. Under the circumstances it is difficult to sympathize with his complaints against the ingratitude of the demos.[4]

This combination of a real political and a bogus economic reform finds a close parallel in the laws carried at Rome in 367 by the tribunes Licinius and Sextius.[5] The plebeian families who extorted their admission to the consulship as the price for their support of the masses were themselves owners of large estates,[6] and it has been plausibly maintained that many of the so-called plebians were local dynasts in the Italian communities which had been incorporated in the Roman state, and that they were

---

[1] Woodhouse (*Solon*, especially c. 14) attributes to Solon a thoroughgoing solution of the agrarian problem; this view is hard to reconcile with the rapid growth of the revolutionary party in the years after Solon's reforms.

[2] See below, pp. 307 f.

[3] This is a possible inference from fr. 24 (Diehl), ll. 13–15.

[4] Fr. 25 (Diehl); cf. *A.P.* 12. 5.

[5] Described as their programme in Livy, vi. 35. 4–5.

[6] Cf. the story in Livy, vii. 16. 9.

connected by political and matrimonial alliances with some of the old patrician families.[1] So the Solonian reforms appear to be the work of an alliance between the local magnates in the out-lying districts of Attica which had been incorporated in the state later than the rest, and some of the Eupatrid families which were trying to establish their supremacy on a new foundation. The council as well as the chief magistracies had to be thrown open to the non-Eupatrid members of this alliance, and as the Roman plebeians who were elected to the consulship secured admission to the Senate, so Solon enacted that the Areopagus should in future be recruited from those who under the new conditions created by his law were elected to the archonship.

In both the Roman and the Greek reform popular discontent due mainly to economic causes was exploited to transfer to new hands the control of the machine of government. But when we consider the sequel to the reform in the two cases, the parallel breaks down. The explanation of this must be sought in the greater difficulties of the economic situation at Athens, and in the instability of the alliance between the two most influential sections of Solon's supporters. In Solon, who was by tempera-ment and conviction averse to radical economic change, the Eupatrid members of the coalition found a leader after their own heart. But though the new families had acquiesced in the programme of their Eupatrid allies, since admission to office was their first objective, some of them determined to take advantage of the economic grievances which Solon's half-measures had failed to remedy. They saw that under the changed political conditions created by Solon the formal sovereignty of the people might be made a reality, since the old nobility was now split into rival factions and the competition of conflicting aspirants to power made the ekklesia the arbiter of the strife. The demos itself was not yet sufficiently organized and self-conscious to assert its dominance, but it was now in a position, under the direction of powerful leaders who were ready to champion its cause, to achieve the realization of the reforms which it desired.

[1] Cf. F. Münzer, *Römische Adelsparteien und Adelsfamilien* (Stuttgart, 1920), *passim*, also H. H. Scullard, *Roman Politics, 220–150 B.C.* (Oxford, 1951), 10.

V. FROM SOLON TO KLEISTHENES[1]

BEFORE Solon the government of Athens had always been based on a religious sanction, on the divine right to rule possessed by the basileus or the Aristoi in virtue of their birth.[2] Solon discarded this sanction and substituted for it the principle that office should be the prerogative of those who held the largest stake in the country. Thereby he admitted the landed proprietors who were not Eupatridai to share the magistracies and the council with the members of the old aristocracy. Yet this great political revolution, which was the necessary prelude to the later developments of the Athenian constitution, was characterized by the same spirit of compromise as Solon's other measures. Though he destroyed the aristocratic monopoly of office, he retained the organs of the aristocratic state, and left them with the same functions and powers which they had enjoyed before. Apparently he thought that the old machinery of government, if entrusted to new men, would be adequate to the needs of the state.

This expectation might have been realized if Solon had dealt more drastically with the agrarian problem, and if the demand of the landed proprietors for office had been the only political problem awaiting solution. But there were other political problems which Solon ignored. The failure of the aristocrats to maintain their power had been due to the internal dissensions which destroyed their solidarity,[3] and the anarchy which the central government was unable and perhaps unwilling to suppress had been heightened by the feuds of the noble houses. In vain Solon preached to the Athenian magnates on the virtues of justice and moderation;[4] the only remedy was a government in which the executive had powers sufficient to suppress disorder and establish the rule of law throughout Attica,[5] but Solon was more concerned to impose checks on the competence of the executive than to extend it. He seems never to have realized that the usefulness of his new code would be severely limited in

---

[1] The reconstruction in the first part of this chapter is based on two main presuppositions: (1) that Solon's legislation is to be dated not long before 570, and (2) that the Philaïds and Peisistratos were political allies. See below, Appendixes III and V.

[2] Cf. Wade-Gery in *C.Q.* xxv, 1931, 89.

[3] BS 800.   [4] e.g. frr. 3 and 4 (Diehl).   [5] Cf. de Sanctis, 258.

practice if the magistrates on whom its enforcement depended
lacked the authority to secure the obedience of the local dynasts.

It was fortunate for Athens that the Solonian revolution was
not followed by a political reconciliation between the *novi
homines* and those who had previously held the monopoly of
power. Most of the Eupatrids remained bitterly hostile to the
interlopers, and united to form a party which came to be known
as the Pedieis,[1] from the πεδίον, the plains in the vicinity of
Athens and Eleusis where the estates of the great aristocratic
families were situated.[2] They can hardly have hoped to secure
the repeal of Solon's laws which had admitted the new families
to office and the council. Probably the chief purpose of their
combination was to exclude their hated rivals as far as possible
from election to the archonship.[3]

Those who were opposed to the Pedieis were organized in a
party called the Paraloi,[4] men of the coast. This would appear to
have included at first all the leading men who had supported
Solon's reforms. The meaning of their party-name is obscure.
In the *Athenaion Politeia*[5] the names of all the parties are said
to have been derived from the regions in which lay the lands
tilled by their members. At a later date the Paralia was identical
with the south-eastern triangle of Attica,[6] but the opponents of
the Pedieis cannot have been confined to this region; they
included aristocratic familes which had quarrelled with their
peers, such as the Alkmaionidai. The true significance of the
name is now lost, but the explanation in the *Athenaion Politeia*
does at least discredit the modern hypothesis[7] that the party
derived much of its support from wealthy traders and manufacturers. It was an association of renegade nobles and 'plebeian'
landowners, backed by their dependents and by the freehold
farmer who had benefited from the Seisachtheia.

The party of the Paraloi had originally been formed to defend
Solon's legislation against reaction, but before long there was
a split within its ranks. Some of its members, including the
Alkmaionidai, were entirely satisfied with Solon's economic and

---

[1] Plut. *Solon* 13. 2; Hdt. i. 59. 3 calls them οἱ ἐκ τοῦ πεδίου.
[2] BS 779 and n. 1 and 860.   [3] Cf. Wade-Gery, op. cit. 79.
[4] Hdt. i. 59. 3 and Plut. *Solon* 13. 2 (παράλιοι in *A.P.* 13. 4).
[5] 13. 5 (end).
[6] Thuc. ii. 55. 1 and 56. 1; cf. Cornelius, 14–15. For a different view cf. P. N.
Ure, *The Origin of Tyranny*, 312–13.
[7] e.g. in Busolt, ii². 305 and *C.A.H.* iv. 60–61.

political reforms and were not prepared to go beyond them,[1] but
an influential section of the party regarded them as merely provisional and no more than the first step to their ultimate goal.
The leaders of this section were patriotic enough to resent the
impotence to which Athens, with a larger territory and population than any state in Greece except Thessaly and Sparta, was
reduced by the weakness of her government,[2] and had a confidence in their own ability which encouraged them to demand
a revision of the Solonian settlement. This wing of the Paraloi
therefore decided to break away from their former political
allies and create a new party, the members of which were called
the Hyperakrioi. The nucleus was supplied by their friends and
retainers, and the support of the discontented poor was secured
by the promise of a new agrarian reform more thorough than
Solon's.[3]

This revolutionary party was led by Peisistratos son of
Hippokrates. Herodotus says[4] that he created it when the other
two parties were already in existence, and this testimony is to
be preferred to that of Plutarch,[5] who makes the three parties
contemporary in origin and prior to Solon's reforms. In Herodotus the adherents of Peisistratos are called Hyperakrioi.
Elsewhere[6] Herodotus uses the adjective to mean the hill
country as opposed to the plain, and later writers call the new
party Diakrioi[7] or Epakrioi,[8] the men of the hills. But it is
possible that the original name of the party, preserved by
Herodotus, meant something different, 'the men beyond the
hills'.[9] If this suggestion is correct, the term must have been
used in Athens with reference to the nucleus of the new party,
the henchmen and neighbours of Peisistratos, who lived at
Brauron in east Attica.[10] Brauron was also the home of the
powerful family called the Philaïdai, who were closely associated
with Peisistratos.[11]

---

[1] Megakles seems to have led the party continuously from before its split
down to 546.

[2] This may safely be inferred from the 'Panathenaïc' propaganda of the
party; see below, p. 330.   [3] Cf. Plut. *Solon* 29. 1.

[4] i. 59. 3.   [5] *Solon* 13. 1–2.   [6] vi. 20.

[7] *A.P.* 13. 4, Plut. *Solon* 13. 2 and 29. 1.   [8] Plut. *Moralia* 763 D.

[9] I owe this suggestion to a course of lectures by the late J. A. R. Munro.

[10] See above, p. 103, n. 4.

[11] The name Philaïdai was later given to one of the demes into which Brauron
was divided by Kleisthenes; cf. Plut. *Solon* 10. 3 and see below, pp. 135 f. On the
alliance of the family with Peisistratos cf. Appendix V.

Although the new party bore a name derived from a particular locality, its adherents must have been drawn from all parts of Attica. The author of the *Athenaion Politeia* says[1] of the three parties before the tyranny that the Pedieis desired an oligarchy, the Paralioi aimed at a μέση πολιτεία, while the third party was headed by Peisistratos, who was thought to be δημοτικώτατος. Plutarch says[2] that his party included ὁ θητικὸς ὄχλος καὶ μάλιστα τοῖς πλουσίοις ἀχθόμενος, and Aristotle in the *Politics*[3] agrees that it was based on enmity to the rich. The Thetes mentioned by Plutarch must be the landless citizens, composed of the small-holders expropriated before the Seisachtheia and the former Hektemoroi, who had failed to obtain from Solon the redistribution of land which they desired, and were now encouraged by Peisistratos to expect from him the satisfaction of their demands. This class of adherents cannot have been limited to the hill country, and it is possible that many of them lived in the πεδίον.[4]

The author of the *Athenaion Politeia* says nothing about the main body of Peisistratos' party, which he calls the Diakrioi, but he notes[5] that its ranks were swelled by those whom Solon's legislation had deprived of the debts due to them, and also by those of doubtful citizenship, οἱ τῷ γένει μὴ καθαροί. Both halves of this statement are open to suspicion. The creditors who suffered from the Seisachtheia were probably rich men who before Solon's reforms had been adding field to field; it is unlikely that they would have been so impoverished by the loss of their outstanding debts as to be ready to join in an agrarian revolution. On the inclusion of the second group in the Diakrioi the author cites as evidence the διαψηφισμός (revision of the list of citizens) held by the Athenians after the expulsion of the tyrants; the object of this revision was in his opinion to expel from the citizen-body those who had secured admission to it illegally. From this he concludes that the tyrants were supported by some citizens whose claim to Athenian citizenship was disputable, and that this class of citizens had existed in Attica before the tyranny.

It has been suggested[6] that this class of citizens who were not of pure Athenian descent owed its origin to the law of Solon,

---

[1] 13. 4.
[2] *Solon* 29. 1.
[3] 1305[a]22–24.
[4] So Busolt, ii[2]. 309, n. 3.
[5] 13. 5.
[6] By E. M. Walker in *C.A.H.* iv. 145.

mentioned by Plutarch,[1] which offered citizenship to all alien craftsmen who settled permanently in Attica. But the ascription of this law to Solon may be erroneous, and even if it is really Solonian, it does not justify the proposed inference. The citizenship of aliens enfranchised under the provisions of this law could not have been disputed, since it was derived from a law which had been approved by the people.

Whatever may have been the significance of the διαψηφισμός held in the year 510 or soon after,[2] it is likely that Peisistratos and his sons had conferred the citizenship on some of their supporters, such as the Akarnanian seer Amphilytos.[3] Greek tyrants often created new citizens in large numbers; Gelon of Syracuse is said[4] to have given citizenship in Syracuse to over 10,000 of his mercenaries. The enfranchisement of aliens by the Athenian tyrants must have been on a much smaller scale, as they showed far more respect than the Sicilian tyrants for public opinion. But it is possible that Peisistratos gave the full citizenship not only to aliens[5] but also to part of the population of Attica which had previously possessed an imperfect citizenship or none at all. These new citizens, whether of alien origin or natives of Attica, would naturally be regarded as γένει μὴ καθαροί by the opponents of the tyranny, especially by the aristocrats. The author of the *Athenaion Politeia* may easily be wrong in his assumption that these people had possessed the citizenship before the tyranny was established.[6]

In the economic and political programme of the Hyperakrioi the appeal to patriotism was the dominant note.[7] Attica was to be effectively unified by the subjection of the local dynasts to the central executive and to be strengthened in man-power by an increase in the number of her freehold farmers, the backbone of the army. By these measures the Athenian state was to be reorganized drastically and thereby enabled to pursue a vigorous foreign policy directed to the control of the lands adjacent to Attica.

A reorganization of the Solonian state on this model could only be effected by a dictator backed by the majority of the people. But Athens was pledged to give Solon's laws a trial for

[1] *Solon* 24. 4.   [2] See below, pp. 132 f.
[3] Hdt. i. 62. 4 with the note in How and Wells.   [4] By Diod. xi. 72. 3.
[5] BS 861, n. 4 (with ref. to Ar. *Knights* 447 ff.).
[6] Busolt, ii². 310, n. 2.
[7] The programme here attributed to the Hyperakrioi is a reconstruction.

ten years,[1] and the interval was used by the leaders of the new
party to popularize their programme and enhance their prestige,
while it revealed more clearly the deficiencies of the Solonian
settlement. In 566/565 the chief archonship was held by the
Philaïd Hippokleides,[2] who was probably a member of the new
party. His year of office was marked by the transformation of
the Panathenaia, one of the state festivals in which was commemorated the unification of Attica by Theseus. In this year it
was celebrated with special splendour, and athletic contests were
for the first time included in the festival; in future the new type
of celebration was held every four years and called the Great
Panathenaia.[3] This reorganization of a festival traditionally
founded or remodelled by Theseus was evidently intended to
lay fresh emphasis on his great achievement, the unification
of Attica, which the new party proposed to restore in a more
effective form.

Soon after the archonship of Hippokleides war broke out
between Athens and Megara.[4] During the struggle there must
have been a truce to the strife of the political factions. Athenian
patriotism, already roused by the propaganda of the Hyperakrioi, was stimulated by Solon, now returned from his travels.
In a stirring poem[5] he called on his countrymen to wrest the fair
isle of Salamis from their hated Megarian neighbours. The
strength of Megara had declined in the severe internal conflicts
which followed the end of the tyranny of Theagenes,[6] and was
no longer a match for the superior man-power of Athens. By the
treachery of some Megarian exiles Salamis was surrendered to
the Athenians,[7] who followed up this success by the capture of
Nisaia, the seaport of Megara on the Saronic gulf. The Athenian
army which captured Nisaia was commanded by Peisistratos,[8]
who was presumably polemarch at the time.[9] By this and other

---

[1] Hdt. i. 29. 2.   [2] Evidence in Cadoux, 104.

[3] Cf. Busolt, ii². 344, n. 2 (also 93, n. 1); see below, p. 330.

[4] Hdt. i. 59. 4 shows that the war occurred not long before Peisistratos first
became tyrant.

[5] Cf. fr. 2 (Diehl). I agree with Toepffer (*Q.P.* 51) that this poem was written
by Solon in his old age, and that the alleged earlier war in which Solon is said
to have led the Athenian forces is unhistorical, as Daïmachos of Plataiai saw
(*F.H.G.* ii. 44; Jacoby, *F.G.H.* ii A, no. 65, fr. 7); cf. also Toepffer, *Q.P.* 39 ff.

[6] Cf. Plut. *Q. Gr.* 18.

[7] Pausanias i. 40. 5; cf. Toepffer, *Q.P.* 56–57.   [8] Hdt. i. 59. 4.

[9] So de Sanctis, 270. Herodotus says ἐν τῇ πρὸς Μεγαρέας στρατηγίῃ, but the
last word cannot be used in its strict sense; if the στρατηγοί existed at all in this

feats of arms he acquired fame and popularity, and before long he was able with the support of his party to seize the Acropolis and establish 'tyranny' in Athens (561/560).[1]

The new government was anathema to the noble families, and on two occasions they were able by temporary alliances with the Paraloi to overthrow it. On the first occasion Peisistratos merely withdrew from Athens to Brauron,[2] but in 556 after a second brief tenure of power he had to leave Attica altogether and his property was confiscated. It was purchased by Kallias son of Phainippos, head of the Eleusinian genos of the Kerykes and one of the bitterest enemies of the tyrant.[3] Representatives of other old families were among the opponents of Peisistratos, such as Lykourgos son of Aristolaïdas, leader of the Pedieis[4] and probably head of the clan of the Eteoboutadai, and Leogoras, ancestor of the orator Andokides and member of one of the oldest houses in Athens.[5] The Alkmaionidai under their chief Megakles were at first less uncompromising in their hostility but in the end made common cause with their fellow nobles.[6]

Peisistratos spent ten years in exile before he ventured to return. During his exile he had acquired wealth in the mines of Pangaios[7] and useful friendships in many states of northern Greece.[8] Meanwhile, renewed anarchy in Athens had convinced many of the citizens that tyranny was to be preferred to such a freedom, and when Peisistratos landed at Marathon in 546 he easily overcame the resistance offered by his adversaries and established his power so securely that the régime lasted for thirty-six years.[9]

Some of the families opposed to Peisistratos, including the Alkmaionidai, left Attica on his final triumph.[10] This enabled him to solve the agrarian problem without a general redistribution of land. He seems to have provided some of his landless

period they must have been merely commanders of tribal regiments (see above, p. 77, n. 9).

[1] For the date cf. the careful discussion in Cadoux, 104-9.

[2] This is a fair inference from the statement of Herodotus (i. 61. 2) that on his second loss of power ἀπαλλάσσετο ἐκ τῆς χώρης τὸ παράπαν.

[3] Hdt. vi. 121. 2.   [4] Hdt. i. 59. 3 and 60. 1.

[5] Andok. ii. 26. The story given by Andokides in i. 106 is difficult; cf. Busolt, ii². 325, n. 3.

[6] Hdt. i. 61. 2 and 64. 3.   [7] A.P. 15. 2; cf. Hdt. i. 64. 1.

[8] Thebes, Eretria, Thessaly, and Macedonia; cf. Hdt. i. 61. 2-3, v. 63. 3 and 94. 1.

[9] Hdt. v. 65. 3; I agree with the view that Herodotus here means 36 years of *continuous* rule.   [10] Hdt. i. 64. 3.

supporters with farms carved from the estates of the exiled nobles.[1] Others were settled overseas in Sigeion, which was now recovered from Mytilene,[2] or joined in the new state which was founded in the Thracian Chersonese by Miltiades,[3] the nephew or cousin of Hippokleides[4] and apparently a member of the tyrant's party. To those who received freeholds in Attica Peisistratos advanced loans for the development of their farms.[5] The prosperity of the farmers was promoted by a foreign policy which maintained peace between Athens and her neighbours and by a domestic policy which suppressed the ruinous feuds of the great families.

Peisistratos enforced the authority of the executive over the local dynasts. Those who had remained in Attica were compelled to surrender to him their sons as hostages for their good behaviour.[6] He appointed district judges (δικασταὶ κατὰ δήμους) who went on circuit through the rural parishes.[7] The author of the *Athenaion Politeia* believes that the object of this innovation was to keep the rustic population away from the city, but it is more probable that the courts of the tyrant's nominees were intended to supersede the hereditary jurisdictions of the great nobles,[8] just as the new state coinage may have replaced the heraldic issues bearing the badges of the aristocratic clans.[9] Possibly the old naukraries were now remodelled to provide a local administration for the whole of Attica which should be responsible for executing the orders of the central government, including the collection of the direct tax on produce introduced by Peisistratos.[10]

Herodotus says[11] that Peisistratos did not interfere with the existing magistracies or alter the laws; Thucydides agrees that the tyrants observed the laws already in force, but adds[12] that they took care to secure the tenure of the chief magistracies by their own supporters. Probably the Solonian code was

---

[1] This is only a hypothesis, but it fits the facts better than the alternative view (cf. Woodhouse, 193 ff.) that it was Solon who solved the agrarian problem; cf. BS 864 and n. 1.　　　　　　　　　　[2] Hdt. v. 94. 1.

[3] Hdt. vi. 35–36; see below, Appendix V.

[4] Cf. Cadoux, 104, n. 173 and see below, pp. 327 f.

[5] *A.P.* 16. 2.　　　　　　　　　　　　　[6] Hdt. i. 64. 1.

[7] *A.P.* 16. 5.　　　　　　　　　　　　　[8] Cf. Cornelius, 53.

[9] So Cornelius, 53 (cf. 52). I find his view attractive but doubt whether all numismatists would accept it.　　　　　　　[10] See above, p. 70.

[11] i. 59. 6 (but with reference to Peisistratos' *first* tenure of power).

[12] vi. 54. 6.

supplemented by fresh laws such as the νόμος ἀργίας,[1] but the statement in the *Athenaion Politeia*[2] that many of Solon's laws lapsed under the tyranny is refuted by the testimony of Herodotus and Thucydides. The control exercised by the tyrants over the elections to the archonship served a double purpose, for not only were the archons the chief magistrates of the state but at the end of their year of office they became members for life of the council. Within a few years of his return Peisistratos must have been sure of a majority in the council, as the ex-archons admitted to it since 546 were all his nominees, and of the old members those most hostile to him had fallen in battle or left Attica, while the rest were pledged to submission by the surrender of their sons. Hence when Peisistratos was prosecuted for murder he could appear confidently before the Areopagus to stand his trial like an ordinary citizen.[3] By 510 the council must have been almost entirely composed of partisans of the Peisistratidai.

Although the tyrants could count on the support of the executive and the council and could to this extent use the organs of the Solonian state as the instruments of their personal rule, they could not include their authority completely within the framework of the Solonian constitution. Thucydides[4] says that they levied a tax of one-twentieth on crops, commanded in war, and offered state sacrifices. Possibly the tax was authorized by the ekklesia, and this and other revenues may have been administered by the ordinary officials, though in practice their conduct of the finances must have been controlled by the tyrants. But the other activities mentioned by Thucydides were in strict law reserved for magistrates, and they must have been quietly usurped by Peisistratos with popular consent. His command of the army is significant. The office usually held by the tyrants of Syracuse later was that of general with plenary powers, στρατηγὸς αὐτοκράτωρ. It has been suggested that the competence of the tribal στρατηγοί was increased under the tyranny to the detriment of the polemarch and that this change initiated the subsequent development of the στρατηγία.[5] This suggestion is unsupported by evidence, and the control of the

---

[1] Theophrastos in Plut. *Solon* 31. 5; see above, p. 19, also below, pp, 307–8.
[2] 22. 1.   [3] *A.P.* 16. 8.
[4] vi. 54. 5 (on the amount of the tax cf. Cornelius, 53, n. 5).
[5] De Sanctis, 311–12 and 346. The view of Beloch (i[2]. 2. 327) is that the military powers usurped by the tyrants were transferred after their fall to the στρατηγοί.

military power of the state by the tyrants must have been unconstitutional. They respected the laws which guaranteed the private rights of the citizens and preserved as far as possible the machinery of the old government, but their executive powers were not in fact compatible with the Solonian constitution.[1] The real foundation of their authority was the support of a party which seems to have included a majority of the citizens.

What proportion of the citizen-body consisted of new citizens who owed their citizenship to the tyrants? Before Solon possession of full citizen-rights almost certainly depended on the ownership of a plot of land.[2] At some date during the sixth century the possession of land ceased to be a condition of full citizenship. It has usually been supposed that this innovation was due to Solon. The Atthidographers and Aristotle[3] imply that he conferred full citizenship on the Thetes, in the sense that he admitted them to the ekklesia as well as the private rights of citizenship, though they were still excluded from the magistracies. If membership of a phratry continued to be a condition and criterion of citizenship, Solon must have insisted on the admission of the Thetes to the phratries, and some have found confirmation of this in the law quoted by Philochoros[4] which binds the members of the phratries to admit orgeones as well as gennetai.

The ascription to Solon of the law in Philochoros is open to question,[5] but even if it were certain the inference drawn from it is at variance with the known facts. It cannot have enacted for the first time that those who were not members of any genos should be admitted to the phratries,[6] since Drakon's law proves that in the pre-Solonian state a phratry might include other than aristocratic members.[7] Perhaps during the agrarian crisis before Solon's legislation the aristocrats had been able to expel from the phratries those plebeian members who had lost their freeholds, and consequently their title to full citizen-rights. But there were many farmers left who had avoided or resisted expropriation, and these must have been numerous enough to ensure the failure of any attempt to limit membership of the

---

[1] De Sanctis, 311, suggests that the powers mentioned in Thuc. vi. 54. 5 were conferred on the tyrants by laws voted in the Assembly.
[2] See above, p. 79.   [3] *A.P.* 7. 3; *Politics* 1274ᵃ15 ff.
[4] Fr. 94 (35a in Jacoby, *F.G.H.* iii B).   [5] See below, Note C.
[6] As stated by Jacoby in *C.Q.* xxxviii, 1944, 70; cf. his *Atthis* (middle of 318).
[7] *I.G.* i². 115 (Tod, 87), 16 ff.

phratries to gennetai. Solon's law (if it was his) was therefore not the declaration of a new principle but the reaffirmation of an old one to which recent events may have given a greater significance; no support can be found in it for the view that it was Solon who altered the conditions of citizenship.

It is difficult to believe that Solon gave full citizenship to the Thetes (including the former Hektemoroi). Had he done so he would have been compelled either to swamp the phratries with the new citizens or to divorce the possession of full citizenship from membership of a phratry. The former procedure seems alien to the cautious temperament revealed in his poems, and the latter would have been impossible for a reformer so conservative as Solon. A large increase in the number of Athenian citizens is more credible during the tyranny than at any other time in the sixth century. The ascription of this enfranchisement to the tyrants is not disproved by the contrary testimony of the Atthidographers,[1] for they have no clear or consistent ideas about the problems of citizenship in this period.

What, then, was the position after Solon's legislation of the landless men, the Thetes and the former Hektemoroi? As they were not full citizens (since they did not own land)[2] they could not attend the ekklesia, but probably they possessed the private rights of citizenship, and though their exclusion from the phratries debarred them from the protection conferred by membership Solon had given them a different guarantee against oppression in his provision that in certain types of cases any citizen could initiate a prosecution on behalf of another.[3]

Within this class of half-citizens, of whom all or most naturally joined the revolutionary party of Peisistratos, two groups can be distinguished. One consisted of labourers who worked on the land and wanted farms of their own. The second was composed of craftsmen and other town-dwellers; it may have been a comparatively small group at first, which increased during the tyranny with the development of trade and industry and was then probably augmented by alien immigrants. Although those in the first group who received allotments of land from Peisistratos were thereby put in a position to satisfy the condition which connected citizenship with ownership of land, it is unlikely that Peisistratos solved the problem by transforming

---

[1] Implicit in *A.P.* 13. 5.   [2] See above, p. 98.
[3] *A.P.* 9. 1; cf. Bonner and Smith, 169 ff.

all his Thetic supporters into freeholders. It was a simpler solution to abolish the connexion between citizenship and ownership of land, a solution which enabled him to satisfy the political demands of both his agrarian and his urban supporters.

Before the tyranny citizenship had depended on two conditions, membership of a phratry and ownership of land. Did Peisistratos cancel the first condition as well as the second, or did he compel the phratries to find room for his new citizens? The previous organization of the citizen-body had doubtless favoured the aristocrats, since the genē possessed considerable influence in the phratries. Aristotle in the *Politics*[1] mentions the creation of new and more numerous tribes and phratries as one of the most efficient means for destroying the power of an aristocracy. There is little evidence for the policy of the early tyrants with reference to the subdivisions of the citizen-body in the aristocratic states which they superseded, but what we know of Corinth suggests that its Kypselid tyrants replaced the four old birth-tribes by eight new local tribes.[2] Beloch maintained that a similar reorganization took place in Attica under Peisistratos, that it was he who replaced the four old Attic tribes and the phratries for political purposes by the system of ten new tribes composed of local units, the demes, which has usually been ascribed to Kleisthenes.[3]

This hypothesis raises two problems: who replaced for political purposes the four old tribes by the ten new tribes, and who made citizenship depend on membership of a deme rather than of a phratry? It has usually been supposed that Kleisthenes was the author of both these changes. Beloch ascribed them both to Peisistratos. But despite the possible parallel from Corinth, he must have been wrong in crediting Peisistratos with the creation of the ten tribes found later in Athens. Herodotus states definitely[4] that it was Kleisthenes the Alkmaionid who gave the Athenians ten new tribes in place of the four 'Ionian' tribes, and on such a point he cannot have been mistaken. But although the *Athenaion Politeia*[5] attributes to Kleisthenes the creation of the demes as well, Herodotus does not say so, nor does he say that Kleisthenes was the first to base citizenship on membership of a deme; he knew that the demes existed before Kleisthenes,

---

[1] 1319ᵇ19 ff.   [2] Busolt, i². 215; Beloch, i². 1. 363, n. 1.
[3] Ibid. 2. 328 ff., followed by Kahrstedt in *R.-E.* xi. 621. See below, pp. 135 f.
[4] v. 66. 2.   [5] 21. 5.

and in this connexion he merely remarks[1] that the new tribes were composed of groups of demes. His account does not exclude the possibility that the change which based citizenship on the deme rather than the phratry may have been earlier than the reforms of Kleisthenes.

Beloch believed that the later principle which made citizenship depend on membership of a deme could be traced back to the tyranny. It is generally agreed that the demes existed as local divisions in the countryside of Attica long before they were used for political purposes, and Herodotus in his account of the final return of Peisistratos contrasts them with the ἄστυ,[2] the town of Athens. Herodotus also notes that Phye, the sham Athena who brought Peisistratos back to Athens for his second tyranny, was a woman from the deme of Paiania.[3] But the deme of Philaïdai, to which Peisistratos himself is said to have belonged, was apparently an artificial creation, formed by dividing the old deme of Brauron.[4] Hence Beloch argued that the reorganization of the demes and their political functions must be as early as Peisistratos. It is, however, doubtful whether so much can be extracted from this evidence; possibly it amounts to no more than this, that the estate of Peisistratos was situated in that part of Brauron which later fell within the deme of Philaïdai. What is needed to prove Beloch's case is an instance prior to the reforms of Kleisthenes in which the deme is found as the basis of citizen-rights or in which a citizen is officially described by his deme-name.

Plutarch in his *Life of Solon*[5] says that those responsible for the massacre of the Kylonians were eventually persuaded to have their case tried by a court of 300 members chosen from the aristocrats (ἀριστίνδην), and that they were accused before this court by Myron of Phlya, Μύρων Φλυεύς.[6] In Plutarch's version the trial is prior to the archonship of Solon, but Beloch[7] connects it with the later expulsion of those who were descended from the murderers of the Kylonians and were often described as 'the polluted' (ἐναγεῖς).[8] This second expulsion, which took place soon after the end of the tyranny and is attested by

---

[1] v. 69. 2.   [2] i. 62. 1.   [3] i. 60. 4; cf. Jac. 368.
[4] Plut. *Solon* 10. 3; cf. Wil. *Aus Kydathen*, 110 and n. 22, also Beloch, i². 2. 330–1 and *I.G.* i², p. 273, col. 1.   [5] 12. 3–4.
[6] Solon's part in this version is clearly unhistorical; cf. Busolt, ii². 209–10, n. 1.
[7] *G.G.* i². 2. 302–3 and 331.
[8] Hdt. v. 70. 2, Thuc. i. 126. 11.

Thucydides,[1] was the work of the Spartan king Kleomenes and of Isagoras, the leader of the Athenian oligarchs and opponent of the Alkmaionid Kleisthenes. Herodotus says[2] that Kleomenes attempted to abolish the old council and substitute for it one composed of 300 partisans of Isagoras; this has been identified with the Court of Three Hundred mentioned by Plutarch. The account in Plutarch must be derived from the Atthis,[3] and Beloch maintained[4] that the source here employed by the Atthis was an inscription which recorded the second banishment of the Alkmaionidai and that Μύρων Φλυεύς was the description given of the prosecutor in this official record.

If the reorganization of the citizen-body is assigned to Kleisthenes and not to Peisistratos, it is possible that it preceded by a few weeks or months the intervention of Kleomenes and the second trial of the ἐναγεῖς. But Busolt, who adopted this view, must surely have been wrong when he tried to combine with it the belief that the ultimate source of Plutarch's account was an official record of the trial of the ἐναγεῖς in 508/507.[5] The aristocrats opposed to Kleisthenes would not have described the prosecutor by his deme-name in a public document if the principle which made membership of a deme the criterion of citizenship had only just been introduced by Kleisthenes.

The weak point in Beloch's argument is his assumption that the account of the trial and the description of the accuser as Μύρων Φλυεύς must have been obtained by the Atthis from an official inscription. This is contrary to all probability. If the aristocrats recorded the result of the trial on stone or bronze, the record must surely have been destroyed when Kleomenes was ignominiously expelled and the ἐναγεῖς returned in triumph. But the Alkmaionidai were so prominent in politics and so hated by their opponents that the discreditable incidents in their history were carefully saved from oblivion; thus the account of their trial, which must be dated before the legislation of Solon, may have been derived from an oral tradition.[6] It is perhaps significant that Phlya, the deme of Myron, was also associated with the Lykomidai, the genos to which Themistokles belonged; the chapel of this genos, rebuilt by Themistokles after

---

[1] Ibid. 12; cf. Hdt., loc. cit.   [2] v. 72. 1.
[3] Cf. A.P. 1 for traces of the same account, also Jac. 367, n. 81.
[4] Op. cit. 331.   [5] ii². 209–10, n. 1.
[6] Cf. Jac. 186–8 and the notes on 366 ff. (especially the authors cited in n. 79).
See below, pp. 334 f.

the repulse of the Persian invasion, was situated in Phlya,[1] which was presumably the original home of the Lykomidai. These facts may account in part for the later hostility between the Alkmaionidai and Themistokles.[2]

Though Beloch's arguments are inconclusive, it is a possible hypothesis that citizenship was based on membership of a deme, not of a phratry. But if Peisistratos was the author of this innovation, we must suppose that he distributed his new citizens over the four Attic tribes, which retained their political importance till the time of Kleisthenes.[3] And if Peisistratos ignored the phratries, the attempt to expel the new citizens which followed the overthrow of the tyranny in 510 may have been justified by a revival of the old rule that membership of a phratry was an essential condition of citizenship.

This hypothesis is attractive, but it cannot be proved, and the evidence which we possess for the reaction in and after 510 is on the whole unfavourable to it. We must therefore suppose that the tyrants either insisted on the admission of their new citizens to the old phratries or created additional phratries for them; of these alternatives the first is the more probable. The tyrants are more likely than Solon to have carried through such a radical transformation of the membership of the phratries. But their action was challenged when the tyranny was overthrown, and as their work had to be done again by Kleisthenes, the credit of the achievement was naturally assigned to him in the tradition.[4] Yet it was due to the tyrants that the Thetes were first admitted to full citizenship, and during the tyranny their citizenship was so firmly established by prescriptive right that the subsequent attempt to deprive them of it ended in the decisive defeat of the reactionaries.

As the powers exercised by the tyrants were outside the constitution and never received legal confirmation, they did not in any way affect the form of the constitution. Nor were any significant changes introduced into the constitution under the rule of the tyrants. The importance of the tyranny in the constitutional development of Attica was that it hastened and facilitated the transition from the aristocratic state to demo-

[1] Plut. *Them.* 1. 4.
[2] Cf. end of the long note in Busolt, ii². 209–10.
[3] On the view that the authority of Hdt. v. 66. 2 is decisive for the Kleisthenic authorship of the ten tribes.
[4] Ar. *Politics* 1275^{b}35 ff.; cf. *A.P.* 21. 2 and 4.

cracy. By the admission of the Thetes to full citizenship the plebeian element in the citizen-body was strengthened, and by the solution of the agrarian problem many of its members were provided with a stake in the country and acted in future as a stabilizing force. But the greater achievement of Peisistratos was the effective unification of Attica. The Attica of Solon was not a centralized state governed by democratic institutions and subject to the rule of law, but a confederacy of local dynasts,[1] like Scotland in the sixteenth century, a unity in little more than name. Peisistratos was the historical Theseus who brought about the second and truer συνοικισμός,[2] and his democratic monarchy is reflected in that of Theseus as described by Euripides in the *Supplices*. He saw that in his state and generation strong government was more necessary than new constitutional machinery.[3] The local influence of the great families which had promoted disunion was broken, and respect for the law was enforced on members of all classes. This levelling policy prepared the ground for the democracy which was established by Kleisthenes.[4]

[1] Hdt. vi. 35. 1 uses ἐδυνάστευε to describe the position in Attica of Peisistratos' ally the elder Miltiades.   [2] Cf. Meyer, *G.A.* iii². 718.
[3] So de Sanctis describes Peisistratos' accession to power in the title of his eighth chapter as 'the end of the anarchy'.   [4] Cf. BS 868.

VI. KLEISTHENES

Kleisthenes and the struggle for power

TYRANNY in Greece was a transitional form of government and seldom endured to the third generation.[1] The new monarchy lacked the legitimacy of the old, and though the first tyrant could claim to represent the popular will, he had received no mandate from the people to hand on his position like an estate to his heir,[2] who was always inferior in prestige and usually in ability to his predecessor. Moreover, the tyrant had been supported by the people as the champion of their cause, and when under his leadership they had secured their objectives they began to resent their dependence.[2] It is, however, doubtful whether these causes played any part in the overthrow of the tyranny at Athens. Hippias, the eldest son of Peisistratos and his successor in the government, seems to have maintained the conciliatory policy of his father. He was assisted in the administration by his brother Hipparchos, and Thucydides declares[3] that their rule was distinguished by virtue and wisdom. When Hipparchos was murdered in 514 by Harmodios and Aristogeiton, Hippias is said to have ruled with greater severity and executed many of the citizens.[4] But the victims of his harshness probably belonged mainly to the upper classes, for when the exiled Alkmaionidai invaded Attica with a small force and occupied a strong position at Leipsydrion their demonstration received no popular support and ended in failure.[5]

The Alkmaionidai had great influence at Delphi, and the Delphic oracle now recommended the Spartans to free Athens from the tyrant.[6] Policy as well as piety decided the rulers of Sparta to obey; they were opposed in principle to tyranny, and the Athenian tyrants by their alliance with Argos, the traditional enemy of Sparta, had incurred their special disfavour.[7] But they underrated their task, and their first invasion of Attica was easily repulsed. Then they sent a larger force under their king,

---

[1] Ar. *Politics* 1315ᵇ11 ff.　　　　　　[2] Glotz and Cohen, i. 250.
[3] vi. 54. 5.　　　　　　　　　　　　　[4] Thuc. vi. 59. 2.
[5] Hdt. v. 62. 2; cf. *A.P.* 19. 3, where the exiles are said to have been joined by τινὲς τῶν ἐκ τοῦ ἄστεος. The occupation of Leipsydrion may have been in 513, in spite of Wil. i. 34, n. 10.
[6] Hdt. v. 62. 3–63. 2.　　　　　　　　[7] *A.P.* 19. 4.

Kleomenes, which in the early summer of 510 expelled the Peisistratidai from Attica.[1]

Kleomenes had been supported by 'those of the Athenians who wished to be free'.[2] These were probably the exiles for the most part, as the mass of the people seem to have been apathetic. The hoplites had been disarmed by Hippias as a precaution after the murder of Hipparchos,[3] but had good reason to be suspicious of the real intentions of their aristocratic 'liberators'. Prominent among these were Kleisthenes, the chief of the Alkmaionidai, and Isagoras son of Teisandros,[4] a member of an old family which had apparently remained in Attica during the tyranny, and therefore denounced as a friend of the tyrants by the returned exiles.[5] A struggle for power between these two dynasts was the sequel to the liberation of Athens. But the Alkmaionidai were always unpopular with their peers, and Isagoras had secured the ear of Kleomenes. In the summer of 508 Isagoras won the first round by his election to the archonship.[6]

According to Herodotus it was when Kleisthenes was being worsted in the struggle for power that he 'took the demos into partnership'.[7] This statement indicates that Kleisthenes had not been in alliance with the demos before, and Herodotus says later that Kleisthenes took over the demos of the Athenians entirely into his own party, although previously he had spurned them. The Alkmaionidai who seized Leipsydrion had been fighting for their own ends, and the drinking-song which celebrates their exploit is wholly aristocratic in tone; it praises the Eupatridai who proved by their valour the nobility of their birth.[8] From this evidence it is clear that when Kleisthenes first came back from exile he was not planning a democratic reform. He had no ties with the demos which he found on his return, for it was largely the creation of the tyrants and bound by gratitude to them. But when his own personal following was overmatched by his opponents he decided to take a leap in the dark and appeal to the demos. This demos must have been mainly composed of supporters of the Peisistratidai, who now combined with the

---

[1] Hdt. v. 63. 2–65. 2; on the date cf. Cadoux, 112–13.   [2] Hdt. v. 64. 2.
[3] Thuc. vi. 58. 2. The precaution is wrongly attributed to Peisistratos in *A.P.* 15. 4–5 (followed by Wil. i. 269–72); cf. Busolt, ii². 326, n. 1 and 383, n. 1.
[4] Hdt. v. 66. 1.
[5] Hdt. v. 70. 1 and *A.P.* 20. 1; cf. Busolt, ii². 401, n. 2 and Wade-Gery in *C.Q.* xxvii, 1933, 19, n. 4.   [6] Evidence in Cadoux, 113.
[7] v. 66. 2; cf. 69. 2.   [8] *A.P.* 19. 3.

former enemy of Hippias against the peril of an oligarchic reaction.[1]

Herodotus does not mention Isagoras' election to the archonship of 508/507; the fact and the date are supplied by Dionysios of Halikarnassos.[2] But when he says[3] that Kleisthenes was getting the worse of his struggle with Isagoras, it is reasonable to assume that the reverse to which he is referring was the election of Kleisthenes' opponent to the chief magistracy. Probably the same assumption is the source of the statement in the *Athenaion Politeia*[4] that Kleisthenes became the recognized champion of the people in the archonship of Isagoras.

Kleisthenes' sensational volte-face may therefore be dated to the second half of the year 508, perhaps not long after Isagoras had taken over the archonship. By his alliance with the demos he obtained a majority in the ekklesia, and his next step was to submit to it far-reaching proposals for the reform of the constitution. Herodotus implies that these proposals were sanctioned by the assembly before Isagoras called on the Spartans to intervene. It has, however, been maintained that at this stage the proposed reforms were only brought before the people, not carried, and that they did not actually become law till after the expulsion of Isagoras and the final victory of the demos.[5] This view was suggested by the account contained in the *Athenaion Politeia*, but the interpretation of that account is disputed. In any case, as the narrative which it gives is clearly dependent on that of Herodotus, it is unlikely that its author had better information than Herodotus concerning the precise order of events.

On these grounds the ratification of the new constitution by the ekklesia must be dated with Herodotus before the Spartan intervention. But as Isagoras was then archon, and as the archon at this time was still the president of the ekklesia, it is difficult to see how the proposals of Kleisthenes could have been put to the vote without violence to the existing constitution. Some have supposed that Kleisthenes, like Solon, was given plenary powers for the drafting of a new constitution,[6] or that a legislative commission was appointed of which he was the chief

---

[1] Cf. Macan's note on Hdt. v. 66. 2.

[2] *A.R.* i. 74. 6 and v. 1. 1.   [3] v. 66. 2.   [4] 21. 1.

[5] Cf. Meyer, *G.A.* iii². 740–1, n. 1; for a discussion of the various views see below, Appendix VI, also Busolt, ii². 402, n. 6.

[6] Cf. the end of the long note 6 in Busolt, ii². 402–4.

member.[1] These suggestions are exposed to the same difficulty:
how could Isagoras have been induced to put to the vote proposals which conferred such dangerous powers on his chief
opponent? The only possible explanation is that Kleisthenes
was so strongly supported by the ekklesia and the popular
enthusiasm evoked by his programme was so intense that Isagoras was daunted and gave way. In normal times the archon
might be free to decide whether he would put a particular proposal to the vote or not, but it was a right which could not be
maintained with safety against the peremptory insistence of an
overwhelming majority.[2]

As the distinction between laws and decrees was unknown or
ignored in this period,[3] there is no reason why the measures of
Kleisthenes should not have been moved by him as a private
citizen in the ekklesia; the procedure seems to have been the
same when on the motion of Aristion a bodyguard was permitted to Peisistratos by the people.[4] There was no probouleutic
council,[5] and the assembly was still competent to pass decrees
by which the constitution was altered, provided that the archon
was willing to put them to the vote. Solon had bound the
Athenians to observe his laws for ten years, but the ancient
authorities give no support to the modern notion that he must
have provided permanent guarantees against any alteration in
the constitution created by him.[6] Modern parallels prove that
a rigid constitution can be drawn up which is intended to be
unalterable but provides no adequate machinery to prevent the
violation of its fundamental provisions.[7]

Some scholars have supposed that laws contrary to the constitution could be quashed by the Areopagus,[8] but there is no
evidence that this power was comprised in the guardianship
of the laws ascribed by ancient writers to the Areopagus; the

---

[1] So Beloch, i². 1. 395, n. 2; cf. F. Schachermeyr in *Klio*, xxv, 1932, 335.

[2] Cf. the way in which the assembly overrode the opposition of the prytaneis
in 406 (Xen. *Hell.* i. 7. 12–15).

[3] Xen. *Mem.* i. 2. 42; see below, p. 300. Cf. also Kahrstedt in *Klio*, xxxi,
1938, 8 and 17–18.

[4] *A.P.* 14. 1. But see below, Note F.   [5] See above, pp. 92 ff.

[6] Wil. ii. 193–4 maintained that the γραφὴ παρανόμων was Solonian. Busolt,
iii. 279, n. 3 thought that the thesmothetai could indict unconstitutional measures
before the Areopagus.   [7] Cf. A. V. Dicey, *Law of the Constitution*⁸, 127 ff.

[8] Wade-Gery in *C.Q.* xxvii, 1933, 24, n. 3 describes the νομοφυλακία of the
Areopagus as 'probably in effect a *veto*'. De Sanctis, 356, claims that the Areopagus
could intervene 'as supreme tribunal' against the proposal of unconstitutional
decrees or of new laws.

νομοφυλακία of the Areopagus was probably limited to judicial prosecution before its own tribunal of individuals charged with violation of the laws.[1] As Kleisthenes was not a magistrate, the only way in which the Areopagus could have exercised its νομοφυλακία against him would have been by an impeachment for attempted subversion of the existing constitution.[2] But at this time the Areopagus was composed of ex-archons who had almost all been appointed under the tyranny,[3] and was therefore as a body favourable to the Peisistratid party, with which Kleisthenes was now co-operating against the oligarchic reactionaries. It may therefore be presumed to have supported his reforms, as it was almost certainly the council which soon after offered vigorous resistance to his opponents.[4]

The ratification of Kleisthenes' proposals by the people was a decisive defeat for the oligarchs. Isagoras, realizing that his party could never hope to regain power under the new constitution, decided to secure its overthrow by foreign intervention.[5] On his appeal Kleomenes sent a herald ordering the Athenians to expel Kleisthenes and the other Athenians who were under the curse of Kylon. Kleisthenes at once retired from Attica, but the other ἐναγεῖς apparently did not. Kleomenes then arrived in Athens with a small force to complete the expulsion, and banished 700 families. But when he tried to establish an oligarchy by the creation of a new council of 300 members, partisans of Isagoras, he met with a vigorous resistance from the old council, the Areopagus. The people rose against the oligarchs and the Spartans, who were compelled to take refuge on the Acropolis, but they were unprepared for a siege and after two days agreed to retire from Attica. Kleisthenes and the 700 families were promptly recalled (perhaps early in 507). His reforms, which had already been sanctioned by the ekklesia, could now be carried out.

[1] See above, p. 91.
[2] Under the law cited in *A.P.* 8. 4 (if it is pre-Kleisthenic, but cf. Gilliard, 281 and 57, n. 2).
[3] Cf. Thuc. vi. 54. 6. Kleisthenes himself would be a member of the Areopagus if, as seems probable, he is to be identified with the archon of 525/524; cf. Cadoux, 109–10.
[4] See above, p. 94. For a defence of the old view that the council of Hdt. v. 72. 2 was the 'Solonian' Council of Four Hundred cf. P. Cloché in *R.E.G.* xxxvii, 1924, 1–26.
[5] For the details here given cf. Hdt. v. 70–73. 1; on the additions to his narrative supplied in the *A.P.* cf. Wade-Gery in *C.Q.* xxvii. 18–19.

The ancient authorities

Herodotus gives only a brief and incomplete summary of the reforms.[1] He says that Kleisthenes created new tribes with new names, more numerous than the old, made the phylarchs ten instead of four, and divided the demes into ten groups, assigning one of these groups to each tribe. Aristotle in the *Politics* refers to Kleisthenes twice;[2] both passages are controversial and must be reserved for fuller discussion later, but it may be noted that both presuppose a large increase in the number of citizens by Kleisthenes. The fullest account of the reforms is supplied by the *Athenaion Politeia*,[3] but much of it is taken up with the author's speculations about their purpose. If we ignore these we get the following description of the laws of Kleisthenes:

Kleisthenes created ten tribes, each of which supplied fifty members to his new Council of Five Hundred. He divided the demes into thirty groups, of which ten were taken from the city of Athens (and its neighbourhood), ten from the coast, and ten from the inland region. These groups Kleisthenes named trittyes. Each of the ten new tribes was composed of three trittyes selected by lot from the three different regions, town, coast, and inland. Kleisthenes abolished the naukraries and substituted for them the demes, which he created and provided with names; the demarchs took over the functions of the old naukraroi. In future an Athenian was to be designated not by the name of his father but by that of the deme in which he lived; this and the tribal reform facilitated *Kleisthenes' admission of new citizens*. The old genē, phratries, and hereditary priesthoods were not interfered with by Kleisthenes.

On the discovery of the *Athenaion Politeia* the chapter which describes the reforms of Kleisthenes was greeted with special enthusiasm as a new revelation.[4] It is therefore essential to remember that the value of this as of all parts of the *Athenaion Politeia* is entirely dependent on the value of its source. Was the description of Kleisthenes' reforms derived, directly or indirectly, from the text of the laws? Some have believed that the laws of Kleisthenes were still extant in the fourth century,[5] but the grounds of this belief are weak and unconvincing. The laws of

---

[1] v. 69. 2 (reading the word after ἐποίησε as δέκαχα; see below, p. 134).
[2] 1275ᵇ34-37, 1319ᵇ19 ff.　　　　　[3] 21. 2–22. 1.
[4] e.g. Wil. ii. 146: 'it is all pure gold'.
[5] So Wade-Gery in *C.Q.* xxvii. 19–20. But cf. Jac. 385, n. 36.

Kleisthenes are never cited by the orators.[1] In the *Athenaion Politeia*[2] we read that the laws of Solon had become obsolete from disuse under the tyranny, and that Kleisthenes to please the people made new laws, including the law of ostracism. It will be shown later that the law of ostracism was not Kleisthenic,[3] and the statement that Solon's laws lapsed under the tyranny is refuted by Herodotus[4] and Thucydides.[5] The *Athenaion Politeia* records the proposal made by a certain Kleitophon before the revolution of 411 that the commissioners who had just been appointed to draft a new constitution should be instructed to examine for their guidance the laws made by Kleisthenes when he established the democracy.[6] This motion certainly implies that though the laws of Kleisthenes were not generally known in the last decade of the fifth century they were still extant in the archives. But Kleitophon was a reactionary, and whether he was a moderate or an extreme oligarch it is not likely that the constitution of Kleisthenes would have been acceptable to him. Wade-Gery suggests[7] that in 411 Kleisthenes' laws were to be studied from the point of view of procedure, as the oligarchs wished like him to create a new constitution by psephismata, but this explanation is contradicted by the wording of Kleitophon's motion.[8] It is simpler to assume that the motion was merely a skilful piece of propaganda, that Kleitophon neither knew nor cared whether Kleisthenes' laws were still preserved in the archives or not, but calculated that the changes proposed by his party might be camouflaged as a revival of the constitution of Kleisthenes.[9]

Even if it could be proved that the laws of Kleisthenes were still extant in the fourth century, the description of the laws in the *Athenaion Politeia* cannot have been taken from an official record, for it contains some statements which are manifestly incredible. Kleisthenes did not create the demes nor did he give them their names; the country demes at least had existed before his time.[10] It is unlikely that he abolished the naukraries; Klei-

---

[1] Cf. Ehrenberg, *Neugründer*, 60.   [2] 22. 1.
[3] See below, pp. 159 ff.   [4] i. 59. 6.
[5] vi. 54. 6.   [6] *A.P.* 29. 3.   [7] Op. cit., p. 21.
[8] This contention is still valid even if (as is probable) the words after τὸ ἄριστον represent someone's comment (possibly Androtion's; cf. Jac. 384, n. 30) on Kleitophon's motion.
[9] See above, pp. 15 f. and cf. Ledl, 24. Ehrenberg (op. cit. 61) says that 'the motion meant no more than a return to the pre-Periklean state'.
[10] Hdt. i. 60. 4 and 5, also 62. 1; cf. Jac. 368, n. 81, section (2).

demos[1] asserts that he retained them and changed their number to fifty. The summary of Kleisthenes' legislation given in the *Athenaion Politeia* is probably a reconstruction from the materials available in the fourth century. These consisted of the brief account preserved in Herodotus and a tradition, recorded by Aristotle in the *Politics*,[2] that Kleisthenes had admitted to the citizen-body many who were previously outside it, and that their admission had been facilitated by a reorganization of the tribes and the phratries.

Herodotus supplied the evidence that it was Kleisthenes who created the ten tribes, each composed of a group of demes. From this it was assumed that the use of the deme-name started now, that Kleisthenes created the demes, and that he abolished the naukraries; of these assumptions the second and third are certainly false and the first is at least doubtful. Further it was natural to ascribe to Kleisthenes the origin of the institutions which were closely connected with the ten tribes. So Grote[3] believed that Kleisthenes had created the Council of Five Hundred and the ten στρατηγοί, whereas the Atthidographers credited him with the one but not with the other, since they had reason to date the first board of ten strategoi to the year 501/500.[4] The genē, phratries, and hereditary priesthoods were obvious survivals from the aristocratic state which had presumably persisted unchanged throughout their history.

The account of Kleisthenes' reforms in the Atthis contains two items of independent value. One is the description of the way in which the demes were distributed among the tribes, and of the function of the trittyes as the link between them. Doubtless this was based on the organization of the ten tribes in the fourth century, the origin of which was correctly referred to Kleisthenes. The second is the statement, probably derived from the oral tradition, that the eponymous heroes of the ten new tribes were chosen by the Delphic priestess from a list of 100 Attic heroes (ἀρχηγέται). This detail is very significant; it proves that Kleisthenes procured for his new constitution the blessing of Delphi.[5]

---

[1] Fr. 8; see above, pp. 68 and 73.
[2] 1275^{b}36–37 and 1319^{b}21–22.
[3] Grote, iii. 115–16 (abridged ed. 64–65).
[4] Cf. *A.P.* 22. 2; see below, pp. 169 f.
[5] *A.P.* 21. 6; cf. H. W. Parke, *A History of the Delphic Oracle*, 166–7.

The reorganization of the citizen-body by Kleisthenes

Herodotus does not mention the creation of new citizens by Kleisthenes, but his silence does not disprove the evidence of the *Politics* on this point. His references to the history of the sixth century are always selective, and he may have thought it tactless to remind the Athenians that many of them belonged to families which had only possessed the citizenship for two or three generations. The author of the *Athenaion Politeia* declares that the tribal reform was intended to smooth the way for the admission of new citizens, and that the use of the deme-name was introduced to conceal the origin of these νεοπολῖται.[1] It is therefore beyond any doubt that he, like Aristotle, accepted the tradition which attributed to Kleisthenes the enfranchisement of a large number of non-citizens. But if the tradition is correct, what explanation can be offered of the revision of the citizen-list which followed the expulsion of the tyrants? This revision is recorded by the author of the *Athenaion Politeia*[2] to support his speculations on the composition of Peisistratos' party, and he does not attempt to explain how it was related to the enfranchisement policy which he ascribes to Kleisthenes.

It is not necessary to suppose[3] that the revision was recorded in an extant decree. These revisions of the list of citizens were rare in Athenian history, and probably the occasions on which they had occurred would be remembered as precedents. Many scholars,[4] however, have been reluctant to accept as a fact the holding of such a διαψηφισμός in or soon after 510. To some it seems incompatible with Kleisthenes' creation of new citizens. Others believe that it was subsequent to his reforms and amounted to nothing more than the verification by each deme of its own citizens,[5] since the demes were to be responsible in future for the keeping of the lists. Wilamowitz[6] tried to identify it with the expulsion of 700 families by Kleomenes, but this expulsion as described by Herodotus bears no resemblance to the procedure of a διαψηφισμός.[7]

At Syracuse on the overthrow of the tyranny established by Gelon the old citizens proceeded to exclude from office the new

---

[1] *A.P.* 21. 2 and 4.   [2] 13. 5.
[3] As Wade-Gery does in *C.Q.* xxvii. 25.   [4] e.g. Beloch (i². 1. 396, n. 2).
[5] So de Sanctis, 337 (who wrongly says that *A.P.* 13. 5 attributes it to Kleisthenes) and so apparently Busolt, ii². 416. Cf. BS 224, n. 1.
[6] *A.A.* i. 31–32.   [7] Cf. Busolt, ii². 310, n. 2.

citizens who owed their citizenship to the tyrants.[1] This analogy supports the tradition that in Athens after the expulsion of Hippias many who had previously possessed the citizenship were deprived of it, since their right to it was in some way defective. It is probable that the διαψηφισμός recorded in the *Athenaion Politeia* was held in 510 soon after the end of the tyranny, and that it was effected by a combination of all who were opposed to the tyrants, the Alkmaionidai as well as the oligarchs. The new citizens who were excluded on this occasion from the list of citizens were apparently restored to the list two years later by Kleisthenes after he had joined forces with the demos.[2]

To what category did these new citizens belong? Aristotle in the *Politics*[3] says that Kleisthenes admitted to the tribes many foreigners and slave metoikoi; if the text is correct the latter must be former slaves who on their emancipation received the status of metics. We have already seen[4] that the number of those who received full citizenship from the tyrants was probably greater than has usually been supposed, and that the new citizens were composed of two groups. Those natives of Attica who had obtained allotments of land from Peisistratos were in a stronger position than the rest of the new citizens. Possibly the revision in 510 was combined with a revival of the old principle which made citizenship dependent on the ownership of land. On this view the revision must have been directed against the town-dwellers who had been enfranchised by the tyrants. This group may have included alien craftsmen who had settled in Athens during the tyranny as well as the former Hektemoroi and their children who had found employment in the city; the latter would naturally be described as 'serfs who had become metics' by those who regarded their citizenship as invalid.

Though the enfranchisement by Kleisthenes of those who had been excluded from the citizenship in 510 was incidental to his main reforms, it was made easier by them, and its significance must not be denied or underrated. It was for Kleisthenes the support of a numerous body of voters[5] in the ekklesia who had a personal interest in the maintenance of his reforms. Moreover, as they were mainly resident in Athens, the legal ratification of

[1] Diodoros, xi. 72. 3.   [2] Cf. Wade-Gery, op. cit. 25–26.
[3] 1275^{b}36. The objections of Busolt (ii². 409, n. 5) are unconvincing.
[4] Above, p. 112.
[5] Aristotle, loc. cit., says that Kleisthenes admitted many (πολλούς) to the tribes.

their status marks the definitive affirmation of the new principle that the ownership of land was not a necessary condition of citizenship.

With his admission of new citizens Kleisthenes combined a drastic reorganization of the citizen-body. For political purposes the old tribes were replaced by the ten new tribes created by Kleisthenes, each composed of a number of local units, the demes. Our manuscripts of Herodotus[1] credit him with the statement that Kleisthenes assigned ten demes to each tribe. If the reading is correct, Herodotus must have believed that there were precisely 100 demes at that time. In the late fourth century there were at least 150.[2] Some scholars have believed that there really were 100 demes in 507, but that local interests caused the subdivision of many of them before the end of the fifth century.[3] This hypothesis is unconvincing,[4] and we must suppose either that Herodotus made a mistake or that the manuscripts are corrupt. It has been suggested[5] that what he wrote was δέκαχα δὲ καὶ τοὺς δήμους κατένειμε ἐς τὰς φυλάς: Kleisthenes divided the demes into ten groups, assigning one group to each tribe.

From the *Athenaion Politeia*[6] we learn that each tribe was composed of three groups of demes taken from three different regions of Attica, and that these groups were called trittyes, since three of them formed a tribe. Now it is true that no tribe contained two trittyes from the same region in the sense that none contained two trittyes from the Paralia or two from the Mesogeios, but it might and did happen that in a particular tribe the coast trittys adjoined the inland trittys. So in the Marathonian district, usually believed to have been a stronghold of the Peisistratid party, two trittyes of the tribe Aiantis formed a compact block of territory, and in the east of Attica the inland and coast trittyes of the tribes Aigeis and Pandionis, possibly of Akamantis also, were contiguous.[7]

---

[1] v. 69. 2.

[2] Cf. BS 873 and n. 5, and the article on 'Demoi' in *R.-E.* v (1903), 1 ff.

[3] BS 873–4; cf. Jac. 128 and 317.

[4] It is rejected by Wil. ii. 148 ff. and Busolt, ii². 405, n. 3.

[5] By H. Lolling in Δελτίον ἀρχ. v, 1889, 31 (cf. A. Wilhelm in BS 873, n. 4); the word δέκαχα is used in a similar context in *I.G.* ii². 1 (Tod, 96), l. 34. For another suggestion cf. J. L. Myres in *Mélanges Glotz* (1932), ii. 665 (he proposes to read δέκα δέκα δέ: Kleisthenes distributed the demes, ten and ten).   [6] 21. 4.

[7] So Busolt, ii². 421 and Ehrenberg, *Neugründer*, 90 (who rightly points out in 131, n. 15 that Loeper was surely justified in his refusal to admit enclaves in the trittyes). Cf. the map in Loeper or the one at the end of Gomme, *Population*.

These facts were adduced by Beloch[1] in support of his contention that the tribal reorganization must have been the work not
of Kleisthenes but of Peisistratos. He argued that the composition of these four tribes was intended to favour the tyrant's
supporters, who lived in eastern Attica, and he saw in it an early
example of 'electoral geometry'. But though the following of
Peisistratos was strong in Brauron and possibly in Marathon
also, it is unlikely that it was confined to the east part of Attica.
Moreover, Beloch's theory presupposes a system of group voting
similar to that employed in the Roman *comitia tributa*, whereas
in the Athenian ekklesia questions were decided by a majority
of the individual voters present, not by a majority of the tribes.
In the *Athenaion Politeia*[2] it is stated that Kleisthenes drew lots
to decide the allocation of the trittyes to the tribes, but this may
be a later conjecture to account for the anomalies of the allocation. It must be admitted that if these anomalies were deliberately planned by Kleisthenes their purpose can no longer be
discerned, but it is possible that they were accidental.

The inhabitants of certain territories adjacent to Attica and
controlled by Athens were not included in this organization.
They were the people of Oropos and Eleutherai,[3] and the old
inhabitants of Salamis who remained in the island side by side
with the Athenian cleruchs.[4]

In the *Athenaion Politeia*[5] Kleisthenes is said to have created
the demes and given them their names. Herodotus presupposes
the existence of demes in an earlier period, but as he contrasts
them with the ἄστυ in his account[6] of Peisistratos' return from
exile, he must be referring only to the rural demes. The demes
into which the town of Athens was divided seem to have been
created by Kleisthenes.[7] Those who follow the account in the
Athenaion Politeia[8] admit that Kleisthenes based his rural demes
on the village communities which he found in existence, and that
some of these, such as Acharnai, formed a single deme, but
they maintain that most of his demes were new units formed

---

[1] *G.G.* i². 2. 329 ff.; Beloch's view is criticized in BS 870, n. 3. Cf. also Ehrenberg in *Klio*, xix, 1923, 108 ff. and F. E. Adcock in *C.A.H.* iv. 71.
[2] 21. 4.
[3] Cf. Busolt, ii². 405, n. 2 and BS 871, n. 1, also Tod, p. 102 and the full discussion in Kahr. i. 346 ff.
[4] Cf. Pausanias i. 35. 2 and Kahr. i. 355 ff., also BS 871–2, n. 1.
[5] 21. 4–5.   [6] i. 62. 1.
[7] Busolt, ii². 406 and n. 2.   [8] e.g. BS 872–3.

by the division of large villages or the combination of small hamlets, and that these new units received their official names from him. This reconstruction is contrary to Herodotus and goes far beyond the statement in the *Athenaion Politeia* on which it claims to be based, a statement which is probably no more than an ill-founded conjecture. The great disparity between the demes in population which is found later must also have existed in the last decade of the sixth century, and supports the conclusion that with very few exceptions the rural parishes of Attica were taken over without alteration by Kleisthenes into his new tribes.

Henceforward each deme kept a register (the ληξιαρχικὸν γραμματεῖον)[1] of all its male members over eighteen years of age who were citizens, and the full citizenship possessed by these members depended on their membership of a deme. All citizens who at the time of Kleisthenes' reforms had their regular abode in a district which formed a Kleisthenic deme were now enrolled as members on the register of that deme. As the demes were local units, the Kleisthenic organization was to this extent based on the principle of locality. Yet Kleisthenes made membership of a deme hereditary for the future;[2] the direct descendants in the male line of a man who had been entered in 507 on the deme-list of Acharnai continued to be members of the deme of Acharnai whether they lived in the deme or not. So later movements of population produced the distinction[3] between demesmen residing in their own deme and ἐγκεκτημένοι, residents in a deme who belonged by descent to another deme.

In the fourth century the demes had their own local government.[4] Each was under the control of a demarchos, appointed for a year, probably by election in the deme-assembly,[5] and assisted by treasurers and other officials. He had charge of the details of administration within his deme, including the maintenance of public order, and was also responsible for carrying out the commands of the central government. Final decision in all important matters concerning the deme was reserved for the assembly of the demotai, which met in the deme, not in Athens.

---

[1] Cf. *I.G.* i². 79, l. 6, Isaios vii. 27, and [Dem.] xliv. 35; cf. also de Sanctis, 336, n. 1.   [2] Cf. BS 875 and n. 2.   [3] Cf. Gilbert, 204.

[4] Details in Busolt, ii². 412 ff. and the article 'Demos' by B. Haussoullier in Daremberg–Saglio, ii. 1. 83 ff.; cf. Gilbert, 204 ff.

[5] Gilbert, 205, n. 1, accepts the inference of Müller from *I.G.* ii². 1172, ll. 12–14 and Dem. lvii. 25 that he was appointed by lot, but cf. Busolt, ii². 412, n. 7.

Although the list of its members was kept by the demarch, membership could only be conferred by the vote of the assembly. Admission, for those who were members' sons, took place at the age of eighteen. As membership of a deme had been made an essential condition of citizenship by Kleisthenes, safeguards were provided against a biased verdict of the demotai. In the fourth century unsuccessful applicants could appeal to the law-courts, and all admissions had to be ratified by the Council of Five Hundred.[1]

The trittyes served as the connecting link between the demes and the tribes; the number of demes included in a trittys varied with the population of the demes, and a trittys might even be composed of a single large deme.[2] In themselves the trittyes had little importance and were apparently named after the principal demes in each. They were sometimes used as convenient sub-divisions of the tribes, as when citizens were conscripted for public works, and Plato[3] mentions the command of a trittys as an example of a minor military post. Stones have been found in the Piraeus and in Athens which mark boundaries between trittyes,[4] and it has been suggested that those in the Piraeus were intended to mark the stations to be occupied by men called up for service in the fleet; so proposals made by Demosthenes[5] include a proviso that each tribe and each trittys should have their definite stations in the dockyards. But apart from these minor functions the trittyes had no importance except as deter-mining the allocation of the demes to the ten new tribes.[6]

In his allocation of demes to tribes Kleisthenes endeavoured to make the new tribes equal not in area but in population.[7] As each tribe was to enjoy equal representation in the new Council of Five Hundred and to supply a regiment of infantry to the Athenian army it was necessary to make sure that the tribes would remain approximately equal in the future. In this need

---

[1] Cf. *A.P.* 42. 1–2.

[2] Cf. H. Hommel in *R.-E.* vii A, 1. 359 ff., also Gilbert, 209–10.

[3] *Republic* 475 A. Wil. ii. 164 thinks that the trittyarchs may have been concerned with the mobilization of the army but E. Harrison denies that they were military at all (*Proc. Camb. Phil. Soc.* 1911, 3–5); cf. Hommel, 364.

[4] *I.G.* i². 897–901. See also 883–5 and the stones published by Meritt in *Hesperia*, viii, 1939, 50–51 and ix, 1940, 53–57.

[5] xiv. 23. See, however, Gomme, *Population*, 49, n. 2.

[6] The prytaneis of the council were subdivided by trittyes (cf. *A.P.* 44. 1); the fifth-century boards which had thirty members may have been composed of one member from each trittys.   [7] Wil. ii. 148; cf. Gomme, op. cit. 49.

may be found the reason why Kleisthenes made membership of a deme hereditary, since membership of a tribe depended on membership of a deme.

The members of a Kleisthenic tribe formed a corporation under the presidency of ἐπιμεληταί; in their meetings, which were held in Athens, they passed decrees on matters which fell within their competence.[1] They served together in the army in their tribal regiment, and had an additional bond of union in the cult of their eponymous hero. The statues of these ἐπώνυμοι stood on the south side of the agora at Athens, but each of them had also a separate shrine and a priest.[2]

Though some of the details in the preceding description may represent subsequent alterations and additions, Kleisthenes must have been responsible for the principal elements in the later organization of the citizen-body which was based on his ten tribes. The purpose of the reforms can only be deduced from their content, since the explanations of Kleisthenes' motives propounded by the ancient authorities are unsatisfactory. Herodotus says[3] that Kleisthenes was imitating his mother's father, Kleisthenes the tyrant of Sikyon, and that he substituted his ten tribes for the four Ionian tribes from contempt for the Ionians. It is possible that Kleisthenes was to some extent indebted in his reorganization of the tribes to the example of his grandfather, but the motive suggested by Herodotus cannot be taken seriously; he brings it in because he always enjoys a fling at the Ionians and because it improves his parallel between Kleisthenes of Athens and Kleisthenes of Sikyon.

In the *Athenaion Politeia*,[4] as in the *Politics*, the reform of the tribes is connected with the extension of the citizen-body; Kleisthenes divides the Athenians into ten tribes instead of four in order to remove the barriers between the different classes and thereby make easier the admission of new citizens. Moreover, it is assumed by the author that as Kleisthenes based his new tribes on the demes he introduced the practice of describing a citizen by the name of his deme as a substitute for the previous

[1] Details in Busolt, ii[2]. 422 ff., de Sanctis, 344–5, and Gilbert, 200 ff. On the official order of precedence of the new tribes cf. [Dem.] lx. 27–31 and the evidence cited in Gilbert, 200, n. 2.

[2] Busolt, ii[2]. 423 and Gilbert, 201. It is significant that though there was also a cult of the eponymous hero in each deme (Busolt, ii[2]. 407, n. 5) there was no such cult for the trittyes.

[3] v. 67. 1 and 69. 1.

[4] 21. 2; cf. *Politics* 1319[b]19 ff.

custom of adding his father's name, which would have revealed too clearly the alien parentage of the new citizens.[1] On this view, whereas Themistokles had previously been known as Θεμιστοκλῆς Νεοκλέους, his official designation was henceforth Θεμιστοκλῆς Φρεάρριος. The use of the deme-name by the Athenians in private life is regarded as the consequence of the official usage.

The practice of describing a citizen by his deme-name (demotikon) is found early in the fifth century,[2] and its origin is probably to be connected with the Kleisthenic reorganization. But it needs no other explanation than the fact that citizenship had been linked by Kleisthenes with membership of a deme, that a man who could boast a deme-name was *eo ipso* proved to be a full citizen.[3] Moreover, the evidence which we possess from the fifth century does not support the assumption made in the *Athenaion Politeia* about the employment of the demotikon. The personal name alone seems to have been used in some official records, such as decrees and casualty lists. In other official documents from the second half of the fifth century the demotikon occurs but sometimes[4] it is combined with the patronymic. The inscriptions in general suggest that there was no official nomenclature which was universally observed, and the same conclusion is to be drawn from the extant ostraka,[5] which frequently contain only the personal name and the patronymic, though the deme is sometimes added. These fluctuations indicate. that official documents merely reflected the variations common in everyday speech. In private life the patronymic continued to be used by the upper classes, and the same practice is observed by Herodotus and Thucydides, whereas Aristophanes often employs the deme-name without the patronymic.

Hence the inferences drawn by the author of the *Athenaion Politeia* from the use of the demotikon are unsound. It may nevertheless be argued that although he got hold of the wrong end of the stick he was right in his assumption that the part assigned to the demes by Kleisthenes was intended to promote his enfranchisement policy. In other words, Kleisthenes ordained

---

[1] 21. 4.

[2] The two examples in Hdt. viii. 93. 1 are perhaps from an official record; cf. Wil. ii. 172, n. 6.

[3] Cf. Wil. ii. 171 ff., BS 876, n. 1, and the elaborate discussion in Kahr. i. 199–214.

[4] *I.G.* i². 82, ll. 1–2, 84, ll. 1–2; for inconsistencies of nomenclature within the same inscription cf. i². 324 and 302 (= Tod, 64 and 75).

[5] Examples in Tod, 15 and 45.

that in future Athenian citizenship should depend on membership of a deme rather than on membership of a phratry, on a local unit instead of a kinship unit, because it was his intention, as the evidence of the *Politics* shows, to make extensive additions to the citizen-body.[1]

The flaw in this contention is that it exaggerates the difficulty of introducing new citizens into the phratries in this period; the law admitting foreign craftsmen to citizenship[2] shows that foreigners could be admitted to the old phratries. Further, it ignores the fact that Kleisthenes secured for his new citizens admission to the phratries as well as to the demes;[3] if he could do this, the previous conditions of citizenship did not constitute a real obstacle to his proposed creation of new citizens. A different explanation must be found for the importance of the deme in the Kleisthenic system.

That the substitution of the ten new tribes for the four Attic tribes was connected with the extensive enfranchisements of Kleisthenes is affirmed in the *Politics*[4] as well as in the *Athenaion Politeia*. It may be allowed that the admission of new citizens was simplified by the tribal reform, but it does not account for the peculiar character of the Kleisthenic tribes. Other Greek states in the archaic period replaced their old birth-tribes for political purposes by new local tribes. But why was each of the new local tribes of Athens composed of three parts taken from three different regions of Attica?

These three regions, the ἄστυ, παραλία, and μεσόγειος, from which the three trittyes of a Kleisthenic tribe were drawn, have apparently nothing to do with the three political parties, the Pedieis, Paraloi, and Hyperakrioi, which had existed in Attica before the tyranny.[5] The old parties, though each may have had a nucleus in a particular district, were not regional in character, with the possible exception of the Pedieis. Moreover, the three Kleisthenic regions did not correspond strictly to their names. The Asty included most of the coastal strip between Hymettos

---

[1] So E. M. Walker in *C.A.H.* iv. 144–6.

[2] Plut. *Solon* 24. 4. See above, pp. 111 f.

[3] Even if the law quoted in Philochoros 94 (Jacoby, 35*a*), is Solonian, its principles must have been reaffirmed by Kleisthenes; that admission to a phratry was a concomitant of a grant of citizenship in the late fifth century is proved by *I.G.* i². 110 (Tod, 86), ll. 15–17. Cf. also Francotte, 80 and Greenidge, 158.

[4] 1319^{b}19 ff. (if read in conjunction with 1275^{b}35–37); cf. *A.P.* 21. 2.

[5] The old view was refuted by Walker in *C.A.H.* iv. 146–7; cf. Ehrenberg, *Neugründer*, 88–89.

and Aigaleos. Part of the plain north of Athens belonged to the
Mesogeios, and the plain west of Aigaleos was assigned to the
Paralia, which here included the hilly country north and north-
west of the plain to the Attic frontiers.[1]

The inclusion by Kleisthenes of part of the Asty in each of the
new tribes has been attributed[2] to personal motives; as most of
the new citizens enfranchised by him probably resided in Athens
and could more easily attend the assembly than the tribesmen
of the Paralia or the Mesogeios, Kleisthenes thereby secured a
strong body of voters to further his interests in each of the ten
tribes. This suggestion recalls Beloch's argument for ascribing
the creation of the ten tribes to Peisistratos, and is open to the
same objection that it presupposes a system of group-voting
which was unknown in the Athenian ekklesia. In any case the
Asty included more than the city of Athens, which was not
represented in some of the trittyes of which the Kleisthenic
Asty was composed.

There are three main peculiarities in the composition of the
Kleisthenic tribes; the members of each are drawn from three
different regions of Attica, the Asty forms one of the three
regions, and the coast and inland trittyes are contiguous in some
tribes but not in others. For the third no satisfactory explanation has been offered, but it is a fact which does at least rule out
the supposition[3] that the construction of the new tribes was
intended to weaken the local influence of the old families. The
other characteristic features of the Kleisthenic tribe may have
been intended to transcend local barriers by bringing together
men from urban, coastal, and rural districts and to develop
a sentiment of union and fellowship between its members, who
henceforth fought side by side in the same regiment.

Thus the peculiar composition of the new tribes was the
instrument devised by Kleisthenes to preserve and strengthen
the unity which had been imposed on Attica by the tyrants and
to preclude for the future any growth of regional interests to the
detriment of the whole. Such a threat to the balance of the state
was latent in the development of the urban population in
Athens, and this was probably the reason why Kleisthenes provided no local administration for the town of Athens as such
but divided it into several demes, each with its own officials,

---

[1] Cf. the map at the end of Gomme, *Population.*
[2] By Walker in *C.A.H.* iv. 147–8.   [3] Ibid. 147.

and assigned these demes to various tribes.[1] But Athens retained
its privileged position as the centre of the state government and
naturally was chosen to be the headquarters for the administration of the new tribes.[2]

Athens was not the only state in which the old tribal divisions
were later replaced by tribes based on the new principle of
locality, but the peculiar composition of the Kleisthenic tribes
seems to have had no parallel elsewhere in Greece. Yet they
proved permanent, despite their artificial character, because
they were composed of local units which with few exceptions
were natural and well established. As village communities the
rural demes must have existed long before Kleisthenes, and in
them he found the firm foundation which he required for his
reorganization.

Kleisthenes and the old organization of the citizen-body

The use of the demes as organs of local administration was
apparently Kleisthenic,[3] and the democratic nature of their
institutions was a microcosm of the new δημοκρατία established
by Kleisthenes for the government of the state. It is doubtful
whether the naukraries had ever been responsible for local
government, and they have sometimes been regarded as groups
of taxpayers analogous to the later symmoriai with which they
were compared by Kleidemos.[4] Direct taxation, introduced by
the tyrants, had presumably lapsed or been abolished on the
overthrow of the tyranny, but the naukraries may have been
retained for naval purposes until 483/482,[5] when the reorganization of the fleet by Themistokles made a new system necessary.
Kleidemos may be right in his statement that the number of the
naukraries was raised by Kleisthenes to fifty in order to bring
them into relation with his ten new tribes.

Kleisthenes also retained the four Solonian property-classes
and the Solonian system which made the political privileges of
a citizen depend on the importance of the class to which he
belonged. As before, the treasurers of Athena were chosen only
from the Pentakosiomedimnoi[6] and the archons only from the
members of the first two classes.[7] It is probable that the Thetes

---

[1] Ehrenberg, op. cit. 89–90.   [2] Cf. BS 878.   [3] Cf. Francotte, 49.
[4] Fr. 8; cf. Beloch, i². 2. 325. BS 881 maintained that the naukraries were
groups of taxpayers after Kleisthenes' reforms, but local divisions before them.
[5] Beloch, i². 2. 325–6 and Wil. ii. 165.
[6] A.P. 8. 1.   [7] See above, pp. 101 f.

were still excluded from minor offices, perhaps also from membership of the new Council of Five Hundred,[1] but Kleisthenes, unlike Solon, admitted the Thetes to the ekklesia and finally broke with the old principle which made attendance at the assembly dependent on the ownership of a plot of land.[2]

Some scholars[3] have maintained that though Kleisthenes preserved the Solonian classes in form he radically altered their character by a provision which permitted income in money as well as income in kind to count for membership of a telos; hence the possession of real-estate ceased to be necessary for membership of the three highest classes, and a rich merchant could now stand for the archonship without landed property. But though it is usually assumed that at some date between Solon and the fourth century[4] income from movable as well as from real property was included in the calculation of a man's telos, the evidence on which this assumption was based is inconclusive,[5] and even if the alleged innovation is accepted as a fact, it is more likely to have been introduced by Perikles than by Kleisthenes.

Kleisthenes did not abolish the four Attic tribes and their subdivisions the twelve trittyes,[6] but the functions which he left to them were merely ceremonial and religious, as his creation of a new political organization had deprived the old of its political importance. It is implied in the *Athenaion Politeia*[7] that the phratries and the genē were reduced to similar insignificance by the reform which made membership of a deme the condition of citizenship. There is some truth in this opinion, but it is not the whole truth. Membership of a phratry was still a condition of citizenship after Kleisthenes, and decrees which confer citizenship stipulate that the recipient shall be admitted to a tribe, deme, and phratry.[8] There may have been a few citizens who for one reason or another had failed to obtain admission to a phratry, but they were apparently exceptional.[9] These facts prove that although Kleisthenes connected citizenship with

---

[1] Even if membership of the 500 was legally open to the Thetes they would not be eager to serve in this period, when pay for service had not yet been introduced. Cf. de Sanctis, 359, and see below, pp. 157 and 220.

[2] See above, pp. 117 ff.   [3] e.g. BS 837.

[4] Beloch, ii². 1. 89 and n. 2, is inclined to date the change to the period of the Persian Wars.

[5] Cf. Kahr. i. 255 ff.   [6] See above, pp. 71–72.   [7] 21. 6.

[8] See above, p. 140, n. 3, and cf. Francotte, 53 ff.

[9] See above, pp. 59 f., and cf. Wade-Gery in *C.Q.* xxvii, 1933, 27 and n. 2.

membership of a deme, he maintained the old rule that a citizen must be a member of a phratry.

How did Kleisthenes effect the admission of his new citizens to the phratries? The author of the *Athenaion Politeia*, despite his insistence on the creation of new citizens by Kleisthenes, ignores the problem, and merely states that he allowed everyone to remain in his former phratry. A passage in the *Politics*[1] has been cited as evidence that Kleisthenes increased the number of the phratries and altered their character, but Aristotle is there speaking of Kyrene as well as Athens, and the reference to the phratries may apply only to Kyrene.[2] If Kleisthenes had broken up the old associations and remodelled the phratries he would have given a severe and unnecessary shock to popular feeling; if he had left the old phratries untouched and simply created additional phratries for his νεοπολῖται, he would have emphasized the distinction between the new citizens and the old. The most probable view is that he compelled the old phratries (which at this date must have numbered far more than twelve)[3] to admit those whom he had enfranchised, and that these new members formed fresh thiasoi within the phratries side by side with the previously existing thiasoi and genē.[4]

Different explanations have been suggested for Kleisthenes' action in making citizenship depend on membership of a phratry as well as on membership of a deme. Some deny that it had any logical justification, and see in it merely a tactful concession to the religious conservatism or the social snobbery of the Athenians.[5] It is, however, worth noting that the overlap between the new system and the old was not complete, since children under eighteen and women could be members of a phratry,[6] but only male citizens over eighteen could be members of a deme and exercise the full rights of citizenship,[7] including the right to sit and vote in the ekklesia. The deme-lists have therefore been compared with the modern electoral-rolls, while the phratry-lists were analogous to our registers of births.[8] Membership of

---

[1] 1319[b]19 ff.

[2] Cf. Sandys' note on *A.P.* 21. 6 and Wade-Gery, op. cit. 26–27.

[3] See above, pp. 59 f.

[4] Or possibly secured admission to the existing thiasoi.

[5] So Francotte, 80.

[6] Cf. Francotte, 79, and on the position of women the articles by Ledl cited in the Bibliography.

[7] *A.P.* 42. 1.   [8] Toepffer, *A.G.* 17 (criticized by Francotte, 73).

a phratry was evidence of the status of those who enjoyed it, the only decisive evidence in the case of women and minors. Even citizens over eighteen possessed in it an additional guarantee of their citizenship, and this may be the principal reason for its retention by Kleisthenes. By basing the rights of his new citizens on the phratry as well as the deme, he linked his reconstruction of the citizen-body with the past and the present at once and thereby provided greater security for its permanence.[1]

It must, however, be admitted that the retention by Kleisthenes of the old criterion of citizenship alongside the new was to some extent a temporary expedient dictated by the peculiar character of his problem. When he made full citizenship depend on membership of a deme he must have expected and intended that the old political importance of the phratries would be undermined by the change.[2] He could therefore afford to tolerate the continuance of the aristocratic genē in their old form. They might retain their social pre-eminence within the phratries,[3] but their political influence had been shattered by the tyrants, and any danger of its revival had been forestalled by the transference of emphasis in the Kleisthenic reorganization from the phratry to the deme.

The councils, the magistrates, and the ekklesia

If we collect the ancient evidence on the constitutional reforms of Kleisthenes we find that it amounts to very little, apart from his creation of the ten tribes and his reorganization of the citizen-body, and even this little may be due wholly or in part to conjecture. Institutions of the fifth century which were closely connected with the ten Kleisthenic tribes would naturally be presumed to owe their origin to Kleisthenes. So Grote, writing before the discovery of the *Athenaion Politeia*, ascribed to him the creation of the ten στρατηγοί and the replacement of the Solonian Council of Four Hundred by the later Council of Five Hundred.[4] In the *Athenaion Politeia*, although the latter reform is definitely attributed to Kleisthenes, the former is dated to the year of Hermokreon (apparently 501/500)[5] and its

---

[1] So Ehrenberg, *Neugründer*, 94–95.
[2] At a later period we find that enrolment in a phratry was delayed or omitted altogether as a superfluous formality; cf. Francotte, 81–82.
[3] Cf. Aischines, ii. 147.   [4] Grote, iii. 115–16 (abridged ed. 64–65).
[5] 22. 2; on the date see below, Appendix VII, and cf. Cadoux, 115–16.

ascription to Kleisthenes seems to be denied by implication. Androtion[1] credited Kleisthenes with the introduction of the ten ἀποδέκται, Herodotus with that of φύλαρχοι δέκα, but the statement of Herodotus is false[2] and that of Androtion is far from certain. Apart from these items we have no evidence for the alterations made by Kleisthenes in the Solonian constitution, and it is obvious from the *Athenaion Politeia* that the Atthidographers had no clear ideas about the nature and the working of the Athenian constitution during the period 507–462.

Confronted with these lacunae, modern scholars have tended to fill in the gaps by ascribing to the Kleisthenic consitution without any warrant features borrowed from the constitution of Periklean Athens. For example, it is usually assumed that Kleisthenes must have played some part in the development of the popular courts, must have introduced some reform which bridged the gap between the Heliaia of Solon and the dikasteries of Perikles.[3] One suggestion is that magistrates now had to secure the approval of a popular court for their verdict in all cases, not merely in those wherein they wished to exceed the legal penalty. But though Kleisthenes may have reserved to the ekklesia the trial of capital charges,[4] there is no evidence that he altered in any way the functions of the Heliaia as defined by Solon,[5] and doubtless he relied on the judicial powers vested in the Areopagus to enforce on the magistrates and people respect for the laws.

Modern reconstructions of the Kleisthenic constitution on the Periklean model leave little or no place for the Areopagus. In justification it is maintained that the Areopagus could not be trusted with its former powers because at this time a majority of its members were adherents of the Peisistratidai.[6] The argument is inconclusive. Some of the majority may have been passive rather than active supporters of the tyrants. Moreover, we have seen that Kleisthenes on the occasion of his political conversion formed an alliance with the party of Hippias, and that it was the Areopagus which led the opposition to the oligarchic reaction attempted by Isagoras. Finally, there is evidence[7]

---

[1] Fr. 3 (5 in Jacoby, *F.G.H.* iii B).
[2] J. L. Myres in *Mélanges Glotz*, ii. 664–5 suggests that Herodotus in v. 69. 2 was using φυλάρχους in a non-technical sense and meant the ten στρατηγοί; cf. Macan's note on the passage.   [3] So de Sanctis, 356.   [4] See below, pp. 154 f.
[5] Cf. Bonner and Smith, 200, n. 4.   [6] So de Sanctis, 353.
[7] Cf. Cadoux, 109–10 and p. 71, n. 6.

that Kleisthenes himself had held the archonship during the tyranny and must therefore have been a member of the Areopagus at the time of his reforms. As membership was for life it is unlikely that Kleisthenes diminished the powers of the council, since his seat in it gave him a permanent position in the state.

Plutarch, in a passage[1] probably derived from Theopompos, says that the later reforms of Ephialtes by withdrawing the cognizance of all cases from the Areopagus transformed the government into a radical democracy, and that Kimon's attempt to repeal the reforms was intended to restore to the Areopagus its former jurisdiction and thereby revive 'the aristocracy of Kleisthenes'. The presuppositions of this account are that the constitution of Kleisthenes was far less democratic than that of Periklean Athens,[2] and that its moderate character (exaggerated in the description of it as an 'aristocracy') was due to the judicial authority of the Areopagus, an authority which had been preserved undiminished by Kleisthenes as a bulwark against further change.

There was, however, another view current in the fourth century, summarized in the statement of Aristotle[3] that the Areopagus was able συντονωτέραν ποιῆσαι τὴν πολιτείαν after the Persian War of 480–479 because it had won prestige by its patriotic conduct during the crisis. That this view was derived from an Atthis is shown by the fuller statement of it in the *Athenaion Politeia*. We read there[4] that after the Persian invasion the Areopagus acquired control of the state, and that this control was not conferred by any decree but was the consequence of its patriotism before Salamis, when it supplied eight drachmas apiece to the sailors and so made possible the manning of the fleet. This version is refuted by the silence of Herodotus and by the anachronism of its details, which reflect the conditions of a later age.[5] It was apparently invented by Kleidemos,[6] though in his account Themistokles, not the Areopagus, was the hero of the story. The alleged recovery of power by the Areopagus in the Persian War must be regarded as an unsound hypothesis based on false presuppositions. As the Atthidographers accepted the view that the radical democracy had been established by

---

[1] *Kimon* 15. 2–3.
[2] Cf. the comment at the end of *A.P.* 29. 3 (see above, p. 15, n. 2).
[3] *Politics* 1304ª20–21.   [4] 23. 1.
[5] Cf. the refutation by Walker in *C.A.H.* v. 472–4, also Busolt, iii. 27, n. 2.
[6] Fr. 13 (21 in Jacoby); cf. Jac. *Atthis*, p. 75.

Solon and restored by Kleisthenes they had to account for the
fact that the Areopagus was deprived of substantial powers by
Ephialtes. The only solution available to them was that the
Areopagus must have regained its old powers or usurped new
ones in the period between Kleisthenes and Ephialtes, and the
occurrence of the Persian invasion within this period suggested
a suitable occasion. But the problem which they tried to solve
by this hypothesis was non-existent, as Theopompos realized,
for the judicial powers taken from the Areopagus by Ephialtes
were those which it had possessed since the days of Solon.

It may be objected that even if the judicial powers of the
Areopagus were left substantially unaltered by Kleisthenes, his
creation of a new council, the Council of Five Hundred, must
have diminished its authority in other respects, especially if it
had hitherto been the sole council in the state. The validity of
this objection depends on the answers given to some very
difficult questions. What precisely were the powers of the Areopagus before Kleisthenes? What were the powers conferred by
him on his new council? Which of the previous organs of government was most affected by these innovations, the old council,
the magistrates, or the popular assembly?

Any account of the powers vested in the Areopagus under the
Solonian constitution must be largely conjectural, but the reconstruction of them attempted in an earlier chapter[1] pointed to the
conclusion that those powers were mainly religious and judicial,
and that it retained them without much alteration until the
revolution of Ephialtes. As there is no valid evidence for the
financial functions sometimes attributed to the Solonian Areopagus, there is no reason to believe[2] that the creation of the
ἀποδέκται by Kleisthenes (if he did create them) was designed to
limit its authority. We have seen that the control exercised by
the Areopagus in the aristocratic state over the initiative of the
magistrates had probably lapsed before the time of Solon, and
the conditions of the sixth century were not favourable to its
revival. Hence the establishment of a new council by Kleisthenes
would seem to have been intended to provide for a closer supervision and control than had previously existed over the magistrates, and possibly over the ekklesia as well.

Our information about the Council of Five Hundred is very

---

[1] See above, pp. 89 ff.
[2] As de Sanctis does (*Atthis*, 353–4). See above, p. 91.

scanty for the period between Kleisthenes and Ephialtes. It is doubtful whether it is mentioned by Herodotus at all, for the βουλή which opposed Isagoras was almost certainly the Areopagus, which may also have been the βουλή that exercised probouleutic functions in 479.[1] The earliest inscriptions which prove the existence of the new council cannot be dated with certainty before the reforms of Ephialtes and may easily be later. Philochoros says[2] that whenever an ὀστρακοφορία took place ἐπεστάτουν οἵ τε ἐννέα ἄρχοντες καὶ ἡ βουλή, but although the procedure may go back to 488, the date at which the law establishing ostracism was passed, the part played in it by the boulē may have been taken over by the 500 from the Areopagus later. The only witness who attests unambiguously the existence of the new council in the period before 462 is the author of the *Athenaion Politeia*. Even he has nothing to tell us about its duties and its powers in this period. He merely states that Kleisthenes substituted for the Solonian Council of Four Hundred a new Council of Five Hundred, fifty from each tribe, and that in the year of Hermokreon they (i.e. the Athenians) drew up the oath for the new council which is still taken by its members.[3] His warrant for the date of the original oath is uncertain, but his implication that it had continued unchanged to his own day is improbable and is contradicted by other ancient writers.[4]

On these grounds the evidence for the creation of the new council by Kleisthenes cannot be regarded as beyond dispute, and the statement in the Atthis that it was instituted at the same time as the ten tribes may be no more than a plausible conjecture. But the alternative hypothesis, that the Council of Five Hundred was created by Ephialtes, is improbable; had its origin been so recent the fact would surely have been remembered. Hence it seems safer to ascribe its institution to Kleisthenes and to suppose that there was documentary authority for its existence in the year of Hermokreon.

If the new council was Kleisthenic, we may perhaps identify it with the council mentioned in the ninth book of Herodotus,[5] and conclude that from its inception it exercised the probouleutic function which belonged to it in the later fifth century. This

---

[1] Hdt. ix. 5.   [2] Fr. 79b (30 in Jacoby).   [3] 21. 3 and 22. 2.
[4] Details in BS 1023, n. 1; cf. Wade-Gery in *B.S.A.* xxxiii, 1932–3, 117–19.
[5] ix. 5. 1–2.

function may have belonged to the Areopagus in the aristocratic state, but had probably lapsed in the course of the sixth century, if not earlier. When Kleisthenes entrusted it to his new boulē he was not encroaching on the authority of the Areopagus but providing a necessary safeguard against the abuse of power by the magistrates and the popular assembly.

With this possible exception it is impossible to decide with any certainty which of the later characteristics and functions of the Council of Five Hundred belonged to it from the beginning. It has usually been supposed that the use of the solar year as the official year observed by the council, the so-called conciliar year, owed its invention to Kleisthenes, but Meritt has now shown[1] that this was not introduced until the middle of the fifth century. The original method of appointment to the council is unknown. In the fourth century the fifty members supplied by each tribe were chosen from the demes of that tribe in proportion to their population.[2] Each deme appointed a number of its members as πρόκριτοι (perhaps twice as many as its quota on the council); from these the councillors were selected by lot, while the rest were available to fill any vacancies which might occur during the year.[3]

From the start the council contained fifty members from each of the ten tribes. In Periklean Athens each tribal group served in turn for a tenth part of the conciliar year as a business committee of the council; during this period they were called πρυτάνεις, and each of the periods was a πρυτανεία.[4] The prytaneis had a president (ἐπιστάτης) who was chosen by lot from the prytaneis and changed every day.[5] He presided over the meeting of the whole council, which in the later fifth century had a session every day except on festivals, and also acted as president of the ekklesia if it met during his day of office.[6]

Although in the second half of the fifth century this system was connected with the conciliar year it does not necessarily presuppose it; the system continued after the conciliar year was abolished and may therefore have existed before its introduc-

[1] In *Hesperia*, v, 1936, 370; cf. Kahr. ii. 88. M. Giffler in *A.J.Phil.* lx, 1939, 436 ff. thinks that the independent conciliar year was not introduced till 432.

[2] Cf. *S.I.G.* iii. 944 and the note in Sandys (p. 246) on *A.P.* 62. 1.

[3] Headlam, *Election by Lot²*, 53–56 (with Macgregor's notes in the second edition, 196 ff.).   [4] Cf. Tod, i *passim*.

[5] Tod, pp. 106–7 and the important note of Sandys on *A.P.* 44. 2.

[6] Sandys, loc. cit., and Gilbert, 274, n. 3.

tion. But if, as is generally supposed,[1] Kleisthenes transferred the presidency of the ekklesia to the epistates of his new council, he must to that extent have limited the authority of the chief archon, to whom the privilege had hitherto belonged.[2] It has, however, been inferred from the passage of Philochoros already mentioned that as the ballot in an ὀστρακοφορία was presided over by the nine archons (assisted by the council) the archons must have still presided over the ekklesia in 488.[3] The validity of this inference may be doubted in view of the exceptional character and importance of the assembly in which the vote on an ostracism was taken. Nevertheless it must be remembered that we do not really know who presided over either the council or the ekklesia in the early fifth century; possibly the chief archon continued to preside over the ekklesia until the reform of 487, which deprived the archons of their former prestige by altering the method of their appointment.

Of those Greek states which possessed a popular probouleutic council there were some in which the president of the ekklesia was not chosen from the members of the council. Although such a council must have existed in Syracuse at the time of the Sicilian Expedition,[4] the presidency of the Syracusan assembly then belonged to the chief executive magistrates, the στρατηγοί,[5] and some scholars, while accepting the tradition that Solon created a popular council with probouleutic functions, have believed that the archon continued to preside over the assembly until the last decade of the sixth century.[6] But in a constitution of the Kleisthenic type there must surely have been some provision for collaboration and exchange of views between the magistrate who presided over the assembly and the council which prepared its agenda. In Syracuse the difficulty may have been overcome by making the generals *ex officio* members of the boulē, as they probably were in Periklean Athens.[7] So Kleisthenes may have made provision for the co-operation of the chief archon with the boulē in its probouleutic function.

This cannot have been the only function of the new boulē, and modern writers have assumed on the analogy of its later powers that from the first it had the right of participating with the magistrates in the general administration of the state. De

---

[1] Cf. de Sanctis, 352.   [2] See above, pp. 98 f.
[3] So Kahr. i. 124.   [4] Cf. Beloch, iii². 2. 195.   [5] Thuc. vi. 41. 1.
[6] So Greenidge (*Handbook*, 153).   [7] See below, p. 245.

Sanctis holds[1] that it was empowered by Kleisthenes 'to give instructions to the magistrates, to supervise them and co-operate with them, to direct diplomatic negotiations, and to control the finances of the state'. In his opinion the creation of a new council with these functions was an attempt to strike a reasonable compromise between the growing insistence of the demos on full sovereignty and the retention by the executive of the wide powers left to it by Solon; the activities of the executive were thereby subjected not to the intermittent and capricious censures of a mob but to the steady and intelligent control of a council which was the representative of the communes, and in composition and character better qualified than the ekklesia to act as the mouthpiece of the general will. The aggrandizement of the new council was prevented by the combination of sortition with election in its appointment[2] and by the rules which governed its membership. These limited the term of office to one year; though re-election was permitted, the second term was never continuous with the first, and appointment for a third term was absolutely prohibited.[3]

If we ascribe to Kleisthenes the creation of the Council of Five Hundred we must assume a definition of its competence similar to that proposed by de Sanctis. The centralizing policy of the tyrants had been made possible in part by the creation of new officials[4] but must also have involved an increase in the administrative duties of the ordinary magistrates. Moreover, on the downfall of the tyranny the magistrates had also to take over the duties hitherto performed by the tyrant, and may therefore have welcomed the assistance of the new council in their task. Further, as suggested above, the participation of the boulē may have been intended as a substitute for a greater measure of direct control by the ekklesia. Consultation of the assembly by the executive, rare in the aristocratic state, had doubtless become more frequent since Solon, and especially under the rule of the tyrants, who could rely on a majority in the ekklesia and had an interest in parading the popular character of their rule. Provision for regular meetings of the ekklesia had to be made by Kleisthenes, but he seems to have kept their number down to a minimum, and in the strict control over the

---

[1] *Atthis*, 347.   [2] See below, pp. 227 ff.
[3] *A.P.* 62. 3 with Sandys' comments. Cf. BS 1022 and n. 5.
[4] e.g. the deme-judges (*A.P.* 16. 5).

agenda of all meetings of the ekklesia which he gave to the boulē he established a further safeguard against the abuse by the demos of its sovereignty.

Although the creation of the new council may have limited the former competence of the magistrates, there can be no doubt that in the period 507–487 the archons held a position of great dignity and importance in the state.[1] Their powers had naturally revived with the expulsion of the tyrants, who had overshadowed the ordinary magistracies, and their authority was enhanced by the fact that they owed their election to the direct vote of the citizens. The prestige of the chief archonship in these years is attested by the eminence of some of its holders, such as Hipparchos the relative[2] of Peisistratos, Themistokles, and Aristeides;[3] its influence is indicated by the passage of Thucydides in which the inauguration by Themistokles of the fortifications of the Piraeus is connected with his tenure of the archonship.[4] In this period also the polemarch had regained his former importance, and was still commander-in-chief of the Athenian army.[5] The judicial functions of the nine archons were probably the same as they had been under Solon's code; there is no evidence that Kleisthenes had imposed any limitations on the magistracy in this respect.

For the Kleisthenic ekklesia there is little direct evidence. An attempt has been made[6] to pierce the darkness by the suggestion that a law from the last decade of the fifth century preserved in a mutilated inscription[7] is simply a re-enactment *totidem verbis* of a law of 502/501. The law limits the powers of the boulē and defines those of the ekklesia. It reserves sovereignty for the δῆμος πληθύων (probably a quorum of 6,000) in all cases involving the death penalty or the imposition of fines; presumably the last clause refers to fines over a certain amount, as the boulē could later impose fines up to 500 drachmas.[8] Archaic expressions

---

[1] Ehrenberg in *Klio*, xix, 1923, 107 and 110. Rosenberg in *Hermes*, liii, 1918, 314 unduly minimizes the power of the chief archon in this period.

[2] *A.P.* 22. 4 says he was one of Peisistratos' συγγενεῖς, but the precise connexion between them is obscure; cf. Kleidemos, fr. 24 (15 in Jacoby) and Kirchner, *P.A.*, no. 7600.

[3] The dates are 496/495, 493/492, 489/488; cf. Cadoux, 116–17 and n. 254.

[4] i. 93. 3; cf. Cadoux, 116, n. 252.   [5] *A.P.* 22. 2; see below, pp. 170 ff.

[6] P. Cloché in *R.E.G.* xxxiii, 1920, 1–50 (especially pp. 28 ff.).

[7] *I.G.* i². 114. Cf. Bonner and Smith, 201–5, also Wade-Gery in *C.Q.* xxiv, 1930, 114–16 and 38 and in *B.S.A.* xxxiii. 113–22.

[8] *I.G.* i². 76 (Tod, 74), ll. 57–59 and [Dem.] xlvii. 43.

in the law suggest that it was to some extent a copy of an
earlier law, and the restoration of the radical democracy in 410
was certainly followed by a codification of the laws. But even if
this law reproduces verbatim the text of a previous law, the
original may have been no earlier than the revolution of
Ephialtes in 462; of that revolution the boulē and the ekklesia
were the beneficiaries, and a legal definition of their respective
shares of the spoils must have been necessary. It is, however,
incredible that in 410, when the full democracy had just been
restored after an oligarchic interlude, a law on this subject
should have been no more than a faithful copy of a previous law;
some additional safeguards suggested by recent experience must
have been inserted. Fragments of the ὅρκος βουλευτικός seem to
occur in the law, and some alterations were certainly introduced into this in the year 410/409.[1] Whether the archaisms are
due to legal conservatism or to borrowings from an earlier law,
there is not sufficient ground for regarding this law as a faithful
transcript of a Kleisthenic original.

Nevertheless the constitution of Kleisthenes must have defined the powers of the boulē and the ekklesia, and Kleisthenes
was probably the first to enact the clause in the law of 410 which
reserved to the people the final verdict in all cases involving the
death penalty.[2] The jurisdiction of the homicide courts was not
subject to this limitation, but it must have applied to all other
capital trials, including those on the charge of attempting to
subvert the constitution, which had hitherto been conducted by
the Areopagus. If Kleisthenes allowed it to retain this privilege
we must suppose that those found guilty by the Areopagus on
this charge could not be executed until the verdict had been
confirmed by the ekklesia. In the period between Kleisthenes
and Ephialtes we find some examples of capital charges tried
by the people; Miltiades, after his failure at Paros in 489, was
prosecuted before the demos on a charge of 'deceiving the Athenians',[3] and Themistokles during his ostracism was impeached
in absentia for treason.[4] It has been suggested[5] that the transference to the ekklesia of jurisdiction in such cases was effected
by the decree of Kannonos, and that the decree must be assigned

---

[1] Philochoros, fr. 119 (140 in Jacoby); cf. I.G. i². 114, ll. 28 ff.
[2] l. 37; cf. Bonner and Smith, 208–9 and Busolt, ii². 438–9.
[3] Hdt. vi. 136. 1. Cf. Berve, Miltiades, 99–100.
[4] Plut. Them. 23. 1 and Krateros, fr. 5 (11 in Jacoby, F.G.H. iii B, p. 202).
Cf. Bonner and Smith, 299.   [5] By Bonner and Smith, 208 and n. 1.

to the period of Kleisthenes' ascendancy. According to the account given by Xenophon[1] the decree ordained that if anyone was accused of 'doing wrong to the Athenian people' he should make his defence in fetters before the demos, and if convicted should be hurled into the Barathron. This decree may, however, be a later modification of the law under which Miltiades was tried.[2]

Herodotus[3] implies that the peace-offer of Mardonios in 479 was submitted to the boulē and that it was competent to reject it without consulting the ekklesia. If his account is true to the facts, it can only be explained by the hypothesis that the people had authorized the boulē to reject all proposals from Persia for a separate peace. It has been assumed that the right of making peace was conferred on the ekklesia by Kleisthenes,[4] but even in the aristocratic state the assembly of the armed men must have been consulted on such questions, and Solon probably confirmed by law its right to a final voice on all important issues such as those of peace, war, and alliance.[5] In these respects Kleisthenes merely confirmed powers which had legally belonged to the ekklesia since Solon, and the same is true of its right to appoint the magistrates. He may, however, have been the first lawgiver to make provision for regular meetings of the ekklesia. Probably he ordained that it should always meet once in every prytany,[6] the meeting which was distinguished as κυρία later when there were four meetings in each prytany.[7] In addition to the ten regular meetings in each year there would also be one for the election of magistrates and a number of special meetings convened on the request of the magistrates. But though Kleisthenes may have widened the competence of the ekklesia and by these regulations guaranteed to it the exercise of its legal rights, the ekklesia with only eleven regular meetings a year could do no more than maintain a general control over its partners in the work of government. It had the last say on important questions, and could turn down proposals submitted to it by the council, but it is unlikely that in this period it was free to amend these proposals and still more unlikely that it now possessed the power which

---

[1] *Hell.* i. 7. 20.   [2] See below, pp. 304 f.   [3] ix. 5. 1–2.
[4] This seems to be the inference of Cloché (op. cit. 33 and 34) from *I.G.* i².
114, l. 36. But the right may have been merely reaffirmed in 501/500.
[5] See above, pp. 96 f. and cf. Wade-Gery in *C.Q.* xxvii, 1933, 22 ff.
[6] Cf. de Sanctis, 355.
[7] *A.P.* 43. 4–6 and 44. 4.

later belonged to it of recommending the council to submit a probouleuma drafted in accordance with its instructions.[1]

Conclusion

The account of Kleisthenes' political conversion given by Herodotus proves that he became champion of the people by an afterthought, and consequently that his constitution was not inspired by any doctrinaire conviction of the superiority of democracy as such to all other forms of government.[2] He was driven by his failure in the struggle against Isagoras to appeal to the demos, and to secure his position he completed the work begun by the tyrants. They had destroyed the political influence of the noble families; he reorganized the citizen-body in such a way as to prevent any revival of that influence. They had relied on the support of the people; Kleisthenes revived the sovereignty of the ekklesia. But the demos had now shown that it could assert its rights, and its new champion was far more dependent on its favour than the tyrants had ever been.

Kleisthenes, like Solon, denied the divine right of the nobles to rule, but this denial did not entail acceptance of the thesis, developed later by the radical democracy, that the average citizen was competent to undertake any office in the state.[3] His conception of democracy seems to have resembled that which Thucydides[4] puts into the mouth of Athenagoras: the people may be the best judges of all important questions, but they must be guided to a right decision by the advice of the wise and must leave the guardianship of the public purse to the rich. Accordingly he left unaltered the regulations laid down by Solon for eligibility to the executive offices. Only Pentakosiomedimnoi could be appointed to the chief financial posts, and the nine archons (and consequently the members of the Areopagus) were still chosen only from members of the first two property-classes. We have seen that membership of these classes probably continued to depend, as in Solon's time, on the ownership of land. Thus the landed gentry of Athens were left by Kleisthenes in control of the executive and of the important judicial functions vested in the Areopagus.[5]

---

[1] See below, p. 243, n. 4.
[2] Cf. Bonner and Smith, 196: 'nothing that is known of Kleisthenes justifies the belief that he was a man with a mission.'
[3] See below, pp. 231 f.   [4] vi. 39. 1.
[5] Cf. de Sanctis, 358–9, also BS 887 and n. 1.

In these respects then his constitution was identical with that
created by Solon. And though in others it was more truly a
δημοκρατία than Solon's, it was more democratic in form than
in practice. As Aristotle observes,[1] the government of a Greek
state was usually conditioned by the character of its principal
military force, and while the main strength of Athens still lay
in its hoplites the democracy of Kleisthenes was in fact controlled by the ὅπλα παρεχόμενοι.[2] They probably outnumbered
the Thetes in the ekklesia at this time. Even in the period just
before the Peloponnesian War more than half of the citizens
lived in the countryside of Attica,[3] and the proportion must
have been greater in the time of Kleisthenes. Moreover, the
sovereignty of the ekklesia was limited by the control of the
boulē, and though there is no evidence that the Thetes were
excluded by Kleisthenes from his new council, it is unlikely that
they were represented on it in proportion to their numbers. The
principle of payment for state service had not yet been accepted
by the Athenians, and so long as membership of the boulē and
other functions of state remained unpaid they must have been
undertaken mainly by members of the propertied classes.[4]

Kleisthenes had based his constitution on the firmest possible
foundation, the support of a strong and vigorous middle class.
The members of this hoplite democracy still looked up to the
members of the great families for leadership and guidance, but
they were fully conscious of their own powers and were prepared to exact a heavy reckoning from statesmen who forgot
that they were now no more than servants of the demos. A new
order of society had been founded in which distinctions of rank
still persisted but had lost most of their political importance.[5]
The watchwords of this citizen society were ἰσονομία and ἰσηγορία,[6] and the popular enthusiasm which they evoked in the first
flush of the democratic triumph still lives in the sympathetic
record of Herodotus.[7] Nor is Herodotus far wrong when he sees
in this enthusiasm the motive force which impelled the Athenians
to rise to their opportunities in the crisis of the Persian Wars.

If Kleisthenes borrowed some of his ideas from the previous

---

[1] *Politics* 1321[a]5–14 (cf. 1297[b]16–28).   [2] See below, Note G.
[3] Thuc. ii. 14. 2.   [4] Cf. de Sanctis, 359.
[5] So Ehrenberg, *Neugründer*, 97–98.
[6] ἰσηγορία appears in Hdt. v. 78. ἰσονομία is a concept as well suited to moderate
oligarchy as to moderate democracy; hence the adjective ἰσόνομος occurs in
Thuc. iii. 62. 3 and the skolion on the tyrannicides (cf. Jac. 160).   [7] v. 78.

political experience of the Greeks, the use which he made of them was peculiarly his own, and unlike many innovators he produced a constitution which was admirably suited to the needs and circumstances of his own polis. He cannot therefore be blamed if his work was assailed when circumstances changed. That he recognized in the landless members of the citizen-body a possible menace in the future to the stability of his constitution may be inferred from the policy, probably his, of planting citizen colonies in Salamis and Euboia,[1] which allayed the discontent of the poor by turning them into freeholders. But he could not foresee the danger of the Persian invasion which made Athens a great naval power and transformed the lower classes into the ναυτικὸς ὄχλος, the saviours of the state. Radicals of a later generation who disliked the moderate democracy of Kleisthenes ignored its author and reserved their praises for the imaginary democracy which they fathered on Solon, but the memory of his achievement was rescued from oblivion by Herodotus and the Atthidographers.

[1] Cf. de Sanctis, 359, also *I.G.* i². 1 (Tod, 11) and Hdt. v. 77. 2.

VII. FROM KLEISTHENES TO EPHIALTES

The date and provisions of the law on ostracism

THE law which instituted ostracism at Athens is often attributed to Kleisthenes on the testimony of the *Athenaion Politeia*.[1] It is, however, unlikely that its author had documentary evidence in favour of this attribution. He includes the law almost by an afterthought among the laws of Kleisthenes, and his language gives no support to the hypothesis[2] that he had before him a source in which the law was dated precisely to the year 505/504. Moreover the Kleisthenic authorship of the law was not admitted by all the Atthidographers. Androtion, as we learn from Harpokration,[3] maintained that the date of its passing was only a short time before its first application, when Hipparchos the son of Charmos was ostracized. This event is dated to the year 488/487 by the author of the *Athenaion Politeia*,[4] who agrees with Androtion that it was the first occasion on which the law was applied. As the accuracy of Harpokration's statement has been challenged it is necessary to quote his exact words : περὶ δὲ τούτου (Hipparchos) Ἀνδροτίων ἐν τῇ β΄ φησὶν ὅτι συγγενὴς μὲν ἦν Πεισιστράτου τοῦ τυράννου καὶ πρῶτος ἐξωστρακίσθη τοῦ περὶ τὸν ὀστρακισμὸν νόμου τότε πρῶτον τεθέντος διὰ τὴν ὑποψίαν τῶν περὶ Πεισίστρατον, ὅτι δημαγωγὸς ὢν καὶ στρατηγὸς ἐτυράννησεν. The reason given in this passage for the invention of ostracism is almost verbally identical with the reason alleged in the *Athenaion Politeia*. This coincidence suggested the hypothesis[5] that Harpokration's citation is merely a confused recollection of the *Athenaion Politeia*, and this is backed up by the argument that whereas the words τότε πρῶτον are naturally used in the *Athenaion Politeia* of the first application of the law they have no meaning in the alleged extract from Androtion.[6] The obvious objection to this hypothesis is that Harpokration refers definitely to Androtion, Book II, which implies direct consultation of Androtion's work. By his use of the expression τότε πρῶτον Androtion presumably intended to dismiss briefly the

---

[1] 22. 1 and 4. [2] Of Schachermeyr in *Klio*, xxv, 1932, 347.
[3] s.v. Ἵππαρχος = Androtion, fr. 5 (6 in Jacoby, *F.G.H.* iii B). [4] 22. 3–4.
[5] So Kaibel (quoted with approval in BS 884, n. 2); cf. Wil. i. 123, n. 3.
[6] BS, loc. cit.

view of a predecessor (possibly Kleidemos) who had attributed
the invention of ostracism to Kleisthenes. The verbal coincidence
with the *Athenaion Politeia* proves nothing, as its author certainly consulted the Atthis of Androtion; probably he followed
Androtion closely on the motive for the introduction of ostracism,
while rejecting his date.

Since there is no valid reason for rejecting the evidence of
Harpokration, it follows that Androtion dated the law on
ostracism to the year 488. The ascription to Kleisthenes in the
Athenaion Politeia was probably derived from another Atthidographer, whose dating seemed to the author more plausible than
Androtion's. Busolt's contention that it was derived from a
documentary source rests on the mistaken assumption that the
laws of Kleisthenes were still extant in the fourth century.[1]
Moreover, Busolt has to explain away the evidence of Harpokration, which he has signally failed to do. The only possible
conclusion from the disagreement of the Atthidographers is that
they had no documentary evidence for the date of the law, and
that the different dates given by different writers are all due to
conjecture.

This conclusion must be true of Androtion's date no less than
of that given in the *Athenaion Politeia*, which was followed by
later writers such as Philochoros and Aelian.[2] Androtion's reason
for dating the law to 488 may have been the same as Beloch's:[3]
'such a weapon is not forged to be left for twenty years in the
sheath.' If the law was first applied early in 487, the obvious
inference is that it had been passed not long before, and as the
law contained provision for its regular annual application within
a fixed period soon after midwinter the date of its passing must
have fallen somewhere inside the year 488. A practical statesman
like Androtion could come to no other conclusion on the evidence
before him. Nor can we, once we realize that the ascription to
Kleisthenes is as conjectural as Androtion's dating.

Even if Kleisthenes retained his ascendancy in Athens from
the archonship of Isagoras till 500 and passed the law on
ostracism towards the end of this period, an interval of at least
thirteen years[4] must be postulated by those who attribute the

---

[1] BS, loc. cit.

[2] Philochoros 79 B (30 in Jacoby); Aelian, *V.H.* xiii. 24. 3. Both presumably
followed the account in *A.P.* 22; cf. Kahr. i. 123, n. 3.

[3] *G.G.* i². 2. 332.   [4] Seventeen, on Schachermeyr's view.

law to Kleisthenes between its passing and its first application.
The author of the *Athenaion Politeia* has made this position
more difficult to defend by his assertion[1] that the chief motive
of Kleisthenes in passing the law was to get rid of Hipparchos,
who was in fact the first victim of the law but was not ostracized
till 487; clearly the attribution of this motive to Kleisthenes is
no more than a conjecture which deduces the purpose of the law
from its results.

In the *Athenaion Politeia*[2] the long delay before the application of the law is explained partly by the customary moderation
of the demos, partly by the assumption that the Athenians did
not dare to use the law until their victory at Marathon gave
them confidence. These explanations are not entirely consistent.
And if the campaign of Marathon, fought in the summer of 490,
filled the demos with courage and provoked its anger against the
friends of the tyrants, why did it not apply the law at the next
opportunity, early in 489? Why wait till 487? Busolt, refining
away the crudities of this explanation, surmised that though the
law was passed soon after 506 the parties were so evenly balanced
then and afterwards that for many years no statesman dared
advise the people to demand an ὀστρακοφορία.[3] This sounds
plausible but makes Kleisthenes' conduct very strange; why did
he propose the law at all if his political position was so uncertain
that he dared not risk its application?

Carcopino has proposed a more attractive solution of the main
difficulty.[4] He sees in the law, which he ascribes to Kleisthenes,
a modification of the severity of earlier legislation. The earlier
law ordained that if anyone tried to make himself tyrant or
helped another to do so he should be ἄτιμον καὶ αὐτὸν καὶ γένος.[5]
To the author of the *Athenaion Politeia*, misled by the later
meaning of ἄτιμος, this proved the mildness of the Athenian law
against tyranny in the time of Peisistratos. Actually the ἄτιμος
of the sixth century was an outlaw from the commonwealth who
could be killed with impunity.[6] Carcopino believes that under
the old law Hipparchos, son of Charmos, might have been declared ἄτιμος in this sense, as being one of the συγγενεῖς of the
tyrants and after their expulsion leader of the party friendly to

---

[1] 22. 4; the assertion is challenged by Schachermeyr as a later invention
(op. cit. 347; cf. Wil. ii. 87, n. 28).

[2] 22. 4 and 3.   [3] BS 886.

[4] *Ostracisme*, 28 ff. [108 ff. in first edition].   [5] *A.P.* 16. 10.

[6] Cf. Kahr. i. 118–19, who cites the laws in *A.P.* 16. 10 and Dem. xxiii. 62.

them in Athens.ᵃ Kleisthenes, however, by his invention of ostracism transferred to the people the discretion to proceed against Hipparchos and his associates as soon as they threatened to become a menace to the public safety. In this way the old νόμος ἐπὶ γένει was replaced by a series of ψηφίσματα ἐπ᾽ ἀνδρί.[1] The leaders of the Peisistratid party took the hint and kept quiet; hence they were able to remain securely in Athens until the renewal of their intrigues with Hippias and Persia during the campaign of Marathon exhausted the long patience of the demos.

This ingenious hypothesis is based on a false premiss. No attempt is made by Carcopino to prove that γένος in a sixth-century context would naturally have the meaning which he attaches to it. Whatever γένος may have included in earlier times, it is clear from Thucydides that only the direct descendants of Peisistratos were included in the ban inscribed on the στήλη ἀτιμίας[2] in 510. So in the condemnation of Antiphon and Archeptolemos in 411 it was decreed that they should be put to death and their property confiscated, also that each should be ἄτιμος and likewise the γένος τὸ ἐκ τούτοιν.[3] Carcopino himself calls attention to the evidence of Thucydides and regards the procedure of 510 as a modification of earlier practice.[4] It is difficult to see how he can reconcile with this view his statement that Kleisthenes might have outlawed Hipparchos as a kinsman of the tyrants.[5] He has not substantiated his contention that the penalty provided in the earlier law was different from that enforced in 510, but, even if he had, the procedure of 510 had on his own showing created a new precedent. Hipparchos was now exempt from the ban and could not have been outlawed unless detected in a new conspiracy. Carcopino, like Busolt, ignores the difficulty that over two years separate the discovery of Hipparchos' treason in 490 from his ostracism in 487.

All the attempts to explain away the hiatus between the passing of the law and its application are unsuccessful. The only alternative compatible with the ascription of the law to Kleis-

---

[1] Carcopino, 35–36.

[2] ἀτιμίας, proposed by van Herwerden in *Mnemosyne*, viii, 1880, 156, seems a necessary emendation for the ἀδικίας of the manuscripts in Thuc. vi. 55. 1; cf. Busolt, ii². 398, n. 2 and Carcopino, 32, n. 2.

[3] Cf. the end of the life of Antiphon in [Plut.] *Moralia* 834 B.

[4] Op. cit. 32.

[5] Anyhow it is doubtful whether Hipparchos was connected *by blood* with the Peisistratidai; see above, p. 153, n. 2.

thenes is to suppose that there was no such hiatus, and consequently that the ostracism of Hipparchos was not the first. Seeck,[1] observing that the notices of ostracisms from Hipparchos to Aristeides all come from the period 490–480, concluded that they were taken from the decree of recall passed in 481/480. As the Atthidographers had no evidence of any ostracism earlier than that of Hipparchos, they naturally assumed that his was the first, but the law may have been applied earlier, against other friends of the tyrants. Indeed Aelian[2] asserts that the law was first applied against its author, Kleisthenes himself.

The flaws in this explanation are obvious. If there was evidence that Kleisthenes was the first victim of his own law, why does it not appear in our sources until Aelian? Why was it unknown to the Atthidographers? Androtion and the author of the *Athenaion Politeia* agree in the statement that Hipparchos was the first to suffer ostracism. Is it reasonable to suppose that they would have affirmed this so positively if they had no other evidence before them than the decree of 481/480? For the author of the *Athenaion Politeia*, who thought that ostracism was invented by Kleisthenes, the belief that it was not used till 487 offered serious difficulties. If it was based merely on a weak *argumentum a silentio*, why did he accept it without question?

Further, although it is not easy to suggest a source from which the Atthidographers obtained their precise information about the ostracisms of the decade 490–480, Seeck's hypothesis is untenable. It is unlikely that the amnesty-law of 481/480 mentioned by name all who had been ostracized since 490; that it should have contained the date at which each of them had been ostracized is simply incredible.[3] The amnesty decree proposed in 405 by Patrokleides refers explicitly in its first paragraph to the precedent of 481/480.[4] From this we may infer that in 481/480 the recall of those who had been ostracized was included in a general amnesty similar to that of 405.

It is, however, implied in the *Athenaion Politeia*[5] that the decree which recalled them included a proviso that in future those who were ostracized must live outside limits defined by the promontories of Geraistos in Euboia and Skyllaion in the Argolid, and that violation of this rule should be punished with

---

[1] In *Klio*, iv, 1904, 300–1; cf. Glotz and Cohen, i. 479, n. 254 and *C.A.H.* iv. 152.
[2] *V.H.* xiii. 24. 3.   [3] So Beloch rightly in i². 2. 333.
[4] Andok. i. 77–79 and 107.   [5] 22. 8 (with the emendation ἐκτός).

perpetual ἀτιμία. This suggests that the recall of the *ostracisés* in 481/480 was effected by a separate measure distinct from the general amnesty.[1] Even if this inference were sound, why should the bill have included a detailed survey of the ostracisms of the past ten years, as postulated by Seeck? But the argument for assuming a separate decree on this subject may be questioned.[2] The statement of the *Athenaion Politeia* that the conditions of residence were first added to the ostracism law in 481/480 is inherently improbable. In this crisis of their history the Athenians were anxious to promote the unity of the state and to appease the rancours of the internal strife which had raged during the last decade; is it credible that at this moment they should have shown such cynical forethought for the possibility of its revival in the future? The residence clause must have been included in the law from the first; possibly it was post-dated by the Atthidographers under the mistaken belief that Aristeides during his ostracism had resided in Aigina.[3]

In view of the shipwreck of all hypotheses which in one way or another have tried to maintain the ascription of ostracism to Kleisthenes, the only possible conclusion is that Kleisthenes was not its author and that the ancient writers who attributed it to him had no warrant for their assertion.[4] We are therefore free to accept Androtion's conjecture that the authors of such a law cannot have intended to let it remain a dead letter, and that on this ground it must have been passed not long before its first application. Who its authors were, and what the purpose was of their strange innovation are questions which cannot be answered until the political history of the period has been examined. It is, however, convenient to consider here the provisions of the law.

The later procedure,[5] which probably went back to the original law, was that the people were asked in the κυρία ἐκκλησία of the sixth prytany (approximately the beginning of the Julian year) whether they desired to have an ὀστρακοφορία that year or not. No debate was allowed on the question; according to the *Athenaion Politeia* it was settled by ἐπιχειροτονία, which in the

---

[1] Carcopino, 45 ff. argues unconvincingly that the amnesty of 481/480 was limited to those who had been ostracized; he rejects the evidence of Andok. i. 107.

[2] Cf. Busolt, ii². 660, n. 1.

[3] Suggested by the story in Hdt. viii. 79. 1, on the difficulties of which cf. Macan, ad loc., and J. B. Bury in *C.R.* x, 1896, 414–18.

[4] Cf. Macan's edition of Herodotus iv–vi, vol. ii, 142–5.

[5] Described in *A.P.* 43. 5; cf. Philochoros 79 B (30 in Jacoby).

fourth century was the technical term for a decision without debate.[1] If the people voted to hold an ostracism the decisive vote was taken soon after. In a fragment of Philochoros it is stated that the first vote took place before the eighth prytany, but Carcopino[2] seems to be right in assuming that the excerptor has telescoped the text and that Philochoros was really referring to the final vote. He explains the vagueness of Philochoros' date by reference to a passage in the *Athenaion Politeia*[3] which states that the ἀρχαιρεσίαι for the military posts, including those of the ten generals, were held by οἱ μετὰ τὴν ἕκτην [πρυτανείαν] πρυτανεύοντες ἐφ' ὧν ἂν εὐσημία γίγνεται. As this shows that the date of the elections to the strategia was not absolutely fixed, Carcopino believes that the date of the ὀστρακοφορία fluctuated with it, and that if an ostracism was held the vote was always taken before the election of the στρατηγοί in order to clarify the political situation.

A rhetorical composition formerly attributed to Andokides[4] purports to be a speech delivered shortly before an ὀστρακοφορία. But its author betrays the fictitious character of his theme when he complains that under the law on ostracism no accusation or defence was permitted before the voting.[5] This proves that the final vote, like the preliminary decision, was taken without debate. The proviso was a safeguard against the inflammation of party passions by oratory and compelled the voters to decide for themselves whom they wished to be ostracized, although the interval between the two votes opened the way in a later age to sinister intrigues.[6]

There was a further device to protect the institution from abuse, contained in the clause which declared an ostracism invalid if the total number of citizens who registered their votes was less than 6,000. Such is the explicit assertion of Plutarch in his *Life of Aristeides*.[7] The theory that a man could not be ostracized unless 6,000 votes contained his name is derived from the fragment of Philochoros already mentioned. There are, however, indications in the citation that at this point also the text has been telescoped by the excerptor.[8] Even if Philochoros

---

[1] Carcopino, 62 and n. 4; cf. Wil. ii. 256.   [2] Op. cit. 69–70.   [3] 44. 4.
[4] Printed in texts of And. as [And.] iv. On this speech see below Note H.
[5] [And.] iv. 3; cf. Carcopino, 65.   [6] Carcopino, 72.   [7] 7. 6.
[8] Cf. BS 885, n. 2. This argument is not decisive, as the version in our text of the fragment reappears in Pollux, viii. 20 and the scholion on Ar. *Knights* 855; cf. Carcopino, 97–98.

actually held this view his evidence would be far from decisive, for he is also credited with the statement, certainly false, that the original ten-year exile imposed by the law was later reduced to five years.[1] Plutarch's statement that 6,000 was the quorum for a valid ostracism is supported by the analogy of other νόμοι ἐπ' ἀνδρί and of votes conferring ἄδεια.[2] The texts referring to these show that the 6,000 mentioned in them must be a quorum, for ἐὰν μὴ ἑξακισχιλίοις δόξῃ can mean nothing else,[3] unless we are to suppose that every decree which contains the words ἔδοξε τῷ δήμῳ was carried by a unanimous vote of the ekklesia.

The voter wrote the name of the person whom he wished to ostracize on a potsherd,[4] hence the voting was called ὀστρακοφορία and the penalty ὀστρακισμός. Plutarch says[5] that the ostraka were not sorted by the magistrates until they had counted them to see if the quorum had been reached. Although the procedure may seem cumbrous to us, it had the advantage that if the ostraka fell short of 6,000 no one knew how many votes had been cast against any one man, and there is no valid reason for rejecting Plutarch's testimony on this point. If the ostracism was valid, the man against whom most votes were cast (not necessarily an absolute majority of the total) had to leave Attica within ten days and remain in exile for ten years, but he was allowed to retain control of his property and its revenues.[6]

The constitutional innovations at the end of the sixth century

Of these a curt account, apparently derived from the Atthis, has been preserved in the *Athenaion Politeia*.[7] 'In the archonship of Hermokreon [501/500] the Athenians fixed the terms of the oath which was to be sworn by the members of the Council of Five Hundred, which they still swear. Then they began to appoint the στρατηγοί by tribes, one from each tribe, but the polemarch continued to be the leader of the whole army.'

The formulation of the ὅρκος βουλευτικός must have helped to define and limit the powers of the boulē, but nothing more can be said of it with certainty. All our evidence for the content of

---

[1] Carcopino, 41–42.
[2] Cf. R. J. Bonner in *C.P.* viii, 1913, 223–5 and Bonner and Smith, 194–5.
[3] In spite of the ingenious arguments of Carcopino, 99 ff.
[4] Carcopino, 78 ff.   [5] *Arist.* 7. 6.
[6] Philochoros 79 B (30 in Jacoby); cf. Carcopino, 51.
[7] 22. 2; on the date cf. Cadoux, 115–16.

the oath is later in date than the revolution of 462, and the implication in the *Athenaion Politeia* that the wording had never been altered is demonstrably incorrect.[1] Hence the attempts which have been made to reconstruct the original oath are inconclusive.[2] Presumably it contained the later proviso that the βουλευτής would exercise his functions in accordance with the laws. But these functions must have been less extensive at the outset than later. Sokrates cited this part of the oath in justification of his refusal to submit an illegal proposal to the vote of the ekklesia.[3] It has, however, been argued above that in 501/500 the presidency of the ekklesia may still have belonged to the archon. At whatever date it was transferred from him to an ἐπιστάτης chosen from the boulē, a clause referring to its exercise must have been added to the ὅρκος βουλευτικός, and this clause is perhaps traceable in the fragments of the constitutional law of 410 still extant.[4] In the later part of the fifth century the oath of the bouleutai that they would not bring before the ekklesia any illegal proposal was an important safeguard of the existing constitution, as is shown by the history of the oligarchic revolution of 411.[5] There is, however, no need to assume that this particular safeguard is anterior to 462. Kleisthenes had probably relied on the Areopagus to protect his new constitution; when this duty was taken from the Areopagus in 462 a greater responsibility rested on the members of the boulē of Five Hundred, who by that date supplied the sovereign ekklesia with its president.

A more comprehensive duty to defend the constitution has been attributed to the boulē of 501/500 and its successors.[6] In the year 410 the Athenians decreed that every citizen must take an oath of loyalty to the restored democracy; by this oath he was bound to treat as an outlaw anyone who tried to subvert the democracy in any way. The ways specified include 'ἐάν τις τυραννεῖν ἐπαναστῇ ἢ τὸν τύραννον συγκαταστήσῃ'.[7] It has been argued that by 410 the fear of tyranny had become an anachronism, and that the clause must have been taken over from an earlier oath, probably the original ὅρκος βουλευτικός.[8] So in

---

[1] See above, p. 149.

[2] The evidence is given in BS 1023, n. 1; cf. Wade-Gery in *B.S.A.* xxxiii, 1932–3, 118–19.   [3] Xen. *Mem.* i. 1. 18.

[4] *I.G.* i². 114, ll. 28–29; cf. Bonner and Smith, 204.

[5] *A.P.* 29. 4; cf. Wade-Gery, op. cit. 119 (on his 'fragment 10').

[6] BS 848–9, n. 3; cf. Wil. i. 54 and n. 23.   [7] Andok. i. 97.   [8] BS, 848–9.

the time of Demosthenes[1] the oath recognized the right of the bouleutai to imprison anyone who was detected in a conspiracy ἐπὶ προδοσίᾳ τῆς πόλεως ἢ ἐπὶ καταλύσει τοῦ δήμου. 'Subversion of the democracy' is certainly the wider concept which envisages tyranny as well as oligarchy, and the fear of tyranny admittedly goes back to the sixth century. Thucydides, however, says[2] that tyranny as well as oligarchy was a danger feared by the Athenians in 415 after the mutilation of the Hermai. Further, the Areopagus had been entrusted by Solon with the duty of dealing with conspiracies against the constitution, and there is no ground for assuming that it had been deprived of this duty by Kleisthenes, although he may have reserved the final decision to the ekklesia.[3] It is more probable that the initiative in this type of prosecution was transferred to the 500 from the Areopagus in 462, and that on this occasion a relevant clause was inserted into their oath.

We do not know the ground on which the Atthidographers dated the original oath to the year of Hermokreon. Perhaps the oath in the fourth century contained some reference to his archonship,[4] just as that of the archons still mentioned Akastos. If such was the ground, it suggests the conjecture that the Council of Five Hundred was first instituted in 501/500. This conjecture conflicts with the evidence of the *Athenaion Politeia*, which ascribes the institution of the 500 to Kleisthenes but by implication excludes him from any part in the reforms of 501/500. The implication may, however, be traceable to the limitations of the sources possessed for this period by the Atthidographers; they knew, or thought they knew, that Kleisthenes had created the new boulē, but had no evidence for his activity in 501/500. It is true that Herodotus records no event in the life of Kleisthenes subsequent to his final victory over Isagoras, and as Kleisthenes must then have been over sixty years old his death or retirement may have followed soon after.[5] But in the case of Herodotus the argument from silence is very dangerous, and Kleisthenes may have continued to play a prominent part in Athenian politics until the end of the sixth century.[6]

---

[1] xxiv. 144. [2] vi. 53. 3 and 60. 1.
[3] Cf. Bonner and Smith, 197 ff. on cases tried by the ekklesia in this period.
[4] So Seeck in *Klio*, iv, 1904, 302.
[5] Cf. Macan's edition of Herodotus, iv–vi, vol. ii, 142, n. 10.
[6] That Kleisthenes 'lost power *c.* 499 B.C.' was suggested by Wade-Gery in *C.Q.* xxvii, 1933, 28.

Whether Kleisthenes was or was not the author of the innovations of 501/500, they must be regarded as supplementary to and framed in the same spirit as his main reforms. Even if the Council of Five Hundred had been created a few years earlier, the definitive formulation of its oath would promote its conscientious and efficient exercise of the functions assigned to it by Kleisthenes. So, too, the reorganization of the strategia was a logical consequence of Kleisthenes' reforms, as Grote realized.[1] The effect of this second innovation cannot be inferred with certainty from the laconic statement in the *Athenaion Politeia*. As the polemarch had previously been commander-in-chief of the army, the final clause of the statement must mean that his position was not affected by the change. In what, then, did the change consist?

Some have supposed[2] that the author of the *Athenaion Politeia* is describing the institution of the στρατηγία, and that there were no στρατηγοί before 501/500, but this cannot have been his meaning, since he believed that they had existed in the time of Drakon ;[3] moreover the turn of the sentence indicates that it is a change in the method of their appointment to which he is referring. The most probable view of their origin is that as colonels of the tribal regiments they had replaced the φυλο-βασιλεῖς in the aristocratic state.[4] On that view their increase in number to ten must have been contemporaneous with the Kleisthenic reorganization of the tribes; it could hardly have been deferred for six years. They would naturally be members of the tribes which they commanded; during the fifth and most of the fourth century the στρατηγός of each tribal regiment was usually a member of the tribe,[5] and if this was the rule in the artificial tribes created by Kleisthenes, *a fortiori* each of the four birth-tribes of pre-Kleisthenic Athens must have been commanded by one of its own members. On this ground the natural meaning of the passage in the *Athenaion Politeia*, that this rule was first introduced in 501/500, cannot be accepted. The passage also implies that the body which elected all and each of the

[1] iii. 116 (abridged ed. 65).
[2] The supposition is implicit in the statement of Wade-Gery (loc. cit.) that 'Kleisthenes created the Strategoi *c.* 500 B.C.'.
[3] Unless we assume that the 'constitution of Drakon' was a last-minute addition to the *A.P.*, unknown to the author when he was writing 22. 2.
[4] Schwahn, 1072.
[5] *A.P.* 61. 1 with Sandys' note; cf. Wade-Gery in *C.Q.* xxiv, 1930, 38.

generals was the whole people. In the second half of the fifth century the people chose a general for each tribe from the members of that tribe who offered themselves for election.[1] It has been suggested that this method of appointment was introduced in 501/500;[2] before then each of the generals was perhaps chosen by the members of his own tribe.

If the essence of the reform was a change not in the body from which the στρατηγοί were chosen but in the body by which they were chosen, it has been strangely obscured in the *Athenaion Politeia*. There is the further difficulty that on this interpretation the change must have increased the prestige of the strategoi, and this can only have been at the expense of the polemarch. It is therefore tempting to assume that the change really belongs to the second decade of the fifth century, when the strategoi displaced the archons as the chief executive of the state. The solution adopted by Busolt[3] is to retain the dating of the change to 501/500 and to reject the statement in the *Athenaion Politeia* that the strategoi continued to be subordinate to the polemarch.

Busolt's view of the relations between the strategoi and the polemarch in the early years of the fifth century is based on remarks made by Herodotus in his account of the campaign of Marathon. In Herodotus the polemarch Kallimachos presides over the board of strategoi and holds the post of honour on the right wing of the army in battle, but the supreme command of the army seems to belong to the strategoi, who hold it in rotation, each for one day. Busolt infers from this[4] that in 501/500 the ἡγεμονία of the polemarch became merely nominal and honorary, and that the transference of the real power to the strategoi and the rotation between them of the supreme command were measures to avert the danger which might threaten the infant democracy from the concentration of military authority in the hands of a single ambitious polemarch.

The statement in the *Athenaion Politeia* on the position of the polemarch in this period may be no more than a fourth-century rationalization of Herodotus' account,[5] but it appears to be true to the facts. Busolt's explanation ignores the inconsistencies

---

[1] Xen. *Mem.* iii. 4. 1; cf. Hdt. vi. 104. 2.

[2] This is the solution usually accepted; cf. BS 881. Beloch, i². 1. 398, n. 1, admits an alteration in the method of election in 501/500 as one of the possibilities.

[3] BS 881 and n. 3; further references in Berve, *Miltiades*, 79, n. 2.

[4] BS 881.   [5] Cf. Macan, op. cit. ii. 198–200.

contained in the Herodotean narrative.[1] Herodotus is careless
about the minutiae of the Athenian constitution, as is shown by
his statement[2] that the polemarch at Marathon was appointed
by lot, and his account of the relations between the strategoi and
the polemarch is confused. He describes the polemarch as an
ordinary member of the military council along with the ten
strategoi, as ἐνδέκατος ψηφιδοφόρος. Yet the strategoi debate
without him, and when a majority of them reject Miltiades'
proposal to fight at once, Miltiades appeals to the polemarch,
who by his decision in favour is apparently able to override the
vote of the majority. This suggests[3] that the strategoi were at
this date merely an advisory body and that the polemarch was
not bound to follow their advice. He must in that case have been
superior to them in authority, must in fact have been commander-in-chief, and as such commanded the right wing in
battle, the position once held by the king.[4]

Herodotus asserts[5] that each strategos held the πρυτανηίη in
turn for one day, and implies that this gave its holder supreme
command of the army; so Miltiades began the battle when the
day of his πρυτανηίη came round. This part of his account seems
traceable to a 'Philaïd' source, anxious to emphasize the constitutional propriety of Miltiades' behaviour and to vindicate
for him the chief credit of the victory.[6] If the πρυτανηίη is
historical at all it may have meant merely the presidency of the
board of generals; its importance in the field may then be explained by the assumption that the prytanis for the day would
be the chief assistant and adviser of the polemarch.[7] Possibly,
however, Herodotus was simply transferring to 490 the conditions of his own age, for according to Diodoros[8] each of the
strategoi present with the fleet in 406 held the supreme command in turn for one day at a time.

The tenure of the strategia by Miltiades in 490 might be
regarded as a proof that the office was more important than that
of the polemarch. Miltiades was now the most influential man
in Athens; if the polemarch retained his old powers, surely

---

[1] Cf. ibid. 156 ff. and Berve, op. cit. 78 ff.
[2] vi. 109. 2; cf. Berve, 80 (also Grote, iii. 126, n. 2).
[3] So Berve, loc. cit.; cf. W. W. How in *J.H.S.* xxxix, 1919, 52.
[4] Hdt. vi. 111. 1; cf. Euripides, *Supplices* 656–8.
[5] vi. 110; cf. 111. 1. [6] Berve, 81. [7] Berve, 83.
[8] xiii. 97. 6 (cf. 106. 1) accepted by Schwahn, 1080. But I doubt whether this
evidence is trustworthy; see below, p. 247, n. 3.

Miltiades would have secured his own election to the position. The argument is not conclusive. It is possible that Miltiades had already held the archonship; a Miltiades who may be the same man had been chief archon in 524/523.[1] But even if we deny the identity and assume that there was no legal bar to his election, he may have refused to stand for the polemarchia on personal grounds. In view of his past history and his present wealth and influence, his tenure of the chief military command would have given a handle to his enemies and enabled them to represent his ambition as a menace to the democracy. For this reason it was better for Miltiades to keep out of the limelight and to secure the chief military command for Kallimachos, who was probably one of his supporters and might be expected to follow his advice.

If the election of the strategoi really was transferred from the tribes to the whole people in the year 501/500, we must suppose that this did not at first affect the relations of the strategoi to the polemarch. Wade-Gery has suggested[2] that this innovation, which he attributes to Kleisthenes, was the creation of the strategoi 'as a secular executive destined to displace the archons'; Kleisthenes' method in this reform, as in his reorganization of the citizen-body, was 'to make the religious structure politically insignificant by creating alongside it a secular structure'. Yet the reform was not carried through at once to its logical conclusion, the degradation of the archonship, and for this Wade-Gery finds an explanation in the hypothesis that Kleisthenes lost power soon after. This hypothesis provides a neat solution for the main difficulty, but the interpretation of the reform suggested by Wade-Gery is open to criticism in other respects. We have already seen that the authority of the *Athenaion Politeia* cannot be claimed for the view that the strategia was first instituted in 501/500, and although the positive evidence is weak the strategoi must have existed in the Solonian state, if not earlier.[3] Moreover, although Kleisthenes in his tribal reform replaced a religious by a secular structure, there was no need for him to apply this method to the executive. The archonship had been secularized by Solon and deprived of its religious connexion with the Eupatridai,[4] and there was therefore no reason why the powers of the archon and pole-

---

[1] Cf. Cadoux, 110 and n. 217. [2] *C.Q.* xxvii, 1933, 28.
[3] Cf. Schwahn, 1071–2 (also How and Wells on Hdt. i. 59. 4).
[4] Cf. Wade-Gery in *C.Q.* xxv, 1931, 89.

march should have been deemed by Kleisthenes incompatible with his new constitution. Perhaps the assumption by the ekklesia in 501/500 of the right to elect the generals was simply a fresh affirmation of the sovereignty of the demos, and the consequent increase in the prestige of the generals was an unexpected by-product of the change.

Whatever may be the true nature and explanation of the reform of 501/500, the polemarch must have retained till after Marathon the supreme command of the army. In the period between the expulsion of Hippias and the reform of the archonship in 487/486 the old magistracies, partially eclipsed under the tyranny, regained much of their former importance. As the chief archon resumed the direction of internal affairs, so the polemarch recovered his old control over the armed forces of the state.[1] The archon and polemarch seemed to have retained the old powers which had reverted to them on the downfall of the tyranny until the reforms of 487/486.

The reforms of the year 487/486 and the political history of Athens during the Persian Wars

Our only direct evidence for the reforms of 487/486 is contained in a single sentence of the *Athenaion Politeia*:[2] 'in the year of Telesinos [487/486] they appointed the nine archons, one from each tribe, by sortition from 500 men previously chosen by the demes, for the first time since the tyranny; the archons before this had all been elected.' The natural implication of the last clause is that the archons had never before 487/486 been appointed by κλήρωσις ἐκ προκρίτων, and this was probably the version of the Atthis. As the author of the *Athenaion Politeia* believed that this method of appointment was introduced by Solon, he was driven to the hypothesis that it had lapsed under the tyranny. The notice which he has taken over from the Atthis runs more smoothly if his insertion μετὰ τὴν τυραννίδα is removed. Possibly the words τότε πρῶτον were also inserted by him;[3] if they appeared in the Atthis they must have come earlier in the sentence.

It is not explained in the notice how nine archons could be chosen κατὰ φυλάς from ten tribes; the problem may be solved by reference to another passage of the *Athenaion Politeia*[4] in

---

[1] So Ehrenberg in *Klio*, xix, 1923, 110.   [2] 22. 5.
[3] Cf. de Sanctis, 242, n. 3; Ledl, 349–50 is unconvincing.   [4] 55. 1.

which the tenth tribe is said to supply the γραμματεύς of the
Thesmothetai. A more serious difficulty is raised by the number,
500, given in the papyrus for the πρόκριτοι. In the fourth century,
when the preliminary choice from the tribes was made by
sortition, ten candidates were chosen by lot from each tribe.[1]
It may be objected that under the system introduced in 487/486
the preliminary selection took place not in the tribes but in the
demes; if the πρόκρισις for the archonship was modelled on that
for the boulē, and if the demes were represented among the
πρόκριτοι in proportion to their population, the number of
πρόκριτοι could not be far below 500.[2] But even if the Atthis
really ascribed the preliminary prokrisis to 'the demotai' or 'the
demes',[3] it is idle to speculate on the way in which they performed their task. The analogy of the council is misleading,
since the number of persons qualified for membership was so
much greater. There cannot have been more than 1,500 citizens
at the most in 487 who satisfied the conditions of eligibility to
the archonship, and it is hardly credible that from this small
number 500 πρόκριτοι were selected every year. If the system
was ever tried it must speedily have been abandoned as unworkable. It is, however, more probable that the text is corrupt;
perhaps ἑκατόν was the original reading.[4]

There is no need to suppose that this reform in the method of
appointing the archons was accompanied by a change in the
conditions of eligibility. The Hippeis had probably been eligible
since the introduction of the property-qualification by Solon,[5]
and the Zeugitai were not made eligible until 457/456.[6] Some of
those who hold that the archonship was confined by Solon to the
Pentakosiomedimnoi have conjectured that it was the law of
487/486 which first opened the office to the Hippeis;[7] others
maintain that this step was not taken till about nine years later,[8]
relying on the story in Plutarch of the decree proposed after the
Persian invasion by Aristeides that everyone might share in the
government and the archons be chosen out of the whole body of
Athenians. But the decree as given by Plutarch[9] cannot be

---

[1] *A.P.* 8. 1.   [2] Cf. Busolt, ii². 639 and 417, n. 1.
[3] There is some doubt about the reading. Emendations which limit the
archonship to the Pentakosiomedimnoi (cf. the textual note ad loc. in Sandys)
are to be rejected.
[4] As Kenyon suggested (p. 60 of his *editio princeps* of the *A.P.*).
[5] See above, pp. 101 f.   [6] *A.P.* 26. 2.   [7] e.g. BS 888 and n. 2.
[8] So Sandys in his note on *A.P.* 26. 2.   [9] *Arist.* 22. 1.

historical, and may be pure invention;[1] it recalls the oligarchic misrepresentations of Aristeides' career which have left traces in the *Athenaion Politeia*.[2] If there was definite evidence available for the admission of the Hippeis to the archonship in the second or third decade of the fifth century it must have been preserved by the author of the *Athenaion Politeia*, who took a particular interest in the history of the archonship.

The curt reference in the *Athenaion Politeia* to the law of 487/486 merely chronicles it as a fact, and offers no suggestion concerning the purpose or the results of the reform. It is, however, obvious that the part played by sortition in the new method of appointment was bound to entail a decline in the prestige and a limitation in the competence of the archonship. The offices of chief archon and polemarch had hitherto been filled by election from the ablest men in the state; they could not retain their previous functions undiminished when their holders were taken by lot from a 'short list' of one hundred candidates.[3] Naturally the polemarch now lost the command of the army, which passed to the strategoi, and retained only his religious functions and the conduct of cases affecting non-citizens.[4] The effect of the reform on the position of the chief archon is harder to estimate, since there is greater uncertainty about his previous functions. If he had not already lost the presidency of the ekklesia he must have been deprived of it now. It may have been transferred at once to an epistates chosen from the boulē, or there may have been an intermediate stage during which it was vested in the strategoi, as at Syracuse in 415.[5]

In any case there is no doubt that the strategoi not only took over the command of the army but eventually replaced the archon as the chief executive in the internal administration; this may have been a gradual development brought about by circumstances unforeseen in 487/486. As the strategia was henceforth the only important office to be filled by direct election, its prestige increased at the expense of the older magistracies. This, however, was due in part to the course of events during the next decade which both enlarged the competence of the strategoi and

---

[1] Cf. Wil. i. 124, n. 4; Busolt, iii. 31, n. 4, attributes it to Idomeneus.
[2] e.g. 24. 1. Cf. Busolt, iii. 28 and BS 888, n. 6.
[3] Cf. BS 888.   [4] *A.P.* 58.
[5] See above, p. 151. Macan in his edition of Hdt. vii–ix, vol. ii, p. 202 even suggests that the archon may have had the presidency of the Council of Five Hundred until this reform.

made their powers more important. When Athens, on the eve of
Xerxes' invasion, became a great naval power, the strategoi
acquired the command of the fleet as well as the army, and on
the foundation of the Delian League they became the leaders of
the naval and military forces of the new confederacy.[1] Not only
did they come to exercise the functions of ministers of war and
marine, but in view of the connexion of finance with their
departments they acquired a share in the financial administration also. It is not known when they were relieved of their
original task, the command of the tribal regiments; either in
487/486 or at some later date this was transferred to ten ταξίαρχοι
chosen by the people.[2]

The first appointment of archons by κλήρωσις ἐκ προκρίτων is
dated in the *Athenaion Politeia* to the archonship of Telesinos,
487/486. From this it follows that the reform must have been
carried after the election of Telesinos and his colleagues and
before the election of their successors.[3] It is, therefore, not far
removed in time from the introduction of the law concerning
ostracism. But before we consider the nature of the connexion
between the two measures we must examine in more detail our
information on the political history of this period.

There has occasionally been a controversy about the rise of
the polis, the date at which it began to be recognized by the
Greeks as a religious and political community of fellow-citizens.[4]
But the question of origins is surely less important than that of
the content which the idea of the polis possessed in Greece and
especially in Athens at different periods. The concept was certainly familiar in Athens as early as the later phases of the
aristocratic state since it appears without comment in the
poems of Solon, but whatever it may have been as an ideal, in
practice it was hardly more than a façade for the warring ambitions of the great nobles who exploited the authority of the
state for their own ends. During the sixth century Solon and the
tyrants prepared the hoplite demos to take its part in the polis,

---

[1] Wil. ii. 108–9 and BS 890–1.

[2] Wil. ii. 88, n. 29 dates the institution of the taxiarchoi soon after 479; they
are first mentioned in Aischylos (fr. 182 in Sidgwick's text).

[3] The account of the *A.P.* here (22. 5) is more precise than that of the reform
of 457 given in 26. 2, with which it is unfairly compared by Beloch (ii². 2. 139).
Beloch dates the reform of *A.P.* 22. 5 to 489/488, and Macan (op. cit. ii. 201–2)
does the same.

[4] Cf. W. Jaeger, *Paideia*, vol. i (E.T., Oxford, 1939), cc. 5–8 *passim*.

and Kleisthenes finally established on a firm foundation the organization of the citizen society, more effectively comprehensive than ever before. Yet the demos was still politically immature, still swayed by the prestige of the leading men and susceptible to their influence.

In such a state the time was not yet ripe for the formation of organized political parties. The *Athenaion Politeia* represents the political history of the fifth century as a recurring conflict between the champions of the demos and the leaders of the γνώριμοι.[1] In the generation after Kleisthenes Miltiades is said to have been at the head of the γνώριμοι, while Kleisthenes' position as προστάτης τοῦ δήμου is assigned to Xanthippos, who is later replaced by Aristeides and Themistokles as joint leaders of the popular party. This reconstruction is too schematic to deserve any serious consideration. It is sufficiently discredited by the fact that when political parties made their appearance in Athens during the fifth century there were not two but three parties, oligarchs, moderates, and radicals.

After the expulsion of the extreme reactionaries under Isagoras there was probably no further strife for some time about the form of the constitution, for the innovations of 501/500 did not at first affect the balance of power in the state. Modern writers have assumed the existence at Athens in the early fifth century of an oligarchic party bent on the subversion of the Kleisthenic constitution and looking to Sparta for the realization of its purpose,[2] but the assumption is unsupported by evidence.[3] In the struggle of the δυνατοί Kleisthenes had triumphed by taking the demos into his following, and the lesson had not been lost on his fellow nobles. Accepting the Kleisthenic constitution, they seem to have decided to exploit in their own interest the new openings which it had created for those who could win the confidence of the demos. Why should they have desired to abandon the fascinating and profitable pursuit of popular favour in order to restore an oligarchy which would have limited their opportunities?

Nevertheless the opposition of the rival leaders was no mere conflict of personalities and family groupings. As the constitutional issue was in abeyance, this opposition was concerned with questions of foreign policy, which had acquired a new and

[1] 28. 2–3.   [2] e.g. J. A. R. Munro in *C.A.H.* iv. 231.
[3] Cf. the criticisms adduced by Rosenberg in *Hermes*, liii, 1918, 311 ff.

unpleasant urgency.[1] Kleisthenes, confronted with the menace
of a Spartan invasion in support of Isagoras, had sought Persian
protection from Artaphernes, the satrap of Lydia. Herodotus
says that the Athenian envoys were asked by Artaphernes for
earth and water, the tokens of submission, that they decided on
their own initiative to consent to this unexpected demand, but
that they incurred severe censure on their return home.[2] This
account frees Kleisthenes from direct responsibility for the surrender, but it is difficult to believe that the envoys really
exceeded their instructions, as Kleisthenes must have known
that Persia would demand it as the price of her protection, nor
is it expressly affirmed by Herodotus that the submission was
disavowed by the ekklesia. The full implications of this step did
not become evident until the end of the century, when Hippias
obtained the goodwill of Artaphernes and induced him to send
the Athenians an ultimatum demanding the restoration of
Hippias if they wished to avoid incurring the hostility of Persia.

Herodotus indicates that the ultimatum was sent shortly
before the outbreak of the Ionian revolt; he says[3] that the
indignation excited by it in Athens was still fresh when Aristagoras of Miletos, the leader of the revolt, applied to Athens for
help (winter 499/498). The policy of reliance on Persia was now
discredited and the Athenians sent twenty ships to help
Aristagoras. These returned home at the end of the campaigning season of 498, and despite renewed appeals from Aristagoras
Athens took no further part in the revolt.[4] When the dramatist
Phrynichos produced early in 493 a topical play on 'The Capture
of Miletos' the Athenians fined him 1,000 drachmas 'for remind-
ing them of their misfortunes'.[5]

In these critical years the Athenians had done too much and
too little. They had alienated the Persians by their rejection of
Artaphernes' ultimatum and had provoked Persian resentment
by their participation in the burning of Sardis, but as soon as
they had committed themselves beyond recall they had held
aloof from the revolt, although its success would have provided

---

[1] On what follows cf. the article by M. F. McGregor in *Ferguson Studies*,
71–95, A. W. Gomme in *A.J.Phil.* lxv, 1944, 321–31, and C. A. Robinson in lx,
1939, 232–7 (also lxvi, 1945, 243–54).

[2] v. 73 (cf. E. M. Walker in *C.A.H.* iv. 157–8); I find Gomme's attitude to
this account (op. cit. 322) hard to understand. Jac. 340, n. 61 identifies this embassy with that in Hdt. v. 96. 2, which, however, was clearly sent some years later,
c. 500.   [3] v. 97. 1.   [4] Hdt. v. 103. 1.   [5] Hdt. vi. 21. 2.

the best guarantee of their own safety. These vacillations may have been the hot and cold fits of a popular assembly incapable of framing a long-term policy in foreign affairs, but it is more likely that they reflect a struggle between the policies of the leading men. Kleisthenes' policy of reliance on Persia against Sparta had been wrecked on the ultimatum of Artaphernes, and it is possible that Kleisthenes himself was involved in its ruin.[1] For a time the leaders who were hostile to the Persian connexion gained the upper hand, but they were unable to maintain their ascendancy.

Unfortunately we have only one significant clue to the internal history of Athens in these years, the election of Hipparchos, son of Charmos as archon in 496,[2] and its interpretation is disputed. Although he was connected by marriage[3] and perhaps by birth with the family of the tyrants, the facile assumption that he was now the leader of their party in Athens cannot be proved, for his inclusion among 'the friends of the tyrants' in the *Athenaion Politeia* may be guesswork or an echo of partisan malice. The statement in the same chapter that Kleisthenes passed the law on ostracism for use against Hipparchos is incredible even if Kleisthenes really was the author of the law.[4] Moreover, Hipparchos had not been connected so closely with the tyrants in 510 as to be involved in their expulsion, and since then he had given no further handle to his political enemies. Finally, the existence of a strong Peisistratid party in Athens at this time is not only pure hypothesis but improbable in itself.[5] Fourteen years had elapsed since the expulsion of the tyrants, and at least eleven since Kleisthenes by his reforms had confirmed the craftsmen and freehold farmers in the possession of the political and economic advantages which they had received from the tyranny. There was no sentimental glamour in the memory of the exiled tyrant, and there was now no political or economic discontent which he could exploit in his own interest.

These arguments are not absolutely decisive. The election of Hipparchos may have been effected by a political coalition of

---

[1] So Jacoby (*Atthis*, 161); he believes that the silence of Herodotus was deliberate. Cf., however, Macan's view cited above, p. 168, n. 5.

[2] Dion. Hal. *A.R.* vi. 1. 1; cf. Cadoux, 116.

[3] Cf. Kleidemos, fr. 24 (15 in Jacoby). The existence of a connexion by birth is implied in the συγγενῶν of *A.P.* 22. 4, but see above, p. 153, n. 2.

[4] See above, p. 161, n. 1.

[5] Cf. the observations of Gomme (op. cit. 318).

groups which separately were in a minority. If Kleisthenes had
solved the internal problems of Athens, his foreign policy had
broken down. The consequences of the recent breach with Perisa
must have seemed more serious to the Athenians after the
campaigning season of 497, during which the Persian forces had
made rapid progress towards the subjugation of the Ionian
revolt. In the panic produced by this revival of Persian power
it was natural that the party favourable to an accommodation
with Persia should gain ground and that some tentative moves
should be made to a reconciliation with Hippias, the protégé of
Artaphernes.[1] Even if Hipparchos was not the avowed leader
of the Peisistratid party in Athens, his connexion with Hippias
must have been a political handicap, and his election to the
archonship may therefore be regarded as an indication that in
the spring of 496 the prejudice against the Peisistratidai was
overriden by other considerations.

It has been suggested[2] that Hipparchos owed his election to
the support of the Alkmaionidai, and the evidence for the part
played by their leaders in these years affords some support to
the suggestion. Kleisthenes had initiated the policy of reliance
on Persian protection, which was beginning to revive in 496.
After his death or retirement the leadership of the clan seems to
have passed to Megakles the son of his brother Hippokrates.[3]
Megakles' sister Agariste was the wife of Xanthippos, father of
Perikles[4] and probably a political ally of Megakles. Another
member of the group may have been Alkibiades, grandfather of
the famous Alkibiades,[5] although the only known marriage connexion between his house and the Alkmaionidai belongs to a
later date. That this group inherited the pro-Persian policy of
Kleisthenes may be inferred from the following facts. Miltiades,
the leader of the anti-Persian party in Athens during the years
493–489, was prosecuted after his failure at Paros by Xanthippos.[6] Further, there was a tradition at Athens in the time of
Herodotus that the Alkmaionidai were engaged in treasonable

---

[1] Cf. Hdt. v. 96.

[2] By Walker in *C.A.H.* iv. 169; cf. Busolt, ii². 567 and n. 2.

[3] *A.P.* 22. 5 and Hdt. vi. 131. 2; it is a curious fact that Megakles' father bore
the same name as Peisistratos' father (Hdt. i. 59. 1).

[4] Hdt. vi. 131. 2.

[5] On the family of Alkibiades cf. Dittenberger in *Hermes*, xxxvii, 1902,
1–13. Beloch, ii². 2. 139–40, argues that the Alkibiades prominent in the early
fifth century was the great-grandfather of the famous Alkibiades (Isokrates
xvi. 26), but he is refuted by Hatzfeld, 13, n. 3.   [6] Hdt. vi. 136. 1.

intrigues with Hippias during the campaign of 490 and that they had displayed a shield on Mount Pentelikon as a signal to the Persian forces at Marathon.[1] The importance of this tradition is proved by Herodotus' anxiety to refute it, its feasibility by the weakness of the arguments which he brings against it.

Herodotus produces no warrant for his assertion[2] that no family in Athens at the time of Marathon was more respected or enjoyed greater honour than the Alkmaionidai, and it is refuted by other evidence. If, as seems probable, the trial of Phrynichos early in 493 was political,[3] his condemnation was the last success gained by the coteries which were hostile to the Ionian revolt and favourable to Persia. The subsequent elections to the archonship resulted in the victory of Themistokles, the advocate of a resolute anti-Persian policy, and also a member of the clan of the Lykomidai,[4] which perhaps had a special reason for antagonism to the 'accursed' Alkmaionidai.[5] In the summer of 493 the return of Miltiades, chief of the Philaïd family, provided the occasion for a fresh trial of strength. He was promptly prosecuted on the charge of his 'tyranny' in the Chersonese—by his enemies, adds Herodotus, preserving a discreet silence on their identity.[6] There can, however, be no doubt that the prosecution was brought or inspired by the pro-Persian groups, since the arrival of Miltiades at this juncture, in view of his great wealth, military ability, and inflexible hostility to Persia constituted a serious menace to their policy and a valuable accession of strength to their rivals. Miltiades' acquittal was a decisive triumph for the anti-Persian movement in Athens, and was followed by the renewal of Athenian friendship with Sparta and her king, Kleomenes. Kleomenes had no cause to love the Alkmaionidai, and his renewed goodwill to Athens is sufficient proof that they were no longer supreme there.

The main argument adduced by Herodotus in his defence of the Alkmaionidai is that no family in Athens had shown more hostility than they to the tyrants, since they had been in exile throughout the tyranny and were mainly responsible for the expulsion of Hippias.[7] Herodotus here omits certain facts in the

---

[1] Hdt. vi. 121 and 123–4.   [2] vi. 124. 1.
[3] Cf. Meyer, *G.A.* iii[1]. 312–13.
[4] Plut. *Them.* i. 4; on the date cf. Cadoux, 116 and n. 252.
[5] See above, p. 121.
[6] vi. 104. 2. Cf. Berve, *Miltiades*, 66–67.
[7] vi. 123. 1.

past history of this family of μισοτύραννοι which run counter to his thesis; he does not remind us in this context that Megakles the father of Kleisthenes had not only married the daughter of the tyrant of Sikyon but had played the main part in Peisistratos' recovery of the tyranny after his first loss of power.[1] A hostile analysis of Herodotus' argument produces the following result: before 510 the Alkmaionidai had sometimes opposed, sometimes supported the tyrants, but in 510 they secured their expulsion. Herodotus never faces the possibility that the policy of the family might have changed again between 510 and 490. Some modern historians argue that after the part played by the Alkmaionidai in 510 they could never hope for reconciliation with Hippias.[2] This contention does less than justice to the adaptability of Greek politicians[3] and is refuted by the career of Megakles. It must also be remembered that by 496 the main obstacle to a *rapprochement* between the two families had been removed by the death or disappearance of Kleisthenes, the chief opponent of Hippias.

We may, therefore, accept the ancient evidence for the existence in 490 of an understanding between the Alkmaionidai and the groups favourable to the return of Hippias. Whether this coalition dated from the election of Hipparchos in 496 is a question which cannot be answered and anyhow is not of great importance. The hopes of the pro-Persian factions were dashed by the Athenian triumph at Marathon, which further enhanced the popularity of Miltiades, and although Xanthippos in the next year secured his condemnation for his failure at Paros[4], it is doubtful if the revulsion of feeling against Miltiades produced any further advantage for the groups opposed to his policy. Their leaders certainly suffered most from the applications of the law on ostracism during this decade; Hipparchos was ostracized in 487, Megakles in 486, an unknown (Alkibiades?) in 485, and Xanthippos in 484.[5] In the *Athenaion Politeia*[6] the first

[1] vi. 130. 2 and i. 60. 2.

[2] So McGregor (op. cit. 86) says that the return of tyranny 'spelled ruin for the Alkmaionidai'. Contrast Meyer, *G.A.* iii[1]. 316–17.

[3] For an outstanding example cf. Thuc. viii. 73. 2. English statesmen of all parties were in correspondence with the exiled James II after the 'Glorious Revolution' of 1688.

[4] Hdt. vi. 136.

[5] Cf. Carcopino, *Ostracisme*, 145–8. The tradition on the ostracism of the elder Alkibiades is rejected by Meyer (*G.A.* iii[1]. 341 n.) and by Dittenberger (op. cit. 7).

[6] 22. 6.

three are distinguished from Xanthippos as 'friends of the tyrants', which may only mean that they were more deeply implicated than Xanthippos in the intrigues with Hippias.

Of the other statesmen prominent in this period the most important are Themistokles and Aristeides. Themistokles has often been described on slender evidence as an upstart or a *novus homo*.[1] He was in fact a member, probably the head, of the aristocratic genos of the Lykomidai, and his election to the archonship in 493 proves that he was not a poor man; if his mother was a foreigner,[2] so were the mothers of Kleisthenes and Kimon. In external affairs he was at this time in favour of resistance to Persia, and strenuously advocated measures which were calculated to increase Athenian preparedness for the coming struggle. Of his domestic policy, apart from those items in it which were connected with his foreign policy, nothing is known. The view that he was a radical democrat is no more than a deduction from his authorship of the navy bill, and confuses results with motives. Although the bill made the Thetes important in the state and so brought nearer the advent of radical democracy, no further explanation need be sought for its introduction and adoption than the imminence of the Persian peril.[3] Naturally Athenian statesmen cannot have been blind at the time to the political consequences which might follow the transformation of Athens into a great naval power; the bitter opposition, led by Aristeides,[4] which the bill provoked was probably due to the fear that it might imperil the predominance of the hoplites in the state. Themistokles' insistence on his bill does not show that he either minimized or welcomed this possibility; in his mind all other considerations were overruled by the urgency of the military situation. Nor have we sufficient reason to see in him with Beloch[5] the successor to Miltiades in the leadership of the γνώριμοι; despite the *Athenaion Politeia* the γνώριμοι cannot be said to have existed as a party in this period. It is, however, true that Themistokles continued

[1] Meyer (*G.A.* iii[1]. 310) alone tries to justify the application to him of the term in its correct Roman sense, but how can he know that 'his ancestors had played no important part in the state'?

[2] Plut. *Them.* 1. 1–2 (cf. Busolt, ii[2]. 640, n. 1). Strange conclusions are drawn from this by Meyer, loc. cit., and Hatzfeld, 2, n. 2.

[3] Cf. Beloch, ii[2]. 2. 134–5.

[4] This is a hypothesis, but a probable one; cf. Beloch, ii[2]. 2. 142 and de Sanctis, 377, n. 2.

[5] ii[2]. 2. 134. Beloch was answered by Rosenberg in *Hermes*, liii, 1918, 310–13.

Miltiades' policy of resistance to Persia abroad and opposition to the Alkmaionidai at home.

With both aspects of this policy Aristeides was probably in agreement. He was strategos in the year of Marathon and was elected to the chief archonship in the following spring, when the popularity of Miltiades was still undiminished.[1] These facts suggest that he was one of Miltiades' supporters and, like him, anti-Persian in foreign policy. He was probably of noble birth and was connected with the Eleusinian genos of the Kerykes.[2] His property was sufficient in 489 to qualify him for the archonship; if the circumstantial stories[3] about his poverty at the time of his death are true, he may have been impoverished by the Persian invasion.

Wilamowitz asserted[4] that Aristeides was an out-and-out democrat, who had as little to do with Philaïdai as with Alkmaionidai. He rejected, with good reason, Plutarch's opposition of him to Themistokles as conservative versus radical, and claimed that his προστασία τοῦ δήμου[5] was proved by his policy. There is, however, nothing in the facts of Aristeides' career to justify the claim,[6] apart from his share in the foundation of the Delian Confederacy. Later conservatives, whose views are reflected in the *Athenaion Politeia*,[7] made Aristeides as the founder of the confederacy responsible for all the political consequences of the Athenian Empire, but this is a glaring example of the fallacy *post hoc ergo propter hoc*. Aristeides' part in the creation of the Delian League shows that after the Persian War he accepted the implications of Themistokles' naval policy, but the same is true of Kimon, and no one has ever suggested that Kimon was a radical democrat.

De Sanctis,[8] unlike Wilamowitz, accepts Plutarch's statement[9] that Aristeides had been a friend of Kleisthenes, and maintains

---

[1] Beloch, ii². 2. 137; on the date cf. Cadoux, 117 and n. 254.

[2] Plut. *Arist.* 25. 6 makes Kallias ὁ δᾳδοῦχος (= Kirchner, *P.A.*, no. 7825) his ἀνεψιός; cf. Busolt, iii. 111, n. 6. The name of Aristeides' father Lysimachos is borne by a member of the Tamiai of Athena, *c.* 550; cf. *I.G.* i². 393.

[3] Plut. *Arist.* 27; cf. de Sanctis, 368, n. 3. The Alkibiades who proposed the grant for Aristeides' son Lysimachos (Plut. 27. 2 and Dem. xx. 115) may be the one ostracized in 485; cf. Hatzfeld, 15 and n. 4.

[4] *A.A.* ii. 87 and n. 27.   [5] For which cf. *A.P.* 23. 3 and 28. 2.

[6] If we reject as unhistorical the story in Plut. *Arist.* 22. 1.

[7] 24. 1 and 3; cf. Busolt, iii. 28–29 n.

[8] *Atthis*, 368 and n. 2.

[9] *Arist.* 2. 1; cf. Wil. ii. 87, n. 27.

that he was a political ally of Xanthippos,[1] apparently for the same reason as Walker, who describes Aristeides as sharing the good and evil fortunes of the Alkmaionidai.[2] But although Aristeides and Xanthippos were both strategoi in 479[3] and were in command of the military and naval forces respectively, the Persian invasion had produced a reconciliation of opposing groups, and despite the silence of Herodotus Themistokles may have been strategos in the same year.[4] The correct date for the ostracism of Aristeides is early in 482;[5] his ostracism has therefore nothing to do with that of Xanthippos, which was two years earlier, and is to be explained by his opposition to the navy bill of Themistokles. Aristeides' election as archon in the spring of 489, before the disgrace of Miltiades,[6] proves that he was not a political ally of the Alkmaionidai, and also throws doubt on the dogmatic assertion of Wilamowitz[7] that he had no connexion with the Philaïdai.

Aristeides and Themistokles may therefore be regarded as the joint heirs of the foreign policy of Miltiades and also of his vendetta against the Alkmaionidai and their allies. It is possible that the introduction of ostracism belongs to the first half of the year 488, while Aristeides was still archon. Anyhow the law on ostracism must have been promoted by the anti-Persian leaders, since three at least of the first four victims were their opponents. Suspicion of the δυνατοί is given by the Atthis[8] as the motive for the passing of the law; possibly their intrigues with Hippias and Persia were urged as a justification for the institution of this abnormal procedure. It was essential for the anti-Persian leaders, as for Demosthenes in the struggle with Philip, to ensure the solidarity of the state and the application of their policy by the removal of the leaders of the opposition. Unlike Demosthenes they were not strong enough to silence them by prosecutions. Ostracism was an ingenious expedient which enabled them to exploit the unpopularity of their opponents, whose removal from the scene for ten years was a compromise which gave the

---

[1] Cf. op. cit. 367–8: Aristeides became archon for 489/488 as the candidate of the Alkmaionid party.

[2] In *C.A.H.* iv. 266; cf. Macan, edition of Hdt. vii–ix, vol. ii, p. 206.

[3] Possibly in 480 also; cf. J. B. Bury in *C.R.* x, 1896, 418.

[4] Cf. de Sanctis, 385.   [5] So Wil. i. 25–26, followed by Cadoux, 118.

[6] It is surely impossible to date Miltiades' attack on Paros to the campaigning season of 490 unless we accept for Marathon Munro's date of 491 (against which see Cadoux, 117, n. 253).

[7] *A.A.* ii. 87.   [8] In *A.P.* 22. 3.

chiefs of the anti-Persian party sufficient time for their preparations and lulled to rest the consciences of the voters in the
ekklesia.

Ancient writers in discussing the purpose of ostracism treat it
in too abstract a manner and without sufficient consideration of
the special circumstances in which it originated. Aristotle, who
refers to it more than once in the *Politics*,[1] explains it as a
clumsy method of securing equality among the citizens, a device
to prevent the undue eminence of an individual. On his view
its employment by political leaders for the removal of their
opponents was an abuse of its proper function, an exploitation
for party purposes of a weapon forged for the protection of the
state. In fact it was invented and used from the start as a party
weapon by the anti-Persian leaders, but the end which they had
in view, the salvation of Athens and of Greece, was patriotic,
and to that end the banishment of their political rivals was a
necessary preliminary.

The first application of the new law, early in 487, resulted in
the ostracism of Hipparchos, and this was followed early in 486
by the ostracism of Megakles, the chief of the Alkmaionid clan.
De Sanctis has brought the second ostracism into connexion
with the passing of the law which reformed the method of
appointment to the archonship. He sees in it evidence of a
reaction against the Alkmaionidai and suggests[2] that its object
was to prevent them and their friends from monopolizing the
chief offices of state. Some of the details in this hypothesis cannot be accepted; in particular the motive alleged for the introduction of the law seems far-fetched. Moreover, all that we know
about the date of the law is that it must have been passed
between the spring of 487 and the spring of 486, and this dating
is not precise enough to establish a connexion between the
passing of the law and the ostracism of Megakles.[3]

Yet the proximity of these events is close enough to throw
doubt on the hypothesis that the Alkmaionidai, not their
opponents, were the promoters of the law. Those who hold this
view seem to start from a false conception of the political

[1] 1284[a]17 ff., 1284[b]15 ff., 1302[b]15 ff. The last sentence refers to ostracism as
existing in Argos, which (in spite of Wil. ii. 87) presumably copied ostracism from
Athens when it adopted democracy.   [2] Op. cit. 374.

[3] Beloch (ii[2]. 2. 139) was perhaps trying to meet this objection when he insisted, in defiance of *A.P.* 22. 5, that the reform of the archonship must have been
carried in the year before Telesinos' archonship. See above, p. 176, n. 3.

struggles of the period. They see in them a conflict of principles between conservatives and radicals, a conflict in which the Alkmaionidai inherit the leadership of the radical party. For them the reform of the archonship is in accord with the radical programme and entirely in the spirit of Kleisthenes' legislation;[1] radical democracy, always suspicious of its executive, prefers the collegiate principle to the concentration of wide powers in a single magistracy, and the essence of this reform was the transference of the most important functions previously vested in the archon and the polemarch to a board of ten equal members.

This interpretation of the reform has a superficial plausibility. It must, however, be remembered that whereas the archon and polemarch held office for one year only and were not re-eligible the strategoi could be re-elected year after year so long as they retained the confidence of the people; in this respect the reform had merely substituted a new and more insidious danger for the old. A strategos who was trusted by the demos and had held office for many years must have enjoyed greater authority in practice on the board of generals than his theoretically equal colleagues. Moreover, as early as the invasion of Xerxes the precedent was set for conferring supreme command in an emergency on a particular general.[2] Above all, the motive alleged by this interpretation for the reform is too doctrinaire and negative, too remote from the conditions and problems of the time.

There is much that is obscure about the reform. What arguments were used to connect with the reform in the appointment of the archons a measure to transfer their chief powers to another magistracy?[3] Although the author of the *Athenaion Politeia* stresses the first to the exclusion of the second, the essence of the reform is undoubtedly to be found in the creation of a new executive in which were vested the chief powers, civil and military, of the old. The main advantages of the new system over the old were the combination of the various executive powers within a single board and the possibility of continuity of direction contained in the fact that the members of this board could be re-elected. Lack of sufficient provision for continuity

[1] So Macan (op. cit. 207).
[2] Cf. Schwahn, 1079 and see below, p. 353.
[3] Possibly the reformers, having decided on a new executive, abolished popular election for the archonship in order to avert the danger of a conflict between two boards of executive officials both created by direct election.

has been urged[1] as a criticism against the government instituted by Kleisthenes; this deficiency was in part made good by the reform of 487/486.

The new organization proved its worth within a few years; it enabled the Athenians before and during the Persian invasion to derive the maximum advantage to the state from the talents of their generals and statesmen. Is it credible that this result of the reform should have been unforeseen by its promoters? Surely such a view is no more tenable than Herodotus' assertion[2] that the creation of a great Athenian navy was due to the accident of war with Aigina. The reform of 487/486 must therefore have been intended to increase the political and military efficiency of the Athenian state against the menace of a fresh Persian attack, and its authors must have been the leaders of the anti-Persian party, Themistokles and Aristeides.

This conclusion might be challenged[3] on the ground that the conservatives, who must have formed the bulk of the anti-Persian party, would never have sponsored a reform which was bound to lower the prestige of the Areopagus. The objection is not cogent. As we have seen, the labels 'conservative' and 'radical' have little meaning in this period, when the Kleisthenic constitution was taken for granted by all the rival politicians and the problems of foreign policy dominated the minds of the voters. It is true that the archonship was stripped of its old importance by the reform and henceforth ceased to attract the ablest men in the state, who were in consequence no longer to be found in the Areopagus, recruited as it still was from ex-archons. But the decline in the average level of ability among the Areopagites during the years 487–462 has been exaggerated,[4] and there is no ground for assuming that it contributed in any degree to the attack made in 462 on the powers of the Areopagus. Even if it did, the danger must have seemed very remote in 487.

The programme of the anti-Persian party in these years evinces a fertility in expedients and a brilliance in the adaptation of means to ends which point to Themistokles as its originator. By the device of ostracism he and his collaborators

---

[1] e.g. by de Sanctis, 346 ff.

[2] vii. 144. 1–2, refuted by Thuc. i. 14. 3; the compromise proposed by Plut. *Them.* 4. 1–2 is untenable.

[3] Cf. Headlam, *Election by Lot*[2], 45–46 and 185, also Beloch, ii[2]. 1. 26–28. Note on the other side the cogent arguments of Walker in *C.A.H.* iv. 155.

[4] As Wil. noted (ii. 92–93).

eliminated their chief opponents one by one, and by the reform of the executive they reorganized the antiquated machinery of the magistracy so that the energies of the state might be exerted effectively and without restraint in the impending crisis. One item in Themistokles' brilliant plan still remained unrealized, the creation of a great Athenian navy. As archon he had started the building of its harbour, the Piraeus,[1] and ten years later the funds for its construction were provided by the opportune discovery of a new vein of silver in the state-owned mines at Maroneia.[2] Themistokles proposed to devote these resources to the building of 200 warships on the latest model; these 'triremes' were intended to supersede the existing navy which was composed entirely of 'penteconters'.

Themistokles' proposal split the ranks of the anti-Persian party. Aristeides, who had probably co-operated with him in his previous measures, now offered vigorous opposition to his naval plans.[3] Possibly he was alarmed by the political consequences which might follow from the transformation of Athens into a sea-power. But the insistence of Themistokles and the imminence of the peril bore down all opposition; the bill was carried, and Aristeides was ostracized. Although he was the first of the anti-Persian leaders to suffer this fate, his ostracism should not be regarded as a new departure. The law on ostracism, introduced to combat the intrigues of the pro-Persian party by removing its chiefs from the state, was rightly invoked against Aristeides after his ill-timed opposition to the proposal on which depended the salvation of Athens in the impending war with Persia. Nor is there any cause for surprise in the fact that the amnesty-law passed in the archon-year 481/480[4] included the *ostracisés* among the exiles whose return it authorized. Thereby they were given a chance to acknowledge their former errors and to share in the defence of Athens against the barbarian attack which was now certain. Hipparchos apparently did not come back and was later condemned to death in absence as a traitor,[5]

---

[1] Thuc. i. 93. 3; on the date see above, p. 181, n. 4. The objections raised by Gomme (*Thucydides*, i. 261–2) are not decisive.

[2] *A.P.* 22. 7 and Hdt. vii. 144. 1; cf. Thuc. i. 14. 3.

[3] See above, p. 183, n. 4.

[4] *A.P.* 22. 8 (archonship of Hypsichides); Plut. *Arist.* 8. 1 dates it inaccurately to August 480. Carcopino's attempt (op. cit. 153–6) to date the year of Hypsichides to 482/481 cannot be accepted.

[5] Lykourgos, *Against Leokrates*, 117. Cf. Busolt, ii². 660, n. 1 and 398, n. 2.

but Aristeides and Xanthippos returned to place their services at the disposal of the state.

Their relations with Themistokles during the war are obscure. In 479, when they play a prominent part in the campaigns on land and sea, Themistokles is not mentioned. After the war there is some evidence for a renewed collaboration between Aristeides and Themistokles.[1] But the ascendancy of Themistokles was short-lived. When the Persian invasion had been repelled he ceased to be indispensable and his self-laudation became irksome.[2] He may also have changed his policy, advocating the suspension of hostilities against Persia and the overthrow of Spartan hegemony in the Peloponnese;[3] the cynical realism of such a programme could be contrasted unfavourably with the Panhellenic idealism of his new rival, Kimon the son of Miltiades. His growing unpopularity was exploited by the noble families which resented the supremacy of the Lykomidai and their chief. A temporary truce in the long feud between Alkmaionidai and Philaïdai had been brought about by the marriage of Kimon with Isodike, whose father Euryptolemos was a member of the Alkmaionid clan.[4] The coalition of the great houses triumphed; Themistokles was ostracized.[5] A year or two later he was condemned to death in absence on a charge of high treason brought against him by an Alkmaionid, Leobotas son of Alkmaion.

Of Aristeides little is known after his participation in the foundation of the Delian League.[6] Xanthippos is never mentioned after 479, and Perikles, his son by the Alkmaionid Agariste,[7] does not become prominent till 463. The descendants of the Alkmaionidai in the male line henceforth played no important part in politics. On the fall of Themistokles the leadership of the state fell to Kimon. Though his family may

[1] Thuc. i. 91. 3; cf. *A.P.* 23. 3 (on which cf. Busolt, iii. 63, n. 3). Plutarch says (*Kimon* 5. 6) that Aristeides favoured the rise of Kimon as a counterpoise to Themistokles, but this may be pure guesswork.

[2] Plut. *Them.* 22. 1–3; Busolt, iii. 109, n. 1.

[3] Meyer, *G.A.* iii[1]. 511–12.

[4] Plut. *Kimon* 4. 10 and 16. 1. See below, Note J.

[5] Plut. *Them.* 22. 4 (cf. Thuc. i. 135. 3). I am inclined to accept the view (cf. Carcopino, op. cit. 160–1) that 471/470 was the year of Themistokles' condemnation on the charge brought by Alkmaion (Plut. *Them.* 23. 1); possibly he was condemned in the spring of 470. His ostracism may have been early 472 (Carcopino dates it early 471).

[6] Cf. Meyer, *G.A.* iii[1]. 507 n. for criticism of the ancient evidence on Aristeides' later years.   [7] Hdt. vi. 131. 2.

have belonged to the new nobility which owed its rise to the tyrants[1] it made good its position among the dynastic houses of Athens. Moreover Kimon was connected with the old nobility through his wife Isodike and his half-sister Elpinike[2] who had married Kallias, the wealthy head of the Kerykes, one of the families connected with the Eleusinian cult. Himself possessor of a princely fortune, Kimon employed it in a princely manner, in benefactions to the state and in generosity to individual citizens.[3] His popularity with the masses was strengthened by the appeal of his frank and genial personality and his soldierly qualities. Even the idealism of his foreign policy suited well the temper of Athens in the seventies.

Kimon's popularity was reflected in his frequent election to the strategia, which he probably held without a break from 477 to 461.[4] His long tenure, which foreshadows that of Perikles, is significant for the prestige acquired by this magistracy since the reform of 487/486. The functions conferred on it by the reform were in themselves important, and may even have included the presidency of the ekklesia,[5] but their scope had been greatly augmented by the development of Athenian resources and ambitions. When Athens was transformed into a great naval power the strategoi became admirals of the largest navy in Greece. During the Persian invasion it was found necessary to confer supreme command on one of the generals, who represented Athens on the war-council of the Hellenic League. After the war Athens acquired the hegemony of the Delian Confederacy, and in consequence her strategoi assumed the command of its fleets and armies. Well might Wilamowitz say[6] that the stratégia had provided a new and congenial field of action for the members of the great families. It is not certain that there was a property qualification for the office,[7] but the gifts of political leadership

---

[1] See above, p. 104.

[2] Nepos, *Cimon* 1. 2 suggests that Elpinike was the daughter of Miltiades by his first marriage (for which cf. Hdt. vi. 41. 2). On her marriage with Kallias cf. Plut. *Kimon* 4. 8.

[3] *A.P.* 27. 3; fuller discussion in Plut. *Kimon* 10.

[4] Gomme (*Thucydides*, i. 386, n. 3) says that 'there is no evidence at all for this'. There is, however, evidence that Kimon was general in ten of these sixteen years and no evidence that he was not general in the other six.

[5] See above, p. 175. [6] *A.A.* ii. 88.

[7] Such a qualification is alleged by Deinarchos i. 71, but this evidence, though accepted by many scholars (e.g. Schwahn, 1074) is not above suspicion; cf. Kahr. ii. 23 and n. 3.

and military capacity which it required were in any case only to be found among the rich landowners.

For a decade and a half after Plataiai the leading families were left undisturbed by the demos in control of Athenian policy. It was the Indian summer of the Athenian aristocracy and the true zenith of Athenian glory in Greece. For so long the Kleisthenic constitution, buttressed by the reforms of 487/486, remained intact. But Athens had experienced such a transformation in the forty years since the legislation of Kleisthenes that his hoplite democracy had become a manifest anachronism. Its foundations were undermined and the inevitable collapse could not long be delayed.

VIII. THE REVOLUTION OF 462

KIMON'S long predominance came to an abrupt and disastrous end early in 461,[1] when he was ostracized and had to leave Attica for ten years. The ultimate cause of this catastrophe is to be found in the fatal contradiction between his foreign and his domestic policy. His maintenance of the war against Persia and its corollary, the suppression of revolts within the Delian League, increased still further the importance of the fleet and of the Thetes who manned it.[2] As the safety and welfare of the state depended to an ever greater degree on their exertions, it was natural that they should demand the lion's share of the government. Kimon had set his face against any change in the constitution,[3] but the measures by which he averted for a time the imminent danger were merely makeshifts. Following the example of the tyrants, he tried to distract the Thetes from political agitation by promoting their material well-being. Possibly his lavish generosity was influenced by this motive.[4] He also revived Kleisthenes' expedient of providing poorer citizens with freeholds in 'cleruchies' outside Attica. When he conquered Skyros the original inhabitants were driven out and the island was occupied by Athenian settlers. A more ambitious project was the planting of 10,000 colonists, Athenians and allies, at Ennea Hodoi (465/464) ;[5] these soon met with a disaster at Drabeskos in the interior which dealt a serious blow to Kimon's popularity.

This disaster occurred while Kimon was engaged in the siege of Thasos, which kept him away from Athens for over two years.[6] His absence and his growing unpopularity were exploited by the opposition, now directed by able leaders. Foremost among these was Ephialtes son of Sophonides. His talents and achievements have been overshadowed in the ancient tradition by the fame of his friend Perikles who succeeded him in the leadership of the radical party. Of his family nothing is known except his father's name,[7] and his first recorded exploit is his conduct as strategos

---

[1] On the date cf. Busolt, iii. 258, n. 1 and Carcopino, *Ostracisme*, 161–8. See below, pp. 337 f.   [2] Ar. *Politics* 1304ª22–24.
[3] Cf. Plut. *Kimon* 15. 1.
[4] *A.P.* 27. 3. Cf. the discussion in G. Lombardo, *Cimone* (Rome, 1934), 39–45.
[5] Thuc. i. 98. 2 (Skyros) and 100. 3 (Ennea Hodoi).
[6] On the length of the siege cf. Thuc. i. 101. 3.   [7] *A.P.* 25. 1.

of an expedition of thirty ships to the eastern Mediterranean,[1] probably in one of the years 465–463. His tenure of the strategia is sufficient to disprove the later legend of his poverty,[2] and suggests that he belonged to one of the noble families of Athens.

By this time the aristocracy was no longer united in support of Kimon; his attempt to combine the great houses in defence of the existing constitution had been thwarted by new quarrels and the revival of old antagonisms. The marriage between Kimon's half-sister Elpinike and Kallias seems to have been ended by divorce,[3] and Kallias is later found in the ranks of the opposition.[4] Through his wife Kimon was connected with the Alkmaionidai and therefore with Perikles, the younger son of Xanthippos and the Alkmaionid Agariste,[5] who was just beginning his political career. But although Xanthippos had co-operated with Kimon in 479[6] he had prosecuted his father Miltiades a decade before,[7] and the ancient feud was revived when Perikles took a prominent part in the prosecution directed against Kimon on his return from Thasos.[8]

Ephialtes saw in the powers still retained by the Areopagus the chief bulwark of the existing order and therefore determined to make their abolition his first object. In the *Athenaion Politeia*[9] he is alleged to have prepared the way for his reforms by attacks on individual Areopagites for their official conduct. So Plutarch[10] says that he was dreaded by the oligarchs and in connexion with euthynai and public prosecutions was an inexorable foe to those who had wronged the demos. These statements raise serious difficulties. It is doubtful whether the Areopagus had financial duties as a council, and even if it had, how could individuals have been prosecuted in connexion with

---

[1] Kallisthenes, fr. 1 (16 in Jacoby, *F.G.H.* ii B, p. 646) quoted in Plut. *Kimon* 13. 4; cf. Meyer, *Forsch.* ii. 3 and n. 2.

[2] Cf. Busolt, iii. 246, n. 1. Hatzfeld, 2 and n. 3, is sceptical.

[3] Meyer, *Forsch.* ii. 27 and n. 3, infers this from the fact that Elpinike's tomb was near that of the historian Thucydides (Plut. *Kimon* 4. 3: ἐν τοῖς Κιμωνείοις). Beloch, ii². 2. 45, denies the validity of the inference.

[4] On the assumption that the Kallias who went to Sousa *c.* 461 (Hdt. vii. 151; for the date cf. Walker in *C.A.H.* v. 470) is identical with Elpinike's husband and not with the Kallias, probably his nephew (cf. Beloch, ii². 2. 44–45) who helped to negotiate the peace with Sparta in 446 (Diod. xii. 7).

[5] Hdt. vi. 131. 2; see above, p. 180.

[6] On the embassy to Sparta; cf. Plut. *Arist.* 10. 10.

[7] Hdt. vi. 136. 1.

[8] *A.P.* 27. 1 and Stesimbrotos in Plut. *Kimon* 14. 5 (fr. 5 in Jacoby, *F.G.H.* ii B).

[9] 25. 2.　　　　　　　　　　[10] *Per.* 10. 8.

them? Busolt suggested[1] that individual Areopagites may have
been responsible for paying into the treasury of Athena the fines
imposed by the Areopagus in certain cases and that the trans-
action offered opportunities for peculation. A more probable
explanation[2] is that the members of the Areopagus singled out
for attack by Ephialtes were prosecuted not for their actions as
Areopagites but for misconduct in some other office. Plutarch's
reference to euthynai raises a special difficulty if, as some
believe,[3] the Areopagus itself was the body which dealt with the
euthynai of officials before 462. Yet our ignorance of the details
of the constitution in this period is such that the tradition may
be founded on fact. The qualities attributed to Ephialtes in the
tradition, his incorruptibility and his ruthless elimination of his
principal opponents, have prompted a comparison between him
and another revolutionary statesman, Robespierre.[4]

The revolution of 462 had presumably been preceded by a
long agitation against the privileges of the Areopagus. One
argument used by the radical spokesmen was that these privileges had not belonged to the Areopagus from the beginning
but had been acquired later by usurpation;[5] the Areopagus had
at first been merely a court for the trial of homicide cases and
ought to be restricted once more to its original function. Some
scholars[6] have maintained that the prestige of the Areopagus
had suffered a steady decline since the reform of 487, because in
consequence of that reform the ex-archons from whom the
Areopagus was recruited had ceased to include the ablest men
in the state, and of those who had been appointed by direct
election earlier than 486 the number sank year by year. This
explanation does not touch the real cause. The archons were
still drawn from the first two of the Solonian property-classes,
and a study of the names of the chief archons in this period
shows that some at least belonged to distinguished families.[7]
It was not the unworthiness of the Areopagites to exercise their
powers which was denounced by the radicals but the retention
of such wide powers in a progressive state by a council whose
members were appointed for life.

[1] iii. 263, n. 1 (cf. A.P. 8. 4).
[2] Wil. ii. 94; cf. Bonner and Smith, 256.
[3] e.g. Meyer, G.A. iii². 609 and Kahr. ii. 177–8; cf. Bonner and Smith, 164–6.
[4] Made by Swoboda in R.-E. v. 2. 2850.
[5] Cf. A.P. 25. 2 and Wil. ii. 186–7.
[6] So de Sanctis, 401.   [7] Wil. ii. 93; cf. Busolt, iii. 262, n. 1.

After the disaster at Drabeskos, Ephialtes and Perikles thought that the time had come to strike a blow at Kimon himself, rightly regarding him as the most formidable champion of the existing constitution. Accordingly they prosecuted him as soon as he returned from Thasos on a charge of accepting bribes from Alexander, the King of Macedonia.[1] But they had underestimated his popularity. Not only was he acquitted but he was still influential enough a few months later to gain a signal success over his rivals on a momentous question of foreign policy. When Sparta appealed to Athens in 462 for aid against the revolted Helots Ephialtes urged the ekklesia to refuse. He is said to have warned them 'not to raise up again a state which might prove a dangerous rival, but to allow the pride of Sparta to fall and be trampled in the dust'.[2] This is simply an appeal to power-politics, but probably Ephialtes also realized that Sparta, the defender of conservative interests throughout Greece, was bound to be alienated if Athens adopted a more radical form of democracy.

Against these narrow arguments of self-interest Kimon urged the claims of Panhellenic patriotism, and by his vigorous eloquence persuaded his hearers to give a favourable answer to the Spartan appeal.[3] His triumph was complete, but it was destined to play into the hands of his political enemies and to end before long in the ruin of the conservative cause at Athens. In his previous expeditions Kimon had taken with him many of the Thetes who served in the fleet, while most of the hoplites stayed in Attica. But when he marched to Ithome he left the fleet and the Thetes at home and took with him 4,000 of the hoplites,[4] who were the chief supporters of the Kleisthenic democracy. The result was a temporary shift in the balance of parties in the ekklesia. Ephialtes seized the opportunity to renew his agitation against the Areopagus, and laws were proposed by him and by Archestratos which transferred most of its privileges to the boulē of Five Hundred and the Heliaia.[5] These laws were perhaps moved in the form of psephismata.[6] The Areopagus did not venture to exercise the indirect powers for the defence of the

---

[1] Plut. *Kimon* 14. 3; cf. Wil. ii. 245.   [2] Plut. 16. 9.
[3] Ibid. 9–10 (with quotations from Ion).
[4] Aristophanes, *Lysistrata* 1143.
[5] *A.P.* 25. 2; cf. 35. 2 (with Kenyon's note). On the chronology see below, Appendix VIII.
[6] As Wade-Gery believes those of Kleisthenes to have been; see above, p. 15.

constitution which it possessed; a prosecution of Ephialtes would have been bound to fail, and the Areopagus was in a very invidious position, as its own powers were in question.

Naturally Kimon challenged the validity of this 'snap vote' on his return, when he tried to get the obnoxious laws repealed and the old jurisdiction of the Areopagus restored.[1] But his position in Athens had been undermined during his absence. Sparta, alarmed by the revolution of Ephialtes, had requested the Athenian force to leave Messenia. As the other allies of Sparta remained at Ithome, the dismissal of the Athenians could be represented by the radicals as an intolerable affront. When Kimon tried to undo the recent revolution they delivered a vigorous attack on his philo-Laconian policy. An appeal to ostracism early in 461 ended in the banishment of Kimon. But the triumph of Ephialtes was brief. The opposition, weakened by the removal of their leader, were driven to desperate courses, and before the eventful archonship of Konon reached its end, Ephialtes was assassinated.[2]

His fate is sufficient to prove that the conservatives saw in him their chief enemy. In some ancient accounts the principal role in the revolution of 462 is assigned to Perikles, and Ephialtes becomes merely his collaborator or the instrument employed by him to carry out his plans.[3] These accounts are refuted by the more trustworthy version of Theopompos[4] and antedate the beginning of Perikles' ascendancy; in the sixties his position in the radical party was subordinate to that of Ephialtes. Perikles must have taken part in the agitation against the Areopagus, but the statement in the *Athenaion Politeia*[5] that 'he took away some of the powers of the Areopagites' looks like a desperate attempt to reconcile conflicting traditions. The laws curtailing the powers of the Areopagus which were repealed by the oligarchs in 404 are described[6] as the laws of Ephialtes and Archestratos, not as the laws of Ephialtes and Perikles.

Wilamowitz, relying on the evidence of Plutarch that Perikles frequently used other orators and friends as the official sponsors

---

[1] Plut. *Kimon* 15. 3.
[2] By Aristodikos of Tanagra according to *A.P.* 25. 4; Antiphon, v. 68 (cf. Diod. xi. 77. 6), says that the assassins were never discovered.
[3] Plut. *Per.* 9. 3–5; cf. 7. 7–8. The words καὶ Περικλῆς in Ar. *Politics* 1274ᵃ8 may be an interpolation; cf. de Sanctis, 410, n. 1.
[4] In Plut. *Kimon* 15. 2; cf. Philochoros, fr. 141b (Jacoby, 64b).
[5] 27. 1.   [6] In *A.P.* 35. 2.

of his plans, suggested[1] that Archestratos was the spokesman employed by Perikles for his legislation against the Areopagus, and that he was to be identified with an Archestratos son of Lykomedes who was a general in 433/432.[2] Hence it has been argued that the laws of Archestratos may have been subsequent to those of Ephialtes and may represent a later attack on the Areopagus ending in a further curtailment of its powers.[3] But nothing is known of the reformer Archestratos except his name, which is fairly common at Athens in this period,[4] and in the passage of Plutarch cited by Wilamowitz it is Ephialtes, not Archestratos, who is named as typical of the agents employed by Perikles. There is, therefore, no adequate ground for rejecting the usual view that the laws of Archestratos were carried, like the laws of Ephialtes, in the archonship of Konon ;[5] probably he was one of Ephialtes' supporters and undertook the responsibility for some of the laws in the party programme.

We have no detailed account of these important laws, which deprived the Areopagus of all but a remnant of its ancient powers. This is not surprising; as the Atthidographers had no clear ideas about the nature and working of the Kleisthenic constitution, they were naturally unable to describe the revolution by which it was overthrown except in vague and general terms. The author of the *Athenaion Politeia*, reproducing the radical version of the reform, says that the powers taken from the Areopagus, which had made it the guardian of the state, were powers which had not originally belonged to it ;[6] this version, with its implication that Ephialtes was only restoring the πάτριος πολιτεία, is refuted by his earlier testimony[7] that the guardianship of the laws was the function of the Areopagus in the pre-Solonian state. He does not describe the powers taken from the Areopagus, but gives a clue to their nature in his comment[8] that they were transferred either to the Council of Five Hundred or to the demos and the popular courts. For Theopompos, whose account seems to be Plutarch's ultimate

---

[1] *A.A.* i. 68, n. 40, citing Plut. *Per.* 7. 7–8.

[2] Thuc. i. 57. 6; Wil. also identified the general with the proposer of the rider in *I.G.* i². 39 (Tod, 42), ll. 70 ff. Cf. de Sanctis, 416, n. 2.

[3] Bonner and Smith, 253, suggest that he may have been the official proposer of some laws of Periklean authorship which they date on very slender grounds (270 ff.) to 452 or 451. [4] Cf. Busolt, iii. 270, n. 1.

[5] So de Sanctis, 415–16. [6] See above, p. 195.

[7] 3. 6. [8] 25. 2.

authority,[1] the essence of the reform was a transference of jurisdiction; the Areopagus was deprived of all its former jurisdiction except the trial of homicide cases, with the result that the demos in the popular courts practically monopolized the administration of justice and thereby transformed the state into a radical democracy. Hence Kimon's attempt to secure the repeal of Ephialtes' laws was described by Theopompos as an attempt to restore to the old council its former jurisdiction and so revive the aristocracy of Kleisthenes.

Theopompos was certainly right in maintaining that the revolution of 462 transferred to other bodies extensive judicial powers which had previously belonged to the Areopagus, but his account of the reforms, though a striking testimony to his historical insight, is not the whole truth; among other omissions he failed to notice the important authority possessed by the Areopagus before 462 in the sphere of religion. It may be doubted whether he or any other fourth-century historian was in a position to describe in detail the powers which had been vested in the Areopagus by Solon and left untouched by Kleisthenes. A reconstruction of these powers, indispensable for a proper appreciation of the reforms of 462, has been attempted above in the chapter on Solon. If the conclusions there reached may be taken for granted here, we obtain the following picture of the reforms.[2]

Jurisdiction in most cases connected with religion, notably in prosecutions for impiety, was transferred from the Areopagus to the popular courts. But some jurisdiction in this department was retained by the Areopagus;[3] for example, it continued to try cases arising out of the destruction of any of the sacred olive trees.[4] In all such cases, whether they were tried before the Areopagus or before a dikastery, and also in all homicide cases, the basileus as head of the state religion still presided. Religious conservatism was strong enough to deter the radical reformers from any interference with the ancient jurisdiction of the Areopagus in cases of deliberate homicide and arson, which it retained in the fourth century.[5] By then the Ephetic courts which dealt with certain types of homicide cases had ceased to

[1] *Kimon* 15. 2; cf. Busolt, iii. 239, n. 4 and 261, n. 1.
[2] Cf. also Wil. ii. 8 and Bonner and Smith, 257–70.
[3] Cf. Bonner and Smith, 260.
[4] *A.P.* 60. 2; [Dem.] lix. 79–80 gives other examples of its religious jurisdiction and proves that its authority was limited.   [5] *A.P.* 57. 3.

be composed of the Fifty-one (chosen from the Areopagites) and were selected from the ordinary dikasts. It has been argued[1] that this minor reform was carried by Perikles in the decade after Ephialtes' death, but the evidence for this view is unconvincing, and the reform was more probably introduced in 403.

The secular jurisdiction in various departments which the Areopagus had previously possessed was now taken away from it entirely and divided between the Council of Five Hundred, the ekklesia, and the popular courts. It is doubtful whether the Areopagus had retained till now the right conferred on it by Solon to try those who were accused of conspiracy against the constitution; possibly this right may have been subjected to some limitation towards the end of the sixth century.[2] However that may be, cases of this type and all others which were tried by the process of eisangelia came henceforth to the 500 or the ekklesia, the final decision being reserved for the ekklesia or the law-courts.[3] In the other departments of its secular jurisdiction the Areopagus seems to have maintained its former competence till 462. Thus it could take action against a magistrate who was guilty of exceeding his legal powers in his official capacity, and it could prosecute any citizen who had broken the laws.[4] The right of hearing complaints against the magistrates was apparently transferred by Ephialtes to the 500.[5] Andokides quotes a decree of 403 which empowers the Areopagus to watch over the laws and to ensure that the magistrates observe them;[6] this, however, was a clause in a provisional constitution and was probably abrogated when normal conditions were restored.

Offences against the laws committed by private citizens could be dealt with in various ways. If they affected the person or property of another citizen, the injured party could bring a charge against the offender before the appropriate court.[7] In some types of cases an action could be brought by any citizen who chose to do so; in these cases the right to prosecute was not limited to the injured party or his kinsmen.[8] The object of this

---

[1] By Bonner and Smith 270–5; cf. the article by Miss Smith in *C.P.* xix, 1924, 353 ff.

[2] See above, pp. 154 f. and cf. Busolt, iii. 125, n. 4.

[3] Wil. ii. 189–90; Bonner and Smith, 300 ff. Cf. *X.A.P.* 3. 5, Ar. *Wasps* 590–1, and *A.P.* 59. 2.　　　　　　　　　　　[4] See above, pp. 90 f.

[5] Wil. ii. 192 and Bonner and Smith, 262; cf. *A.P.* 45. 2.

[6] And. i. 84.　　　　　　　　　　　[7] Cf. de Sanctis, 423–4.

[8] Cf. Bonner and Smith, 167 ff.

innovation, which is attributed to Solon, is doubtful. According to one suggestion[1] it was designed by Solon to supplement the lacunae and imperfections which were to be found in the jurisdiction of the Areopagus. In the *Athenaion Politeia*[2] there is no hint of any limitation on the right of the Solonian Areopagus to initiate action against wrongdoers and to try them in its own court. But in practice, unless the attention of the Areopagus was directed by a complaint to a particular case, its initiative must have been limited in the main to the enforcement of laws which were the concern of the state rather than the individual, for example the νόμος ἀργίας; all prosecutions under this law were at one time tried by the Areopagus.[3]

The rights of initiative and jurisdiction possessed by the Areopagus in connexion with this and other laws conferred on it an extensive control over the lives and morals of the citizens. But the existence of a censorship such as that attributed by Isokrates[4] to the Solonian Areopagus must have become irksome to the developing democracy, especially as the main tendency of this supervision was to maintain the old order in political and social life. It was the weakness of the Areopagus that the action left to it under the constitution of Kleisthenes was mainly obstructive and repressive.[5] Moreover, its jurisdiction was not subject to the rules of the ordinary courts; if the testimony of the *Athenaion Politeia*[6] may be accepted, the Areopagus could impose fines without stating the precise ground for their imposition. Hence its opponents could arouse popular resentment against its censorial powers; the motto of the radical democracy was to be 'live as you please',[7] and when the *praefectura morum* of the Areopagus was destroyed no attempt was made to provide a substitute.

Some departments, however, of the secular jurisdiction formerly vested in the Areopagus were transferred in 462 to other bodies. For example, its old power to hear complaints against the magistrates seems to have passed now to the Council of Five Hundred.[8] Our evidence for the jurisdiction exercised by this council in the second half of the fifth century is imperfect, and there is wide disagreement on the conclusions to be drawn from

---

[1] Made by de Sanctis, 424.   [2] 8. 4; cf. 3. 6.
[3] Plut. *Solon* 22. 3 and Athenaios 168 A (citing Phanodemos and Philochoros).
[4] vii. 46.   [5] Cf. de Sanctis, 425–6.   [6] 8. 4.
[7] ζῆν ὡς βούλεταί τις (Ar. *Politics* 1317ᵇ12).   [8] *A.P.* 4. 4 and 45. 2.

it. The most probable view is that the council was not permitted even in this period to impose a penalty of more than 500 drachmas;[1] it could try any case which fell within its competence and register its verdict, but if the penalty proposed exceeded the legal maximum the case had to be referred to the ekklesia or the popular courts.[2] In such cases the council's verdict had no legal effect, but it might as a *praeiudicium* have some influence on the final decision.

Within the sphere of its jurisdiction the council was not limited to the trial of charges brought by magistrates or private persons; it could take action on its own account. Thus it could initiate a prosecution against a trierarch who had failed to do his duty,[3] or against tax-farmers and state contractors who had not fulfilled their obligations to the treasury.[4] It could also call to account any magistrate for irregularities in the discharge of his legal or administrative duties.[5] The initiative of the council in these instances is connected with its general supervision of the administration and its special concern with the financial and naval departments. Normally, however, its attention must have been drawn to such cases by the zeal of voluntary prosecutors. Moreover, its jurisdiction was restricted in the main to offences which affected the interests of the state; it did not extend to offences against individuals, except those committed by magistrates in their official capacity.

These limitations on the judicial initiative of the council show that the extensive powers in this respect previously vested in the Areopagus, which had largely compensated for the absence of a public prosecutor, were not made over to the Lower Council by the revolution of 462. Presumably the radical reformers, suspicious of powers which had enabled the Areopagus to maintain a close control over the conduct and morals of the citizens, were determined not to transfer them in their entirety to any other organ of government, even to one so democratic as the 500. They preferred instead to give a wider field to the activities of the voluntary prosecutor and to increase the number of cases in which his intervention was permitted. It is possible that the right ἐξεῖναι τῷ βουλομένῳ τιμωρεῖν ὑπὲρ τῶν ἀδικουμένων may

---

[1] *I.G.* i². 76 (Tod, 74), ll. 57–59; cf. [Dem.] xlvii. 43.

[2] *A.P.* 45. 1. Cf. the discussion in Bonner and Smith, c. 14.

[3] [Dem.] xlvii. 41 ff. and *I.G.* ii². 1629, ll. 242–6 (date 325/324); cf. BS 1049, nn. 3 and 4.   [4] Dem. xxiv. 96; cf. Gilbert, 279–80.

[5] *A.P.* 45. 2; cf. Gilbert, 278 and n. 1.

have been recognized to some limited degree in the laws of Solon, to which its origin was ascribed by tradition,[1] but its later extension seems to be subsequent to and produced by the Ephialtic revolution.[2] In the developed form of the system its inevitable result was the emergence of the professional accuser, who under the name of συκοφάντης speedily became a characteristic feature of the radical democracy.

It has been suggested that until 462 the Areopagus had some share in the εὔθυνα of the magistrates.[3] This was the examination of their administration which the magistrates had to undergo at the end of their term of office. Under the radical democracy it consisted of two parts. The first part was the verification of the magistrate's accounts.[4] These he submitted to the careful scrutiny of the public accountants (λογισταί); if they were dissatisfied he was prosecuted in a dikastery presided over by them.[5] Even if they found no ground for complaint they had to bring him before their court, since his final discharge was dependent on its verdict.[6] Magistrates who had not handled public money were naturally exempt from this part of the examination,[7] but all had to submit to the second part, to which the term εὔθυνα must originally have been confined. In this the retiring magistrate had to face charges which might be brought against his conduct while in office; the charges were presented by the aggrieved persons to the ten εὔθυνοι, who passed on any charge which seemed well-founded to the appropriate authority, the 'deme judges' in private, the thesmothetai in public suits.[8] Charges of this kind received by the thesmothetai were referred by them to a dikastery for decision. Thus most magistrates had to pass a twofold examination, first the λόγος, then the εὔθυνα, but either name could be applied to the examination as a whole.[9]

From the two distinct stages of this curious procedure it is

---

[1] *A.P.* 9. 1 and Plut. *Solon* 18. 6–7. The tradition is accepted by Bonner and Smith, 168.   [2] So de Sanctis, 426.

[3] Cf. Bonner and Smith, 164 and n. 1, also Meyer, *G.A.* iii². 609 and Kahr. ii. 177–8.

[4] Cf. Bonner and Smith, ii. 34 ff. and Gilbert, 226–8, also Wil. ii, c. 12, de Sanctis, 436–7, and BS 1076 ff.   [5] *A.P.* 54. 2.

[6] Cf. Bonner and Smith, ii. 35 and n. 1, and BS 1077 and n. 3.

[7] Each, however, had to submit a written statement in which he certified that he had not received or spent any public money (Aischines iii. 22).

[8] *A.P.* 48. 4–5.

[9] εὔθυναι in Lys. xxx. 5 (cf. xxv. 30), λόγος in Dem. xix. 211, both together in *I G.* i². 91 (Tod, 51 A), ll. 25–27 and Aischines, iii. 26. Cf. de Sanctis, 436, n. 1 and BS 1080, n. 2.

reasonable to infer an historical development in which one stage was superimposed on the other. That the procedure before the euthynoi was the more primitive is probable in itself, and is supported by the comparative unimportance of the financial functions of the magistrates in the archaic state. Moreover, an inscription of the deme Skambonidai proves that εὔθυνοι were a regular institution of local government in Attica before 462.[1] It is implied by the author of the *Athenaion Politeia*[2] that the εὔθυνοι of the central government were appointed in his time from, as well as by, the boulē of Five Hundred. Those who ascribe their institution to the Solonian period see in this an indication that the εὔθυνοι were originally chosen from and by the Areopagus. De Sanctis[3] finds confirmation of this view in the fact that they did not possess the power (which belonged to most magistrates in a similar position) of presiding over the court which examined the charges received by them. He ascribes the establishment of the logistai-procedure to Kleisthenes and suggests that its object was to make the magistrates responsible to the people as well as to the Areopagus.

The date proposed by de Sanctis for the creation of the board of logistai cannot be accepted. Their existence is not attested before 454, and the more probable view is that they were instituted at the time of Ephialtes' reforms or soon after; Ferguson maintains that until then the λόγοι of the magistrates came before the Areopagus.[4] The institution of the εὔθυνοι was earlier, as we have seen, but there is no evidence that it was Solonian. Aristotle speaks in the *Politics*[5] of the power τὰς ἀρχὰς εὐθύνειν in connexion with Solon's legislation, but he states that Solon entrusted this power to the ekklesia. Moreover, it is clear from other references in the *Politics* that in this passage he must be using εὐθύνειν in a wider sense; he cannot have meant to restrict it to the procedure initiated by the εὔθυνοι. It is, however, not clear whether he ascribed to the Solonian period anachronistically the examination of magistrates as it was conducted under the radical democracy, or whether (as some believe)[6] he was thinking of the ἔφεσις εἰς τὸ δικαστήριον; in either event his testimony is irrelevant to the present problem.

[1] *I.G.* i². 188. 30 ff. (Wil. ii. 239–40, n. 30 dismisses it too easily).
[2] 48. 3–4; cf. Wil. ii. 234, n. 14 and de Sanctis, 437.   [3] *Atthis²*, 437.
[4] *Klio*, iv, 1904, 4–5; cf. Kahr. ii. 178.
[5] 1274ᵃ15–17 and 1281ᵇ32–34.   [6] Bonner and Smith, i. 164–5.

Busolt surmised that under the Solonian constitution the magistrates on laying down office had to submit to an examination of their administration before the popular assembly.[1] But the imposition of this obligation on all retiring magistrates as a regular routine is a characteristic of a fairly advanced democracy; the introduction of the εὔθυνα in this form at Athens cannot be carried back to the age of Solon. Admittedly there must be some provision for enforcing magisterial responsibility under any settled government. But it may be doubted whether in the Solonian state this provision went beyond the powers vested in the Areopagus to hear complaints against the magistrates and to prosecute those who plotted against the constitution,[2] and these powers, however admirable in theory, must often have been defied in practice by the powerful dynasts who struggled for supremacy in the post-Solonian period. The government of Peisistratos was probably the first which was strong enough to enforce on the magistrates respect for the laws. Peisistratos is more likely to have been responsible for the institution of the εὔθυνοι than Solon. The Areopagus, from which they were chosen, was composed of his supporters, and the deme judges to whom they referred private suits owed their origin to him.[3] The suits which in later times were sent by the εὔθυνοι to the thesmothetai must at first have been submitted by them to the Areopagus. This practice and the selection of the εὔθυνοι from the Areopagites were presumably left unaltered by Kleisthenes and went on until the reforms of Ephialtes.

Did the Areopagus before 462 play any part in the δοκιμασία of the magistrates? In the Periklean democracy and later the δοκιμασία was an examination which the magistrates (and also the members of the boulē) had to undergo between their selection and their entry on office. It consisted of a number of questions designed to test whether the magistrate-elect possessed the legal qualifications required for the office to which he had been appointed.[4] For most offices the inquiry was held before a dikasterion, but the dokimasia of the nine archons belonged to the Council of Five Hundred, which was also responsible for the dokimasia of its successors, the members-elect of

[1] BS 847.   [2] See above, pp. 90 f.
[3] A.P. 16. 5; they are usually assumed to have lapsed after the fall of the tyranny until their reinstitution in 453/452 (A.P. 26. 3; see below, pp. 218 f.).
[4] BS 1072–3; cf. Headlam, 96–102.

the next year's council.[1] In both cases a negative decision of the council had at one time been final, but at a later period the rejected candidate could appeal to a dikasterion; this limitation of the council's powers may be earlier than the end of the fifth century. The author of the *Athenaion Politeia* asserts[2] that in his time the nine archons were always subjected to a double dokimasia, first before the council, then in a law-court, and though his testimony has been questioned (on the ground that such a system would reduce the dokimasia before the council to an empty form) it is confirmed by a passage of Demosthenes.[3]

Attempts to deduce the historical development from these facts have produced a number of conflicting hypotheses. Wilamowitz, ascribing the institution of the procedure to Solon, supposed that from the first the dokimasia of the archons-elect was assigned to the Lower Council,[4] while the Areopagus, which had formerly nominated the minor magistrates, received instead from Solon the right to test their qualifications; when Ephialtes transferred this right to the popular courts in 462 he left to the Lower Council the dokimasia of the archons, for whom special guarantees were still required. This view assumes that the Lower Council was first created by Solon, and does not explain why the dokimasia of the strategoi, whose political importance was far greater by 462 than that of the archons, was held in a dikasterion.

De Sanctis maintains the opposite thesis, that the Areopagus was never concerned with the dokimasia of the minor magistrates but possessed that of the archons until 462, when it was transferred to the 500.[5] He notes that although the γραμματεὺς τῶν θεσμοθετῶν was closely associated with the nine archons his dokimasia was held not before the boulē but before a dikasterion, and assuming that his office was created by Kleisthenes he sees in the difference between his dokimasia and that of the pre-Kleisthenic archons a proof that the latter had at one time belonged to the Areopagus.[6] But though the addition of a secretary to the nine archons formed a board of ten in which all the Kleisthenic tribes were represented, the addition need not be contemporaneous with the creation of the ten tribes; it may belong to 487/486 or may even be as late as 462.

[1] *A.P.* 45. 3 and 55. 2.   [2] 55. 2.
[3] xx. 90; cf. BS 1045, n. 2 and Wil. ii. 189, n. 3.
[4] *A.A.* ii. 189.   [5] *Atthis*², 435.   [6] Ibid. 150.

Wilamowitz and de Sanctis have rightly seen in the anomalies
of the later procedure a proof that the dokimasia must have
been instituted before 462, but their hypotheses are both vitiated
by the assumption that its origins must be carried back to Solon
or earlier. For this assumption there is no satisfactory evidence.
We may admit that the questions put to the archon-elect at
the dokimasia, as quoted in the *Athenaion Politeia*,[1] may have
been modified with time and so cannot safely be used to date the
beginnings of the procedure. It is, however, significant that they
contain no reference to the possession of the requisite $\tau\acute{\epsilon}\lambda o s$,
which, together with Athenian citizenship, must have been the
most important qualification for all offices under the Solonian
constitution. In an earlier chapter of the *Athenaion Politeia*[2] we
read that the question '$\pi o \hat{\iota} o \nu$ $\tau\acute{\epsilon}\lambda o s$ $\tau \epsilon \lambda \epsilon \hat{\iota}$' was put to everyone
who was intending to draw lots for any office, consequently
before his appointment, whereas the dokimasia came between
his appointment and his entry on office. This suggests that the
dokimasia was the later and more elaborate procedure, and
though certainty is impossible the most probable view is that it
was instituted by Kleisthenes.

The duty of verifying the $\tau\acute{\epsilon}\lambda\eta$ of candidates may have been
entrusted by Solon to the Areopagus, but it is more probable
that he assigned it to the magistrates who presided at the
elections. When $\kappa\lambda\acute{\eta}\rho\omega\sigma\iota s$ $\acute{\epsilon}\kappa$ $\pi\rho o\kappa\rho\acute{\iota}\tau\omega\nu$ was substituted for
$a\acute{\iota}\rho\epsilon\sigma\iota s$ in the appointment of archons, the verification of the
telos must have become part of the prokrisis;[3] by the fourth
century it had been reduced to a meaningless formality.[4] The
dokimasia was probably instituted by Kleisthenes in connexion
with his new Council of Five Hundred, and from the start the
outgoing boulē must have held the dokimasia on its successors.
In their case the old test was superfluous, as no property
qualification was required for membership of the boulē. But
elsewhere it must have been retained as a necessary preliminary
when the newer test of the dokimasia was applied to the
magistracy by Kleisthenes or one of his successors.

It is possible that of the magistrates the archons alone, as the
chief executive of the state, were subjected to the new test by
Kleisthenes, and that their dokimasia was from the first assigned
to the 500. The difference between the archons and the other

[1] 55. 3.
[2] 7. 4 (end).
[3] On the $\pi\rho\acute{o}\kappa\rho\iota\sigma\iota s$ cf. Kahr. ii. 52 ff.
[4] *A.P.* 7. 4.

magistratés in the later procedure may perhaps be taken to show that the dokimasia was not extended to the other magistrates until 461, when it would naturally be entrusted to the popular courts. If these suggestions are correct, the Areopagus had never held any share in the dokimasia of the magistrates; in this respect the revolution of 462 made no difference to its powers. It had the right to subject the archons to a searching examination at the end of their term as a test of their fitness to enter the Areopagus,[1] but this was not a dokimasia in the strict sense and may have been instituted by Solon when he restricted membership of the Areopagus to ex-archons.

In the ancient sources there are several references to the guardianship of the laws exercised by the Areopagus before 462. Plutarch[2] says that it was made φύλαξ τῶν νόμων by Solon, but the author of the *Athenaion Politeia*[3] sees in τὸ νομοφυλακεῖν a function which had belonged to the Areopagus in the aristocratic state and was merely confirmed by Solon. Neither source supplies precise information about the scope or operation of this νομοφυλακία. Grote[4] believed that it empowered the Areopagus to exercise a supervision over the proceedings of the ekklesia and to take care that none of them 'should be such as to infringe the established laws of the country'. Others think that before 462 the Areopagus probably had the right to declare invalid any resolution of the people which contravened existing laws.[5]

These views seem to be based on the assumption that there must have been some constitutional safeguards in Athens before 462, an assumption which is quite arbitrary and finds no real support in the ancient evidence. Although Kleisthenes in 508 and Ephialtes in 462 proposed far-reaching alterations in the existing constitution, nothing is heard of any such safeguards on either occasion. Moreover the guardianship of the laws seems to be connected in one passage of the *Athenaion Politeia*[6] with the supervision exercised by the Areopagus over the magistrates and its right to try any of them who was accused of action contrary to the laws. Hence the νομοφυλακία should not be interpreted as a specific authority to quash illegal decrees; it is merely a comprehensive name for the exercise by the Areopagus

---

[1] Cf. Gilbert, 250, n. 4 and BS 795, n. 3.   [2] *Solon* 19. 2.
[3] 3. 6 and 8. 4.   [4] iv. 104 (abridged ed. 316).
[5] This seems to be the view of de Sanctis, 439, n. 2, and of BS 895. See above, p. 127 and n. 8.
[6] 4. 4 (in 'the Constitution of Drakon'); cf. Bonner and Smith, 262.

of certain judicial functions through which it enforced respect for the laws. These were three in number:[1] the right to hear complaints against the official conduct of magistrates, the right to punish transgressors in general, and the right to try those who were prosecuted on the charge of conspiracy to overthrow the demos. We have seen that these functions were taken from the Areopagus by the revolution of 462 and transferred to other bodies, the boulē, the ekklesia, and the popular courts.

On this interpretation the constitutional safeguards found in existence later must have been a new creation, not a substitute for some power previously vested in the Areopagus. They were presumably invented by reformers who saw the need to provide the radical democracy with some stronger guarantee against an oligarchic reaction, but when was the need realized? In 462, or some years later? Philochoros is credited with the statement that when Ephialtes carried his reforms the nomophylakes were instituted; they are described as a board of seven who compelled the magistrates to observe the laws.[2] But nothing is heard of them in Athenian history after this until a reference to them in a speech delivered by Deinarchos shortly before 322.[3] Most scholars have assumed that the nomophylakes were instituted between 329 and 322, and that the ascription of the reform to 462 was due not to Philochoros but to the lexicographer, who misunderstood some allusion made by Philochoros to the events of 462 in his description of the creation of the nomophylakes.[4]

In connexion with the oligarchic revolution of 411 we hear of two guarantees against constitutional change, the γραφὴ παρανόμων,[5] and the clause in the ὅρκος βουλευτικός by which the members of the boulē pledged themselves not to put to the vote any proposal contrary to the laws.[6] The latter must have been included in the oath of the bouleutai when the president of the ekklesia first began to be chosen from the boulē. This innovation can hardly be later than 462 but it need not be earlier; the presidency of the ekklesia may have belonged to the archons till

---

[1] *A.P.* 3. 6, 4. 4, 8. 4.
[2] Philochoros, fr. 141b = 64b (a) in Jacoby, *F.G.H.* iii B, p. 117.
[3] Cited by Harpokration, s.v. νομοφύλακες. Cf. Philochoros 141a (Jacoby, 64a).
[4] Cf. de Sanctis, 439, n. 3. Ferguson suggested (in *Klio*, xi, 1911, 272–3) that they were instituted by Ephialtes but were mere caretakers until late in the fourth century, when they were raised to a position comparable with that of the ephors at Sparta.   [5] Thuc. viii. 67. 2, *A.P.* 29. 4.
[6] Ibid. 29. 4; see above, p. 167.

487, to the στρατηγοί from 487 to 462. Hence the inclusion of the clause in the oath may be due to Ephialtes. But it was not an effective guarantee against illegal decrees. The responsibility which it imposed on the πρυτάνεις and especially on the ἐπιστάτης was too heavy for them to bear in a constitutional crisis, and their opposition could always be borne down by the tumultuous insistence of the ekklesia, as at the trial of the six generals in 406.[1] Although the oligarchs in 411 were careful to secure the suspension of this particular guarantee, they did so not because they doubted their ability to override it,[2] but because they wanted to regularize their proceedings as far as possible.

By the institution of the γραφὴ παρανόμων all the citizens were made responsible for the defence of the laws and the constitution. There are very few references to its use in the period 462–404, and none of them need be earlier than 415. In the fourth century its frequent employment became an abuse; the orator Aristophon once boasted that he had been prosecuted and acquitted seventy-five times on this charge.[3]

The procedure in the fourth century[4] was that any citizen could object to a motion proposed in the boulē or ekklesia on the ground that it was invalid in form or contrary to an existing law in substance. His objection could be raised before or after the voting and took the form of a sworn statement (ὑπωμοσία) that he intended to bring a γραφὴ παρανόμων against the proposer. Thereby the vote, if not yet taken, was postponed and the proposal, if already carried, was suspended until the question had been decided by a dikastery. If the proposer was condemned his proposal lapsed and he was sentenced to a fine fixed by the court; three condemnations on this charge entailed loss of civic rights. It is probable that if the proposal was not attacked within a year of its adoption the proposer ceased to be personally responsible, though the measure could still be attacked in the courts.

Particular details of this procedure may well be due to later elaboration, but most scholars agree that the γραφὴ παρανόμων goes back in some form to the fifth century. Wilamowitz even traced it as far back as the time of Solon;[5] he assumed that it

---

[1] Xen. *Hell.* i. 7. 14–15.
[2] Thuc. viii. 66. 1–2 shows that they had complete control over the boulē and the ekklesia.   [3] Aischines iii. 194.
[4] Cf. Greenidge, 170–1, BS 1014–15.   [5] *A.A.* ii. 193–4.

was brought before the thesmothetai, who originally decided it
on their own authority but as time went on had to refer the
decision to a popular court. Busolt also referred the institution
to Solon, but maintained[1] that from the first the final decision
in such cases must have been reserved for the Areopagus, of
whose members two-thirds had been thesmothetai. These
speculations seem to be based partly on the references in ancient
writers to the νομοφυλακία of the Areopagus, partly on the
assumption that Solon must have provided some regular
machinery to protect his constitution from alteration. But the
creation by Solon of any such safeguard as the γραφὴ παρανόμων
is excluded by the tradition, recorded in Herodotus,[2] that Solon
imposed on the Athenians an oath to observe his laws for ten
years, and the guardianship of the laws by the Areopagus can be
adequately explained, as we have already seen, by the powers
which are known to have belonged to it.

The nature of the procedure in the γραφὴ παρανόμων, which
entrusted the defence of the constitution to the initiative and
public spirit of the individual citizen, indicates that this type of
prosecution was first instituted by the radical democracy.
Hence it cannot be earlier than the revolution of Ephialtes. But
was it instituted then, or later? Grote, believing that the right
of veto on unconstitutional legislation had previously been
vested in the Areopagus, seems to have seen in the γραφὴ
παρανόμων a new safeguard devised by Perikles to replace that
which Ephialtes had abolished.[3] There is, however, no satisfactory evidence for the possession of any such veto by the
Areopagus before 462, and it is possible that the γραφὴ παρανόμων
was not introduced until a later date, when experience had
shown the dangers of uncontrolled legislation.

Kahrstedt indeed maintains[4] that the γραφὴ παρανόμων was not
introduced until 403/402, the year of Eukleides, since it presupposes a distinction between ψηφίσματα and νόμοι which was
not in fact recognized until the codification of the laws in
Eukleides' archonship. Moreover, the law which was alleged to
have been violated had to be cited by the prosecutor, and this,
Kahrstedt argues, would not have been possible until 403/402,

---

[1] *G.G.* iii. 279, n. 3.   [2] i. 29. 2.
[3] iv. 118 (complicated by Grote's ascription of the nomothetai procedure to
Perikles). Grote's editors are more cautious (abridged ed. 323 and n. 1).
[4] i. 128 and n. 1.

when the code of laws was first fixed and made accessible to all. Prosecutions earlier than 403 described in our sources as γραφαὶ παρανόμων are explained away by Kahrstedt on the hypothesis that until 403 the term was used to describe the type of case which was later known as γραφὴ νόμοις μὴ χρῆσθαι, a prosecution directed against an official for exceeding his powers or for failing to perform his duties.[1]

This hypothesis, which is essential to Kahrstedt's case, cannot be regarded as satisfactory. It is improbable but perhaps not impossible that the term applied originally to one type of prosecution should have been transferred in 403 to another. But surely Andokides, referring in 399[2] to a case of the old type brought in 415, would never have described the indictment as παρανόμων if the term had recently been transferred to a different type of prosecution of which there had been numerous instances in the four years preceding the delivery of his speech.[3] Moreover the attempt to prosecute Kallixenos παρανόμων at the trial of the generals in 406[4] was directed against the proposal which he had made in the boulē, and the charge was therefore of the same type as the later γραφὴ παρανόμων; Kahrstedt's contention, that the real question was the extent of the powers possessed by the prytaneis,[5] is refuted by the plain narrative of Xenophon, who proves that this question was not raised until later in the trial. Hence it is unnecessary to examine the general arguments adduced by Kahrstedt in support of his theory; they are incapable of proof, and any plausibility which they possess is due to the scantiness of our evidence for the use of the γραφὴ παρανόμων before 403.

The first case recorded in our sources which can be dated is the prosecution of Speusippos in 415 by Leogoras, the father of Andokides.[6] It is not certain whether the speech of Antiphon on a παρανόμων charge against the famous general Demosthenes[7] was earlier than this or a little later. The absence of any reference in our sources to earlier cases may be accidental, but suggests that the introduction of the γραφὴ was considerably later than 462. Possibly it was one of the safeguards introduced by Perikles in the period of his unchallenged ascendancy to protect

---

[1] Cf. *A.P.* 45. 2.   [2] And. i. 17 and 22.
[3] Aischines iii. 191; for a well-known example cf. *A.P.* 40. 2.
[4] Xen. *Hell.* i. 7. 12.   [5] *Klio*, xxxi, 1938, 22.
[6] And. i. 17.   [7] *Life of Antiphon*, § 20 ([Plut.] *Moralia* 833 D).

the state against abuse of the legislative sovereignty of the ekklesia either by the demos itself or by its secret enemies.

Our survey of the powers vested in the Areopagus before 462 has shown that although less extensive than those attributed to it by some historians they were important enough to impose an effective limitation on the sovereignty of the people, and the revolution which transferred them to more democratic bodies may fairly be regarded as a turning-point in the history of the Athenian constitution, the political counterpart of the great innovation which had transformed Athens from a land-power to the leading sea-power in Greece.[1] Yet although the revolution of 462 was the decisive stage in the development of the constitution from a moderate to a radical democracy, much remained to be done. In our authorities Ephialtes is credited only with the reform which deprived the Areopagus of its ancient privileges. He may have realized that further measures were necessary to give full effect to the sovereignty of the demos, but the dagger of the assassin removed him from the struggle in the hour of his triumph, and the completion of his work was reserved for others.

[1] Ar. *Politics* 1304^{a}22–24; cf. de Sanctis, 421–2, also Jac. 294, n. 29.

IX. RADICAL DEMOCRACY

Introduction

ARISTOTLE in the *Politics*[1] gives a list of the regulations conducive to the maintenance of a radical democracy. First come numerous precautions against the aggrandizement of the various magistracies. Their holders are to be chosen by the people and from the people; if a property qualification is needed for any office it must be kept as low as possible. Appointment must be made by sortition to all offices, or at least to all those not requiring special experience or technical qualifications. The term prescribed for the tenure of office must be brief, and re-election must be forbidden altogether or restricted to a second term for almost all except military offices.

These rules are followed by others calculated to ensure the supremacy of the people in the assembly and the law-courts. All judicial business, or the greater part of it (including the audits of the magistrates, constitutional questions, and all cases of private contracts), is to be decided by all the citizens or by a body chosen from all. Sovereignty in all questions is to be reserved for the ekklesia; all independent authority must be taken from the magistrates or confined within the narrowest limits. In a radical democracy the only body that can be trusted to share power with the ekklesia is the popular council. There must be provision for state payment of the magistrates, council, law-courts, and if possible the ekklesia as well. No claim to privilege based on superiority of birth, wealth, or culture can be admitted. Finally there must be no ἀρχή whose members hold office for life; if any such has survived previous changes in the constitution, its powers must be curtailed to a minimum, and appointment to it must be made by sortition rather than direct election.

In this description Aristotle has done little more than reproduce the characteristic features of Athenian democracy as he knew it from his own experience. But though the regulations he describes are those of the fourth century, they are in the main (apart from payment for attendance at the ekklesia)[2] the same

---

[1] 1317^{b}17–1318^{a}10 (the version in the text is based on Welldon's translation); cf. 1298^{a}26–28.　　[2] On the μισθὸς ἐκκλησιαστικός see below, Note K.

as those in force at the time of Perikles' death in 429. Many of
them, as we have seen, had had a much longer history. Some of
the limitations imposed on the tenure of magistracies carry us
far back into the past, for they were no less characteristic of
oligarchy than of democracy, and were taken over by Solon and
Kleisthenes from the aristocratic state. Sortition had already
been used since the reforms of Kleisthenes.[1] Yet the differences
between Aristotle's account and the moderate democracy of the
early sixties are as striking as the resemblances. The change in
the method of appointment brought about by the introduction
of κλήρωσις ἐκ προκρίτων was only partial, the property qualification for office was probably the same in 463 as that established
by Solon,[2] and there is no evidence that the authority of the
magistrates had been appreciably modified between the reforms
of Kleisthenes and those of 462.

If we compare the conclusions reached in the preceding chapters with the constitution as it was in 429 we see that the principal
changes introduced between the revolution of Ephialtes and the
death of Perikles were: the development of the popular courts;
the introduction of pay for dikasts and other civilian officials;
the abolition or reduction of property qualifications for magistracies; the use of sortition for most appointments; the strict
limitation of the competence of the magistrates; the acquisition
of full sovereignty by the people and its realization in the three
popular bodies, the ekklesia, the boulē, and the dikasteria.

Of these important innovations, which completed the transformation of the Kleisthenic constitution into a radical democracy, there is no connected account in any ancient writer. Our
knowledge of them is based partly on the combination of scraps
of information taken from various sources, partly on constructive
inference. Owing to the defects of our evidence it is impossible
to date any of these changes with certainty or even to fix their
chronological sequence. In the *Athenaion Politeia* we have dated
notices, probably taken from an Atthis, of three laws carried in
the decade 459–450, but of these laws only one, that which made
Zeugitai eligible for the archonship, is directly relevant to the
history of the constitution. Theopompos seems to have assigned
the introduction of jury-pay by Perikles to the lifetime of
Ephialtes,[3] and it has been suggested[4] that the limitation of the

[1] See above, p. 150.   [2] See above, pp. 101 f.   [3] See below, Appendix IX.
[4] By Wade-Gery in *B.S.A.* xxxvii, 1936-7, 267-8.

judicial powers of the magistrates was included in the legislation proposed and carried by Ephialtes, but it is more probable that both these reforms were subsequent to his death. As the sequence of the innovations adopted in the generation between the death of Ephialtes and that of Perikles is uncertain, they will here be classified for convenience according to their content.

The dikasteria and the introduction of μισθός

At the end of the sixth century there was probably only one popular court, the Heliaia.[1] There were at least five others when Aristophanes wrote the *Wasps*,[2] in addition to the ἡλιαία τῶν θεσμοθετῶν which had nothing in common with the Solonian Heliaia except the name and the place of meeting. The super-session of the old Heliaia by a number of δικαστήρια was doubt-less necessitated by a great increase in the cases brought before the popular courts. Under the new system courts seem to have been manned by panels of jurors drawn from the body of 6,000 dikasts[3] chosen annually from those who volunteered[4] for service. An inscription[5] proves that in the fifth century 600 were chosen from each of the ten tribes, but there is no evidence for the view that the jurors of each tribe were selected from the demes in proportion to their population.[6] The choice of the number 6,000 for the dikasts seems to be connected with the quorum required for a meeting of the δῆμος πληθύων,[7] but only one occasion is known on which the whole 6,000 sat together to try a case.[8] Each of the dikasteries into which the jurors were divided was conveniently deemed to be representative of the whole people, and so their decisions were not subject to appeal or revision.[9]

At what point did the many dikasteria replace the single Heliaia? The ancient authorities who speak of dikasteria in the plural as part of the Solonian constitution must be guilty of an anachronism.[10] Modern scholars usually connect the change with an increase in the business brought before the popular court, but

---

[1] Cf. Bonner and Smith, 195 ff. and 224 ff.
[2] 119–20 and 1108–9; cf. Bonner and Smith, 234 and 156.
[3] For the total 6,000 cf. *Wasps* 662 and *A.P.* 24. 3.
[4] *A.P.* 27. 4; cf. also Bonner and Smith, 232–3.
[5] *I.G.* i². 84, l. 20; cf. de Sanctis, 445 and n. 4.
[6] Wil. i. 201 and Bonner and Smith, 230; there is an unsatisfactory compromise in de Sanctis, 445–6.   [7] Cf. Bonner and Smith, 202 and 211 ff.
[8] Andok. i. 17 (but cf. de Sanctis, 453, n. 2).
[9] Bonner and Smith, 226; cf. BS 1166.
[10] Cf. Bonner and Smith, 151–4.

disagree on the date. One suggestion[1] is that it took place soon after 477 and was necessitated by a growth of litigation consequent on the foundation of the Delian League,[2] but our knowledge of the relations between Athens and the members of the League during the first fifteen years of its history is too fragmentary to justify this hypothesis. It is more probable that the cause of the change was internal, the transference to the popular court of jurisdiction formerly belonging to others, the magistrates or the Areopagus or both. Hence the most likely occasion for the change would be the legislation of Kleisthenes or that of Ephialtes.

The decision between these two possibilities depends on the extent of the judicial powers left to the magistrates by Kleisthenes. Those who believe that it was one of the fixed principles of every Greek democracy to limit the judicial independence of the magistrates naturally suppose that Kleisthenes as the founder of Athenian democracy must have included such limitations in his legislation, and if he did so he must have instituted the dikasteria; Busolt's assumption that he did the one but not the other is surely untenable.[3] There is, however, no evidence that he did either; his moderate democracy was far removed from the radical democracy of Perikles. He did not interfere with the jurisdiction of the Areopagus, and it is unlikely that he made any alteration in the powers of the magistrates as defined by Solon.[4] The most probable conclusion is that the later limitation of their competence in jurisdiction was the work of one of the radical reformers who were associated with Ephialtes.

Ephialtes himself was apparently not the author of this reform, for ancient accounts imply that the judicial powers of the Areopagus alone were attacked by him in 462. His laws against the old life-council were the first item in the radical programme. They effected a transference of jurisdiction from the Areopagus to the Heliaia so extensive that it created a need for new popular courts.[5] When the dikasteria had been instituted, the realization of the programme could be carried a stage farther

---

[1] Made by Bonner and Smith, 221-3.   [2] Cf. BS 1152.

[3] This results from a comparison of BS 883 and 897-8.

[4] See above, p. 146.

[5] Hence there is no need to infer (as is done by Bonner and Smith, 221) from the use of the plural δικαστήρια in *A.P.* 25. 2 that their creation was prior to Ephialtes' reforms.

by a reform authorizing them to decide most of the cases that had formerly been reserved for the decision of the magistrates; this reform was probably carried by one of Ephialtes' collaborators not long after his death.

By this reform the amount of judicial business that came before the dikasteria, already considerable under the legislation of Ephialtes, must have been greatly augmented. The number of cases now tried in the popular courts was still further increased in the generation after Ephialtes' death by the rapid economic development of Athens and the Piraeus[1] and by the steady growth of Athenian interference in the jurisdiction of the allied states. So many courts were necessary that there were not enough magistrates to supply presidents to all, and two new boards had to be created for this purpose, the ναυτοδίκαι and the εἰσαγωγεῖς. The ναυτοδίκαι,[2] as their name indicates, dealt mainly with maritime cases,[3] but there is evidence[4] that they also tried those who were charged with illegal usurpation of Athenian citizenship; possibly the ναυτοδίκαι were called in to try these cases in the spate of litigation which followed the διαψηφισμός of 445/444.[5] All that is known of the εἰσαγωγεῖς in the fifth century is that they presided over the court which reviewed the assessments of tribute imposed on the allied states; in the fourth century they dealt with many (but not all) types of ἔμμηνοι δίκαι, cases which had to be settled within a month.[6]

To these innovations may be added the law of 453/452[7] which created the thirty δικασταὶ κατὰ δήμους. Peisistratos had created deme-judges for the country districts of Attica, probably to replace the local jurisdiction of the great nobles by the courts of his own nominees,[8] but the institution had apparently been allowed to lapse on the fall of the tyranny. Now it was revived, and the new deme-judges at first went on circuit like the old, though at a later date they ceased to do so and held their courts

---

[1] On this development cf. Beloch, ii[2]. 1. 77 ff.

[2] First mentioned in *I.G.* i[2]. 41 (soon after 446).

[3] So the lexicographers; cf. Lysias, xvii. 5 (dated 397) and BS 1114–15.

[4] Harpokration, s.v. ναυτοδίκαι; cf. Aristophanes, fr. 225, and Krateros (Jacoby, *F.G.H.* iii B, no. 342), fr. 4.

[5] Körte suggested (in *Hermes*, lxviii, 1933, 238 ff.) that they took over this function soon after 440 from the ξενοδίκαι (on whom cf. *I.G.* i[2]. 342–3, ll. 38 and 89).

[6] *I.G.* i[2]. 63 (Tod, 66), 7 ff. and *A.P.* 52. 2; cf. BS 1113 and n. 4.

[7] *A.P.* 26. 3 (archonship of Lysikrates).

[8] See above, p. 115 and cf. Bonner and Smith, 184.

in Athens.[1] They were competent to decide on their own authority any case involving a sum of less than 10 drachmas; the rest were referred by them to the public arbitrators, the διαιτηταί, and only those in which the decision of the arbitrators were not accepted by both parties to the suit were brought to a dikastery.[2] The motive for this revival of the deme-judges is not stated in the *Athenaion Politeia*. It may have been an attempt to decentralize jurisdiction in order to relieve in some measure the pressure of business on the dikasteria and the magistrates,[3] or it may have been a concession to the rural population, so that they could get their disputes settled on the spot and need no longer make the journey to Athens.

Aristophanes[4] calculated that on the average the dikasts were actively employed in the courts for 300 days of each year. The estimate may be slightly exaggerated, but citizens who volunteered to serve as jurymen must have been prepared to neglect their normal occupations for the greater part of the year. As poor men could not afford to do so without compensation, and as the radical leaders, who found their main support in the proletariat, could not allow the new courts to become the private preserve of the middle and upper classes, the next step was bound to be the introduction of state-payment for service on juries. This reform may have been carried at the same time as the institution of the dikasteria, but since its authorship is always ascribed to Perikles[5] and the name of Ephialtes is nowhere mentioned in connexion with it, the more likely view is that it was introduced by Perikles soon after Ephialtes' death.[6]

Soldiers and sailors had received pay in Kimon's time, but this was only an allowance for maintenance.[7] Such an allowance may have been paid before 462 to the members of the boulē of Five Hundred or at least to the representatives of each tribe in turn during their πρυτανεία, but perhaps the πρυτάνεις were merely fed and lodged at the expense of the state.[8] When once the principle of payment for state service had been established, it was given a wider application. The amount paid to soldiers

---

[1] Cf. *A.P.* 53. 1 and Sandys' note. [2] *A.P.* 53. 1–3.
[3] So de Sanctis, 136 and 444; cf. Bonner and Smith, 229.
[4] *Wasps* 661 ff.
[5] Ar. *Politics* 1274ᵃ8–9, *A.P.* 27. 4, Plut. *Per.* 9. 2–3; cf. Plato, *Gorgias* 515 E.
[6] See Appendix IX. The rate of pay was 2 obols a day; cf. BS 898, n. 4.
[7] Plut. *Kimon* 9. 6.
[8] Wil. ii. 95 and n. 33.

and sailors in the Peloponnesian War seems to have fluctuated,[1] but was always more than a maintenance allowance. Under the radical democracy all members of the boulē of Five Hundred met every day (except holidays and days of ill omen)[2] and therefore had to be paid: the existence of the βουλευτικὸς μισθός in 411 is attested by Thucydides.[3] There is no evidence for its amount in the fifth century; perhaps, as in the fourth century, the πρυτάνεις alone got a drachma, the rest 5 obols a day.[4] Some time before 411 pay had been introduced for the nine archons,[5] possibly by Perikles, but it may have done no more than cover their expenses; the amount received by each in the fourth century was only 4 obols a day, and out of this he had to maintain a κῆρυξ and an αὐλητής. Probably payment had been extended before Perikles' death to all officials appointed by lot. Members of the Areopagus were apparently not paid.[6] It is disputed whether the military officials were entitled to payment or not; probably they were not, as they differed in many respects from the ordinary magistrates. Aristophanes,[7] however, describes the general Lamachos as μισθαρχίδης, and it has been suggested[8] that generals and hipparchs were entitled to pay, but as most of them were wealthy men they seldom troubled to draw it.

Payment of officials by the state, as Aristotle notes,[9] is one of the essential features of a radical democracy, and its adoption by Athens after 462 enabled the lower classes to play a greater part in political life than had been possible for them in practice under the democracy of Kleisthenes. Hence the disfavour with which it was regarded by the conservatives; the gist of Plato's criticism[10] is that it encouraged the rabble to meddle with matters which ought to have been reserved for their betters. To what extent it altered the composition of the boulē we cannot judge; our evidence for the fourth century indicates that the upper and middle classes then formed a large proportion of its members,[11] but the position may have been different in the second half of the fifth century.[12] Whatever may have been the percentage of

[1] Cf. Tod in *C.A.H.* v. 23–4, also G. F. Hill, *Sources* (1907), 215 f. (edition of 1951, p. 350).   [2] *A.P.* 43. 3; cf. BS 517, n. 2 and 1025, n. 1.
[3] viii. 69. 4.   [4] *A.P.* 62. 2; cf. Xen. *Hell.* ii. 3. 48 and BS 899, n. 3.
[5] *A.P.* 29. 5; cf. 62. 2.   [6] Cf. Kahr. ii. 182 and n. 6.   [7] *Acharnians* 597.
[8] By Kahr. ii. 182–3.   [9] *Politics* 1317^b35 ff.   [10] *Gorgias* 515 E.
[11] Cf. T. Sundwall cited by Macgregor in Headlam[2], 200.
[12] As suggested by Theramenes' criticism in Xen. *Hell.* ii. 3. 48.

poorer citizens in the boulē during this period, it is certain that
they held the majority in the dikasteria,[1] and as the control
exercised by the people in the law-courts extended to all departments of political life, the introduction of payment for the
dikasts completed the revolution which the creation of the
dikasteria had begun and crowned the transfer of power from
the middle classes to the proletariat; the supremacy of the
demos in the courts guaranteed its predominance in the state.[2]

The magistracies: rotation and sortition

The triumph of radical democracy at Athens, as elsewhere in
Greece, entailed a curtailment of the powers and a decline in the
prestige of the magistrates.[3] A drastic limitation of their competence in jurisdiction was facilitated by the institution of the
dikasteries, but the precise extent of this limitation is uncertain.
We have seen[4] that Solon had probably defined the amount of
the penalties which each magistrate could impose on his own
authority. An archaic law preserved in a speech of the fourth
century[5] ordains that the chief archon shall be competent in
certain cases which belong to his jurisdiction to impose a fine
within the limit ($\kappa\alpha\tau\grave{\alpha}$ $\tau\grave{o}$ $\tau\acute{\epsilon}\lambda o\varsigma$); if the offence seems to deserve
a higher penalty he is to fix the amount and bring the case
before the Heliaia. Under the radical democracy we find a
similar distinction between the fine which a magistrate is competent to inflict and the higher penalty which he has to refer to
the courts for confirmation; in the second type of case the
magistrate is himself a party to the suit when it comes before
a dikastery.[6] A good example of this distinction appears in a law
on the powers of the $\pi\rho\acute{o}\epsilon\delta\rho o\iota$,[7] who replaced the $\dot{\epsilon}\pi\iota\sigma\tau\acute{\alpha}\tau\eta\varsigma$ $\tau\hat{\omega}\nu$
$\pi\rho\upsilon\tau\alpha\nu\acute{\epsilon}\omega\nu$ as presidents of the boulē and ekklesia in the fourth
century. For any disorderly behaviour by a speaker in either
assembly they can impose fines up to 50 drachmas for each
offence; in these cases they simply notify the Praktores, who
collect the amount. If they wish to impose a higher fine they
bring the case before the boulē or ekklesia.

There is, however, an important difference to be noted between
the grounds of action under the two laws. The penalties imposed
by the $\pi\rho\acute{o}\epsilon\delta\rho o\iota$ are of the type called by German writers

---

[1] Cf. *A.P.* 27. 4 ($o\dot{\iota}$ $\tau\upsilon\chi\acute{o}\nu\tau\epsilon\varsigma$).   [2] *A.P.* 9. 1.   [3] Cf. Kahr. ii. 196–9.
[4] Above, p. 97.   [5] [Dem.] xliii. 75.
[6] Cf., for example, *A.P.* 52. 4 on the Apodektai.   [7] Cf. Aischines i. 35.

Ordnungsstrafen, penalties imposed by magistrates on those 'who interfere with their administration or judicial functions by disobedience or opposition',[1] whereas the other law empowers the chief archon to take action against all who transgress its provisions. So the power of the boulē in the fourth century to impose fines up to 500 drachmas was directed against those who were guilty of offences against the laws, not merely those who impeded the boulē in the exercise of its functions.[2]

Aischines says[3] that Demosthenes as τειχοποιός imposed fines like other magistrates. It is certain that in the fourth century a magistrate could by means of this power set on foot a prosecution in a dikastery and might even preside over the court which tried the case.[4] But what happened if he imposed a fine below the limit? Our evidence on this point is scanty and its interpretation disputed. The extreme view is that in the fourth century no magistrate was competent to settle any case within his own jurisdiction except the Apodektai and the Forty, and they only in cases involving a sum of 10 drachmas or less.[5] Fines could not be imposed by magistrates at all except as *Ordnungsstrafen*, and against these, even when they were below the legal limit, the person fined had the right of appeal to a dikastery.[6] Lipsius and Busolt inferred from the language of the *Athenaion Politeia* that fines imposed by the boulē within the maximum of 500 drachmas were subject to appeal in the fourth century.[7]

It is dangerous in this matter to infer the practice of the fifth century from that of the fourth, for the tendency in the fourth century was to limit as far as possible the judicial powers of the magistrates. This is proved by the decline in the competence of the στρατηγοί; late in the fifth century they still possessed the right to inflict the death penalty in the field,[8] but by the Demosthenic period they had lost it,[9] and even their power of imposing fines was rarely exercised. An inscription of the late fifth century[10] shows that the ἱεροποιοί were competent to impose *Ordnungsstrafen* up to 50 drachmas, and in the same period the boulē

---

[1] Quoted from Bonner and Smith, 279.
[2] *A.P.* 45. 1, supplemented by [Dem.] xlvii. 43.　　　　[3] iii. 27.
[4] So in [Dem.] xliii. 75; cf. Kahr. ii. 233 and 226–7.
[5] Cf. Bonner and Smith, 283.
[6] BS 1054; cf. Bonner and Smith, ii. 245–6.
[7] BS 1046 and n. 2.
[8] Xen. *Hell.* i. 1. 15 and Lys. xiii. 67.
[9] *A.P.* 61. 2; cf. Kahr. ii. 245 ff.　　　　[10] *I.G.* i². 84, ll. 26 ff.

could impose fines up to 500 drachmas[1] which were apparently not subject to appeal. Aristophanes' statement[2] that cases involving a penalty of 1 drachma were tried by the dikasteria must surely be an example of comic exaggeration, and it is possible that in the fifth century at least the magistrates could still give a final verdict in trivial cases.

Whether this was so or not, the judicial independence of the magistrates was narrowly limited by the radical democracy. All important cases were reserved for the ekklesia or the dikasteria, and the duties retained by the magistrates were almost purely formal. A magistrate had to receive suits which fell within his jurisdiction. He conducted the preliminary hearing,[3] but his main function in this was simply to establish whether the case was admissible or not, and he could not refuse a suit unless the legal requirements were not fully satisfied.[4] At the trial he presided over the court, but he did not expound the laws or direct the jury; questions of law as well as fact had to be decided by the dikasts, who had nothing to guide them but their own superficial knowledge of the law and the grounds put forward in the speeches delivered by the parties to the suit.[5]

In the sphere of administration also the competence of the magistrates was curtailed by the radical democracy. The supervision exercised by the boulē over their activities became closer and more effective when it met daily, and when the ekklesia began to reserve to itself the final decision in all questions of administration which were of more than routine importance. Moreover the radical leaders fully realized the truth of the political maxim that limitation of the magistracy in respect of its functions is favourable to democracy, and accordingly created numerous boards of officials to superintend the different departments of the administration.[6] This reform not only circumscribed the activities of the older magistracies; it also increased the efficiency of the administrative machinery in general. The new boards were so numerous that the duties assigned to each could be restricted in range and carefully defined, with the result that any negligence or irregularity was more easily detected. Each

[1] I.G. i². 76 (Tod, 74), ll. 57–59 and 114, l. 32.   [2] Wasps 764–70.
[3] ἀνάκρισις; cf. Bonner and Smith, 283 ff. and Wade-Gery in B.S.A. xxxvii, 1936–7, pp. 266–7. On the problems raised by I.G. i². 16 (Tod, 32) see below, Note L.   [4] Cf. Bonner and Smith, 289 ff. and Headlam, 147, n. 1.
[5] De Sanctis, 449–52.
[6] On what follows cf. the admirable account in Headlam, c. 6.

board was composed of several members, usually ten, and as the members of most boards were chosen by lot for one year only and were not re-eligible they had little temptation to favour at the expense of the state the private interests of those whom they had to supervise. Any official who exceeded or abused his powers was liable to immediate deposition and prosecution,[1] and we have seen[2] that at the end of their term all had to submit to a close scrutiny of their whole conduct in office; this strict enforcement of their responsibility before the popular courts provided the most effective guarantee of their good behaviour.

Any citizen over thirty years of age was legally qualified for membership of the dikasteria[3] and the boulē.[4] The same qualification may by analogy be assumed for all the magistracies, including the strategia;[5] for some of them a property qualification was required as well. According to an oligarchic pamphlet of the late fifth century included among the works of Xenophon,[6] it was thought right that all citizens should be eligible for the magistracies whether their holders were appointed by direct election or by lot, but in practice, as the author admits, the proletariat had the sense to realize that they did not possess the special talents required in the chief military posts, and limited their ambition to the tenure of those offices which brought pay or personal profit. This implies that certain offices were reserved to the upper classes *de facto* rather than *de iure*. We know, however, that the treasurers of Athena continued to be chosen from the richest class, the Pentakosiomedimnoi,[7] and the same rule probably applied to the Hellenotamiai also. Democratic principles were here overruled by expediency; the chief financial offices were left in the hands of the rich because their wealth provided the state with the necessary guarantees against peculation.[8] A passage in Deinarchos declares that the strategoi had to possess landed property in Attica;[9] this is not improbable, as their office was now the most important in the state.[10]

---

[1] BS 1006.   [2] Above, pp. 203 ff.   [3] *A.P.* 63. 3, Dem. xxiv. 150.

[4] The passages cited by BS 1022, n. 3 refer to Athens when ruled by an oligarchy (so de Sanctis, 348, n. 4) but the evidence of Xen. *Mem.* i. 2. 35 is supported by *I.G.* i². 10. 9 f. (the constitution of Erythrai, presumably on the Athenian model, now dated 453/452 [= Tod, 29]).

[5] Kahr. ii. 18.   [6] *X.A.P.* i. 2–3.

[7] *A.P.* 47. 1.

[8] Headlam, 93; cf. Beloch, ii². 1. 124 and the law in Aischines iii. 21.

[9] i. 71; cf. *A.P.* 4. 2 and Ar. *Politics* 1282ª25–32.

[10] The testimony of Deinarchos is rejected by Kahr. ii. 23 and n. 3, also by

The decline in the powers of the archonship is reflected in the lowering of the property qualification. Solon had limited the right of candidature to the Pentakosiomedimnoi and Hippeis,[1] but it was extended to the Zeugitai soon after 460, perhaps in 458/457.[2] Passages in the orators[3] have been cited to prove that subsequently Thetes must have been made eligible for the archonship, but the author of the *Athenaion Politeia* remarks[4] that in his time each candidate was asked at the prokrisis ποῖον τέλος τελεῖ and that no one would answer θητικόν. The wording of the question suggests that the property qualification was retained in form, the evasion in the answer that it was by then no more than a legal fiction. But although the archonship had lost its old importance it retained some of its old dignity, and Athenian conservatism excluded from it (and from all the state priesthoods) those citizens who had acquired their citizenship not by birth but by vote of the people.[5]

If Solon's conditions for membership of the τέλη had remained unchanged they would have become increasingly stiffer in terms of money during the fifth century, which witnessed a great rise in the prices of agricultural produce and livestock.[6] A law quoted in one of the private speeches of Demosthenes[7] ordains that in certain circumstances an orphan girl is to be provided by her nearest of kin with a dowry, 500 drachmas if he is a Pentakosiomedimnos, 300 if a Hippeus, 150 if a Zeugites. It has been supposed[8] that these sums are roughly equivalent to the value of a year's income in each case, and that they postulate a transformation of the Solonian τέλη by a new calculation in terms of money income on the basis of an equation of one measure of corn or oil with 1 drachma. This change has been connected by Beloch[9] with the development from the old natural economy

Colin (Daremberg–Saglio, iv. 2. 1524 A and n. 3); it is accepted by de Sanctis, 387, n. 2 and Kalinka (commentary on *X.A.P.*, p. 103).

[1] See above, pp. 101 f.

[2] *A.P.* 26. 2 dates the reform 457/456 but inconsistently adds that the archon for 457/456 was the first Zeugite archon.

[3] Lys. xxiv. 13 is the most relevant; Isokrates, xx. 20 proves no more than *X.A.P.* 1. 2. [Dem.] lix. 72 is indecisive, as in the fourth century a Zeugite might be a poor man.   [4] 7. 4 (end); on the πρόκρισις see above, pp. 173 f.

[5] [Dem.] lix. 92 and 106; cf. *A.P.* 55. 3 and BS 947, n. 4. Cripples also were excluded (Lys. xxiv. 13).   [6] Beloch, ii². 1. 94; cf. Tod in *C.A.H.* v. 25–26.

[7] [Dem.] xliii. 54.   [8] BS 822, n. 1.

[9] *G.G.* ii². 1. 89 and n. 2. Beloch, however, held that membership of the classes was defined not by income but by the ownership of capital, and that the highest class was composed of those who had a capital of not less than 1 talent.

to the new system based on coinage, and is ascribed by him to the period of the Persian Wars, by Busolt[1] to Kleisthenes. It is, however, possible that the older classification, which restricted office to holders of land in Attica, was successfully maintained by the conservatives till 462.

Kahrstedt denies that the incomes required for the τέλη were ever calculated in drachmas. He maintains[2] that the τέλη became obsolete when the state developed out of primitive conditions, and that their retention in the prokrisis of some magistrates[3] was an empty form. This hypothesis is refuted by the facts, which show that Athenian citizens in the second half of the fifth century were still grouped in the property classes to which they belonged.[4] Moreover, the author of the *Athenaion Politeia* says that in his day the treasurers of Athena continued to be chosen from the Pentakosiomedimnoi under the provisions of Solon's law, although those appointed to the office might be quite poor. The natural inference from this is not that Solon's law was practically obsolete,[5] but that by 330 membership of the highest class was no guarantee of wealth. This is quite feasible if the condition of membership had been changed in the fifth century to possession of an income of 500 drachmas. In a speech almost contemporary with the *Athenaion Politeia* it is asserted[6] that it is not easy to live on a property of 45 minas (the annual income from which at the normal rate of 12 per cent. would have been 540 drachmas).

The purpose of the original reform may have been to destroy the monopoly of office previously enjoyed by owners of land and to open the older magistracies to the growing class of citizens whose income was not derived from land. But if ownership of land continued to be a necessary qualification for the strategia, the scope of the reform cannot have been very great, as most offices, including the new administrative boards, were now open to all citizens, and its ultimate result, owing to the rapid decline in the purchasing power of the drachma, was to deprive the Solonian classification of all importance.

There was also during the Periklean period an alteration in the method of appointment to office. Kleisthenes and his suc-

---

[1] BS 880.   [2] i. 251–2.   [3] *A.P.* 7. 4 and 47. 1.
[4] *I.G.* i². 45 (Tod, 44), ll. 39–41; cf. Thuc. iii. 16. 1 and *I.G.* ii². 30*a*. 12.
[5] So Sandys on *A.P.* 47. 1; but 7. 4 is not a valid parallel.
[6] [Dem.] xlii. 22.

cessors had instituted κλήρωσις ἐκ προκρίτων for the selection of
the boulē and the archons,[1] perhaps for most other officials as
well. In 458/457 the archons were still chosen in this way,[2] but at
a later date the only two methods of appointment in use were
direct election and pure sortition.[3] Direct election by the people
was retained in the choice of officials who had to possess technical
qualifications, such as the generals and other important officers,
architects, envoys, and members of special boards for the super-
intendance of public works.[4] All officials not elected by the
people were chosen by lot, either in the tribes or in the demes,
from those whose names had been submitted. Candidature may
have been voluntary in most instances,[5] but compulsion was
perhaps necessary to fill the chief financial posts. The usual
method of selection by lot was a single sortition; thus for the
boulē each deme selected by lot as many candidates as its quota
on the boulē and an equal number of reserves to fill any vacancies
which might occur during the year.[6] In the appointment of the
archons there was a double κλήρωσις,[7] the first stage of which
represented the earlier πρόκρισις. Ten candidates were chosen
from each tribe as before, but by sortition instead of election,
and from these the nine archons and the secretary of the
thesmothetai were chosen by a second sortition.

At Athens the tenure of all offices which were filled by sortition
was governed by the principle of rotation, an institution taken
over by the democracy from the aristocratic state. It was indeed
common in oligarchies[8] as well as democracies;[9] in both it distributed the offices more evenly among those qualified to hold
them, and in both it expressed the jealousy felt towards the
executive officials by the real sovereign, which in a democracy
was the popular assembly and in an oligarchy the council or
senate. The bogus constitution of Drakon, which embodies the
aims of Athenian oligarchs towards the end of the fifth century,
expresses the principle of rotation in its purest form; no one
is to hold office for a second term until all who possess the

---

[1] See above, pp. 150 and 173.   [2] A.P. 26. 2; cf. BS 898.
[3] Evidence in BS 898, n. 6. Kalinka, 99, infers from X.A.P. 1. 2 that the
abolition of prokrisis was recent when the author wrote, but the inference depends
on the reading τῷ νῦν κλήρῳ, which is doubtful.   [4] Headlam, 102 ff.
[5] Cf. Macgregor in Headlam², 196–7, also BS 1022 and n. 6.
[6] A.P. 62. 1; cf. Aischines iii. 62 and BS 1022, n. 7.
[7] A.P. 8. 1 and 55. 1.
[8] e.g. Sparta (notably in the ναυαρχία) and Rome; cf. Ar. Politics 1308ª3 ff.
[9] Politics 1317ᵇ23–24.

necessary qualifications have served once.[1] It is obvious that if the supply of persons eligible to a particular office exceeded the demand, the desired rotation could be achieved more simply by an absolute veto on reappointment. At Athens the law that no one could hold the same office twice[2] applied to all regular magistracies except the military commands. Reappointment to the boulē was permitted for a second term but not for a third.[3] The reason for this relaxation of the normal rule must have been a shortage not of qualified candidates (since all citizens were eligible) but of those who were willing to serve. Probably many of the poor were reluctant to undertake the duties of a bouleutēs, and it was not thought desirable to compel them to take their turn.

The purpose and the effect of selection by lot cannot be stated in general terms; they are always conditioned by the particular circumstances of its application.[4] Fustel de Coulanges maintained that the use of the lot for the appointment of magistrates was religious in origin.[5] Sortition was always one of the recognized methods by which the will of heaven could be discovered by men. Throughout the classical period priests and temple officials were still appointed by lot so that the final choice might be left to the gods. In the aristocratic state the magistrates had possessed religious as well as secular functions, and the former had been at least as important as the latter. Hence the magistrates must always have been appointed by lot.

This hypothesis is untenable. The history of sortition in Athens is not free from difficulties, but the evidence that the archons were chosen by lot in pre-Solonian times[6] is late and untrustworthy. Many scholars believe on the authority of the *Athenaion Politeia* that the use of sortition for political appointments was introduced by Solon, but it is more probable that no officials (with the possible exception of the treasurers of Athena) were selected by lot until after the expulsion of the tyrants.[7] Even if the premises of the hypothesis were sound, it would not follow that the democratic statesmen who developed the institu-

[1] *A.P.* 4. 3; cf. *Politics* 1298ª15 ff. [2] Dem. xxiv. 150; *A.P.* 62. 3.
[3] Ibid. Sandys' note here is misleading; the two terms could almost certainly not be held consecutively (BS 1022 and n. 5). Kahr. ii. 135–6 argues that the original rule merely forbade, as at Erythrai (*I.G.* i². 10, l. 11), the holding of more than one term in four years.
[4] Cf. Headlam, 80–81. [5] *La Cité antique*, 212–13.
[6] Op. cit. 213, n. 1 (Plut. *Per.* 9. 4 says that the archonships in Perikles' time had been κληρωταὶ ἐκ παλαιοῦ; cf. Pausanias iv. 5. 10).
[7] See below, Appendix IV.

tion were influenced by the same religious motives as its originators; the language of the orators proves that in the classical period the political use of sortition had no religious associations for the Athenians.[1] De Coulanges asserted that, whereas the magistrates with priestly duties continued to be chosen by lot under the democracy, those who had merely secular functions were all elected by the people;[2] this is manifestly untrue and shows the shifts to which he was reduced by an untenable theory.

Isokrates argues in one passage[3] that whereas a demos which elected its officials by open voting would invariably choose professed democrats, the use of sortition often resulted in the selection of men favourable to oligarchy. Hence some have supposed[4] that the object of the institution was to prevent the tyranny of the majority by making provision for the proper representation of minorities. It is true that the lot was used by some Greek oligarchies,[5] but the part which it played in them was politically less important than its role in the Periklean democracy and in the constitutions of other Greek states which took that democracy as their exemplar. When Herodotus contrasts the three main types of government it is of democracy, not oligarchy, that he says[6] πάλῳ τὰς ἀρχὰς ἄρχει, and Aristotle writing a century later includes the use of the lot in his picture of a radical democracy.[7] The contention of Isokrates is a shallow paradox which has no relation to the realities of Athenian political life.[8] However radical the demos might be, it was still susceptible to the influence of birth and wealth, and the offices to which their possessors were appointed were precisely those which were still filled by direct election.

In an oligarchy sortition may be used to decide the order of promotion within the small circle of those who are admitted to office. Aristotle says[9] that the lot was introduced at Heraia (which was probably governed by an oligarchy) to put an end to the dissensions produced by the rivalries of competitors for

---

[1] Cf. Headlam, 10–11.
[2] Op. cit. 389 and conclusion of n. 1 on pp. 213–14.
[3] vii. 23; cf. Headlam, 13, n. 1 and 39–40.
[4] Cf. Glotz, *La Cité grecque*, 249 (E.T. 213).
[5] The evidence is given by Macgregor in Headlam[2], 201–2.
[6] iii. 80. 6.   [7] *Politics* 1294[b]7 f., 1317[b]20 f.
[8] Cf. Kalinka in his edition of *X.A.P.*, 99, n. 1.
[9] *Politics* 1303[a]15 f.; cf. Headlam, 38 and n. 1.

office. It is unlikely that this was the motive for its introduction at Athens, for the chief magistracy there was always elective (the archonship before, the strategia after 487/486). Moreover, the offices appointed by lot in Athens were open to all the citizens, in practice if not in strict law, by the middle of the fifth century. As most of these appointments were subject to the principle of rotation it has been supposed[1] that one of the motives for the use of the lot at Athens was to make the rotation of offices work more smoothly.

There is some truth in this view, but it overestimates the difficulty of combining rotation with election. In oligarchies, as for example Sparta and Rome, the combination was easier because the offices to be filled were few. At Athens, however, it was not because the number of officials was large but because their functions were so unimportant that they had to be appointed by lot.[2] All officials appointed in this way had merely routine duties which were supposed to be well within the capacity of the ordinary Athenian. It would have been absurd to select them on grounds of character or talent. The decision was so unimportant that it might be left to the lot.

Was this the cause or the effect of the introduction of sortition? Historically the institution first appears as a political device at Athens in the democracy of Kleisthenes, and then in the form of κλήρωσις ἐκ προκρίτων. This method of appointment is a hybrid;[3] it indicates that its authors, though anxious to introduce sortition, were not prepared to press it to its logical conclusion, and maintained preliminary election as the guarantee of a certain minimum of ability in those finally chosen by the lot. Hence it follows that in the Kleisthenic democracy the functions of the officials were still fairly important. The radicals by increasing the number of officials were able to limit the competence of each of the executive boards; they could then safely take the final step and do away with the safeguard contained in the prokrisis.

This leaves us with the question: Why did the statesmen of the Kleisthenic period think it necessary to introduce the lot in the appointment of the magistracies and the boulē? The answer must be that they wished to prevent them becoming too powerful. As sortition carried with it no religious sanction in political

---

[1] By Headlam, 92-93.   [2] Headlam admits this (p. 93).
[3] Cf. Ledl, 371 and 376-7.

appointments, an official selected by the chance of the lot could not enjoy the same prestige as one chosen by the will of the people. This is proved by the history of the archonship. After κλήρωσις ἐκ προκρίτων had been substituted for αἵρεσις as the method of appointment, the archonship at once declined in importance and ceased to attract the ablest men in the state.[1] Sortition, like rotation, was a device to protect the sovereign demos against the acquisition by its potential rivals, the boulē and the magistrates, of an authority and influence which might threaten its own sovereignty.[2]

The two safeguards were complementary. Although the use of the lot sometimes had as its result the appointment of prominent politicians,[3] it ensured that the average level of ability among the bouleutai and in the various boards of officials should not be much above that to be found in the ekklesia, while rotation guarded against the danger that by long continuance in the same functions they might acquire the authority of permanent officials. If the boulē and the magistracies had been filled by the ablest men in the community, the government would have been oligarchic in fact if not in form.[4] Hence the importance attached by the Athenians to the maintenance of sortition. One of the gravest charges against Sokrates was that he had criticized the use of the lot and had argued that government should be the business of a class of experts.[5]

Both rotation and sortition presuppose that the persons legally eligible for a particular office all possess approximately the same capacity to perform the duties belonging to it, and that no special ability is required beyond the average level of capacity within the circle of qualified persons. These presuppositions may pass unchallenged in an oligarchy, where the offices are confined to a small and homogeneous body, but in a democracy like that of Athens, which admitted all citizens to the boulē and to most of the magistracies, they seem at first sight indefensible. Where the range of selection is so wide, the gap between the average capacity and that of the individual, and with it the margin of error in the working of the lot, must be far greater and far more disastrous.

---

[1] See above, pp. 175 and 188.   [2] Cf. Headlam, 28–32 and *passim*.
[3] e.g. Kleon in 427/426 (see below, p. 262, n. 3) and Demosthenes in 347/346 (Aischines iii. 62); cf. Headlam, 54–55.
[4] Cf. Headlam, 48.   [5] Xen. *Mem.* i. 2. 9.

For this reason some have supposed[1] that the most unsuitable of those who had been chosen by the lot were weeded out at the δοκιμασία, which thus protected the state against the worst consequences of the institution. There is, however, no evidence that the δοκιμασία was used in this way. Its purpose was not to test the candidate's capacity but to make sure that he possessed the legal qualifications for the office to which he had been appointed.[2] When an appointment was challenged, advocates sometimes argued that the candidate's past life should be examined or that he was a notorious oligarch unworthy of the people's confidence,[3] but these arguments, employed to bias the minds of the jury, were irrelevant, like so many of the arguments addressed to Athenian courts.

Sokrates' criticism of the Athenian use of sortition was superficial. Nearly all the officials chosen by lot were members of administrative boards; in each of these boards decisions were usually taken by the whole board, and little scope was left for individual initiative or error. Although the total amount of work performed by these boards was considerable, they were so numerous that the functions assigned to each were fairly simple and such as could be performed by the ordinary citizen.[4] The Athenians had unusual opportunities for acquiring a practical knowledge of public business, and the problems with which they had to deal were far less complex and technical than those which arise in a modern state. Moreover they did recognize that the holders of offices on which the safety of Athens depended must not be chosen by lot or from the mass of the people. For these offices, notably the strategia, they accepted the principle of government by a ruling class with expert knowledge, ἐὰν τοὺς δυνατωτάτους ἄρχειν.[5] For the rest they preferred a method of appointment which at the cost of a slight sacrifice in efficiency guaranteed them against the danger of an over-powerful bureaucracy.

The ekklesia and the boulē

The ekklesia was open to every man in possession of full citizen rights who had completed his eighteenth year.[6] It sat

[1] e.g. BS 1072.   [2] Cf. Headlam, 97 ff.
[3] Headlam cites Lys. xvi. 9 and xxvi. 9.
[4] Headlam, c. 6, especially p. 161.   [5] X.A.P. i. 3.
[6] This was the age when he was enrolled on the register of his deme (A.P. 42. 1). Glaukon tried to harangue the ekklesia before he was 20 (Xen. Mem.

more frequently now than in the time of Kleisthenes, for in addition to special meetings it had four regular meetings in every prytany.[1] The checks previously imposed on its sovereignty by the powers of the executive officials and the Areopagus were removed by the reforms of Ephialtes and his collaborators. The laws which established the radical democracy were the only authority to which it was subject, for there was no constitutional method by which they could be repealed or altered.[2] Within these limits the demos was now supreme and irresponsible, like an absolute monarch.[3] As a fourth-century orator said,[4] the people had the right to do what it pleased, and all parts of the state were subject to its control.

For Aristotle it was characteristic of democracy that all things should be decided by the popular assembly, and among its prerogatives he mentions[5] that it declares war and concludes peace, makes and dissolves alliances, passes laws, inflicts sentences of death, exile, and confiscation, elects magistrates and audits their accounts. Radical democracy at Athens did not exactly conform to this pattern, for though the ekklesia still chose the most important magistrates by direct election, it had in the interests of true equality waived its right to apply the same method of choice in the selection of the minor magistrates,[6] and the audits of all magistrates had been entrusted to the dikasteria,[7] together with final jurisdiction in all cases of any importance, including all that involved the penalties of death, exile, or disfranchisement. Actually this limitation on the sovereignty of the demos was only apparent; payment for jury service ensured that the dikasts were genuinely representative of the people[8] and that to them final authority could safely be delegated in judicial questions. The only serious exceptions to the jurisdiction of the dikasteria were the homicide trials, which were still left to the Areopagus, and cases tried by the ekklesia itself.

Important political cases came under the category of εἰσαγγελίαι.[9] Such cases, in which the activity of the boulē was merely preparatory to that of the ekklesia, were sometimes referred to

iii. 6. 1). After 336/335 the ἐφηβία monopolized the time of the young Athenian from 18 to 20 (A.P. 42. 2–5; cf. BS 966, n. 2).

[1] A.P. 43. 4 and 6. [2] Glotz, C.G. 211–12 (E.T. 180); cf. BS 457.
[3] Ar. Politics 1313ᵇ38; cf. Headlam, 29–31. [4] [Dem.] lix. 88.
[5] Politics 1298ᵃ3 ff. [6] BS 1006. [7] See above, pp. 203 ff.
[8] Bonner and Smith, 248; cf. Headlam, 37.
[9] Cf. the discussion in Bonner and Smith, 294 ff.

the popular courts; when this course was taken the people fixed the penalty and sometimes the size of the court which was to try the case. On other occasions, when the offence alleged was unusual or popular feeling aroused, the ekklesia might decide to try the case itself, instructing the boulē to prepare the pro-bouleuma. Both types of procedure were employed in the fifth century; the best-known example of the first is provided by the trial of Perikles,[1] of the second by that of the generals who fought at Arginousai.[2] Eisangelia was a procedure obligatory for certain offences, but could apparently be extended to others in which the safety of the state was threatened.[3] Before the invention of ostracism and again after its decline, eisangelia was the weapon used by the demos against statesmen who had forfeited its confidence.

Since Solon, if not earlier, the most important questions, such as war, peace, alliances, legislation, and the conferment of citizenship, had been reserved for the decision of the ekklesia,[4] but under the radical democracy it exercised a close control over the whole administration.[5] Its supremacy in questions of foreign policy and national defence is illustrated by the fifth-century historians, who frequently mention its activity but hardly ever refer to the boulē. Envoys from other states, after presenting their credentials to the boulē, had to explain the purpose of their mission to the ekklesia,[6] to which Athenian envoys sent abroad had to report on their return.[7] All naval affairs were subject to its supervision, since on the fleet depended the food supply of Athens and the maintenance of the Empire.[8] In time of war the ekklesia fixed the size of an expedition, chose the generals who were to command it, and gave them detailed instructions for its conduct.[9] When the Sikeliot allies of Athens concluded peace with their enemies in 424, the three Athenian generals on the spot signified their consent, but for this action, taken without previous consultation of the assembly, two were banished on their return and the third fined.[10] Any agreements made by

---

[1] Plut. *Per.* 32. 3–4 and 35. 4–5; cf. Ar. *Wasps* 590–1.
[2] Xen. *Hell.* i. 7. 7 ff. [3] Cf. Bonner and Smith, 295.
[4] See above, pp. 96 f.
[5] Cf. Glotz, *C.G.*, part ii, c. 3 and BS 1005 ff.
[6] Thuc. v. 45; cf. Headlam, 67 and BS 1016.
[7] Thuc. vi. 8. 2; other examples in BS 1016, n. 3.
[8] *A.P.* 46. 1; cf. BS 1018. [9] Thuc. vi. 8. 2; cf. BS 1017.
[10] Thuc. iv. 65. 2–3. In the circumstances a consultation of the assembly

generals in the field had to be referred to the people for confirmation.[1]

When the Delian League was transformed into the Athenian Empire the ekklesia naturally controlled all dealings between Athens and the subject states.[2] Possibly in the early years of the League its interference was limited to regulating the position of new members or of states which had been subdued after a revolt, but soon it extended to all the tribute-paying states of the Empire. In a decree passed before 430[3] it enacted that all these states must henceforth use Athenian currency, weights, and measures, and a later decree[4] imposed on them the offering of first fruits to the goddesses of Eleusis. Special privileges were conferred on states and individuals in the Empire who steadfastly maintained their loyalty to Athens in difficult times.[5] The ekklesia was also the final authority for the finances of the Empire; it decreed a new and stiffer assessment of the tribute, and although it was the council that fixed the assessments of the several states and the dikastery that heard appeals against them, only the ekklesia could grant a state complete exemption from tribute.[6]

In the internal administration of the state the supremacy of the ekklesia was nowhere more clearly manifested than in the sphere of religion. The radical democracy left the old hereditary priesthoods to the noble families which had always held them,[7] but in all departments of the state religion it had a decisive voice, and the business arising out of them occupied a prominent place in its agenda.[8] It alone could authorize the building of new temples and the inclusion of foreign deities among the official cults of the city. One decree authorizes the appointment of a life-priestess for the worship of Athena Nike and defines her salary and perquisites, while a second, passed some years later, makes provision for the punctual payment of her salary.[9] When

would have been a futile waste of time. I cannot accept the view of H. Stein in *Rh. Mus.* lv, 1900, 533-4, n. 1 (repeated by Cloché in *R.E.A.* xxvii, 1925, 103-4). See below, pp. 263 f.

[1] Cf. Kahr. ii. 258 and *I.G.* i². 116 (Tod, 88).   [2] BS 1017 and n. 4.

[3] *A.T.L.* ii. 61-68 and iii. 281, n. 29; on the date cf. Tod in *J.H.S.* lxix, 1949, 105.

[4] *I.G.* i². 76 (Tod, 74).

[5] States: e.g. Neapolis and Archelaos of Macedon (*I.G.* i². 108 and 105 = Tod, 84 and 91). Individuals: *I.G.* i². 118 (Tod, 90) and 56.

[6] Cf. *I.G.* i². 63 and 57, ll. 29-32 (Tod, 66 and 61).

[7] See above, p. 129.   [8] Cf. BS 1015-16.

[9] *I.G.* i². 24-25 (Tod, 40 and 73).

regulations had to be made for the offering of the first fruits to Eleusis they were drafted by συγγραφεῖς, commissioners specially appointed by the people, and had to be submitted to the council and assembly for ratification; although the recommendations of the commissioners were apparently adopted without modification, the people in its final decree supplemented them with additional proposals moved by Lampon, one of the professional expounders of the traditional sacred lore.[1] All details of the financial administration of the state cults, such as the leasing of temple lands and expenditure on sacrifices and festivals, were controlled by the people.

The *Athenaion Politeia* shows[2] that in the fourth century the corn-supply was one of the chief preoccupations of the ekklesia. In the fifth century, when the Athenian fleet was supreme in the Aegean, this gave less cause for anxiety, but in wartime at least Athenian officials stationed in the Hellespont maintained a close control over the export of corn from the Pontos, and a subject state wishing to obtain its corn direct from the Hellespont had to secure a special authorization from the ekklesia.[3]

Details of the financial administration were left to the council acting in co-operation with the appropriate officials,[4] but though provision of funds to meet expenditure had to be devised by the council all but the routine items of expenditure had to be sanctioned by the people. A special quorum of 6,000 was necessary, as for ostracism, when the ekklesia voted the imposition of a property tax or authorized an individual proposer to move the use of funds from temple treasuries for secular purposes.[5] The same quorum was needed for the conferment of citizenship on states and individuals,[6] and it is practically certain that it was required for the conclusion of peace and the declaration of war.[7] This requirement ensured that the ekklesia should be adequately attended when it voted on questions of special importance. A further safeguard against hasty or ill-considered decisions was provided by the constitutional principle that no business whatever could be brought before the ekklesia for final decision without previous consideration by the council.[8]

---

[1] *I.G.* i². 76 (Tod, 74).   [2] 43. 4.
[3] *I.G.* i². 57 (Tod, 61), ll. 34–41.   [4] Cf. Headlam, 121–3.
[5] *I.G.* i². 92 (Tod, 51 B), ll. 12–19 combined with Dem. xxiv. 46.
[6] [Dem.] lix. 89.
[7] δῆμος πληθύων in *I.G.* i². 114 (*passim*) presumably means a quorum of 6,000; cf. Bonner and Smith, 211 ff.   [8] Dem. xxii. 5–7; cf. Headlam, 58 ff.

In a radical democracy the popular council was the most democratic of all the ἀρχαί.[1] At Athens the Council of Five Hundred, which after the revolution of 462 replaced the Areopagus as the chief council and was henceforth officially described as ἡ βουλή, was always closely associated in democratic sentiment with the ekklesia and the dikasteria.[2] It was open to all male citizens over thirty years of age, and its members were drawn from all the demes of Attica in proportion to their population.[3] Moreover, the application of the principles of sortition and rotation to the selection of the bouleutai made them a representative cross-section of the whole community and prevented them from acquiring the permanence and authority of an oligarchic life-council. These considerations were doubtless responsible for the application of the same principles to the internal organization of the boulē.[4] The bouleutai of each tribe served as πρυτάνεις for one-tenth of the year and the order in which the ten tribes held the πρυτανεία was determined by lot.[5] From the πρυτάνεις was chosen, also by lot and for one day only, the ἐπιστάτης who presided over the boulē, and also over the ekklesia if it met during his day of office.[6] The secretary of the boulē was appointed by election but only for the duration of a single prytany, and he was always chosen from those members of the council who did not belong to the φυλὴ πρυτανεύουσα.[7]

Ephialtes had divided between the dikasteria and the boulē the functions which he took away from the Areopagus.[8] But the prominence of the boulē after 462 cannot be explained by its acquisition of these new functions; it is rather to be connected with the triumphant affirmation by the radicals of the sovereignty of the demos. The ekklesia was now supreme, and as the business brought before it increased, the preparation of its agenda by the boulē became more complex and more important. Moreover, although the ekklesia could make decisions it was too unwieldy to superintend their execution, and so delegated the

---

[1] Ar. *Politics* 1317ᵇ30–31.

[2] Cf. Glotz, *C.G.* 237 and n. 3 (E.T. 202 and n. 3).

[3] See above, p. 150, n. 3, also p. 224.   [4] Cf. Headlam, 51–52.

[5] Probably lots were drawn before each prytany up to the ninth to decide which tribe should preside in the coming prytany; cf. T. Nicklin in *Journal of Philology*, xxiv, 1896, 76 (citing *I.G.* ii². 109ᵇ, ll. 16 ff.) followed by Ferguson, *The Athenian Secretaries* (New York, 1898), 21 ff.

[6] Cf. *A.P.* 44. 1 and Sandys' note on *A.P.* 44. 2.

[7] Cf. *A.P.* 54. 3 and the long note in BS 1034 (n. 1; also BS 478).

[8] *A.P.* 25. 2.

task to the boulē, which as the representative committee of the ekklesia was the obvious body to undertake it.[1] The exercise of these functions gave the member of the boulē a valuable training in public business and the working of the principle of rotation extended this experience to a large proportion of the citizen-body.

In administration it was the business of the boulē to make sure that the wishes of the people as expressed in the decrees of the ekklesia were fulfilled, and that no magistrate or private citizen neglected or exceeded the functions imposed on him by the state. It supervised the magistrates, assisted them with its advice, and co-operated with them in the exercise of their official duties.[2] As the work of the executive at Athens was divided between numerous boards, each with its own carefully defined sphere, some central authority was needed to co-ordinate the work of the various departments. This role was performed by the boulē, which through its control over the magistrates gave unity to the whole administration.[3] Its task was facilitated by the work of special commissions chosen by lot or election from the boulē itself. So there were ten τριηροποιοί[4] and ten ἐπιμελόμενοι τοῦ νεωρίου[5] for naval affairs, ten εὔθυνοι[6] to hear complaints against magistrates at the end of their term, and commissions of ἱεροποιοί for the conduct of religious ceremonies.[7]

Inscriptions provide the best illustration of the part played by the boulē in administration. In religion it superintended the officials responsible for the treasuries of the various temples. The basileus brought the leases of temple lands before it and reported to it any offences against the temples or the state religion.[8] When the ekklesia ordered a public sacrifice or laid down new regulations for an official cult, the boulē was made responsible for the execution of the decree.[9] Plans for a temple of Athena Nike were drawn up by the architect Kallikrates in

---

[1] Cf. Headlam, 64–65 with illustrations from *I.G.* ii². 1629 (Tod, ii. 200).
[2] *A.P.* 47. 1; cf. BS 475 and 1045, also Glotz, *C.G.* 227 (E.T. 193).
[3] Cf. de Sanctis, 346–8.
[4] *A.P.* 46. 1; cf. Tod, pp. 223–4 and Glotz, 223 (E.T. 189–90).
[5] *I.G.* i². 73, ll. 4 and 19; cf. Macgregor in Headlam², 205–6 and BS 1032.
[6] *A.P.* 48. 4; cf. BS 1033, n. 1.
[7] *I.G.* i². 84 and *A.P.* 54. 7; cf. Tod, p. 182, Glotz, 223–4 (E.T. 190), and BS 1031–2.
[8] *A.P.* 47. 1 and 4, *I.G.* i². 76 (Tod, 74), ll. 57 ff., And. i. 111.
[9] *I.G.* i². 76.

conference with three members of the Council and were then referred to the whole council for its approval.[1]

Diplomatic relations between Athens and other states were also controlled by the boulē. It received foreign envoys and obtained information from them about their business and their instructions before it introduced them to the ekklesia.[2] When a treaty was ratified by the ekklesia, the oath to observe it was sworn on behalf of Athens by the members of the boulē, together with the generals and other magistrates.[3] The boulē was also bound to watch over the interests of individual foreigners recommended to its protection by the ekklesia.[4] But during the period of the Empire the most important and exacting of its duties in this sphere were those arising out of the relations of Athens with the states under her sway.[5] Here it had to co-operate with the magistrates who were specially concerned with the administration of the Empire, such as the strategoi and Hellenotamiai. When a decree of the ekklesia imposed on all the tributary states of the Empire the obligation to adopt Athenian currency, weights, and measures, a special clause was added to the usual oath taken by members of the boulē which bound them to enforce the provisions of the decree.[6]

The στρατηγοί who commanded the fleets and armies of Athens were, as *ex officio* members of the boulē,[7] in close contact with it and made regular reports to it. In the organization of the land forces the part played by the boulē was small;[8] its particular concern was the fleet. The whole boulē was responsible for the maintenance of the warships and dockyards, but the work of supervision in detail was entrusted by it to two special commissions chosen from its members.[9] When a naval expedition was required, it had to control the necessary preparations and make sure that the trierarchs had duly fitted out their ships.[10] After the great expedition to Sicily had been decreed in 415, the prytaneis had to convene an assembly at the docks in the Piraeus when the fleet was ready, and had to confer there with the generals, treasurers, and trierarchs.[11] A few years later a new

---

[1] *I.G.* i². 24 (Tod, 40), 15 ff.; cf. *A.P.* 49. 3.   [2] Thuc. v. 45.
[3] Thuc. v. 47. 9, *I.G.* i². 90 (Tod, 68), ll. 8–9; cf. BS 1048, n. 2.
[4] *I.G.* i². 118 (Tod, 90), ll. 16 ff.   [5] Cf. Glotz, *C.G.* 227–8 (E.T. 193–4).
[6] Tod, 67, ll. 11 ff. = *A.T.L.* ii. 61–68.
[7] See below, p. 245.   [8] Cf. BS 1050.   [9] *A.P.* 46. 1; see above, p. 238.
[10] *I.G.* ii². 1629 (Tod, ii. 200); cf. [Dem.] xlvii. 41–42 and l. 6.
[11] *I.G.* i². 98 (Tod, 77 A).

fleet was being built in Macedonia; the generals were made responsible for its construction, the boulē for its conveyance to Athens and from there to Ionia.[1]

In the department of finance the work performed by the boulē was indispensable. It has been well said[2] that only its super-vision prevented pure anarchy in the financial administration of the state. The magistrates who handled public money had to keep it informed of all their transactions, and if guilty of fraud or neglect were liable to prosecution by it.[3] When Kallias pro-posed the repayment of the debt to the 'Other gods', the boulē was instructed to convene the thirty λογισταί who had to calcu-late the amount due, and its prytaneis had to pay back the debts in association with the rest of the boulē, which was also present at the transference of the treasuries from the various local sanctuaries to the new ταμίαι τῶν ἄλλων θεῶν.[4] All tax-farmers and lessees of other state-contracts were subject to the surveillance of the boulē, which could throw defaulters and their sureties into prison.[5] When the tribute payable by the subjects of the Empire was due for reassessment, it was the boulē which fixed the amount to be paid by each state in the new assessment.[6] In war-time it was also concerned with the provision of fresh revenues to meet the increased expenditure.[7] Lysias asserted that when it was pressed for money it showed a greater readiness to receive denunciations against the rich and confiscate their property.[8]

The control of the boulē over the officials and others who came under its supervision was strengthened by its authority to receive and hear charges against them. Prosecutions before it could be initiated either by one of its own members or by a private citizen.[9] These judicial powers must have been a valu-able asset to the boulē even if its verdict was in more important cases subject to confirmation by the ekklesia or the popular courts.[10] The author of the *Athenaion Politeia* asserts[11] that the boulē had once been competent to impose fines, to imprison, and

---

[1] *I.G.* i[2]. 105 (Tod, 91).   [2] By Glotz, *C.G.* 229 (E.T. 195).
[3] *A.P.* 47. 2, 47. 5–48. 2, 45. 2.   [4] *I.G.* i[2]. 91 (Tod, 51 A).
[5] And. i. 134 and 93; Dem. xxiv. 144.
[6] *I.G.* i[2]. 63 (Tod, 66), ll. 16–20. Cf. *X.A.P.* 3. 2 which says that the boulē also had the duty φόρον δέξασθαι; on this cf. BS 1049, n. 1.   [7] *X.A.P.* 3. 2.
[8] Lys. xxx. 22.   [9] *A.P.* 45. 2. Cf. Glotz, 233–4 (E.T. 198–9).
[10] The severity of the control over financial officials is illustrated by the con-demnation to death of nine Hellenotamiai in a single year under false suspicion (Antiphon v. 69).   [11] 45. 1.

even to pass sentence of death. Those who accept this statement find in the possession by the boulē of this wide competence in jurisdiction the secret of the efficiency of the democracy in the second half of the fifth century.[1] But the evidence of inscriptions and of contemporary writers affords no trace of the possession of such powers by the boulē; they indicate that in the fifth century, as later, the fines imposed by it without appeal were limited to a maximum of 500 drachmas, that its right to imprison was restricted to certain special cases, and that the power to inflict higher penalties, including sentence of death, was strictly reserved for the ekklesia or the dikasteries.[2] For the strict limitation of the council's judicial powers by the people it is significant that although its decisions in the dokimasia of the archons and bouleutai were originally final, the people before long enacted that those rejected by the boulē could appeal to the courts.[3] The reference in the *Athenaion Politeia* to the wide powers of jurisdiction formerly vested in the boulē is not above suspicion, for it serves to introduce an anecdote, almost certainly apocryphal, that professes to explain why it had lost them. If it had ever exercised these powers, the most plausible explanation[4] is that it had illegally usurped them on the instigation of Archinos after the restoration of 403 and had retained them until the demos took them away again.

It is clear from the preceding survey that little scope was left for the exercise of initiative by the boulē in administration. This part of its work was mostly a matter of routine; it had to keep watch over the machine of government and see that all its parts were working properly.[5] If fresh orders were issued to the departments by decree of the ekklesia, the responsibility for their execution rested with the boulē. In this sense it is correct to say[6] that the boulē was concerned with business, not with policy. But it was also a deliberative as well as an administrative body. In this capacity it drafted decrees which were divided into two categories. The first was composed of decisions which the boulē

[1] So de Sanctis, 429 ff.
[2] See especially *I.G.* i[2]. 114, passed after the radical restoration of 410 but presumably in part repeating earlier provisions; cf. also Cloché in *R.E.G.* xxxiii, 1920, 1–50 and Bonner and Smith, c. 14.
[3] *A.P.* 45. 3; the earlier practice is reflected in *I.G.* i[2]. 10 (Tod, 29), ll. 8–9.
[4] Cf. Cloché, op. cit. 36 ff. But the whole account in *A.P.* 45. 1 is scouted as worthless by Swoboda in *Hermes*, xxviii, 1893, 597; cf. BS 1046, n. 1.
[5] Cf. Headlam, 64.
[6] As Headlam did (p. 57).

was wholly competent to make on its own authority; such decrees were final and did not require confirmation by any other body.[1] More important were the decrees of the second category, the drafts or probouleumata which were submitted by the boulē to the ekklesia for its consideration; these dealt with questions which the people alone was competent to decide. No question could be submitted to the ekklesia unless it had been included in its agenda by the prytaneis after previous discussion in the boulē.[2] What was the significance of the council's probouleutic activity? Did it confer on the council any control over the policy of the state?

A minimizing view was maintained by Headlam.[3] He claimed that the main function of the boulē in this sphere was not to influence the decision of the ekklesia but to explain clearly in its probouleuma the questions which the ekklesia had to settle and to see that the motion was properly worded. Headlam called attention[4] to the activity of the συγγραφεῖς, and pointed out that the regulations drafted by them were brought before the ekklesia by the boulē without modification. He also contended[5] that every citizen had access to the boulē and that consequently popular leaders did not need to have a seat in it, since they could introduce motions which, thanks to their influence with the people, were adopted by the boulē without alteration for submission to the ekklesia.

This interpretation of the evidence is open to criticism. Although Headlam's account of the relations between the συγγραφεῖς and the boulē was correct, his suggestion that they may have been permanent officials cannot be accepted; they seem to have been appointed *ad hoc* whenever their services were required.[6] Moreover access to the boulē was rarer and more difficult than Headlam realized.[7] Any citizen, even a magistrate, who was not a member of the boulē had to obtain a permit of admission (πρόσοδος) from the prytaneis.[8] Presumably this was granted as a matter of course to a magistrate, but applications from ordinary citizens might be rejected; a special

---

[1] Cf. Glotz, *C.G.* 226–7 (E.T. 192–3) and BS 1027 and n. 4.

[2] See above, p. 236, n. 8. [3] Op. cit. 56 ff.

[4] Op. cit. 60–61; cf. *I.G.* i². 76 (Tod, 74), ll. 2–4 and 48 ff. and Tod, p. 181, also *I.G.* i². 22 and 45 (Tod, 44), ll. 15–17. [5] Op. cit. 69–72.

[6] Cf. BS 460–1 and Glotz, 208–9 (E.T. 177–8).

[7] As Macgregor pointed out in the second edition (Headlam², 200–1).

[8] Scholion on Aristophanes, *Pax* 908 (Dindorf 907); cf. And. i. 111.

recommendation to the prytaneis to give audience to a particula‸ citizen was sometimes voted by the ekklesia.[1] When the applicant had been admitted to the boulē he could make a statement but could not propose a motion; further action could not be taken unless a member of the boulē introduced a proposal with reference to his report and undertook the responsibility for the authorship of the decree.[2]

The possession of these powers by the boulē and its prytaneis might have constituted a serious limitation on the freedom of the ekklesia. But in the Periklean Age the people were no longer compelled to accept or reject a probouleuma as it stood; they could modify it by means of amendments.[3] Nor was this all; they could even initiate a motion by instructing the boulē to submit a probouleuma on a particular subject for their decision.[4] Despite these facts, Headlam's view that the probouleutic function of the boulē was merely a matter of drafting and clarification is untenable. Elaborate decrees such as those regulating the status of Chalkis and the reassessment of the tribute,[5] which contain important provisions affecting the relations of Athens with her subject allies, were adopted with only minor alterations by the ekklesia in the form submitted to it by the boulē. On such questions the boulē must have been guided by the opinion of the στρατηγοί who shared its deliberations, and until the time of Kleon the men recognized by the people as their spokesmen[6] usually held the στρατηγία. This close connexion and co-operation between the boulē and the popular leaders made it an effective instrument of government in the Periklean period and enabled it to direct successfully the energies and the policy of the state. Its later decline may have been due in part to the divorce between the στρατηγία and the προστασία τοῦ δήμου.[7] But a leader of the demos could always find in a body as numerous as the boulē many who were willing to sponsor the measures that he thought desirable. Owing to the nature of its composition the boulē shared the sympathies and

---

[1] *I.G.* i². 45 (Tod, 44), ll. 32–39; cf. *I.G.* i². 108 (Tod, 84), ll. 28–30.

[2] The evidence was collected by Swoboda in *Rh. Mus.* xlv, 1890, 288 ff. (especially 296–8).

[3] Or adopt a solution different from that recommended by the boulē (Xen. *Hell.* vii. 1. 1–14); cf. BS 454 and Gilbert, 295, n. 3.

[4] BS 449–50 and Gilbert, 295, n. 4; cf. *I.G.* ii². 360, ll. 46–50.

[5] *I.G.* i². 39 and 63 (Tod, 42 and 66).

[6] Including Ephialtes; cf. Plut. *Kimon* 13. 4.

[7] So de Sanctis, 350–1, citing Beloch, *Attische Politik*, 16–17.

the ekklesia[1] and could therefore be trusted not to
vileges to the detriment of the ekklesia.

The strategia

der the radical democracy most officials were
ᵣᵣᵤᵢᵢₜₑd by lot, the people chose some by direct election, either
in the ekklesia or in the tribal assemblies. Extraordinary officials
were usually elected,[2] such as architects and the ἐπιστάται who
supervised them, also envoys chosen for important missions;
these special appointments could be combined with the tenure
of an ordinary magistracy, for example the strategia,[3] and were
not subject to the normal rule that forbade anyone to hold two
offices simultaneously.[4] The holders of the special financial
offices created in the second half of the fourth century were also
appointed by direct election,[5] and the same is probably true of
the fifth-century Hellenotamiai, for they were from the start
officials of the Delian League as well as Athenian magistrates.[6]
In the fifth century the secretary of the boulē was elected, either
by the boulē itself or by the assembly, but he held office merely
for the duration of a single prytany and was always chosen from
a tribe different from that which was presiding for that prytany.[7]

Among the officials directly elected by the assembly the
holders of the chief military posts occupied a special position.
Although they were appointed only for a year they could be
reappointed for a fresh term and there was no legal limit to the
number of such reappointments.[8] If the people showed its confidence in a military official by re-electing him, the usual audit
may have been little more than a formality, especially for a
general conducting operations in a theatre of war far distant
from Athens.[9] Elections to the military posts were normally

[1] Glotz and Cohen, ii. 291; cf. Glotz, *C.G.* 237 (E.T. 201–2).
[2] Cf. Headlam, 72–74 and 104–8, Glotz, 250–1 (E.T. 213–14), BS 1064 ff.
[3] Cf. BS 1069 and n. 2, where it is pointed out (also 896, n. 8) that Perikles
combined the στρατηγία with membership of various special boards.
[4] Dem. xxiv. 150 (heliastic oath).
[5] *A.P.* 43. 1; on the position of Lykourgos after 336 cf. BS. 1147, n. 4.
[6] I think Loeschcke's conclusion was right although his argument was unsound; cf. Kahr. ii. 43–45, and for a different view Macgregor in Headlam², 204–5.
[7] *A.P.* 54. 3 with Sandys' note; cf. BS 1033–4 and 1034, n. 1.
[8] *A.P.* 62. 3; BS. 1069 and n. 1.
[9] Wil. ii. 243 ff. (especially 249) and Swoboda in *Hermes*, xxviii, 1893, 554;
cf. also BS 1069–70, Kahr. ii. 174–5, and Glotz, 267 (E.T. 228). Dissent is expressed
by de Sanctis, 438, n. 1.

held in the seventh prytany[1] (February–March), and some
have supposed that this was done to enable the new officials to begin their duties with the campaigning season,[2] but
the evidence available indicates that they entered on office,
like most of the other magistrates, in midsummer.[3] The military
and political inconveniences of this practice are obvious, but
a partial parallel is found in the Spartan ναυαρχία.

Candidates for the strategia had to possess some aptitude for
leadership in war,[4] but it is unlikely that they were always
chosen in the fifth century for their military qualifications alone.
Since the reform of 487 the strategia had political importance
as well, and there is some evidence that it conferred positive
political advantages on its holders. Plutarch's references to
Perikles and Nikias show both in close contact with the boulē,
and in his biography of Nikias[5] Plutarch associates this contact
with his hero's tenure of the strategia. Was this merely a matter
of special facilities for access to the boulē? Doubtless a magistrate
would always be granted prompt audience for the discussion of
special problems arising out of his official duties.[6] It might be
argued that the business of the strategoi was so important that
it multiplied occasions for consultation with the boulē, so that
they were almost continuously in contact with it and yet not
members of it.[7] This hypothesis, however, does not explain
their right to propose motions in the boulē, either as a board or
individually. The first clear instance of this right comes from
the first decade of the fourth century,[8] but if the right existed
at that date it is a reasonable inference that it goes back to the
fifth century. If Hartel was correct in his contention[9] that only
a bouleuēts could propose a motion in the boulē, the conclusion
to be drawn is that the strategoi must have been *ex officio*
members of the boulē.[10] Kahrstedt assumes that private citizens

---

[1] Cf. *A.P.* 44. 4 with Sandys' note; the relevance to this matter of Ar. *Clouds*
581 ff. has been questioned (*J.H.S.* lix, 1939, 63, n. 3).

[2] So H. B. Mayor in *J.H.S.* lix. 45–64.

[3] Cf. W. K. Pritchett in *A.J.P.* lxi, 1940, 469–74.

[4] *X.A.P.* 1. 3 implies this; cf. the fate of Kleon before Amphipolis in 422.

[5] 5. 1; cf. *Per.* 7. 5.   [6] See above, p. 242 and n. 8.

[7] So apparently Headlam, 72.

[8] *I.G.* ii². 27 (*S.I.G.* 132); cf. the restoration of *I.G.* i². 71, l. 47 in *A.T.L.* iii.
313, n. 61, and the note on l. 47 in *S.E.G.* x. 86.

[9] Cf. his article 'Demosthenische Anträge' published in *Commentationes philo-
logicae in honorem Th. Mommsen* (Berlin, 1877), 518–36.

[10] So Swoboda in *Rh. Mus.* xlv, 1890, 299 ff. (especially p. 302); cf. BS 474 and
1026, n. 5.

who had obtained access to the boulē could move the adoption of a probouleuma on their proposal, but the only cases he cites[1] are motions proposed by leading orators in the Demosthenic period and after, and he produces no evidence that this was possible in the Periklean Age.

Theoretically it might seem desirable that in a radical democracy any citizen should be able to initiate a proposal, but in the generation after Ephialtes' reforms the demos was probably content to leave the initiative to its leaders. Moreover, Themistokles had apparently intended the generals to be the supreme political as well as military executive of the state, and if he transferred to them the presidency of the ekklesia[2] he must have made provision for close contact between them and the boulē; to make them *ex officio* members of it would be the obvious solution. The value of this privilege to the generals was enhanced when the growth of the Empire increased the range and importance of their duties, and this would explain why the privilege was left to them in 462 by the radicals when they took from them the presidency of the ekklesia.

After 462 the generals could not convene the ekklesia; this mattered little, as its presidents, the πρυτάνεις, were bound to convene it on the request of the generals,[3] and an inscription of 426[4] shows that they had to include in its agenda any urgent business raised by the generals. Thucydides[5] says that Perikles in 431 did not allow the people to come together either in the ekklesia or in a more informal meeting. Although Attica was then the scene of military operations the passage can hardly be explained by the assumption that Perikles kept the able-bodied citizens busy with military duties and so debarred them from attendance at any political assembly.[6] Nor is it likely that the people, who had conferred some special powers on Perikles in this crisis, would have included in them authorization to suspend its own normal meetings if he should think fit.[7] If Thucydides merely meant that he prevented any *extraordinary* meetings of the ekklesia he failed to express his meaning clearly. It seems

[1] ii. 291–2 and 292, n. 1 (on Kahrstedt's examples cf. Hartel in *S.-B. Wien*, 88, 1877, 365 ff.).　　　[2] See above, p. 175.　　　[3] Cf. Thuc. iv. 118. 14.

[4] *I.G.* i². 57 (Tod, 61), ll. 55–56.　　　[5] ii. 22. 1.

[6] Kahr. ii. 267–8 assumes that Perikles could do this while the enemy were still in Attica.

[7] BS 1062, n. 2 apparently follows the view expressed by Swoboda in *Rh. Mus.* xlv, 1890, 308.

better to interpret his words strictly and to assume that the prestige Perikles enjoyed as a statesman rather than any powers vested in him as general enabled him to prevail on his fellow-generals and the council to postpone all meetings of the people until the immediate danger of the Spartan invasion was over.[1]

Originally the generals had probably been a board of colleagues with equal authority, and there is evidence that even in the second half of the fifth century generals in the field decided the allocation of their tasks by lot[2] or made provision for the necessity of supreme command by the equalitarian expedient of rotation, each acting in turn for one day as commander-in-chief.[3] But the principle of strict collegiality was early violated, for the needs of the Persian War compelled the Athenians to confer supreme authority within the board for a whole campaign on a single general,[4] who then acted as the representative of Athens on the war-council of the patriotic Greeks. Later in the fifth century the generals sent on an expedition, who rarely if ever included all the members of the board, might either have equal powers or be subject to the overriding authority of one of their number nominated to the chief command by the people.[5]

It is not known whether in the meetings of the board of generals the presidency was held by the same man throughout the year,[6] but even if it was, it need not have conferred on its holder more than the rights of an ordinary chairman. Even Beloch, who maintained that the presidency throughout the year was vested in a single general, admitted that the constitutional powers of the supposed πρύτανις did not differ essentially from those of his colleagues, although his eminence and the peculiar method used (according to Beloch) in his appointment gave him a *de facto* supremacy within the board.[7]

A general might be superior in competence to his colleagues *de iure* in one of two ways. He could, as we have seen, be nominated by the people to exercise supreme command in a particular

---

[1] So Kahr. ii. 268. [2] Thuc. vi. 62. 1.

[3] Diod. xiii. 97. 6, but this evidence is rejected by Kahr. ii. 152, n. 1 and certainly seems inconsistent with Xenophon's account of the same events in *Hell.* i. 6. 29 ff. Hdt. vi. 110 (though anachronistic) may be relevant, but Kahr. ii. 164 refers this to the presidency of the board of generals.

[4] Cf. BS 891, n. 2 and Schwahn, 1079.

[5] See below, Appendix XI.

[6] A president may be indicated by the wording of *I.G.* i². 324 (Tod, 64), l. 3; cf. also Colin in Daremberg–Saglio, iv. 2. 1524 B and Macgregor in Headlam², 194.

[7] *Attische Politik*, 288.

expedition,[1] or he could receive from the people a grant of special powers; by this grant, which in certain respects (apparently defined in the grant) freed him from his customary dependence on the ekklesia, he was given greater freedom of action, made αὐτοκράτωρ.[2] Some scholars have erroneously spoken of 'the office of *strategos autokrator*'.[3] There never was any such office; a general was αὐτοκράτωρ in virtue not of an office but of special powers conferred on him by the people, which need not be and usually were not conferred at the time of his election to the strategia. In most years they were probably not conferred at all, and, when they were, the grant was not necessarily limited to one member of the board; it was conferred on all the three generals who commanded the Sicilian Expedition in 415.[4]

These grants were not limited to generals; they could be made to others, for example envoys, and even the Council of Five Hundred.[5] It has been suggested that the power common to all grants made to generals was competence to conclude an alliance without reference to the ekklesia.[6] They may have tended to follow the same pattern, but the assembly probably defined the powers afresh on the occasion of each grant. It is clear from Thucydides that the grant originally made to the three generals in 415 was limited in scope, since it was only by a subsequent grant that they were empowered to decide the size of the forces required and the conduct of the whole expedition.[7]

If special powers were conferred on a single general, the man so honoured would be the most important member of the board; in 407 Alkibiades, then the leading man in Athens, received them, and Xenophon shows[8] that the grant was made some time after his election and to him alone. According to Plutarch[9] Themistokles was στρατηγὸς αὐτοκράτωρ in 480, Aristeides in 479. No other instance is known of the grant of special powers to a single general in the fifth century, but despite the silence of Thucydides they were perhaps conferred on Perikles in 431 and again in 430/429. Since Thucydides describes him as δέκατος αὐτὸς in 431,[10] it is possible that the Athenians had not only given

---

[1] See below, Appendix XI.
[2] Beloch, *A.P.* 285-6; cf. Greenidge, *Handbook*, 255.
[3] e.g. Walker in *C.A.H.* iv. 266.   [4] Thuc. vi. 8. 2.
[5] And. iii. 33 and i. 15; on the latter cf. Kahr. ii. 277-8 and also *I.G.* i². 91 (Tod, 51 A), l. 9.   [6] Kahr. ii. 265-6.   [7] vi. 8. 2 and 26. 1.
[8] *Hell.* i. 4. 10 and 20.   [9] *Arist.* 8. 1 and 11. 1.   [10] ii. 13. 1.

him greater freedom from the control of the ekklesia but had also subordinated his colleagues to his authority.

The powers conferred on Perikles in the early years of the Peloponnesian War and on Alkibiades in 407 were clearly exceptional and reflected the seriousness of the crises with which Athens was then faced. But even in less abnormal conditions a general might hope to be nominated to the chief command of an expedition and so obtain a military reputation that would strengthen his popularity with the people, and the political privileges enjoyed by the generals associated them with the activities of the council. Through their membership of it they were not only acquainted with all the details of the routine administration, but as leaders of the armed forces they could exercise a special influence in naval and financial questions and in virtue of their right to initiate probouleumata could exert a positive influence on the shaping of policy. Hence it is not surprising that the political supremacy of Perikles in the period 443–430 is expressly connected by Plutarch[1] with his continuous tenure of the strategia throughout those years, or that the office was held by all the statesmen who enjoyed the favour of the demos from the reform of 487 to the rise of the demagogues.

In the Periklean Age the demos was so conscious of its own strength that it could allow its leaders to be re-elected year after year to the strategia and thereby to enjoy a comparative freedom from accountability. It knew well that if they dared to abuse its confidence they could soon be deposed and disgraced.[2] Accordingly it was not afraid to take its leaders from the higher ranks of society, from families distinguished by noble birth, landed possessions, and a tradition of activity in the public service.[3] In addition to these qualifications the general who aspired to lead the people needed some military talent and particularly the gift of ready speech indispensable to a popular leader in a radical democracy. Kimon had possessed a vigorous natural eloquence that could sway the ekklesia by a happy phrase,[4] but since then the art of rhetoric had been elaborated. Perikles had profited by the new learning, and although few fragments of his oratory have survived its power is sufficiently attested.[5]

[1] *Per.* 16. 3.　　[2] As Perikles was in 430. Cf. Thuc. viii. 54. 3 and Kahr. ii. 105 ff.

[3] Cf. Aischines i. 27 on those who can claim πρόγονοι ἐστρατηγηκότες. On wealthy men as generals cf. Ar. *Politics* 1282ª25–32 and Eupolis, fr. 117.

[4] Plut. *Kimon* 16. 10 (from Ion).

[5] e.g. by Eupolis, fr. 94 in Hill's *Sources*, p. 285 (116 in 1951 edition).

Admittedly the authority enjoyed by a statesman as eminent as Themistokles or Perikles depended less on his tenure of the strategia than on his retention of the people's confidence.[1] It was nevertheless a useful weapon in the hands of an able and popular leader, whose popularity with the ekklesia enhanced his authority on the board of generals or in the council, and it was the outward expression of the influence he enjoyed in the state, just as the loss of that influence was made manifest by his deposition or failure to secure re-election.[2]

The radical democracy created by Ephialtes and Perikles was a bold experiment in direct rule by the people. The powers of the Areopagus and the magistrates had been curtailed, and payment for state service had for the first time made it possible for the Thetes to play an active part in the government. These developments, in which some scholars have seen the triumph of the proletariat over the bourgeoisie,[3] naturally aroused the suspicion of the more conservative states in Greece, especially Sparta. It must be admitted that Periklean democracy when transplanted to the soil of other communities sometimes produced strange fruits. Its success at Athens in the generation after 462 must largely be ascribed to the peculiar qualities of the Athenian people. Their history shows that they had a special aptitude for the successful working of popular government,[4] and this aptitude, first provided by the tyrants with the possibility of growth, had been further developed by the judicious innovations of Kleisthenes and his successors.

In the famous panegyric on Athenian democracy attributed by Thucydides to Perikles the function of the popular leader is ignored, but elsewhere Thucydides states plainly[5] his conviction that an irresponsible democracy must rely on its accredited leaders for guidance and the initiation of policy if it is not to relapse into anarchy, and that the people's function should be limited to deciding on the proposals originated by the statesmen, the men who had the ability to discern the proper policy

[1] Cf. Headlam, 30–31.

[2] Perikles was apparently deposed in 430; Alkibiades failed to be re-elected in 406.

[3] e.g. de Sanctis, 418.

[4] Cf. the important defence of Athenian democracy by M. Cary in *History*, xii, 1927, 206–14.

[5] vi. 39. 1; cf. the definition in ii. 60. 5 of the qualities desirable in a leader of the people, and on the omission of the προστάτης τοῦ δήμου from the Funeral Speech see BS 901.

and to expound it to the masses. The political maturity of the Athenian demos in the Periklean Age was nowhere more clearly shown than in their readiness to trust leaders who had earned their confidence, and from the strategia the foresight of Themistokles had fashioned an instrument that enabled those leaders to make an effective use of their talents in the service of the state.

X. THE DECLINE AND FALL OF THE ATHENIAN EMPIRE

The supremacy of Perikles

'A NEW constitution does not produce its full effects as long as all its subjects were reared under an old constitution, as long as its statesmen were trained by that old constitution. It is not really tested till it comes to be worked by statesmen and among a people neither of whom are guided by a different experience.' These words, in which Walter Bagehot[1] explained why the real consequences of the Reform Act of 1832 were not revealed till many years after its passing, apply equally to the history of Athens during the three decades that followed the reforms of Ephialtes.[2] If during this period the Athenians were able to enjoy the benefits of radical democracy without suffering unduly from its defects, it was because they had learnt under the moderate democracy to entrust the shaping and direction of policy to statesmen chosen from the old and wealthy families with a tradition of leadership. This dependence on aristocratic leaders long survived the revolution of 462, for at first the demos was still overawed by the talents and social prestige of its champions and submissive to their control, and when a new generation was growing up, the pre-eminence of Perikles in his own party was such as to exclude that fierce competition between rival politicians for popular favour which under his successors proved so disastrous for Athens.[3]

Member of an aristocratic and distinguished family,[4] rich, eloquent, and endowed with respectable if not outstanding military talents, Perikles was obviously marked out for a political career. His father Xanthippos had been one of the foremost men in the state during the period of the Persian Wars,[5] and his mother Agariste a member by birth of the great Alkmaionid house, a niece of Kleisthenes the founder of Athenian democracy.[6]

---

[1] *The English Constitution²*, introduction, p. ix.
[2] Cf. Wil. ii. 111.   [3] Thuc. ii. 65. 8–10.
[4] Its name is unknown; the assertion of the scholiast in Aelius Aristides ὑπὲρ τῶν τεττάρων (Dindorf, iii. 473) that Perikles belonged to the Bouzygai is of very doubtful value (cf. Wil. ii. 86, n. 25).
[5] Hdt. viii. 131. 3, ix. 114. 2, *A.P.* 22. 6.
[6] Hdt. vi. 131. 2.

But it was probably not so much the traditions of his mother's clan as his hereditary feud with the family of Miltiades[1] that caused Perikles to join the ranks of the radical democrats. In him they found an inspiring leader who completed the unfinished work of Ephialtes and carried the constitutional revolution to a triumphant conclusion. The force of his oratory is attested by Eupolis,[2] his patriotism and incorruptibility by Thucydides.[3] Moreover, he had developed his natural gifts by association with some of the principal philosophers of his time, who began to make their home in Athens when it became the political centre of the Aegean area, notably Anaxagoras of Klazomenai and Protagoras of Abdera.[4] From them he acquired the philosophical bent of thought and detachment from popular opinions which earned for him the nickname of 'the Olympian'.[5] When he had attained the fullness of his powers his almost inhuman superiority to passion and prejudice was combined with a clarity of intellectual vision which enabled him as a statesman to see all sides of a question and to shape his policy accordingly.

Plutarch implies that Perikles' political life fell into two parts, before and after his pre-eminence was assured. He began as a radical politician and in a subordinate position,[6] and it was fortunate for him that Ephialtes was removed by death from the leadership of the radicals when Perikles was probably still in his early thirties. Plutarch[7] attributes to him a primacy of forty years in the political life of Athens, but here he seems to follow the view which dated the beginning of Perikles' supremacy from the death of Aristeides. Moreover he goes on to imply that his supremacy in the last fifteen years of his life, after the ostracism of Thucydides the son of Melesias, was more marked than in the previous period. There are really two questions involved: How long was Perikles leader of the Athenian people as a whole, and how long was he the most influential statesman of the radical party? The answer to the first question is that he was the undisputed leader of the state during the ten years

---

[1] Hdt. vi. 136. 1, Plut. *Kimon* 14. 5.
[2] See above, p. 249, n. 5. Cf. de Sanctis, 419, n. 2.
[3] ii. 60. 5.
[4] Plut. *Per.* 4. 6–5. 1; 6; 36. 5. Perikles' Athenian teacher Damon (on whom see Tod, pp. 92–93) is associated with Anaxagoras in Isokrates xv. 235.
[5] Plut. 8. 3–4; cf. Aristophanes, *Acharnians* 530.
[6] See above, pp. 197 f.   [7] 16. 3.

between early 443, when Thucydides was ostracized, and the revival of the opposition in 433.

The second question is more difficult. We have already seen that Ephialtes must have been the leader of the radical party until his death in 461. Archestratos, who proposed some of the measures against the Areopagus, is a shadowy figure to us.[1] One of the most characteristic features of Periklean democracy is the payment of citizens for civilian service, inaugurated by the law which introduced pay for jurors. This law was proposed by Perikles himself,[2] and the most probable date for it is soon after Ephialtes' death. On the whole it seems reasonable to suppose that while Ephialtes was alive Perikles held the second place in the radical party, and succeeded to the leadership on Ephialtes' death. But the frequent assumption that he was responsible for the whole domestic and foreign policy of Athens between 460 and 446, apart from the brief period when Kimon was back in Athens, presumes too much on the argument from silence, as we know so little about the internal history of Athens in this period. It is unlikely that Perikles' leadership of the radicals was as unchallenged now as it was to be later, and Plutarch[3] records the failure of his opposition when Tolmides advocated an immediate attempt to re-establish Athenian control in Boiotia. Perikles is usually saddled with the responsibility for the creation of an Athenian land empire in central Greece, but in the period before 446 he may not yet have had sufficient authority to withstand the territorial ambitions of the other prominent men in the radical party.

Who were Perikles' rivals? In addition to Ephialtes Plutarch[4] mentions Leokrates, Myronides, Kimon, Tolmides, and Thucydides. Of these, Thucydides son of Melesias succeeded Kimon in the leadership of the moderate democrats. The other three are known chiefly as generals who played a prominent and successful part in the wars waged by Athens from 458 to 454. Myronides belonged to an older generation[5] and may have been a moderate in politics; he was the most successful commander of this period

---

[1] See above, pp. 197 f.
[2] A.P. 27. 4; Ar. Politics 1274ᵃ8. On the date see Appendix IX.
[3] Per. 18. 2.   [4] Per. 16. 3.
[5] Cf. Plut. Arist. 10. 10 (the story in 20. 1 is probably apocryphal). The identity of the general of the fifties with the envoy of 479 has been questioned (by Ehrenberg in R.-E. Supplbd. vii, 1940, 510 ff.) on grounds which appear to me inadequate.

in land operations. In the fifties the hoplites of Athens were still doughty fighters, worthy to rank with the men who had triumphed at Marathon. Their victories in war should have increased the prestige of the moderate party to which they belonged, but Kimon, the leader of that party, was in exile during most of the decade 460–451, and it was the paradox of his career that he should have won military renown as the admiral of the 'sailor rabble' rather than as general of the hoplites who were his political supporters. Moreover the hoplites suffered heavy losses in the land fighting of the fifties, as shown by the stelē[1] which records the death of 177 men from one tribe in a single year, and these casualties were regarded by oligarchic critics later as contributory to the decline of conservative influence.[2] Hence the land campaigns of this period may be attributed to the expansionists in the radical party, of whom Tolmides was perhaps the foremost.[3]

To the earlier phase of Perikles' career, when he was still only the leader of a party, probably belong those of his measures which have a specifically radical flavour. He had at the beginning of his leadership proclaimed his political faith by the introduction of jury-pay, and he must have approved if he did not actually sponsor the proposals which extended the principle of state payment to other forms of civilian service. Must we then suppose that he was acting as a party leader when he proposed the only other bill in this period that is definitely attributed to his authorship, the famous law of 451/450 which restricted the citizenship to those who had an Athenian mother as well as an Athenian father? The assumption is easy and popular, but doubt is thrown on it by a closer examination of the law and the circumstances of its passing. Conservatives must surely have commended the purpose of the law, to preserve the purity of the citizen stock from contamination by undesirable alien elements. Moreover their old leader Kimon was now back in Athens, and there is some evidence that since his return he was acting in co-operation with Perikles.[4] Hence the law may have been an agreed measure acceptable to moderates and radicals alike.[5]

If Kimon's return was accompanied by a pact between the

---

[1] *I.G.* i². 929 (Tod, 26). [2] *A.P.* 26. 1.
[3] If the story in Plut. *Per.* 18. 2 is to be trusted.
[4] Plut. *Per.* 10. 4–5 (antedated to 457 by Plutarch's sources).
[5] See below, Appendix X.

moderates and radicals, the political truce did not long survive his death. After the return of his fleet from Cyprus the Athenians undertook no further operations against Persia and may even have concluded a formal peace. This sudden cessation of the anti-Persian crusade may have alienated the moderates; it certainly aroused great discontent in the states of the Delian League,[1] which had thereby been deprived of its justification. Perikles adopted various expedients to tide over this crisis, but he had made up his mind to maintain Athenian control over the allies even at the cost of transforming the League into an Empire. His determination to exploit the League in the service of purely Athenian interests was revealed in his proposal to use for the building of the Parthenon the surplus funds which had accumulated in the treasury of the League since its foundation.

It was on this issue that the Opposition challenged his policy. Plutarch[2] calls them the aristocratic party, but his views on Athenian political history are distorted by the conditions of his own day, and he habitually fails to realize that in the fifth century there were not two but three parties in Athens. The new leader of the Opposition, Thucydides the son of Melesias, is called Kimon's κηδεστής and may have been his brother-in-law,[3] and his adherents were probably composed in the main of Kimon's old following, the hoplite class. He was a more adroit politician than Kimon and showed great skill in his reorganization of the moderates, training them to act together as a party in the ekklesia.[4] Yet the ground of his challenge to Perikles was badly chosen and does more credit to his heart than to his head. The average Athenian voter was not likely to be moved by the wrongs of the allies or appeals to Panhellenic sentiment. Moreover there was a lack of political realism in the belief that Athens could put the clock back to where it had been in the seventies and ignore the developments of the last thirty years. The intensity of the party struggle culminated in an appeal to the verdict of ostracism; it was adverse to Thucydides, and early in 443 he went into exile.[5]

Plutarch[6] asserts that after this triumph Perikles' position

[1] Cf. Thuc. iii. 10. 4, also de Sanctis, 466 and 474.
[2] Per. 11. 1.
[3] Cf. the genealogical table given by Wade-Gery in J.H.S. lii, 1932, 210.
[4] Plut. Per. 11. 2.
[5] On the date cf. Wade-Gery, op. cit. 206 and Carcopino, Ostracisme, 168 ff. Busolt, iii. 495, n. 3, argues for 442.   [6] 15. 1.

was so secure that he no longer needed to court popular favour. The failure of the land empire had allowed him to concentrate the energies of Athens on the consolidation of her naval supremacy. Moreover, his greater prestige in the years after 443 enabled him to maintain for the next ten years the peace made by Athens with Sparta in the winter of 446/445, while the strength of his position in Athens gave confidence to the states-men who led the peace parties in Sparta and other Peloponnesian states. When Alkibiades later claimed for himself and his family that they were the leaders of the whole people,[1] he was perhaps thinking of the influence exercised by Perikles at the zenith of his career. If Perikles in the decade after 443 became a national rather than a party leader, the transformation must be mainly credited to his pacific policy during these years. From the end of 446 to the end of 434 Athens enjoyed twelve years of peace, broken only by the brief interlude of the Samian revolt. This was the culmination of the Periklean Age, and its artistic and cultural achievements are rightly credited to Perikles' leader-ship. The peace and prosperity ensured by his conduct of affairs and the firmness of his control over the assembly must have done much to remove the misgivings of the middle classes and reconcile them to radical democracy. In this period the prestige of his statesmanship was so high that he even won over some of the aristocrats, notably the historian Thucydides.

For Thucydides[2] the recurrence of party strife and the ruin of Athens were disasters due to Perikles' death, since among his successors none was found who combined, as Perikles had done, the intellectual and the moral qualities required in a democratic statesman. Plato[3] thought that Perikles himself had by his demagogic innovations contributed more than anyone to the subsequent deterioration of the Athenian people. Neither view does full justice to the complexity of the historical factors. It is easy to say that Ephialtes and Perikles, by destroying the Kleisthenic constitution under which Athens had become the leading state in Greece, had started a movement which was to lead to her decline and fall, but the beginning of the process must surely be sought earlier, in Themistokles' decision to turn Athens into a great naval power. Once the safety and welfare of the state had begun to depend on the ναυτικὸς ὄχλος, it was inevitable that political power should pass sooner or later from

---

[1] Thuc. vi. 89. 6.   [2] ii. 65. 8–12.   [3] *Gorgias* 515 E.

the middle classes to the proletariat.[1] The main charge which can be brought against Ephialtes and Perikles is the charge brought by conservatives against all radical reformers, that they should have helped to retard the natural trend of the historical process in their own state instead of doing all in their power to accelerate it.

There was, however, in Perikles' whole policy a latent contradiction which was fraught with disastrous consequences. At first sight there would seem to be a logical connexion between his two main ideas, the establishment of radical democracy in Athens and the maintenance of the Empire. The proletariat certainly came to believe that the perquisites they enjoyed under the radical democracy depended on the retention of their subjects; this belief may explain why in the Ionian War they opposed any peace which required territorial sacrifices. Perikles' own imperialism was less crude. He appears to have held that important advances in civilization could only be achieved by great and wealthy states whose power and resources were based on their rule over others. The buildings on the Acropolis were an essential part of his plan to make Athens the cultural capital of Greece, and he was not to be deterred from his purpose by scruples about the use of the reserves in the League treasury. Moreover the greatness and wealth of Athens must depend on the maintenance of her naval supremacy in the Aegean, in other words, on the discipline and skill of the Athenian sailors. As these were drawn from the proletariat, the government of imperial Athens must be a radical democracy, in accordance with the maxim that the permanence of a constitution in a state depends on the nature of the armed forces on which the state mainly depends for its survival.[2]

The inference seemed cogent to oligarchs as well as radicals,[3] but in application it was exposed to the fatal objection that a radical democracy was incapable of governing an empire.[4] At first this was not realized, for several reasons. As we have seen, the reforms of Ephialtes and Perikles were slow to produce their full effects. In the decade from 443 to 433 the government of Athens, in form a radical democracy, was in fact a principate controlled by its leading citizen.[5] Throughout the same decade Perikles pursued a cautious and conciliatory policy which

---

[1] See above, p. 193.   [2] Ar. *Politics* 1321[a]5 ff.
[3] Cf. *X.A.P.* i. 2.   [4] Thuc. iii. 37. 1.   [5] Thuc. ii. 65. 9.

shunned unnecessary adventures abroad and preserved peace at home. Thereby he reassured the farmers, who had every reason to dread war with Sparta, and secured a wider basis of support for his ascendancy. But the development of Athens into the centre of a great empire had produced a shift of population from the countryside to the town. Whereas in the time of Kleisthenes the urban population numbered not more than one-third of the whole citizen-body, by 431 nearly half the Athenians lived in Athens itself or the Piraeus,[1] and as the seat of the government was in Athens the influence exercised by the urban voters in the assembly and the law-courts was far greater than that of the country-folk. They had much less to fear from the renewal of war with Sparta, and they had assimilated only too well the gospel of imperialism as preached by Perikles.

Foreign trade was largely in the hands of the resident aliens, but many of the citizens who lived in Athens and the Piraeus may have profited indirectly from it and favoured its increase. Whatever may have been their motives, the extremer elements in the radical party saw no reason why any halt should be called to the aggrandizement of Athens, and if Perikles refused to further their ambitions they could find other leaders who would. In effect the expansionists were merely pushing Perikles' imperialism to its logical conclusion. His pacifism in the period 445–434 is so much at variance with the rest of his career that it has been suspected as insincere, as an expedient to secure for Athens a breathing-space until she was ready to begin a fresh struggle with Sparta for supremacy in Greece.[2] It may be, however, that after 446 Perikles genuinely believed that a limit must be set to the growth of Athens, and that he was eventually forced to abandon this position by the growing alienation of the extremer members of his own party.

Perikles' difficulties were aggravated by the rise of the demagogues. In a radical democracy the gift of eloquent speech is indispensable to a popular leader, and Perikles himself was the foremost orator of his day. But the Sophists had so elaborated the technique of public speaking that it could be mastered by any man of fair ability who was able to pay their fees. The result was the emergence of a new class of politicians, drawn perhaps at first from the ranks of the rich industrialists,[3] whose influence

---

[1] Ibid. 14. 2. [2] Wade-Gery in *J.H.S.* lii, 1932, 215.
[3] Cf. Wil. i. 129, n. 11 and Busolt, iii. 986 ff., also 1183, n. 3 and 1535, n. 3.

was derived mainly from their oratory. Their background and interests naturally led them to join the expansionist wing of the radical party, and the obvious way to make a name for themselves was to attack Perikles' conduct of affairs. As they had no sense of responsibility they appealed without scruple to the baser passions of the mob. The loud voice and coarse abuse of a Kleon, whose demeanour and gestures on the Bema showed no respect for the old traditions of order and decorum,[1] provided an agreeable novelty for the jaded palates of the speech-tasters in the assembly. But though the demagogues probably joined in, if they did not initiate, the attacks on Perikles' friends,[2] his own position was unshaken as long as the peace endured. Why he decided in 433 and 432 to take steps which inevitably precipitated war with the Peloponnesian League was a riddle to his contemporaries and still is to us, but need not be discussed here. What is certain is that the hardships and disasters incurred in the first two years of the war undermined his power and hastened his fall. The demagogues who thought themselves qualified to take his place merely revealed the incapacity of a radical democracy to conduct a great war when deprived of the guidance of conscientious and far-sighted leaders.

The rule of the demagogues

The chief effect of the Archidamian War on the Athenian democracy was to destroy the unity of the state by sharpening the latent antagonism between the different classes in the citizen-body. At Athens there were no parties in the modern sense, since every citizen could influence policy directly by his vote in the assembly. It is, however, convenient to divide the Athenians at this period into three main sections, oligarchs, moderates, and radicals, who may be regarded as roughly equivalent to the rich, the rural population, and the urban proletariat. This classification was also reflected in the military organization of the state, for the rich served in the cavalry, the freehold farmers as the hoplites, and the Thetes as marines or as rowers in the fleet.

Perikles' strategy had entailed the evacuation of Attica in the

---

[1] *A.P.* 28. 3.

[2] Cf. Diog. Laertius ii. 12 and E. Derenne, *Les Procès d'impiété* (Liège, 1930), 35–36. Kleon certainly joined in the attacks on Perikles in 430; cf. Hermippos in Plut. *Per.* 34. 8.

weeks before and during the Peloponnesian invasions, and the concentration of the population within the fortifications of Athens and Piraeus and the Long Walls which connected the two towns. On military grounds his decision was undeniably sound, for the land forces of Athens alone would have been no match for the army of the Peloponnesian League, and she dared not rely on the contingents of her subjects to supplement them. Nevertheless his strategy had grave consequences, so grave that he should have striven earnestly to preserve peace rather than risk war at such a cost.

The open avowal that Athens could no longer face Sparta on land had the worst possible effect on the morale and discipline of the Athenian army. The cavalry were allowed to skirmish with detached forces of the enemy in attempts to limit the scope of his ravages, but the hoplites were cooped up within the walls during the invasions, and doomed to look on helplessly while their farms were destroyed. It is hardly surprising that when they landed on Sphakteria six years later they were panic-stricken at the prospect of coming to close quarters with the dreaded Spartans.[1] A contemporary says that the hoplites were the worst part of the Athenian forces,[2] and the aristocratic Xenophon contrasted the insubordination of the cavalry and the hoplites with the excellent discipline that prevailed in the fleet.[3]

Much more serious was the fact that the sacrifices caused by the war fell very unequally on the different classes of the community. It would be unfair to say that the Thetes did not suffer at all, and they certainly sustained heavy casualties in the plague, but their material losses were hardly comparable with those inflicted on the rich and the hoplites, who saw their estates and farms ravaged year after year by the enemy.[4] This disparity of sacrifice inevitably widened the breach between the urban and the rural population. For the rich as a class there could never have been any reconciliation with the radical democracy, though some of them might consent to serve the state as generals or hipparchs, and not all were prepared to go to such lengths as the extremists, who did not shrink from plotting the overthrow of the constitution with the aid of a Spartan army.[5]

---

[1] Thuc. iv. 34. 1.   [2] X.A.P. 2. 1.
[3] *Mem.* iii. 5. 18–19.   [4] X.A.P. 2. 14; cf. BS 903.
[5] Thuc. i. 107. 4 and X.A.P. 2. 15.

The farmers, however, had been prepared to tolerate the radical democracy until their losses in the Archidamian War converted them to the desirability of a peace by negotiation. When their hopes were dashed by the opposition of the demagogues, their discontent began to be directed against the régime.

It is true that the damage inflicted on the Attic country-side by enemy action was much less serious in this war than it was to be in the Dekeleian War of 413–404.[1] But Attica had not been ravaged by a foreign enemy since the withdrawal of the Persians in 479, apart from the abortive Spartan invasion of 446, and the exasperation of the country-folk was heightened by the contrast of their lot with that of the urban proletariat. The nervous tension produced by a long and bitter war intensified political discord. To these causes of growing demoralization were added the horrors of the plague. The war and the plague cast their shadows over the bright picture of Athenian democracy painted by Perikles in the Funeral Oration. As Thucydides clearly shows,[2] private morality was undermined by the plague, public morality by the war. The patriotism and solidarity of an earlier age were dead. In such an atmosphere the middle classes felt no obligation of loyalty either to the upstart leaders who now had the ear of the Assembly or to the constitution which had given them their opportunity.

The rise of the demagogues had not brought about any change in the chief executive of the state. Kleon's tenures of the strategia in 425 and after were exceptional, and after his defeat and death at Amphipolis his successors were not minded to repeat the experiment. Normally the board of generals was still composed of men from the same social class as before, but after Perikles' death its members began to lose to the demagogues the decisive voice in the shaping of policy. The demagogue owed his power not to any office he might hold but to the influence he wielded over the people by his oratory. He was not, like the generals, an *ex officio* member of the boulē. By the accident of the lot he might be chosen as an ordinary member in a particular year,[3] and during this year he could use his position to initiate

---

[1] Thuc. vii. 27. 4; cf. 'Kratippos' (Jacoby, *F.G.H.*, no. 66) 12. 3–5.

[2] ii. 53 and iii. 82–83.

[3] As Kleon apparently was in 427/426 (Ar. *Knights* 774 and Wil. i. 129, n. 11). The view of Busolt (end of n. 6 in iii. 994–6), repeated by Kahrstedt in *R.-E.* xi. 714, that Kleon was Hellenotamias in 427/426 and must therefore have been bouleutēs in 428/427, rests on a misdating of *I.G.* i². 297.

motions in the boulē, but he could not hold the position for more than a year at a time or for more than two years in all. This handicap might, however, be circumvented to some extent. The demagogue could usually find someone in the boulē to initiate the measures he favoured, and he could also exploit the Assembly's prerogative to remodel freely the decrees submitted to it by the boulē.

It is true that the power of the chief adviser of the people had always rested primarily not on any office he might hold but on the confidence which the demos felt in his leadership. Yet as long as it had chosen its leaders from the men who held the strategia, it had always been able to hold them accountable in their official capacity for the failure of the policies they had advocated in the ekklesia. But when the favourite of the sovereign people began to be merely its most persuasive orator, who did not necessarily hold any office, he could not technically be called to account for the miscarriage of any scheme which he had persuaded the demos to adopt. Doubtless his opponents would be encouraged to attack him on some trumped-up charge if the collapse of his policy had been sufficiently catastrophic; so the oligarchs during the horrors of the siege that followed the disaster at Aigospotamoi could exploit Kleophon's mounting unpopularity by a prosecution for neglect of his military duties and thereby destroy him.[1] But although Thucydides[2] says that after the calamitous ending of the Sicilian Expedition the people were angry with the orators who had joined in promoting it, we do not hear that any were condemned. Androkles, a leading demagogue in 415, was still in Athens and still prominent in 411.[3]

Moreover it was always easy for the demagogue, when one of his projects failed, to throw the blame on the generals or other officials who had been responsible for its execution. So when the Athenian forces failed to reduce by blockade the Spartans cut off on Sphakteria, Kleon sought to divert the censure of the Assembly from himself to Nikias and the other generals.[4] A year later, when the Greek states in Sicily agreed to a peace sponsored by the Syracusans, the three Athenian generals on the spot concurred. It would have been useless to continue the war in Sicily without allies, and a futile waste of time and money to wait for the authorization of the ekklesia. Nevertheless, on their

---

[1] Lys. xiii. 12 and xxx. 10–11.   [2] viii. 1. 1.
[3] Andok. i. 27 and Thuc. viii. 65. 2.   [4] Thuc. iv. 27. 4–5.

return two of them were banished and the third fined. Presumably they were made the scapegoats when the extravagant hopes of western expansion aroused by the demagogues were disappointed.[1]

This divorce between influence and responsibility was an ominous development, destined to prove one of the principal causes for the decline of Athens.[2] The dangers inherent in the sovereignty of a mass-meeting were intensified when the demos, in the middle of a struggle for its very existence, turned for guidance to leaders who like itself were technically accountable to no other authority. Only men of exceptional gifts could have been trusted not to abuse such power. The demagogues had great financial ability and were less corrupt than their enemies alleged;[3] they were also patriotic after their own fashion. Where they fell lamentably short of the standard set for the popular leader by Perikles was in their lack of his ability $\gamma\nu\tilde{\omega}\nu\alpha\iota$ $\tau\grave{\alpha}$ $\delta\acute{\epsilon}o\nu\tau\alpha$,[4] to discern the proper policy for Athens. They throve on the unhealthy excitement produced by a great war, and posed as the watch-dogs of the people, hot on the scent of plots against the democracy. When the Syracusans were warned in 415 by Hermokrates that the Athenians were about to sail against Sicily with a great armada, the popular leader Athenagoras scouted the report as a trick of oligarchs conspiring to subvert the constitution.[5] Rich men in the states of the Athenian Empire were harried by vexatious charges set on foot by the demagogues,[6] many of whom had started their political career as professional prosecutors.[7] The continuance of the war affected their supporters less than other classes in the state, and proposals to end it could be denounced as sinister intrigues intended to rob the demos of the full fruits of its victories.

Intoxicated by their own eloquence and the plaudits of their adherents, the demagogues lost sight of the realities, and constantly failed to discern the limits of the attainable. In their insistence on the continuance of the war they grotesquely overrated the real power of Athens. As Meyer said,[8] Kleon thought he had beaten the enemy when he had shouted down his opponents in the ekklesia. When the tide of war began to turn in

---

[1] Thuc. iv. 65. 3–4; see above, p. 234, n. 10.
[2] Cf. Walker in *C.A.H.* v. 108–9.   [3] Cf. BS 903, n. 2.
[4] Thuc. ii. 60. 5.   [5] Thuc. vi. 38.   [6] Cf. Ar. *Pax* 635–40.
[7] e.g. Phrynichos; cf. [Lys.] xx. 11–12.   [8] *Forsch.* ii. 350.

favour of Athens, Kleon merely became more extravagant in the terms he sought to extort from the enemy. In 425 he persuaded the people to throw away the best opportunity that occurred during the war to conclude a durable peace with Sparta, an incident which Thucydides rightly made one of the turning-points of his History.[1] When peace was finally signed in 421 after Kleon's death, both sides had been exasperated by the reverses they had sustained during the last four years and were more reluctant to trust each other in future.

Even so the peace might have endured for many years. Kleon's place in the Pnyx had been taken by the lamp-maker Hyperbolos, whom Thucydides dismissed scornfully as 'a rascally fellow'.[2] He was clearly inferior to Kleon in ability, and the stock of the war-party was low. Unfortunately the wealthy Nikias, whose policy gave him a better claim than any other statesman to be regarded as Perikles' political heir,[3] did not possess Perikles' personality or his oratorical gifts. But he enjoyed the respect and confidence of the people, and he might have kept a difficult situation under control had it not been further complicated by the intervention of a new and incalculable factor.

Noble, rich, and handsome, Alkibiades was just over thirty years old at the conclusion of the peace, and therefore qualified to stand for the strategia.[4] His ambition prompted him to aim at a constitutional primacy such as that once enjoyed by Perikles, his arrogance to expect that he could reach it without serving a long political apprenticeship. His good looks and unconventional audacities won him friends in strange quarters, and he knew how to exploit to the full the charm of his youth. He had won distinction as a soldier, and the future was to prove him a brilliant commander who never lost a battle.[5] His diplomatic talents were no less remarkable, and as a negotiator he showed himself a match for the greatest variety of persons and circumstances.[6] Of his oratorical gifts we know nothing in detail, but in combination with the glamour of his personality

---

[1] Cf. F. E. Adcock in *C.A.H.* v. 233–4 and J. H. Finley, *Thucydides*, 193–5.
[2] viii. 73. 3 (a curious echo of Ar. *Knights* 1304); cf. Ar. *Pax* 679–81 and Busolt, iii. 1183–5.
[3] Cf. A. B. West in *C.P.* xix, 1924, 124 ff. and 201 ff. (especially 134–8).
[4] Cf. Hatzfeld, *Alcibiade*, 27–28.
[5] Cf. Thuc. vi. 15. 4 (which I take to refer to the years 411–406).
[6] Like Perikles' ideal Athenian (Thuc. ii. 41. 1).

they were sufficient to hold a crowd spellbound, and like Perikles he could expound a policy clearly and persuasively to the Assembly.

Yet Alkibiades was not the man to fill the gap left by Perikles' death. Although he had many of Perikles' gifts and some which Perikles had never possessed, he was deficient in the strength of character and firmness of purpose which are so prominent in the portrait of Perikles drawn by Thucydides.[1] In many respects his personality recalls that of Philip V of Macedonia. Incredibly fertile in expedients when confronted with an apparently hopeless situation, Alkibiades showed at his best in a tight corner, but when he had to deal with the problem of framing a long-term policy, he lacked Perikles' talent for seeing a situation in all its bearings. The schemes with which his name is chiefly associated, the Argive alliance and the Sicilian Expedition, were showy but unsound. The license and extravagance of his private life were a grave error which a statesman living in a democracy could not afford to commit.[2] Moreover they made such inroads on his property that he became seriously embarrassed for funds, and this handicap in turn reacted on his policies and on his reputation. As for his patriotism, it was of the new-fangled type which was soon to make its appearance in aristocratic Sparta no less than in democratic Athens. Alkibiades, like Lysandros, desired his city to be great, but only if its greatness could be reconciled with and made the instrument of his own ambition.[3]

In the early part of his career Alkibiades had perhaps flirted with the radicals[4] and certainly with the moderates. But Spartan statesmen had repelled his advances and had preferred to negotiate the peace through Nikias whom they knew and trusted.[5] Alkibiades was piqued, but even without this rebuff he must have made common cause with the radicals sooner or later, for he needed an adventurous foreign policy to display his diplomatic skill and a renewal of the war to prove his military abilities. The radicals welcomed a recruit with so many advantages who could hold the strategia, but the demagogues were envious of his brilliance, which quite eclipsed their own mediocrity, and mistrustful of his ultimate designs. After the

[1] Cf. Finley, op. cit. 203.
[2] Thuc. vi. 15. 3–4; cf. Grote, v. 491 (abridged ed. 743).
[3] Cf. Meyer, *G.A.* iv. 630.
[4] So Beloch (*A.P.* 50), partly relying on Ar. *Acharnians* 713–16.
[5] Thuc. v. 43. 2.

failure of Alkibiades' Argive policy Hyperbolos decided to get rid of him, and to this end revived the obsolescent weapon of ostracism, which had been rusting in the political armoury since 443.[1] His move was ingenious, but Alkibiades countered it by proposing to Nikias an alliance against Hyperbolos, who was as a result the victim of the ostracism held early in 417.[2] Plutarch's account of this curious incident,[3] which discredited ostracism for ever, reveals that the followers of Nikias and Alkibiades could be drilled to follow the orders of their leaders in something like the discipline of a modern political party, and that the number of those prepared to obey such orders was considerable enough to decide the issue of the ostracism.

Alkibiades had escaped, but at a heavy cost. The demagogues were exasperated at what they regarded as the betrayal of Hyperbolos, and more than ever determined to eliminate their rival for the leadership of the people.[4] At first fortune seemed to favour Alkibiades. In the winter of 416/415 an appeal from Egesta enabled him to press successfully for a fresh Athenian intervention in Sicily on a big scale. The Sicilian Expedition was linked by various threads with the history of the previous years, but for Alkibiades it was above all a political expedient. He had quarrelled with all parties and was trusted by none; it was now his cue to claim that he stood above all parties for the unity of the whole state.[5] His policy of western expansion was designed to create for him a new following of the young and adventurous in all classes and so cut across the old party alliances.[6]

For the moment he succeeded. Not only the young but many of the older people rallied round him,[7] fascinated by the glamour of this novel and grandiose project. But his triumph was brief. The city was thrown into a fever of excitement and apprehension by the mutilation of the Hermai. The demagogues, full of envy and rancour against Alkibiades and perhaps genuinely apprehensive of what he might do if he returned victorious from Sicily, determined to exploit the crisis for their own ends and remove him for ever from their path.[8] By this reckless manœuvre they deprived the fleet of the one commander who could lead it

---

[1] Plut. *Alk.* 13. 6 says that the initiative came from Hyperbolos.
[2] On the date see below, Note H.   [3] *Nik.* 11. 5.
[4] Cf. Beloch, *A.P.* 61.   [5] Thuc. vi. 89. 6.
[6] Plut. *Nik.* 11. 3; cf. Thuc. vi. 13. 1 and 18. 6.
[7] Ibid. 24. 3.
[8] Ibid. 28. 2; cf. viii. 65. 2.

to victory, and so alienated Alkibiades from his country that
he threw in his lot with her foes.

Thucydides has perhaps exaggerated the effects of this action.
It was a great advantage to the Spartans to have at their disposal full and accurate information about the weaknesses of
Athens, but they naturally mistrusted Alkibiades in view of his
past record and were slow to take his advice.[1] He did, however,
help to persuade them to send to Sicily a Spartan commander,
Gylippos, who with the energetic support of the Corinthians
saved Syracuse from destruction at the eleventh hour. Gylippos
then induced the Syracusans to overhaul and enlarge their fleet.
The large urban population supplied the rowers; skilled Corinthian pilots trained the crews and suggested improvements in
the construction of the ships.[2] These improvements had been
recently tested in the Corinthian Gulf, where they had enabled
a Corinthian squadron to fight a drawn battle with a slightly
larger Athenian force. In the confined waters of the Great
Harbour at Syracuse the new type of ship proved irresistible,
and though the Athenians had been reinforced in July 413 by
a large fleet under Demosthenes, they were overwhelmed in two
great battles. The legend of their invincibility at sea was shattered, and their enemies prepared to consummate their ruin.

The oligarchic revolution of 411

The victory of Syracuse had been achieved by its rowers, with
the result that in less than three years the Syracusans replaced
the moderate democracy under which they had triumphed by
a radical democracy closely modelled on that of their defeated
enemy.[3] Meanwhile the converse had happened in Athens. The
defeat of the 'sailor rabble' had discredited radical democracy
there. All classes had lost heavily in Sicily, but the losses of the
Thetes had been especially severe. Moreover, the Spartans had
been provoked by a futile invasion of Lakonia in 414 to start
a fresh war in Greece, and in the early spring of 413 had established a permanent post in Attika at Dekeleia.[4] The countryside
was systematically ravaged, and the farmers were compelled
to make their home for the duration of the war in the city,
where they were needed to guard the walls against the danger

---

[1] Cf. Hatzfeld, 213–14.   [2] Thuc. vii. 36. 2 (cf. 34. 5) and 39. 2.
[3] Diod. xiii. 34. 6; cf. Ar. *Politics* 1304ª27–29.
[4] Thuc. vii. 18–19. 1; cf. vi. 105. 1–2.

of a surprise attack from Dekeleia.[1] When the naval war flared up on the coast of Ionia in the summer of 412, the Thetes of military age had to serve abroad continuously until the summer of 410 with the fleet, and as the hoplites were now concentrated in the city there was a change in the balance of the groups in the ekklesia. The hoplites, who formed the bulk of the moderate party, had been left leaderless by the death of Nikias, and in their resentment against the existing régime were easily induced to support a revolution.

In the autumn of 413, when the news of the catastrophe in Sicily reached Athens, the first step was taken on the road of constitutional change. A committee of ten probouloi was appointed from men over forty years old,[2] apparently for an unlimited period. Aristotle says in the *Politics*[3] that where probouloi and boulē exist in the same state the probouloi are a check on the boulē, and that as the probouloi are always few in number this check must be oligarchic in tendency. The higher age qualification fixed for these Athenian probouloi and the absence of any time limit for their tenure of office were also oligarchical features.[4] The prytaneis perhaps continued to convene and preside over the ekklesia, but they must have acted under the direction of the probouloi, who were mainly responsible for the drafting of the agenda of both the boulē and the ekklesia.[5] One of the probouloi was the poet Sophokles, now eighty-two years old, and another was Theramenes' father Hagnon, who was probably over sixty.[6] The existence of this committee facilitated the revolution of 411, and its members were not strong enough to resist the pressure of the extreme oligarchs.[7]

The revolution did not actually mature until the situation abroad became more desperate. Before the demagogues lost power they had embroiled Athens with Persia as well as with Sparta by giving support to the rebellion of Amorges in Karia against the Great King.[8] After the Syracusan disaster the Persian satraps in the west of Asia Minor, Tissaphernes and Pharnabazos, made overtures to Sparta for common action.[9] They offered the

---

[1] Ibid. 28. 2.   [2] Thuc. viii. 1. 3 and *A.P.* 29. 2.
[3] 1299b36 ff.   [4] Meyer, *G.A.* iv. 557–8.   [5] Cf. Busolt, iii. 1409, n. 2.
[6] Ar. *Rhetoric* iii. 18. 6 (1419a) and Lys. xii. 65.
[7] Cf. Wil. i. 102, n. 6 and Meyer, *Forsch.* ii. 417–18.   [8] And. iii. 29.
[9] Thuc. viii. 5. 4–6. 1. *The account of Thucydides in Book VIII is the foundation of most of the narrative in the rest of this section.*

subsidies which were indispensable if Sparta was to maintain a large fleet on a war footing throughout the year. So Sparta could at last offer a serious challenge to the naval supremacy of Athens in the Aegean. By using the special reserve of 1,000 talents set aside by Perikles in 431 the Athenians were able to make headway against their foes, but at the end of the campaigning season of 412 their position was still critical and their prospects gloomy. It was in October or November 412[1] that Alkibiades, who had by now quarrelled with the Spartans and taken refuge with Tissaphernes, opened negotiations with some prominent Athenians serving in the Athenian fleet at Samos. He had made a great impression on Tissaphernes and seems to have genuinely believed that he could persuade him to arrange peace between Persia and Athens on terms. So Alkibiades promised his anti-democratic friends that he would secure for Athens peace with Persia in return for the overthrow of the radical democracy.

This proposal has stimulated modern scholars to extravagant speculations[2] but its explanation is simple. Alkibiades knew that the leaders of the radicals, especially Androkles, were inflexibly opposed to his return to Athens, so the present form of government must be replaced by one which would recall him.[3] His offer was accepted with enthusiasm by the conspirators at Samos. They sent a deputation to Athens headed by Peisandros, who with the versatility shown by other Greek politicians in these troubled times, had recently moved from the extreme left to the extreme right.[4] He extorted from the ekklesia its reluctant consent to negotiate with Tissaphernes and Alkibiades, and if necessary to promise that an oligarchy would be set up in Athens. But Alkibiades now found that he had over-estimated his influence with Tissaphernes and that he was unable to fulfil his part of the bargain. He vainly tried to throw the blame for this breakdown on the Athenian negotiators, who went away in a rage. The break between Alkibiades and the oligarchs was complete (February 411).

While Peisandros was in Athens he had got into touch with all the oligarchic clubs and exhorted them to combine for concerted

---

[1] On the chronology see below, Appendix XII, especially p. 363.

[2] e.g. A. Holm, *History of Greece* (E.T.), ii. 487; cf. B. W. Henderson, *The Great War between Athens and Sparta*, 415.   [3] Thuc. viii. 65. 2; cf. 48. 4.

[4] Cf. And. i. 36, also the references given by Busolt in iii. 1291, n. 3 and 1461, n. 1.

action against the democracy.[1] After the fiasco with Alkibiades he and the other oligarchs at Samos decided to persevere with their design. The hope of peace with Persia, by which the people had been induced to consent to an alteration of the constitution, had vanished, and with it any prospect of setting up an oligarchy by agreement. But the enemies of the democracy decided that they had gone too far to draw back. If the people would not give their voluntary consent to the institution of an oligarchy they must be overawed by force. The oligarchic clubs instituted a reign of terror in Athens and brought the boulē and ekklesia under their control. The most prominent of the radicals, including Androkles, were removed by assassination. Meanwhile Peisandros and his friends, still in Samos, converted some three hundred Samian democrats to the oligarchic cause.[2] These Samians agreed to set up an oligarchy in Samos at the crucial moment and so secure for the oligarchs in Athens control over the Athenian fleet based on Samos.

This attack on the unity of the state in the crisis of its struggle for existence was certainly ill advised, but the follies of the radical democracy had so exasperated even its more moderate opponents that they were prepared to run great risks in order to overthrow it. They knew that while the war lasted the safety of the state depended on the fleet, but they expected that the sailors would be cowed for the moment by the double coup to be carried out simultaneously in Athens and in Samos, and that afterwards their attitude would not matter. The opponents of the democracy had changed their foreign policy; disappointed by Persia, they now hoped that their other enemy, Sparta, would be more willing to grant peace to Athens if it was ruled by an oligarchy. From the beginning of their intrigues with Alkibiades the oligarchs had included in their programme the replacement of democracies by oligarchies in all the subject-states of the Empire.[3] The original aims of this policy were to conciliate the upper classes in those states and secure their support for the new oligarchy that was to be set up in Athens, but it could be fitted in with the new plan as a proof that the conversion of the Athenians to oligarchical principles was sincere.

Clear-sighted politicians such as Phrynichos, who had gone over to the oligarchs after their quarrel with his enemy

---

[1] Thuc. viii. 54. 4.   [2] Ibid. 73. 2.
[3] Ibid. 48. 5 and 64.

Alkibiades,[1] realized the fallacy of such reasoning. But until the revolution was consummated it was necessary to produce a policy that could be approved by the moderates, whose co-operation was indispensable in the early stages. The moderates wanted a mild oligarchy that would exclude the Thetes from the ekklesia, but they were not prepared to abandon the Empire. Phrynichos had seen from the start that the establishment of oligarchies in the subject-states would merely facilitate their revolt from Athens,[2] but when he threw in his lot with the oligarchs he probably decided that if Sparta proved unwilling to grant peace on any terms short of the surrender of their empire by the Athenians, even this sacrifice would be worth making to ensure the permanence of the oligarchy.

The moderates seem to have had no recognized leaders at this time; Laches, Nikostratos, Nikias were all dead. They gave their support to the anti-democratic movement, but its real promoters were the extreme oligarchs, whose adherents were mainly supplied by the aristocratic Hippeis. The Athenian nobles had had their country houses destroyed and their estates ravaged in the war. For countless generations their lives had been bound up with the land. Now that they had been uprooted from their ancient setting, they turned their energies to plots against the democracy.[3] Some of their abler members had sat at the feet of the Sophists in order to equip themselves for the political struggle by a training in the weapons provided by the New Learning, oratory and dialectic. Chief of these was the sinister Antiphon, who shunned publicity as far as possible under the democracy but was always ready to place his talents at the disposal of its enemies. With him Thucydides[4] associates as the moving spirits in the revolution the two renegades from the radical party, Peisandros and Phrynichos, and the enigmatic Theramenes, who comes to the front in 411 as a politician without a past.[5] His father Hagnon is probably to be identified with the strategos who had been Perikles' colleague in 430[6] and was now

---

[1] Thuc. viii. 68. 3.   [2] Ibid. 48. 5.

[3] Cf. the admirable sketch by G. Méautis in L'Aristocratie athénienne (Paris, 1927).   [4] viii. 68.

[5] The punctuation and with it the interpretation of Xen. Hell. ii. 3. 30 is doubtful ,but a comma after Ἅγνωνα (as in Marchant's text) would seem to suit better both the facts and Kritias' argument.

[6] The strategos is known to have belonged to the same deme as Theramenes (Steiria); see below, Appendix XI, p. 351.

one of the ten probouloi. Thucydides' whole account[1] implies
that Theramenes was closely associated with the extreme oligarchs and gives no support to the modern view that he was
the accredited leader of the moderates before the revolution
of 411.

Both the extreme and the moderate oligarchs professed that
their objective was the restoration of an older and sounder
form of the democracy.[2] Their favourite slogan was the πάτριος
πολιτεία, the constitution of their ancestors. But where in the
past could they find the realization of their ideal? Their proposal
to exclude the Thetes from the ekklesia was perhaps only a
reversion to what had been the norm under Solon,[3] but they
could not contemplate a genuine restoration of Solon's constitution as a whole, for it would have necessitated first and foremost
a revival of the authority of the Areopagus. A publicist like
Isokrates later might advocate such a revival, but how could
practical politicians propose the transference of supreme power
to a body to which they themselves did not belong? The ideal
of the oligarchs was a Council of Four Hundred which was to
be the real ruler of the state, and they boldly postulated its
existence in the past, though its relation to the Areopagus was
carefully left obscure. As the average Athenian had little
acquaintance with and even less interest in the constitutional
history of the past, it was easy for the oligarchic pamphleteers to
father such a council on Solon,[4] or, better still, to ascribe to his predecessor Drakon a detailed constitution on the required model.

These propagandist fictions incidentally betray the fundamental divergence between the moderates and the extremists.
In Plutarch[5] the first Council of Four Hundred is chosen by
Solon himself, and its members seem to hold office for life, but
in the 'Constitution of Drakon' preserved in the *Athenaion
Politeia*[6] the Council of Four Hundred and One is chosen by lot,
its members hold office for one year only, and no one can serve
on the council for a second term until every member of the body
of full citizens has had his turn. The first version reflects the
ideas of the extremists, the second those of the moderates. Both
desired the limitation of full citizenship to those of hoplite

---

[1] Especially viii. 89. 2–4; cf. Lysias, xii. 65–66.
[2] Cf. Kleitophon's rider in *A.P.* 29. 3; see above, pp. 15 and 130.
[3] See above, p. 98.   [4] *A.P.* 31. 1.
[5] *Solon* 19. 1.   [6] 4. 3.

census and upwards, the ὅπλα παρεχόμενοι, but the moderates intended that they should form a purified ekklesia possessing the final voice on all important questions, and that they should take their turn in regular rotation as members of an annually changing council.[1] In the programme of the extremists real sovereignty was to be vested in the Council of Four Hundred which was to be permanent and irresponsible, while the rest of the qualified citizens must be kept in the background as far as possible.

These differences did not appear clearly at first, for the extremists were careful to conceal their real aims from the moderates. They secured their support by a programme which included the abolition of state pay for all except men in the armed forces and the limitation of citizenship to a body of 5,000 men.[2] The choice of this figure was a brilliant stroke, for it suggested that the number of those privy to the designs of the oligarchs was much larger than it was in reality. Suspicion and uncertainty were heightened by the success of the oligarchs in securing the most unlikely persons as converts to their cause. The younger members of the radical party were absent in Samos with the fleet, and the older men were confused by the propaganda of the oligarchs or intimidated by the terrorism of the clubs.

When Peisandros and his friends returned from Samos in the second half of May 411, they found the ground fully prepared for the final assault on the constitution. An assembly was promptly convened, at which they carried a decree for the appointment of a special commission to be composed of the ten probouloi and twenty other members; these commissioners (ξυγγραφεῖς) were given plenary powers to draft proposals for the reform of the constitution, and were instructed to present them, on a day fixed in the decree, to another meeting of the ekklesia.[3] In this way the conspirators were able to side-track the council and override its customary right to examine beforehand all proposals that were to be admitted to the Assembly; they did not want their plans to become common knowledge until they were ready for the decisive coup.

On the appointed day they arranged that the Assembly should be convened at Kolonos, a mile outside the walls of

---

[1] As on the usual interpretation of *A.P.* 30.   [2] Thuc. viii. 65. 3.
[3] Ibid. 67. 1; on the discrepancies between his account of the revolution and that in the *A.P.* see below, Appendix XII.

Athens. It was necessary to avoid the associations of the usual meeting-place in the Pnyx, and a rendezvous outside the city-walls, exposed to the danger of a sudden attack from the enemy, would ensure the absence of most citizens of the Thetic class;[1] practically all the members of this class between the ages of twenty and forty would be serving with the fleet. Presumably the citizens of the middle and upper classes who attended the meeting at Kolonos took their arms with them.

When the commissioners were asked to present their report, they had no recommendation to make except the abolition of the existing constitutional safeguards contained in the Councillors' Oath and the Graphē Paranomon. Of this fact, stressed by Thucydides,[2] there can be only one explanation; some members of the commission had refused to agree to the positive proposals advocated by the extremists. Naturally the conspirators had concerted their plans to overcome this obstacle, and when the abolition of the safeguards had been duly approved by the assembly at Kolonos they took control of the proceedings. Peisandros now moved that all existing offices should be superseded, that pay for all forms of civilian service should be abolished, and that the old council should be replaced by a new Council of Four Hundred, to be chosen in the following manner: the Assembly was to appoint five proedroi, who were to select one hundred men inclusive of themselves, and of the hundred so chosen each was to co-opt three more. The five proedroi must have been the leaders of the oligarchs and the one hundred men their most trusty supporters, though they may have been selected by the proedroi for the sake of appearances from lists of prokritoi in each of the ten tribes, lists previously compiled by the oligarchs but formally approved by the tribesmen present at Kolonos. Peisandros' final proposal was that the 400 should take over the Council-chamber and govern with plenary powers, and that they should convene the 5,000 when they thought fit.

The extremists had laid their plans carefully and the moderates had no leaders. Even so it is surprising that the proposals of Peisandros should have been accepted by the assembly at Kolonos without opposition. The success of the revolution was largely due to the sedulous preservation by its promoters of the fiction that there was already in being a body of 5,000 supporters. Peisandros spoke of them at Kolonos as *the* 5,000, thereby taking

[1] Cf. Busolt, iii. 1478 and n. 2.   [2] viii. 67. 2; see below, pp. 361 f.

their existence for granted,[1] although by the decree that post-poned their participation in the government to a future date and gave the 400 full discretion to fix that date he safeguarded the oligarchs against any demand for the immediate publication of the list of the 5,000.

Although the supporters of the radical democracy present in Athens had been effectively intimidated, it was obvious that the extremists, once they had shown their hand plainly, could no longer count on the support of the moderates. Hence they could not afford to wait for long after Kolonos before they took the final step. It was perhaps later on the same day as the meeting at Kolonos[2] that the 400, each armed with a concealed dagger, presented themselves to the members of the old boulē in their council chamber and ordered them to withdraw, taking their pay for what remained of their year of office. As the 400 were backed by a special band of 120 young men who had played a prominent part in the previous reign of terror, the former councillors abdicated without making any protest. No signs of opposition appeared elsewhere in the city, and the 400 took over the control of the government. So on 7 June 411[3] the Athenian democracy, after a glorious career of nearly a century since its triumphant establishment by Kleisthenes, was overthrown and replaced by a comparatively narrow oligarchy.

The downfall of the 400 and the rule of the 5,000[4]

In Athens the extremists had carried out their plans without a hitch, but in Samos, where success was almost equally impor-tant to them, their friends failed miserably. The Samian con-spirators, aided by some of the oligarchs in the Athenian armament at Samos, including the general Charminos, achieved the assassination of the Athenian demagogue Hyperbolos who was living in exile at Samos, but the Samian democrats took alarm and appealed to the radicals in the Athenian fleet. Prominent among these were the generals Leon and Diomedon, the trierarch Thrasyboulos, Thrasyllos who was serving as a hoplite, and a certain Chaireas. Hostility to oligarchy was already strong in the fleet, notably in the crew of the state

---

[1] Thuc. viii. 67. 3; cf. Grote, v. 385 (abridged ed. 700).
[2] See below, pp. 359 f. and cf. Meyer, *Forsch.* ii. 424–5.
[3] 14th Thargelion, 412/411; cf. *A.P.* 32. 1.
[4] *The narrative in this section is mainly derived from Thuc. viii. 73–98.*

trireme, the Paralos; it was further stimulated by the leaders of the radicals, who took suitable precautions against the impending revolution in Samos, and when it did occur the oligarchs were easily crushed.

The victorious Samian democrats and their Athenian allies now sent Chaireas on the Paralos to Athens to announce their success. The news of the events at Kolonos had not reached Samos when Chaireas started,[1] but on his arrival he found the 400 already established. He contrived to escape, and on his return inflamed the armament against the oligarchs by a highly coloured denunciation of the iniquities of the new régime. Thrasyboulos and Thrasyllos took advantage of the indignation aroused by Chaireas' report to ensure the predominance of the radicals in the fleet. All its members, including the oligarchic-ally minded, had to take an oath to be loyal to the radical demo-cracy, to continue the war with Sparta, and to refuse to have any dealings with the 400. All generals and trierarchs who had incurred suspicion were deposed and others were appointed. Thrasyboulos and Thrasyllos were among the new generals. Whether Thrasyboulos had previously been on friendly terms with Alkibiades is not known, but he certainly took the lead in urging the fleet to recall him.[2] Despite considerable opposition he persisted in his purpose, and at last Alkibiades was invited to return. On his arrival Alkibiades harangued the Athenians at Samos and was so successful in persuading them of his influence with Tissaphernes that they promptly appointed him general and gave him their whole confidence. So great was his prestige that both on this occasion and on another a few days later he dissuaded them from their impulse to sail forthwith against the Piraeus to put down the oligarchy.

There was indeed a real danger that the extremists among the 400 might betray the city to Sparta. It is possible that when the new Athenian government heard of their failure in Samos they may have promulgated the two documents preserved in the *Athenaion Politeia*, one to regularize their rule, and the other containing a constitution more acceptable to the moderates which was to come into force in the not too distant future.[3] If any such gesture was ever made it produced no impression at Samos. The inflexible hostility of the fleet to the 400 made their

---

[1] Thuc. viii. 74. 1.   [2] Ibid. 81. 1.
[3] See below, Appendix XII, pp. 360 and 373 f.

position desperate from the outset. How could they hope to negotiate a peace with Sparta on tolerable terms when they could offer the Spartans no guarantee that it would be accepted by the fleet? How could they carry on the war if the fleet was hostile? How could they hope to feed the population at home if the new harvest from South Russia should be intercepted by the fleet? Confronted with these difficulties, the extremists decided that the sacrifice of the Empire was preferable to the alternative, surrender to Alkibiades and the fleet, and prepared to betray the Athens–Piraeus fortress to Sparta.

Alkibiades saw the danger. He saw also that he could not meet it by sailing to Attica with the fleet, for he could not force an entry into the fortress from the sea, and in his absence the enemy would have had a free hand in Ionia and the Hellespont. But he had persuaded the sailors to give a hearing to the envoys of the 400, and to these envoys he made the reply that he had no objection to the abolition of pay for civilian service or to the establishment of the 5,000, but that the 400 must go and the old Council of Five Hundred be restored.[1] This message was admirably calculated to produce a split in the ranks of the government at Athens. Some members of the 400, led by Theramenes and Aristokrates the son of Skelias, deserted their former associates; acting upon the hint suggested by Alkibiades they began to clamour for the immediate appointment of the 5,000 and denounced the treasonable schemes of the extremists. At first this propaganda was confined to a few, but after the murder of Phrynichos the dissidents came out into the open and persuaded the hoplites to demolish the fort at Eëtioneia which the extremists were building to facilitate the eventual admission of Spartan ships into the Piraeus. Soon after, when the defeat of a hastily raised Athenian fleet had been followed by the loss of Euboia, the 400 were deposed (September 411); they had ruled for less than four months,[2] but their policy of encouraging oligarchies in the subject-states produced a crop of revolts in the Empire under their successors.[3]

Thucydides affirms that the real motives which caused the dissidents to break away from the oligarchy were disappointed ambition and fear of Alkibiades' power;[4] he does not consider that they may also have been patriotic enough to resent the

---

[1] Thuc. viii. 86. 6–7.   [2] *A.P.* 33. 1; cf. Busolt, iii. 1508, n. 3.
[3] e.g. in Thasos; cf. Thuc. viii. 64. 3–5.   [4] Ibid. 89. 2–4.

treasonable courses of the extremists. In accordance with their programme they proceeded to carry a decree to entrust the government to the 5,000 and another to reaffirm the abolition of pay for civilian services.[1] They could claim that both proposals had been sanctioned in advance by Alkibiades, and they based the new government as broadly as possible by admitting to the 5,000 all who could provide their own equipment as hoplites;[2] an almost contemporary speech tells us that the total number was 9,000.[3] Apart from these few details we have no other certain knowledge of the new constitution, but it may be surmised that as a gesture to Alkibiades and the fleet the Kleisthenic Council of Five Hundred was restored, although for the present its members may have been chosen not by lot but by direct election.[4]

Most of the extremists had made good their escape to Dekeleia, but they were outlawed and their property confiscated.[5] The corpse of Phrynichos was disinterred and cast outside the borders of Attica.[6] Only Antiphon and Archeptolemos remained to stand their trial, thereby causing great embarrassment to Theramenes who would probably have preferred their escape.[7] The last embassy to Sparta was chosen as the ground for the prosecution, and the accused were found guilty of treason and executed, after Antiphon had made the greatest speech of his life on his defence.[8] These proceedings naturally alienated the goodwill of all convinced oligarchs from the new government, and its continuance depended on the tolerance of the fleet. Thucydides gives it high praise as a judicious compromise between oligarchy and radical democracy, and says that it was the best constitution ever enjoyed by Athens in his lifetime.[9] It certainly restored harmonious relations between the city and the fleet and helped to promote the recovery of Athens in the naval war. But while Athens still depended on her ships and rowers for the maintenance of her empire, a constitution which excluded the Thetes from the active

---

[1] Ibid. 97. 1 and *A.P.* 33. 1.
[2] Cf. the parenthesis in Thuc., loc. cit.
[3] [Lys.] xx. 13; see below, pp. 366 f.
[4] Cf. Meyer, *G.A.* iv. 599 and note on p. 600. See below, p. 378.
[5] Thuc. viii. 98. 1; cf. Lykourgos, *Against Leokrates*, 121.
[6] Ibid. 113–15.   [7] Cf. Lys. xii. 67.
[8] Cf. the *Life of Antiphon*, 22–24 (= [Plut.] *Moralia* 833 D–834 B) and Thuc. viii. 68. 2. Fragments of the speech are printed in the Budé edition of Antiphon by L. Gernet (pp. 165–6).   [9] Thuc. viii. 97. 2.

rights of citizenship could only be tolerated as a temporary expedient. In the spring of the next year (April or May 410) the confidence of the seamen was revived by the crushing victory which they gained at Kyzikos under the brilliant leadership of Alkibiades. The enemy fleet was completely destroyed, and within a few weeks (towards the end of June 410) the rule of the 5,000 came to an end.[1] The 'best constitution' had lasted less than ten months, and the old radical democracy was restored.

The radical democracy after the first restoration

Soon after the restoration, in the first prytany of the year 410/409 (July 410) Demophantos carried a decree[2] that all Athenians should testify their allegiance to the democracy by an oath, under the terms of which they were to bind themselves to regard as an enemy anyone who joined in an attempt to overthrow the democracy or held office in any government which superseded the democracy; the oath, which was to be taken by every Athenian before the next Dionysia (spring 409), stated that any enemy of the democracy who had committed one of the above offences could be put to death with impunity and that his slayers were to be deemed free from any taint of blood guilt. This uncompromising oath, perhaps modelled on that sworn earlier by the armament at Samos, proves that the government which imposed it can only have been the old radical democracy, and is sufficient to disprove the view[3] that its restoration was a gradual process, not completed till Alkibiades' return in 407.

Our information on the internal history of the restored democracy is derived mainly from the orators, whose evidence is not always trustworthy.[4] It is, however, certain that the triumph of the radicals was followed by a war of prosecutions, and that leading demagogues were active in the law-courts.[5] The persons against whom these attacks were directed were not merely staunch oligarchs; they included even the more moderate men who had taken part in the revolution of June 411 or had served in any way under the oligarchy. Membership of the 400

---

[1] On the date cf. B. D. Meritt, *Athenian Financial Documents*, 106-9.

[2] And. i. 96-98, dated by the name of the secretary Kleigenes; he recurs in *I.G.* i². 304 (Tod, 83), which shows that the tribe Aiantis held the first prytany in the year 410/409.

[3] Accepted by G. E. Underhill in his edition of Xenophon's *Hell.* 314-16.

[4] Cf. the critical analysis given by Cloché in *Mélanges Octave Navarre* (Toulouse, 1935), 81-94.   [5] Cf. Busolt, iii. 1540-6.

was the favourite charge brought by the prosecutors, and Lysias[1] satirically remarked that if all accused on this charge had been really guilty, the 400 must have numbered more than a thousand. Kritias, who had been closely associated with Theramenes and had in autumn 411 moved the decree for the recall of Alkibiades,[2] was one of the accused. His case received the personal attention of Kleophon himself,[3] the most important of the demagogues after the restoration. Kritias was condemned and withdrew to Thessaly, cherishing in exile an undying enmity against the demos which had banished him.[4]

Many of those convicted were sentenced to pay heavy fines, and if they were unable to pay them out of their property they were entered on the list of state debtors and thereby forfeited their citizen rights.[5] Such forfeiture might be complete or partial. Some, like the soldiers who had remained faithful to the 400 till the end, were forbidden to address the ekklesia or to become members of the boulē. A man might be forbidden to go to Ionia or to the Hellespont, or might not be allowed to enter the Agora at Athens. The number of those who had suffered complete or partial loss of citizen rights grew in a way which alarmed all patriots. Nearly five years after the restoration, Aristophanes[6] appealed to the people to grant pardon for their former errors to the unfortunates who had been 'tripped up by the tricks of Phrynichos', but in vain; nothing but the appalling catastrophe of Aigospotamoi could persuade the Athenians to restore the disfranchised to their citizen rights.[7] Yet the radical prosecutors are alleged to have been so venal that in return for bribes they often allowed the really guilty to escape, while bringing vexatious charges against the innocent, especially if they were wealthy.[8] One rich man, Kriton, made friends with a prominent radical, Archedemos the Blear-eyed, and thereby secured his protection against the other demagogues.[9]

Lysias[10] says that the prosecutors exploited the misfortunes of the state for their own private profit. Even if the charge is false and due to the malice of their enemies, their activities were undeniably a source of great evils to Athens. What she

---

[1] xxx. 7. [2] Plut. *Alk.* 33. 1; cf. Lykourgos, 113.
[3] Ar. *Rhetoric* i. 15. 13 (1375[b]). On Kleophon cf. the article by Swoboda in R.-E. xxi. 792-6. [4] Xen. *Hell.* ii. 3. 15 and 36.
[5] On this paragraph cf. And. i. 73-79. [6] *Frogs* 689.
[7] Xen. *Hell.* ii. 2. 11; cf. And. i. 73 and the text of the decree in 77-79.
[8] Lys. xxv. 25-26, cf. xx. 7. [9] Xen. *Mem.* ii. 9. [10] xxv. 25.

needed above all at this stage was a respite from political agitation. The radical democracy had triumphed and its leaders
could afford to be generous; if they had had any real insight
they ought to have proclaimed an amnesty for all political
offences during the last two years. Instead they preferred to
show to all the world that they had learnt nothing and forgotten
nothing. They carried the intemperance of party strife no less
far than their oligarchic opponents, and like them undermined
the unity of Athens at a time when the energies of all the citizens
should have been concentrated on the struggle against the
external enemies of the state.[1] So they stirred up against the
restored democracy numerous enemies who were powerless for
the moment but waited with the patience of mortal hatred for
their hour to come.

Some reforms were carried in this period. The powers of the
boulē were carefully defined and limited,[2] and Philochoros tells
us[3] that in 410/409 a new regulation was introduced for the seating arrangements in the boulē. His language is obscure, but as
the councillors henceforth had to swear in their oath that they
would observe the new regulation, it must in some way have
been directed against anti-democratic intrigues. Possibly it was
intended to defeat such tactics as those of Thucydides the son of
Melesias, who had disciplined his supporters and made them sit
together in the ekklesia.[4] Syngrapheis seem to have been appointed to draft new laws, and Anagrapheis to make official
copies of these laws and to re-copy the old laws still in force.[5]
Kleophon was at least in two respects like Perikles; he was an
able financier and he did not take bribes.[6] The strain on the
state's resources had been eased by the victory of Kyzikos, and
he was able to introduce the so-called 2-obol payment, probably
a measure of poor relief for those impoverished by the war who
were not already receiving state payment.[7]

Kleophon certainly, and the other demagogues presumably,
had spoken against acceptance of the peace-offer made by the
Spartans after Kyzikos.[8] As they were apparently unwilling to

---

[1] Cf. Busolt, iii. 1542 and de Sanctis, *Storia dei Greci*, ii. 385.

[2] As shown by an inscription of this period, *I.G.* i². 114. See above, p. 153.

[3] Fr. 119 (140 in Jacoby, *F.G.H.* iii B).   [4] See above, p. 256.

[5] *I.G.* i². 115 (Tod, 87), ll. 4 ff. and And. i. 96 (συνέγραψεν). Cf. Busolt, iii.
1538 and BS 910, also Tod, 215 and Underhill, op. cit. 315.

[6] Lys. xix. 48; cf. Busolt, iii. 1535–6 and BS 903, n. 2.

[7] *A.P.* 28. 3; cf. Wil. ii. 212 ff. and Tod, 206–7.   [8] Cf. Diod. xiii. 53. 2.

explore the possibilities of obtaining better terms, they m̲
have set their hopes no lower than the full restoration of the
Empire.[1] Actually they were on the horns of a dilemma, for
whether Athens lost or won the war they would forfeit their
power. If Athens lost the war their ruin was certain, but if she
was to win the war she could only do so if she retained Alkibiades
in supreme command of her forces. The demagogues had always
been jealous of Alkibiades' influence over the people, and now
they were afraid, perhaps not without reason, that if he brought
the war to a triumphant conclusion he might be strong enough
to make himself supreme under a semblance of democratic
forms, as Dionysios was soon to do at Syracuse. This fear might
have proved unfounded in the sequel, for the Athenians did not
usually tend to overrate the services of their great men, and the
very ambiguous reception which they gave to Alkibiades on his
return home in 407[2] showed that his eight years of absence had
not effaced from their minds the bitter memory of the great
misfortunes which he had brought on the state. The demagogues,
dazzled by the successes of the last three years, were too short-
sighted to realize that with the appearance of Lysandros and
the Persian prince Cyrus on the scene the war had taken a
dangerous turn for Athens which made Alkibiades more than
ever indispensable. Thucydides sums up the situation in a few
words:[3] 'the people thought that he was aiming at a tyranny
and set themselves against him. And therefore, although his
talents as a military commander were unrivalled, they entrusted
the administration of the war to others, because they personally
objected to his private habits; and so they speedily shipwrecked
the state.'

The final defeat at Aigospotamoi was so sudden and so complete that the suspicion of treachery came naturally to the
Athenians. In fact the demoralization of the fleet, due to the
irregularity with which the crews were paid and the incompe-
tence of their leaders, is quite sufficient to account for the final
collapse. After such a catastrophe the downfall of the democracy,
whose statesmen were directly responsible for it, was as inevitable as the overthrow of the Third Empire in France after
Sedan and could not possibly have been averted. Kleophon, like

---

[1] Meyer, *G.A.* iv. 610 n. On the policy of the demagogues cf. A. B. West in
C.P. xix, 1924, 124 ff. and 201 ff., also Glotz, *C.G.* 208 (E.T. 177).
[2] Xen. *Hell.* i. 4. 13-19.   [3] vi. 15. 4 (Jowett's translation).

the advisers of James II in 1688,[1] lacked the patriotism to accept
the facts of the situation, for what sort of miracle could save
Athens now? When the city had already begun to suffer from
the effects of the siege and Sparta had offered terms which
under the circumstances were moderate, Kleophon wrecked all
hope of peace, for he persuaded the people to pass a decree
which forbade the discussion of any conditions including a
proviso for the demolition of the Long Walls.[2] Thereby he forfeited any claim to be regarded as a statesman or even as a true
lover of his country. His selfish folly doomed Athens to several
months of useless suffering,[3] and only the far-sighted policy of
the Spartan leaders saved her in the end from the destruction
for which their infuriated allies clamoured.[4] The bankruptcy
of radical democracy under the contemptible Epigoni who had
aspired to wear the mantle of Perikles was apparent to all. It
remained to be seen whether their opponents were better
qualified to rule the state.

[1] Cf. F. C. Turner, *James II* (London, 1948), 418.
[2] Lys. xiii. 8; cf. Aischines ii. 76.
[3] It is unfair to blame Theramenes for this, as Schwahn does (*R.-E.* v A, 2.
2320) following Lys. xiii. 11. He had no choice but to spin out his mission until
the Athenians were brought to their senses by famine (cf. Xen. *Hell.* ii. 2. 16).
[4] Ibid. 19–20; cf. Plut. *Lys.* 15. 3.

XI. THE OLIGARCHIC REVOLUTION OF 404 AND THE SECOND RESTORATION[1]

THE Spartans had not included in the peace treaty any stipulation for the replacement of the Athenian democracy by a moderate or extreme form of oligarchy;[2] the statement in the *Athenaion Politeia* that they insisted on the restoration of a *patrios politeia* seems to be a fabrication traceable to the writers who sought to excuse the part played by Theramenes in the subsequent events.[3] After all that had happened the overthrow of the democracy was inevitable, and Theramenes had presumably given assurances to the Spartans that as soon as the peace was signed steps would be taken to remodel the Athenian constitution and produce a form of government more acceptable to Sparta.

In many respects the situation was more favourable to the opponents of the radical democracy in 404 than it had been in 411. The fleet had been cut down to twelve ships in the final version of the peace treaty;[4] anyhow it had ceased to matter now that the Empire was lost. As a result the Thetes who manned the fleet could no longer claim to exercise a decisive influence on the form of the state; their numbers had been greatly reduced by the execution of the 3,000 Athenian sailors captured at Aigospotamoi[5] and by their losses from starvation during the siege. All that had happened in the history of Athens since her transformation into a great naval power by Themistokles was to be forgotten.

The natural sequel, in a state where democratic traditions had

---

[1] *All references to Xenophon in the notes on this chapter will be to his* Hellenika. On the modern literature see Lenschau's introduction to his long article on οἱ τριάκοντα in *R.-E.* vi A, 2 (1937), 2355–77. Although I agree with him on many points his views on the details of the chronology seem to me impossible.

[2] The silence of Xen. ii. 2. 20 on any such stipulation is confirmed by Plut. *Lys.* 14. 8 (And. iii. 12 is clearly selective).

[3] *A.P.* 35. 3. Diod. xiv. 3. 2 reproduces the same version, but in xiii. 107. 4 agrees fairly closely with Xenophon; cf. Meyer, *G.A.* v. 18. The compromise proposed in BS 911, n. 1 (cf. *C.A.H.* v. 366) is untenable; there is no evidence that the peace was followed by an alliance between Sparta and Athens (Xen. ii. 2. 20 makes the Athenian obligation to supply military aid an integral part of the peace-treaty).

[4] So Xen. ii. 2. 20, Plut. *Lys.* 15. 1 (cf. 14. 8); Diod. xiii. 107. 4 says ten ships.

[5] Plut. *Lys.* 13. 1 (Pausanias ix. 32. 9 gives 4,000).

had such a long and vigorous existence, would have been a revival of the hoplite democracy of Kleisthenes, possibly accompanied by the disfranchisement of the Thetes, as under the rule of the Five Thousand. But it was unlikely that events should be allowed to take their natural course. Democracy, even in this moderate form, was not acceptable to the Spartan conquerors, and their victorious admiral Lysandros was a zealous champion of extreme oligarchy. Moreover, all the Athenian exiles had been restored to Attica under one of the clauses in the treaty;[1] they could claim the special favour of Sparta, as many had fought with her against their fellow citizens, and they came back full of hatred against the democracy and in no mood to tolerate any form of compromise with its adherents.

Theramenes had skilfully kept the door open for negotiations with Sparta when Kleophon's motion had threatened to shut it,[2] and by his patient diplomacy he had achieved for Athens the best terms that could be hoped for after her crushing defeat. When he brought peace back from Sparta he was the leading statesman in Athens. Naturally his position was to some extent affected by the return of the exiles, but there is no reason to believe that he disagreed with them at this stage on the solution of the constitutional problem. Later he was to claim[3] that he had always been opposed to extreme oligarchy as well as extreme democracy, but the claim was hard to reconcile with the part he had played in the first revolution of 411 and was made at a time when the course of events had taken a turn unfavourable to his schemes. Nor can it be urged[4] that the solution which he advocated did at least save Athens from the menace of a Lysandrian dekarchy. The Spartan government allowed Lysandros to set up dekarchies composed of his partisans in the states of the former Athenian Empire, but it is improbable that they would have permitted him to bring Attica itself under the control of his creatures. Moreover, Xenophon's narrative proves that in the early days of the oligarchy Theramenes was in agreement and on friendly terms with Kritias, the chief of the restored exiles.[5]

---

[1] Xen. ii. 2. 20; cf. Plut. *Lys.* 14. 8 and And. iii. 12. Diodoros (xiii. 107. 4) omits this proviso.   [2] Xen. ii. 2. 15–16; cf. Beloch, ii². 1. 427.

[3] Xen. ii. 3. 48; Theramenes' reference a little earlier in the same speech (§ 45) to his part in the overthrow of the democracy in 411 is very disingenuous.

[4] As is done by the editors of the abridged Grote (p. 792).

[5] Xen. ii. 3. 15. On Kritias cf. Meyer, *G.A.* v. 16–17 and Wade-Gery in *C.Q.* xxxix, 1945, 24–26 and 32–33.

After the peace was signed and the blockade was raised the opponents of the radical democracy intensified their activities. An unofficial committee to direct these activities was set up by the extremists; it was composed of five members named Ephoroi in imitation of Sparta.[1] The shape of things to come was so ominous that a number of respectable democrats, led by some of the generals and taxiarchs, formed a conspiracy to save the régime. Lysias is discreetly silent about the methods by which they proposed to attain their end; perhaps they intended to assassinate their most dangerous opponents. The plot was divulged by a traitor Agoratos and the conspirators arrested.[2] But its discovery alarmed the oligarchs and they decided to make haste.

A Peloponnesian garrison was still in the Piraeus,[3] where the ekklesia was convened for the crucial meeting. Lysandros, still engaged on the siege of Samos, came to Piraeus for the occasion.[4] In the meeting Drakontides[5] proposed the appointment of thirty Syngrapheis who should draft a new code of laws (including laws on the constitution) and act in the meantime as the heads of a provisional government.[6] Theramenes spoke in support of this proposal, and in answer to objectors claimed that it had the approval of Lysandros and the Spartans.[7] Finally Lysandros addressed the assembly: he pointed out that the Athenians had violated the terms of the peace by their failure to demolish the Long Walls within the time specified in the treaty, and warned them that they would have to pay the penalty unless they accepted Drakontides' motion. The motion was then carried and the Thirty duly appointed; they were composed of ten men chosen by the 'Ephors', ten nominated by Theramenes, and ten

---

[1] Lys. xii. 43–44; his dating is vague, but the creation of the Ephors must have been after the return of the exiles if Kritias was one of them.

[2] Cf. Meyer, v. 18–19. Details are supplied by Lys. xiii. 13–15 but he seems to have deliberately confused the chronology of these events. Colin, *Xénophon historien*, p. 30, n. 4, has failed to realize this; cf. Beloch, ii². 1. 430, n. 1.

[3] This is the most probable explanation of the reference in Lys. xii. 71 to the presence of a Spartan army; cf. Beloch, iii². 2. 207.

[4] Lys. xii. 71; cf. Appendix XIII.

[5] *A.P.* 34. 3; cf. Lys. xii. 73.

[6] For the powers conferred on the Thirty cf. *A.P.* 35. 1, Diod. xiv. 4. 1, and Xen. ii. 3. 11; see also Appendix XIII, pp. 382 f.

[7] On the parts played by Theramenes and Lysandros in this assembly cf. Lys. xii. 74. The account in Diod. xiv. 3. 5–7 is a more blatant form of the apologia presented by the 'Theramenes-legend', which is implicit in the more insidious version followed in *A.P.* 34. 3.

ostensibly selected 'from those present',[1] who in the sequel showed themselves no less oligarchically minded than the rest.

After ensuring the success of this coup, which placed Athens under the control of a narrow oligarchy bound by gratitude to himself, Lysandros returned to Samos, and the Peloponnesian garrison could now be safely withdrawn from the Piraeus. The existing officials had continued to function after the end of Alexias' year until the constitutional question had been settled, but once the Thirty were installed (July or early August 404) they appointed an archon, Pythodoros,[2] a new Council of Five Hundred,[3] and other officials. They also associated with themselves in their rule a new board of 10, whose special duty was to watch over the population of the Piraeus, suspected by the new rulers for its radical sympathies, and the old board of 11, now manned by their most trusty supporters, who were headed by the brutal Satyros[4] and were supported in their police duties by 300 scourge-bearers.[5] The democratic conspirators, who were still in prison, had been promised a trial in a dikastery of 2,000 members, but the Thirty soon settled their fate. They were brought to trial before the new boulē, and as the voting was open they were condemned and promptly executed.[6] They could hardly have expected any other result when once their plot had been detected.

At first the government of the new rulers was mild.[7] They modified the laws of Solon by the removal of clauses which had given rise to litigation, and they repealed the laws of Ephialtes and Archestratos against the Areopagus;[8] this was mere propaganda, for they had no serious intention of restoring the Areopagus to its old predominance in the state. The most detested of the professional accusers who had been prominent in the

----

[1] Lys. xii. 76. The names of the Thirty in the (interpolated) list of Xen. ii. 3. 2 are given in the official sequence of the ten Kleisthenic tribes, three from each tribe; cf. Lenschau, op. cit. 2363–4.

[2] A.P. 35. 1 is refuted on this point by the interpolation in Xen. iii. 3. 1. On the chronology cf. BS 912, n. 7 and see below, Appendix XIII.

[3] Xen. ii. 3. 11; cf. Lys. xiii. 20. The reference in A.P. 35. 1 to the method of selection of this council is unfortunately corrupt; BS 913, n. 2 suggest that the Thirty were responsible for the prokrisis.

[4] Cf. Xen. ii. 3. 54. Satyros as councillor in 405/404 had been mainly instrumental in procuring Kleophon's condemnation (Lys. xxx. 10).

[5] A.P. 35. 1.   [6] Lys. xiii. 35–37.

[7] A.P. 35. 2, Diod. xiv. 4. 2. Xenophon's account of the early measures of the Thirty (ii. 3. 12) is brief and his approval tepid.

[8] A.P. 35. 2 is our only source for these two measures.

radical democracy were put to death, and their execution was approved by most of the citizens. But Kritias and the most extreme oligarchs did not propose to stop here. They were determined to establish a despotism and to strike from their path all influential citizens who were likely to resist their programme. Realizing that they were not strong enough to achieve their object with their present forces, they applied to Sparta for a garrison, whereupon Kallibios arrived with 700 men, probably at the end of September 404.[1] The upkeep of this force imposed an additional strain on the finances of the Thirty, who were driven to a policy of further executions and confiscations to meet it.[2]

Theramenes had disapproved of the application for the garrison[3] but he was outvoted in the Thirty. From now on he made up his mind to resist the extremists, but the arrival of the garrison had cut the ground from under his feet. The presence of these foreign troops in the city gave the extremists a firm support for their rule, and goes far to explain why this revolution followed a different course from that of the 400. After the troops arrived the extremists began a reign of terror in which several respectable citizens were put to death, in spite of Theramenes' protests.[4] He next complained that the basis of the government was too narrow. Kritias replied by producing a list of 3,000 who were to enjoy full citizen rights including the privilege of trial before the boulē ; all outside this privileged body could be put to death by the Thirty without trial.[5] When Theramenes objected that the privileged were so few that they were outnumbered by the rest, the extremists disarmed the unprivileged by a trick. They now felt absolutely secure, and embarked on a second reign of terror, in which they killed their personal enemies and many others whose wealth aroused their cupidity.

Kritias decided that the time had come to settle with his old ally Theramenes. Thirty of the metics were marked down for destruction, and the extremists proposed that each of the Thirty

---

[1] Xen. ii. 3. 13–14, Diod. xiv. 4. 3–4. *A.P.* 37. 2 supplies the size of the garrison but wrongly dates its arrival after Theramenes' death; see below, Appendix XIV, p. 387, also Meyer, v. 24. For a story (perhaps apocryphal) about Kallibios cf. Plut. *Lys.* 15. 7.   [2] Xen. ii. 3. 21.   [3] Ibid. 42.

[4] The narrative which follows is based mainly on Xenophon; on the sequence of events see below, Appendix XIV.

[5] Expulsion or exclusion from the 3,000 might be followed by enrolment on the 'black list'; see Appendix XIV, p. 388. The ἱππεῖς, apparently distinguished from the 3,000 in Xen. ii. 4. 2 (contrast ii. 4. 9) may have been a cadet corps of young oligarchs under thirty.

should confiscate the property of one of the metics. When Theramenes refused to compromise himself the extremists plotted his ruin. As soon as they had made their preparations Kritias accused Theramenes in the boulē of plotting against the oligarchy, but Theramenes' speech in his defence was so successful that it made a great impression on the councillors. Kritias, however, intimidated them with the threat of armed force, and by a dramatic gesture struck the name of Theramenes off the list of the 3,000. He then proclaimed sentence of death on Theramenes in the name of the Thirty and handed him over to the Eleven for immediate execution.[1] Before his death he displayed a fortitude and sense of humour which extorted the reluctant admiration of the unsympathetic Xenophon. He achieved something of the reputation of a martyr by the constancy he showed in his end, but the reputation was as little merited as that of Charles the First. His justest obituary is contained in the dry remark of Holm:[2] 'it is a pity that his conduct was not more satisfactory in the earlier part of his career.'

The death of Theramenes freed the Thirty from their last restraint. All who were not on the list of the 3,000 were forbidden to enter the city of Athens, and those of them who lived in the country-side were expelled from their farms, so that they could be appropriated by the Thirty and their friends. The dispossessed fled to Piraeus, and from there many made their way to Megara, Thebes, and other places. Alkibiades was now living in the satrapy of Pharnabazos. Although he was no longer at the head of a great fleet as in 411, his daring and resourcefulness were still dreaded by the oligarchs, who did not feel safe so long as he was alive. They applied to Lysandros, who welcomed the excuse to get rid of his old rival.[3] Pharnabazos dared not resist his demand, and Alkibiades was assassinated.

Sparta had instructed her allies not to harbour the Athenian exiles but Thebes and Megara disobeyed.[4] They had been disillusioned by the results of victory and in their revulsion against Sparta were in no humour to help the pro-Spartan government of Athens. Argos[5] and Elis also gave shelter and help to the

---

[1] Xen. ii. 3. 50–51; see Appendix XIV, p. 389.

[2] *History of Greece* (E.T.), ii. 529–30.

[3] Plut. *Alk.* 38. 4–6; cf. Isokrates xvi. 40. On the place of Alkibiades' death (antedated by Hatzfeld, 340–1) in the sequence of events cf. Meyer, v. 25.

[4] Diod. xiv. 6. 1–3 and Justin, v. 9. 4 (the Spartan decree is not mentioned by Xen.); cf. Plut. *Lys.* 27. 5–6 and Deinarchos, i. 25.   [5] Dem. xv. 22.

fugitives. Thrasydaios, leader of the Eleian democracy, was persuaded by his friend Lysias, who had lived as a metic in Piraeus and had had a narrow escape from the emissaries of the Thirty, to support the banished Athenian democrats with a loan of two talents.[1] The most prominent of the exiles went to Thebes. It was the obvious base for an invasion of Attica, and Ismenias, the leader of the anti-Spartan party, was favourable to the cause of the refugees.[2]

Even so the prospects of a successful restoration seemed bleak except on the improbable supposition that Sparta and Lysandros would refrain from intervention or fail to intervene until it was too late. If we recall the evidence for the awe inspired in Greece by Spartan power at this time, the seizure of Phyle, a strong position near the frontier between Attica and Boiotia, by seventy men under Thrasyboulos seems an even more desperate venture than that with which Plutarch[3] compares it, the plot of Melon and Pelopidas against the Theban oligarchy in 379. The first intention of the Thirty, to blockade Phyle, was baffled by an unexpected snowstorm, but they posted some troops about two miles away to keep watch. When Thrasyboulos' men had increased to 700 he surprised this enemy force one day at dawn and routed it. The Thirty then took fright and resolved to prepare a refuge for themselves at Eleusis. They arrested the inhabitants of Eleusis, and next day compelled the 3,000 to pass a motion to put all the prisoners to death.[4]

This was the last of their atrocities, for on the fourth night after this victory Thrasyboulos marched to the Piraeus.[5] As his little army was not strong enough to defend the whole circuit of Piraeus, he concentrated it on the hill of Mounychia. The Thirty promptly led out their forces to attack him, but the natural strength of the position gave a decisive advantage to the defenders. The oligarchs were routed, and among the slain were Kritias himself and Charmides, one of the ten governors of Piraeus and uncle of the philosopher Plato. Discredited by this reverse and discouraged by the loss of Kritias, the Thirty could not maintain their power against the growing opposition in

---

[1] [Plut.] *Moralia* 835 F (= the *Life of Lysias*, c. 7).

[2] Justin, v. 9. 8.   [3] *Pelopidas* 7. 2.

[4] Xen. ii. 4. 8–9; Lysias twice mentions in this connexion the execution of Salaminians (xii. 52 and xiii. 44).

[5] Xen. ii. 4. 13. Piraeus at this time was full of fugitives expelled by the Thirty from the Attic country-side (ibid. 1).

Athens. On the day after the battle they were deposed, but allowed to retire with their supporters to Eleusis.

Under these circumstances it is curious that the Thirty should have been replaced by an even narrower oligarchy, the Ten. But the Ten seem to have been supported throughout the events that followed by a majority of the 3,000 in their resistance to Thrasyboulos and the radical democrats, and as 'the men in the city' had made up their minds to continue the civil war they probably thought that a small executive would be more likely to ensure its vigorous prosecution.[1] If this was their hope they were doomed to disappointment. At first Thrasyboulos was not strong enough to take the offensive, but fresh supplies of men and arms came in steadily; Lysias, who had perhaps been sent by Thrasyboulos on a special mission to those Greek states which were well-disposed to the exiles,[2] raised 300 mercenaries, and himself supplied 2,000 drachmas and 200 shields to the cause.[3] Finally 'the men of Piraeus' were able to bring up siege-engines against the walls of Athens.

During this period the Spartans had taken no action to help their friends in Attica, although their intervention would have been decisive. Even if they disapproved of the overthrow of the Thirty, the government of the Ten must surely from the Spartan point of view have been preferable to the restoration of the radical democracy. Yet even when the Thirty and the Ten, alarmed by Thrasyboulos' progress, both sent envoys to Sparta to ask for aid, the Spartans did not intervene with their land forces.[4] However, Lysandros championed the cause of the Athenian oligarchs and persuaded his own government to lend them 100 talents, with which to raise mercenaries to supplement their armies. He also secured his own appointment as director of the land operations, and, more important still, persuaded the ephors to instruct his brother Libys, who was nauarch for the year 404/403, to blockade Piraeus with a Spartan fleet.[5]

The effects of this blockade were soon felt in Piraeus, but the democrats were saved from ruin by internal dissensions in

[1] The statement in *A.P.* 38. 1 (cf. Lys. xii. 58) that the Ten had been appointed ἐπὶ τὴν τοῦ πολέμου κατάλυσιν is certainly false; cf. P. Cloché, *Restauration*, 76–85 and 120 ff.   [2] Cf. Cloché, 467.

[3] [Plut.] *Moralia* 835 F; for loans raised in this period by the exiles cf. Lys. xxx. 22 and Dem. xx. 149.

[4] Lys. xii. 59 suggests religious motives for the Spartan attitude; for a more plausible view cf. Cloché, op. cit. 195–7.   [5] Xen. ii. 4. 28.

Sparta. A party there, led by King Pausanias, viewed with jealousy and alarm the power and ambitions of Lysandros.[1] This party seems to have disapproved of the excesses into which the new imperialism had led their country, and to have deplored the unpopularity which Sparta had incurred by her support of the extreme oligarchs in Athens and elsewhere.[2] The precise chronology at this point is uncertain; the Spartan year 403/402 may have started in August 403 and with it a new board of ephors, less favourable to Lysandros than those of the previous year,[3] or possibly the growing reaction against him had affected the ephors as well. Whatever the explanation, Pausanias, as we learn from Xenophon,[4] persuaded a majority of the ephors to send him to Attica with an army, the usual levy of the Peloponnesian League.

On his arrival in Attica Pausanias first inspired in 'the men of Piraeus' a wholesome respect for his army and then persuaded them to open negotiations with him and with Sparta. He also got into touch with a party in Athens itself which was favourable to a policy of reconciliation and encouraged them to send representatives to Sparta,[5] but the majority of the 3,000 were still opposed to any compromise with their opponents. The Spartans appointed fifteen[6] commissioners to arrange with Pausanias on the spot the terms of a settlement between the different parties. The commissioners confirmed the separation of Eleusis under its present rulers from Athens, but sanctioned the reunion of the rest of Attica under a single government, which like that of Eleusis was to be bound to Sparta by an alliance.[7] Taking warning from the events of the past year, they made no stipulation about the form of this government, but drafted, possibly with the assistance of leading statesmen in Athens and Piraeus, the terms of a reconciliation between the two parties, and stipulated that as soon as the men of Piraeus returned to Athens all citizens should bind themselves by an oath to observe its provisions.[8]

[1] Ibid. 29.
[2] This motive is indicated in Diod. xiv. 33. 6. The motive given in Justin, v. 10. 7 is less probable (Pausanias . . . misericordia exulis populi permotus).
[3] So Beloch, iii². 2. 210–11.
[4] ii. 4. 29, cf. 36.
[5] Ibid.; cf. Cloché, op. cit. 234–9.
[6] So Xen. ii. 4. 38; *A.P.* 38. 4 gives δέκα which some emend.
[7] *A.P.* 39. 2; cf. Xen. iii. 2. 25.
[8] *A.P.* 38. 4 (followed by Cloché, 243 ff.) distinguishes the εἰρήνη from the

This settlement is variously described in our authorities as the reconciliation, the oaths, the covenant, or 'the oaths and the covenant'.[1] The version in the *Athenaion Politeia*,[2] after detailed clauses on the relations between the inhabitants of the Athenian state and those of Eleusis, ordains a general amnesty for all that had happened, an amnesty which was to apply to everyone except the Thirty, the Ten, the Eleven, and the ten magistrates in Piraeus, and even those excepted were to be included in it if they were willing to submit to the customary inquiry on their conduct in office, but in contrast to the usual procedure it was laid down that the former governors of Piraeus should be examined by a court composed of inhabitants of Piraeus, the other officials by a court composed of citizens with a property qualification. From other sources we learn that the reconciliation also dealt with the thorny problem raised by claims to property after a series of political revolutions.[3] Much property had changed hands during the recent troubles. It was decided that all which had been duly sold was to remain the property of the purchasers, while that which had not been sold should revert to its former owners; there seems also to have been a provision, presumably to cover sales where the price paid had been low, that the original owner could recover his property from the purchaser if he was prepared to offer him the price of its purchase.

Many of the returned exiles, especially those whose property had been confiscated by the state, must have suffered financially by this settlement. Two of the radical leaders, Thrasyboulos and Anytos, are praised by Isokrates[4] for having made no attempt to recover the great wealth of which they had been deprived. Although Thrasyboulos after the triumphant return of the exiles to Athens (October 403) had sternly rebuked the men of the city for the part they had played, he ended his speech with an exhortation to his followers to observe the amnesty faith-

διαλύσεις, but cf. G. Colin, *Xénophon historien*, 85. It is obvious that the oath was a condition imposed by Sparta; cf. Colin, 87.

[1] διαλλαγαί in *I.G.* ii². 10 (Tod, ii. 100), l. 8 and Lys. xiii. 80 (διαλύσεις in *A.P.* 39. 1), ὅρκοι in Xen. ii. 4. 43 (cf. Andok. i. 90), συνθῆκαι in *A.P.* 39. 1, ὅρκοι καὶ συνθῆκαι in Lys. xiii. 88, xxv. 23, &c.

[2] c. 39, discussed in Cloché, 251–77.

[3] Cf. the fragment of Lysias, *Against Hippotherses*, published in *Ox. Pap.* xiii. 48 ff. (no. 1606) and the comments of Reinach in *R.E.G.* xxxii, 1919, 443–50; see also the Budé edition of Lysias by Gernet and Bizos, ii. 227 f.

[4] xviii. 23.

fully.[1] A provisional government of twenty,[2] perhaps composed of ten representatives of the restored exiles and ten of the 3,000,[3] was chosen; it presumably arranged for the appointment of a Council of Five Hundred and the other officials of the old democracy, including a new archon Eukleides, who gave his name to the whole year although not appointed till October.[4] The codification of the laws, which had been dragging on since 410, was resumed,[5] and in them the year of Eukleides was named as the date of a new era, which was also marked by the adoption of the Ionic alphabet for all official documents.[6]

Thrasyboulos was more of a soldier than a politician, and after the restoration the leadership of the state fell mainly to Archinos. The fact that he had been one of the stalwarts of Phyle[7] placed the purity of his democratic sentiments beyond suspicion, and he was able to use his prestige to enforce a strict observance of the amnesty. When one of the returned exiles brought a prosecution contrary to the amnesty, he induced the boulē to convict the man and order his immediate execution;[8] legally the boulē of the democracy had no power to inflict the death penalty, and the precedent set by this case had to be disallowed by later legislation,[9] but for the present this high-handed action intimidated the radical malcontents. Archinos followed it up by a law authorizing any defendant who claimed that the charge against him was a violation of the amnesty to dispute its admissibility by a special plea (paragraphē);[10] thereby the court was compelled to decide this issue first, and if its decision was favourable to the defendant, the original charge was quashed.

By his vigorous defence of the amnesty Archinos did much to reconcile the former members of the 3,000 to the restoration. Soon after the return from Piraeus, when many of them were preparing to migrate to Eleusis, he arbitrarily cut down the

---

[1] Xen. ii. 4. 40–42. On the date (Boedromion 12th) cf. Plut. de gloria Ath. 7 (Moralia 349 F).   [2] And. i. 81.

[3] BS 918; Cloché, 409, doubts the inference.

[4] This follows from Xen. ii. 4. 43; cf. Colin, 87–88. A.P. 41. 1 would imply that Pythodoros was nominally still archon at the time of the restoration; contrast A.P. 39. 1.

[5] See below, Appendix I.   [6] See above, p. 18, n. 1.

[7] Dem. xxiv. 135; cf. Kratippos, fr. 2 (T 2 in Jacoby, F.G.H. ii A, no. 64) in Plut. Moralia 345 E.

[8] A.P. 40. 2.   [9] See above, p. 241.

[10] Isokrates xviii. 2; cf. Cloché, 276. G. M. Calhoun in C.P. xiii, 1918, 169–85 (especially 179 ff.) argues that Archinos' law applied only to civil suits which contravened the amnesty.

time allowed in the covenant for the migration, and by forcing
them to remain in Athens strengthened the moderate element
in the state.[1] In pursuance of the same policy, when Thrasyboulos had carried a measure to confer the citizenship on all who
had fought for the democracy, Archinos attacked the decree as
unconstitutional, because it had never been submitted to the
council, and persuaded the jurors to cancel it.[2] We know of it
only from a hostile source, and it may be doubted whether
Thrasyboulos really proposed to enfranchise slaves as well as
metics. The proposal has been described[3] as a return to the
liberal tradition, set by Kleisthenes in 508, of strengthening the
citizen-body by new blood, while the restrictive tradition of
Perikles was revived by Aristophon, who reaffirmed the law of
451/450 by a statute which declared illegitimate the offspring
of a union between an Athenian man and a foreign woman.[4] This
rule had probably been relaxed during the Peloponnesian War,
and Nikomenes carried a decree, possibly as a rider to Aristophon's law, which limited its application to those born after the
archonship of Eukleides and affirmed that those born earlier
from foreign mothers should be allowed to retain the citizenship.[5]
Economy may have been the reason for the Bill of Theozotides,
which excluded adopted and illegitimate children from the
benefits of public maintenance given to orphans whose fathers
had been killed in war.[6]

It was perhaps the cancellation of Thrasyboulos' decree that
encouraged Phormisios, one of the restored exiles, to propose the
limitation of full citizenship to those who held some form of
landed property.[7] He may have included those who owned a
house,[8] as we are told that only 5,000 citizens would have been
disfranchised by his proposal.[9] It must have been supported by
those who had belonged to the 3,000, and its advocates claimed
that it had the approval of the Spartans. Its fate turned on the

---

[1] *A.P.* 40. 1.

[2] *A.P.* 40. 2, Aischines iii. 195, and *Ox. Pap.* xv. 142 (no. 1800, frr. 6 and 7);
cf. Cloché, 447 ff., also Meyer, *Forsch.* ii. 175–6 and *G.A.* v. 221 (but his dating
of the decree to 401/400 is rightly challenged by Cloché, 449). Beloch, iii². 1. 13,
takes a cynical view of the reasons for the rejection of the decree.

[3] By Cloché (op. cit. 452).   [4] Athenaios 577 B–C.

[5] Cf. the scholion on Aischines i. 39. On these two measures cf. Colin, 97–98
and Cloché, 468.   [6] *Hibeh Pap.* i. 49 ff. (no. 14); cf. Gernet–Bizos, ii. 234–5.

[7] Cf. Dionysios' ὑπόθεσις to Lys. xxxiv, and Cloché, 420 ff.

[8] BS 920, n. 2; cf. Wil. ii. 229 and Meyer, *Forsch.* ii. 177, n. 1.

[9] Dionysios, loc. cit., and Cloché, 430.

votes of the small farmers who had been ejected from their
holdings after the death of Theramenes,[1] and it is to them that
Lysias appeals in the speech he wrote against the bill. As it was
rejected, they must have decided to defend the citizenship of the
artisans and sailors who had been their comrades-in-arms against
the oligarchy. Nothing is recorded of Archinos' attitude towards
it, but it is almost certain that he must have spoken against
a measure which would have been fatal to the restoration of
harmony between the citizens.[2]

Many Spartans must have regretted the failure of Phormisios'
proposal,[3] but their misgivings may have been allayed by the
success with which the restored democracy had been controlled
by its leaders and induced to respect scrupulously the terms of
the covenant and the obligations of its alliance with Sparta.[4]
When Eleusis was incorporated again in the Athenian state a
few years later (401/400) by a mixture of treachery, force, and
persuasion, the Spartans made no protest.[5] Now that the
moderate element in the citizen-body had been strengthened
by the inclusion of the Eleusinians,[6] Archinos brought forward
a decree making tardy recompense to the metics who had
fought for the democracy. Though the stone which contains the
text of his proposal[7] is grievously mutilated, it is probable that
it gave the reward of full citizenship only to those metics who
had served with Thrasyboulos before or during his march on
Piraeus, and that those who joined him later received lesser
privileges;[8] it has been estimated that on this assumption the
number of those who obtained the citizenship under this decree
was less than 200.[9]

Under the wise guidance of Archinos, Anytos, and Thrasyboulos Athens made a steady recovery from the terrible wounds
inflicted on her by foreign wars and civil strife, and the trade of

---

[1] Xen. ii. 4. 1; cf. Cloché, 423–4.

[2] Meyer, *G.A.* v. 216. Cloché is too ready to accept the tainted evidence of
A.P. 34. 3 that Archinos, Anytos, and Phormisios were all Theramenists; this is
refuted by the fact that none of the three appeared among the Thirty although
ten of the Thirty had been nominated by Theramenes (so Meyer, v. 18).

[3] Cloché, 440–4.   [4] Cf. Xen. iii. 2. 25 (401 B.C.).

[5] Xen. ii. 4. 43; *A.P.* 40. 4 supplies the date but no details.

[6] Cf. Colin, 99.

[7] *I.G.* ii². 10 (Tod, ii. 100). The name of the proposer does not appear on the
stone; the assumption that it was Archinos is based on the identification (denied
by Cloché, 463) of this decree with that mentioned by Aischines iii. 187.

[8] See the discussion in Tod, ii. 11–13 and the bibliography on p. 8.

[9] Cf. the authors cited by Tod (ii. 13).

Piraeus rapidly revived.[1] The demos of Athens, purified by the trials through which it had passed, refused to violate the spirit of the amnesty by insistence that all candidates for office should be democrats decidedly preferring radical democracy to any other régime,[2] and freely admitted its former opponents to the council and the magistracies. It was fortunate after the restoration in the leaders in whom it had put its trust, and though some of the spokesmen of the demos in the fourth century were led astray by the mirage of the old imperialism, most of them showed themselves worthy of the people's confidence. Certainly the restored democracy was remarkably successful in its internal affairs, and if it was less successful abroad, that was due largely to circumstances beyond its control.

From one preoccupation its statesmen were free; the constitutional question had been finally settled. Isokrates[3] claimed that after the madness of the Thirty all the Athenians had become more loyal to the democracy than those who had occupied Phyle, and even Plato[4] admitted that the excesses of the oligarchs had caused the former government to appear by comparison as pure gold. The Athenians of the restoration would probably have agreed that the radical democracy was the constitution which divided them least, and as at any rate more tolerable than any other form of government it endured without serious opposition until it was again overthrown by a foreign conqueror.

[1] As shown by the evidence of Andok. i. 133–4.
[2] Lys. xvi. 8. The sentiments expressed by Lysias in xxvi. 9 seem to be approved by Cloché (op. cit. 393–4).
[3] viii. 108.   [4] *Letters*, vii. 324 D.

APPENDIX I

The Revision of the Laws

In the Demosthenic period there were two recognized forms of procedure. One, described by Aischines (iii. 38–39), depended on the initiative of the thesmothetai. It was part of their official duties to examine the laws, presumably with special reference to recent legislation, and if they found any law which was either ἐναντίος ἑτέρῳ νόμῳ or ἄκυρος ἐν τοῖς κυρίοις, or more than one law dealing with the same subject, they had to post up in public the laws to which they objected and had to request the prytaneis to call an assembly; the people then decided on the appointment of nomothetai who voted on the rejection or retention of the laws concerned. This procedure, usually known as the διόρθωσις τῶν νόμων, must have been mainly a matter of form, the removal of discrepancies in the existing laws; possibly it had at one time concerned the thesmothetai alone, and ratification by nomothetai had been added later.

The other procedure, the ἐπιχειροτονία τῶν νόμων, plays a prominent part in Demosthenes' speech against Timokrates (= Dem. xxiv; cf. also xx. 89–92 and 99 and Aischines iii); the substantial authenticity of the documents inserted in that speech was demonstrated by Schoell (*Gesetzgebung*, 83 ff.). In the first law quoted by Demosthenes it is laid down that in the first ekklesia of each year, on Hekatombaion 11th, the people were to have the laws submitted to them by groups, and were to vote on each group whether the laws in it seemed to them adequate or not. If the people voted against some of the existing laws, the prytaneis had to put the appointment of nomothetai at the top of the secular agenda for the last regular meeting of the first prytany. During the interval any citizen who wished to propose a new law must display his proposal in a specified place for general inspection. The Assembly which appointed the nomothetai fixed their terms of reference and their pay, and possibly their number as well. On the occasion discussed by Demosthenes this was fixed at 1,001 (xxiv. 27), which indicates that it varied with the importance of the measures submitted to their judgement; moreover a decree in Andokides (i. 84) speaks of 500 nomothetai (really 501?). The law in Demosthenes (xxiv. 21) says that they had to be chosen from those who had sworn the heliastic oath; they were evidently a section of the heliasts empanelled for this special purpose. Resolutions of the nomothetai are preserved in *I.G.* ii². 140 and 244 (= *S.I.G.* 200 and Michel, 1465) and we have psephismata referring to their activity (*I.G.* ii². 222 and vii. 4254 = *S.I.G.* 226 and 298).

Demosthenes (xx. 89) describes the law which governed new legislation as ὁ παλαιὸς νόμος and indeed attributes it to Solon, but until the close of the fifth century there is no trace of the procedure which it prescribes. New laws to supplement the existing laws could be drafted by special commissions (boards of syngrapheis; see above, p. 242) or by an individual acting on the instructions of the people, or could be simply enacted by the people in the Assembly, voting on proposals submitted to it by the boulē (cf. *X.A.P.* 3. 2); as Perikles is made to say by Xenophon (*Mem.* i. 2. 42), πάντες γὰρ οὗτοι νόμοι εἰσίν, οὓς τὸ πλῆθος συνελθὸν καὶ δοκιμάσαν ἔγραψε. Hence the fourth-century distinction between νόμοι and ψηφίσματα was not yet known. It is doubtful whether any provision was made for revision of the laws in the Periklean democracy; certainly fundamental laws could not be altered without a revolution. The oligarchs in 411 proposed the appointment of syngrapheis with special powers (Thuc. viii. 67. 1; cf. Isokrates vii. 58), and syngrapheis seem to have been appointed after the restoration of the radical democracy in 410 to superintend a general revision of the existing code (Busolt–Swoboda, 910 and n. 2; cf. Tod, 215). Thucydides (viii. 97. 2) says that the moderate democracy which was set up in the autumn of 411 after the overthrow of the 400 appointed νομοθέται, but these were presumably a legislative commission akin to the syngrapheis found before and after them, not the nomothetai of the Demosthenic Age (so Kahrstedt in *Klio*, xxxi, 1938, 9, answering the argument of Meritt in *A.J.Phil.* lvi, 1935, 323; for a non-technical use of νομοθέτης K. compared Xen. *Mem.* i. 2. 31).

The first clear example of the later procedure is found in the decree of Teisamenos, quoted in our texts of Andokides (i. 83–84) in the course of his account of the events in 403/402 following the second restoration of the radical democracy. This decree mentions two kinds of nomothetai: (*a*) a body chosen by the boulē, and (*b*) οἱ νομοθέται οἱ πεντακόσιοι chosen by the δημόται; the latter seem to have been recently chosen as they have not yet taken the oath. Two problems are raised by the decree as it stands in our manuscripts of Andokides: is it a faithful transcript of the original, and what is its relation to the surrounding text?

After the customary reference to the demos (but not the boulē) and the proposer's name, the decree ordains that the Athenians shall πολιτεύεσθαι κατὰ τὰ πάτρια and observe the laws and measures and weights of Solon and also the θεσμοί of Drakon, as in the former time; ὁπόσων δ' ἂν προσδέῃ, οἵδε ἡρημένοι νομοθέται ὑπὸ τῆς βουλῆς ἀναγρά-φοντες ἐν σανίσιν ἐκτιθέντων πρὸς τοὺς ἐπωνύμους σκοπεῖν τῷ βουλομένῳ, καὶ παραδιδόντων ταῖς ἀρχαῖς ἐν τῷδε τῷ μηνί. The word οἵδε is clearly unsatisfactory, and the explanations suggested by Schreiner and Elter (cf. Schreiner, 96) are inadequate. Either we must write οἱ δέ and assume the existence after προσδέῃ of a lacuna of uncertain length, or we must emend οἵδε; we may then adopt one of the sug-gestions which give the size of the legislative commission (either as ten members, reading οἱ δέκα, or as fifty, reading οἱ Ν=πεντήκοντα or οἱ ΔΕ=δεκάκις πέντε) or we may adopt Dobree's suggestion, οἱ ἤδη ᾑρημένοι, and assume that, as the existence of both kinds of nomothetai is presupposed in this decree, their numbers had been already fixed in an earlier decree (in this decree the second board are called 'the 500' as well as 'those chosen by the demotai' from an excess of caution, to distinguish them beyond any doubt from the legislative commission).

The rest of Teisamenos' decree raises further difficulties. Before the νόμοι drawn up by the first board of nomothetai are handed over to the magistrates they must be subjected to a scrutiny by the boulē and the 500 nomothetai; at this stage any private citizen can submit suggestions to the boulē. When the laws are duly set up, the Council of Areopagus is to superintend the observance of the κείμενοι νόμοι by the magistrates. The decree ends with a provision on the publication of the laws: τοὺς δὲ κυρουμένους τῶν νόμων ἀναγράφειν εἰς τὸν τοῖχον, ἵνα περ πρότερον ἀνεγράφησαν, σκοπεῖν τῷ βουλομένῳ. There is an obvious inconsistency between the earlier and the later halves of the decree, since the former seems to be concerned merely with the addition of necessary supplemental legislation to the pre-existing code of Solon and Drakon (which is taken for granted), but the duty of the Areopagus to ensure the observance of the laws by the magistrates manifestly refers to all the laws, and therefore ἐπειδὰν τεθῶσιν οἱ νόμοι must do the same. Moreover, the reference to τοὺς κυρουμένους τῶν νόμων in the last sentence suggests a general revision of the existing laws in which some were expected to be rejected.

Andokides himself asserts (i. 81–82) that a general revision of the laws had been ordered after the second restoration. After mentioning the amnesty he says that the people chose twenty men to look after the state ἕως [ἂν] οἱ νόμοι τεθεῖεν, and decided that for the present (τέως) they would observe the laws of Solon and Drakon. When they had appointed a boulē by lot and had chosen nomothetai, they found that many citizens were liable to prosecution for past offences under the existing laws, and after deliberation voted to examine all the laws, and to write up in the Stoa (i.e. the Stoa Basileios, which must be the locality of the τοῖχος at the end of Teisamenos' decree) only those laws which were approved. He then asks the clerk to read the psephisma, and in our texts the decree of Teisamenos follows. Schreiner (p. 96) followed Droysen's view that the decree was wrongly inserted here by some ancient editor who took it from a collection of decrees; he thought that it was passed at an earlier stage when the necessity for a general revision of the laws had not yet become apparent. This hypothesis is ingenious but does not meet the main difficulty, for as we have seen the decree presupposes the general revision as well as the supplemental legislation.

The epigraphic evidence, unknown when Schreiner wrote (see above, p. 17), points to the conclusion that the general revision in 403 was the continuation and completion of the revision begun in 410; naturally it was resumed after the second restoration. Teisamenos 'the son of Mechanion' is scornfully classed with Nikomachos and other ὑπογραμματεῖς by Lysias (xxx. 28). These were the legal experts on whom the syngrapheis and other legislative commissions relied for advice, and in 403 they would seize the occasion to press for the completion of the revision already begun. Lipsius seems to have assumed a lacuna before ὁπόσων ἂν προσδέῃ, but as Schreiner pointed out (p. 95) the detailed proviso which follows suggests that the procedure had not been mentioned before. Ferguson (in *Classical Studies Presented to E. Capps*, 1936, 146) thinks that the main text of the new edition had been inscribed on the wall of the Stoa Basileios before 404; 'what was feasible in 403 was to supplement it by the measures called for' by recent events. But Ferguson himself has to admit later (pp. 150–1) that although the codifiers had already started work on the regulations for sacrifices before 404 they later scrapped their first draft and drew up the entire calendar afresh. He infers (p. 144) from Lys. xxx. 20–22 that the revision was completed in 401. We may suppose that a large part of the new codification had been completed between 410 and 405 and that the result could be described as 'the laws of Solon and Drakon'; hence ὁπόσων ἂν προσδέῃ might conceivably be held to include any modifications in the unrevised sections of the old code.

Andokides (i. 81) represents the decision at the second restoration to observe the laws of Solon and Drakon as a temporary measure ἕως ἂν οἱ νόμοι τεθεῖεν (ἂν is obviously wrong and was bracketed by Dobree; others emend to αὖ or δή. Stahl's ἕως ἄλλοι νόμοι τεθεῖεν is too violent). But there was no need to overhaul again the laws already revised and published in the Basileios Stoa in the years 410–405. The law of Diokles (Dem. xxiv. 42), probably passed in 403/402 or soon after, affirms the validity of (*a*) the laws passed before 403/402 under the democracy and (*b*) those which had been passed in 403/402 and were ἀναγεγραμμένοι; the first group is presumably identical with the revised laws published between 410 and 405. These facts are obscured by Andokides. He carefully refrains from giving any indication that the revision of 403 was a resumption of that begun in 410, for it was his purpose in this part of his speech to emphasize the break with the past made by the Athenians in the amnesty of 403 (so Schreiner, 92–94). Hence the motive alleged by him (§ 82) for the revision of 403 is false; offences committed before the restoration (with certain exceptions stated in the second law in § 87) were covered by the indemnity. Andokides' prosecutors had claimed that his return was contrary to the decree of Isotimides, which had excluded from the temples all who had been guilty of impiety and had confessed their guilt (Andok. i. 71). This decree, passed in 415 after Andokides had by his disclosures secured his own release from prison (cf. Busolt, *G.G.* iii. 1316) had been the cause of his first exile. Like all legislation prior to the revision of 410–401 it would have been abrogated by the new code unless its provisions had been embodied in a new statute by the codifiers, and even if that had been done Andokides would still have been covered by the amnesty. But in fact his position was vulnerable, as his past record laid him open to the malicious attacks of his enemies. Hence he decided to meet this particular charge by the long survey of recent history in §§ 71–103. Much of it is irrelevant to his case, but it provides a valuable supplement to our knowledge of the internal history of Athens in these years.

Among the enactments carried after the second restoration Andokides mentions a law that no ἄγραφος νόμος was to be recognized as valid; this is connected with the publication of the revised code in the Basileios Stoa (i. 85; wrongly rejected by Schreiner, 103). Kahrstedt (*Klio*, xxxi, 1938, 32) sees in this measure, combined with the publication of the code and the creation of the state archives in the Metroön (above, p. 14) an attempt by the legislative commission of 403 to clear up the prevailing chaos which had facilitated the revolutions of 411 and 404. They presumably inspired another law of this period quoted by Andokides (i. 87) that no decree of boulē or demos should be superior to a νόμος. From now on, in the words of Kahrstedt (op. cit. 16) νόμοι are all the regulations which either (*a*) appeared in the revised code of 410–401 or (*b*) had been approved later by the heliastic νομοθέται under the procedure laid down in Dem. xxiv. 20–23. The latter might be supplementary to the former or might replace an existing νόμος, rescinded at the same time by the nomothetai. All enactments not included in either of the above groups henceforth count as ψηφίσματα.

There is no direct evidence for any revision of the Athenian code earlier than that of 410–401, but Schreiner maintained that there had been more than one such revision before 410. Schoell had already pointed out (op. cit. 88 ff.) that Solon's laws seem to have been grouped not according to their subject but under the magistrate who was concerned with them. From this Schreiner inferred (pp. 40–41) that any fundamental change in the constitution must have necessitated a revision of the laws, and therefore (pp. 47–48) revisions must have been the logical consequence of the reforms carried by Kleisthenes and Ephialtes. But as the post-Solonian codifiers preserved many of Solon's laws (with the necessary modifications and adjustments) and retained his arrangement by assigning these and their own new laws to the appropriate magistracies (p. 49), it was always possible to keep the name of Solon as the author of the Athenian code. Hence any reference to the laws of Solon in the period 450–410 must mean the laws included in the code at the time of its last revision, on the occasion of Ephialtes' reforms in 462 (p. 64). Any enactment of a date later than the last revision must be in the form of a decree and must be cited by the name of its author, and any decree cited in this way must be later than the last codification of the law.

The silence of our ancient sources need not be taken to disprove the hypothesis that Solon's code had undergone at least one revision before 410, but Schreiner's version of this hypothesis is open to grave objections. His view that every change in the constitution necessitated a revision of the whole code of law was no more than an assumption. The statute in Dem. xxiv. 20 gives four groups of laws: (1) βουλευτικοί, (2) κοινοί, (3) concerning the nine archons, (4) concerning other magistracies. If we grant that the classification was made in a post-Solonian revision of the code, it would be possible thereafter to alter the laws in one or both of the first two groups without touching the rest. Schreiner was curiously vague about the date of the last revision before that of 410; sometimes he connected it with Ephialtes' reforms (p. 48), sometimes with the later reforms of Perikles (p. 64).

Although it is true in the period 401–322 that a psephisma cited as the existing law must be later than the last codification, there is nothing to prove that the same criterion is valid for the fifth century, and Schreiner's insistence that it was seems incompatible with his view that there was a fresh codification at some date between 463 and 450. Xenophon (Hell. i. 7. 20) mentions the decree of Kannonos, which has been dated on internal evidence to the time of Kleisthenes (Bonner and Smith, 205–8, cf. Busolt–Swoboda, 884, n. 1) and Andokides (i. 43) cites the rule of Athenian law which forbade the torture of citizens as τὸ ἐπὶ Σκαμανδρίου ψήφισμα; this has usually been translated, and rightly, as 'the decree in the archonship of Skamandrios' (the explanation, given by Schreiner, 64, that Skamandrios was the secretary of the Council of Five Hundred is untenable). If Skamandrios was the archon who gave his name to the year in which the decree was passed, the decree must belong to one of those years between 510 and 480 for which the archon's name has not been preserved, for all the archon-names from 480 to the end of the century are known, and that of Skamandrios is not among them. His archonship may be just after the fall of the tyranny, in 510/509, or a few years later (cf. H. T. Wade-Gery in C.Q. xxvii, 1933, 23 and T. J. Cadoux in J.H.S. lxviii, 1948, 113 and n. 240).

Schreiner himself pointed out (op. cit. 15–16) that in the fifth century new laws could be made by psephismata (see above, p. 300). Whether they were cited as such and by the name of their author only when subsequent to the last codification is uncertain. Perhaps the decree of Skamandrios was exceptional in this respect; it might be

regarded as a palladium of Athenian freedom, and so its date might
have been preserved in popular memory, together with the fact that
it was a later addition to the original code. We must remember that
ἐπὶ Σκαμανδρίου gives the date, not the mover of the decree. The
decree of Kannonos is easier to explain, as it is not necessarily
Kleisthenic; it may be as late as the sixties of the fifth century (cf.
Lipsius, *A.R.* i. 43 and n. 132). Kahrstedt, i. 156, even dates it between
415 and 406. But if it could still be referred to in 406 as 'the decree of
Kannonos', we must either assume that the codifiers who began their
revision in 410 had not yet reached it, or that although already incorporated in the revised code it was still known by the old name. As
Schreiner's position on the fifth-century citation of psephismata is so
insecure, we cannot fairly combine it with Andok. i. 43 to prove that
there had been no revision of Solon's code later than the end of the
tyranny, and consequently none at all, till the revision of 410.

Peisistratos probably added new laws to the Solonian code
(Herakleides certainly credited him with the one for the support of
war invalids, and Theophrastos assigned to him and not to Solon the
νόμος ἀργίας; cf. Plut. *Solon* 31. 3–5 [but see below, p. 308]). Herodotus
says (i. 59. 6) that Peisistratos did not change the existing laws, but
the author of the *Athenaion Politeia* asserts that many of Solon's
laws lapsed from disuse during the tyranny (22. 1). He adds that
Kleisthenes enacted new laws to secure the favour of the masses, but
he was probably thinking mainly of laws modifying the constitution,
and the solitary example which he gives, the ostracism law, throws
doubt on the accuracy of his general statement. A revision of Solon's
code in the time when Kleisthenes was establishing the democracy
(Hdt. vi. 131. 1) is not impossible, but on the whole I prefer to believe
that there had been only one revision of the code between its enactment by Solon and 410, a revision which should be dated either to
479/478 with Linforth (see above, p. 20) or, less probably, in the
decade following the revolution of 462. It is an interesting fact that
the popular tradition at the end of the fifth century (cf. Lys. xxx. 28)
regarded as the outstanding legislators of the past Solon, *Themistokles*, and Perikles.

APPENDIX II

Problems of the pre-Solonian state and of its organization

(a) Drakon's code and the Ephetai

IN the fourth century there were at Athens five courts which dealt
with different types of homicide cases. We have already discussed the
ceremonial jurisdiction of the basileus and the four phylobasileis.

Trials for deliberate murder, wounding, poisoning, and arson were held before the Areopagus. The Palladion court tried cases of involuntary homicide, and of instigation to homicide (βούλευσις); to its competence also belonged all prosecutions for the murder of a slave, a resident alien, or a foreigner. Cases in which the defendant could plead that the homicide was accidental or that it was justifiable were heard in the Delphinion court. Finally, anyone previously exiled for involuntary homicide who during his exile had incurred the charge of wilful murder was tried before the court at Phreatto, which held its sessions in the Piraeus on the seashore; the defendant, who could not set foot on Attica, had to make his defence from a boat moored near the land (*A.P.* 57, §§ 3–4).

It is usually assumed that the jurors in the last three courts were originally the Ephetai, and though the restoration δικάζουσι δ' οἱ λαχόντες ταῦ[τα ἐφέται] in the *A.P.* 57, § 4 is doubtful the assumption may be accepted. The statements of Harpokration and Pollux that the Ephetai also formed the jury in the Prytaneion court may be due to misunderstanding or conjecture; they thought that there must have been a jury in this court, and as it was not the Areopagus it could only have been composed of the Ephetai (cf. Ledl, 305–6).

An inscription of 409/408 (*I.G.* i². 115 = Tod, 87), which contains a copy of a law described as Drakon's, mentions the Ephetai as the jurors in trials for involuntary homicide, and also refers to the Fifty-one. An equation of these with the Ephetai is suggested by line 17 of the inscription as restored from the text of this law preserved in [Dem.] xliii. 57. But Isokrates (xviii. 52–54), referring to a trial in the Palladion court soon after 403 for the murder of a female slave, says that it was heard by 700 dikasts. The usual explanation (e.g. Busolt–Swoboda, 1092 and n. 6) is that the fifty-one Ephetai must have been replaced by dikasts in the Palladion court, and possibly also in those at the Delphinion and at Phreatto, on the revision of the laws in 403. This explanation is open to two objections: if the law had been copied out in 409/408 why was it altered again in the revision of 403 (which was really only a continuation of that begun in 410) and why does the author of Dem. xliii quote the 409/408 version as the contemporary law on the subject? Miss G. Smith has met these difficulties by the suggestion that the change to the later system occurred before the death of Perikles (*C.P.* xix, 1924, 353 ff.; cf. Bonner and Smith, i. 270–5).

Fifty-one was presumably the number of the original Ephetai, as stated by Pollux, viii. 125 (though his ultimate source may only have been *I.G.* i². 115). Before we can decide who they were we must examine what is known of Drakon and his legislation. Ancient writers affirm that he drew up a comprehensive code but that all of it was repealed by Solon except the laws on homicide (*A.P.* 7. 1, Plut.

Solon 17. 1). So the decree of Teisamenos (above, p. 300) ordained that the Athenians should continue to use as before the θεσμοί of Drakon and the νόμοι of Solon (on the significance of these two terms see Jacoby, *Atthis*, 309, n. 64) ; this proves that part of the code in force at Athens before 403 was ascribed to Drakon, and if Solon had repealed the rest of Drakon's laws, that part must have consisted of the homicide laws included in the Athenian code.

This conclusion, however, seems to conflict with the evidence of the inscription already mentioned. It begins with a decree instructing the ἀναγραφεῖς to make a copy of Drakon's law on homicide ; this is followed by the heading πρῶτος ἄξων on a separate line, and then, starting on the next line, the text of the law. Although this text is very defective, enough of it survives to show that it began with the word καί and dealt in the opening clauses with involuntary homicide. These facts have led some to suppose that the provisions of Drakon's code dealing with deliberate homicide had been repealed by Solon (Busolt, *G.G.* ii². 139, n. 1 ; cf. Ledl, 293–6). But Demosthenes (xxiii. 51) definitely attributes to Drakon all the laws quoted earlier in the same speech, which include those on deliberate homicide (cf. Dem. xx. 157–8). Whatever may be the explanation of the inscription, it is clear that the Athenians in the fourth century ascribed all their homicide laws to Drakon, just as they ascribed the rest of their code to Solon (cf. Schreiner, 78–79).

There must have been some historical foundation for this distinction within the Athenian code, and the obvious explanation is that the Athenian laws on homicide really did go back to a pre-Solonian original. If this is admitted, there is no valid reason for doubting the tradition that they were drafted by a single lawgiver called Drakon ; the arguments against his historical existence adduced by Beloch (*G.G.* i². 2. 258 ff.) are arbitrary and unconvincing. The Atthidographers (cf. *A.P.* 4. 1) seem to have dated his legislation to the archonship of Aristaichmos, possibly 621/620 (cf. Jacoby, 308, n. 58, but note the caution on p. 94) ; hence Drakon was not archon when he drew up his code. Pausanias ix. 36. 8 perhaps suggests that he was one of the thesmothetai for the year, but it is more probable that he was given special powers (Jacoby, 94).

Did Drakon undertake a general codification of the laws? Fourth-century writers claim to know of laws of Drakon other than his homicide laws (e.g. Xen. *Oikonomikos* 14. 4 and Ar. *Politics* 1274ᵇ 15) but this alleged knowledge can for the most part be reduced to the single statement that Drakon's laws imposed the death penalty for all offences, including trivial thefts (Plut. *Solon* 17. 2, probably from an Atthis). This cannot be true, as Solon's poems show that before his own legislation enslavement was the legal penalty for debt. Nor is it easy to see on what authority Lysias and others (Busolt, *G.G.* ii².

149, n. 1) affirmed Drakon's authorship of the so-called νόμος ἀργίας, which Herodotus assigned to Solon (ii. 177. 2); its ascription to Peisistratos by Theophrastos may have been pure guesswork (cf. Busolt–Swoboda, 815, n. 1). The fourth-century tradition that Drakon promulgated a general code of great severity might be derived from a popular memory of the severe punishments inflicted by the magistrates in the pre-Solonian period. Linforth (pp. 275–6) argues from a passage in Solon's poems (Diehl, fr. 24, ll. 18–20) that Solon was the first lawgiver to draw up a comprehensive code, and believes that Drakon 'had done nothing but formulate and possibly record in writing the laws relating to bloodshed', but his interpretation of the poem seems forced, and his conclusion is therefore not beyond dispute. Moreover if the words πρῶτος ἄξων in *I.G.* i². 115 (l. 10) are taken from Drakon's own law, his code must have covered more than one axon and therefore must have dealt with other topics as well as homicide.

For our purpose it is sufficient to state that Drakon was an historical figure, a pre-Solonian lawgiver who first codified the rules governing procedure in homicide cases. But although the homicide laws in the Athenian code of the fourth century were attributed to him, and although some of their provisions go back to an archaic original, it is impossible to believe that they had not been modified, at least in details, since Drakon's time. The application of the word δικάζειν to the jurors in the law quoted by Dem. xxiii. 22 is later than its use to describe the part played by the president of the court, as in *I.G.* i². 115, 11–12 and the amnesty law in Plut. *Solon* 19. 4 (cf. Busolt–Swoboda, 793, n. 1 and the end of the long note on pp. 811–13).

Schreiner, therefore, contended (pp. 79 ff.) that Drakon's homicide laws, after their incorporation by Solon in his legislation, shared the vicissitudes of the Solonian code and were modified like Solon's own laws in subsequent revisions of the code. He then proceeded to explain the peculiarities of *I.G.* i². 115 on this assumption: when the code was revised in 410–401 the provisions of the law on involuntary homicide must have been altered, and on that account a copy of this (altered) part of the homicide laws was set up outside the Stoa Basileios. Schreiner believed that copies on stone of all the homicide laws had previously stood there on two stelai, and that the stone containing the provisions on deliberate homicide was not recopied because that part of the code had not been altered in the revision (op. cit. 88 ff.).

Plutarch (*Solon* 19. 3), discussing the origin of the Areopagus, says that Drakon in his homicide laws nowhere mentions the Areopagus but always speaks of the Ephetai. On what version of Drakon's laws is this assertion based? Clearly it cannot be derived from the fourth-century code, for the law on deliberate homicide quoted by Demosthenes and attributed by him to Drakon (xxiii. 22, cf. 51) prescribes trial by 'the council on the Areopagus'. One solution is that Plutarch's authority was using the inscription of 409/408 and assumed that the law of Drakon preserved on it represented the whole of his homicide legislation, but we have already noted the objections to any such solution (see above, p. 307). Schreiner suggested (p. 91) that the pronouncement in Plutarch was ultimately derived from a collection of the old laws of Drakon accessible to Alexandrian scholars.

Schreiner did not follow up the implications of his suggestion, but Kahrstedt, who holds the same view as Schreiner on Plutarch's source, has used it to revive the old theory that the Ephetai formed the council of the aristocratic state (*Klio*, xxx, 1937, 10–33). I have argued above (p. 80) that Plutarch's evidence, even if sound, would merely prove that the Areopagus had as such no judicial functions in the period between Drakon and Solon. This argument, though technically correct, is not in fact decisive. If it could be proved that the Ephetai alone were the jurors in homicide trials during the period, the case for their identification with the council would certainly be strengthened. Kahrstedt adduces in confirmation the evidence of Pollux, viii. 125 : ἐφέται τὸν μὲν ἀριθμὸν εἰς καὶ πεντή-κοντα, Δράκων δ' αὐτοὺς κατέστησεν ἀριστίνδην αἱρεθέντας. ἐδίκαζον δὲ τοῖς ἐφ' αἵματι διωκομένοις ἐν τοῖς πέντε δικαστηρίοις. Σόλων δ' αὐτοῖς προσκατέστησε τὸν ἐξ Ἀρείου πάγου βουλήν. But the assertion in this passage that the Ephetai sat in all the five homicide courts cannot be accepted. As Ledl pointed out (p. 304) Aristotle would never have concluded that the Areopagus was pre-Solonian if he had known that the Ephetai tried homicide cases on the hill of Areopagus before Solon. The amnesty law quoted by Plutarch (*Solon* 19. 4) proves that the Ephetai did not sit in the Prytaneion court during the period immediately preceding the passing of the law, and this period must be that between Drakon and Solon for those who accept, as Kahr-stedt does, the Solonian authorship of the amnesty law. Kahrstedt is therefore driven to suggest that the Ephetai must have sat in the Prytaneion court earlier, but how could Pollux or anyone else, even in the fourth century, have discovered a function of the Ephetai which they had already lost in the pre-Solonian period? The state-ment of Pollux may represent the conjecture of a scholar based on the same elements as those contained in the discussion reproduced by Plutarch (*Solon* 19), as Ledl suggests (p. 306).

The assumption of Schreiner and Kahrstedt that the original text of Drakon's laws was preserved in the fourth century is improbable (cf. Ledl, 289–90). After the comprehensive codification of the laws by Solon there was no reason, practical or sentimental, for preserving the short-lived code of Drakon. And if the homicide laws had been taken over into the new code word for word, why should the

Athenians have troubled to keep the wooden tablets on which Drakon had presumably inscribed them?

Plutarch answers the argument from Drakon's law by adducing the evidence of the amnesty law to show that the Areopagus had been one of the homicide courts in the period before Solon. The validity of this contention depends on the dating of the law (see below, p. 313). Kahrstedt, however, does not question its attribution to Solon, and can only suggest that the name Areopagus may have been adopted by the Ephetai between Drakon and Solon; this is a counsel of despair, for the wording of the amnesty law would be meaningless if the Areopagus and the Ephetai were the same court under different names.

In the law on deliberate homicide as quoted by Demosthenes (xxiii. 22) not only the word δικάζειν but the addition of τὴν ἐν Ἀρείῳ πάγῳ to qualify βουλήν must be post-Drakonian; there would be no need for the addition at a time when the Areopagus was the only council in Athens. But Plutarch's statement that Drakon never mentions the Areopagites by name cannot be explained by the suggestion that the copy of Drakon's homicide laws consulted by Plutarch's source referred merely to τὴν βουλήν, as Plutarch continues (Solon 19. 3) ἀλλὰ τοῖς ἐφέταις ἀεὶ διαλέγεσθαι περὶ τῶν φονικῶν. Those who believe that Plutarch's authority had before him a complete copy of Drakon's own laws must suppose that cases of deliberate homicide were tried by the aristocratic council before Drakon, transferred to the Ephetai by Drakon, and restored to the council by Solon (so Gilbert, Greek Constitutional Antiquities, 122 ff.) but the supposition is most improbable (cf. Bonner and Smith, 93). I find equally incredible the explanation that the writer followed by Plutarch had no other evidence for Drakon's homicide legislation than the extant inscription of 409/408 (see above, p. 307). As the Atthidographers accepted the legends that made the Areopagus a homicide court in the monarchical period, it is hard to believe that they denied to it the exercise of this function in the period between Drakon and Solon. Either the discussion in Plutarch is due to the misplaced ingenuity of some Hellenistic scholar or Plutarch himself has misunderstood the problem (cf. Jacoby, 316, n. 137).

The council at Athens in the aristocratic period had probably tried all homicide cases at an earlier stage (for the exercise of criminal jurisdiction by the council in an aristocracy compare the Spartan γερουσία). As the homicide cases tried by the Ephetai later in their three courts were less important than those still reserved for the Areopagus, it is possible that the Ephetai were originally appointed to relieve the Areopagus, which as a council had other duties as well, of some of the burden of jurisdiction. Probably the innovation had been introduced before Drakon's time; the text of his law given in

I.G. i². 115 presupposes the existence of the Ephetai and does not mention the different sites of their courts, apparently because the competence of these had already been defined and was taken for granted by Drakon (cf. Ledl, 332–3). The etymology of their name is obscure; the explanations suggested are numerous and unconvincing (Bonner and Smith, 101 and n. 2). Pollux says that they were appointed ἀριστίνδην. This may be only a guess based on a false reading in [Dem.] xliii. 57 (τούτοις for τούτους in O.C.T., l. 16) but such a body would certainly in the aristocratic state be chosen from the Eupatrids; homicide raised complicated questions of law and religion which could only be dealt with by the experts. Perhaps they were drawn from the older members of the Eupatrid order, but no confidence can be placed in the assertion of the lexicographers that they had to be over fifty years old. After Solon (but not necessarily before Solon) they were presumably chosen from the Areopagus until the law was enacted under which juries in the Ephetic courts were chosen from the dikasts.

(b) *The evidence of the amnesty law ascribed to Solon*

It has long been recognized that the account given by Herodotus (v. 71) of the Kylonian affair was taken over by him, probably in good faith, from informants who had a personal interest in the falsification of the facts (see now Jacoby, *Atthis*, 187 and 368, n. 84) and that the most suspicious feature of their version is the statement that Athens at the time of the affair was governed by οἱ πρυτάνιες τῶν ναυκράρων. Unless there is an error in our manuscripts of Herodotus, an error which must be earlier than Harpokration, this presupposes the existence at Athens in the late seventh century of a *council* of ναύκραροι under the presidency of πρυτάνεις. But the evidence is tainted, and we have already seen (above, p. 81) the objections to Meyer's view that this naukraric council was the counterpart in pre-Solonian Athens of the Homeric γερουσία. Meyer, however, claimed for his view the support of the amnesty law ascribed to Solon, from which he inferred the existence at Athens in Kylon's time of a court, presided over by the basileus and the four phylobasileis, which sat near the Prytaneion and tried those who were accused of insurrection or of attempting to set up a tyranny. There is nothing in the text of the law to indicate that the jurors in this court were identical with the naukraroi, but as some of those who reject Meyer's conclusions have maintained that the court of the basileus and phylobasileis, which was little more than an antiquarian survival in the fourth century, had once possessed a wide jurisdiction (e.g. Busolt–Swoboda, 792) it is necessary to re-examine the law which they cite in support of their view.

The text of the law, as given by Plutarch (*Solon* 19. 4), is as follows:

ἀτίμων ὅσοι ἄτιμοι ἦσαν πρὶν ἢ Σόλωνα ἄρξαι ἐπιτίμους εἶναι, πλὴν ὅσοι
ἐξ Ἀρείου πάγου ἢ ὅσοι ἐκ τῶν ἐφετῶν ἢ ἐκ πρυτανείου καταδικασθέντες
ὑπὸ τῶν βασιλέων ἐπὶ φόνῳ ἢ σφαγαῖσιν ἢ ἐπὶ τυραννίδι ἔφευγον ὅτε ὁ
θεσμὸς ἐφάνη ὅδε. The provisions of the law are repeated with slight
variations in the decree of amnesty proposed by Patrokleides and
accepted by the ekklesia in 405 (quoted by Andok. i. 77–79). Plutarch
in his comments on the law (*Solon* 19. 5) refers to cases tried by
Ἀρεοπαγῖται καὶ ἐφέται καὶ πρυτάνεις. As the last term seems to correspond with the words καταδικασθέντες ὑπὸ τῶν βασιλέων in the text
of the law, Meyer supposed that the phylobasileis were identical with
the Herodotean πρυτάνιες τῶν ναυκράρων. But Plutarch's reference to
the prytaneis is surely no more than a hasty deduction from the name
of the court which enabled him to give a neat summary of the law
(cf. Ledl, 311).

As de Sanctis showed (*Atthis*, 187), there is no need to assume that
the three types of crimes described in the law correspond precisely to
the three courts mentioned, and the Prytaneion court is probably
identical with the ceremonial court composed of the basileus and the
four phylobasileis which continued to sit in the fourth century (*A.P.*
57. 4, Dem. xxiii. 76; cf. Pollux, viii. 90 and 120). As the cases tried by
it included those in which the slayer was unknown, it was necessary
that these undetected homicides should be formally excluded from
the amnesty in order that the state should be technically free
from the guilt incurred by them (this explanation seems to have been
first suggested by H. Gleue, *De homicidarum in Areopago iudicio*,
Göttingen, 1894, p. 13; cf. Ledl, 312–13). The same provision is found
in the decree of Patrokleides (Andok. i. 78) and that context is
decisive for its meaning; a Prytaneion court possessing the powers
attributed to it by Meyer could not have existed as late as 405.

A few words may here be added on the interpretation of the law
preserved in Plutarch. The phrase καταδικασθέντες ὑπὸ τῶν βασιλέων
must be connected with all the preceding words from the second ὅσοι
onwards, as the king presided in all the homicide courts. Some have
seen in the word βασιλέων a reference to the phylobasileis alone (Wil.
A.A. i. 94) or to the phylobasileis and the basileus together. The latter
seems to be the fashionable explanation now (cf. Busolt–Swoboda,
793, n. 1 and Tod, 216) but the plural occurs also in *I.G.* i². 115 (Tod,
87), l. 12, and as there is no other evidence that the phylobasileis were
associated with the basileus in the presidency of the ephetic courts,
I prefer the old view that the plural in this inscription (and in the
amnesty laws quoted by Plutarch and Andokides) means all those
who in the previous years have held the office of basileus, the successive holders of the office. This is the view accepted by de Sanctis
(p. 142 and n. 2), who cites parallels for this use of the plural from
I.G. ii². 1174 and Michel, 998, l. 46; cf. Ledl, 308 and Miss G. Smith (in

C.P. xvi, 1921, 352 f.). In the amnesty law σφαγαί seems to be used of massacres committed in political conflicts, as in Isokrates iv. 114 and xii. 259 (cf. Ledl, 103); probably the council, in addition to its jurisdiction on the Areopagus in homicide cases, also acted as a supreme court for the trial of those responsible for such massacres and of those who had attempted to set up a tyrant.

I have assumed above that the amnesty law in Plutarch is Solonian, but there are some reasons for doubting its authenticity. Not only does the language suggest a post-Solonian date, but ἄτιμος is used in its later sense, in which it denotes a man deprived of the active rights of citizenship, whereas in earlier times it seems to have meant an outlaw, one who could be killed with impunity (this must surely be its meaning in the law quoted in *A.P.* 16. 10; cf. also Kahrstedt, i. 118 ff.). Further, it is a disquieting fact that Patrokleides, in the preamble of his decree, cited as a precedent the decree carried in 481/480 (Andok. i. 77; cf. *A.P.* 22. 8) but said nothing about an earlier Solonian precedent. Plutarch certainly cites the law as the eighth on Solon's thirteenth axon; possibly he or his authority got it from Demetrios of Phaleron, who may have translated the archaic language of the original into the terminology of his own age. The alternative is to suppose that the law was taken from a later revision of Solon's code, and that the reference in it to Solon was an editorial interpolation.

(c) *The name of the phratry in* I.G. *ii². 1237*

The first two of the three decrees contained in this inscription have been translated and discussed by Wade-Gery in *C.Q.* xxv, 1931, 131 ff. His article and the commentary in Dittenberger, *S.I.G.* iii (on no. 921) may be recommended as an adequate introduction to the problems of the inscription. The purpose of this appendix is not to re-examine the two decrees as a whole, but to consider whether the phratry responsible for the decrees was called Demotionidai, as Wilamowitz argued, or Dekeleieis, as Wade-Gery maintains.

Wade-Gery argues that Theodoros, the priest secretary and treasurer of the phratry, is also priest of ὁ τῶν Δεκελειῶν οἶκος. He translates this phrase as 'the Dekeleia Lodge' and regards it as synonymous with the phratry, whose members must have been called Dekeleieis (cf. 1. 64 of the inscription).

The Demotionidai are mentioned four times in the inscription; their νόμος prescribes the rules for the scrutiny of the phrateres, they keep a list of the members of the phratry, they are to hear appeals from candidates for admission against an adverse vote, and failure in such an appeal involves the payment by the appellant of a fine of 1,000 drachmai. It is not stated in ll. 26 ff. who is to hold the scrutiny in future, in other words, what is the body whose adverse decision may be followed by an appeal to the Demotionidai.

On Wade-Gery's view 'the unexpressed subject . . . is the body which votes the decree', and therefore the phratry itself. If appeal is allowed from the phratry to the Demotionidai, the latter cannot be identical with the phratry, as Wilamowitz believed. Wade-Gery concludes that they must have been a small committee of experts, who were the final court of appeal in questions relating to the phratry and expounded its laws; he compares them with the exegetai, and regards their privileged position as a pale reflection of that possessed by the members of the council in the aristocratic state.

Such a survival of privilege at Athens, even within a phratry, as late as 396 is difficult to accept. The crucial contention in Wade-Gery's theory, that the unexpressed subject of the verb in line 29 must be the phratry, cannot be proved. It must be remembered that the two decrees with which this inscription begins are merely supplementary to the nomos of the Demotionidai, and the second decree refers to 'the former decrees' about the introduction of new members; thus the reason why the body voting in line 29 is not mentioned may well be that it had been specified in the nomos or in a previous decree and so everyone knew what it was.

In the second decree, which modifies the first, the appeal is from thiasos to phratry; presumably the appeal to the Demotionidai in lines 30–31 is also from thiasos to phratry. The mover of the first decree had imposed a fine of 1,000 drachmai on the unsuccessful appellant; this was perhaps impracticable, and the second decree (probably proposed in a subsequent meeting, though not long after the first) transferred the responsibility to the members of the same thiasos as the candidate's introducer and made them liable to a fine of 100 drachmai (despite Wade-Gery, 136, n. 4, this must surely mean 100 each). Hence the difference in the two regulations does not prove that the nature of the appeal in the two cases is different.

Wade-Gery really begs the question by his misleading translation of ὁ τῶν Δεκελειῶν οἶκος as 'the Dekeleia Lodge'; what other evidence is there that the Greek term οἶκος was ever used as a synonym of φρατρία? Probably the οἶκος in question was part of an ancient genos whose members occupied a position of such importance within the phratry that their priest was *ex officio* priest of the phratry. The Δεκελειεῖς of line 66 were apparently the members of the deme of Dekeleia; as Wade-Gery admits, 'the deme and the phratry had much the same personnel'.

But the decisive objection to Wade-Gery's hypothesis is the reference to the nomos of the Demotionidai (l. 14). This nomos laid down the rules for the scrutiny of those seeking admission to the phratry. We know that Athenian corporations had the right to legislate for themselves provided that their rules were not in conflict with the laws of the state, but it is obvious that the body which laid

down such rules must have been the whole, therefore the Demotionidai
are the phratry, and so the list of members is kept in their archives.
Wade-Gery says (p. 141): 'The law of the Phratry perhaps still
resides unwritten in their breasts; if not, it resides written in their
keeping.' But there is nothing to show that the nomos in question
was unwritten, and the reference to it in line 14 makes it clear that
the Demotionidai were its authors, not merely its guardians or
exponents, and if they legislate for the phratry they must be identical
with the phrateres. [The above arguments are in the main those
adduced by Kahrstedt, i. 234, n. 1.]

(d) The interpretation of a fragment of Polemon

The scholiast on Sophocles, O.C. 489 (Müller, F.H.G. iii. 131) refers
to the part played in the official worship of the Eumenides by the
Hesychidai. After citing Polemon as his authority he quotes from
Polemon the statement τὸ δὲ τῶν Εὐπατριδῶν γένος οὐ μετέχει τῆς
θυσίας ταύτης. The Hesychidai were clearly a genos, and were so
described in a further passage cited by the scholiast, which mentions
their offerings to their mythical ancestor Hesychos at his shrine near
the entrance to the Acropolis. As the Hesychidai were a genos, it is
natural to assume that the Eupatridai were a genos in the same
sense, and that they were mentioned in this connexion by Polemon
because they were associated with the Hesychidai in the state cult of
the Eumenides, although the conduct of the sacrifice was reserved
for the Hesychidai alone.

Wade-Gery, however, sees in the evidence of Polemon a decisive
proof that non-Eupatrids were included in the genos of the Hesychidai (C.Q. xxv, 1931, 82–85 and 129). His case rests on the postulate
that Eupatridai always means the order, the aristocratic caste, and
that there is no warrant for the existence of a genos of Eupatridai
bearing the same name as the order. If this postulate is granted, then
the only possible meaning for the passage of Polemon already quoted
is 'members of the aristocratic order are excluded from this sacrifice';
hence the conclusion follows that the Hesychidai must have been
composed in part of non-Eupatrid members. Obviously if this was
true of one genos it might be true of all, and Meyer's theory that the
genē were composed exclusively of Eupatrids would be invalidated.

As the fragment of Polemon makes perfectly good sense on the
usual assumption that the Eupatridai specified in it were a genos of
that name, the cogency of Wade-Gery's proof depends on his contention that the word Eupatridai must always mean the caste. No
one doubts that Eupatridai sometimes means the aristocratic order
as a whole, and it is possible that, as Wade-Gery argues, the ἐξηγηταὶ
ἐξ Εὐπατριδῶν mentioned in inscriptions were so called because they
belonged to the order, not to the genos. But it is questionable whether

an Athenian would ever have referred to the order as τὸ τῶν Εὐπατριδῶν γένος; the passage quoted in this sense from the *Life of Andokides* is confused and full of historical errors, and the relevant words do not form part of the citation from Hellanikos. Even if the text is correct, the obvious interpretation seems to be that Andokides belonged to the genos of the Eupatridai but was also connected (perhaps in the female line) with that of the Kerykes. We have no other evidence for the genos of Andokides, but there are strong reasons against the view, still frequently expressed, that he was a member of the genos of the Kerykes—see Wil. *A.A.* ii. 74, n. 5.

Further, the existence of a genos of Eupatridai within the order seems to be supported by a passage in Isokrates (xvi. 25) which describes the ancestry of the younger Alkibiades. ὁ γὰρ πατὴρ πρὸς μὲν ἀνδρῶν ἦν Εὐπατριδῶν, ὧν τὴν εὐγένειαν ἐξ αὐτῆς τῆς ἐπωνυμίας ῥᾴδιον γνῶναι, πρὸς γυναικῶν δ' Ἀλκμεωνιδῶν. It has usually been assumed that in this passage Eupatridai and Alkmaionidai are both names of genē. Wade-Gery believes that Isokrates is mixing his categories, that the Eupatridai are the aristocratic order, and that the Alkmaionidai were not a genos but an oikos, whose members were all descended from Alkmaion the contemporary of Solon. Pausanias, however, says (ii. 18. 9) that they were a genos descended from a much earlier Alkmaion, presumably mythical. It is conceivable that the house descended from the sixth-century Alkmaion was the only branch of the genos to attain distinction later; cf. Ferguson in *Hesperia*, vii, 1938, 43, n. 3.

Isokrates' reference to the Eupatridai seems to have more point if he is speaking of a particular genos called by the same name as the order than if he merely means the order as a whole. Nor can it be proved that Alkibiades in fact belonged to a different genos; his claim to descent from Eurysakes (Plato, *Alkibiades* i. 121) may be explained by the assumption that one of his ancestors took a bride from the genos (perhaps Salaminioi—cf. Wade-Gery, op. cit. 85 and n. 3) which traced its ancestry in the male line to Eurysakes (cf., however, Meyer, *Forsch.* ii. 532, n. 3 for a different explanation).

On these grounds I accept with Toepffer and others the existence of a separate genos of Eupatridai, and believe that they, not the order, are indicated in the relevant fragment of Polemon. I am therefore unable to agree with the conclusions drawn by Wade-Gery from this fragment.

APPENDIX III

The date of Solon's legislation

SOSIKRATES (in Diog. Laertius i. 62) gave Olympiad 46 (596–592) as the date of Solon's ἀκμή and 594/593 as that of his archonship; the

latter date was almost certainly derived from Apollodoros, and therefore ultimately from the official archon-list (cf. Jacoby, *Apollodors
Chronik*, 165 ff. and T. J. Cadoux in *J.H.S.* lxviii, 1948, 93 ff.). But in
the *Athenaion Politeia* (14. 1) Komeas is said to have been archon ἔτει
δευτέρῳ καὶ τριακοστῷ μετὰ τὴν τῶν νόμων θέσιν; the last four words
refer to Solon's legislation, presumably dated to the year of his
archonship. As Plato (*Hippias* i. 285 E) proves that the names of all
the eponymous archons from his time up to Solon were known,
Apollodoros must have been able to fix precisely the year in which
Solon had been archon. Hence the reading of the papyrus of
the *Athenaion Politeia* must be corrected by the alteration of
τετάρτῳ for δευτέρῳ, since Komeas was probably archon in 561/560
(Busolt, *G.G.* ii². 311, n. 2; cf. long discussion in Cadoux, op. cit.
104 ff.); Pomtow's objection to the emendation has been answered
by Cadoux (p. 83, n. 50). Busolt suggested (op. cit. 258, n. 3) that there
were in antiquity two calculations of Solon's archonship, one of
which did not allow for the two years of ἀναρχία in the second decade
of the sixth century, while Beloch tried to solve the supposed difficulty by the hypothesis that Solon remained in office for several
years (*G.G.* i². 2. 165); both these suggestions were untenable (cf.
Cadoux, 95–96; Jacoby, *Atthis*, 346–7, n. 22). Hence the date of
Solon's archonship is securely anchored to the Athenian year
594/593.

Plutarch, however (*Solon*, 14. 3; 16. 3–5), while ascribing the
σεισάχθεια or cancellation of debts to Solon's archonship, believed
that an interval of some duration ensued between the Seisachtheia
and Solon's codification of the laws; in this interval the people, at
first disappointed by the results of the Seisachtheia, learnt to appre-
ciate the benefits that they had received from it, and in consequence
appointed Solon τῆς πολιτείας διορθωτὴν καὶ νομοθέτην. From this
account it has been inferred (by N. G. L. Hammond in *J.H.S.* lx,
1940, 71–83) that although the Seisachtheia and the economic reforms
(including the monetary and other reforms described in *A.P.* 10
and dated there πρὸ τῆς νομοθεσίας) belong to the year of Solon's
archonship, correctly identified with 594/593, the 'constitutional'
legislation of Solon should be ascribed to 592/591, the date given in
A.P. 14. 1. Hammond's thesis has been criticized in a detailed
examination by Cadoux (op. cit. 96–98), whose arguments seem to me
unanswerable. I would certainly agree that most ancient accounts
concur in attributing Solon's achievement to the year of his archonship (so *A.P.* 5. 1; the same view is implied in Plut. *Solon* 14. 3).
Androtion seems to have been used by the third-century writer
Hermippos, one of Plutarch's sources for the life of Solon, but the
separation of the Seisachtheia from the rest of Solon's legislation by
a considerable interval of time is almost certainly a conjecture later

in date than the earlier Atthidographers and possibly due to Hermippos himself.

Hence the Atthidographers were probably right in connecting the Seisachtheia closely with the rest of Solon's legislation. But Hammond has made an important contribution to the subject by his suggestion that Solon need not have been eponymous archon for the year in which he carried his legislation (op. cit. 82). As he points out, the view that Drakon held any of the ordinary offices for the purpose of enacting his code is improbable (see above, p. 307) and 'it is more likely that he held an extraordinary position of which we do not know the title. Similarly, Solon . . . was appointed to some extraordinary office, of which the title is equally unknown to us. If we desire an analogy, the position of Sulla *dictator reipublicae constituendae causa* may afford one.'

It is true that the fourth-century Atthidographers ascribed Solon's legislation to the year of his archonship (cf. διαλλακτὴν καὶ ἄρχοντα in *A.P.* 5. 2) but the ascription may have been a mere conjecture; in their time the details of his appointment had been forgotten, and as they found his name in the official archon-list they naturally assumed that he had carried his laws in his archonship. Possibly the conjecture had already been made by Hellanikos; Plato's words (*Hippias* i. 285 E) might be taken to imply that Solon's archonship was regarded as the beginning of a new era. Jacoby's assertion (*Atthis*, 175) that the information in *A.P.* 5. 2 'definitely appears documentary' is hard to understand, still more so his inference that Solon was described in a note appended to the official archon-list as διαλλακτής in the year of his archonship. Jacoby has presumably realized the fact stated in the following words by Cadoux (op. cit. 97): '*even for historians of the late fifth century B.C. there is not likely to have been any evidence for the date of Solon's reforms, other than the archon-list itself*' (italics mine). This is what Cadoux rightly says when he is arguing against Hammond, but a little further on he speaks of 'a unanimous and reasonable tradition . . . that Solon's economic reforms and the main bulk of his legislation fell in his archonship'. Why 'reasonable'? Drakon had not been chief archon (if archon at all) and even Jacoby admits (*Atthis*, 352, n. 54) that Solon was no ordinary archon. 'Unanimous' significantly ignores Herodotus, who was the most likely person to report the popular tradition if it existed on this point, and simply means that after some intelligent person hit upon the idea (later than the publication of the archon-list which Herodotus had not seen) it was duly parroted by all subsequent writers.

Busolt argued (*G.G.* ii². 258–9, n. 3) that the legislation of Solon must have been carried in his archonship because the amnesty law quoted by Plutarch (*Solon* 19. 4) contains the words πρὶν ἢ Σόλωνα ἄρξαι. But we have already seen (above, p. 313) that the law as quoted by Plutarch cannot be an exact transcript of a Solonian law, and that it is doubtful whether Solon passed an amnesty-law at all. Even if the law in Plutarch was derived from a Solonian original from which the words just quoted were taken over without alteration, the ἀρχή of Solon there mentioned may have been the special appointment in virtue of which he was legislating; the fact that he had held another ἀρχή earlier need not have caused any practical difficulty in the application of the law. Busolt did not call attention to the fact that another 'Solonian' law (Plut. 23. 3) referred to the Isthmian Games, the foundation of which is usually dated to 582; the attempt of Cadoux (op. cit. 98 and n. 140) to deal with this awkward fact suggests that silence may have been the wiser course for those unwilling to accept the obvious possibility (above, p. 313) that this law may not be Solonian at all.

When we have once realized that the connexion between Solon's legislation (including his Seisachtheia) and the year of his archonship is probably an hypothesis and not a fact, we are free to find a more suitable date for the former. The second decade of the sixth century was a period of acute internal conflict in Athens. For the years 590/589 and 586/585 the archon-list contained the entry ἀναρχία; probably an archon was elected in each of these years but the appointments were later ignored as irregular (cf. Xen. Hell. ii. 3. 1 on the archon of 404/403). Finally Damasias, archon for 582/581, continued to hold the archonship throughout 581/580 and the first two months of 580/579, until he was forcibly deposed; on the chronology see Jacoby, Atthis, 351, n. 46 and Cadoux, op. cit. 93–95 and 102–3. During the remaining months of the year 580/579 the chief archonship seems to have been handed over to a commission of ten composed of five εὐπατρίδαι, three ἄγροικοι, and two δημιουργοί, who may have acted jointly as a board or held office in turn, each for one month.

For these events our sole authority is the account in A.P. 13, §§ 1–2, apparently taken from the Atthidographers and perhaps ultimately derived from official records (cf. Jacoby, Atthis, 175); this would explain how the details of the ephemeral compromise of 580 were preserved. Yet the terms of that compromise seem anachronistic; surely Solon had transformed the qualifications for the archonship fourteen years earlier. For those who accept the Atthis date for Solon's legislation the only escape from this impasse is by the assumption that there must have been a reaction against Solon's political reforms in the following decade (cf. Sandys on A.P. 13. 2). So Wade-Gery has suggested (C.Q. xxv, 1931, 79) that the Eupatrids were trying to annul Solon's admission to the archonship of those who were not Eupatrids. He conjectured that the three ἄγροικοι and the two δημιουργοί possessed by inheritance or purchase property in land sufficient to make them members of the Solonian class of

Hippeis, and were thereby qualified under Solon's law to be archons, although the Eupatrids had been agitating to deprive them of their legal rights.

The alternative is to suppose that the compromise of 580 preceded Solon's reform of the constitution, and that it was a revolutionary measure adopted to unite all classes in the defence of order after the usurpation of Damasias; the previous ἀναρχίαι may then have been merely the products of the strife between the various Eupatrid factions. On this view Solon's legislation must be dated to the seventies and as near to 570 as possible in order to suit the indications in Herodotus (cf. T. Case in *C.R.* ii, 1888, 241–2). The statement in Herodotus (ii. 177. 2) that Solon borrowed the νόμος ἀργίας from an Egyptian law of Amasis would date Solon's legislation later than 570, but the law in question was attributed by others to Peisistratos (see above, p. 307), and probably Herodotus was here misled by the tendency of the Athenians to attribute to Solon all the laws of the fifth-century code. Elsewhere Herodotus says of Solon that he made laws for the Athenians at their request and then left Attica for ten years in order that he might not be compelled to alter any of his laws, as the Athenians had sworn to observe them for ten years (i. 29; the sobriety of this account contrasts favourably with the '100 years' of *A.P.* 7. 2). During his travels Solon visited Philokypros the ruler of Soloi in Cyprus, and wrote an elegy on him which is quoted by Plutarch (*Solon* 26. 2–4). The visit and the elegy are mentioned by Herodotus (v. 113. 2) in connexion with the death of Philokypros' son Aristokypros, who was King of Soloi when he was killed at the battle of Cyprian Salamis in 497. Even if we assume that he was about seventy years old at the time of his death and that his father was a young man when Solon was his guest, Solon's travels and consequently his legislation cannot be earlier than the seventies of the sixth century. [Those who date the legislation to 594/593 are driven to reject the tradition about its connexion with his travels (found also in *A.P.* 11. 1); so Cadoux, op. cit. 98 and Jacoby in *J.H.S.* lxiv, 1944, 50, n. 64.]

Further, it is improbable that a period of over thirty years elapsed between Solon's legislation and the acquisition of the tyranny by Peisistratos. Solon admitted in his poems that the masses had expected a redistribution of land and were disappointed by his reforms (*A.P.* 12. 3 = Diehl, fr. 23, ll. 16 ff.). The Seisachtheia apparently did nothing for the farmers who had already alienated their farms to pay their debts. Moreover no provision seems to have been made for the former serfs, the ἐκτήμοροι, who were now freed, or for those who had been ransomed from slavery abroad (on all these points I disagree with the conclusions of W. J. Woodhouse, *Solon The Liberator*). This multitude of landless freemen obviously constituted a grave danger to the stability of the Solonian settlement. Peisistratos was the champion of the poor, and the party which supported him was probably an agrarian party (see above, p. 110). These facts suggest that the poor who rallied round Peisistratos were the same as those who had failed to obtain from Solon the freeholds that they desired. If the inference is sound, the interval between the Seisachtheia and the tyranny cannot have been thirty-three years but may be eleven or twelve. On the traditional chronology the history of the agrarian agitation becomes unintelligible, and it is impossible to explain what happened to it between Solon and Peisistratos.

For these reasons I believe that Solon carried his laws not in his archonship but late in the third decade of the sixth century, and that he received from the people for this purpose special powers under an extraordinary appointment as διαλλακτὴς καὶ θεσμοθέτης ; like Drakon he was not a thesmothetes in the ordinary sense but a lawgiver with plenary powers. He had held the archonship some twenty years or more before, and was now chosen to frame the first complete code of laws for Athens as one of her elder statesmen who was known to be favourable to some measure of reform.

In my fourth chapter I have assumed that some of the families active in politics during the fourth decade of the sixth century had been in alliance with Solon at the time of his legislation ; this assumption is partly connected with my hypothesis about the date of the legislation. But even if it could be proved to have been carried by Solon in his archonship, the proof would not in any way invalidate my contention that Solon must have been supported by a coalition between discontented Eupatrids and landed proprietors who were members of 'new families' excluded from office. The chronological controversy that I have revived does not materially affect what I have said about the antecedents, the content, and the significance of Solon's political reforms ; all that I would claim in favour of the later date is that it throws new light on the political history of Attica in this period and makes the course of events more intelligible.

APPENDIX IV

The method of appointment in the sixth century to the archonship and other magistracies

I HAVE stated in the text that in the aristocratic state the chief magistrates were elected by the popular assembly, and that Solon made no change in the method of their appointment. This is the account given by Aristotle; he says in the *Politics* that Solon took over without alteration from the previous constitution the council and the election of magistrates, and also that under Solon's constitution the people elected the magistrates (1274ᵃ1 ff. and 15 ff.). The Atthis seems to have held that the archons were appointed by popular election in the period between Solon's reforms and the tyranny, as is shown by its reference to the election of Damasias ($A.P.$ 13. 2). Thucydides (vi. 54. 6) says that the tyrants observed the laws previously established, but took care that office should always be held by men of their own party. In the years between the expulsion of Hippias and 487 the archons must have been appointed by direct election, as the chief archonship was held during this period by some of the leading statesmen of the time (Isagoras, Hipparchos son of Charmos, Themistokles, Aristeides). A reform carried in 487 or early in 486 ordained that in future the archons should be chosen by lot from 100 candidates previously elected by the demes (the reading πεντακοσίων in $A.P.$ 22. 5 must be a mistake). This method of appointment was called κλήρωσις ἐκ προκρίτων. Later the prokrisis by the demes was abolished. Instead, the 100 candidates were chosen by lot, 10 from each tribe, and from these 100 candidates the archons were chosen by lot; thus there was a double sortition ($A.P.$ 8. 1).

The evidence cited in the preceding paragraph presents a steady and logical development in the method of appointment to the archonship; popular election, more or less modified in practice during the period of the aristocratic state and again under the rule of the tyrants, appears to continue without a break from the institution of the archonship until the reform of 487/486.

In the *Athenaion Politeia*, however, the law of 487/486 is implied to be merely a revival of a change first introduced by Solon. It lapsed under the tyrants, who allowed many of Solon's laws to become obsolete by disuse, and was not revived when the tyrants were expelled. Hence the archons appointed during the tyranny and in the subsequent years to 487 were directly elected by the people (8. 1, 22. 1 and 5). The author must have believed that direct election was first introduced by Peisistratos, since he holds that in the pre-Solonian period the magistrates were appointed by the Areopagus (8. 2).

This account cannot have been taken from the Atthis; there is no trace of it in Plutarch's *Life of Solon*, which is based on the Atthis, and it is inconsistent with the reference in the Atthis to the election of Damasias. To what extent does it represent a genuine tradition? Some ancient authorities say that sortition was applied to the archonship from an early date (Plut. *Per.* 9. 4, Pausanias iv. 5. 10) but they are speaking of simple κλήρωσις, not κλήρωσις ἐκ προκρίτων, and their statements are simply examples of the common popular tendency to claim an early origin for the institutions of the developed democracy. So Demosthenes asserts (xx. 90) that Solon was responsible not only for the κλήρωσις of the Thesmothetai but also for the double scrutiny to which they were liable in the fourth century, and Herodotus (vi. 109. 2) is under the impression that the polemarch was appointed by lot in 490, which is certainly false. It is true that Isokrates in one passage (vii. 22) regards κλήρωσις ἐκ προκρίτων as a characteristic feature of 'the democracy established by Solon and restored by Kleisthenes', but elsewhere (xii. 145, cf. 130 and 148) he ascribes it to a mythical period of good government which is presumed to have endured from Theseus μέχρι τῆς Σόλωνος μὲν ἡλικίας Πεισιστράτου δὲ δυναστείας. The existence of the second passage (which is ignored by Ehrenberg, *Losung*) obviously discounts the evidence of the first. Probably Isokrates had no warrant for either statement, and merely invented an origin in the remote past for an institution which seemed to him essential to an ideal democracy. Those who follow Isokrates in his ascription of the procedure to the pre-Solonian period are bound to reject on this point the evidence of the *Athenaion Politeia*, the principal authority for its inclusion in the reforms of Solon.

Aristotle in the *Politics* declares that Solon made no change in the αἵρεσις τῶν ἀρχῶν, whereas the author of the *Athenaion Politeia* maintains that he transferred the election from the Areopagus to the tribes; thus there is a fundamental discrepancy between the two accounts. Ehrenberg, who evades this difficulty by the assertion that nothing is known of the method of election in the pre-Solonian period (op. cit. 1469 and 1474), has revived the view of Wilamowitz that αἵρεσις in the *Politics* is opposed not to sortition in general but to pure sortition, and therefore can include κλήρωσις ἐκ προκρίτων (op. cit. 1469 and 1472–3). To refute this amazing doctrine it is sufficient to quote the decisive passage in the *Politics* (1298b8): ἐὰν δ' ἐνίων μὲν αἱρετοὶ ἐνίων δὲ κληρωτοί, καὶ κληρωτοὶ ἢ ἁπλῶς ἢ ἐκ προκρίτων. The divergences between the two accounts cannot be explained away, but they are less surprising if Aristotle was not the author of the *Athenaion Politeia*.

Apart from the dubious testimony of Isokrates the account in the *Athenaion Politeia* stands alone, and we must now examine it more closely. In the crucial passage (c. 8) the author says that under Solon's law each tribe chose ten candidates, that from these forty πρόκριτοι the nine archons were selected by lot, and that the two stages of this procedure were reflected in the double sortition of his own time. He then cites the law still in force for the appointment of the treasurers of Athena, ordaining that they should be chosen by lot from the Pentakosiomedimnoi. As this law is alleged to have remained unchanged since Solon's time (cf. *A.P.* 47. 1), he sees in it a proof that Solon made all magistracies, including the archonship, κληρωτὰς ἐκ τῶν τιμημάτων.

Lehmann-Haupt maintained (*Klio*, vi, 1906, 306 f.) that the law concerning the treasurers was cited only to prove the imposition of a property-qualification by Solon on candidates for office, but the run of the sentence implies that it was cited for the use of κλήρωσις as well. In any case, this passage proves that Solon's law on the appointment of the archons was not available to the author; otherwise he could have proved his point by direct quotation from it, which would have been more convincing than his inference from the law on the treasurers. But that law apparently did not mention κλήρωσις ἐκ προκρίτων. How then did he know that it was the method prescribed by Solon for the appointment of archons? His language suggests that he or his source saw in the double sortition of his own time an anomaly which required explanation, and correctly inferred that it represented an original κλήρωσις ἐκ προκρίτων. But he failed to realize that this original procedure was not earlier than 487, and, possibly under the influence of Isokrates' picture of the primitive democracy, traced its institution back to Solon. In order to account for its disappearance during the subsequent period he assumed that it was allowed to lapse by the tyrants. He would have escaped one inconsistency had he realized that the archonship of Damasias was probably earlier, not later, than Solon's reforms (above, p. 320). But at least he avoided the fantasies of some of his modern followers, who assume that κλήρωσις ἐκ προκρίτων went on without a break from Solon till after 487 (Cavaignac in *Revue de philologie*, xlviii, 1924, 146–7; cf. Glotz and Cohen, *Histoire grecque*, i. 477–8); he did realize that for half a century and more before 487 the archons had been αἱρετοί.

The conclusion of our analysis must be that the account in the *Athenaion Politeia* is founded not on the text of Solon's law or on a trustworthy tradition, but on an argument from survivals in which the conclusion does not follow from the premisses. As it is irreconcilable with the Atthis and with the logical development, it must be rejected.

It has been suggested that the introduction of κλήρωσις ἐκ προκρίτων for the archonship by Solon was intended to prevent stasis (so Ehrenberg, who cites Plato, *Laws* 757 D–E and Ar. *Politics* 1303ª13 ff.) or that it was a concession to religious scruples; when the archonship was thrown open to men who lacked the divine sanction of Eupatrid birth, this sanction was replaced in a new form by the introduction of sortition, which was believed to reflect the will of the gods (Wade-Gery in *C.Q.* xxv, 88). But stasis continued after Solon's reforms, and especially in connexion with the archonship (*A.P.* 13. 2) and at Rome, where the religious sanction of the patriciate was emphasized no less than in Athens, the opening of the consulship to the plebeians was not followed by a change in the method of election. Moreover, nothing can be decided either way by purely *a priori* arguments; thus it is futile to argue on the other side that partial sortition could not have been employed in the appointment of the chief magistrates of the state. The problem can only be solved by an examination of the ancient evidence, and the result of that examination is fatal to the alleged reform.

We must now consider whether sortition was prescribed by Solon for magistracies other than the archonship. The author of the *Athenaion Politeia* attributes to Solon a law still in force in his own time, under which the treasurers of Athena were to be chosen only from the Pentakosiomedimnoi and by lot, one treasurer from each tribe. There is no mention of prokrisis; the treasurers appear to be chosen by pure sortition from qualified candidates (*A.P.* 8. 1 and 47. 1, cf. *I.G.* i². 91, l. 14). If the law is genuinely Solonian, it disproves the general statement (8. 1) that Solon applied κλήρωσις ἐκ προκρίτων to 'the magistracies'. But probably the Solonian authorship of the law was not certain in the fourth century and merely inferred from the reference in it to the first of the Solonian property-classes. If the wording of the law had not been changed since Solon's time there could only have been four treasurers until Kleisthenes replaced the four tribes for political purposes by his ten new tribes, but an inscription on a bronze tablet (*I.G.* i². 393) seems to show that there were eight treasurers about the middle of the sixth century. If the law is not Solonian, nothing can be proved from it for Solon; if it is Solonian, the conclusions to be obtained from it apply only to the treasurers.

Ledl (pp. 364 ff.) maintained that the introduction of κλήρωσις ἐκ προκρίτων, which he rightly attributed to Kleisthenes, presupposes the separate existence at an earlier stage of both the modes of appointment which it combines, and as he denied that pure sortition was used by Solon in the appointment to any magistracy (even the treasurers), he concluded that it must have been used for the Council of Four Hundred. This solution is not open to those who deny the existence of the alleged council. Are they then compelled to postulate the existence of pure sortition somewhere else in the Solonian constitution? The difficulty is unreal, for Ledl's major premiss is not true in the sense required to justify his conclusion. Sortition was familiar in sixth-century Greece and had been used before the time of Kleisthenes for political purposes in some Greek states, though probably not in Athens. Presumably Kleisthenes borrowed it from another state when he introduced it into the Athenian constitution, but he thought it advisable to limit its application to his new Council of Five Hundred, and even there combined the innovation with the older method of direct election, which was retained in the form of prokrisis (see above, p. 150).

It is possible that in the appointment of the treasurers, who were so closely connected with the patron goddess of the city, the use of the lot was pre-Solonian and was simply confirmed by Solon. The archons were appointed under Solon's laws as before by direct election in the popular assembly, and the minor magistrates may still have been nominated by the Areopagus. When sortition came to be regarded as the foundation of democracy, its institution was ascribed to Solon, but there is no valid evidence that he made any use of it, except perhaps in the appointment of the treasurers, and even that may be explained as the retention of an earlier custom.

APPENDIX V

Peisistratos and the Philaïdai

WILAMOWITZ, discussing the objectives of the Diakrioi, asserted that these were secured for them 'by their leaders, Peisistratos of Brauron and Miltiades the Philaïd' (*A.A.* ii. 66). A few pages later (73–74) he expresses his view at greater length. Peisistratos lived close to the Philaïdai in the neighbourhood of Brauron and therefore both belonged originally (von haus aus) to the same party of the Diakrioi. Only five years before Peisistratos' first tyranny a Philaïd, Hippokleides, had been archon and had founded the festival of the Panathenaia. But he was no formidable competitor for power since he lacked seriousness and steadiness (οὐ φροντὶς Ἱπποκλείδη became proverbial). A more important member of the family had founded a colony in the Chersonese. The Philaïds and Peisistratos were not always friends (cf. Hdt. vi. 103) but they ended with mutual recognition. Even when the head of the Athenian branch of the Philaïds was murdered and gossip made the tyrants responsible there was no breach between them.

It must be admitted that Herodotus insists on the hostility of the Philaïds to the tyrants (vi. 35. 3 and 103. 1) and accepts as true the report that Kimon the half-brother of Miltiades I had been murdered on the orders of Peisistratos' sons after their father's death (103. 3). Modern scholars who accept these statements at their face value naturally conclude that the Philaïdai must have belonged to the party of the Pediakoi (so Busolt, ii². 304). The novel hypothesis of Wells (*Studies in Herodotus*, 112–14) that they sided with the Paraloi has not found favour. Busolt had earlier (ii². 304, n. 4) ruled out this solution on the ground that they were old enemies of the leaders of the Paraloi, the Alkmaionidai, but there is no evidence that the feud between the two families existed so early. Wells stressed the marriage alliance of the Philaïds with the Kypselid tyrants of Corinth (proved by the name Kypselos given to the father of Miltiades I in Hdt. vi. 35. 1 and by the statement on the ancestry of Hippokleides in vi. 128. 2) and their friendship with Lydia, but these data would obviously fit in just as well with the view of Wilamowitz, and the other arguments produced by Wells are too slender to prove his case. Nevertheless even those scholars who reject the idea that the Philaïds were Peisistratos' political allies have been forced to admit that as rulers of the Chersonese they were to some degree dependent on the goodwill of the tyrants (cf. the list of references in Berve, *Miltiades*, 9, n. 1); this culminates in the assertion of Meyer (*Forschungen*, i. 17) that the colonization of the Chersonese was an enterprise inspired by Peisistratos, who deliberately put in command of it the head of a family opposed to him, knowing that they could only maintain themselves in Chersonese as long as they had the government of Athens at their back and that they would thereby be forced into dependence on the support of the tyranny.

Before we re-examine these theories we must first consider the place of Miltiades the oikist in the family tree of the Philaïdai. Such a tree is given by Markellinos in his life of Thucydides (§ 3) on the authority of Didymos, who quoted a passage from Pherekydes (Jacoby, *F.G.H.*, no. 3, fr. 2). This extract is unfortunately corrupt in places but ends with the statement that the Miltiades who settled the Chersonese was son of the Hippokleides in whose archonship the Panathenaia was founded. As Herodotus says (vi. 35. 1) that the father of Miltiades I was Kypselos, this statement has been generally rejected, except by Wade-Gery (*C.A.H.* iii. 764–5; cf. table II on 570) who equates Hippokleides with Kypselos; he also distinguishes Hippokleides the archon from Hippokleides the suitor (Hdt. vi. 127. 4), but this seems unnecessary, as the suitor was of marriageable age in 576 or 572 and would therefore be old enough in 566 to hold the archonship. Toepffer (*A.G.* 279) accepted Vömel's insertion of the words καὶ Κύψελος before τοῦ δὲ Μιλτιάδης, but Jacoby (*F.G.H.* i. 388) rightly objects that this reading (which makes Miltiades' father the archon's brother) is improbable in view of the fact that these family trees always proceed in a straight line. But Jacoby's own proposal, to insert τοῦ δὲ Κύψελος and make Kypselos son of Hippokleides, is impossible on chronological grounds; how could the oikist be grandson of a man who was chief archon in 566/565? The settlement of Chersonese may indeed belong to the forties but cannot be later than 541.

A possible solution of the difficulty is to suppose that Hippokleides was the head of the family in his generation, that Kypselos was his younger brother, and that he adopted Kypselos' son because he had no children of his own. It has been pointed out that the genealogy in Markellinos does not seem to fulfil its function, since it follows on the statement that Thucydides the historian was a descendant of Miltiades the general, i.e. Miltiades II who fought at Marathon. Actually this Miltiades was the son of Kimon Koalemos, who was merely half-brother to Miltiades the oikist; Kimon had the same mother as the

oikist but a different father, who might have belonged to another
genos. Beloch cuts the knot by the assumption (ii². 2. 38) that the
father of Kimon Koalemos was also a Philaïd, but on this hypothesis
it is hard to see why Pherekydes should not have given the pedigree
in the direct line. De Sanctis (*Atthis*, 297) alleges that the second
Philaïd ruler of the Chersonese, Stesagoras, the son of Kimon
Koalemos, had been adopted by the childless Miltiades I, who
certainly bequeathed to Stesagoras his χρήματα as well as his ἀρχή
(Hdt. vi. 38. 1). Perhaps Miltiades I adopted both his nephews (who
on this view need not have been Philaïds before) in order to avert the
extinction of the main branch of the Philaïd house. One of Themistokles' sons was adopted by his maternal grandfather Lysandros
(Plut. *Them.* 32. 1–2) presumably to ensure the continuity of his
family, and the practice was common in the fourth century.

Even if Miltiades I had not been adopted by Hippokleides the
archon, I agree with Wade-Gery that he belongs to the next generation. The assumption, frequently made, that he must have gone to
the Chersonese during Peisistratos' *first* tenure of power is unsupported by direct evidence and rests on unsound chronological
foundations. We must start with the fact (Hdt. vi. 37. 1) that
Miltiades after his arrival in Chersonese was captured in an ambush
by the men of Lampsakos, who were compelled by Kroisos of Lydia
to release him. Peisistratos' final tyranny almost certainly began in
546 (the thirty-six years of Peisistratid rule in Hdt. v. 65. 3 must
surely be years of *continuous* rule). The fall of Kroisos is dated to the
same year by the chronographers who followed Apollodoros (cf.
Busolt, ii.² 458, n. 1 and Jacoby, *Apollodors Chronik*, 177–8, also 153
and 193). But it cannot have been dated by Herodotus to 546, for he
assumed that Peisistratos was in control of Athens when Kroisos sent
messengers to Greece to look for allies (i. 59. 1). Moreover, we know
that the chronologist of the Parian Marble dated the fall of Sardis to
541/540 (cf. Jacoby, *Marmor Parium*, 171, where the facts are need-
lessly complicated by Jacoby's desire to date the archonship of
Euthydemos to 556/555 instead of the correct year 555/554). Although
it is doubtful whether the authority of Xanthos can be claimed for
this date (cf. Pearson, *Early Ionian Historians*, 115 and n. 2) it is in
harmony with Herodotus, and has been accepted by Busolt (loc. cit.);
cf. Toepffer, *Q.P.* 116–20 for a fair statement of the problem.

Hence the incidents recorded in Herodotus vi. 36–37 can be safely
ascribed to the years between 546 and 541; the objection raised by
Cornelius (p. 33), that after the fall of the Median Empire Kroisos
had no time to trouble about such trifles as the capture of Miltiades,
is without weight. Even if Miltiades I had been hostile to Peisistratos
it would be more credible that he should have departed to the
Chersonese after 546, when Peisistratos was at last firmly established

in power, than in his short-lived first tyranny when his position was still insecure. Yet it is natural that the earlier date should have been preferred by the defenders of the Herodotean account (e.g. Berve, op. cit. 2), for that account becomes less plausible if the colonization of the Chersonese is dated after 546; after his final return Peisistratos rooted his tyranny so securely that he had no need to fear the noble families still left in Attica. It is incredible that he should have welcomed the establishment of a political opponent in an independent principality on the Hellespont near the old Athenian possession of Sigeion, which Peisistratos now or soon after brought under his own control. Markellinos may be only embroidering the Herodotean story when he says (vita Thuc. 7; cf. Berve, 11) that Miltiades set out οὐκ ἄνευ γνώμης τοῦ τυράννου and that Peisistratos sent him προσδοὺς δύναμιν, but it is clear that the colony could not have been launched without the approval of the home government or maintained without its support.

Herodotus seems to have followed a Philaïd version of the relations between the Philaïdai and the tyrants, a version which was probably derived from the defence put forward by Miltiades II in 493 (Hdt. vi. 104. 2; cf. Macan's edition of Herodotus iv–vi, vol. 2, p. 46). The items in Herodotus which are pressed by Berve (Miltiades, 9–12) in his attack on Wilamowitz are not decisive. (1) The motive assigned (Hdt. vi. 35. 3) for the departure of Miltiades I from Athens cannot be reconciled with the support that he certainly received from Peisistratos in his enterprise. (2) Berve's assertion (op. cit. 9) that Miltiades' stepbrother Kimon had to live in exile during the tyranny of Peisistratos is too strong. All that Herodotus says (vi. 103. 1) is that Κίμωνα . . . κατέλαβε φυγεῖν ἐξ Ἀθηνέων Πεισίστρατον τὸν Ἱπποκράτεος. This Kimon won three Olympic victories with his four-horse chariot, and as all were won with the same team they can be dated 532, 528, and 524 (since the second was before and the third after Peisistratos' death). It follows from Herodotus that Kimon was in exile by 532, but there is no indication that he had been in exile since 546, and it is certain that in 528 he was anxious to return since he allowed his Olympic victory of that year to be accredited to Peisistratos; thereupon he returned to Attica ὑπόσπονδος. (3) Herodotus (vi. 103. 3) accepts the report that Kimon's murder, soon after his third Olympic victory and presumably in 524, was perpetrated by assassins suborned by Peisistratos' sons, but as the murder occurred at night it is unlikely that the charge could have been substantiated; probably it was the invention of spiteful gossip. How Kimon had quarrelled with the tyrants is not recorded; his nickname Koalemos (Plut. Kimon 4. 4) suggests an unflattering idea of his political sagacity. But if he was not a member of the Philaïd clan his quarrel with Peisistratos need not be decisive for their attitude.

Whatever the gossips might say and Herodotus might repeat, the facts refuted them. Berve may deny the identification of the Miltiades who was archon in 524/523 with Kimon's son Miltiades II (op. cit. 5 and n. 7; see, however, Cadoux, 110 and n. 217), but he cannot deny the damaging admission made by Herodotus that on the death of his brother Stesagoras Miltiades 'was sent in a trireme to the Chersonese to take possession of the government by the sons of Peisistratos who had dealt with him well in Athens also' (vi. 39. 1; Macaulay's translation). This admission is fatal to the picture normally given by Herodotus of the relations between the rulers of the Chersonese and the Peisistratids. Berve's general objection (op. cit. 10) that Peisistratos, like the Kypselidai, would have governed a foreign possession (e.g. Sigeion) by a member of his own family simply begs the question at issue, and the same may be said of his assumption that the other noble families necessarily stood in a relationship of open or latent hostility to the family of the tyrants. His attempt (p. 35) to find support for his view in the relations of the Philaïds and Peisistratids with Lampsakos is no more successful. It is not known when tyranny was set up in Lampsakos; the adversaries of Miltiades I and his nephews are always referred to by Herodotus as οἱ Λαμψακηνοί. But we do know from Thucydides (vi. 59. 2–3) that it was not until after the death of Hipparchos that Hippias sought and obtained a matrimonial alliance with the tyrant of Lampsakos.

In view of his own admission in vi. 39. 1 it is clear that Herodotus derived most of his account of the Philaïd rulers of Chersonese from a source which represented their conduct in the best possible light; it is unfortunate that an Alkmaionid version of it has not survived! I therefore accept as correct the conclusion of Wilamowitz that Miltiades I and his nephews were political allies of Peisistratos and his sons.

Wilamowitz suggested that Hippokleides the archon of 566/565 was a member of the same party. The festival of the Great Panathenaia was founded in the year of his archonship, and Meyer plausibly assigned its foundation to the initiative of Peisistratos (G.A. ii[1]. 665–6 and 785, cf. iii[2]. 617 and n. and 728). His object, according to Meyer, was to transform an older usage 'into a national festival of the whole citizen-body of Attica united into a state, in contrast with the cults and shrines of the particular districts'. Busolt (ii[2]. 344, n. 2) raised various objections to this view: (1) the political unification of Attica had long been completed. Busolt strangely failed to realize that this was true in name only, not in fact. I believe that one of the objects of the Diakrioi was to end the existing anarchy. (2) The establishment of a festival with such a tendency is unsuited to a period of vigorous party struggles; moreover, Peisistratos was then beginning to form his party from the rural poor, who had little interest in γυμνικοὶ ἀγῶνες, and his programme was democratic and agrarian. But Busolt here assumes what he has to prove, that the policy of the Diakrioi was purely agrarian; why should it not have been patriotic as well, an attempt to solve the political as well as the economic ills of Attica? If it was, the foundation of a great festival of national unity might well be a weapon in the party struggle, and the archon in whose term it was founded a supporter of the Diakrioi.

APPENDIX VI

The date of Kleisthenes' reforms

WHEN were Kleisthenes' reforms ratified by the ekklesia? To this question there are two possible answers. One, accepted in the text (p. 126), is that the ratification preceded the intervention of Kleomenes; the other is that at this stage the reforms were merely promulgated and were not ratified until after the expulsion of Kleomenes and Isagoras. The first answer seems to accord better with the evidence of Herodotus, the second with that of the *Athenaion Politeia*. It must, however, be admitted that there is some obscurity on this subject in both accounts, and that neither marks very precisely in the sequence of events the point at which the proposals of Kleisthenes were approved by the popular assembly. Hence the attempts which had been made to resolve the apparent contradiction between them have not settled the controversy, since each party to it has claimed to interpret both the texts in a sense favourable to its own contention. It should also be noted that on the first alternative an interval of some length may have elapsed between the political conversion of Kleisthenes and the Spartan intervention, whereas on the other view the interval is reduced to a minimum; this consideration has played an important part in modern discussions of the problem. As the interpretation of the ancient evidence is disputed we must begin with a detailed examination of the relevant texts.

Herodotus says (v. 66) that the expulsion of Hippias was followed by a struggle for power between Isagoras and Kleisthenes, and that when Kleisthenes was being worsted in the struggle he took the demos into partnership; μετὰ δὲ τετραφύλους ἐόντας Ἀθηναίους δεκαφύλους ἐποίησε. After a digression in cc. 67–68 on Kleisthenes of Sikyon the tribal reform is described in c. 69, which ends with the words ἦν τε [ὁ Κλεισθένης] τὸν δῆμον προσθέμενος πολλῷ κατύπερθε τῶν ἀντιστασιωτέων. The next sentence begins (70. 1) ἐν τῷ μέρεϊ δὲ ἑσσούμενος ὁ Ἰσαγόρης ἀντιτεχνᾶται τάδε, and describes Isagoras' appeal for help to Kleomenes. There is no further reference to the reforms in this section of Herodotus; the final failure of the Spartan

intervention and the return of Kleisthenes is followed by an account
of the Athenian embassy to Sardis (73. 1).

It is nowhere definitely asserted by Herodotus that the tribal
reform was ratified before the Spartan intervention; he merely notes
that it followed (μετὰ δὲ) the conversion of Kleisthenes to the popular
cause. Moreover he gives as the motive of Isagoras' appeal to Sparta
not the tribal reform, which he has just described, but the decisive
supremacy which Kleisthenes had acquired through his alliance
with the demos. Hence his account of the reform has sometimes been
regarded as an anticipation, since it can be removed without leaving
any lacuna in the narrative.

The account in the *A.P.*, cc. 20–21, begins like that of Herodotus
with the struggle between Isagoras and Kleisthenes and its result:
ἡττώμενος δὲ ταῖς ἑταιρείαις ὁ Κλεισθένης προσηγάγετο τὸν δῆμον,
ἀποδιδοὺς τῷ πλήθει τὴν πολιτείαν (20. 1). This sentence is followed by
a description of Isagoras' appeal to Kleomenes and its consequences
down to the return of Kleisthenes (20. 2–3). The position in Athens
after his triumphal return is apparently described in 20. 4: κατασχόντος
δὲ τοῦ δήμου τὰ πράγματα Κλεισθένης ἡγεμὼν ἦν καὶ τοῦ δήμου προστάτης.
To this is appended a digression on the hostility of the Alkmaionidai
to the tyrants, introduced to explain (21. 1) why the demos trusted
Kleisthenes. The main narrative is then resumed with the words
τότε δὲ τοῦ πλήθους προεστηκὼς ἔτει τετάρτῳ μετὰ τὴν τῶν τυράννων
κατάλυσιν ἐπὶ Ἰσαγόρου ἄρχοντος, which introduce the detailed description of Kleisthenes' reforms.

In this account the ratification of the reforms seems at first sight
to be subsequent to the final return of Kleisthenes, and the account
has been interpreted by many in this sense. Those who question this
interpretation usually contend that the author of the *Athenaion
Politeia* accepted for the reforms the date implicit in the narrative of
Herodotus (which he followed closely for the events) but on stylistic
grounds deferred his description of the reforms till the conclusion of
his record of the political struggle. Wade-Gery has supported this
view with the suggestion (*C.Q.* xxvii, 1933, 19) that the words
ἀποδιδοὺς τῷ πλήθει τὴν πολιτείαν (20. 1) which do not occur in Herodotus but are inserted by the *Athenaion Politeia* in the narrative at
the point where Herodotus describes the reforms, are really a shorthand description of the reforms, the fuller account being reserved till
later. He maintains that the dating ἐπὶ Ἰσαγόρου ἄρχοντος was taken
from the actual laws of Kleisthenes (op. cit. 21), which must therefore
have been ratified while Isagoras was still archon, consequently
before his expulsion and Kleisthenes' return in triumph.

There are, however, serious objections (see above, p. 129) to the
hypothesis that the laws of Kleisthenes were still extant in the fourth
century. Moreover, 'the archonship of Isagoras' is mentioned in the

Athenaion Politeia to date not the actual ratification of the reforms but (as the run of the sentence shows) the acquisition by Kleisthenes of the προστασία τοῦ δήμου, which enabled him to carry out his programme. But when did Kleisthenes become προστάτης τοῦ δήμου? He might be deemed to have acquired this position on the morrow of his conversion to the popular cause, but the author of the *Athenaion Politeia* connects his prostasia with the final victory of the people, κατασχόντος τοῦ δήμου τὰ πράγματα; on his view, then, the prostasia and the consummation of the legislation were subsequent to the expulsion of Isagoras.

From this conclusion there is no escape. It follows that when the author dated the prostasia, and consequently the fulfilment of the laws, to the archonship of Isagoras, he cannot have meant that they fell within that part of the archon-year in which Isagoras was still in Athens. There is no evidence that on his expulsion another archon was appointed for the rest of his year, and the Atthidographers, who arranged their material under archon-years, naturally chronicled under the year of Isagoras all the incidents of the struggle between him and Kleisthenes. The words ἀποδιδοὺς τῷ πλήθει τὴν πολιτείαν may well refer, as Wade-Gery claims, to the Kleisthenic reforms as a whole, but the use of the present participle indicates that in the writer's opinion the reforms were at this stage merely promulgated, not yet ratified by the people; his statement is of Kleisthenes' intention, not of his achievement (Wade-Gery, op. cit. 19, leaves this question open). He has in fact not fixed precisely the time at which the proposals of Kleisthenes were approved by the assembly. His language in his description of the legislation is ambiguous; it would suit either the formal ratification of Kleisthenes' programme or the first application of reforms which had previously been voted by the ekklesia but not yet put into practice.

It is impossible to decide whether this ambiguity is deliberate or not. As the author was dependent on Herodotus for his narrative of the events he cannot have been better informed than Herodotus concerning the dates at which the reforms were ratified and carried out (see above, p. 331). He or his source may have assumed that Kleisthenes could not have carried his reforms before the intervention of Kleomenes, and may therefore have corrected the account of Herodotus on *a priori* grounds, in which case the ambiguity in c. 21 is unintentional; this seems to me the more probable alternative. The other is to suppose that he had noted the ambiguity of the Herodotean narrative on this point and was careful to reproduce it in his own account.

In either case Herodotus is our only primary source. And although close scrutiny may detect some obscurity in his statement of the dating of the reforms, the natural implication of his narrative is that they were at least ratified before the appeal of Isagoras to Kleomenes. More than this cannot be affirmed, for the language of Herodotus, like that of the *Athenaion Politeia*, is equally appropriate to the ratification of the reforms or to their application.

The solution of this question, left in doubt by Herodotus, has been sought elsewhere. Plutarch (*Solon* 12), describing the trial of the ἐναγεῖς for the murder of the Kylonians, says that they were prosecuted before a court of 300 by Μύρων Φλυεύς. This account was probably derived from an Atthis (cf. *A.P.* 1) and dated the trial before the legislation of Solon. Against this Beloch maintained (*a*) that the details given by the Atthis really belong to the proceedings against the ἐναγεῖς mentioned in Hdt. v. 72. 1 and (*b*) that the source of the Atthis for these details, including the description of the prosecutor as Μύρων Φλυεύς, was an official record of the trial. It is obvious that (*a*) does not necessarily presuppose (*b*); the source of the Atthis may, for example, have been an oral tradition of the second trial wrongly referred by the Atthis to the first trial. But if (*b*) is true then (*a*) must also be true, for an Athenian could not have been described officially by the name of his deme in pre-Solonian times, and after the reforms of Solon there is no record of any trial of the ἐναγεῖς till after the downfall of the tyranny. As we have seen (see above, p. 120) Beloch concluded from these premisses that the tribal reorganization based on the demes was introduced not by Kleisthenes but by Peisistratos. Busolt (*G.G.* ii². 209–10 and 402, n. 6) accepting Beloch's premisses but rejecting his conclusions, saw in Myron's use of the demotikon a proof that the reorganization of the citizen-body by Kleisthenes had been completed before the trial and therefore before the Spartan intervention.

The difficulties entailed by this hypothesis have already been noted (see above, p. 121). Beloch's construction stands or falls as a whole; if the official use of the demotikon was admitted by the oligarchic friends of Isagoras it could not have been a recent innovation but must have become common form under the tyranny. Nevertheless Busolt's view has been revived by F. Schachermeyr (*Klio*, xxv, 1932, 334–47), who suggests the following chronology:

ratification of Kleisthenes' reforms	autumn 508
application of the reforms . .	winter 508/507–summer 507
intervention of Sparta . . .	autumn 507 or winter 507/506.

This assumption of a considerable interval of time between the promulgation of Kleisthenes' reforms and the Spartan intervention is found already in Grote and other writers who believe that the council which opposed Kleomenes' interference was the new Kleisthenic boulē of Five Hundred (see above, p. 94). But the hypothesis of Busolt and Schachermeyr requires an extension of this period which is scarcely credible; the longer we make the interval, the more incomprehensible becomes the delay in the Spartan intervention. Schachermeyr's attempts (op. cit. 344–5) to explain away this difficulty are inadequate; Kleomenes must have realized that Kleisthenes' democratic reforms were bound to produce a change in the foreign policy of Athens, and the narrative of Herodotus implies that when Isagoras was worsted by Kleisthenes in the party struggle he lost no time in appealing to Sparta.

As Schachermeyr's view is untenable, the assumption on which his chronological scheme is founded must be false. The details on the trials of the ἐναγεῖς given by the Atthides might conceivably belong to a second trial in 508/507, though we must not confuse with such a trial (if it actually occurred) the quite different expulsion of 700 families, supporters of Kleisthenes, recorded by Herodotus (v. 70. 2), but it is more probable that these details belong to a trial in the pre-Solonian period (see the excellent discussion in Jacoby, Atthis, 367, n. 81). On either explanation there is not sufficient ground for Beloch's contention that they must have been derived by an Atthidographer from an official record of the trial. As Meyer pointed out (G.A. ii¹. 638 n. = iii². 591, n. 1), the Κυλώνειον ἄγος retained political importance till long after, since it was revived by the opponents of the Alkmaionidai in 508 and again in 432, and for this reason the details of the original offence and the subsequent trial were carefully preserved. Hence there is no need for the assumption made by Wilamowitz (Hermes, xxxiii, 1898, 122, n. 2) that many of the details were derived from the records of the ἐξηγηταί, such as the statement that the 300 jurors entered on their task καθ᾽ ἱερῶν ὁμόσαντες (for this phrase in a literary context cf. Isaios vii. 28).

There is no reason why the name of the prosecutor should not have been preserved by the oral tradition. Far too much has been made of the fact that he is described in Plutarch (Solon 12. 4) as Φλυεύς; demes existed in Attica before Kleisthenes and their names were used to describe the persons who lived in them (cf. Jacoby, op. cit. 368). Phlya recalls the Lykomidai (see above, pp. 121 f.). Possibly the place-name served to distinguish Myron from a namesake of the same genos.

Herodotus must therefore be regarded as our only trustworthy source for the chronology of Kleisthenes' reforms. His account points to the conclusion that the reforms had already been ratified by the ekklesia before the intervention of Kleomenes, but that the march of events was so rapid that they had not yet been put into force when Kleisthenes was compelled to leave. Their application must as a result have been deferred, as the Athenaion Politeia implies, until after the expulsion of Isagoras and the triumphal return of

Kleisthenes. Cf. Ledl, 282–4 and Wade-Gery in C.Q. xxvii, 1933, 24–25.
[See also the long note 249 by Cadoux in J.H.S. lxviii, 1948, 114–16.
I cannot agree that the dating of Kleisthenes' laws to the archonship
of Isagoras was derived from a copy of the laws; cf. Jacoby, Atthis,
385, n. 36.]

APPENDIX VII

Chronological problems in the history of the years 506–480

A SKETCH of the constitutional and political history of these years
is contained in the Athenaion Politeia, c. 22. In that part of the
chapter which deals with the decade after Marathon three archons
are mentioned, Telesinos, Nikodemos, and Hypsichides; of these
Telesinos and Hypsichides are not mentioned elsewhere. The archonship of Telesinos is dated to the year after the ostracism of Hipparchos, which is said to have been two years after the battle of
Marathon. Telesinos must, therefore, have held the office in the
archon-year 487/486; the archons for the two preceding years are
known (Aristeides and Anchises) and a date later than 487/486 is
excluded by the evidence of the Athenaion Politeia. The ostracism of
Hipparchos must belong to the year 488/487, and it was followed in
three successive years by the ostracisms of Megakles, an unknown
'friend of the tyrants' (probably the elder Alkibiades—cf. Lys. xiv.
39 and [Andok.] iv. 34), and Xanthippos the father of Perikles. Thus
the ostracism of Xanthippos is dated to 485/484. Since the archonship
of Nikodemos is dated to the third year after the ostracism of
Xanthippos it must coincide with the Athenian year 483/482, as
Dionysios says (A.R. viii. 83. 1). To this year the Athenaion Politeia
assigns the navy bill of Themistokles and the ostracism of Aristeides.

Then follows the statement that 'in the fourth year . . . in the
archonship of Hypsichides' they recalled all those who had been
ostracized. The fourth year from the archonship of Nikodemos should
be 480/479, but the archon for that year was not Hypsichides but
Kalliades (Hdt. viii. 51. 1). Sandys in his note on the passage (A.P.
22. 8) assumes that the year 481/480 is meant, and that the date is
reckoned from the ostracism of Aristeides, which he assigns with
Jerome to 484/483. But the reference to this ostracism in the Athenaion
Politeia is parenthetical, so that it cannot be regarded as the natural
terminus a quo; moreover, the clear implication of the passage is that
the ostracism occurred in the same year as the navy bill. Carcopino
suggests that the reference in τετάρτῳ ἔτει is to the ostracism of
Xanthippos, and that the year of Hypsichides is therefore to be
equated with 482/481. The names of the archons for 482/481 and

481/480 have not been preserved, but Carcopino's view conflicts with the evidence of Plutarch (*Arist.* 8. 1), who says that Aristeides was recalled in the third year of his banishment. Although Plutarch is certainly wrong in his comment that the recall was voted 'when Xerxes was advancing through Thessaly and Boiotia', which would date it to 480/479, the words τρίτῳ ἔτει must come from a good source. Hence the τετάρτῳ ἔτει of the *Athenaion Politeia* must be rejected as an error of the author or a scribe, and the archonship of Hypsichides must be identified with the year 481/480. The decree of recall was probably carried early in the year 480.

In the account of the period before Marathon the reorganization of the strategia, which is dated to the twelfth year before the battle, seems to belong to the same year as the formulation of the ὅρκος βουλευτικός, which is dated to the year of Hermokreon. On this calculation the archonship of Hermokreon should correspond to the year 501/500. But it is also described as ἔτει πέμπτῳ μετὰ ταύτην τὴν κατάστασιν. These words ought to refer to the reforms of Kleisthenes, which have already been dated to 508/507, the archonship of Isagoras. But in addition to the discrepancy between the two methods of dating there is the further objection that the fifth year from Isagoras, 504/503, is already occupied by Akestorides. It has been suggested by Schachermeyr (*Klio*, xxv, 1932, 347) that as the author has referred in the preceding paragraph to the ostracism law he is really calculating in ἔτει πέμπτῳ from the date of this law, which may therefore be regarded as the last of Kleisthenes' reforms and ascribed to the year 505/504. This explanation is untenable. The author of the *Athenaion Politeia* believed that the legislation of Kleisthenes was carried in 508/507. If he had known that the ostracism law was not passed till 505/504 he would certainly have said so. Moreover, the law is mentioned only incidentally, as an example of the new laws introduced by Kleisthenes. Finally, it is incredible that ἔτει πέμπτῳ could be used by the author with reference to a date which had been neither mentioned nor suggested in the preceding paragraphs. The words must represent a copyist's error for ἔτει ὀγδόῳ; this date, calculated from 508/507, the year of Isagoras' archonship, gives 501/500 for Hermokreon's year, in harmony with the alternative method of dating which makes it the twelfth year before that of Marathon, 490/489. [See also T. J. Cadoux in *J.H.S.* lxviii, 1948, 115–19.]

APPENDIX VIII

The date of the Ephialtic revolution

THE author of the *Athenaion Politeia* states (25. 1–2) that Ephialtes prepared the ground for his attack on the Areopagus by a series of prosecutions directed against individual Areopagites, and dates to the archonship of Konon (462/461) the passing of the laws by which Ephialtes took away from the Areopagus most of its powers, but he does not relate this legislation to other events of Athenian history in the same period. It seems reasonably certain (cf. Busolt, iii. 1. 258, n. 1) that the battle of Tanagra was fought in the campaigning season of 457, and we know from Theopompos (fr. 88 in O.C.T. and Jacoby) that at the time of the battle Kimon had been in exile for less than five years; hence we may safely conclude (in view of *A.P.* 43. 5) that Kimon was ostracized early in 461, in the year of Konon's archonship. His ostracism was therefore not far removed in time from the overthrow of the Areopagus, but as the archon-date is the same for both events it cannot tell us which of the two came first.

For the answer to this problem we must turn to Plutarch, who in his *Life of Kimon* (henceforth cited as PK) informs us that Kimon's opponents stirred up the anger of the people against him when he tried to secure the repeal of Ephialtes' laws, which had been carried while Kimon was absent from Athens on a naval expedition (PK 15. 2–3). From this it follows that the original authority for this account dated Kimon's ostracism after the legislation of Ephialtes. Those who believe that it must have occurred before the fall of the Areopagus are forced to discredit Plutarch's evidence, and this can only be done by the assumption that the account here given by him was not based on fact but was merely constructive inference, to provide an 'explanation' for Kimon's absence from Athens at the time when Ephialtes carried his laws (so Walker in *C.A.H.* v. 468). But if, as seems likely, Theopompos was Plutarch's ultimate source here, he was not content to assume that Kimon 'was absent on one of his numerous expeditions'; he proceeded to pile hypothesis on hypothesis by his assertions that Kimon on his return promptly tried to get the reform repealed, that he was met with a campaign of calumny by the radicals, and that he was ostracized in consequence.

I cannot believe that all these details were supplied by Theopompos from constructive inference, and the grounds produced by Walker and Beloch for believing that they were are unconvincing. Beloch's arguments (*G.G.* ii². 2. 197–8) are as follows: (1) even in Athens an alteration of the constitution was something which required considerable time and could not be carried through in a day, and as Kimon was not far away (Beloch thought he was at Ithome in 462) he could have returned to Athens at any moment to resist the proposals of Ephialtes. (2) Kimon's popularity was shaken when the Spartans dismissed the Athenian contingent from Ithome, but Ephialtes' laws cannot have been carried before Kimon was ostracized; otherwise the ostracism would have been *post festum*. The second argument rests on a misunderstanding of the purpose of ostracism. There was no reason why the issue of *policy* should not be decided before an ostracism; by removing the defeated leader from the scene ostracism ensured the smooth execution of the victorious party's programme (so the ostracism of Aristeides probably took place after the adoption of Themistokles' navy bill by the ekklesia). The first argument is still weaker. Kimon had been sent to Messenia, presumably with his own consent, as strategos in charge of the Athenian force; how could he throw up his command and return to Athens before the expedition was over, however much the political situation at home might call for his presence there?

Walker also attacked Plutarch's testimony on *a priori* grounds. He claimed that it was 'most improbable' that 'the democrats, after sustaining two such reverses as those involved in the acquittal of Cimon and the sending of a contingent to Ithome should have ventured once more to try conclusions with the conservatives. . . . No ground could have been chosen less favourable to the democratic cause than the question of the Areopagus.' Surely this last statement is the direct opposite of the truth. The radicals had previously made the mistake of attacking Kimon personally, but it was easy to represent the privileges of the Areopagus as a usurpation (*A.P.* 25. 2) and their survival as an intolerable anachronism in a progressive state. Perhaps Ephialtes had begun his war of prosecutions against the Areopagites while Kimon was absent so long in Thasos with no other intention than to weaken the prestige of leading conservatives, but he had thereby undermined the resistance of the Areopagus as a whole. In reply to Walker's first point we may say that the absence of Kimon with 4,000 hoplites (who would naturally be supporters of moderate democracy) offered an opportunity to Ephialtes which must have seemed to him too good to be missed.

It must, however, be admitted that there is some confusion in Plutarch's narrative. After mentioning that Kimon's attempt to get the reforms reversed was met by the radical leaders with a campaign of defamation (PK 15. 3), he goes off into a long digression on their calumnies under the two headings of (*a*) incest of Kimon with his sister Elpinike and (*b*) his Lakonism. The first was perhaps an almost contemporary charge; on its origins it is sufficient to refer to Beloch, ii². 1. 159, n. 1 and Wells, *Studies in Herodotus*, 128. Plutarch's discussion of the second charge fills the whole of his sixteenth chapter, ending with Kimon's success in persuading the Athenians to help the Spartans at Ithome. PK 17 begins with a further digression on a Corinthian attempt to bar Kimon's march, which must clearly be his return march from Ithome to Athens, although Plutarch has not yet told us how he fared at Ithome. This last digression following on the others has caused Plutarch to lose the thread of his narrative, and this may be the reason (cf. Busolt, iii. 1. 260–1, n. 3) why he now speaks of a second Spartan request for help and a second expedition to Ithome of the Athenians, who, however, are soon sent away ὡς νεωτεριστάς. They returned full of anger against Kimon, and seizing on a trifling pretext ostracized him for ten years (PK 17. 3).

In this last sentence it seems clear that the ostracism is regarded as following closely on the (second) expedition to Ithome. Thucydides shows plainly (i. 102) that there was only one expedition, and the assumption of a second may well have been made by Plutarch himself. But was Plutarch's ultimate source for this passage (probably Ephoros) correct in his view that the Ithome expedition closely preceded the ostracism (and therefore took place in the campaigning season of 462), and why did his source in 15. 2 say that the Areopagus was overthrown ὡς (Κίμων) πάλιν ἐπὶ στρατείαν ἐξέπλευσε?

The first of these two questions cannot be conclusively solved. Meyer, whose views (Forsch. ii. 50–55) I have in the main accepted, makes his task too easy by assuming that the fall of Thasos is firmly dated to 463. I think that the great earthquake at Sparta may safely be assigned to the summer of 464 (possibly to the first half of that summer, in spite of Pausanias iv. 24. 5) and the catastrophic fate of the colonists of Ennea Hodoi to the Athenian year 465/464 (on the assumption that Thucydides is calculating by archon-years in iv. 102. 2–3; cf. Gomme, Thucydides, i. 392–3), but the precise relation of these two events to the revolt and subjugation of Thasos must remain uncertain (for a discussion of the chronology of those years see Gomme, op. cit. 390–1 and 401 ff.). If the τρίτῳ ἔτει of Thuc. i. 101. 3 is a calculation based on archon-years and if, as Gomme says and I believe, Thasos fell in the archon-year 463/462, then its revolt must have begun in the archon-year 465/464, i.e. in the second half of the year 465, and Kimon's trial on his return from Thasos (PK 14. 3) must have been in the autumn or winter of 463/462. Although this is the chronology that I prefer, I must admit that there is no insuperable objection to the view of Beloch (ii². 2. 195) that the revolt of Thasos began in the first half of 466/465 and ended in the first half of 464/463, though no argument can safely be drawn from the fact that Diodoros (xi. 70. 1) records under 464/463 both the revolt and the subjugation of Thasos.

Beloch himself dated Kimon's Ithome expedition to 462, but others (notably von Domaszewski, Die attische Politik in der Zeit der Pentekontaetie, SBHeidelberg 1924/5) have used his chronology of the Thasian revolt to date to 463 Kimon's march to Ithome. This leaves Kimon free for an expedition by sea in 462, which is assumed to have been that to Cyprus mentioned in Thuc. i. 104. 2, and the conclusion then follows that it was during this expedition (hence the ἐξέπλευσε of PK 15. 2) that the Areopagus lost its powers (op. cit. 11). It is difficult to believe that the events in Thuc. i. 104. 2 can be as early as 462, but the source of PK 15. 2 might have been referring to an otherwise unrecorded naval expedition of Kimon, and the close connexion of the Ithome affair with his ostracism might be 'explained' by the hypothesis that this was the principal charge made against him (PK 16. 4) when his opponents were stirring up popular feeling against him, although it had occurred over a year earlier.

But although it is chronologically tenable, von Domaszewski's reconstruction lacks plausibility. How could Ephialtes carry his proposals when the rowers, the main support of the radical party, were absent from Athens on a great naval expedition? This is to make too much of the mysterious ἐξέπλευσε in PK 15. 2. It cannot be referred to the Ithome expedition by the facile assumption that Kimon and his 4,000 hoplites went to Messenia by sea. If they returned by land (PK 17. 1–2) they presumably went by land. It is obvious that there are two different sources behind Plutarch's main narrative here, (A) in 15. 1–3 and (B) in 16. 4–17. 3, and it is usually supposed that A = Theopompos and B = Ephoros. The first preserved the fact that Kimon was absent from Athens when Ephialtes carried his reforms and that his ostracism was due to his attempt to get them repealed on his return, but gave only a vague explanation for his absence from Athens at the critical moment. Perhaps Theopompos, unwilling to refer directly to the Ithome expedition because of the inglorious part played in the affair by Kimon and by Sparta (cf. Busolt, iii. 1. 242, n. 2) merely said that he was absent from Athens on a στρατεία, and this was carelessly transformed by Plutarch's intermediary source into a naval expedition. It cannot be asserted that B definitely connected the fall of the Areopagus with Kimon's absence at Ithome, but he certainly linked his ostracism closely with his ignominious return from Ithome.

Meyer is surely right in dating the Ithome expedition to 462 (this follows from B in PK 17. 3) and in accepting the evidence of A (PK 15. 2–3) that the successful attack on the powers of the Areopagus occurred during Kimon's last absence from Athens before his ostracism. This view alone explains convincingly (a) why Ephialtes was able to carry his reforms; 4,000 hoplite voters were away with Kimon while most of the rowers were presumably at home in 462, (b) why the Spartans sent the Athenians away from Ithome ὡς νεωτεριστάς (PK 17. 3); they had just heard of the radical revolution in Athens, (c) why the Corinthians adopted a hostile attitude to the Athenian contingent on its return march; they must have anticipated that the revolution in Athens would be followed by a complete change in her foreign policy.

APPENDIX IX

The institution of δικαστικὸς μισθός

PLUTARCH, apparently on the authority of Theopompos, dates the introduction of jury-pay by Perikles before the legislation of Ephialtes, and implies that this and other measures were designed to gain the favour of the masses in preparation for the attack on the Areopagus (*Per.* 9. 2–3). In this connexion he cites the evidence of 'Aristotle' for the story that jury-pay was introduced by Perikles on the suggestion of his friend Damonides to win popularity in his struggle with Kimon; when Kimon had secured the goodwill of the poor by his generous largesses from his private property, Perikles overtrumped him by bribing the people with their own money. In the *Athenaion Politeia* (27. 4), which is obviously Plutarch's ultimate source for this spiteful tale, we find a version even more hostile to Perikles than that in Plutarch. Its malicious colouring is obvious; unscrupulous as the innovation was, Perikles could not hit upon the idea himself but borrowed it from his music-master! Hence it is probable that this account was first popularized in the oligarchic pamphlet of the late fifth century which underlies chapters 23–28 of the *Athenaion Politeia*, chapters marked by a denigration of almost all Athenian statesmen from Aristeides to Kleophon (see above, pp. 5–6).

A source of this type cannot safely be used as evidence for the date of the event which it describes. It may in strict logic imply that the measure was carried when Perikles was at the head of the radical party and Kimon was leader of the conservative party and when both were present in Athens, but such rigour of interpretation (on which Walker in *C.A.H.* v. 101 relies to prove that the date of the reform must be 451 or 450) is out of place here. The author of the pamphlet knew that jury-pay was a reform introduced by Perikles, and never stopped to consider whether the bill was carried during the lifetime of Ephialtes and before Kimon's ostracism. In *A.P.* 27. 4 the story is timeless; it occurs in a digression on the career of Perikles, not in the preceding chapter, which preserves the dates in archon-years (presumably from the Atthis) of three laws carried in the fifties. From these facts it is a fair conclusion that no date was given in the Atthis for the introduction of jury-pay and that none was known to the author of the *Athenaion Politeia*.

As Theopompos followed the source which lies behind *A.P.* 27. 4, his ascription of the innovation to a period before the attack on the Areopagus (cf. Wade-Gery in *A.J.Phil.* lix, 1938, 131 ff.) must be based on conjecture, a conjecture which simply ignored the subordination of Perikles to Ephialtes at the time. It is more probable that the date was later than the revolution of 462; when much jurisdiction which had previously belonged to the Areopagus had been transferred to the popular courts it might reasonably be maintained that the jurors should henceforward be paid. Whether the reform was carried before Ephialtes' death is doubtful; the fact that such an important measure was sponsored by Perikles suggests that Ephialtes was no longer alive, but it was a logical consequence of the revolution of 462 and cannot have been long delayed.

APPENDIX X

The citizenship law of 451/450

UNTIL 451/450 Athenians could intermarry freely with members of other states; the children born of such unions were legitimate and were citizens of the state to which the male parent belonged. The law of 451/450 limited the citizenship of Athens to τοὺς ἐκ δυεῖν Ἀθηναίων γεγονότας (Plut. *Per.* 37. 3; cf. *A.P.* 26. 4). Presumably it also enacted that henceforth no Athenian man could contract a valid marriage with a woman who was not an Athenian citizen; it is certain that in the time of Aristophanes (cf. *Birds* 1649 ff.) the children of an ἀστός by a ξένη were not only excluded from the citizenship but also ranked in law as νόθοι. At some date before 413 (Lys. xxxiv. 3) the law of 451/450 was modified by the grant of ἐπιγαμία to the Euboians. It has been plausibly suggested by de Sanctis (*Atthis*[2], 470) that the reasons for this concession were the close proximity to Athens of Euboia and the settlement there of large numbers of Athenian cleruchs; if this is correct, the concession cannot be earlier than 446, when the revolted Histiaians were expelled from their territory in north Euboia and replaced by a settlement of Athenian cleruchs known as Oreos (Thuc. i. 114. 3, viii. 95. 7).

The only provision of the law of 451/450 cited in the *Athenaion Politeia* is: μὴ μετέχειν τῆς πόλεως ὃς ἂν μὴ ἐξ ἀμφοῖν ἀστοῖν ᾖ γεγονώς. There is nothing in this clause as we have it to exclude from the citizenship those whose parents were both Athenian citizens but had never married, and it is usually assumed that, as being of pure Athenian descent, they were not excluded from the citizenship either before or after the law of 451/450. This assumption has been held to be inconsistent with a later passage in the *A.P.*, 42. 1. We read there that when an Athenian male reached the age of eighteen and applied for enrolment on the register of his deme, the demesmen had first to verify whether he really was over eighteen, then whether ἐλεύθερός ἐστι καὶ γέγονε κατὰ τοὺς νόμους. The last four words could be interpreted as a reference back to *A.P.* 26. 4, the law enacting that both the parents must be citizens, not to a requirement that they should have been united in marriage before the applicant's birth. Wyse objected (*The Speeches of Isaeus*, 281) that here and in other fourth-century contexts ἐλεύθερος must be translated 'of citizen birth', and that γέγονε κατὰ τοὺς νόμους must therefore mean something different, 'born in lawful wedlock'. His argument is unconvincing, as the four words might be pleonastic and explanatory of the term ἐλεύθερος.

In strict law the validity of all marriages (except those of ἐπίκληροι; cf. Wyse, 501) depended on the ceremony called ἐγγύησις, usually translated 'betrothal'. The translation is misleading because the contract was made by the suitor not with his future bride but with her legal representative (cf. Wyse, 289 ff., also for the suggestion that ἐγγύησις originated in marriage by purchase). A citation in [Dem.] xlvi. 18 from a law in force during the fourth century but almost certainly older shows that only the children of an ἐγγύησις marriage were recognized as legitimate, and presumably they alone were qualified to inherit property. But if the children of an Athenian father and an Athenian mother who were not born in lawful wedlock were not regarded as γνήσιοι, it does not necessarily follow that they were thereby excluded from the citizenship.

This controversy is summarily dismissed by some scholars on the ground that irregular unions of Athenian men with Athenian women were rare (cf. Wyse, 281–2 and Wade-Gery in *C.Q.* xxv, 1931, 2, n. 3). So they may have been in the middle and upper classes, to which most of the evidence in the orators applies, but modern analogies might suggest a doubt whether they were equally rare among the proletariat. The children of these unions must have ranked legally as νόθοι. It is impossible to say whether their status or their legal rights would have been altered by the subsequent marriage of their parents. The children of Mantitheos and Plangon were perhaps adopted by their father before he died, but our information on this famous case (Dem. xxxix and xl) is one-sided; cf. Wil. *A.A.* ii. 179, n. 24.

Isaios vi. 47 quotes a law, cited also in [Dem.] xliii. 51, that νόθοι were excluded from the right to inherit the family cult and the family property. In both texts the law is said to be valid from the archonship of Eukleides, 403/402, but a similar disqualification was in force in the second half of the fifth century and was attributed to Solon by Aristophanes; in the *Birds* (1649 ff.) he makes Peisthetairos explain to Herakles that as a νόθος he has no share whatever in his father's estate. Perhaps this did not matter to the children of the proletariat who had little or no property to inherit. The special clause in the law of 403/402 may indicate that the earlier law was not strictly enforced during the later years of the Peloponnesian War, and that bastards, at least those of pure Athenian blood, had been allowed to inherit. (Müller's view, derived from the alleged double marriage of Sokrates in Diog. Laertius ii. 26, that bigamy was

legalized by the Athenians during the years 411–403, has been refuted
by Ledl in *Wiener Studien*, xxx, 1908, 38–46; cf. Wyse, 279–80).

Even if the interpretation of *A.P.* 42. 1 given by Wyse is the only
possible one, it is valid only for the fourth century. The main object
of the law of 451/450 was probably to preserve the racial purity of the
citizen-body (see below, pp. 346 f.); hence it is possible that Perikles
was not concerned to word the law in such a way as to exclude from
the citizenship those born out of lawful wedlock, although they were
still excluded from ἀγχιστεία by the pre-existing 'Solonian' law.

A more important problem raised by the law of 451/450 is whether
it was retrospective, whether it deprived of citizenship and legitimacy
the offspring of all unions between Athenian men and foreign women
contracted before the passing of the law. It is hard to believe that it
did, on two grounds. Before 451 an Athenian who wished to marry
a foreign woman would presumably do so by the ceremony of
ἐγγύησις which guaranteed the validity of an Athenian marriage; it
would have been an intolerable injustice that these unions, contracted
in good faith by the parties, should have been denounced later as
illegal by retrospective legislation. Moreover Kimon himself was the
son of a foreign woman; can we believe that the law deprived him of
his citizenship and his property? If he had ceased to be a citizen he
would have been unable to hold the στρατηγία, but in fact he was still
general at the time of his death in 449 or late in 450.

To get over this difficulty it has been assumed that the law was
not made retrospective till 445/444, when there was a revision of the
list of citizens (διαψηφισμός) on the occasion of a gift of corn to Athens
by Psammetichos (Philochoros, fr. 90 [119 in Jacoby], Plut. *Per.* 37. 4).
The number 14,240 given by Philochoros for those who received the
corn, probably all or nearly all Thetes, may well be genuine, but the
number 4,760 for those deprived of citizenship is suspicious and was
perhaps obtained by simple subtraction of the figure for the recipients
from 19,000, which has been regarded as Philochoros' estimate for
either the total number of the citizens or the Thetes only in 445 (see
Gomme, *Population of Athens*, 16–17 and Busolt–Swoboda, 766, n. 1).
Moreover, the men now struck off the rolls are described by Philochoros as ξένοι παρεγγεγραμμένοι, and this ought to mean aliens whose
names had been fraudulently inserted on the deme-lists, not sons of
Athenian citizens and foreign mothers, since these sons had been
legally qualified for inclusion on the lists before 451/450. The conclusion must be that the διαψηφισμός of 445/444 had no close connexion
with the Periklean law of 451/450. It doubtless revealed many abuses
in the deme-lists, but the number 4,760 for those now excluded from
the lists must be an exaggeration.

In the *Athenaion Politeia* the motive alleged for the law of 451/450
is 'the great increase in the number of citizens' (26. 4—Kenyon's

translation), and from this Gomme has inferred an anxiety that the citizen-body might grow so rapidly as to make the constitution unworkable (*J.H.S.* l, 1930, 106, repeated in *Essays*, 87, though with a caution in the footnote that really contradicts the text). But if the law was not retrospective this explanation is untenable, unless we are to suppose that if Athenian men were not allowed to marry foreign wives they would not marry at all. The obvious gainers from the law were the unmarried women of Athens, since it improved their chances of obtaining husbands. If the law did not diminish the number of citizens we must also reject Walker's contention (*C.A.H.* v. 103) that it was due to the selfishness of a demos careful to limit the number of those who shared the perquisites of empire. Apart from the exclusion of fraudulent claimants on the one hand and the natural growth of population on the other, the citizen-body had remained constant.

Gomme also suggested (*Essays*, 87) that popular sentiment disapproved of intermarriage with aliens and that the law was therefore an attempt to restore what was regarded as normal by the many. It is certainly reasonable to suppose that the law was an attempt to preserve the purity of the citizen stock, but can we be sure that anxiety to do so was either confined to or shared by the common people? Our knowledge of previous marriages is naturally confined mainly to those of Athenians in the upper classes, and it is known that many of these had mothers or wives who were foreigners, but why should the same not be true of the lower classes as well, especially the urban proletariat? Athens had admitted foreign immigrants under Solon and Peisistratos, and since the growth of Piraeus a large alien population had been residing there. These aliens included not merely Greeks from the Athenian Empire and the rest of Greece, but non-Greek elements and even Orientals. To allow citizens to intermarry with such might entail a debasement of their racial purity that would be viewed with alarm by conservatives, and the alarm might be shared by progressive statesmen who could take a long view. These considerations suggest that the law of 451/450 was a measure on which Perikles and Kimon would have been in full agreement.

The political situation at Athens in 451/450 is obscure. Walker (*C.A.H.* v. 101–3) thought that Kimon had not come back to Athens until the full term of his ostracism had run out, early in 451, and that Perikles proposed the citizenship law to restore his own popularity, which had presumably waned with Kimon's return to the political scene. It is true that Plutarch's account of Kimon's recall in 457, soon after Tanagra, raises almost insuperable difficulties, but his assertion (*Kimon* 17. 8) that he was recalled before 451 by a decree of the people proposed by Perikles may possibly have been derived from the text of an actual decree; we must then suppose that Plutarch's authority

was unable to date the decree on internal grounds and wrongly connected it with the defeat at Tanagra.

Wade-Gery has conjectured that the decree should be dated to 452
and perhaps connected with the story in Plutarch's *Life of Perikles*
(10. 5) that Kimon's recall was due to a secret compact negotiated by
his sister Elpinike, under which he was to resume the war against
Persia with a large fleet and allow Perikles to retain control in
Athens (*Hesperia*, xiv, 1945, 221–2, nn. 21 and 22). The role here
ascribed to Elpinike arouses suspicion, and it is not certain that
Plutarch's statement about the decree is based on epigraphic evidence.
Yet even if it was not, and even if Kimon did not return till 451,
these stories point to some kind of understanding reached by Perikles
with Kimon either before or soon after his return. Plutarch's moraliz-
ing (*Kimon* 17. 9) may not be so far from the truth after all; both
statesmen were patriotic enough to subordinate their private quarrels
to the welfare of Athens. If this was the setting of the citizenship law
it must have been either a concession to the conservatives or a
measure on which both they and the radical leaders were in agreement.

APPENDIX XI

The strategia: some problems

GENERALS and other military officials were elected by the ekklesia in
the manner prescribed by the people and regulated by a Probouleuma;
it was ordained that the elections should be held by the first board of
prytaneis ἐφ' ὧν ἂν εὐσημία γίγνηται after the sixth prytany. Hence
the elections would take place in the seventh prytany if the omens
were favourable; if not, they might be delayed till later in the year.
Such was the procedure at the time when the *Athenaion Politeia* was
written (cf. 44. 4). It is probable that in the fifth century also the
elections to the strategia were normally held in the seventh prytany,
for the natural inference from Aristophanes (*Clouds* 581 ff.) is that
Kleon's election as general for 424/423 fell shortly before the eclipse
of the sun on 21 March 424 (so Busolt–Swoboda, 990, n. 2) though the
inference has been queried (by H. B. Mayor in *J.H.S.* lix, 1939,
63, n. 3).

The date at which the generals entered on office is more controversial. It is clear that if they were elected in February or March
they would be ready to take over the command at the beginning of
the campaigning season, and at first sight this seems a more sensible
arrangement than that their predecessors should have remained in
office till July or August. The argument from convenience is strongly
urged by Mayor in his attempt (op. cit.) to revive the old view that
the term of the generals began in early spring, but parallels from the

practice of other ancient states show that the argument need not have appeared so cogent to the Athenians as it does to us, and Mayor has been no more successful than Müller-Strübing in his attempt to find support for his view in Thucydides; see the reply by W. K. Pritchett in *A.J.P.* lxi, 1940, 469–74.

We are therefore left with the usual assumption that the generals, like most Athenian officials, entered on office at the beginning of the Athenian year. But in the later part of the fifth century there were two Athenian years, the archon year and the conciliar year. When the latter was believed to have been instituted by Kleisthenes, it was perhaps a natural assumption that the strategoi, who were also believed to have been created or reorganized by Kleisthenes, should have had their term fixed by the conciliar year (cf. Wade-Gery in *C.Q.* xxvii, 1933, 28). This assumption has ceased to be tenable since Meritt proved (*Hesperia*, v, 1936, 376) that the conciliar year was not introduced till about the middle of the fifth century; others would ascribe its institution to a still later date, about 432 (see M. Giffler in *A.J.P.* lx, 1939, 444). If the conciliar year was not introduced till fifty years and more after the Kleisthenic reforms, there is less need to suppose that it was applied to the tenure of the military posts as well as to the council. Hence we may conclude that the term of the Strategoi, like that of the archons and most other officials, began on the first day of Hekatombaion.

According to the author of the *Athenaion Politeia* (61. 1) the Athenians had formerly chosen the ten generals by tribes, one from each tribe (cf. 22. 2), whereas in his own day they chose them ἐξ ἁπάντων. He goes on to describe how five of the generals were now assigned to specific duties by the people. There is no evidence for such assignment before the middle of the fourth century (Ferguson in *Klio*, ix, 1909, 320 ff.), and it is perhaps significant that in an inscription of 357/356 we find a list of eight generals belonging to seven different tribes (*I.G.* ii². 124 = Tod, ii. 153; on the problem created by the erasure of Chabrias' name see S. Accame, *La lega ateniese*, 253). It is, however, possible that the fourth century had reverted to a practice of election by tribes which had been discontinued at some date in the fifth century. When the taxiarchs were instituted, simultaneously with or soon after the reforms of 487/486 (see Busolt–Swoboda, ii. 891, n. 1) the strategoi had ceased to be commanders of the tribal regiments. Yet there is evidence that some regard continued to be paid to the tribes in their appointment. The story in Plutarch's *Life of Kimon* 8, §§ 7–9, which may come from Ion (Busolt–Swoboda, ii. 891–2, n. 3) proves that each of the tribes supplied one member to the board of generals for 469/468. It is usually believed that in the second half of the fifth century the system was so far modified that in a particular year (not necessarily in every year) two generals might be chosen from a single tribe; this innovation is assumed to have been subject to two limitations, (1) that no tribe supplied more than two generals in a single year, and (2) that the privilege of providing two generals was never granted to more than one tribe at a time. Thus in every year nine at least of the ten tribes had a representative on the board and in a particular year all might be represented.

The *terminus ante quem* for this innovation has been found in the year 441/440, for which we have a list of generals recorded by Androtion and preserved in the scholia of Aelius Aristides. According to the readings of Wilamowitz, who discovered a more complete text of the scholion in a manuscript at Venice, the fragment of Androtion, headed τῶν δέκα στρατηγῶν τῶν ἐν Σάμῳ τὰ ὀνόματα κατ' Ἀνδροτίωνα, named ten generals and the deme to which each belonged. Of these generals the first eight are given (in the correct official order of the tribes) as from Tribes I–VII, Tribe V (Akamantis) having two representatives, Perikles and Glaukon. The eighth name, Xenophon of Melite (Tribe VII) was followed, according to Wilamowitz, by Γλαυκέτης Ἀθηναῖος and Κλειτοφῶν Θοραιεύς, of whom Kleitophon belonged to Tribe X. Wilamowitz emended the meaningless Ἀθηναῖος to the rather improbable Ἀζηνιεύς (Tribe VIII). This emendation was generally accepted (cf. Beloch, *G.G.* ii². 2. 261), and it was supposed that Tribe IX had no representative on the board for 441/440. In four other years Perikles had a colleague from his own tribe, Glaukon in 439/438 (*I.G.* i². 50 as restored by Wade-Gery in *C.P.* xxvi, 1931, 309 ff.; cf. *A.T.L.* ii. 73) and in 433/432 (*I.G.* i². 295 = Tod, 55), Karkinos of Thorikos in 432/431 (*I.G.* i². 296) and probably in 431/430 also (cf. Accame in *R.F.* xiii, 1935, 347, n. 1).

After Perikles' death we occasionally find two generals from the same tribe in a particular year down to 357/356. The only certain instance in the period 429–404 is provided by the board for 407/406, in which Leontis had two representatives, Alkibiades and Adeimantos, both from the deme Skambonidai. There is a possible instance in 415/414 or 414/413; the date depends on whether we date the invasion of Lakonia recorded in Thuc. vi. 105. 2 before or after 27 July in 414 (the date of Hekatombaion 1st in the Attic year 414/413). Pythodoros, one of the Athenian generals responsible for the invasion, has been identified with the son of Epizelos (Thucydides does not give his patronymic) who was choregos in 415/414 for Tribe II, Aegeis (cf. *I.G.* i². 770a). Aegeis was also the tribe of Nikias, who was general both in 415/414 and in 414/413. It used to be assumed that Nikias also had a colleague from his own tribe in 427/426, but Hipponikos probably came from Alopeke (Tribe X); see Meritt in *Hesperia*, v, 1936, 410.

Some have denied the second of the limitations assumed above (ll. 3–5). So Stuart Jones maintained (*Philologus*, lv, 1896, 749) that in 433/432, when Akamantis was represented by Perikles and Glaukon, Kekropis also provided two generals, Proteas and Archestratos. The name Proteas and his membership of Tribe VII are supplied by a combination of Thuc. i. 45. 2 and *I.G.* i². 295 (Tod, 55); Archestratos is more doubtful. That he was one of the generals for 433/432 seems certain (cf. Gomme in *C.R.* lv, 1941, 64–65), but Stuart Jones's contention that he belonged to the deme of Phlya (and therefore to Tribe VII) is not compelling. He is described by Thuc. i. 57. 6 as son of Lykomedes. A Lykomedes, son of Aischraios, who distinguished himself at Artemision (Hdt. viii. 11. 2) is connected with Phlya in Plutarch (*Them.* 15. 3). One of the two generals in command of the expedition to Melos in 416 was Kleomedes the son of Lykomedes (Thuc. v. 84. 3), who seems to have belonged to Phlya (see the almost certain restorations in *I.G.* i². 302 [Tod, 75], ll. 30 ff.). But if the general of 433/432 is identical with the Archestratos who in 446/445 proposed a rider to the Chalkis decree (*I.G.* i². 39 = Tod, 42) it is unlikely that he was, as Stuart Jones supposed, a brother of Kleomedes. The fact that a Lykomedes occurs under Kekropis in a casualty-list of the Archidamian War (*I.G.* i². 949, l. 14) is not mentioned by Stuart Jones and is clearly irrelevant, for Herodotus is sufficient evidence that the name Lykomedes was borne by some members of an important family in Phlya. What is needed is proof that Archestratos, a common name at Athens, was also used by the same family, and this proof is lacking. As an Athenian might bear the name of his maternal grandfather there is no need to suppose that the father of Archestratos belonged to the same genos as the father of Kleomedes. The chief treasurer of Athena in 429/428 was an Archestratos with a deme-name of six letters (*I.G.* i². 237), but he need not be identical with the general of 433/432, and even if he was, Φλυεύς is not the only possible restoration of his deme-name, as Stuart Jones admitted.

Other attempts have been made to prove that in one of the years when Akamantis supplied two generals there were also two generals from another tribe, but they all fail to produce convincing proofs of the deme-attributions which they postulate. Busolt held (BS 891–2, n. 3; cf. Krause, 8) that in 432/431, when Akamantis supplied two generals, Kekropis also was represented by two generals, Proteas (Thuc. ii. 23. 2) and Eukrates (*I.G.* i². 296, l. 5). This view was based on a double assumption, that Eukrates was the demagogue Eukrates (see Gomme in *C.R.* lv, 1941, 61B, n. 1) and that because the demagogue is referred to as Μελιτεύς κάπρος in Aristophanes, fr. 143 ([O.C.T.] cf. Busolt, iii. 987, n. 3) his deme must have been Melite. But he may merely have had a house in Melite, like Hipponikos, and the first assumption is equally hazardous; who was the Eukrates who is mentioned as father of Diodotos in Thuc. iii. 41?

Another pair of generals in the thirties of the fifth century who

have been cited in this controversy are Hagnon and Phormion.
Hagnon, son of Nikias, the founder of Amphipolis (Thuc. iv. 102. 3),
was general in 431/430 (Thuc. ii. 58. 1) and probably in 440/439 (Thuc.
i. 117. 2). Beloch (*A.P.* 333-4) identified him with Hagnon the father
of Theramenes (Xen. *Hell.* ii. 3. 30) who must have belonged to the
deme of Steiria (Tribe III, Pandionis), and though the identification
was queried by Busolt (iii. 1. 517, n. 2) it has now been proved by a
new fragment of Kratinos (see Page, *Greek Literary Papyri*, Loeb
edition, vol. 1, p. 200) that the Hagnon prominent in the thirties was
from Steiria. But the ascription of Phormion to the same tribe as
Hagnon depends on the assumption that his deme was Paiania, and
for this there is no more evidence than for the assumption that Melite
was the deme of Eukrates. All that is proved by the story in Pausanias
i. 23. 10 is that Phormion had a house in Paiania, but in the second
half of the fifth century there must have been many Athenians, as
there were in the fourth, who made their home in a deme other than
that to which they belonged by descent. Apart from this there is
nothing but the purely conjectural restoration of Phormion as the
general of Pandionis in *I.G.* i². 50 (Wade-Gery in *C.P.* xxvi, 1931, 312,
repeated in *A.T.L.* ii. 73) or the complete restoration of his name and
deme in two lacunae of *I.G.* i². 296 (ll. 13 and 23). These restorations
indicate the danger of such supplements in fragmentary inscriptions,
and Gomme has rightly queried the restorations proposed in the
second inscription (*C.R.* lv, 1941, 62, n. 2).

The only possible conclusion is that we do not know to what deme
and tribe Phormion belonged. It is possible that further discoveries
may prove what Stuart Jones and Busolt tried to establish, that in
a year when Akamantis supplied two generals another tribe did the
same, and that as a result there might be two tribes without a representative on a particular board, but until decisive evidence can be
produced for this thesis it seems advisable to exclude it. The same
judgement may be passed on another contention, that even in the
period of Perikles' principate the privilege of supplying two generals
was not always reserved for his own tribe, Akamantis, and that he
might be its sole representative in a year when some other tribe provided two generals for the board (cf. Accame in *R.F.* xiii, 1935, 341-55
and Ehrenberg in *A.J.P.* lxvi, 1945, 113 ff., especially his conclusion
on p. 132).

This contention that during the years of Perikles' ascendancy the
στρατηγὸς ἐξ ἁπάντων might be someone other than Perikles seems
to me less plausible than that of Busolt and Stuart Jones, which
Ehrenberg emphatically rejects (op. cit. 128), and is based on nothing
but the unproved assumption that Phormion belonged to the same
tribe as Hagnon. If he did, then Pandionis had two generals in
431/430 when Akamantis was represented by Perikles and Karkinos;

Phormion was general for 431/430 (Thuc. ii. 29. 6) and Hagnon almost certainly was, for he went on an expedition which must be earlier than 23 July 430, when the Attic year 431/430 ended. To escape from this impasse Ehrenberg has recourse to the assumption that the generals began their term at the same time as the council, that Hagnon was general for 430/429 but not for 431/430, and that his strategia began on Prytany i. 1 of the conciliar year 430/429 (2 July 430). I have already stated the objections to this view. Moreover, the description of Hagnon and his colleague Kleopompos in Thuc. ii. 58. 1 as ξυστράτηγοι ὄντες Περικλέους seems to refer back to the expedition led by Perikles against Epidauros (Thuc. ii. 56); Ehrenberg's explanation (op. cit. 129) is improbable.

In the present state of our knowledge it is justifiable to conclude that the list preserved by Androtion for the year 441/440 is typical, that nine generals were always chosen with reference to the tribes, one from each tribe, but the tenth might be chosen ἐξ ἁπάντων. This tenth general seems always to have been Perikles during his principate; the view of Ehrenberg and Accame that it was Phormion [Why not Hagnon?] in 440/439 and 430/429 lacks confirmation. On the other two occasions in the fifth century after Perikles' death on which we find a board containing two generals from a single tribe, in 415/414 (or 414/413) and 407/406, one of the two generals is a leading statesman, Nikias in the first instance, Alkibiades in the second.

The natural inference from our evidence is that the election of one of the ten generals without reference to the tribes was an innovation introduced during the ascendancy of Perikles to overcome the difficulty created by his continuous tenure of the strategia for several years (so Wade-Gery in C.Q. xxiv, 1930, 38). As long as he monopolized the representation of Akamantis on the board, other candidates from his tribe, however worthy, would find the strategia barred to them; this reform enabled them to serve on the same board as Perikles. We do not know enough about the election of strategoi to say how the details of the reform were worked out; perhaps the people fixed the procedure each year (cf. A.P. 44. 4 and Wade-Gery's restoration of I.G. i². 114, ll. 43-45 in C.Q. xxiv, 1930, 118). When this scheme was adopted one tribe each year had to forgo its right to be represented on the board; for suggestions on the method by which it was chosen see Wade-Gery in C.Q. xxv, 1931, 89 and Accame, op. cit. 352. I agree with Accame's conjecture (op. cit. 348) that the same tribe could not be debarred from representation on the board for two years in succession.

If the above explanation is correct, the choice in any particular year of a single general ἐξ ἁπάντων was simply an expedient to surmount the difficulty created by the continuous re-election of Perikles. It presumably enhanced the prestige of the general so chosen, but there is nothing to indicate that it carried with it any augmentation of his legal powers. Taken by itself this method of election is not sufficient ground for Beloch's hypothesis that it reflects the regular subordination of the generals to one of their number who was president of the board and retained his presidency throughout the year, and the other arguments adduced by Beloch are inconclusive.

We have seen (above, p. 247) that when several generals were sent on an expedition they might be subordinated to one of their number by a vote of the people giving him supreme command of the expedition; such supremacy is indicated in Thucydides by the use of the phrase αὐτός with an ordinal numeral, e.g. τρίτος αὐτός in iii. 3. 2 (cf. i. 61. 1). But the phrase δέκατος αὐτός, applied to Perikles twice in Thucydides (i. 116. 1 and ii. 13. 1), can hardly be explained in this way, for in the first instance it is unlikely that all the generals were with Perikles in the battle against the Samians, and in the second, when Perikles was at Athens in the early summer of 431, some of them were certainly absent in Chalkidike. Now although Attica, then threatened with invasion by the enemy, might be regarded as the main theatre of war (Kahr. ii. 267–8) it remains true that, if the phrase used in ii. 13. 1 is to have any meaning, all the generals, even those in Chalkidike, must have been subordinated to the overriding authority of Perikles. This may be admitted, and we may also admit that the conferment of the supreme command on a single general dates back to the years 480 and 479, but what of it? It merely proves that the position of commander-in-chief could be given to a single member of the board in a crisis, it does not prove that it was regularly conferred every year. The phrase 'to the generals Hippokrates of Cholarges and his colleagues' in *I.G.* i². 324 (Tod, 64), l. 3 may indicate that Hippokrates was president of the board, but there is nothing to show that he retained his presidency throughout the year.

Beloch rightly called attention to the passages which imply the possession of supreme authority by Perikles in 431 and 429 (Thuc. ii. 22. 1 and 65. 4) and by Alkibiades in 407 (Xen. *Hell.* i. 4. 20), but although the second passage might be taken to show that the authority was conferred at the time of the election, this is unlikely in the first instance (since Perikles at the time, early summer 431, was holding an office to which he had been elected in March or April 432, before the passing of the Megarian Decree), while in the third Xenophon's narrative shows plainly that Alkibiades was elected some time before his return to Athens, and not proclaimed ἁπάντων ἡγεμὼν αὐτοκράτωρ until after his arrival and his speech in the ekklesia (*Hell.* i. 4. 10 and 20).

What precisely Xenophon meant by the phrase just quoted is obscure. Beloch has explained clearly that the powers of the στρατηγὸς αὐτοκράτωρ are not necessarily connected with the supposed position

A a

of the στρατηγὸς ἐξ ἁπάντων, since the former represent a heightening
of the general's competence in his dealings with the ekklesia and
might be conferred on more than one general in the same board,
whereas the other, restricted to one general each year, makes the
holder (on Beloch's view) superior in authority to his colleagues. If
plenary powers were conferred on only one member of the board by
the ekklesia, it is reasonable to assume that the general with the
greatest reputation, military or political, would be chosen as the recipient of those powers. But he is αὐτοκράτωρ merely in virtue of the
special grant voted by the people, not as a constitutional consequence
of any special position he may hold on the board of generals. All this
has been pointed out by Beloch himself, but he failed to see that it
made his hypothesis superfluous. If the outstanding general is not
necessarily invested with plenary powers every year, why suppose
that in every year he is δέκατος αὐτός, i.e. that the other members of
the board are subject to his overruling authority? The peculiar
system under which one general could be elected ἐξ ἁπάντων was
indeed connected with the eminence of the general so chosen, but it
was connected as result, not as cause. Precisely because he over-
topped the rest of his fellow-citizens this method was designed to give
an opportunity of election to competent candidates from his own
tribe. It may have heightened his prestige; it did not increase his
legal powers.

The position held by Perikles in 431 and 429 and by Alkibiades in
407 was clearly exceptional. On each occasion the chief member of
the board of generals had a decisive superiority in prestige over his
colleagues, and we may therefore suppose that his position was
strengthened both by the conferment of the plenary powers on him
alone and (as indicated by the δέκατος αὐτός of Thuc. ii. 13. 1) by a
vote of the people subordinating his colleagues to his authority; presumably this carried with it his right to preside over their meetings
throughout the rest of the official year. But it does not follow from
this that the presidency was held throughout the year by a single
general in normal times. The circumstances in 431, 429, and 407 were
very abnormal, and we may assume that the plenary powers conferred on the chief general in these years were unusually extensive to
match the gravity of the crisis, but even so the ekklesia can hardly
have abdicated its own functions; hence if Perikles was able to suspend its meetings in 431 during the Spartan invasion (Thuc. ii. 22. 1;
see above, p. 246) it was probably his prestige rather than his emergency powers that enabled him to do so.

ADDENDUM

In the above account I have accepted the report of the Aristides
scholion given by Wilamowitz. It is only fair to add that it has been

queried by F. W. Lenz (in *T.A.P.A.* 72, 1941, 226–32) who points out
that the Venice manuscript (Marcianus Graecus 423) has not ten
names but eleven. He says (op. cit. 228) that it has been collated both
by Bruno Keil and by himself, and that on this passage they are in
complete agreement: between the names of Xenophon and Glauketes
there is clearly another entry in the manuscript, Λαμπίδης Πειραιεύς,
who must be the representative of Tribe VIII. For the corrupt deme-
name of Glauketes Lenz proposes Ἀφιδναῖος, which would make him
a member of Tribe IX and is certainly more plausible than the
Ἀζηνιεύς of Wilamowitz. Thus all the tribes were represented on the
board of generals for 441/440, and as Akamantis supplied two generals
the total number for the year was eleven.

This conclusion would have interesting implications if it could be
firmly established, but it is not free from difficulties. The heading
τῶν δέκα στρατηγῶν in the scholion might be due to the carelessness of
the scholiast (Lenz, 227, n. 9), but there is no parallel for a board of
eleven strategoi, and Lenz's attempt to find one in 433/432 is unconvincing, since the passage of Thucydides on which he relies (i. 57. 6)
must be corrupt as it stands in our manuscripts; whatever Lenz may
say, it is flatly impossible that all the members of the board of
generals should have served on the expedition against Perdikkas
(see Ehrenberg in *A.J.P.* lxvi, 1945, 118). The description of Perikles
as δέκατος αὐτός in Thuc. i. 116. 1 and ii. 13. 1 proves that in 440/439
and 432/431 there were only ten strategoi. Lenz tries to evade this
difficulty by saying that 'if in 441/40 and 433/32 eleven strategoi
were elected, this does not exclude the possibility that in other years
their number was only ten, either of equal rank or nine under a commander-in-chief' (op. cit. 232). But he has just said that 'all the other
nine tribes were represented by a strategos when Perikles and his
special proxy who was taken from the fifth Phyle belonged to the
strategoi'. This seems to exclude the possibility of Akamantis having
two representatives on the board in any year in which the total
number of generals is known to have been ten. But Karkinos of
Thorikos (*I.G.* i². 296, ll. 36 and 38) certainly represented Akamantis
in 432/431, in which year Perikles was the chief of the *ten* generals.
Hence Akamantis could supply two generals in a year when there
were only ten in all, and almost certainly had done so in 439/438 also
(cf. *A.T.L.* ii. 73).

It is just conceivable that there was a board of eleven generals in
441/440 and that this was the first tentative solution (abandoned by
440/439; cf. Thuc. i. 116. 1) of the problem created by the repeated
re-election of Perikles, but we cannot exclude the possibility that
there has been some error in our manuscript tradition of the Androtion fragment. Ehrenberg (op. cit. 114, n. 5) mentions a suggestion
made by Wade-Gery that Πειραιεύς might have got into the text

as a 'tentative correction' of the already corrupt Ἀθηναῖος, but though
Ehrenberg believes that 'Lampides' was added to the list of names at
an earlier stage he makes no attempt to explain why it should have
been added, while the fact that this name is otherwise unknown in
Athens would make the supposed addition rather more than less
mysterious. Yet the assumption of some flaw in the tradition is still
tenable, even if the attempt to trace its origin has so far proved
unsuccessful. [See now Jacoby, *F.G.H.* iii B, p. 69, n. on l. 19.]

APPENDIX XII

The revolutions of 411

(a) *The* Athenaion Politeia *and Thucydides, Book VIII*

THE account given in the text of the events leading up to the revolution of the 400 is almost entirely derived from Thucydides. In the
A.P., cc. 29–32 we find an historical framework which is indeed based
on Thucydides but contrives by skilful omissions to give an impression more favourable to the promoters of the revolution. Thus the
author states correctly that the people were persuaded to accept the
proposed modification of the constitution by the hope of securing
the alliance of Persia, but he fails to add that this hope was disappointed at an early stage. He never mentions Alkibiades, and says
nothing of the reign of terror which cowed the people into submission.
When he discusses the appointment of the Syngrapheis he is probably
correct (as against our texts of Thuc. 67. 1; cf. p. 274, n. 3) in stating
that they were to be thirty in number including the ten probouloi,
but he does not disclose that they were αὐτοκράτορες and that their
report had to be presented on a fixed day (Thucydides is obviously
right on both these points).

Whether the author consulted Thucydides at first or second hand,
his account certainly contains some items from another literary
source, such as the statement that the decree of Pythodoros (= A
below) was preceded by a commendatory harangue delivered by
Melobios; presumably this and the dates in 32. 1 were derived from
an Atthis. But the peculiarities of the account are mainly due to the
use made of documentary material by the author. The documents he
abridges or quotes in full might have been taken direct by him from
the archives, but it is more likely that he found them in a literary
source, which may also have provided the connecting passages of
narrative between them. In all there are four documents:

(A) The motion of Pythodoros to appoint thirty Syngrapheis to draft
proposals περὶ τῆς σωτηρίας, with a rider by Kleitophon instructing
them to search out the πάτριοι νόμοι proposed by Kleisthenes (29. 2–3).

(B) The proposals actually made by the Syngrapheis. These fall into two parts: (a) a more detailed version (29. 4) of the proposal for the abolition of constitutional safeguards given in Thuc. 67. 2, and (b) three proposals (29. 5) introduced by the words μετὰ δὲ ταῦτα διέταξαν τὴν πολιτείαν τόνδε τὸν τρόπον. These proposals were: (1) money to be spent only on military objects and pay for civilian services (except the archons and prytaneis) to be abolished; (2) full citizenship to be restricted for the duration of the war to not less than 5,000 Athenians, to whom is reserved the sole power to conclude treaties; (3) ten men are to be chosen from each tribe, *though it is not stated who is to choose them*, and the 100 so chosen are to act as cataloguers to enrol the 5,000.

(C) A draft constitution (30. 2–6).

(D) Another draft (31) concerned mainly with the appointment and powers of a new council of 400 members.

The last two documents are apparently quoted in full. The author of the *Athenaion Politeia* describes the first draft as 'the constitution for the future', the second as 'the constitution for the present' (31. 1). As for their provenance, he claims that when the proposals of the Syngrapheis (B*a* and B*b*) had been ratified, the 5,000 (whose enrolment by the 100 cataloguers is simply taken for granted) appointed 100 men to draw up the new constitution, and that the results of their labours were drafts C and D (30. 1 and 32. 1). These drafts were then ratified by τὸ πλῆθος at a meeting presided over by Aristomachos (otherwise unknown) whereupon the old βουλή of 500 for the year of Kallias, 412/411, was dissolved on Thargelion 14th, just a month before the end of its official term. The new Council of Four Hundred entered upon office on Thargelion 22nd (32. 1).

The difficulties of this account are notorious. Its author admits later that the 5,000 λόγῳ μόνον ᾑρέθησαν (confirmed by Thuc. 92. 11). If they never became a reality until after the downfall of the 400 they could not have appointed 100 ἀναγραφεῖς before the installation of the 400. It is also surprising that the draft constitutions of cc. 30–31 are ratified by the πλῆθος, not by the 5,000, who are assumed earlier (30. 1) to have superseded the πλῆθος. The narrative of cc. 29–32 really presupposes four meetings of an assembly, in each of which a definite proposal was carried, in the following order:

(1) it is decided to appoint 30 Syngrapheis;
(2) the proposals of the Syngrapheis are approved;
(3) it is decided to appoint 100 Anagrapheis;
(4) the drafts produced by the Anagrapheis are approved.

Of these the first and second and apparently the fourth are meetings of the ekklesia, while the third is alleged to be a meeting of the 5,000. The first is found in Thuc. 67. 1, the second in his Kolonos meeting (67. 2–3 and 69. 1), while the third and fourth are peculiar to the *Athenaion Politeia*.

Thucydides does not mention the drafts C and D at all, but the suggestion that they were merely paper constitutions drawn up by some political theorist is improbable, as they seem to be closely related to the historical background of the revolution of 411. The possibility that they were abortive proposals (perhaps put forward by the moderates) cannot be dismissed on the ground that such would not have been preserved in the archives, for it is by no means certain that C and D were obtained from official records. Most scholars, however, would agree that they were certainly submitted to a legislative assembly in the course of the year 411 (cf. the verdict of Miss Lang in *A.J.P.* 69, 1948, 286) though they would disagree on the precise occasion of their submission.

The main possibilities are that they were first promulgated (1) during the meeting at Kolonos; (2) a few days after the meeting, when the news reached Athens that the Samian oligarchs had failed and that the democratic counter-revolution had triumphed at Samos and in the Athenian fleet there; (3) shortly before the fall of the 400—cf. Cary in *J.H.S.* 56, 1936, 57 n.; (4) under the rule of the 5,000, in September 411. The last possibility, supported by Beloch, is discussed below (pp. 367 ff.); it presupposes that the words ἐπικυρωθέντων δὲ τούτων, which begins the second sentence of *A.P.* 32, came immediately after the end of c. 29 in the original account, the documents in cc. 30–31 having been inserted in the wrong place by the author of the *Athenaion Politeia* or his source (Beloch, *G.G.* ii². 2. 311–13). Curiously enough Beloch failed to notice that on this view part of the original account must have fallen out, for as reconstructed by him it contains no mention of the decree providing for the appointment of the 400. It is important to remember that each of the four possible solutions entails considerable violence to the narrative of the *Athenaion Politeia*; this is inevitable, since the author was committed to the belief that the 400 were appointed under the provisions of *A.P.* 31 *and* that this document was approved before the dissolution of the old boulē recorded in Thuc. 69. (The second opinion might be correct, but it is impossible that both should be true unless we disregard the evidence of Thucydides.)

On Beloch's view the second sentence in *A.P.* 32 refers to Kolonos, and the assembly over which Aristomachos presided was the one held at Kolonos (Thuc. 67 and 69. 1); hence it is rightly described in *A.P.* 32. 1 as a meeting of τὸ πλῆθος. In this the holders of the first view concur; they suppose that the oligarchs had got these constitutions ready beforehand and induced the Assembly to ratify them before it dispersed. This meeting, from which most of the Thetes were probably absent (cf. p. 275) was regarded as *de facto* representative of the 5,000, although *de iure* they had not yet been enrolled by the Katalogeis. It is presumed that Thucydides omitted the acceptance of these constitutions from his account of the meeting because he regarded them as mere propaganda to delude the moderates and because they were never carried into effect. Wilcken, who held this view (*Berl. SB* 1935, p. 47) suggested that Peisandros' motion on the appointment of the 400 (Thuc. 67. 3) was carried after the two constitutions and as an amendment to the second. This is ingenious, but if the document in question (*A.P.* 31) was ultimately derived from the archives, why did it not contain the presumed rider as well as the original motion? (Kahrstedt in his *Forschungen*, 243, had already made this point against the similar theory of Kuberka.)

There is the further objection to the first view (as also to the third and fourth) that it is difficult to reconcile it with the dates in *A.P.* 32. The word κατελύθη used there for the dissolution of the old boulē might conceivably refer to the decision approved at Kolonos to replace it by a new council, but it is much more natural if used to signify its enforced abdication, described in Thuc. 69. Those who attempt to square the two dates in the *Athenaion Politeia* with the narrative of Thucydides must suppose that the first is the date of the Kolonos meeting and the second the date of the physical removal of the old boulē from the Bouleuterion, and that these two events were separated by an interval of eight days. But the assumption of such an interval is open to very serious objections (cf. Meyer, *F.* ii. 424–6). Hence it has been suggested that, as Athens could not carry on without a boulē, the old boulē, despite the decree for its dissolution carried at Kolonos, was allowed to carry on its functions until the 400 were ready to take them over (cf. Beloch, 322–3). According to Ferguson (*C.A.H.* v. 329), the oligarchs even contemplated the possibility that the old boulē or part of it might carry on for another month until the end of its term on Skirophorion 14th.

It is true that before the meeting at Kolonos the old council was subservient to the oligarchs (Thuc. 66. 1), and after Kolonos it was probably in no position to offer resistance by itself, but it might serve as a rallying-point for the enemies of the revolution. We must remember that hitherto the opponents of the radical democracy had been united, but that after the oligarchs had shown their hand openly at Kolonos many of the moderates must have been alienated by the selfishness of their allies and converted into potential adversaries; from now on the extreme oligarchs were menaced by opposition on two fronts. Moreover, at the time when they committed themselves at Kolonos they were still without news of the fate of their plot to control Samos, and it was therefore all the more urgent that they should seize power in Athens without undue delay.

If Thargelion 14th is the date on which the old boulē was expelled from the Bouleuterion, we have no positive evidence for the date of the meeting at Kolonos, and probability can be the only guide in any

estimate of the time which elapsed between it and the expulsion of
the old boulē. For the reasons given above the interval must have
been very brief, and Meyer may well be right that both events
occurred on the same day. The words τῇ ἡμέρᾳ ἐκείνῃ in Thucydides
(69. 2) have more point if they mean that the expulsion of the boulē
took place on the same day as the proceedings at Kolonos (cf. Cary
in *J.H.S.* 33, 1913, 10, n. 39).

Those who agree with Meyer in this conclusion must suppose that
Thargelion 22nd was the date on which the rule of the 400 began
de iure, was legitimized by the promulgation of a written constitution defining its powers. Some such step was expedient to reassure
public and especially moderate opinion, alarmed by the vague
unlimited authority conferred on the 400 at Kolonos, and the need
to appease the moderates was especially pressing after the fiasco at
Samos.

The objection made by Busolt to this solution is that it cannot be
squared with either Thucydides or the *Athenaion Politeia* (Busolt–
Swoboda, 76; *J.H.S.* 56, 1936, 51). We have already seen (p. 358)
that every reasonable reconstruction is bound to contradict the
Athenaion Politeia. Thucydides (70. 1) says that when the 400 entered
the Bouleuterion 'they elected by lot Prytaneis of their own number
and did all that was customary in the way of prayers and sacrifices
to the Gods at their entry on office' (Jowett's tr.). In spite of Busolt
this is not quite the same as 'constituted themselves with all the
usual formalities'; it certainly does not exclude the hypothesis that
the 400 produced two written constitutions a few days later and
decided to date the inauguration of their rule from the acceptance of
these constitutions by a mass meeting, carefully packed with trusty
supporters of the oligarchy. (Despite *A.P.* 32. 1 this might have been
the meeting at which Aristomachos presided, but certainty is impossible.) Thucydides naturally ignored this meeting as he ignored
those proceedings at Kolonos which, like these, were mere propaganda to delude the moderates. If this explanation of the dates in the
Athenaion Politeia is sound, we may go farther and say that the
written constitution produced on Thargelion 22nd was probably
composed of the two documents contained in *A.P.*, cc. 30–31 (cf.
Lang, op. cit. 284–6); it will be argued below (pp. 367 ff.) that their
provisions are relevant to the situation then existing, and that their
description as a provisional and a more permanent constitution is
correct.

We must now return to the discrepancies between Thucydides and
the author of the *Athenaion Politeia*. Ledl has well said (*Wiener
Studien*, xxxii, 1910, 38) that there are three crucial questions about
the appointment of the 400: (1) In what assembly, (2) Under what
decree, (3) By what method were they appointed? Thucydides

answers: (1) at Kolonos, (2) under a decree moved by Peisandros, (3) that five πρόεδροι should select 100 men who were each to co-opt three more. The author of the *Athenaion Politeia* returns no answer to the first question. He implies that the 400 were appointed under the provisions of c. 31, forty from each tribe, chosen ἐκ προκρίτων οὓς ἂν ἔλωνται οἱ φυλέται, *though he does not state who is to choose them,* for the task of the φυλέται is clearly confined to the selection of the πρόκριτοι. The speech *Pro Polystrato* preserved in the works of Lysias (= XX) tells us that Polystratos was one of the Katalogeis appointed to enrol the 5,000 and was chosen by the members of his tribe; he was also one of the 400. Wilamowitz inferred from § 14 of the speech that Polystratos took a single oath which covered both his functions, as Katalogeus and as member of the 400, and concluded that the 100 Katalogeis were all members of the 400 (but see below, pp. 365 ff.).

Thucydides' statement that the 400 were appointed at Kolonos and his account of the method of their appointment must be accepted as correct. The author of the *Athenaion Politeia* omitted all this from his account of the Kolonos meeting (29. 4–5) because his authority preferred to suggest that the 400 were appointed by the procedure prescribed in c. 31, and this in turn necessitated the contention that the new constitutions were ratified before the old council was dissolved. Probably the 100 Katalogeis of *A.P.* 29. 5 are to be identified with the 100 men selected by the 5 proedroi in Thuc. 67. 3; this supposition would explain the vague statements in *A.P.* 29. 5 and 31. 1 about selection *from* the tribesmen or *from* prokritoi chosen by the tribesmen. Possibly the tribesmen present at Kolonos gave their formal approval to lists of suitable prokritoi previously prepared by the oligarchs), and the 5 proedroi (presumably the innermost clique of the oligarchs) then selected the 100 from these lists, naturally taking care to select their most trusty supporters. This farce enabled Polystratos to say that he had been chosen by the tribesmen, because he had been selected by the proedroi from a list approved by the tribesmen.

Thucydides asserts positively that the Syngrapheis proposed nothing at Kolonos but the abolition of the constitutional safeguards (ἄλλο μὲν οὐδέν, αὐτὸ δὲ τοῦτο) and ascribes to Peisandros the authorship of the proposals subsequently carried at Kolonos (67. 2 and 68. 1). These he gives as (a) all existing ἀρχαί to be abolished, (b) all ἀρχαί to be unpaid, (c) provisions on the mode of appointing a new Council of Four Hundred, (d) the members of this council to take over the Bouleuterion and ἄρχειν ὅπῃ ἂν ἄριστα γιγνώσκωσιν αὐτοκράτορας, (e) they shall summon the 5,000 when they choose. Only the second of these appears in the *Athenaion Politeia* among the proposals carried at this juncture. These in the *Athenaion Politeia* version are introduced by the vague phrase μετὰ δὲ ταῦτα τὴν πολιτείαν διέταξαν τόνδε τὸν τρόπον; the subject of the verb might be 'the Athenians', i.e. the Assembly, but the implication is that the Syngrapheis were responsible. Thucydides' emphatic denial of this proves that he was familiar with some such contention; perhaps he had met it in Antiphon's speech on his defence (Thuc. 68. 2), to which this and other falsifications in the *Athenaion Politeia* account have been traced by Kriegel, *Die Staatsstreich der Vierhundert*, 38.

Thucydides' version of the proposals carried at Kolonos is to be preferred to that in the *Athenaion Politeia*, and we must reject the assertion (*A.P.* 29. 5) that a definite proposal to limit the franchise to 'not less than 5,000 men' was carried there (*Pro Polystrato* § 13 may refer to September 411). Probably the actual decision was that the 400 should summon the 5,000 ὁπόταν αὐτοῖς δοκῇ (Thuc. 67 end) and that when the time arrived the ἑκατὸν ἄνδρες should act as Katalogeis. As the oligarchs never intended to carry this out Thucydides omitted most of it, whereas Antiphon would naturally try to magnify its importance in his defence.

The leaders of the revolution singled out by Thucydides (c. 68) are Peisandros, Antiphon, Phrynichos, and Theramenes. In the parallel passage of the *Athenaion Politeia* (32. 2) Phrynichos is conveniently omitted; the real Aristotle knew better than to conceal the importance of his part in the revolution (*Politics* 1305^{b}27). There is not a shred of evidence in any ancient authority for the view often maintained by modern scholars, that Theramenes was the recognized leader of the moderates before the revolution of 411, entered into a coalition with the extremists and was then tricked by them. The account given by Lysias (xii. 65–66), that he began as a genuine oligarch and deserted the cause of the 400 later from fear and disappointed ambition, is fully confirmed by Thucydides (89. 2–3). There is no reason to believe that he was deceived by all the talk about the 5,000 (Thuc. 65. 3), which was intended to mislead public opinion by exaggerating the amount of support behind the oligarchs but also served as a useful bait to capture the support of the moderates, still without a recognized leader since Nikias' death. It was not till later, when the 400 began to split, that Theramenes and Aristokrates decided to part company with their former associates and lead the opposition to the extremists.

(b) *The reconstruction proposed by Miss Lang*

A fresh attempt to reconcile the accounts of Thucydides and the *Athenaion Politeia* has been made by Miss Mabel Lang in *A.J.P.* 69, 1948, 272–89. She starts with the assumption (made previously by Caspari in *J.H.S.* 33, 1913, 2) that the decree in *A.P.* 29. 2 for the appointment of the thirty Syngrapheis is to be connected with Peisandros' first journey from Samos to Athens; she believes that the decree may have been carried in the same assembly as that which reluctantly approved Peisandros' mission to Tissaphernes and Alkibiades (Thuc. viii. 54. 2). What is novel in Miss Lang's theory on this matter is the assumption that the thirty Syngrapheis presented their proposals (*A.P.* 29. 4–5) to a 'Second Assembly' during Peisandros' absence, and that the Katalogeis were duly appointed and actually started work on their task before his return (p. 287). When he did return he reported to a 'Third Assembly' that the Persians required a stricter oligarchy than that of the 5,000, and carried a proposal that a new committee of Syngrapheis, composed of only ten members, should be appointed with full powers to produce on a fixed day (in the near future, cf. p. 280) suggestions καθ' ὅτι ἄριστα ἡ πόλις οἰκήσεται; this is the proposal recorded in Thuc. viii. 67. 1, which on this theory is different in time, attendant circumstances, and content from the decree in *A.P.* 29. 2.

It is an essential postulate of this reconstruction that the news of the breakdown in the negotiations with Persia (Thuc. viii. 56) was successfully concealed by the oligarchs, so that Peisandros on his return was able to justify his demands by the supposed insistence of the Persians on a closer oligarchy than that proposed by the thirty Syngrapheis. This postulate seems to me irreconcilable with our remarkably detailed chronological information for this period, which is provided by the particulars in Thucydides' narrative (the stages of which are dated by the reference to the winter solstice in viii. 39. 1 and the cross-references between the two parallel sections cc. 29–44 and 45–59, both describing the 'winter' of 412/411) and the precise dates in c. 32 of the *Athenaion Politeia*.

From this information Busolt (*G.G.* iii. 1471–2 and 1476) rightly inferred the following dates, all in 411: (1) the assembly authorizes Peisandros and ten others to negotiate with Alkibiades, towards the end of January; (2) breakdown of these negotiations, before the end of February; (3) conclusion of a fresh treaty between Tissaphernes and Sparta, about the end of February; (4) return of Peisandros to Athens and the decree, recorded in Thuc. 67. 1, to appoint ξυγγραφέας αὐτοκράτορας, towards the end of May. The date given by Miss Lang (p. 288) for the first is 'early spring', which presumably implies a date not earlier than 21 March and is therefore at variance with the evidence of Thucydides. She dates her 'Second Assembly' (*A.P.* 29. 4–5) to 'middle spring' and her 'Third Assembly' to the beginning of Thargelion (p. 289), which equals the last week of May in 411. She seems to imply that her Second Assembly was not very long before Peisandros' return, for of the decree carried in this assembly she says (p. 276) that its 'effectiveness . . . was temporary in the extreme and almost immediately voided by a more effective measure'. This compression of the time scheme is inevitable on her theory. But if in fact

three clear months elapsed between the breakdown of the negotiations with Tissaphernes and Peisandros' return to Athens, how can
we believe that the news of the breakdown was still unknown in
Athens when Peisandros arrived, especially as Persia had long since
made a new treaty with Sparta?

Caspari's contention (loc. cit.) that Thucydides had postdated by
nearly five months the appointment of the Syngrapheis is unacceptable. But Miss Lang's suggestion that their proposal in Thuc. 67. 2
was submitted to an assembly held at least three weeks later than
that which approved of the proposals in *A.P.* 29. 4 is surely impossible.
The version in the *Athenaion Politeia* is fuller than that of Thucydides,
but the kernel is the same, the abolition of the Graphē Paranomon,
and therefore the two accounts, despite the discrepancies between
them, must refer to the same occasion. If the Athenians had already
voted the suspension of the Graphē Paranomon at the 'Second
Assembly' there would have been no need for the Thucydidean
Syngrapheis to propose its suspension again a month or so later.

Miss Lang claims that her reconstruction saves the credit of the
author of the *Athenaion Politeia* (as well as that of Thucydides), but
if her account of how his mind worked (p. 283) could be accepted it
would make him out to be even more incompetent than his sternest
critics had supposed. Although there is much of permanent value in
Miss Lang's paper, the novelties in her reconstruction must be rejected.

(c) *The evidence of the* Pro Polystrato

It is doubtful whether much trust can be placed in the statements
made in this speech (henceforth referred to as P). What is certain is
that the defendant had been a member of the 400 and that he was
later tried twice for his part in the revolution. The first trial seems to
be dated in § 14 soon after his return from Eretria, and must therefore
have occurred very early in the rule of the 5,000; it ended in the
imposition of a heavy fine. The second trial, for which P was composed, seems to belong to the period after the restoration of the radical
democracy, and therefore to a date after the middle of 410. On all
this see the discussion by Wilamowitz (*A.A.* ii. 356–67).

The principal items in the speech are: (1) §§ 1–2. It is not right to
be angry with all the members of the 400, for some of them were well
disposed to the city like Polystratos; οὗτος γὰρ ἡρέθη μὲν ὑπὸ τῶν
φυλετῶν ὡς χρηστὸς ὢν ἀνὴρ καὶ περὶ τοὺς δημότας καὶ περὶ τὸ πλῆθος τὸ
ὑμέτερον. (2) § 13. A clear proof of his friendship for the democracy is
given by the fact that when the demos voted to hand over the government to a body of 5,000, Polystratos καταλογεὺς ὢν ἐνακισχιλίους
κατέλεξεν. (3) § 14. He was not willing either ὀμόσαι or καταλέγειν, but
they [apparently the oligarchs] compelled him by threats of fines and
penalties. When he yielded to compulsion and took the oath, ὀκτὼ

ἡμέρας εἰσελθὼν εἰς τὸ βουλευτήριον ἐξέπλει εἰς Ἐρετρίαν. Wilamowitz
showed that Polystratos must have sailed to Eretria before the
dispatch of the squadron under Thymochares in Thuc. viii. 95. 2 ; he
inferred that as φρούραρχος he carried through an oligarchic revolution in Eretria and could therefore be regarded as responsible for its
subsequent revolt. Incidentally P admits (§ 12) that Polystratos
belonged to the same deme as Phrynichos and was accused of being
hand in glove with him. P's arguments against this are very weak, as
they merely prove that there had been no close friendship between
the defendant and Phrynichos before 411 ; we know from Thucydides
that Phrynichos did not join the oligarchs till 411 (viii. 68. 3).

It is clear from the above that we have only scattered allusions in
P, no connected narrative of the events in which Polystratos was
implicated. The natural inference from the first item is that his
election by the tribesmen was somehow connected with his membership of the 400, whereas in the second and third items he is concerned
with the enrolment of the 5,000. As § 14 connects with his appointment to this function his obligation to take an oath, it is assumed
that he was one of the 100 Katalogeis appointed to enrol the 5,000 by
the decree of *A.P.* 29. 5, who were to begin their task ὁμόσαντες
καθ' ἱερῶν τελείων. Yet the immediate sequel to the taking of the oath
by Polystratos is his entry into the council chamber (§ 14), for the
ὅρκος in line 25 of the Oxford Text must refer to the same thing as the
ὁμόσαι of line 23.

Wilamowitz (op. cit. 357) inferred that the oath in question was
that taken by Polystratos as Katalogeus, but that election as one of
the 100 Katalogeis automatically included membership of the 400 ;
on this view the Katalogeis, appointed before the Council of Four
Hundred, were made the nucleus of the new council by the decree
which created it. Another hypothesis has been suggested above
(p. 362) that the 100 Katalogeis were the 100 men who in Thuc.
viii. 67. 3 certainly formed the nucleus of the 400, but that their commission to act as Katalogeis was an afterthought.

Miss Lang supposes that Polystratos and the other Katalogeis had
been appointed in the spring of 411, and that he had made a beginning
of his task before the return of Peisandros ; he was included in the
400 at the time of their inauguration, but only kept in Athens during
the eight days (presumably Thargelion 14th–22nd) when he might be
dangerous, then sent to Euboia (op. cit. 287). It is not clear whether
she believes that *all* the Katalogeis were included in the 400. Kriegel
also seems to hold (op. cit. 31) that there was no necessary connexion
between the election of Polystratos as one of the Katalogeis and his
inclusion in the 400. He argues that § 2 of the speech must refer to
the choice of Polystratos by his fellow tribesmen as one of the
Katalogeis, on the ground that even if *A.P.* 31. 1 were right and the

400 in some sense chosen by the tribesmen, the choice would not
prove that Polystratos was εὔνους τῷ πλήθει τῷ ὑμετέρῳ. But Kriegel
seems to have misunderstood the passage. The method of election is
not adduced as a *proof*. What we have is a statement that the choice
of Polystratos (as distinguished from other candidates) was due to
his fellow tribesmen's conviction of his loyalty to the demos; this is
pure assertion, and no attempt at verification is offered. Moreover,
Kriegel is clearly wrong when he says that election of the Katalogeis
by the tribes is prescribed in *A.P.* 29. 5. The papyrus merely says
ἑλέσθαι δ κ τῆς φυλῆς ἑκάστης, and whether we read δὲ καί with Kenyon
or δ' ἐκ with Herwerden and others, the meaning is the same: the
Katalogeis are to be chosen *from* the tribes, but it is not stated who
is to choose them.

If the author of P had meant what Kriegel says he meant in §§ 1–2
he would have expressed his meaning with the maximum of obscurity,
for the development of the paragraph suggests plainly that appointment to the 400 is in question, and if the Katalogeis were appointed,
as Kriegel apparently believes, at Kolonos, the part played by the
tribesmen in their appointment can have been little more than
nominal, though P found it convenient for his purpose to make the
most of it. It is surely significant that the decree in *A.P.* 29. 5 does
not explain *how* the Katalogeis are to be chosen from the tribes.

Miss Lang's hypothesis certainly provides a period in which Polystratos could have exercised his activities as a Katalogeus, but it is unacceptable on chronological and other grounds (see above, pp. 363 f.).
Beloch showed (*Bevölkerung*, 107–8) that Polystratos had no time to
carry out his task between his appointment and his departure to
Eretria, and that, if Thuc. viii. 92. 11 is correct, no list of the 5,000 can
have been drafted during the rule of the 400. He inferred from P § 13
that a list of 9,000 full citizens was drawn up after the downfall of the
400, and that Polystratos was one of the Katalogeis chosen (possibly
ten in all, one from each tribe) in September 411. But the second of
these inferences must be false if the first trial and first condemnation
of Polystratos occurred soon after the loss of Eretria, i.e. in the early
days of Theramenes' moderate democracy.

Taeger has classified the statements of P in three groups, (1) trustworthy, (2) misleading, (3) false (*Gnomon*, xiii, 1937, 352, n. 1). I am
inclined to agree with him that the description of Polystratos'
activities as Katalogeus should be included in the third group.
Ferguson (*Mélanges Glotz*, 359, n. 2) rightly objected to Beloch's view
that if Polystratos had been chosen as Katalogeus by the 5,000 P
'would certainly have brought the fact out clearly in his defence of
him'. But Ferguson's own inference from P § 13 that the Katalogeis
appointed under the 400 remained in office after the deposition of the
400 seems contrary to all probability. There must have been at least

a reappointment, and if that is admitted Ferguson's argument against Beloch turns against himself. The narrative of P is so incomplete and misleading that it is doubtful whether any valuable conclusions can safely be drawn from it. Even Wilamowitz's inference from § 14 may be false if P for his own purpose was deliberately confusing Polystratos' two functions as Katalogeus and as member of the 400.

(d) *The documents in chapters 30 and 31 of the* Athenaion Politeia

The curiously abrupt transition from the provisions in 29. 5 to the two documents (labelled C and D above, p. 357) in cc. 30–31 suggested to Beloch (*G.G.* ii². 2. 311 ff.) the hypothesis that these two documents, discovered in the archives by the author or his source, were headed by some such rubric as: τάδε οἱ ἑκατὸν ἀναγραφεῖς οἱ ὑπὸ τῶν πεντακισχιλίων αἱρεθέντες ἀνέγραψαν. The mention in the second document of a Council of Four Hundred suggested the erroneous conclusion that the documents had been carried before the installation of the well-known 400, but the rubric should have warned the reader that when the documents were approved the 5,000 were a reality. As these, the ὅπλα παρεχόμενοι, were not properly constituted till the downfall of the 400 (Thuc. 97. 1), the two documents must have been carried in autumn 411. On this view they can only be regarded as complementary parts of one and the same constitution; it is to be noted that D contains a clear reference to C (*A.P.* 30. 3) in the clause arranging for the subsequent distribution of the 400 between the four λήξεις (31. 3). Beloch argued that the ascription of the two documents to two separate constitutions, one permanent and one temporary, was a blunder committed by the author who first used the documents.

Beloch's view has been subjected to a careful re-examination by G. H. Stevenson (*J.H.S.* lvi, 1936, 48–57). He argues that some of the provisions of D are incompatible with its description as a temporary constitution, since they seem intended to remain in force for several years, and that the type of constitution obtained by a conflation of C and D, in which a boulē of 400 exists side by side with an ekklesia of 5,000, is presupposed as a constitution likely to be acceptable to the moderates in Thucydides (93. 2). Stevenson, however, ends with a refusal to commit himself to belief in Beloch's view (p 57).

The possibility of the combination proposed by Beloch depends on the interpretation of C. Its principal provisions are: (1) the council is to be composed of men over thirty, holding office for a year and serving without pay. (2) Certain officials, apparently numbering 100 in all (cf. Sandys on *A.P.* 30. 3) are to be chosen [*by whom?*] from πρόκριτοι who must be members of the council. (3) The control of domestic as well as imperial revenues is entrusted to the

Hellenotamiai [there is some uncertainty about the text here], who are henceforth to number 20 instead of 10, while the two sacred treasuries, Athena's and that of the Other Gods, are to be managed by a single board of 10 instead of two separate boards. (4) All officials other than those specified in clause 2 are to be chosen by lot from citizens who are not members of the council. (5) The Hellenotamiai actually administering the funds (presumably this was done by sections of the board in rotation) are not to sit with the council. (6) For the future four councils are to be formed from the citizens over thirty and each is to hold office in turn. (7) A special provision on financial administration, which comes in oddly here, has perhaps been wrongly transposed from the end of clause 5; see Munro in *C.Q.* viii, 1914, 13–15. (8) The council is normally to meet every five days and is to be convened (reading πληροῦν in 30. 5) by the nine archons; five men are chosen by lot from the council, and from these the president of the council is selected, also by lot. Provisions follow for the order of business in the council meetings (with special facilities for the generals) and for fines to be imposed on councillors absent without excuse.

Controversy centres on the meaning of the sixth clause: βουλὰς δὲ ποιῆσαι τέτταρας ἐκ τῆς ἡλικίας τῆς εἰρημένης (i.e. over thirty) εἰς τὸν λοιπὸν χρόνον, καὶ τούτων τὸ λαχὸν μέρος βουλεύειν, νεῖμαι δὲ καὶ τοὺς ἄλλους πρὸς τὴν λῆξιν ἑκάστην. τοὺς δ' ἑκατὸν ἄνδρας (unexplained; possibly the 100 καταλογεῖς of *A.P.* 29. 5. See Busolt–Swoboda, i. 75, n. 4, and Beloch, 315–16) διανεῖμαι σφᾶς τε αὐτοὺς καὶ τοὺς ἄλλους τέτταρα μέρη ὡς ἰσαίτατα καὶ διακληρῶσαι, καὶ εἰς ἐνιαυτὸν βουλεύειν. The obvious interpretation is that all members of the 5,000 who were over thirty years of age were to be divided into four λήξεις or sections, each of which was to act in turn as βουλή for one year. If those under thirty numbered at least 30 per cent. of the whole body of full citizens, the annual council would contain 875 members, an unwieldy body to meet every five days, especially as non-attendance was to be discouraged by fines.

Sandys supposed that the four councils were to contain 400 members each, and explained in his note on 30. 3 that 'the one hundred who had drawn up the constitution [i.e. the 100 Anagrapheis of 30. 1] were to divide themselves and "the rest", i.e. the rest of the 5,000 above the age of thirty, into four divisions of 400 each'. But how could this be done unless the members of the 5,000 over thirty numbered no more than 1,600, only 32 per cent. of the whole? This is inconceivable, and Sandys's explanation must therefore be rejected.

Beloch's interpretation is more elaborate. He believes, like Sandys, that the βουλή of C was to contain 400 members as prescribed in D, but he thinks that the τέτταρες βουλαί of C (30. 3) are to be regarded as four subdivisions of the full council. Each subdivision is composed of 100 men, and each acts in turn for a quarter of the year in an order fixed by lot (cf. 30. 3) as the inner council, on the model of the local constitutions of the Boiotian states in this period (cf. the 'Oxyrhynchus historian' [Jacoby, *F.G.H.*, no. 66] c. 11). As Beloch explains, these four smaller councils together form the full council, and it is merely the presidency that rotates, so that the relation between the smaller council and the whole forms a close parallel to that between the Prytaneis and the Kleisthenic boulē.

These subdivisions of the full council are described by Beloch as 'sections', a term which has been carefully avoided in the above description. It is used by Beloch in two quite different senses within a few lines (p. 317). After his account of the 'four councils' he continues: 'and indeed the members of the Commission and "the rest", i.e. all members of the Five Thousand over thirty, were to be divided into *the four sections* [italics mine] in such a way that each section contained the same number of members; from these sections the councillors, who remained in office a year, were then chosen by lot' [Beloch thinks this last proviso was altered in D; see below, p. 371]. Thus Beloch's sections are (*a*) the four committees, each 100 strong, of the boulē of 400, or (*b*) the four divisions or λήξεις into which all the 5,000 over thirty are divided. We have already met the second view in the usual interpretation of document C, but whereas on that interpretation each of the four sections acts in turn as council for the year, all its members being bouleutai, on Beloch's view each annually supplies 100 members chosen by lot to a boulē of 400.

In what follows the term 'section' will be confined to the second sense only [= (*b*) above], whether the usual view or Beloch's is under discussion. I cannot help feeling that Beloch's use of it in two senses is deliberate and calculated to enable him to make the best of both worlds. He needs the sections (in the normal sense) to cover certain lacunae in his explanation of the documents, and so he glides from one sense to the other in his interpretation of clause 6. But he has really cut himself off from the normal view (even more completely than Sandys had done) by his version of the first two lines of that clause (down to the first βουλεύειν), and can only get back to it by using the words which I have printed in italics. His expedient is illegitimate; how can he refer to '*the* four sections' when they have never been mentioned in this sense before? On the usual view the creation of the four sections is identical with the creation of the four boulai, and the meaning of τὴν λῆξιν ἑκάστην is obvious from what precedes. On Beloch's view these three words have nothing to do with τὸ λαχὸν μέρος (one of the four subdivisions of his boulē), but suddenly introduce and take for granted a subdivision of the 5,000 which has not hitherto been mentioned at all. It must, however, be admitted that this argument is not absolutely decisive by itself, since all would agree that the legislators who drafted documents C and D performed their task very badly.

Beloch holds that they first laid down their general principles in C, then filled in the details (or most of them, see below, pp. 371 f.) in D. The provisions of D are: (1) the number of the full council is fixed at 400 κατὰ τὰ πάτρια, composed of 40 members over thirty years of age from each tribe, chosen ἐκ προκρίτων οὓς ἂν ἕλωνται οἱ φυλέται; on this clause see above, p. 361. (2) This council is to choose the officials and draft the form of oath to be taken. Wilcken has argued (op. cit. 42 f.; *J.H.S.* 56, 52) that the corrupt reading here in the papyrus should be healed by the omission of γράψαι rather than the introduction of καί suggested by Kenyon, and that consequently the usual interpretation of this clause, which makes the council supreme and irresponsible, is based on a false reading. (3) The council is bound to observe the laws οἳ ἂν τεθῶσιν περὶ τῶν πολιτικῶν and not to modify them by any alteration or addition. (4) Curiously complicated rules are laid down for the military appointments. Three stages seem to be envisaged: (*a*) an immediate election of the strategoi from (and perhaps by) the 5,000. (*b*) when the council has been duly constituted it is to hold a military review and choose ten men (the strategoi are apparently meant) who are to hold office for τὸν εἰσιόντα ἐνιαυτόν as αὐτοκράτορες, with power to join in the deliberations of the council when they wish; the council is also to elect one Hipparch and ten Phylarchs. (*c*) hereafter these officials (τούτων in the last sentence of § 2 presumably includes the strategoi) are to be chosen κατὰ τὰ γεγραμμένα. (5) No office except those of bouleutes and strategos can be held more than once. (6) A final proviso refers to the armament at Samos.

This last clause is extremely difficult. Wilamowitz (*A.A.* ii. 121) rightly defended the papyrus reading τοῖς ἀστοῖς, realizing that the citizens in Athens are here contrasted with οἱ ἄλλοι, i.e. those members of the armament at Samos who possessed the qualification required for membership of the 5,000. Like most scholars he believes that document C rather than D represents the ideal of the moderates, and he detected in this clause their anxiety that the interim Council of Four Hundred should be replaced as soon as possible by the type of council that they preferred. They did not go so far as to say that the provisional constitution must end as soon as the citizens now at Samos could take their place in the council, but they laid down a requirement (the distribution of the 400 among the four sections of *A.P.* 30. 3) which was bound to produce the same result. Beloch assumes that the clause provides for the distribution of the ὅπλα παρεχόμενοι now at Samos among the four sections, and that αὐτούς refers to them and not to the 400, who on his view already belonged to the four sections. He translates: 'to ensure the continuance of the division of the 400 into the four sections after the citizens at Samos are in a position to be represented on the council, the Hundred shall enrol these citizens also in the four sections' (op. cit. 320). I doubt whether this can be fairly extracted from the Greek, but other interpretations of this clause are unsatisfactory and emendations inspire no confidence.

In his examination of document D Beloch supplies the curious gap in the first clause by an assumption that the choice of the councillors from the πρόκριτοι was to be made by the four sections, each voting on the candidates put forward for its section by the tribes (p. 318); he sees in this a modification of the first draft, which had proposed that the councillors should be elected by lot. Clause 2 is supposed to be complementary to clause 2 of C; the elected officials are to be chosen by the council but (as enacted in C) from πρόκριτοι. Beloch suggests that this prokrisis must have been the work of the four sections, but this is rendered improbable by the stipulation in C that the prokritoi are all to be members of the boulē. The crux is rooted in Beloch's interpretation of C as a whole; we have seen that the officials in question probably numbered 100, so that there must have been at least 200 prokritoi, an incredible provision if the whole council was to contain no more than 400 members.

Clause 4 creates fresh difficulties for Beloch. On the usual theories, which date the acceptance of D to the Kolonos meeting or soon after, stage (a) provides for the brief remainder of either the conciliar year or Archon year 412/411, (b) for the ensuing year 411/410, and (c) for the future (see above, p. 370). Beloch, dating D to September or October 411, has to maintain that (a) provides for the rest of 411/410 and (b) for 410/409. This not only presupposes a long interval between the installation of the new council and the adoption of the new method for the appointment of the military officials, but compels Beloch to fuse the two stages distinguished above as (b) and (c). Such a fusion is impossible if κατὰ τὰ γεγραμμένα at the end of the clause refers to the proviso in C that military officials are to be elected from prokritoi who must be members of the body acting as boulē for the time being, for there is no hint in D that the choice of military officials by the boulē is subject to this limitation in stage (b).

Anyone who studes these two documents closely must be struck by their incompleteness. They contain no reference to the new judicial arrangements which would be essential in any transference of political power from the proletariat to the middle and upper classes. Even the topics with which they are mainly concerned, the composition of the council and the appointment of the magistrates, are not adequately treated. Important questions are left unsettled in both documents, and Beloch's hypothesis that D is intended to cover omissions in C is no answer to this objection, for he is still left with some lacunae which he can supply only by conjecture, to say nothing of the fresh cruces appearing in D. Any explanation of the obscurities in these two documents must be conjectural, as we are so utterly in the dark about the circumstances of their origin, but the obvious solution is that they were concocted in a hurry and had to be produced at short notice (cf. Cary, cited on p. 358). Though this conclusion does not enable us to fix the date of their promulgation precisely, it tends against Beloch's view, for there could have been no special need for haste once the 400 had been overthrown.

Beloch's hypothesis really contains two propositions, (1) that documents C and D are complementary parts of the same constitution, and (2) that both were passed after the overthrow of the 400. The possibility of the first does not depend on the truth of the second, for the documents might have been promulgated earlier than September 411 as a draft constitution intended to come into force at some future date, i.e. the description of C in the *Athenaion Politeia* as 'the constitution for the future' might apply to D as well. The second proposition is more open to attack and will be discussed first.

Some have argued that C, as representing the ideal of the moderates, was re-enacted when they acquired power in September 411. But though some provisions from it were probably adopted then, it can be proved that the document as a whole was not (see below, pp. 377 f.), and the proof that 'the constitution of Theramenes' was not identical with C rules out equally Beloch's contention that it was CD. There are two further objections to his view. (1) As Alkibiades in his message to the oligarchs (Thuc. viii. 86. 6) had demanded the restoration of the Council of Five Hundred, Theramenes and the other leaders of the counter-revolution in Athens could hardly have afforded to neglect this demand. It is true that the decree of Demophantos, carried in the first prytany of the year 410/409, soon after the restoration of the radical democracy, refers to ἡ βουλὴ οἱ πεντακόσιοι οἱ λαχόντες τῷ κυάμῳ (Andok. i. 96) and we may agree with Beloch (p. 314) that this description was needed to distinguish it from its predecessors under the oligarchy and the rule of the 5,000. But the carefulness of the description indicates that the restored council had to be distinguished not merely from the hated 400 but from another Council of Five Hundred which had *not* been chosen by lot. We must suppose that on the overthrow of the oligarchy the moderates instituted a Council of Five Hundred to satisfy Alkibiades, but that unlike the old Kleisthenic council it was elected, not chosen by lot (Meyer, *G.A.* iv. 599); it also differed from the old council in being unpaid. (2) It is extremely unlikely that when the 5,000 began to rule they would have fixed the membership of their council at a number which revived all the hateful associations of the régime they had just overthrown. Moreover, the speech *Pro Polystrato*, delivered after the con-

stitution of Theramenes had been superseded by the radical democracy ([Lys.] xx. 22), already uses the term 'the 400' to describe
the oligarchy; it is at least improbable that the term would have
acquired this meaning so soon if the council had still numbered 400
under the rule of the 5,000 (cf. Wade-Gery in Stevenson, op. cit. 57
and n. 37).

It is harder to disprove Beloch's first proposition, for the documents are so obscurely drafted that their interpretation must be
uncertain. But the assumption is at least peculiar that βουλεύειν
could be used in the sixth clause of C (*A.P.* 30. 3) first for the full
council and then for the inner council without any indication of the
change in meaning. The difficulties raised by Beloch's explanation of
clause 4 in D disappear if we abandon his dating of D, and the
ambiguity in his use of the term 'section' should perhaps not be
pressed, but the problem of clause 2 in C remains (above, p. 371) and
it seems to me to be fatal to Beloch's hypothesis. We are therefore
driven back to the view that C is independent of D. It may be presumed to represent the ideal of the moderates, though they must
have exercised some influence over the drafting of D as well; the
clauses of D reveal a determination to limit as far as possible the
powers and the duration of the provisional government, which was
perhaps to be superseded by the beginning of 410/409 (see above,
p. 371 for the interpretation of clause 4 in D).

In my opinion the most likely date for the promulgation of these
documents is Thargelion 22nd (cf. Meyer, *F.* ii. 424–5) eight days
after the expulsion of the old boulē. The 400 must have heard of the
failure of their schemes in Samos within a few days of their occupation of the Bouleuterion, for Thuc. viii. 73. 1 makes the fiasco at
Samos contemporary with the institution of the 400, and 74. 1 shows
that when messengers set out from Samos to announce the triumph
of the democrats, the news of the oligarchical revolution at Athens
had not yet reached Samos. Possibly the 400 had always intended to
legitimize their *coup d'état*, but it was now an urgent necessity to
conciliate the moderates by the promulgation of a written constitution which was supposed to come into force at no very distant date
(see above, p. 370), while the moderates for their part were bound to
co-operate with the extremists in providing a cloak of legitimacy for
their previous proceedings.

It is theoretically possible that after the promulgation of document
D the 400 were regularly reappointed under its provisions (several
days after their irregular designation at Kolonos), from prokritoi
chosen by the tribesmen, in an assembly carefully packed for the
occasion (so apparently Kriegel, *Staatsstreich*, 54–55). Ferguson
(*Treasurers of Athena*, 145, n. 1) supposes that it was to such a regular
re-election that Polystratos referred in [Lys.] xx. 2. The crucial

difficulty in any such view is that the silence of Thucydides about a regular re-election of the 400 would be much harder to understand than in the instances presupposed above (pp. 358 f. and 362). The more probable view is that the promulgation of the document was intended to mislead those who did not know the facts and to suggest that the 400 had in fact been appointed in the manner prescribed (a suggestion actually accepted by the source of the *Athenaion Politeia* —see p. 358 above); this deception was facilitated by the omission to state who was to choose the 400 from the prokritoi.

A gesture to the men of hoplite census serving in the fleet at Samos is contained in the final clause of the provisional constitution, but the rest of it is intended to allay the anxieties of the moderates (cf. p. 360) by carefully limiting the authority of the 400 and providing for their eventual supersession by the 5,000. The plenary powers conferred on the generals for 411/410 probably did not go beyond those conferred on generals under the radical democracy (cf. p. 248).

Some have denied that Thucydides was acquainted with documents C and D, but on insufficient grounds, and he must have known them if they were used by Antiphon in his defence. Others (cf. Stevenson, op. cit. 49–50 for a discussion) have detected references to them in two passages of Thucydides. The later passage (93. 2) is a statement made by representatives of the 400 to individuals among the hoplites at Piraeus who had risen against their rule; the envoys assured them that a list of the 5,000 would be published and that from them the 400 would be chosen ἐν μέρει ᾗ ἂν τοῖς πεντακισχιλίοις δοκῇ. Earlier (86. 3) the emissaries sent by the 400 to the fleet at Samos had announced that the aims of the oligarchs were patriotic, τῶν τε πεντακισχιλίων ὅτι πάντες ἐν τῷ μέρει μεθέξουσιν; the natural interpretation of this is Jowett's, that 'all the Five Thousand in turn were to have a share in the administration' (understanding τῶν πραγμάτων or τῶν τετρακοσίων as the noun to be supplied after μεθέξουσιν, cf. *J.H.S.* 56, 50). Thus the meaning of both passages is roughly the same, though the later one adds that the method of rotation in the choice of the 400 is to be defined by the 5,000. The rotation envisaged seems to be the pure rotation prescribed in the bogus constitution of Drakon (*A.P.* 4. 3), which must represent the ideal constitution of some anti-democratic pamphleteer in the late fifth century; in it no one is to hold for a second time any office, including that of bouleutēs, until all qualified persons have held it once.

This conclusion proves that Thucydides, in those passages which presuppose the co-existence of a Council of Four Hundred with an assembly of 5,000, does not support Beloch's hypothesis that C and D were complementary parts of the same constitution. Though the four sections on Beloch's view have certain functions to perform, these are vested in the four sections *as sections,* and there is no suggestion that their members (who did *not* include those of the 5,000 under the age of thirty) should ever meet together to form an ekklesia. Moreover, it is laid down (*A.P.* 31. 3) that the 400, like the generals, are to be exempt from the rule forbidding re-election.

When the extreme oligarchs triumphed at Kolonos, their success naturally alienated those moderates who had expected the building of a new constitution on a less narrow foundation. As the extremists were now firmly in control of the machine of government they could have ignored the resentment of the moderates if only their plans had been successful at Samos. But when they failed there they were faced by the threat of opposition on two fronts, and knowing that they could not make the concessions needed to satisfy the radicals, they were driven to renew their attempts to conciliate the moderates. The obvious means to this end was an offer to make the 5,000 a reality, and a promise to choose the members of the Council of Four Hundred from all the hoplites in turn; the latter would dispel the suspicion that the present members intended to retain their position indefinitely. But though the extremists professed to be ready to surrender their powers to others, they were unwilling to do more than the bare minimum required to appease the moderates, and presumably were anxious to postpone to a more distant future the replacement of the provisional by the permanent constitution. As Thucydides says (92. 11), they regarded the effective rule of the 5,000 as 'downright democracy'.

(e) The constitution of the 5,000

Thucydides tells us that the assembly which decreed the deposition of the 400 voted to transfer the power to 'the 5,000', who were to include all the ὅπλα παρεχόμενοι, and reaffirmed the abolition of state pay for all civilian services; this assembly was followed by several others, in which the people appointed nomothetai and settled the details of the new constitution (viii. 97. 1–2); presumably the nomothetai were elected to revise the existing code of laws. Apart from the evidence of Thucydides we have little information about the new constitution. A new body of Katalogeis must have been appointed to draw up the list of the new citizens, and we may perhaps infer from the *Pro Polystrato* (§ 13) that when completed the list contained 9,000 names, but it is unlikely that Polystratos had anything to do with their enrolment (see above, p. 366).

The text of a decree belonging to the rule of the 5,000, the decree proposed by Andron for the trial of Antiphon, Archeptolemos, and Onomakles, has been preserved in § 23 of the *Life of Antiphon* contained in the *Lives of the Ten Orators* ([Plut.] *Moralia* 833 E).

Andron proposed that the three men named should be arrested as traitors and brought before the dikasterion, and that the prosecution should be conducted by the generals and by συνήγοροι chosen by them from the members of the boulē (possibly Apolexis was one of these Synegoroi, though he may have been a general; see Harpokration, s.v. στασιώτης). The preamble of the decree describes it as a decree of the βουλή and does not mention the ἐκκλησία; it is also noteworthy that the chairman and the secretary are both members of the same tribe, Antiochis. Under the radical democracy such a coincidence was impossible, since the chairman was chosen from the prytanizing tribe, whereas the secretary always belonged to one of the other nine (see Ferguson in *C.P.* xxi, 1926, 74; in *I.G.* i². 109, the one apparent exception, the reading is doubtful. See now *A.T.L.* i. 168).

Ferguson (in *C.P.* xxi, 1926, 72–75) has tried to supplement our scanty information by the hypothesis that the constitution of September 411 rested on a re-enactment of the document in the *Athenaion Politeia* (c. 30) described as 'the constitution for the future', which has often been supposed to be closer to the ideal of the moderates than 'the provisional constitution' (*A.P.* 31). Ferguson and Wilcken believe that the document in *A.P.* 30 had been approved as a draft constitution in June 411 but had been put into cold storage until the downfall of the 400, when it was revived by the moderates, submitted to the Assembly for confirmation, and accepted without any alteration. So the description of the constitution of September 411 given by Ferguson in *C.A.H.* v (338–40) is mainly derived from *A.P.* 30 and presupposes that the provisions in the draft were taken over without any modification into the constitution when the moderates triumphed.

It may be conceded that some of the proposals contained in *A.P.* 30 were indeed adopted by the framers of the new constitution. (1) The five πρόεδροι of *A.P.* 30. 4, from whom the chairman of the boulē is to be taken, reappear in a decree (*I.G.* ii². 12, ll. 3–7, quoted *I.G.* i², p. 297) assigned to this period by Wilhelm (*Jahreshefte*, xxii, 1924, 147 ff.). (2) *A.P.* 30. 2 proposes that the Hellenotamiai should be raised in number to twenty and should control domestic as well as imperial revenues; in the control of the former they would replace the Kolakretai. There is no direct evidence that this reform was adopted by the 5,000, but it may safely be ascribed to them, as it is found in existence under the restored democracy in 410/409; cf. Meritt, *Athenian Financial Documents*, 98–101 and Tod, 205. Nothing is heard of the Kolakretai after 411, and some at least of their former functions are performed by the Hellenotamiai; compare Tod, 74, l. 52 with Tod, 86, ll. 35–36. (3) The decree cited above from the *Life of Antiphon* mentions the boulē and the dikasterion, but contains no reference to the ekklesia in the preamble. From this fact

Ferguson rather unfairly concluded that 'the Council acts both as council and assembly'. He accepted the usual explanation of *A.P.* 30, that the members of the 5,000 over thirty years old were to be divided into four sections, each of which acts in turn for a year as the boulē, the chief magistrates (including the generals) being eligible only from the members of the section acting as boulē for the year; on this interpretation each section was large enough to represent fairly the opinions of the citizen-body as a whole, and an ekklesia was therefore unnecessary.

Ferguson's proof was inadequate. He himself later demonstrated (*Treasurers of Athena*, 3–7) that though *A.P.* 30. 2 provides for the fusion of the treasury of Athena with that of the Other Gods under a single board of ten, this reform was not adopted until 406/405. Thereby he undermined his whole case, for if one provision of the draft in *A.P.* 30 was rejected by the 5,000, why should they not have rejected the majority of them? Yet Ferguson in his paper on 'The condemnation of Antiphon' (*Mélanges Glotz*, i. 349–66) ignores this objection. His statement that 'the document in question [*A.P.* 30] is not the corpus of the *nomi* under which Athens lived during the period of the Five Thousand' (op. cit. 357), simply means that this draft had to be supplemented by other measures, including one making provision for jurisdiction, a need ignored in *A.P.* 30. This expansion of his earlier theory was forced on Ferguson by the reference to the dikasterion in the decree of Andron, but he still believed that on the downfall of the 400 the programme of the moderates, contained in the 'plan for the modification of the constitution' in *A.P.* 30 became law, though his formulation 'the essentials of the plan were approved by popular vote' might be taken to imply that some inessentials were dropped. But how can we judge what parts of the draft constitution would or would not have appeared inessential to the 5,000 in September 411? Moreover, much had happened since the draft was first prepared, and the wishes of Alkibiades and the armament at Samos had now to be taken into consideration.

On these grounds alone Ferguson's hypothesis seems to me untenable, but there are still weightier objections to it. The draft in *A.P.* 30 is clearly the work of a theorist who had no feeling for the realities of politics; it has rightly been described as 'a pure Utopia', 'a still-born child', and 'a thing incapable of life'. It was certainly not a plan on which the Athenians could have founded their new constitution at such a crisis of their fate as that which they had to face in September 411. Since the discovery of part of the work of the Oxyrhynchus historian (supra, p. 369) we know that the Boiotian constitution, described in his eleventh chapter, was not a true parallel (cf. *J.H.S.* lvi, 1936, 56). Even if a constitution like that of the draft had existed and worked in Boiotia, it does not follow that it would have been adequate to the needs of a great maritime power with an overseas empire. Under the provisions of *A.P.* 30. 2 the generals had to be members of the section acting as boulē for the year, and consequently no one could hold the office of general for more than one year in four, but how could Athens in the middle of a struggle for her very existence afford to forgo for three years out of every four the services of Alkibiades?

Finally, the terms laid down by Alkibiades a little earlier (Thuc. viii. 86. 6) had been the abolition of the 400 and the restoration of the old boulē of 500. The leaders of the government set up after the collapse of the 400 showed themselves anxious to conciliate Alkibiades (Thuc. viii. 97. 3) and they may therefore be presumed to have complied with his second demand. We have seen (p. 372) that in the decree of Demophantos (Andok. i. 96) the careful description of the boulē under the restored democracy of 410 is intended to distinguish it not only from the 400 but also from a previous Council of *Five* Hundred which had not been chosen by lot; this can only have been the boulē under the 5,000, which therefore contained 500 members, and if not chosen by lot was presumably elected.

Thucydides (viii. 97. 2) refers to πυκναὶ ἐκκλησίαι, so the ekklesia must have been revived in September 411, though under the 5,000 membership was limited to the middle and upper classes. No inference can safely be drawn from the non-appearance of the ekklesia in the preamble to Andron's decree (above, p. 376). Although it was probably engraved on the same bronze tablet as the condemnation of Antiphon and Archeptolemos (cf. *Life of Antiphon*, § 24) and was duly recorded by Krateros (Harpokration, s.v. Ἄνδρων), the author of the life did not get it direct from Krateros and it seems to have suffered some mutilation in transmission. Certainly the words μιᾷ καὶ εἰκοστῇ τῆς πρυτανείας are meaningless as they stand, and Ferguson's pronouncement on the matter (*Mélanges Glotz*, i. 354) does not clear up the mystery. Since the preamble of the decree as preserved in the *Life* is defective, it seems unsafe to base any argument on the absence from it of any reference to the ekklesia.

APPENDIX XIII
The installation of the Thirty

[*For details of works cited in this and the next appendix see the Bibliography.*]

THE Spartan peace terms were accepted by the Athenian assembly on the day after Theramenes and his fellow envoys returned from Sparta (Xen. *Hell.* ii. 2. 22). At some unspecified interval after this,

Lysandros made his triumphal entry into the Piraeus, an event dated by Plutarch (*Life of Lysandros* 15. 1) to Mounychion 16th (24 or 25 April 404); this date is usually accepted, although Plutarch's addition that it was the same day as that on which the Athenians defeated the Persians at Salamis is disquieting. In the *Athenaion Politeia* (35. 1) the establishment of the Thirty is dated to the archonship of Pythodoros. To this it has been objected that the Thirty, after their inauguration, appointed the members of the boulē and the other officials, and that according to the interpolation in Xen. ii. 3. 1 the year 404/403 was reckoned as a year of ἀναρχία by the Athenians because Pythodoros ἐν ὀλιγαρχίᾳ ᾑρέθη. We may, however, infer from Lysias (vii. 9) that the archonship of Pythodoros was used for dating the year 404/403, just as that of Eukleides seems to have been used for dating the year 403/402, although Eukleides was apparently not appointed till after the restoration of the democracy and so not till October 403. Hence events which occurred between the end of the year of Alexias (405/404) and the entry on office of Pythodoros would presumably be reckoned to the year of Pythodoros, and unless we throw overboard entirely the evidence of *A.P.* 35. 1 we must assume the author to mean that the appointment of the Thirty did not occur under Alexias but fell inside the hiatus which intervened between the end of his term and the nomination of Pythodoros, and therefore after the beginning of July 404.

What was the length of the hiatus? The solution of this problem is complicated by the present state of our texts of Xenophon at this point. All scholars would agree that there are some later interpolations in Xenophon's original text, but their extent is disputed. In the relevant passage, ii. 2. 23–3. 11, we have the following items: (A) triumphal entry of Lysandros into Piraeus, return of exiles, and start made on demolition of the Long Walls; participants regard that day as the first day of freedom for Greece. (B) Note on Sicilian affairs for 405/404. The next chapter begins with (C) τῷ δ' ἐπιόντι ἔτει. (D) ᾧ ἦν 'Ολυμπιάς, with names of Olympic victor, ephor at Sparta, and archon at Athens. Note on Pythodoros. (E) ἐγένετο δὲ αὕτη ἡ ὀλιγαρχία ὧδε. (F) The people decided to appoint thirty men to draw up the laws. (G) List of names of the thirty chosen. Then we have (H) τούτων δὲ πραχθέντων Lysandros sailed off to Samos and Agis after withdrawing from Dekeleia disbanded the land force. (J) Note on victory of Lykophron in Thessaly, dated by an eclipse of the sun; this was on 3 September 404. Further note on events in Sicily. (K) Reduction of Samos by Lysandros who then disbands his fleet and returns in triumph with the Lakonian ships to Sparta; he also brings with him τὰς ἐκ Πειραιῶς τριήρεις πλὴν δώδεκα and other spoils of war, and (L) hands all these over to the Spartans τελευτῶντος τοῦ θέρους. (M) Length of Peloponnesian War given as 28½ years; this confirmed by a list of twenty-nine ephors. The last one, Eudios, in whose ephorate Lysandros returned to Sparta, was presumably ephor for the Spartan year 404/403, which began in August or September 404; hence the authors of L and M, if not identical, were in agreement. (N) The Thirty were appointed as soon as the Long Walls and the fortifications of Piraeus were demolished (ii. 3. 11).

This last sentence introduces Xenophon's account of the rule of the Thirty, and Beloch believed that it was his first reference to their appointment. He rejected the first reference to them in ii. 3. 2 as an interpolation (Blank, 16, suggested that its insertion there was due to the mention of the demolition of the walls in ii. 3. 11; cf. 2. 23) and cut out all the above sections from B to G. Hence τούτων δὲ πραχθέντων in H referred to the proceedings in A, and there is no evidence that the Thirty were set up before the departure of Lysandros for Samos. The objection of Roos (p. 4) that τούτων πραχθέντων could not grammatically refer to the string of imperfects seems unfounded (cf. Beloch, 206).

The evidence of other interpolations in *Hell.* i–ii would support the excision of D, E, and M and probably the Sicilian notices in B and J (see now Hatzfeld in the Budé edition, 153–8). The list of names in G does not inspire confidence, and the note on Thessaly may also be an interpolation (despite Hatzfeld, 157–8). The crucial passages are C and F, and as C is required to provide the necessary transition if F is retained, it is clear that F stands or falls with C. Blank's careful discussion of the references in *Hell.* i–ii to the beginning of a new year (i. 2. 1, 3. 1, 6. 1; ii. 1. 10, 3. 1) has convinced me that all these formulae were inserted by an interpolator who desired to give a Thucydidean character to Xenophon's 'continuation' of Thucydides. In i. 6. 1 and ii. 1. 10 he equated his new year from the arrival of a new Spartan admiral, and in ii. 3. 1 he calculated from the known date of the fall of Athens. Elsewhere he relied on the indications of the seasons provided by Xenophon himself. But when all these failed he was helpless, and so omitted to record the beginning of a new war-year in i. 5. 11 (Blank, 5–7 and 11–15). I therefore agree with Blank and Beloch that the first reference to the setting-up of the Thirty in ii. 3. 2 is an interpolation, closely modelled on the genuine passage in ii. 3. 11. On this view Xenophon deferred his account of the Thirty until he had finished with the war, and we have no evidence in him for the date of their installation apart from his statement that it followed closely on the demolition of the walls.

Attempts have been made to deduce the date by combining the evidence of Xenophon with that of other authorities. Lysias (xii. 71) says that Theramenes did not allow the decisive meeting of the Athenian assembly to be held until ὁ λεγόμενος ὑπ' ἐκείνου καιρὸς ἐπιμελῶς ὑπ' αὐτοῦ ἐτηρήθη (so the MSS., kept by Colin, 36, n. 1, who refers both ἐκείνου and αὐτοῦ to Theramenes; some accept Markland's

ἐκείνων, which presumably means the oligarchs in general) καὶ
μετεπέμψατο μὲν τὰς μετὰ Λυσάνδρου ναῦς ἐκ Σάμου, ἐπεδήμησε δὲ τὸ
τῶν πολεμίων στρατόπεδον. Diodoros (xiv. 3. 4) says that Lysandros
had just captured Samos when he was invited to intervene in Athens.
Beloch accepted Diodoros' statement as correct, but as he believed
that the Thirty were appointed in June 404 he had to reject τελευτῶντος
τοῦ θέρους in Xen. ii. 3. 9 as due to the interpolator. Others, who agree
with Beloch that Lysandros was on his way home to Sparta, argue
that this reference to the season must be accepted as derived, if not
from Xenophon, from an interpolator who had good sources of
information, and that the appointment of the Thirty must therefore be
dated to September 404 (so Colin, 34, n. 1, though I cannot see how
this is to be reconciled with his acceptance of the earlier reference in
ii. 3. 2).

The assertion in Diodoros seems to me a worthless guess, perhaps
suggested by the passage in Lysias. Diodoros may be right that
a Spartan squadron began the siege of Samos before the fall of
Athens (xiii. 106. 8, though εὐθύς after Aigospotamoi is an exaggeration; see Busolt, iii. 1627, n. 3) and it may be that Lysandros' headquarters were at Samos during the siege of Athens (Colin, 33, n. 1).
If we do not regard the evidence of Diod. xiv. 3. 4 as independent
testimony we may still believe that, though only a guess, it is correct,
or we may adopt the view of Luckenbach and Meyer (v. 20) that
Lysandros after his triumphal entry into Piraeus went off to Samos
(Xen. ii. 3. 3) but came back to Athens with a few ships before the
siege of Samos had finished in order to support the coup of the
oligarchs; he then returned to Samos, finished the siege, and sailed
home to Sparta at the end of the summer. Boerner's objections (pp.
50–51) to this hypothesis are valueless; the καιρός for which the oligarchs were waiting (Lys. xii. 71) need not have been the fall of Samos
and may have been connected with the internal situation in Athens,
while Lysandros may have sent an officer to collect the triremes
from Piraeus which he took home to Sparta. Even if he collected them
himself, there is nothing to show that the Thirty had not already been
installed by this time.

If the siege of Samos was still continuing (despite Diodoros' assertion to the contrary) when Lysandros intervened in the political
struggle at Athens, then we have no evidence to fix the date of this
intervention or its place in the (purified) narrative given in Xen. ii. 3
except (a) the natural inference from A.P. 35. 1 that the Thirty were
created after the end of Alexias' year and (b) the likelihood that the
interval between these two events was fairly brief. Presumably the
political struggle had prevented the appointment of the usual officials
for the next Attic year at the proper time, and those who believe (as I
do) that the creation of the Thirty belongs to the Attic year 404/403 must

suppose that the officials of the previous year had had to carry on until the constitutional question was settled (cf. Blank, 28; Roos, 2). But I cannot agree with Blank and Colin that this arrangement could have continued for nearly three months, and I incline therefore to the conclusion that the Thirty were probably appointed in Hekatombaion 404/403.

Such is the conclusion reached by Roos, but he tries to base it on the text of Xenophon (ii. 3. 2–3) and argues that Lysandros had not yet left for Samos since the fall of Athens. He assumes that τὸ τῶν πολεμίων στρατόπεδον in Lys. xii. 71 is the army of Agis (cf. Xen. ii. 3. 3) but this is as incredible as Blank's view that it is the Spartan fleet returning victorious from Samos (p. 43; he says the expression is an example of the usual rhetorical parallelism which divides a thing into its parts to strengthen the impression). It is more probable that when the Spartan army evacuated Attica a garrison was left in Piraeus to ensure the fulfilment of the peace terms (Meyer, *G.A.* v. 19–20; Beloch, 207). Roos has to suppose that Lysandros had stayed in or near Athens since the capitulation but had sent on part of his fleet to blockade Samos. It is, however, difficult to believe that Lysandros waited nearly two and a half months in Attica at this time.

Scholars who wrote before the discovery of the *Athenaion Politeia* avoided this difficulty, since they were free to date the establishment of the Thirty in the year of Alexias. Schwartz (*Rh. Mus.* xliv, 1889, 118 ff.) assumed a long interval (in which he placed the conspiracy of Strombichides) between the acceptance of the peace by the Athenian assembly (above, p. 378) and the formal 'capitulation' of Athens (including Lysandros' triumphal entry into the Piraeus), and maintained that the installation of the Thirty occurred very soon after the capitulation and before the departure of Lysandros for Samos. Even if we dismiss the evidence of *A.P.* 35. 1, this view is irreconcilable with the statement of Xenophon (ii. 3. 11) that the Long Walls and the fortifications of Piraeus had been demolished before the Thirty were installed; clearly the work of demolition cannot have begun until after the 'capitulation' (cf. Diod. xiv. 3. 6 and Lys. xii. 74).

Munro revived the view of Schwartz in a new form. In a series of articles he argued that the terms brought back by Theramenes from Sparta and accepted by the ekklesia were merely an armistice, that an interval of not less than three or four weeks (*C.Q.* 1937, 37) elapsed between its acceptance by the Athenians and their ratification of the definitive peace treaty on the 16th of Mounychion, that the Thirty were appointed soon after, but only as a legislative commission, and that they were not given the powers of a *government* until after the fall of Samos, in September 404. In maintaining these positions Munro displayed his usual brilliance and ingenuity, but his contention that the notice about the Thirty in [Xen.] ii. 3. 2 refers to an earlier appointment with a more limited scope than that mentioned in Xen. ii. 3. 11 is unacceptable. It is excluded by the remarkably detailed similarity of phrasing between the two passages, which is most easily explained by the hypothesis that the first was the work of an interpolator who followed the second closely in his wording. Moreover, the parallelism between the account in the *Athenaion Politeia* and that in the *Hellenika* is sufficient to show that for the authors of both the Thirty combined from the first the functions of a legislative commission and a temporary government (cf. Diod. xiv. 4. 2). Finally, Munro has to argue that the opposition of Theramenes to Lysandros, recorded in Diodoros and hinted in *A.P.* 34. 3, preceded the supposed first appointment, whereas in both accounts the Thirty proceed to act as a government immediately after their installation.

Colin (pp. 65–66) has attempted to date the appointment of the Thirty from the date of their deposition. The passages in Xenophon on which he relies are two. In the first (ii. 4. 21) the herald Kleokritos says that the Thirty have killed more Athenians ἐν ὀκτὼ μησίν than all the Peloponnesians did in ten years of war; this statement was made on the day before the Thirty were deposed. Less than ten days later the democrats in Piraeus made a foray into the Attic countryside from which they brought back ξύλα καὶ ὀπώραν (ii. 4. 25). Colin rightly argues (p. 66 and n. 3 ; cf. Plato, *Laws* 844 D and Polybius iv. 66. 7) that ὀπώρα points to early June, and by giving an elastic interpretation to the eight months of the first passage he concludes that the second confirms his own date (end of September 404) for the beginning of the oligarchy. But the general assumption that Kleokritos was calculating his eight months from the installation of the Thirty seems to me far from certain. His statement is clearly a rhetorical exaggeration, and for his purpose it was desirable to curtail as far as possible the duration of the period in which the Thirty had committed so many atrocities, and as the end was fixed he may have taken as his starting-point the arrival of the Spartan garrison, when the reign of terror began (Xen. ii. 3. 14). Those who believe that the fall of the Thirty was in March 403 may suppose that the ὀπώρα was the residue of the 404 crops, taken not from the trees but from the farmhouses, or that in this respect Xenophon confused the first raid with others made later in the year (so Roos, 14–15) ; it has also been proposed to emend ὀπώρα to ὄσπρια (Busolt–Swoboda, ii. 912, n. 7).

To sum up, I believe that the Thirty were installed in July 404, and that the popular period of their rule may have lasted until the end of September. If the eight months of Xen. ii. 4. 21 can be calculated from that point, then the fall of the Thirty may be dated to the end of May 403 ; if not, it must be dated to the end of March. On either view there is time for the subsequent events down to the restoration of the democracy.

APPENDIX XIV

The order of events during the rule of the Thirty

THE stages in Xenophon's account may be tabulated as follows: (A) The early measures of the Thirty; execution of 'sycophants'. (B) A garrison of 700 men under Kallibios is obtained from Sparta. (C) First reign of terror. (D) Opposition of Theramenes; after further executions he advises the admission of κοινωνοὺς ἱκανοὺς τῶν πραγμάτων. (E) In reply to this Kritias and the other members of the Thirty compile a list of 3,000, τοὺς μεθέξοντας δὴ τῶν πραγμάτων. (F) Theramenes complains that the number in the list is too small. (G) His colleagues meet his objection by disarming all Athenians not included in the list. (H) Second reign of terror. (J) Decision to put thirty metics to death; Theramenes refuses to compromise himself by taking part. (K) Kritias accuses Theramenes before the boulē of 500. When it seems likely to acquit him, Kritias strikes his name off the list of the 3,000, and in the name of the Thirty orders his execution, in virtue of the καινοὶ νόμοι which authorize the Thirty to put to death without trial anyone whose name is not on the list. Execution of Theramenes. (L) The Thirty feel that they can now τυραννεῖν ἀδεῶς. (M) They forbid all those who are not on the list to enter Athens, and also expel them from the Attic countryside. Those expelled take refuge in Piraeus; from there some proceed to Megara or Thebes. (N) Thrasyboulos starts from Thebes and occupies Phyle with 70 men. (O) An army led against him by the Thirty is driven off from Phyle by an unexpected snowstorm. (P) Thrasyboulos, whose followers now number 700, attacks a force which had been posted about 15 stades from Phyle to watch the exiles; it is surprised at dawn and routed. (Q) The Thirty now prepare a possible retreat for themselves at Eleusis by arresting its inhabitants. (R) On the next day the 3,000 and the Hippeis are compelled by the Thirty to sentence the Eleusinians to death. (S) Thrasyboulos marches his men to the Piraeus by night, and on the next day, after taking up his position at Mounychia, defeats the army of the Thirty in a battle, in which Kritias and Charmides are killed. This battle was fought four days after the victory near Phyle (P above); cf. Xen. ii. 4. 13. (T) On the next day (ii. 4. 23) the Thirty are deposed and retire to Eleusis.

In the *Athenaion Politeia* we have A (in greater detail; cf. 35. 1–3), C, D, E, F (with the curious addition that the Thirty long refused to produce a definitive list of the 3,000). Next comes Thrasyboulos' occupation of Phyle, followed by the decision of the Thirty to destroy Theramenes. They achieve their purpose by the passing of two laws, the law (K above) mentioned by Xen. ii. 3. 51, and another which excluded from the 3,000 all who had helped to overthrow the 400. After

Theramenes' death we get the disarming of all outside the list, and the statement that the Thirty in other respects greatly increased in cruelty and wickedness; it is not clear whether this represents LM in Xenophon or is really H, placed here owing to the postponement of G. Next comes a sentence, without any connecting particle, which says that the Thirty sent envoys to Sparta to accuse Theramenes and to ask for help, whereupon the Spartans sent Kallibios and 700 men. After a version of S, so telescoped that the author is able to avoid any mention of Kritias, he agrees with Xenophon that the Thirty were deposed on the morrow of the battle at Mounychia.

This analysis shows that the author has omitted altogether the items in Xenophon labelled J, L, M, P, Q, R, but a reference to O may be implied in the statement (37. 1) that Thrasyboulos occupied Phyle τοῦ χειμῶνος ἐνεστῶτος; although this has often been regarded as a valuable piece of evidence, I do not believe that the author's source had any warrant for it beyond Xenophon's reference to the snow-storm (see below, p. 386). The most startling novelties in the *Athenaion Politeia* are the placing of B, G, and N with reference to K. Instead of Xenophon's B, G, K, N we have N, K, G, B, a complete inversion of his order on these points.

It cannot be said that the order of events in our later sources supports that of the *Athenaion Politeia*. Diodoros starts with A, B, C, D, then proceeds to K (xiv. 4). He does not mention the occupation of Phyle till xiv. 32, as he has divided his account of the Thirty into two sections, the first placed correctly under the Attic year 404/403, the second under 401/400, which is really the year of the re-incorporation of Eleusis in Athens (*A.P.* 40. 4). Whether the omission of G is due to Diodoros or his source, it is evident that his source followed Xeno-phon in the order B, K, N for the three turning-points in the story. The same is true of Justin (v. 8. 11 and 9. 2–6); his reference in v. 8. 10 to the *tria milia satellitum* appointed *a principio* by the Thirty is prob-ably a rhetorical exaggeration ('quantum ex tot cladibus prope nec civium superfuerat') for the 300 scourge-bearers of *A.P.* 35. 1 rather than an anticipation of the Xenophontic 3,000.

This agreement of the late authorities with Xenophon is the more remarkable because they not only disagree with him on minor details but supply some items which he has omitted, notably the Spartan decree forbidding the Greek states to harbour the Athenian exiles, the death of Alkibiades, and the attempt of the Thirty to bribe Thrasy-boulos after their first failure at Phyle. All three items occur in both Diodoros and Justin; Diod. xiv. 32. 4 (confirmed by Lys. xii. 52) adds that the Salaminians shared the fate of the Eleusinians, and Justin (v. 9. 8) has the probable statement that the Theban Ismenias helped the exiles with his own resources.

Diodoros disagrees with Xenophon in narrating after Theramenes'

death the execution of the Sixty (*sic*!) metics and a fresh reign of terror
(possibly cf. *A.P.* 37. 2). When he resumes in xiv. 32 he has Xenophon's
N, O (with an improbable version of O) then M, Q, R. After this the
Thirty try to bribe Thrasyboulos; when he rejects their offer they send
envoys to Sparta to ask for help and collect a force in the field themselves. Next comes the victory (P in Xenophon, whose evidence in
ii. 4. 4 would put it 15 stades from Phyle) placed by Diodoros at
Acharnai and clearly postdated by him, since in his version it is
followed εὐθύς by the march on Piraeus. Justin agrees with Diodoros
that the expulsion of the unprivileged did not precede the occupation
of Phyle (as in Xen. ii. 4. 1–2) but followed it, and their dating was
preferred by Boerner (p. 57; cf. *C.A.H.* v. 369) who saw in the expulsion a war measure dictated by Thrasyboulos' occupation of Phyle
and directed against his 'fifth column' in Athens and Attica. But it is
hard to believe that Xenophon could have been mistaken on the
order of the two events. Moreover, he says plainly that the expulsion
was due to the cupidity of the Thirty who wanted to appropriate for
themselves and their friends the farms of those whom they expelled
(ii. 4. 1; cf. Meyer, v. 37).

The discrepancies between the *Athenaion Politeia* and Xenophon
are far more serious. Xenophon's evidence on the date of the occupation of Phyle has been explained away by Armbruster (pp. 5 and 20;
cf. Colin, 43) on the ground that Xenophon was dealing with political
events in c. 3 and reserved the military events for the next chapter.
This is not true of ii. 4. 1 (for Colin's difficulties see p. 43, n. 1) or
4. 8–9, and a more absurd reason for scouting Xenophon's authority
would be hard to imagine. It was the death of Theramenes, followed
by the expulsion of the unprivileged, that ended for the present the
political struggle in Athens in favour of the extremists and so
encouraged the exiles to return by increasing their hopes of support
from the discontented. Colin and Armbruster, and others who accept
from *A.P.* 37. 1 the statement that Thrasyboulos occupied Phyle at
the beginning of winter, are compelled to assume a very long interval
between the occupation of Phyle and the march on Piraeus. In my
opinion the date is simply a deduction from Xenophon's reference to
the snowstorm, and therefore valueless as a chronological indication,
for it is certain that there was something peculiar about this particular
snowstorm. Xenophon says that the night in which it occurred had
been preceded by a day of fine weather, and Thrasyboulos, claiming
the support of the gods for the cause of the exiles, uses the words
καὶ γὰρ ἐν εὐδίᾳ χειμῶνα ποιοῦσιν, ὅταν ἡμῖν συμφέρῃ (ii. 4. 14, cf. 2–3).
In view of the recklessness with which chronological inferences have
been drawn from this snowstorm, I venture to add that when I was
in Greece in the spring of 1931 there was a heavy fall of snow in
Attica on 28 March. If we wish to defer the battle of Mounychia to

the end of May we are therefore free to date the occupation of Phyle in March. Colin's view that the two events were separated by nearly five months seems to me impossible.

Xenophon's account is also to be preferred on the other points at issue. Not only does it possess the authority of a contemporary who lived on the spot through the events he describes, but it is decidedly superior to the rival account in internal probability. In Xenophon the first reign of terror follows naturally on the arrival of the Spartan garrison, the second on the disarming of the unprivileged, which in turn was a logical consequence of Theramenes' opposition to the Thirty. The *Athenaion Politeia* makes the course of events unintelligible. Although they have arms in their hands and no Spartan garrison to fear, the moderate Athenians allow themselves to be slaughtered like sheep (1,500 in a short time; cf. *A.P.* 35. 4) and do not stir a finger to prevent the murder of Theramenes; surely it was a work of super-erogation to disarm them after his death.

It is no wonder that earlier scholars sought to remove the main stumbling-block by transferring the last four lines of *A.P.* 37 to an earlier place; their justification was that some dislocation of the text was indicated by the asyndeton. But as these lines presuppose the opposition of Theramenes to the Thirty they must come after the first mention of that opposition in 36. 1, and there is no suitable place for their insertion in the chapter till its end, which is too late; they need to be transposed to the end of c. 35, but clearly would not fit there (Boerner, 59). Faced with this dilemma Armbruster decided to grasp the nettle firmly, accept the text as it stands, and so date the arrival of Kallibios and his garrison after the seizure of Phyle and the death of Theramenes. He alleged (p. 17) that in the *Athenaion Politeia* it is the military situation which necessitates the appeal to Sparta for help, but this is a forced interpretation, and I fail to see why this motive should be regarded as more plausible than that given by Xenophon in ii. 3. 13. When the Thirty turned to extreme courses they were making up their minds to behave like one of the Lysandrian dekarchies, whose usual supports were a garrison and a Spartan harmost. It is true that Diodoros in xiv. 32. 6 records the sending of πρέσβεις περὶ βοηθείας to Sparta by the Thirty after the failure of their attempt to corrupt Thrasyboulos (so too Justin), but both Diodoros and Justin agree with Xenophon that the garrison of 700 arrived before the first reign of terror.

The assumption of a second appeal to Sparta after Theramenes' death and a second sending of help was made by Boerner, who thought that the unknown author (Androtion?) whose account is preserved in the *Athenaion Politeia* had confused the second occasion with the first, but it is more probable that he deliberately post-dated the arrival of the garrison, and that it is an echo of his account that has survived in Diodoros and Justin. As his account shows a marked bias in favour of Theramenes, we may suppose with Meyer (v. 24) that by dating the summoning of the garrison after his death he was trying clumsily to exculpate Theramenes from all responsibility for the step, not realizing that Theramenes' best defence was contained in his statement quoted by Xenophon (ii. 3. 42)—οὐδέ γε τὸ φρουροὺς μισθοῦσθαι συνήρεσκέ μοι.

Why he deferred the disarming of the unprivileged until after Theramenes' death is a mystery; his own account implies (*A.P.* 37. 1) that the Thirty intended it to come first. When once this measure had been removed from its proper place in the narrative it was easy for Diodoros and Justin to drop it out altogether. Its dislocation in the *Athenaion Politeia* is perhaps due to the view (36. 2) that the publication of the list of the 3,000 was long deferred by the Thirty, who kept altering the names on the list; obviously the unprivileged could not be disarmed until the names of the privileged were known. Hence the disarming is transferred after the seizure of Phyle and is directed against the potential adherents of the radical democrats rather than those of Theramenes. But the account in *A.P.* 36. 2 is improbable. The creation of the 3,000 was intended by Kritias as a reply to Theramenes (on this the author of the *Athenaion Politeia* agrees with Xenophon), but any protracted delay in the publication of the list would surely have played into Theramenes' hands. The alterations in the list made by the Thirty, if historical, must have been made after his death, and to the same period may be attributed the drawing-up of the 'black list', mysteriously called ὁ μετὰ Λυσάνδρου κατάλογος by Isokrates (xviii. 16 and xxi. 2; Lys. xxv. 16 calls it ὁ κατάλογος. Did Lysandros visit Athens again now and help the Thirty to draw up the list? Cf. Boerner, 60–61).

To this period between Theramenes' death and the occupation of Phyle may also be ascribed the Spartan decree which forbade the Greek states to harbour the Athenian exiles (Diod. xiv. 6. 1, cf. Justin, v. 9. 4). In both our sources it follows closely the expulsion or flight of many Athenians which took place after Theramenes' death, and its natural place in Xenophon's narrative would be at the end of ii. 4. 1. Perhaps Xenophon was unwilling to record a decree which, although paralleled by the practice of the Athenian Empire, reflected great discredit on Sparta, and his silence about the assassination of Alkibiades may indicate that it was closely connected with the decree against the exiles and that the one could not be mentioned without the other. Justin (v. 8. 12) wrongly makes Alkibiades the first victim of the Thirty. Diodoros (xiv. 11) dates his death to the year 404/403, and puts it after the decree of the Spartans and consequently after the execution of Theramenes; this must be correct, since Xenophon presupposes (ii. 3. 42) that Alkibiades had been exiled but was still alive when Theramenes made his last speech.

One more measure may be assigned to this period, the second of the two laws in *A.P.* 37. 1. In his account of Theramenes' trial Xenophon only mentions the first. The version in the *Athenaion Politeia* is absurd; if the second law had been passed in Theramenes' lifetime, he must have known from the moment of its passing that his fate was sealed. Moreover, if he belonged to a category of persons automatically excluded from the 3,000 by this law, how could he claim the privilege of a trial before the boulē? Kenyon's ingenious suggestion (note on *A.P.* 37. 1 in his edition) that Kritias proposed the second law in the same session of the boulē as that in which Theramenes was tried and 'forced it down the throat of the council by the threat of armed force' will not really bear inspection. At what stage in the session? After it became manifest that the council would not convict Theramenes? For those who rate the *Athenaion Politeia* at its true value, the common-sense solution is that the second law was carried after Theramenes' death. It provided the Thirty with a retrospective justification for his execution and enabled them to strike off the roll of the 3,000 those of his adherents who had been associated with him in the overthrow of the 400.

On these grounds I agree with Meyer against the more recent works of Armbruster and Colin that on all points where the order or the accuracy of Xenophon's narrative is contradicted by that of the *Athenaion Politeia* the preference must be given without hesitation to Xenophon.

SUPPLEMENTARY NOTES

A

The obvious inference from the passage of Kratinos quoted by Plutarch (*Solon* 25. 2) is that in his day the κύρβεις of Solon were treated, perhaps metaphorically, as firewood; so J. H. Oliver says (in *Hesperia*, iv, 1935, 9) that 'the image is of kindling wood'. Some have suggested that Kratinos was thinking of metal plates held over a fire; so W. K. Prentice quoted in Linforth, *Solon*, 281, n. 1. L. B. Holland (in *A.J.A.* xlv, 1941, 346–62) accepts the view that the axones were made of wood, but argues that the kyrbeis (which he distinguishes from the axones and ascribes to Peisistratos) were copper tablets. Holland seems to me to place too much confidence in the explanation of the distinction between the axones and the kyrbeis given by Plutarch (on the authority of ἔνιοι) in *Solon* 25. 2.

B

The ironical suggestion made in the text, that if Aristotle was the author of the *Athenaion Politeia* he must have changed his mind for the worse since he wrote the *Politics*, does not depend on any theory about the date of the *Politics*, for it is my firm belief that the *Athenaion Politeia* was completed at a date not long before that of Aristotle's death and therefore later than the completion of the *Politics*. An attempt to find a *terminus ante quem* for the composition of the *Athenaion Politeia* earlier than 323/322 has been based on *A.P.* 46. 1 (cf. Sandys, ad loc. and Wil. *A.A.* i. 211, n. 43), but the argument is indecisive in view of the remarks on the Athenian quinquereme made by W. W. Tarn, *Hellenistic Military and Naval Developments* (Cambridge, 1930), p. 131. For an example of modern endeavours to find chronological strata in the *Politics* cf. E. Barker in *C.R.* xlv, 1931, 162–72 (Barker has now given up the views he expressed there; see his translation of the *Politics*, Oxford, 1946, introd. xlii, n. 1).

C

The law quoted in Philochoros, fr. 94 (35 in Jacoby, *F.G.H.* iii B), compelling the phratries to admit to their membership both the ὀργεῶνες and the ὁμογάλακτες (equated by Philochoros with the γεννῆται), is cited as from the *fourth* book of Philochoros, which is thought to have opened with the year 461/460 and to have dealt with the Periklean period (so Jacoby in *C.Q.* xxxviii, 1944, 69). As the law is obviously pre-Periklean, Philochoros might have mentioned it either on the occasion of a later re-enactment (e.g. in the codification of 403; cf. de Sanctis, 65, n. 2 and Francotte, 19) or in a digression suggested by Perikles' law of 451/450 on the conditions of citizenship (Busolt–Swoboda, 252, followed by Jacoby, loc. cit.)

Modern scholars agree that the original law must have been enacted by either Solon or Kleisthenes. Most of them tend to ascribe it to Solon, though Busolt (in Busolt–Swoboda, 252; cf. 880) says that the law 'bears the stamp of Kleisthenes'. As we do not possess the context of its mention in Philochoros we can only date it by relating its provisions to an appropriate historical situation. But what precisely is the situation presupposed by its provisions? Some have over-hastily inferred from the law that before its passing membership of the phratries was limited to γεννῆται. Jacoby assumes that the phratries in the pre-Solonian state were formed by the γένη only, and consequently sees in the Philochoran law, which on his view first admitted the non-aristocratic ὀργεῶνες to the phratries, an epoch-making innovation of Solon; Kahrstedt (i. 235 ff.) seems to draw the same inference. The fatal objection to any such hypothesis (as Kahrstedt, 236 half admits) is that, if *I.G.* i². 115 is a replica of a genuine pre-Solonian law, the co-existence in the phratries of both types of members in the generation before Solon is certain.

Wade-Gery has suggested (in *C.Q.* xxvii, 1933, 28) that the situation implied in the law is that the phratry, hitherto composed of γένη and other groups (not united by real or fictitious ties of kinship like the γένη) had been showing 'a tendency to discriminate in favour of the former, and the State hereby forbids such discrimination'. This analysis is almost certainly correct, but the arguments by which Wade-Gery tries to infer Solon's authorship of the law are not cogent. As our ancient source does not tell us who passed the law, the case for its ascription to Kleisthenes is not affected by the contention that there is no direct evidence in its favour. Moreover, although the law does indeed presuppose that 'the citizen-body was the aggregate of the phratries' this was surely as true in Kleisthenes' time as in Solon's.

For those who believe, as I do, that the Kleisthenic reforms included the restoration of citizenship to many who had received it from the tyrants and lost it in 510, the law fits adequately the situation in 508, when the forces of reaction had again showed their strength. It might well have seemed to Kleisthenes less invidious to pass a general enactment compelling the phratries to admit the orgeones to membership, thereby ignoring the circumstance that it was not the old-established plebeian members to whom the aristocratic phratores objected but the intruders foisted upon them by the tyrants. In the pre-Solonian period the freeholders may have been the only plebeians admitted to the phratries, so that those who lost their freeholds might have been in danger of expulsion from the phratries. As I do not agree with the view of the Atthidographers that Solon admitted the proletarians to the ekklesia, I see no reason to assume that he admitted them to the phratries. There are in fact too many unknowns to permit a final solution of this problem. It is safest to conclude with de Sanctis (345 and n. 5) that if the original law was pre-Kleisthenic it was certainly reaffirmed by Kleisthenes.

D

The Athenian genos called Σαλαμίνιοι, which appears in an honorary decree (*I.G.* ii². 1232; cf. Wade-Gery in *C.Q.* xxv, 1931, 85, n. 3) dated towards the end of the fourth century, has been more intensively studied since the discovery by the American excavators in Athens of two decrees specially concerned with the Salaminioi (published by W. S. Ferguson in *Hesperia*, vii, 1938, 1–74) the first dated to the Athenian year 363/362, the second about 250. In the former the genos consists of two distinct branches, οἱ ἀπὸ Σουνίου and οἱ ἐκ τῶν ἑπτὰ φυλῶν, whereas in the second each has become a separate corporation (though both are still called Σαλαμίνιοι). The facts suggest that Sounion was the original nucleus of the genos but that by the time of Kleisthenes some of its members had migrated to other parts of Attica and were to be found in seven of the ten areas which formed the territories of the new Kleisthenic tribes. Such dispersion of the members of a genos by 508/507 has other parallels (cf. Ferguson, op. cit. 45 f.) but naturally presupposes that the genos in question had already been in existence for some time before Kleisthenes' reforms. How long had the Salaminioi been in existence before 508, and what is the relevance of their name to earlier Athenian claims on Salamis?

As the new inscriptions are concerned mainly with the allocation of religious privileges between the two branches of the genos they cannot be said to have thrown much fresh light on these problems, except such as may be derived from the territorial dispersion of the genos or from the fact that one of its cults was a cult of Eurysakes, which was closely connected with Athenian claims to Salamis (Plut. *Solon* 10. 3; cf. Hdt. vi. 35. 1 and Pausanias i. 35. 3). Hence the hypotheses advanced by modern scholars since the discovery of the new inscriptions differ widely. Ferguson suggested (op. cit. 43 ff.) that the group composed of οἱ ἐκ τῶν ἑπτὰ φυλῶν had originally lived in the urban deme of Melite and had about the end of the seventh century (under the stimulus of contemporary Athenian claims to Salamis) identified their cult-hero with Eurysakes and assumed the name Salaminioi. This necessitates the further hypothesis that at the same time or soon after another group of families, living near Sounion, also took the name Salaminioi and (possibly with the encouragement of the central government) decided to combine with the first group to form a single genos with the same genealogical tree; the estates possessed by the Sounion group were thereupon transferred to the new genos and formed its only landed property in the fourth century.

Ferguson claimed that such a merger raises no problems of cult or kin, but his critics find it hard to believe that a genos could be created in this highly artificial manner as late as the beginning of the sixth century, or that two family groups from widely different parts of Attica should almost simultaneously have assumed the name Salaminioi. The territorial name may perhaps be a proof that the birth-ties connecting the original members of the genos were fictitious, but there were other Attic γένη with geographical names which were taken from the particular locality in which the majority of their members had resided at the time of their formation. Hence we must suppose that the Salaminioi, when they first formed a genos, were closely connected with the soil of Salamis itself.

How can this conclusion be reconciled with the later history of the Salaminioi? M. P. Nilsson supposed (*A.J.P.* lix, 1938, 385–93) that they were originally native Salaminians who were transferred to Attica when the Athenians conquered Salamis and received citizenship and lands in Attica in place of their former estates, now taken over by the Athenians for the settlement of Athenian cleruchs in Salamis. This view is improbable; as the members of the genos at the time of the conquest were pro-Athenian, why evict them to make room for Athenian settlers? Moreover, Nilsson does not explain why the newcomers should have been rewarded in Attica with the priesthoods of such ancient cults as those of Aglauros Pandrosos and Kourotrophos.

Miss M. Guarducci in a recent discussion (*R.F.* lxxvi, 1948, 223–37), to which I am greatly indebted, agrees with Nilsson that the genos must have originated in Salamis itself, but her contention that at the time of its origin Salamis must already have been an Athenian possession seems unnecessary. It also has the serious disadvantage that it forces her to postulate an early conquest of Salamis by Athens about the end of the eighth century, followed some time later by a

Megarian conquest; this is assumed to have entailed the expulsion of the Salaminioi, who then found new homes in Attica, principally near Sounion.

The hypothesis of a pre-Solonian conquest of Salamis by Athens is difficult, and Solon's application of the term Σαλαμιναφέται to the Athenians can be explained otherwise. It is more probable that Salamis was an independent state till its conquest by Megara. Some of its nobles, fleeing before the conqueror, may have sought refuge with the rising power of Athens. The exiles could expect a hospitable reception from its rulers, who might hope to use their presence at a suitable moment to support Athenian designs on Salamis; thus their adhesion was so valuable to the Athenians that they may well have been rewarded with grants of citizenship and lands and even with certain priesthoods, while the cults which they brought with them would readily be accepted by the Athenian state. This is in the main Nilsson's theory, with the difference that the migration of the Salaminioi to Attica is transferred to an earlier and more plausible occasion.

E

Foundations of a building dating from the first half of the sixth century have been found in the excavations of the Athenian Agora on a site which Professor Homer A. Thompson believes to have been identical with that of the Bouleuterion built for the Kleisthenic Council of Five Hundred, and he concludes that the earlier building must have been the council chamber used by the alleged Solonian Council of Four Hundred (*Hesperia*, vi, 1937, especially 205-6; cf. *Hesperia Supplement*, iv, 1940, 8-15 and 148-51). Professor Thompson does not rely on this conclusion to demonstrate the existence of a pre-Kleisthenic popular council, which he simply takes for granted, but those of us who are not prepared to accept the 'proofs' usually put forward to establish the existence of such a council must decline to accept his interpretation of the purpose served by the earlier building. It would appear from his later article (*Supplement*, iv, 1940, 148-51) that his identifications of the buildings in this part of the Agora have not found favour with all archaeologists, but even if he has correctly identified the Kleisthenic Bouleuterion it does not follow that an earlier building on the same site must have served a similar purpose.

F

Most scholars have assumed that Kleisthenes must have held some official position at the time when he carried his laws. Yet the author of the *Athenaion Politeia* seems to say (21. 1) that they were carried in 'the archonship of Isagoras'. Wilamowitz, regarding this expression as equivalent to the Athenian year 508/507, maintained (*A.A.* i. 6) that the reforms were carried in that part of the year which remained after the expulsion of Isagoras, 'when a substitute, doubtless Kleisthenes himself', had been appointed for the remainder of the year. Kahrstedt (ii. 108 and 142, n. 1) follows Wilamowitz closely; he claims that Kleisthenes' work was naturally achieved after Isagoras' fall (in the official year at the beginning of which Isagoras was archon, but not while he still had the power in his hands), and if Isagoras was deposed, who more likely than Kleisthenes to have been elected president of the republic in his place? [I cannot understand Ehrenberg's view (in *Klio*, xix, 1923, 107) that Kleisthenes was archon for 509/508 until the intervention of Kleomenes.]

The discovery of the archon-inscription showed that Kleisthenes the lawgiver had probably held the archonship already in the year 525/524 (cf. T. J. Cadoux in *J.H.S.* lxviii, 1948, 109–10) and therefore he presumably could not hold it again in 508/507, even as a *suffectus*. Busolt (ii². 403–4, end of long n. 6) had already criticized the view of Wilamowitz on the ground that the archonship in itself hardly provided the powers required for the enactment of legislation on a large scale. He agreed that Kleisthenes must have held some official appointment, but pointed out that Drakon and even Solon had received an extraordinary position with special plenary powers, and concluded that a similar position must have been conferred on Kleisthenes. Beloch argued (i². 1. 395, n. 2) that the time had gone by for such appointments, and suggested that the Athenians on this occasion appointed a commission of νομοθέται in which Kleisthenes was the leading member.

This discussion would be superfluous if we could accept Wade-Gery's supposition (*C.Q.* xxvii, 1933, 21) that the laws of Kleisthenes were 'common *Psephismata*, moved by Kleisthenes as a private citizen' and carried in the ekklesia. Wade-Gery's attempt to find support for his view in the wording of the motion put forward in 411 by Kleitophon (*A.P.* 29. 3) seems to me unconvincing, but its rejection need not affect the tenability of his main hypothesis, which I adopted in my first draft. After re-examining the question I doubt whether legislation as elaborate as that of Kleisthenes could have been proposed and carried in the ekklesia by a citizen, however eminent, who had no official position, and I am now inclined to believe that Beloch's suggestion (followed by Schachermeyr) provides the true solution.

G

Aristotle in the *Politics* (1297^b16 ff.) discussing the connexion between membership of the armed forces and membership of the citizen-body in the early Greek states, explains that the ancient monarchies were naturally succeeded by aristocracies of ἱππεῖς, since at that time the cavalry were the principal military force. But when states began to increase in size, the hoplite forces acquired tactical skill and experience and claimed a greater share of political power, with the result that the number of those admitted to full political rights was increased.

In Sparta the hoplite-phalanx appears in the poems of Tyrtaios, and there is some evidence that the hoplites there became conscious of their political importance during the Second Messenian War (cf. Ar. *Politics* 1306^b *ad fin.*). Unfortunately it is impossible to trace the same evolution with any confidence in the history of Athens. The levy *en masse* first appears in the story of Kylon's conspiracy (Thuc. i. 126. 7). The Athenian hoplite force presumably became important in the wars with Megara, but the chronology of those wars is very uncertain. One might perhaps expect the hoplites to have supported the rise to power of the popular general Peisistratos, but the insecurity of his first two tenures of power and the fact that in his third he relied on a force of mercenaries tell against the hypothesis that he enjoyed the firm backing of the hoplite class. Nor was its importance as a military force augmented, so far as we can tell, during the period of continuous tyranny from 546 to 510. Thucydides has a reference (vi. 54. 5) to the wars waged by the tyrants, but if (as I believe) the fighting mentioned in Hdt. vi. 108. 4–5 occurred after the expulsion of Hippias, it is hard to see what these wars can have been apart from the struggles with the Mitylenaians for the possession of Sigeion.

Indirectly Peisistratos may have prepared the way for the rise of the hoplite-class to political power, partly by his levelling policy, and partly by his creation of small holdings for impoverished peasants, which would have the effect of increasing the number of freehold farmers and thereby of the hoplites. Anyhow there can be no doubt that the hoplites were the class which finally secured the lion's share of political power in the internal conflict that followed the overthrow of the tyranny, and that their predominance was established at home by the ἀριστοκρατία (Plut. *Kimon* 15. 3) of Kleisthenes, and confirmed by their victories in the field over their Boiotian and Chalkidian neighbours.

H

On the evidence of a fragment of Theopompos (Müller, 103 = 96 *b* in Jacoby, *F.G.H.* ii B, and 98 B in the Oxford Text of Grenfell and Hunt) the ostracism of Hyperbolos has usually been dated to the early months of 417. Theopompos, speaking of Hyperbolos' death, says that they (presumably the Athenians) ἐξωστράκισαν τὸν Ὑπέρβολον ἐξ ἔτη; as no one was ever ostracized for less than ten years, he apparently meant that six full years had elapsed between Hyperbolos' ostracism and his assassination at Samos, which can be dated with fair certainty to May 411. Thucydides, on the occasion of Hyperbolos' death, alludes briefly (viii. 73. 3) to his ostracism without stating the date or the circumstances. Plutarch gives an account of the events leading up to the ostracism (*Nikias* 11 and *Alkibiades* 13), but he is concerned entirely with the internal struggle in Athens and fails to relate the ostracism to the general history of the period.

Plutarch (*Alk.* 13. 3) cites a speech against Alkibiades ascribed to Phaiax, which is identified with a pamphlet preserved among the works of Andokides and cited as [Andok.] iv. As the latest event mentioned in the pamphlet (§§ 22–23) is the fate of the Melians after the capture of their city, the dramatic date intended by the author must be the beginning of 415. This fact has generally been regarded as fatal to the pamphlet's claim to be an authentic speech delivered on a real historical occasion, especially as the author himself admits (§ 3) that no debate was allowed on the occasion of an ostracism (cf. Carcopino, *Ostracisme*, pp. 64 f.). The pamphlet has recently been re-examined by A. E. Raubitschek (in *T.A.P.A.* lxxix, 1948, 191–210). He concludes that it was not, as commonly supposed, a literary exercise, but a work composed shortly before the ostracism to influence public opinion and delivered in an *unofficial* assembly (op. cit. 197); the inevitable conclusion from these premisses is that the true date of Hyperbolos' ostracism is early in 415.

An attempt has been made to provide support for this dating from epigraphic evidence. A. G. Woodhead has published (in *Hesperia*, xviii, 1949, 78–83) a study of *I.G.* i². 95 propounding a new restoration of ll. 9–12 which, if correct, would show that Hyperbolos was in Athens and addressing the ekklesia in the last prytany of 418/417. This does not really support Raubitschek's view, for it would still be possible for Hyperbolos to have been ostracized early in 416, and this could be reconciled with Theopompos' testimony by the supposition that his six years were calculated inclusively. However, Woodhead frankly admits that his restorations are 'highly conjectural', and in my opinion no reliance can be placed on the crucial words ἐπὶ Ἀντιφ[ῶντος ἄρχοντος].

Raubitschek's arguments do not really prove more than what we knew already, that the dramatic date of [Andok.] iv is early 415, and that its author was careful

not to let slip any clear indication of events subsequent to that date. If Raubitschek's defence of the speech as intended for a real occasion is correct, why does
the speaker make no mention of Hyperbolos? Instead he represents himself,
Alkibiades, and Nikias as the only persons affected by the impending ostracism
(§ 2). Moreover it is inconceivable that Thucydides should have omitted to record
Hyperbolos' ostracism in its proper place if it had been so closely related to the
debates on the Sicilian Expedition recorded at the beginning of Book VI. Meyer
(*G.A.* iv. 491 n.), defending a date early in 417 for the ostracism, rightly claimed
that 'the whole political situation' supported such a dating. We know from
Plutarch (*Alk.* 13. 6) that the proposal to hold the ostracism was made by Hyperbolos, and the winter of 418/417, when both Alkibiades and Nikias could be
blamed for the frustration of the high hopes based on the Quadruple Alliance,
afforded the obvious occasion, just as the uneasy alliance of Nikias and Alkibiades
in the years 417 and 416 was the natural outcome of their temporary coalition
against Hyperbolos.

J

Plutarch (*Kimon* 4. 10; cf. 16. 1) describes Kimon's Alkmaionid wife as Isodike
the daughter of Euryptolemos the son of Megakles. Wade-Gery (in *Hesperia*,
xiv, 1945, 221, n. 21) agrees with C. A. M. Fennell (*Pindar, Olympian and Pythian
Odes*, introduction to *Pythian* vii) that Isodike's grandfather is to be identified
with the Megakles ostracized in 486, but this would force us to date the marriage
late in Kimon's life (Wade-Gery dates it to 451) and to deny the accuracy of the
statement attributed by Plutarch (*Kimon* 16. 1) to Διόδωρος ὁ περιηγητής (fr. 37
in Jacoby, *F.G.H.* iii B, p. 238) that Isodike was the mother of Kimon's three
sons. This is dismissed as a late tradition by Wade-Gery (loc. cit.), but is surely
preferable to the malicious fantasies of Stesimbrotos in Plut. *Kimon* 16. 1
(= fr. 6 in Jacoby, *F.G.H.* ii B, p. 517) which are rightly scouted by Jacoby in
his note on this passage (ii D, p. 347); cf. Beloch, ii². 2. 40. Beloch suggests (p. 31)
that Isodike's grandfather may have been an otherwise unknown brother of
Kleisthenes the legislator. Beloch's grounds (pp. 41–42) for dating Isodike's
marriage with Kimon before 480 are flimsy; probably it took place in or soon after
479, as their eldest son Lakedaimonios appears as hipparch in an inscription of
about 446 (*I.G.* i². 400).

K

Our principal evidence on the μισθὸς ἐκκλησιαστικός is supplied by the *Athenaion
Politeia*. In one passage (62. 2), as usually restored, the payment for attendance
at the principal assembly in each prytany (κυρία ἐκκλησία; cf. 43. 4) was 9 obols
for each citizen, whereas the payment at all other assemblies was only a drachma
for each meeting; these were the rates of pay prevailing at the time when the
Athenaion Politeia was written. Elsewhere (41. 3) the author connects the introduction of pay for attendance at the assemblies with the difficulty of obtaining
a quorum. He says that pay was first introduced on the proposal of Agyrrhios
at the rate of 1 obol for each meeting, that this was presently raised to 2 obols
by Herakleides, a Klazomenian who had received Athenian citizenship (on him
see Kahrstedt in *R.-E.* viii. 457) and again to 3 by Agyrrhios. The increase to
3 obols was recent when Aristophanes produced his *Ecclesiazousae* in the spring
of 392, and the whole evolution described in *A.P.* 41. 3 must have occurred within

three years, for in view of the financial difficulties of Athens in and after 403 it is unlikely that pay for attendance at the assembly could have been introduced even at the rate of 1 obol until 395.

L

The stages in the loss of independent judicial authority by the magistrates cannot be clearly determined, but the final step must have been an enactment under which all cases brought before a magistrate were automatically referred to a popular court, so that ἔφεσις in the sense of 'obligatory reference' applied to all such cases and the activity of the magistrate became a mere routine preliminary to the trial before the dikasts. Wade-Gery, whose account of the matter (*B.S.A. Annual*, xxxvii, 1936-7, 266 ff.) I have followed in the above statement, suggested that it was Ephialtes who made the ephesis automatic. He admits that this is not proved by the fact that the judicial role of Athena in the *Eumenides* of Aeschylus is merely introductory, but asks the question: is there in fact any more likely date? I am unable to understand why he decides that 'it cannot surely have been later'. Not much later, certainly, but this reform might have been a few years later than 462, consequential no doubt on Ephialtes' main reform but actually reserved for one of his successors, who by this measure completed the Ephialtic revolution in jurisdiction.

With these possibilities in mind we may approach the famous decree regulating Athenian judicial relations with Phaselis (*I.G.* i². 16 = Tod, 32). This decree enacts that cases arising out of contracts made at Athens between an Athenian and a Phaselite shall be tried at Athens in the polemarch's court and nowhere else (the precise distribution of the emphasis in this sentence does not matter for our purpose). Magistrates who receive suits and pronounce verdicts in contravention of the provisions of this decree are threatened with heavy penalties. The receiving of a suit would indeed be within the competence of a magistrate after ephesis had become automatic, but the reference to his καταδίκη strongly suggests that he still has the power to pronounce a real judgement, and therefore that the reform making ephesis automatic had not yet been carried.

There is so much uncertainty about the date of the Phaselis decree that it might be possible to assume that it was carried before 462. I cannot admit this solution, for I accept the argument (quoted in Tod, p. 59) that the formulae of the inscription point to a time later than the Ephialtic revolution. Yet the inscription need not be as late as 450. It is true that Leon, the mover of the Phaselis decree, was very probably the man who proposed the Athenian treaty with Hermione, apparently between 451 and 449 (cf. J. H. Oliver in *Hesperia*, ii, 1933, 494 ff.), but he may have been active in politics for many years. If the Phaselis decree could be dated somewhere in the early fifties of the fifth century, the difficulty would disappear. The reform which deprived the magistrates of independent judicial authority may seem to us the logical consequence of the affirmation of popular sovereignty implicit in the Ephialtic revolution, but the Athenian radicals may have been slower to react against the jurisdiction of magistrates, holding office for one year only and responsible at the end of it for their official actions, than against the jurisdiction of an irresponsible council whose members held office for life. Hence the law which made ephesis obligatory in all cases brought before a magistrate may perhaps be dated several years after 462.

SELECT BIBLIOGRAPHY

THE works in the following list are, with few exceptions, limited to those which have been mentioned above in the text or the notes. Those marked with a dagger were not read by the author of this book until his own work was already in proof, but where the views expressed in them differ from his own he has seen no reason to change his opinions.

A bibliography entitled *Griechische Staatskunde von 1902–1932*, compiled by Heichelheim, was published in Bursian's *Jahresbericht*, Band 250 (Supplementband), Leipzig, 1935.

ACCAME, S. 'Le archeresie degli strateghi ateniesi nel V secolo', *Riv. di fil.* lxiii (1935), 341 ff.

ARMBRUSTER, O. *Über die Herrschaft der Dreissig zu Athen 404/3 v. Chr.* Diss. Freiburg im Breisgau, 1913.

BELOCH, J. *Die attische Politik seit Perikles.* Leipzig, 1884.

—— *Griechische Geschichte*², i and ii. Strassburg, 1912 and 1916. Vol. iii, Berlin and Leipzig, 1922–3.

—— 'Die zweite Oligarchie in Athen', in *G.G.* iii². 2. 204 ff.

BERVE, H. 'Fürstliche Herren zur Zeit der Perserkriege', *Die Antike*, xii (1936), 1 ff.

—— *Miltiades; Studien zur Geschichte des Mannes und seiner Zeit* (Hermes-Einzelschriften 2). Berlin, 1937.

BLANK, O. *Die Einsetzung der Dreissig zu Athen im Jahre 404 v. Chr.* Diss. Freiburg im Breisgau, 1911.

BLOCH, H. 'Historical Literature of the Fourth Century', *Athenian Studies presented to William Scott Ferguson* (Harvard Studies in Classical Philology, Supplementary Volume I), 341–76. Cambridge (Mass.), 1940.

BOERNER, A. *De rebus a Graecis inde ab anno 410 usque ad annum 403 a. Chr. n. gestis quaestiones historicae.* Diss. Göttingen, 1894.

BONNER, R. J., and SMITH, G. *The Administration of Justice from Homer to Aristotle*, i, ii. Chicago, 1930 and 1938.

BUSOLT, G. *Griechische Geschichte*², i–ii. Gotha, 1893–5. Vol. iii¹ (in 2 parts). Gotha, 1897 and 1904.

—— and SWOBODA, H. *Griechische Staatskunde*, i, ii (IV. 1. i in Iwan Müller's *Handbuch*). Munich, 1920 and 1926.

CARCOPINO, J. *L'Ostracisme athénien*². Paris, 1935.

CARY, M. 'Athenian Democracy', *History*, xii (1927–8), 206 ff.

CHRIMES, K. M. T. 'On Solon's Property Classes', *C.R.* xlvi (1932), 2 ff.

CLOCHÉ, P. *La Restauration démocratique à Athènes en 403 avant J.-C.* Paris, 1915.

—— 'Le Conseil athénien des Cinq Cents et la peine de mort', *R.E.G.* xxxiii (1920), 1 ff.

—— 'La Boulè d'Athènes en 508/507 av. J.-C.', *R.E.G.* xxxvii (1924), 1 ff.

—— 'Les Procès des stratèges athéniens', *R.E.A.* xxvii (1925), 97 ff.

COLIN, G. *Xénophon historien.* Paris, 1933.

CORNELIUS, F. *Die Tyrannis in Athen*. Munich, 1929.

DAREMBERG, C., and SAGLIO, E. (editors). *Dictionnaire des antiquités*. Paris, 1877–1919.

DE SANCTIS, G. *Atthis: Storia della Repubblica Ateniese*[2]. Turin, 1912.

DITTENBERGER, W. 'Die eleusinischen Keryken', *Hermes*, xx (1885), 1 ff.

—— 'Die Familie des Alkibiades', *Hermes*, xxxvii (1902), 1 ff.

EHRENBERG, V. 'Kleisthenes und das Archontat', *Klio*, xix (1923), 106 ff.

—— *Neugründer des Staates*. Munich, 1925.

—— 'Losung', in *R.-E.* xiii. 2 (1927), 1451 ff.

—— 'Pericles and his colleagues between 441 and 429 B.C.', *A.J.P.* lxvi (1945), 113 ff.

FERGUSON, W. S. 'The Athenian Phratries', *C.P.* v (1910), 257 ff.

—— 'The Constitution of Theramenes', *C.P.* xxi (1926), 72 ff.

—— 'The condemnation of Antiphon', *Mélanges Glotz* (Paris, 1932), i. 349 ff.

—— 'The Athenian Law Code', *Classical Studies presented to Edward Capps*, Princeton, 1936.

—— 'The Salaminioi of Heptaphylai and Sounion', *Hesperia*, vii (1938), 1–74.

FRANCOTTE, H. *La Polis grecque*. Paderborn, 1907.

†FRITZ, K. von, and KAPP, E. *Aristotle's Constitution of Athens*. New York, 1950.

GILBERT, G. *The Constitutional Antiquities of Sparta and Athens* (English translation of vol. i of his *Handbuch der Griechischen Staatsaltertümer*). London and New York, 1895.

GILLIARD, C. *Quelques Réformes de Solon*. Lausanne, 1907.

GLOTZ, G. *La Cité grecque*. Paris, 1928 (Eng. trans. by N. Mallinson, London, 1929).

—— and COHEN, R. *Histoire grecque*, i, ii. Paris, 1925 and 1931.

GOMME, A. W. *The population of Athens in the fifth and fourth centuries B.C.* Oxford, 1933.

—— *Essays in Greek History and Literature*. Oxford, 1937.

GREENIDGE, A. H. J. *A Handbook of Greek Constitutional History*. London, 1896 (reprint of 1911).

GROTE, G. *A History of Greece* (edition in 8 vols.). London, 1862.

—— Abridged edition of the preceding in one volume (*From the time of Solon to 403 B.C.*) by J. M. Mitchell and M. O. B. Caspari. London, 1907.

GUARDUCCI, M. 'Orgeoni e tiasoti', *Riv. di fil.* lxiii (1935), 332 ff.

—— 'L'istituzione della fratria nella Grecia antica e nelle colonie greche d'Italia', *Mem. Acc. Lincei*, Ser. vi, vol. vi (1937), 5 ff.

—— 'Le origine e le vicende del γένος attico dei Salamini', *Riv. di fil.* lxxvi (1948), 223 ff.

HASEBROEK, J. *Griechische Wirtschafts- und Gesellschaftsgeschichte bis zur Perserzeit*. Tübingen, 1931.

HATZFELD, J. *Alcibiade*. Paris, 1940 (reprinted, 1951).

HEADLAM, J. W. *Election by lot at Athens*[2] (revised with notes by D. C. Macgregor). Cambridge, 1933.

HILL, G. F. *Sources for Greek History between the Persian and Peloponnesian Wars* (2nd issue). Oxford, 1907.
—— Revised edition of the preceding, by R. Meiggs and A. Andrewes. Oxford, 1951.
HOMMEL, H. 'Die dreissig Trittyen des Kleisthenes', *Klio*, xxxiii (1940), 181 ff.
JACOBY, F. 'Die attische Königsliste', *Klio*, ii, 1902, 406 ff.
—— *Atthis: the local chronicles of Ancient Athens*. Oxford, 1949.
KAHRSTEDT, U. *Studien zum öffentlichen Recht Athens:* i, *Staatsgebiet und Staatsangehörige in Athen.* ii, *Untersuchungen zur Magistratur in Athen.* Stuttgart–Berlin, 1934 and 1936.
—— *Untersuchungen zu athenischen Behörden.* i. 'Areopag und Epheten', *Klio*, xxx (1937), 10 ff. ii. 'Die Nomotheten und die Legislative in Athen', xxxi (1938), 1 ff. iii. 'Einige Instanzen aus der Rechtspflege', xxxii (1939), 148 ff. iv. 'Bemerkungen zur Geschichte des Rats der Fünfhundert', xxxiii (1940), 1 ff.
KEIL, B. *Die Solonische Verfassung in Aristoteles' Verfassungsgeschichte Athens.* Berlin, 1892.
KIRCHNER. *Prosopographia Attica*, i, ii. Berlin, 1901 and 1903.
KRAUSE, A. *Attische Strategenliste bis 146 v. Chr.* Diss. Weimar, 1914.
KRIEGEL, J. *Der Staatsstreich der Vierhundert in Athen 411 v. Chr.* Diss. Bonn, 1909.
LANG, M. 'The Revolution of the 400', *A.J.P.* lxix, 1948, 272 ff.
LEDL, A. 'Das attische Bürgerrecht und die Frauen', *Wiener Studien*, xxix (1907), 173 ff., xxx (1908), 1 ff. and 173 ff.
—— 'Die Einsetzung des Rates der Vierhundert in Athen im Jahre 411 v. Chr.', *Wiener Studien*, xxxii (1910), 38 ff.
—— *Studien zur älteren athenischen Verfassungsgeschichte.* Heidelberg, 1914.
LINFORTH, I. M. *Solon the Athenian.* Berkeley (Cal.), 1919.
LOEPER, R. 'Die Trittyen und Demen Attikas', *Athenische Mittheilungen*, xvi (1892), 319 ff.
LUCKENBACH, H. *De ordine rerum a pugna apud Aegospotamos commissa usque ad triginta viros institutos gestarum.* Diss. Strassburg, 1878.
MÉAUTIS, G. *L'Aristocratie athénienne.* Paris, 1927.
MERITT, B. D., WADE-GERY, H. T., and McGREGOR, M. F. *The Athenian Tribute Lists*, i, ii, iii. Cambridge (Mass.), 1939–50.
MEYER, E. *Geschichte des Altertums*[1], ii–v. Stuttgart and Berlin, 1893–1902. (Vol. iii in the second edition, corresponding to ii of the first edition, was published at Stuttgart in 1937).
—— *Forschungen zur alten Geschichte*, i–ii. Halle, 1892 and 1899.
MUNRO, J. A. R. 'The end of the Peloponnesian War', *C.Q.* xxxi (1937), 32 ff.
—— 'Theramenes against Lysander', *C.Q.* xxxii (1938), 18 ff.
—— 'The constitution of Drakontides', *C.Q.* xxxii (1938), 152 ff.
—— 'The ancestral laws of Cleisthenes', *C.Q.* xxxiii (1939), 84 ff.
MYRES, J. L. 'Cleisthenes and Herodotus', *Mélanges Glotz*, (Paris, 1932), ii. 657 ff.

NIESE, B. 'Über Aristoteles' Geschichte der athenischen Verfassung', *Hist. Zeitschrift* N.F. xxxiii (1892), 38–68.

OLIVER, J. H. 'Greek Inscriptions', *Hesperia*, iv (1935), 5 ff.

†—— *The Athenian Expounders of the Sacred and Ancestral Law.* Baltimore, 1950.

PEARSON, L. *The Local Historians of Attica.* Philadelphia (Pa.), 1942.

†RAUBITSCHEK, A. E. 'The Origin of Ostracism', *A.J.A.* lv (1951), 221 ff.

†ROBINSON, C. A., Jr. 'Cleisthenes and Ostracism', *A.J.A.* lvi (1952), 23 ff.

ROOS, A. G. Chronologisches zur Geschichte der Dreissig', *Klio*, xvii, 1920, 1 ff.

SANDYS, J. E. *Aristotle's Constitution of Athens²*. London, 1912.

SCHOELL, R. 'Über attische Gesetzgebung', *Bayer. S. B.*, 1886, 83 ff.

SCHWAHN, W. 'Strategos', in *R.-E.* Supplementband vi (1935), 1071 ff.

SCHWARTZ, E. 'Quellenuntersuchungen zur griechischen Geschichte', *Rh. Mus.* xliv (1889), 104 ff.

SMITH, G. 'The Prytaneum in the Athenian Amnesty Law', *C.P.* xvi, 1921, 345 ff.

STEVENSON, G. H. 'The constitution of Theramenes', *J.H.S.* lvi, 1936, 48 ff.

SWOBODA, H. 'Bemerkungen zur politischen Stellung der athenischen Strategen', *Rh. Mus.* xlv (1890), 288 ff.

—— 'Über den Process des Perikles', *Hermes*, xxviii (1893), 536 ff.

SZANTO, E. 'Die griechischen Phylen', *Wiener S.B.* cxliv (1901), Abhandlung 5.

TOEPFFER, J. *Quaestiones Pisistrateae.* Diss. Dorpat, 1886.

—— *Attische Genealogie.* Berlin, 1889.

WADE-GERY, H. T. 'Eupatridai, Archons, and Areopagus', *C.Q.* xxv (1931) 1 ff. and 77 ff.

—— 'Studies in the Structure of Attic Society: I. Demotionidai', *C.Q.* xxv (1931), 129 ff.

—— 'Studies in the Structure of Attic Society: II. The Laws of Kleisthenes', *C.Q.* xxvii (1933), 17–29.

—— 'The Charter of the Democracy, 410 B.C.–I.G. I². 114', *B.S.A. Annual*, xxxiii (1932–3), 113 ff. (part of a paper entitled 'Studies in Athenian Inscriptions of the fifth century B.C.').

—— 'Themistokles' Archonship', *B.S.A. Annual*, xxxvii (1936–7), 263 ff.

—— 'Two notes on Theopompos, Philippika X', *A.J.P.* lix, 1938, 129 ff.

†—— 'Miltiades', *J.H.S.* lxxi (1951), 212 ff.

WALKER, E. M. 'The "Athenian Constitution"', in *New Chapters in Greek History* (Powell, J. U. and Barber, E. A.), First Series (1921), 133 ff.

WILAMOWITZ-MÖLLENDORFF, U. von. *Aristoteles und Athen*, i, ii. Berlin, 1893.

—— 'Die lebenslänglichen Archonten Athens', *Hermes*, xxxiii (1898), 119 ff.

WILCKEN, U. 'Zur oligarchischen Revolution in Athen vom Jahre 411 v. Chr.', *Berl. S.B.*, 1935, 34 ff.

WOODHOUSE, W. J. *Solon the Liberator.* Oxford, 1938.

ZIMMERN, A. *The Greek Commonwealth⁴*. Oxford, 1924.

INDEX

Acharnai, 135, 136, 386.
Adeimantos, 349.
Adoptions, in Crete, 58 ; in Athens, 58.
Aelian, on ostracism, 163.
Aelius Aristeides, scholion to, 349, 354–6.
Agariste, mother of Perikles, 180, 190, 194, 252.
Agis, 382.
Aglauros, 392.
agora, see Athens *and* Ekklesia.
Agoratos, 287.
Agyrrhios, 396.
Aiakos, 104.
Aiantis (Tribe IX), 280 n. 2.
Aias, 104.
Aigaleos, 141.
Aigeïs (Tribe II), 134, 349.
Aigikoreis, 50 f.
Aigina, original home of Philaïdai in Herodotus, 104 ; Athenian war with, 188.
Aigospotamoi, battle of, 281, 283, 285, 381.
Aischines, 61, 299.
Aischraios, 350.
Akamantis (Tribe V), 134, 349 f., 352, 355.
Akastos, king of Athens, 38–40, 168 ; possible date of, 45–46.
Akestorides (archon 504/503), 337.
Alexander I, king of Macedonia, 196.
Alexias (archon 405/404), 288, 379, 381–2.
Alkibiades, 265–8, 270, 277–80, 377 f. ; family of, 316 ; character and abilities, 265 f. ; mistrusted by the demagogues, 266–8, 283 ; powers conferred in 407 on him, 248 f., 353 f. ; death, 290 and n. 3, 385, 388 f. ; pamphlet against, preserved among the works of Andokides, 395 f. ; mentioned, 6, 180, 250 n. 2, 257, 352, 356, 363, 372.
Alkmaion (mythical founder of *genos* of Alkmaionidai), 316.
— (contemporary of Solon), 316.
— (father of Leobotas), 190.
Alkmaionidai, probably a *genos*, 63 n. 4, 316 ; names of some inserted in genealogy of Medontidai, 45 ; responsible for the murder of the Kylonians, 69, 86 f., 335 ; tried for the murder, 121, 334 f. ; sentenced to expulsion from Attica, 87, 105 (sentence did not apply to the de-

scendants of the guilty, 105 and n. 6) ; probably adherents of Solon, 105 ; satisfied with Solon's reforms, 107, 109 f. ; attitude to the tyrants, 114, 332 ; retired from Attica in 546, 114 ; attempts to expel the tyrants, 124 f. ; second expulsion from Attica (508/507), 120 f., 128, 132, 334 f. ; attitude in last decade of sixth century, 125 f., 133 ; attitude in early years of fifth century, 180–3 ; coalition with Kimon, 190 ; unimportant after 470 in politics, 190 ; earlier relations with Philaïdai, 326.
Alopeke, 349.
Amasis, 320.
Amnesty of 403, 294 and n. 3 ; faithfully observed by the demos, 298 ; Andokides on it, 302. *See* Law.
Amorges, 269.
Amphilytos, 112.
Amphipolis, 262, 351.
anagrapheis (in 411), 357, 367 f. ; (in 410), 282, 307.
anakrisis, 98, 223 and n. 3.
anarchiai, 4, 317, 319, 320, 379.
Anaxagoras, 253.
Anchises (archon 488/487), 336.
Andokides, 18, 19, 114, 202, 212 ; *genos* of, 316 ; laws quoted by, 300, 303 ; speech falsely attributed to, 165, 395 f.
Androkles, 263, 270, 271.
Andron, 12 and n. 2, 375–7.
Androtion, pupil of Isokrates, 8 ; his *Atthis*, 4, 9, 12 and n. 1 ; use of obsolete laws by, 12, 17, 21 f., 68 f. ; his views on the Areopagus, 8, 80 and n. 7, 81 ; on Solon's Seisachtheia, 8 ; on the *apodektai*, 146 ; on the date of the institution of ostracism, 159 f. ; gave list of generals for 441/440, 17, 349 ff., 354 f. ; on the rule of the Thirty, 387.
Antiochis (Tribe X), 376.
Antiphon, 212, 272, 362, 375 ; decree for trial of, 375–8 ; speech in his own defence, 4, 279 and n. 8, 362, 374 ; condemnation, 162, 279, 378.
Anytos, 294, 297 n. 2.
Apatouria, 57, 60.
apodektai, 146, 222.
Apolexis, 376.
Apollo Patroös, 57, 63.
Apollodoros, 317, 328.
Archedemos, 281.

Archelaos, king of Macedonia, 235 n. 5.

Archeptolemos, 162, 279, 375, 378.

Archestratos, laws of, 13, 196, 198, 254, 288.

— proposer of rider to decree on Chalkis, 198 n. 2, 350.

— (possibly identical with the above), general in 433/432, 198, 350.

— treasurer of Athena in 429/428, 350.

Archinos, 241, 295 ff.; not a Theramenist, 297 n. 2.

archon eponymos, origin of, 41 f., 44 f.; official list of holders of the office, 4 and n. 4, 43; alleged life tenure of early archons, 40–42; decennial archons, 40, 43, 44; powers of, in the aristocratic state, 74 f.; probably presided over the ekklesia till 487, 74, 92, 99, 126, 151; prestige and influence of, revives after expulsion of tyrants, 153 and n. 1, 173; decline in power after reform of 487/486, 175; office handed over to a board of ten in the last 10 months of 580/579, 319. *See* Archons, the nine, *and* Magistrates.

Archons, the nine, did not form a college, 77; oath taken by, 45 f., 91; eligibility to, 78, 101 f., 142 f., 156, 225 and n. 3; appointed by direct election till 487, 79, 97, 321–6; alleged selection by lot in pre-Solonian period, 228 and n. 6, 322; alleged selection by partial sortition under law of Solon, 228, 322 ff.; substitution of partial sortition for election in appointment, 4, 173 ff., 322 (precise date of this reform, 176; its significance, 186–8 and 187 n. 6; its effect, 175, 231); powers of, in pre-Solonian Athens, 42, 74 ff.; received special powers against the Kylonians, 78; office of, secularized by Solon, 172; appointments to, controlled by tyrants, 116; part played by, in holding of ostracisms, 151; double sortition of, 227, 322; *dokimasia* of, 91, 205 ff. *See archon eponymos, basileus*, Magistrates, Polemarch.

Areopagus, Council of, 8 and n. 1; continuity of, with council of aristocratic state, 79–82, 309 ff.; origin of (as aristocratic council), 35 n. 3, 37; original title of, 82; presided over by the chief archon (except in homicide trials), 74 and n. 8, 83, 91 f., 99; powers of, in aristocratic state, 83; probouleutic functions of, 83, 91 f., 150; tried those who con-

spired against the constitution, 90, 147, 168, 200, 205, 313; right of appeal to, against verdicts of magistrates, 74 and n. 7, 78; as homicide court in pre-Solonian period, 80 n. 3, 82, 310; may have appointed minor magistrates before Solon, 79, 322; members of, held their seats for life, 82; recruitment of, in pre-Solonian Athens, 81 n. 2, 83, 103; recruitment of, after Solon, 94, 99 and n. 6, 107, 156; powers of, under laws of Solon, 89–92, 148; guardianship of the laws, 90 f., 127 n. 8, 167, 198, 208 f., cf. 200; alleged veto of, on unconstitutional laws and decrees, 127 and nn. 6 and 8, 208 and n. 5; right to hear complaints against magistrates, 96 f., 200, 205; control over lives and morals of citizens, 201; alleged financial powers, 91, 194 f.; diluted with supporters of tyrants, 116, 146; identified with the council which resisted Kleomenes, 94 f., 128, 146, 149; powers of, under laws of Kleisthenes, 146–8, 156, 167; effect of reform of 487/486 on prestige of, 188, 195; story of part played by it in 480 criticized, 91, 147 f.; alleged recovery of power in 479/462, 6, 147 f.; most of powers of, taken away by the reforms of 462 (on chronology of these reforms cf. 337–41), 13, 147, 198 ff., 217 and n. 5; attitude of radicals to ancient powers of, 195, 198; some judicial privileges retained by, 89 f., 199, 233, 306; members of, unpaid under radical democracy, 219; attitude of oligarchs to, in late fifth century, 273, 288; special powers conferred on, after the restoration of 403, 200, 301; in Isokrates, 8, 80 and n. 6; in Androtion, 8, 80 and n. 7, 81. See *dokimasia*, Ephialtes, *euthynai*.

Arginousai, 234.

Argos, 52, 124, 266 f., 290.

Aristagoras (of Miletos), 178.

Aristaichmos (archon 621/620), 307.

Aristeides, antecedents and policy of, 184 ff.; alleged connexions with Kleisthenes and the Alkmaionidai, 184–5; general at the time of Marathon, 184; archonship (489/488) 153 and n. 3, 184, 185, 322, 336; co-operation with Themistokles, 185 ff.; probably opposed Themistokles' navy-bill, 183 and n. 4, 189; date of his ostracism, 185, 336–7 (its significance, 189, 339); story that during his exile he lived in

Aristeides (contd.)
  Aigina, 163 and n. 3; return from
  exile, 189 f.; general in 479, 185
  (with plenary powers, 248); bogus
  decree attributed to, 174 f.; may
  have renewed his alliance with Themistokles after 479, 190; later
  years of, 190 and n. 1; his poverty,
  101, 184; described as leader of the
  popular party, 177, 184; memory
  of, attacked by oligarchs, 342.
Aristion, 96, 127.
Aristogeiton, 65, 124.
Aristokrates, 278, 362.
Aristokypros, 320.
Aristolaïdas, 114.
Aristomachos, 357, 358, 360.
Aristophanes, on Solon, 3; on Solon's
  law of inheritance, 19, 20, 343 f.;
  on Lamachos, 220; on dikasts, 219,
  223; on pay for attendance at the
  ekklesia, 396; plea for moderation
  in 405, 281; use of demotika in, 139.
Aristophon, 210, 296.
Aristotle, said to have inaugurated
  research into documents, 17; credited with authorship of a work on
  Solon's axones, 25; Politeiai produced by him and his pupils, 29 f.,
  31 n. 2; the Politics of, 29 (modern
  attempts to find chronological strata in, 390); views expressed, in the
  Politics: on the Areopagus, 80, 147;
  on birth as qualification for office in
  aristocracy, 78 n. 6; on concentration of wide powers in a single
  magistracy, 75; on Solon and his
  constitution, 29, 79, 89, 93, 96 f.,
  117, 204, 321 f.; on the followers of
  Peisistratos, 111; on Kleisthenes,
  129, 131 f., 133 and n. 5, 140, 144;
  on devices to destroy power of
  aristocracy, 119; on ostracism, 186;
  on the relation between type of
  government and principal military
  force of a state, 157, 258, 394; on
  regulations conducive to the maintenance of a radical democracy,
  214, 220; on prerogatives of ekklesia in radical democracy, 233; on
  sortition, 229; on probouloi, 269;
  meaning of hairesis in Aristotle,
  323.
Artaphernes, 178 f.
asty, one of the Kleisthenic regions of
  Attica, 140 f.
Athena Nike, 235, 238.
— Polias, 62, 64.
Athenagoras, 264.
Athenaia Phratria, 56 and n. 8.
Athenaion Politeia, 27–30; authorship
  of, 29; date of composition, 1 n. 2,

29, 390; written sources used in
  first part of, (a) democratic, 6–7,
  28, (b) oligarchic, 4–5, 28, 342, (c)
  Kleidemos, 7, 9, (d) Androtion, 9,
  12 n. 3, 30, (e) an unidentified
  Atthis, 356; author alleged to have
  used official copies of the laws of
  Solon and Kleisthenes, 17, 129–31;
  misleading on economic conditions
  in pre-Solonian Attica, 88; views of
  author of, cited on pre-Solonian
  Areopagus, 80 f.; on appointment
  of archons after Solon, 322 ff.; on
  lapsing of Solon's laws during the
  tyranny, 116, 130, 305, 322; on
  Kleisthenes, 20, 129 ff., 305, 331 ff.;
  on jurisdiction of the Council of
  Five Hundred, 241; on the revolution of 411, 356 ff.; documents
  quoted by author of (cc. 30–31),
  357 ff. (Beloch's hypothesis on
  them, 367–73); alleged re-enactment of one of these documents
  (c. 30) in September of 411, 376 ff.;
  order of events in 404/403 given by,
  384 ff.
Athenians, claim to be autochthonous,
  54; special aptitude of, for successful working of popular government,
  250; drift of, from country districts
  to Athens and Piraeus, 259; latent
  antagonism between rural and urban population, 260 ff.
Athens, town of, 120, 135; had as
  such no local administration in
  Kleisthenic system, 141 f.; as centre
  of state and tribal administration,
  141, 259; agora of, exclusion from,
  281 (also American excavations in,
  17, 393).
atimia, types of, in years after 410,
  281.
atimos, 161, 313.
Atrometos, 62.
Atthidographers, 9 ff.; views of, on
  pre-Solonian period, 34, 47–50;
  on Solon's constitution, 16, 25 f.; on
  aristocratic state, 49, 59, 61; had
  no clear views on nature or working
  of the constitution during the
  period 507/462, 146; equally hazy
  about revolution which overthrew
  it, 198; probably did not possess a
  copy of Solon's laws, 25 f.; early ones
  said to have made little use of documents, 25 f.; traces of, in Athenaion
  Politeia, 30.
Atthis, 3, 5, 7 ff.
Attica, political unification of, 34–38.
  See synoikismos.
autokratia (plenary powers), 248,
  353 f., 374.

axones (of Solon), 17, 23, 24 ; originally inscribed on tablets of wood, 12, 24, 390 ; doubtful whether still surviving in the fourth century, 17.

Barathron, 155.
basileus, 39, 238 ; religious privileges and jurisdiction, 75 f. ; presided in trials for impiety, homicide, &c., 89, 199, 312.
basilinna, wife of the *basileus*, 75 f.
Bastards, position of those of pure Athenian descent, 343 ff.
Boards of officials, (*a*) regular, for routine administration, 223, 232, (*b*) special, 227, 244.
Boiotia, local constitutions in states of, 369 ; federal constitution of, 377 ; defeated by Athens, 395.
Boreis 51 f., 54.
Boukoleion, 76.
boulē, see Areopagus, Councils.
Bouleuterion, 14, 276, 359, 360 ; alleged discovery of the Solonian Bouleuterion, 393.
Bouselidai, 63.
Boutes, 65.
Bouzygai, 64, 252 n. 4.
Brauron, 103, 109 and n. 11, 114, 120, 135, 326.
Brytidai, 64.

Chabrias, 348.
Chaireas, 276 f.
Chalkidike, 353.
Chalkis, 243, 395.
Chamaileon, 14 n. 3.
Charmides, 291, 384.
Charminos, 276.
Charon of Lampsakos, 3 n. 2.
Chersonese, Thracian, 115, 181, 326, 330 ; colonization of, 327 ff.
Chios, 62 ; early inscription from, 95, 96 n. 1.
Citizenship, full, conditions of, 79, 84, 98, 117 ff., 122, 133 f., 394 ; dependent after Kleisthenes on membership of a deme, 136 ; conditions altered by law of 451/450, 256, 343 ff. ; exclusion of proletariat from active rights of citizenship (*a*) by the 400, 272, 273 f., (*b*) by the 5,000, 279 f. ; rights of, forfeited by the oligarchs after 410 completely or partially, 281 ; rights of, restricted to the 3,000 by the Thirty, 289, 384, 388.
Code of Athenian laws, revised in 410–401, 17 f., 154, 211 f., 295, 300 ff. (revision possibly begun in autumn 411, 375) ; problem of origins of fourth-century code, 18 ff. ;

alleged existence in fourth century of a compilation of earlier laws, 26 ; first complete codification of law perhaps to be ascribed to Solon, 84, 106, 307 f. ; possible revisions of the code between Solon and 410, 303 ff ; code of Solon perhaps modified in some respects by Peisistratos and Kleisthenes, 116, 19 f. *See* Kleisthenes.
Colonization, 86.
Corinth, tribal organization at, 54 ; Kypselid rulers of, 104 f., 119, 326, 330.
Corinthians, 268, 339, 341.
Council of Four Hundred, attributed to Solon, 92–96, 127, 128 n. 4, 273, 325 ; archaeological argument for its existence, 393.
—— —— set up in 411 by the oligarchs, 274-6, 356–75 ; alleged to be the revival of an earlier 400 (Solonian or Drakonian) 93, 273 ; method of selection of, (*a*) in Thucydides, 275, 360, (*b*) in the *A.P.*, 361 ; possibly promulgated a new constitution after their appointment, 277, 360, 373, 375 ; limitation of their powers in this new constitution, 370, 373 f. ; alleged reappointment of, 373 f. ; hostility of armament at Samos to, 277 f., 370 f. ; collapse of, 278.
Council of Five Hundred (Kleisthenic), 16, 148–53, 155, 237–44 ; date of first creation of, 94, 131, 145, 168, 334 ff. ; ten tribes all equally represented in, 137 ; representation of demes in, 150, 152, 237 ; combination of election and sortition at first in appointment of, 150, 152 (its purpose, 231) ; later selection by lot in the demes, 227 ; minimum age for membership of, 224 and n. 4, 237 ; conditions governing re-election, 152, 228 and n. 3 ; *dokimasia* of members-elect &c., 205 ff. ; composition of, in different periods, 157, 220 f. ; proletariat possibly excluded at first, 143 and n. 1, 157 ; oath taken by members of, 149, 154, 166 ff., 239, 275, 282 ; clause in oath, not to put to vote any proposal contrary to the laws, 167, 209 f., 275 ; motions in, could probably be moved only by a member of the council, 245 f. ; Secretary of, 14, 237, 244, 376 ; presidency of, (*a*) held at first by the chief archon according to Macan, 175 n. 4, (*b*) held by *epistates* of the Prytaneis, 150, 221, 237, (*c*) provided by the *proedroi* later, 221 ; possibly author-

Council of Five Hundred (*contd.*)
ized by the people in 479 to reject peace proposals from Persia, 155; laws relating to, probably remodelled in and after 462, 14; extant law defining powers of, 13, 153 f.; co-operation with leading statesmen in framing of policy, 243 f., 262 f.; co-operation with magistrates in administration, 151 ff., 202, 223, 238 ff.; specially concerned with naval affairs and finance, 202, 240; jurisdiction, 201 f., 240 f.; miscellaneous powers, (*a*) arrest, 90 and n. 5, 240 f., (*b*) fines, 153, 222 f., 241, (*c*) hearing of complaints against magistrates, 90 f., 200 f., 240, (*d*) initiating prosecution in certain types of cases, 202, (*e*) lease of temple lands, 90, 238, (*f*) ratification, in fourth century, of all admissions to deme membership, 137; democratic sympathies of, in Periklean period, 237, 243 f.; types of decree drafted by, 241 f.; dissolved in 411 by the oligarchs, 276, 359; probably restored by the 5,000, 279, 372, 378; restored in 403 (after oligarchy), 295; year of, *see* Year, Conciliar; see also *prosodos*, *prytaneia*, Prytaneis.
—— —— under the rule of the Thirty, 288 and n. 3; used as a law-court, 288, 384.
Cyprus, 256, 320, 340.
Cyrus, son of Darius II of Persia, 283.

Daïmachos of Plataiai, 113 n. 5.
Damasias (archon 582/581), 319 f., 322, 324.
Damon, 253 n. 4 (Damonides, 342).
Deinarchos, 191 n. 7, 209.
Dekarchies, 387.
Dekeleia, deme of, 57, 268, 269, 279.
Dekeleieis, 313 ff.
Delian League, 176, 184, 191, 193, 217, 244, 256.
Delos, Ionian festival at, 75.
Delphi, Athenian embassies to, 36; Alkmaionids and, 124, 131.
Delphinion, 306.
Demagogues, rise of, 259 ff.; attitude of, to Alkibiades, 266 ff., 283; recklessness of, after 410, 280 ff.; policy of, in Ionian War, 282 f.
Demarchs, 129, 136 and n. 5.
Demes, 135–40; names of, 64; number of, 134; rural demes pre-Kleisthenic, 119 f., 130 f., 135 f., 142; city demes apparently created by Kleisthenes, 135; groups of, combined to form trittyes, 134; membership of, made by Kleisthenes a condition of citizenship, 64, 119 ff., 136 f., 343 f. (also made hereditary, 137); residents in, who belonged by descent to other demes, 136, 351; use of, as organs of local administration, 142; choice of prokritoi for Council of Five Hundred by, 150, 227; choice of prokritoi for archonship by, 174; proportional representation of, in Council of Five Hundred, 150, 237; see also *demotikon*.
Demeter Achaia, 65.
Demetrios of Phaleron, 23 and n. 7, 25, 30, 313; on qualification for archonship in 489, 101.
demiourgoi, social division in aristocratic state, 47, 48, 319.
Democracy, Kleisthenic idea of, 156 ff.; radical, *see* Radical democracy.
Demon, 11 n. 6.
Demophantos, decree of, 167 f., 280 and n. 2, 372, 378.
Demosthenes, (*a*) the general, 212, 268, (*b*) the orator, 185, 222.
demotikon, in use in pre-Kleisthenic period, 335; use of, instead of or in addition to patronymic, 138 ff.
Demotionidai, 56, 57, 62, 313 ff.
diaitetai, 219.
Diakrioi, 110, 326, 330 f.; *see also* Hyperakrioi.
diapsephismos, (*a*) soon after expulsion of tyrants, 111, 132 f., (*b*) in 445/444, 218, 345.
Didymos, 23 and n. 7, 25, 327.
dikastai kata demous, instituted by Peisistratos, 115, 152, 205; revived in 453/452, 218 f.; numbered forty in the fourth century, 222.
Dikasteria, 210 f., 216 ff.; creation of, attributed to Solon in the fourth century, 97, 216; alleged innovations of Kleisthenes, 146, 217; after reforms of Ephialtes, 200, 203; responsible for *dokimasia* and *euthynai* of magistrates, 203–5; decisions of, not subject to appeal or revision, 216; predominance of proletariat in, 221; *see also* Homicide cases.
Dikasts, 216 ff.; date of introduction of state-pay for, 219, 254, 342 f. (amount of jury-pay, 219 n. 6); age qualification for, 224; functioned sometimes as *nomothetai*, 299.
Diodoros, of Sicily, on the rule of the Thirty, 385 ff.
— Periegetes, 396.
Diokles, 302.
Diomedon, 276.

Dionysia, 280.

Dionysios of Syracuse, 283.

Dionysos Melanaigis, 56.

dokimasia, 205–8, 241 ; erroneous view of function of, 232.

Drabeskos 193, 196.

Drakon, historical reality of, 307; held special appointment, 307, 318, 321, 394; homicide laws of, 80, (possibly connected with Kylonian affair, 87); legislation on involuntary homicide, 13, 33, 55 (part allotted to phratry in it, 55, 58, 62, 78 n. 6, 117); subsequent history of his homicide laws, 308 ff. ; doubtful whether he codified the whole body of law, 84, 306 ff. (alleged survival of his laws in the fourth century, 309); bogus constitution attributed to, 5 and n. 5, 7, 26, 90, 93, 100, 273 (rotation in, 227, 374).

Drakontides, 287.

Dyaleis, 57.

dynasteia, 103.

Economic development, as cause of constitutional change, 86, 88; as cause of increase in volume of jurisdiction, 218; effect of, on Solon's property-classes, 225 f.

Eëtioneia, 278.

Egesta, 267.

eisagogeis, 218.

eisangelia, law on, attributed to Solon, 90 and n. 8, 128 and n. 2; cases under, tried by ekklesia or dikasteria, 200, 233 f.

Ekklesia, also called *agora*, 79 ; qualification for membership of, (*a*) in aristocratic state, 79, 84, (*b*) after Solon, 98, 117 ff., 273, (*c*) after Kleisthenes, 143 ; age qualification for, 232 and n. 6 ; meetings of, 79, 83 f., 96, 152, 155, 233 ; payment for attendance at, introduced early in fourth century, 214 and n. 2, 396 f. ; group voting not employed in, 135, 141; special meetings of, 153, 233; quorum required for plenary meetings of, 153, 216, 236; agenda of meetings, prepared by the Council of Five Hundred under Kleisthenic constitution, 152 f., 155 f., cf. 236 ff., 242 ff., 263, 274; presidency of, held by (*a*) the chief archon in the aristocratic state, 74, 92, also after Solon, 99, 126, 151, 167, 175, 209, (*b*) possibly the strategoi in 486–462, 175, 191, 209 f., 246, (*c*) the Prytaneis and their *epistates*, after 462 and perhaps earlier, 127 n. 2, 150 f., 167, 175, 209 f., 237,

(*d*) the *proedroi*, in the fourth century, 221 ; in pre-Solonian Athens, 79, 83 f., 92, 97 ; powers of, under Solon's laws, 96–98, 155 ; election of magistrates by, 79, 97, 325 f. ; powers of, under laws of Kleisthenes, 153–8; trial of capital charges (except homicide) probably reserved for it by Kleisthenes, 146, 154 f., 241 and n. 2; powers of, in radical democracy, 233 ff. ; judicial powers of, 153 ff., 200, 233 f. ; sovereignty of, in radical democracy, 233; power to recommend to the Council the initiation of a particular motion, 243.

Election, direct, retained for some appointments under radical democracy, 227.

Eleusis, 35, 37, 44, 64, 235, 236, 291, 384 ; separated in 403 from Athens, 293, 295 ; reunited in 401/400 with Athens, 297 and n. 5, 385 ; plain of, 109.

Eleutherai, 135.

Elis, 34, 290 f.

Elpinike, 191, 194 and n. 3, 339, 347.

Empire, Athenian, 235, 239 f., 243, 264.

Ennea Hodoi, 193, 340.

Enyalios, 75.

Epakrioi, 110.

ephebia, 232 n. 6.

ephesis, 397.

Ephetai, 80, 306 ff.; origin of, 310 f.; assumed by some to have formed the council before Solon, 81 n. 3, 309 ff.; identified with 'the Fifty-one', 306; chosen after Solon from Areopagus, 200, 311; courts of, 199 f.

Ephialtes, 193–213; held office of general, 193 f. ; character of, 195 ; in 462 opposes aid to Sparta, 196; leads attack on Areopagus, 193 f., 339; legislation of, 196–210, 213, 304; suggestion that he made *ephesis* automatic, 396; assassination of, 197 and n. 2, 213; laws of, against Areopagus, repealed by the Thirty, 288; mentioned, 6, 13, 20, 90, 147, 149, 154, 253 f., 396.

ephoroi, at Athens in 404, 287 and n. 1.

Ephoros, the historian, 341.

Ephors, at Sparta, 287, 380.

epicheirotonia, 164 f.

Epidauros, 352.

epimeletai, (*a*) of Kleisthenic tribes, 138, (*b*) *tou neoriou*, 238, 239.

epistatai of public works, 244.

epistates of the Prytaneis, 150, 210, 221, 376.

Epizelos, 349.

Eratosthenes, 40, 43.

Eretria, 114 n. 8, 364, 365, 366.

etai, in Homer, 58, 62.

Eteoboutadai, 62, 64, 65, 114.

Euboia, 163, 343, 365 ; Athenian colonists in, 158, 343 ; inhabitants of, granted right of intermarriage with Athenians, 343.

Eudios (Spartan ephor 404/403) 380.

Eukrates, 350, 351.

Eumenides, worship of, 315.

Eumolpidai, 10, 37 n. 4, 64.

Eupatridai, 47 f., 65 ff ; creation of, as an order, attributed to Theseus, 36 and n. 4, 48, 65 f. ; represented in all four of the 'Ionic' tribes, 50 f ; problem of their relations with the genē, 65 ff., 315 f. ; origin of, 66 f., 103 ; privileges of, in aristocratic state, 47, 311 ; exploitation of state in their own interest before Solon, 80 f. ; monopoly of political power shattered by Solon, 106, 108, 172 ; alleged attempt at reaction after Solon's reforms, 319 f. ; at Leipsydrion, 125 ; revival of leading families after tyranny, 191 f ; *exegetai* of, 315.

— as a distinct genos within the Eupatrid order, 315 f.

Euripides, 50, 123.

Euryptolemos, father-in-law of Kimon, 190, 396.

Eurysakes, 63, 316, 392.

Euthydemos (archon 555/554), 328.

euthynai, 203 ff. ; mentioned, 194 f., 224, 233.

exegetai, 10, 236, 314, 315 ; alleged chronicle of, 10 f., 16, 335 ; thought to have supplied information on the *Synoikismos*, 36.

Five Thousand, the, in propaganda of oligarchs in 411, 274, 275 f., 362, 374 ; in the Constitution for the Future, 368 ff. ; never actually enrolled by the 400, 357, 366, 367 ; government of (September 411), 278 f., 364, 366 ; its institution and character, 279, 375 ff ; Beloch's view on it, 367 ff. ; its constitution sometimes identified with *A.P.* 30, 372 f. ; council under it probably 500, 279, 372 (Ferguson's view on, 376 ff.) ; ekklesia under it, 378.

Forty, the, see *dikastai kata demous*.

Gamelia, 60 n. 2.

Games, Isthmian, 319 ; Olympian, 329.

Geleontes, 50 f., 72.

Gelon, tyrant of Syracuse, 112, 132.

genē, 61–67, 390 f. ; origin of, according to Meyer, 67, 315 f. (different view held by others, 315 f.) ; number of, in Atthis, 49, 59 ; as subdivisions of phratry, 56 n. 3 ; social prestige of members of, in phratry, 61, 64, 119 ; membership of, hereditary in male line, 47 n. 1, 63 ; members called *gennētai* or *homogalaktes*, 56, 61, 117, 390 ; existing genē left alone by Kleisthenes, 129, 131 ; meaning of genos later in a legal context 161 f. ; see also Philochoros.

gennētai, see *genē*.

georgoi, social division in aristocratic state, 47, 48, 319.

Gephyraioi, 65.

Geraistos, 163.

Glauketes (general 441/440), 349, 355.

Glaukon, colleague as general of Perikles, 349.

gnorimoi, leaders of, 177, 183.

Gortyn, code of, 58, 63 n. 1.

graphē paranomon, 127 n. 6, 210–213 ; abolished by the oligarchs, 275, 357, 364.

Gylippos, 268.

Hagnon, 269, 272 f., 272 n. 6, 351, 352.

Hagnous, 36.

Harmodios, 65, 124.

Harpokration, on ostracism, 159 f.

Hekatombaion, first month of Athenian year, 299, 348 f., 382.

Hektemoroi, 84 n. 6, 106, 111, 118, 133, 320.

Heliaia, 97 f., 221 ; functions of, not altered by Kleisthenes, 146 ; superseded by dikasteria, 216.

Hellanikos of Lesbos, history of Athens written by, 3 and n. 6, 5 ; archon-years used for dating by, 4 ; attitude of, (a) to inscriptions, 5 and n. 2, (b) to Solon, 3, 7 ; possibly responsible for invention of decennial archons, 43 ; mentioned, 65 n. 3, 316.

Hellenic League, 191.

Hellenotamiai, 224, 240 n. 10, 308 ; probably appointed by direct election, 244 and n. 6 ; reform of, in 411, 376.

Hellespont, 236, 278, 281.

Helots, 196.

Heraia, 229.

Herakleides, (a) of Klazomenai, 396, (b) author of an epitome of the *A.P.*, 34 and n. 1, 40 n. 5.

Hermai, multilation of, 168, 267.

Hermione, 397.

Hermippos, 317 f.

Hermokrates of Syracuse, 264.

Hermokreon (archon 501/500), 145 and n. 5, 149, 166 ff; date of archonship of, 337.

Herodotus, sources for the period 561–481 used by, 2; value of history of, for political conditions in Greece before 480, 31 f.; on origin of Ionians, 54; on names of Ionian tribes, 50; on colonization of Asia Minor, 51; on conspiracy of Kylon, 67 f., 69, 71, 81, 311 f.; on Solon, 2 n. 7; on duration of tyranny at Athens, 114 n. 9, 328; on events in Athens after expulsion of tyrants, 93–95, 157; on Kleisthenes, 3, 126 ff., 158, 331 ff.; on the number of the demes 134 and n. 5; on the relation of the generals to the polemarchs in 490, 170 ff; erroneous view of, that the polemarch in 490 was chosen by lot, 171, 323; on the Alkmaionidai, 180 ff.; on the hostility of the Philaïdai to the tyrants, 326, 329 f.

Hesychidai, 315 f.

Hesychos, 315.

hetairoi in Homer, 58.

hieropoioi, 222, 238.

Hipparchos, (a) brother of Hippias, 124 f., (b) son of Charmos (archon 496/495), 153 and nn. 2 and 3, 159 ff., 179 n. 3, 182, 189 and n. 5, 322, 336; significance of election as archon, 179 f., 186.

Hipparchs, 220, 261, 370.

Hippeis, 100, 102, 174 f., 225, 272; in early states, 394; at Athens under the Thirty, 289 n. 5, 384.

Hippias, tyranny of, 124 f.; marriage alliance of, with rulers of Lampsakos, 330; expulsion of, 125, 181; in exile, 178, 180; party of, in Athens after his expulsion, 125 f., 146, 161 ff., 179.

Hippokleides (archon 566/565), 104, 105 n. 1, 113 and n. 2, 115, 326 ff.

Hippokrates, (a) father of Peisistratos, 104, 180 n. 3, (b) brother of Kleisthenes, 180.

Hippomenes, 38, 41, 45, 46 and n. 2.

Hipponikos, 349, 350.

Homeric poems, evidence of, on early Attica, 2, 35, 53; on the period of transition from monarchy to aristocracy, 33, 45; on the phratry, 55; on the *hetairoi* and *etai*, 58; on the council of elders and popular assembly, 79.

Homicide cases, courts concerned with trials of, 76, 305 ff.

Homogalaktes, see *genē*.

Hopletes, 50 f.

Hoplite franchise, 273 f.

Hoplites, unimportant in pre-Solonian period, 83; growth in importance of, during sixth century, 176 f., 394 f.; preponderance of, in Kleisthenic Athens, 157, 177, 196, 339, 341; victories of, in middle of fifth century, 255; decline in efficiency of, 261; attitude of, after 413, 269, 273 f.; *see also* Five Thousand, the.

Hymettos, 140.

Hyperakrioi, party of, led by Peisistratos, 103, 110 f., 140; composition of, 111 f., 321; objectives of, 110 and n. 2, 112, 113; meaning of name, 110 and n. 9; *see also* Diakrioi.

Hyperbolos, 265; revived ostracism (winter 418/417), 396; ostracism of, 267 and n. 1, 395 f.; assassinated, 276, 395.

Hypsichides (archon 481/480), 336 f.

Idomeneus, 175 n. 1.

Inscriptions on stone, as evidence, 3; attitude of Atthidographers to, 5 n. 2, 16; few public inscriptions available for period before 462, 12 f.

Ion, mythical figure invented in Asia Minor, 52; tradition that he was polemarch, 42; early organization of Athenian citizen-body ascribed to, in Atthis, 48 and n. 2, 49, 50 and n. 1; this regarded by some as transcript of organization of Kleisthenes' time, 59 and n. 6.

— of Chios, on Kimon, 3, 196 n. 3, 348.

Ionia, ruling families in, 39; colonization of, 51 f.; theatre of war between Athens and Sparta in and after 412, 269, 278; exclusion of oligarchs from, 281.

Ionians, origin of name of, 52; political maturity of, in sixth century, 95; revolt from Persia, 178, 180.

Ionic alphabet, adopted by Athens in 403 for official use, 18, 295.

Isagoras (archon 508/507), 69, 95, 121, 125 ff., 146, 156, 168, 177 f., 331 ff.; archonship of, 125 f., 322, 332 f., 337, 393.

isegoria, 157.

Ismenias of Thebes, 291, 385.

Isodike, wife of Kimon, 190, 396.

Isokrates, 7 f.; date of *Areopagitikos* of, 7 and n. 4; influence of, on Androtion, 8 and n. 6; exaltation of Areopagus in, 8, 78 f., 273; appa-

Isokrates (*contd.*)
  rently attributed creation of Areopagus to Solon, 80 and n. 6; on censorship exercised by Areopagus, 201; on the use of sortition, 229; on combination of sortition with Prokrisis, 323; on Alkibiades' family, 316; on the 'black list', 388; on effect of rule of the Thirty, 298; praises Thrasyboulos and Anytos, 294.

isonomia, 157 and n. 6.
Isotimides, 302 f.
Ithome, 196, 197, 338 ff.

James II of England, 182 n. 3, 284.
Jurisdiction, control of, exploited by Eupatrids before Solon, 84 f.; see *also* Magistrates.
Jury and jury-pay; *see* Dikasteria *and* Dikasts.
Justin, on the rule of the Thirty, 385 f., 387 f.

Kalliades (archon 480/479), 336.
Kallias, (*a*) son of Phainippos, 114, (*b*) cousin of Aristeides and husband of Elpinike, 184 n. 2, 191, 194 and n. 4, (*c*) probably nephew of the preceding, 194 n. 4, (*d*) proposer of financial decrees, 240, (*e*) archon 412/411, 357, (*f*) brother-in-law of Alkibiades, 6.
Kallibios, Spartan harmost, 289 and n. 1, 384 ff.
Kallikrates, 238.
Kallimachos (polemarch 490), 170, 172.
Kannonos, decree of, 154 f., 304 f.
Karkinos, 349, 351, 355.
kasignetoi in Homer, 58 and n. 5, 62.
katalogeis (in 411), 357, 358, 361 ff., 364–368, 375.
Kekropis (Tribe VII), 350.
Kerykes, 36 n. 4, 64, 65, 114, 186 n. 2, 191, 316.
Kimon 'Koalemos', 326, 327, 329.
— son of Miltiades II, 3, 6, 184, 190 ff, 337 ff., 348; marriage of, to Isodike, 190, 396; rise to political influence, 190 and n. 1, 191; frequent tenure of *strategia* by, 191 and n. 4; pro-Spartan, 196 f., 339; Panhellenic policy of, 190, 196; opposed to political change in Athens, 193; prosecuted on return from Thasos, 194, 196, 340; attempted to reverse legislation of Ephialtes, 197, 338 ff.; date of ostracism of, 193, 197, 338; circumstances of his return from ostracism, 255 f.; may have co-operated with Perikles after his

return, 346 f.; his generosity, 191, 193 n. 4, 342; see *also* Ion of Chios.
Kings of Attica, earliest recorded (mythical), 32.
Kingship in Attica, decline of, 39–46.
Kleidemos, 7–8, 147, 160; date of his *Atthis*, 7 and n. 2; its scope, 9; *exegetikon* of, 10; on the naukraries, 22 and n. 1, 68, 70, 73, 130 f., 142 and n. 4.
Kleisthenes of Athens, 125–58 and 331–6; uncle of Perikles' mother, 252; possibly archon 525/524, 128 n. 3, 146 f., 393 f.; political struggle against Isagoras, 69, 125 ff., 156, 168, 177, 331 f.; not 'a man with a mission', 156 and n. 2; method in which his legislation was enacted, 15, 126 f., 130, 393 f.; precise dating of his reforms, 94, 125, 331–6; views of ancient authorities on his reforms, 3, 6, 7, 129 ff., and c. VI *passim*; his reforms, 129–58; names given to his new tribes, 36, 131; creation of new citizens by, 132 ff.; connected citizenship with membership of a deme, 64, 134 ff.; created *apodektai*, 146, 148; enacted or re-enacted a law on the phratries, 61, 140 n. 3, 390 f.; did not increase number of phratries, 59, 60 n. 6, 144; did not abolish the naukraries, 68, 73 (opposite view discussed 20 f., 129 ff.); did not institute ostracism, 159 ff., 305; wrongly connected with institution of Logistai-procedure, 204; possibly instituted the *dokimasia* for councillors and archons, 207 f.; constitutional laws of, 14 f.; doubtful whether they were still preserved in 411, 15 f., 129 ff., 332, 336; lack of sufficient provision for continuity in Kleisthenic constitution, 187 f.; constitution far less democratic than that of Periklean Athens, 147, 156 ff., 217; possible revision of pre-existing code by, 22, 305; fate of, after his legislation, 168 and nn. 5 and 6, 179, 182; possibly responsible for Athenian submission to Persia, 178, 180.
— tyrant of Sikyon, 138, 182, 331.
Kleitophon, (*a*) general 441/440, 349, (*b*) oligarch in 411, 15 and n. 2, 130 and n. 8, 273 n. 2, 356.
Kleokritos, 383.
Kleomedes, 350.
Kleomenes of Sparta, 94 f., 121, 124 ff, 132, 181, 331 ff.
Kleon, 243, 245 n. 4, 260 and n. 2, 263; member of the Council, 262

Kleon (contd.)
n. 2; held strategia, 262; unable to discern the best policy for Athens, 264 f.

Kleophon, 6, 263, 281 ff., 342; prosecutes Kritias, 281 and n. 3; introduces two-obol payment, 282; futile obstinacy of, after Aigospotamoi, 283 f., 286; condemnation of, 263, 288 n. 4.

Kleopompos, 352.

klerosis, see Sortition.

Kodridai, 39, 41.

kolakretai, administered state treasury, 91; possibly pre-Solonian, 78 n. 1; in old law quoted by Androtion, 68; abolished in 411, 378.

Kolias, 68.

Kolieis, 68 n. 11.

Kolonos, 274 ff., 357 ff.

Komeas (archon 561/560?), 317.

Konon, (a) archon 462/461, 197 f., (b) general, son of Timotheos, 6.

Koureion, 60 and n. 2.

Kourotrophos, 392.

Krateros, 13, 14, 30 n. 4, 378.

Kratinos, 351, 390.

Kreon (archon 682/681), 4, 40 and n. 3, 44.

Kritias, 281, 286 n. 5, 289 ff., 384 ff.; suggested as author of the 'oligarchic source' used in the A.P., 6; friendship of, with Theramenes, 281, 286; secures death of Theramenes, 290, 384; killed in battle, 291, 384.

Kriton, 281.

Kroisos, king of Lydia, 328.

Kylon, conspiracy of, 2, 42, 67, 86, 311 (date of, 69 and n. 1); levy of Athenians to suppress it, 394, cf. 71 and n. 3.

Kylonians, slaughter of, and its later repercussions, 2, 77, 86 f., 120, 128, 334 f.

Kypselos, (a) tyrant of Corinth, 105 n. 1, (b) father of Miltiades I, 105 n. 1, 326, 327.

kyrbeis, 24 f., 390.

Kyrene, 144.

Kyzikos, 51, 54; battle of, 280, 282.

Laches, 272.

Lakedaimonios, son of Kimon, 396.

Lakonia, 268, 349.

Lamachos, 220.

Lampon, 236.

Lampsakos, 3 n. 2, 328 ff.

Law, against those who tried to set up a tyranny, 91, 313; against idleness, 116, 305, 307 f., 320; on powers of boulē, 153 f.; law of amnesty,

(a) attributed to Solon, 311–13, 318 f., (b) passed in 481/480, 163 f., 189 and n. 4, 313, (c) passed in 405, 163, 312 f.

Law-courts, popular, see Dikasteria.

Laws, distinguished from decrees, 127 n. 2, 300.

Leagues, see Delian, Hellenic, Peloponnesian.

Leipsydrion, 124 f.

Leobotas, 190.

Leogoras, (a) ancestor of Andokides, 114 and n. 5, (b) father of Andokides, 212.

Leokrates, 254.

Leon, (a) mover of decree on Phaselis, 397, (b) general in 412/411, 276.

Leontis (Tribe IV), 349.

Leukotainioi, 72.

lexiarchikon grammateion, 136.

Libys, Spartan admiral 404/403, 292.

Licinius and Sextius, laws of, 106.

List of suspects, drawn up by the Thirty, 388.

Logistai, 203 f., 240.

Lydia, 86, 178, 326, 328.

Lykomedes, 198, 350.

Lykomidai, 121 f., 181, 183, 190, 335.

Lykophron of Pherai, 379.

Lykourgos, (a) leader of the Pedieis, 114, (b) orator and statesman, 10, 65.

Lysandros, (a) father-in-law of Themistokles, 328, (b) Spartan statesman, 266, 283, 286–93 passim, 379–83, 388.

Lysias, on events of 404, 380 f.; supported Athenian exiles in 403, 291 f; speech against Philon, 27; speech against Phormisios, 297; attack on Nikomachos, 24; on archaisms in extant laws, 18, 21, 97.

Lysikrates (archon 453/452), 218 n. 7.

Macedonia, 114 n. 8, 196, 235 n. 5.

Magistrates, development of, in the aristocratic state, 74; original conditions of eligibility and method of appointment, 78 f.; original jurisdiction, 74 f.; controls over, in the aristocratic state, 78, 83, 91 f.; elected by the ekklesia before and after Solon, 79, 97, 325 f.; conditions of eligibility for, laid down in Solon's laws, 101 f.; powers of, defined by Solon, 98, 108 f.; limits imposed by Solon on their jurisdiction, 97 f., 221; revival of their powers after the expulsion of the tyrants, 153, 273; jurisdiction of, not altered by laws of Kleisthenes,

Magistrates (*contd.*)
146, 153, 215, 217; conditions of eligibility under Kleisthenes and later, 142 f., 174, 225 and n. 2; generals substituted for archons as chief military and civil executive, 187 ff.; decline after 487 in powers and prestige of archonship, 175, 231; limitations on judicial powers of magistrates in Periklean Age, 215 f., 217 f., 221 ff., 397; competence of, in administration, restricted under radical democracy, 223; *dokimasia* of, 91, 205 ff.; provisions for enforcing accountability of, 203 ff.; prosecution of, for exceeding their powers or failing to perform their duties, 96 f., 200, 205, 212; liability to deposition and prosecution, 224; age qualification for, 224; veto on re-election of most magistrates, 214 f., 224, 228; rule against holding two offices simultaneously (did not apply to membership of special boards), 244; *see also* Archons, *prokrisis*, Rotation.

Mantitheos, 344.
Marathon, 35, 114, 134 f.; tetrapolis of, 35 f.; campaign of, 170 f., 181; defeat of Persians at, 161, 182 (date, 185 n. 6, 337).
Mardonios, 155.
Markellinos, life of Thucydides by, 104, 327, 329.
Maroneia, 189.
Marriages at Athens, conditions governing, 343 ff.
Mechanion, 302.
Medeon, 34.
Medontidai, royal family at Athens, 38 f., 41, 43, 76, 104; genealogy of, 45 f.
Megakles, (*a*) archon in the year of Kylon's conspiracy, 69, 77, 86 and n. 5, (*b*) opponent of Peisistratos, 114, 182, (*c*) grandfather of Isodike, 396, (*d*) nephew of Kleisthenes, 180, 182, 186, 396.
Megalopolis, 34 and n. 6.
Megara, 86, 290, 384, 393; war of Athens with, 113 and n. 5, 394; Megarian decree, 353.
Meion, 60 and n. 2.
Melians, 395.
Melite, 349, 350, 351, 392.
Melobios, 356.
Melon, friend of Pelopidas, 291.
Mesogeios, one of the Kleisthenic regions of Attica, 134, 140 f.
Messenia, 197, 339.
Metionidai, 39 n. 4.
metoikoi, 133, 289, 384 ff.

Metroön, archives kept in, after 403, 14, 303.
Miletos, 51 f., 54, 178.
Miltiades, (*a*) archon in 664/663, 104, (*b*) Miltiades I, prince of Chersonese, 105 n. 1, 115, 326 ff., (*c*) Miltiades II, general at Marathon, 154 f., 171 f., 177, 180 f., 183 ff., 185 n. 6, 194, 253, 327 ff. (probably identical with the archon of 524/523, 330).
Mitylene, 115, 394.
Monarchy, *see* Kingship, Tyrants.
Mounychia, 291, 384, 386.
Mounychion (Athenian month), 379, 382.
Myron, prosecutor of those responsible for the murder of the Kylonians, 120, 121, 334.
Myronides, 254 and n. 5.
Myrrhinous, 57.

Naukrariai, 68–74, 77, 115, 129–31; in the *Atthis*, 47, 68; problem of their relation to the four 'Ionic' tribes, 73 f.; possibly local divisions, 68; sometimes compared with demes or with *symmoriai*, 68, 70, 73; may have been remodelled by Peisistratos, 70, 115; date of abolition of, 21 f., 69 f., 129.
Naukraroi, 67–74, 129; meaning of the word, 70; definition of, in lexicographers, 68; as heads of the naukrariai in *A.P.*, 68, 70; functions of, 71; supposed by Meyer to have formed the council in pre-Solonian Athens, 81 f., 311; existed at the time of Kylon's conspiracy, 20, 67, 311; problem of reference in Herodotus to their Prytaneis, 67, 69, 70 f.
Nautodikai, 218 and nn. 3 and 4.
Neapolis, 235 n. 5.
Nikias, (*a*) father of Hagnon, 351, (*b*) opponent of Kleon, 263, 265 ff., 272, 352, 362, 396; tribe of, 349; relations with the council, 245; coalition with Alkibiades, 396.
Nikodemos (archon 483/482), 336.
Nikomachos, 302.
Nikomenes, 296.
Nikostratos, 272.
Nisaia, 113.
Nomophylakes, 209 and n. 4.
nomos argias, *see* Law *and* Peisistratos.
Nomothetai, institution of, attributed to Perikles by Grote, 211 n. 3; board of, possibly appointed to draft laws on occasion of Kleisthenes' legislation, 394; appointed in September 411, 300, 375; concerned later with procedures for

Nomothetai (*contd.*)
revision of laws, 299 ff., drawn from dikasts in the fourth century, 18, 299.

Officials, multiplication of, in radical democracy, 223 f.; *see also* Boards, Magistrates.
oikos, meaning of, 63 and n. 4.
Oinopes, 51 f., 54.
Oligarchs in 411, proceedings of, 210 and n. 2, 356 ff.; programme of, 271; official propaganda of, 274 ff.; scheme to set up oligarchies in subject-states of Athenian Empire, 271 f., 278; envoys sent by, to fleet at Samos, 278, 374; uncertain whether cataloguers were ever appointed by, 357; want of harmony between moderate and extreme oligarchs, 272 ff., 278 f., 359, 373, 375.
Onomakles, 375.
Ordnungsstrafen, 221 ff.
Oreos, 343.
Orgeones, 56, 61, 117, 390.
Oropos, 135.
Ostracism, law on, 16, 130, 159–66, 185 f., 339; procedure under it, 151, 164 ff., 395; dating of law by Schachermeyr, 337.
Ostracisms, quorum for, 165 f.; of Kimon, 193, 338; of Thucydides, son of Melesias, 256 and n. 5; of Hyperbolos, 267, 395 f.
ostraka, 139.
'Oxyrhynchus historian', 369.

Paiania, 120, 351.
Palladion, homicide court at, 306.
Pallene, 36.
Panathenaia, 113, 326 f., 330 f.
Pandionis (Tribe III), 134, 351.
Pandrosos, 392.
Pangaios, 114.
paragraphē, 295.
Paralia, one of the Kleisthenic regions of Attica, 134, 140 f.
Paralioi (or Paraloi), 109, 111, 114, 140, 326.
Paralos, one of the state triremes, 277.
paranomon, see *graphē*.
Paros, 154, 180, 182, 185 n. 6.
Parthenon, 256.
patrios politeia, oligarchic version of, 5, 30, 93, 273, 374; democratic version of, 6, 93; restoration of, falsely alleged to have been included in 404 in the Spartan peace-terms, 285 and nn. 2 and 3.
Patrokleides, amnesty in 405 proposed by, 163, 312 f.
Pausanias, (*a*) king of Sparta, 293, (*b*)

author of a description of Greece, 11, 40 f.
Pay, provided by the state under the radical democracy for (*a*) generals and hipparchs, 220, (*b*) soldiers and sailors, 218 f., (*c*) the nine archons, 220, (*d*) members of the council, 218, 219, (*e*) attendance at the ekklesia, 396; abolition of pay in 411 for civilian services, 275, 279, 357.
Pedieis (or Pediakoi), 109, 111, 114, 140, 326.
Peisandros, 270 f., 274 ff., 359, 361 ff.; proposals made at Kolonos by, 361.
Peisistratidai, 63, 104, 125, 146, 180; relations of, with the Philaïdai, 329 f.
Peisistratos, home and antecedents of, 103, 104 and n. 2; claim of, to be descended from Neleidai of Pylos, 39, 104 n. 2; his rise to power, 110–14 *passim*; becomes polemarch, 113 and n. 9; his supporters before the tyranny, *see* Citizenship, Hyperakrioi; his relations with the Philaïdai, 326 ff.; attitude of hoplite-class to, 394; vote of bodyguard to, 96; his rule as tyrant, 114–23, 395 (chronology 328 f.); his creation of new citizens, 112, 118 f., 133; institution of deme-judges by, 115, 152; may have created the *euthynoi*, 205; probably connected with the reorganization of the Panathenaia, 330 f.; possibly remodelled the naukraries, 70, 115; may have introduced adaptations into the Solonian code, 19, 305; law providing pensions for men disabled in war, 19, 305; law against idleness attributed to, 116, 305, 307 f., 320; Herodotus on, 19, 326 ff.
pelatai, 84 and n. 6.
Pelopidas, Theban statesman, 291.
Peloponnesian League, 190, 261, 293.
Pentakosiomedimnoi, 100 ff., 142, 156, 174 and n. 3, 224 ff., 323, 325.
Pentelikon, Mt., 181.
Perdikkas II, king of Macedonia, 355.
Perikles, son of Xanthippos and Agariste, 180, 190; his antecedents and character, 252 f.; not prominent till 463, 190; associated in a subordinate position with Ephialtes, 193, 197 f., 342; prosecutes Kimon, 194, 196; his career in the radical party, 253 ff; his policy, 254 ff., 260; introduces pay for jurors, 219, 254, 342 f.; proposes and carries a law on the conditions of citizenship, 20, 255, 296, 343–7, 390; possibly re-

Perikles (contd.)
sponsible for introduction of the graphē paranomon, 212; may have modified the telē, 143; his long tenure of the generalship, 191, 352 ff.; difficulty raised by his continuous re-election, 352 ff.; his powers as general, 246 ff.; his relations with the council, 245; exceptional position in 431 and 429, 246, 353 f.; his 'principate', 258, 265; his strategy in the Archidamian War, 260 ff.; deposed in 430 and tried, 234, 260 n. 2; his oratorical gifts, 249 and n. 5, 253, 259; mentioned, 3, 270, 284.

Perinthos, 51.

Persia, becomes a factor in Athenian politics, 178 ff.; war against, abandoned by Athens, 256; Athens again embroiled with, by demagogues, 269; co-operates with Sparta in Ionian War, 269 ff.; hope of peace with, held out to Athenians by Alkibiades, 270 f., 356.

Phainippos, 65, 114.

Pharnabazos, 269, 290.

Phaselis, 397.

Pherekydes, 104, 327 f.

Philaïdai, Athenian family, origins and genealogy of, 104; lived at Brauron, 103; deme named after them, 105, 110 n. 11, 120; relations with Peisistratos, 326 ff.; influence of their historical traditions in our sources, 171 and n. 6, 326 ff; mentioned, 185, 190 f.

Philaios, 104 f.

Philip V, king of Macedonia, 266.

Philochoros, 4, 30 f., 390; law on phratries quoted by, 61, 117, 140 n. 3 (discussed 390 f.); on ostracism, 149; on Nomophylakes, 209; on the introduction of new seating arrangements in the boulē, 282; on the diapsephismos of 445/444, 345.

Philokypros, 320.

Phlya, 120 ff., 334 f., 350.

Phormion, 351, 352.

Phormisios, decree of, 296 f.; not a Theramenist, 297 n. 2.

Phratries, 55–60; origins of, 57–59; alleged subdivision of, into genē, 47 f.; included plebeians as well as nobles in the aristocratic state, 55, 390 f.; probably excluded the landless poor till Solon, 84, 391; may have protected their members against illegal violence in pre-Solonian period, 84; number of phratries in Athens at various dates, 59 f., 144; analogous to Cretan

hetaireiai, 58; uncertain whether landless poor were admitted to them by Solon or by the tyrants, 101, 117, 122; number of, not altered by Kleisthenes, 129, 131; admission of new citizens to, by Kleisthenes, 140 and n. 3, 144; membership of, left a condition of full citizenship by Kleisthenes, 140 n. 3, 143; membership of, still important in fourth century, 55 f.; some citizens not members of any phratry under the radical democracy, 59 f., 145 n. 2; women and children admitted to membership, 56, 60 n. 2, 144; internal organization of, 57; deities worshipped by, 56 f; see also Philochoros, Demotionidai.

Phreatto, homicide court at, 306.

Phrynichos, (a) dramatist, 178, 181; (b) politician, 271 f., 362, 365; murder of, 278; subsequent condemnation, 279; mentioned by Aristophanes, 281.

Phye, 120.

phylai, see Tribes.

phylarchs, 129, 146 and n. 2, 370.

Phyle, 291, 295, 384 ff.

phyletai, in the revolution of 411, 361, 366, 373.

Phylobasileis, associated with the Basileus in the Prytaneion court, 76, 311 ff.; probably declined in importance with the hereditary kingship, 76.

Piraeus, 137, 291, 306; growth of, 218, 346; meetings of ekklesia sometimes held at, 239; large alien population in, 346; garrisoned in 404 by Spartans for a time, 287 and n. 3, 288, 382; fortifications dismantled, 380 ff.; during rule of the Thirty governed by a special board of Ten, 288, 294; filled with fugitives from Attica, 291 n. 5, 384; held as base in 403 by the democrats, 383 ff.; trade of, rapidly revives after 403, 297 f.

Plangon, 344.

Plato, on kings at Athens, 39, 40; on archons from Solon, 4 n. 4, 317 f.; mentioned, 48, 137 and n. 3, 220, 257, 291, 298.

Plutarch, Lives of, as source, 31, cf. 48 and 66 n. 4 (Theseus); on the origins of the Areopagus, 79 f., 308 ff.; on the alleged Solonian Council of Four Hundred, 92; on the Kylonian affair, 86 n. 5, 115, 120; ascribes an unhistorical decree to Aristeides, 174 f.; on the events of 462/461, 338 ff.; on ostracism, 165 f.; on the ostracism of Hyperbolos, 267.

Pnyx, 275.
Polemarch, 39 f., 75, 170–3; office of, subsequent in origin to that of the chief archon, 42, 44; powers of, in aristocratic state, 75; jurisdiction of, 397; held supreme command over the army both before and after the tyranny, 113 and n. 9, 153, 169 ff.; declined in power after reforms of 487/486, 175.
Polemon, 23 n. 2, 25, 65, 315 f.
Polis, content of idea of, 176 f.
Pollux, on the naukraries, 68, 71, 73; on the Ephetai, 309.
Polystratos, speech of, on his defence ([Lysias] xx), 4 n. 1, 364 ff., 373; activities in 411 of, 361, 364 ff.
Pontos, 236.
Poseidon Erechtheus, 64 and n. 7, 65.
Praktores, 221.
Priesthoods of Athenian State, 225; some of, hereditary in certain families, 64, 129, 131, 235.
Probouloi, set up in autumn 413 at Athens, 269, 273; included in the commission of thirty Syngrapheis, 274, 356.
Proedroi, (a) the five men who formed the nucleus of the 400, 275, 361, (b) under the 5,000, 376, (c) presided over the ekklesia during part of the fourth century, 221.
Prokrisis, 207, 225 f., 230, 322, 325.
Prokritoi, (a) for the council, 150, (b) for the archonship, 173 f., (c) in the A.P., 367, 371, 374.
Proletariat, see Thetes.
Propaganda, political, effect on Athenian history of, 5 ff., 93.
Prosecution, right of any citizen to initiate (in certain types of cases), 118, 200 f., 202 f.
prosodos, to council and ekklesia, 242 f., 245 f.
Protagoras, 253.
Proteas, 350.
prytaneia, 150, 155, 237 and n. 5; of generals, 171, 353 f.
Prytaneion, 15, 23, 73; homicide court at, 76, 306, 309, 311 f.
Prytaneis, 150, 237, 239 f., 242, 246, 269, 369; meaning of the term in the seventh century, 81–82; of the Council of Five Hundred, perhaps received maintenance allowance till the introduction of pay for all members of the council, 219; of the 400, 360.
Psephismata, distinguished from Nomoi, 211, 300; legislation by, in fifth century, 304; possible view that the laws of Kleisthenes (and Ephialtes, cf. 196 and n. 6) were carried as Psephismata, 15, 130 (but see 394).
Pythodoros, (a) general in 414, 349, (b) oligarch in 411, 356, (c) archon 404/403, 288, 295 n. 4, 379.

Quadruple Alliance, 396.
Quinqueremes, 390.
Quorum required, for a plenary meeting of the ekklesia, 153, 216; for a valid ostracism, 165 f.

Radical democracy at Athens, 250 f.; motto of, according to Aristotle, 201 and n. 7; decisive stage in establishment of, 213; effect of, on power and prestige of magistrates, 221 ff.; regulations conducive to preservation of, 214; payment of officials an essential feature in, 220; incapable of governing an empire, 258 ff.; gift of eloquent speech indispensable to statesman in, 259; restoration of, (June 410), 280 and n. 1, 373, (in 403), 294 ff.; success of, in the fourth century, 298.
Regions, in the Kleisthenic reorganization of Attica, 129, 134.
Rome, Senate at, 92, 227 n. 8; *comitia tributa* at, 135; plebeians at, 106, 107; mentioned, 230.
Rotation, principle of, in the appointment of officials chosen by lot, 227 f., 230; in the council, 237 f.; in the bogus Constitution of Drakon, 227 f., 374.

Salaminioi, (a) inhabitants of Salamis, 135; executed by the Thirty, 291 n. 4, 385, (b) members of a genos, 316, 391 ff.
Salamis, 104; Athenian claims to, 392; acquisition of, by Athens, 113, 392 f.; Athenian settlers in, 158, 392; battle of, 147, 379.
Samos, 51, 52, 61, 66; revolt of, 257, 353; Athenian base in Ionian War, 276; oligarchic conspiracy in, 271, 359 (its failure, 276 f., 358, 373, 375); siege of, by Lysandros, 287 f., 379 ff.
Sardis, 178, 332; date of its capture by Cyrus, 328.
Satyros, 288 and n. 4.
Sections, the four, mentioned in A.P. 30, 368 ff.
Seisachtheia of Solon, 6–8, 106 f., 317, 320.
Sicily, 379, 380; tyrants in, 112; first

Sicily (*contd.*)
Athenian expedition to, 234 n. 10, 263 f.; expedition of 415 to, 239, 263 f., 267 f., 396.
Sigeion, 115, 329 f., 394.
Sikyon, tribal organization in, 52.
Skamandrios, 304 f.
Skambonidai, 204, 349.
Skirophorion, last month of Athenian year, 359.
Skyllaion, 163.
Skyros, cleruchy at, 193.
Sokrates, 167, 231 f., 344.
Soloi, 320.
Solon, date of archonship of, 317, 321; as *nomothetes*, 103, 317 ff., 320, 394; elected by the people, 79; composition of supporters of, 88 f., 102 ff., 107; poems of, 2, 118; evidence of poems cited on enslavement for debt, 84, on the agrarian troubles preceding his reforms, 87, on power allotted to the demos, 96 f., on the ingratitude of the demos, 106 n. 6; suggestion that poems contained a reference to two councils, 93 and n. 3; exhortations in poems to upper classes, 108; poem on Salamis, 113 and n. 5; called Athenians Salaminaphetai, 393; account given of him in (a) Herodotus and Hellanikos, 2 f., 11, (b) the 'democratic' version of his reforms, 6, 89, (c) fourth-century writers, 7 f., 11, 89.
— legislation of, 89 ff., 117 f., 316 ff.; date of legislation, 108 n. 1, 316–21; varying accounts of his Seisachtheia, 6 ff.; cancellation of debts, 88, 317; attribution of constitutional laws to Solon, 14, 26, 99, (no longer extant in fourth century, 16, 100); history of Solonian code, 19 f., 303 ff.; arrangement of laws in it, 303; attribution to Solon of later laws, 18 f., 322 f.; laws quoted from *axones* by Plutarch, 23, 313; incorporation in code of Drakon's laws on homicide, 308; Solon and the Areopagus, 82, 89 ff., 99 and n. 5; alleged Solonian Council of Four Hundred, 16, 92 ff., 325 (see Council of Four Hundred); law offering citizenship to alien craftsmen, 111 f., 346; law on phratries possibly Solonian, 61, 390 f.; law mentioning Orgeones ascribed to Solon, 61; amnesty-law attributed by Plutarch to Solon, 23, 26, 33, 80, 82 f., 308 f., 311 ff., 318 f.; law on naukraries attributed (by Andration?) to Solon, 21, 69; law on treasurers of Athena, 21, 323, 325;

alleged law directed against neutrality in political strife, 26 f.; alleged introduction of sortition in political appointments, 228, 322 ff.; *graphē paranomon* regarded by some as Solonian, 210 f.; inadequacy of Solon's economic reforms, 106 and n. 1, 107, 320 f.; code guaranteed against alteration for ten years, 97 and n. 3, 112 f., 127 and n. 6, 211, 320; alleged lapse of many of Solon's laws under the tyranny, 116, 130, 305, 322; Solon's laws modified by the Thirty, 288; *see also* Code, Dikasteria, *eisangelia, kyrbeis,* Prosecution.
Sophists, 259, 272.
Sophokles, 269.
Sortition, 228 ff.; purpose of, 230 f., 237; employed for most appointments in radical democracy, 224; used sometimes in oligarchies, 229 f.; regarded by some as a concession to religious scruples, 228, 324; occasionally resulted in the choice of leading politicians, 231 and n. 3; used to decide allocation of tasks between generals, 247; as selection by lot from *prokritoi*, 230; this type of sortition alleged to have been introduced by Solon for the archonship, 173, 228, 322 ff; probably first introduced (for the Council of Five Hundred) by Kleisthenes, 150, 152, 215, 325; extended in 487/486 to the archonship, 173 ff.; replaced at some later date by pure sortition, 227 and n. 3.
Sosikrates, 316.
Sounion, 35, 391 ff.
Sparta, 110, 124, 196 f., 230, 250, 257, 259, 268–98 *passim*, 338 ff., 379 ff.; hegemony of, in Peloponnese, 190; earthquake at, 340; decree of, forbidding Greek states to harbour Athenian exiles, 290, 388; analogies from, 43 (kingship), 54 (tribes), 82 f. and 310 (gerousia), 96 (rhetra), 227 n. 8 and 245 (nauarchia), 287 (Ephoroi); see Ephors.
Speusippos, 212.
Sphakteria, 261, 263.
State pay for military and civilian services, see Pay.
Steiria, 351.
stelai, mentioned by Lysias, 24 and n. 6.
Stesagoras, brother of Miltiades II, 328, 330.
Stesimbrotos, 3, 396.
Stiris, 35.
Stoa Basileios, 25, 76, 302 f., 308.

Strategoi, the, 244–51, 347–56; possibly existed, four in number, in the aristocratic state, 77 and n. 9, 113 n. 9, 169, 172; alleged increase in competence under the tyranny, 116 f.; creation of board of ten, date of, 131, 145 f.; representation of tribes on the board, 348 ff.; possibly numbered eleven for a brief period, 354 ff.; reorganization of, in 501/500, 166, 169 f.; as colonels of tribal regiments, 169; increased in prestige after 487/486, 175 f., 191 f., 245; age qualification, 224; property qualification according to Deinarchos, 191 n. 7, 224 and n. 10, 226; tended to be drawn from old and wealthy families, 249 and n. 3, 252; date of election, 165, 244 f., 347; chosen by direct election, 227; elected in Periklean Athens by whole people, 169 f., 244; *dokimasia*, 206; date of entry on office, 245, 347 f.; re-eligible year after year, 187, 244; perhaps entitled to receive pay, 220; limits on their judical authority, 222; audits, 244 and n. 9; liable to deposition, 249 f.; *prytaneia* of, 171, 354; *prytanis* of, 171, 247, 353; conferment of plenary powers on one or more of, 248, 353 f., 374; single general in supreme command of a particular expedition, 247 f., 353; conferment of supreme command on one general in a crisis, 187, 191 f., 353; members *ex officio* of the Council of Five Hundred, 151, 245 f.; relations of, with the council, 239; exercised control over the meetings and agenda of the ekklesia, 246 f.; importance of the office to leading statesmen in the Periklean Age, 249; later divorce of the office from the leadership of the people, 243, 263 f.
Strombichides, conspiracy of, 287 f., 382.
Sulla, 318.
sykophantai, 203; execution of by the Thirty, 288 f., 384.
symmoriai, naukraries compared with, by Kleidemos, 142 n. 4.
Syngrapheis, 236, 242, 300; in 411, 274, 300, 356 ff., 362 ff. (proposals made by, 361 f.); in 410, 282 and n. 5, 300.
Synoikia, 36.
synoikismos of Attica, 34–37; ascribed to an early date by Meyer, 53; not effectively realized till the tyranny, 123.
Syracuse, 62, 112, 116, 132 f., 263,

268; ekklesia at, presided over by generals in 415, 151, 175; establishment of radical democracy in, 268.

Tamiai, *see* Treasurers.
Tanagra, battle of, 338, 346.
Taxiarchs, 176 and n. 2, 348.
teichopoios, 222.
Teisamenos, 302; decree of, 18, 19, 300 ff., 307.
Teisandros, (*a*) father of Hippokleides, 104, (*b*) father of Isagoras, 125.
telē (property-classes), created by Solon, 99 ff., 100 n. 6; based on landed property, 100–2, 156; used for military purposes, 101; retained as basis of political privileges by Kleisthenes, 142 f., 215; doubtful whether and when income in money was allowed to count for membership, 143 and n. 4, 225 f.; verification of property-classes of candidates for office, 207; obsolescence of, 225.
Telesinos (archon 487/486), 173 ff., 336.
Ten, the, the oligarchic board instituted on the overthrow of the Thirty, 292 and n. 1; appeal of, to Sparta for help against democrats, 292; end of their rule, 293.
Thargelion (month of), 357, 359, 365, 373.
Thasos, 193 f., 339 f.
Theagenes, tyrant of Megara, 86, 113.
Thebes, 114 n. 8, 290, 384.
Themistokles, genos of, 121 f., 183; deme of, 139; antecedents and policy, 183 f., 246; alleged to have been a leader of the popular party, 177; election of, to the archonship, 181, 183, 185, 322; archonship of, 153 and n. 3, 189 and n. 1; co-operates with Aristeides, 185 ff., 190; navy bill of, 183, 189, 336, 339; reorganizes the Athenian navy, 142; anecdote of, in Kleidemos, 147; general in 480 (*autokrator* in Plutarch), 248; possibly general in 479 also, 185; decline of his influence, 190; may have changed his policy after the repulse of the Persian invasion, 190; ostracized, 190 and n. 5; impeached in absence on a charge of treason, 154 (date, 190 n. 5); mentioned, 3, 250, 251, 257, 285, 305.
Theophrastos, collection of laws made by, 25, 30.
Theopompos, 30 and n. 2, 147 f., 198 f., 338 ff.; on introduction of jury-pay, 215, 342; on ostracism of Hyperbolos, 395.

Theozotides, 296.

Theramenes, antecedents of, 272 and nn. 5 and 6, 273, 351; part played by, in oligarchic revolution of 411, 272 f., 286 n. 3, 362; leads movement against extreme oligarchs 278; constitution set up in 411 by; see Five Thousand, the; made unpopular by his prosecution of extreme oligarchs, 279; associated with Kritias in 411 and in 404, 281, 286; alleged literary activity of, 6 n. 1; defended for his behaviour during the siege of Athens, 284 n. 3; terms brought back from Sparta by, 378, 382; alleged opposition to Lysandros, 383; his position and policy after the peace, 286, 287 and n. 7, 378, 380 ff.; his opposition to Kritias and its failure, 289 f; 384, 386 ff; his trial, 290, 389. Holm's obituary on him, 290; later tradition which distorted facts in his favour, 285, 297 n. 2, 387 f.

Theseus, 34, 38, 48 f., 65, 123; alleged abdication of, 37; regarded as founder of Athenian democracy, 48 f.; see also Eupatridai.

Thesmothetai, 76 f.; uncertainty on date of institution of, 76; at least pre-Solonian, 77; doubtful whether they had codified the law before Solon did so, 84; early history of, 77; later functions of, included supervision of the code of law, 20, 299; view that until 462 they could indict unconstitutional measures before the Areopagus, 127 n. 6, 211; choice of, by sortition, 322; grammateus of, 173 f., 206, 227.

Thesmotheteion, 77.

Thessaly, 110, 114 n. 8, 281, 379, 380.

Thetes, in the aristocratic state, 84 and n. 6; as one of the Solonian telē, 100; in post-Solonian period, 98, 101, 117 ff.; as adherents of Peisistratos, 111; probably admitted to full citizenship by the tyrants, 122, 142 f.; in period after Kleisthenes' reforms, 157 f.; importance of, increased by conversion of Athens into a great sea-power, 193, 257 f.; enabled by introduction of state-pay to take an active part in politics, 157, 220 f.; sustained heavy losses (a) in the plague, 261, (b) in Sicily, 268, (c) at Aigospotamoi and after, 285; prestige of, affected by Syracusan disaster, 268; absence from Athens in 412–410 of those of military age, 274, 275; absent in 411 from meeting at

Kolonos, 275, 358; lost political importance in 404 on the surrender of the fleet, 285.

Thiasoi, subdivisions within the phratries, 47, 56, 61 ff.; origin of, 67; number of, probably increased by Kleisthenes, 144.

Thirty, the, appointment of, 287 f., 379–83; list of, in Xenophon, 288 n. 1; powers conferred on, 287 n. 6, 383; rule of, 288–91, 384–9; appointed council and other officials, 288, 379; enacted new laws, 384, 389; drew up list of the 3,000, 289, 384, 388; disarmed all outside the list, 289, 384, 388; excluded unprivileged citizens from the Attic countryside, 290, 386; drew up a 'black list', 388; deposed, 292, 385.

Thorikos, 349, 355.

Thrasyboulos, 276, 277, 291 ff., 384 ff.; friendly with Alkibiades, 277; occupies Phyle, 291, 384 ff.; is offered bribes by the Thirty, 385 ff.; decree to confer the citizenship on all who in 403 had fought for the democracy, 290.

Thrasydaios, leader of democrats in Elis, 291.

Thrasyllos, 276 f.

Three Thousand, the, see Thirty, the.

Thucydides the son of Melesias, 253 f., 256 and nn. 3 and 5, 282.

— the historian, genealogy of, 327 f.; chronology of, in Book VIII, 363; digressions of, into earlier history of Athens, 9; used argument from present to past, 12, 33; criticized Hellanikos, 3 and n. 6, 4; admired Perikles, 257; praised highly the constitution set up on the downfall of the Four Hundred, 279 f.; knew the documents quoted in A.P. 30–31, 374; evidence of, cited on the following topics: the synoikismos, 34 and 36 f.; Kylon's conspiracy, 69 and n. 2, 71; rise of tyrannies in Greece, 86; the tyranny of the Peisistratidai, 115, 116, 117 n. 1, 124, 322; their banishment, 162 and n. 2; Athenian fear of tyranny in 415, 168; Athenian democracy, 250, 257; idea of democracy attributed to Athenagoras, 156, 250 and n. 1; powers of Perikles in 431, 246 f., 354; character of Perikles, 253; sequel of the first Athenian expedition to Sicily, 263; failure of Athenians to make peace in 425, 265; Hyperbolos, 265; revolutions of 411, 269–80, 356–78 passim; motives of those oligarchs

Thucydides (*contd.*)
who broke away from the 400, 278 f.; appointment in 411 of nomothetai, 300; mistrust felt by Athenians towards Alkibiades, 283.

Thymochares, 365.

Timokrates, speech of Demosthenes against, 299.

Tissaphernes, 269, 270, 277, 363 f.

Tolmides, 254, 255 and n. 3.

Tomoi, 51.

Treasurers of Athena, in the aristocratic state, 78; in the sixth century, 325; in 411, 368; conditions of eligibility, 101, 142, 224; method of appointment, 228, 323 ff.

— of 'the Other Gods', 240, 308.

Treasury, (*a*) of the state, 91, (*b*) of Athena Polias, 91, 195, 377, (*c*) of 'the Other Gods', 240, 377.

Tribes, (*a*) the four 'Ionic' or old Attic, 47; creation of, attributed to Ion, 49; origin of, 51–55; names of, not those of occupations, 50 f.; found in Ionia and other places, 51; view that they started as local tribes rejected, 53 ff.; not abolished by Kleisthenes, 143; (*b*) the ten Kleisthenic, 137–42; creation of, attributed by Beloch to Peisistratos, 119 f., 135, 141, 334; really created by Kleisthenes, 119, 129 ff., 134 f.; peculiarities in composition of, 141 f.; choice of some officials in, 227; representation of all ten tribes in (1) the board of generals, 169, 348 ff., (2) the nine archons together with the secretary of the Thesmothetai, 173 f., (3) the Council of Five Hundred, 137, (4) the 6,000 dikasts, 216; (*c*) the three Dorian, 52, 55.

Trierarchs, 239.

trieropoioi, 238, 239.

Trittyes, (*a*) pre-Kleisthenic, 47, 48, 71–72; not identical with phratries, 59 and n. 5; relation of, to phratries, 72 f.; relation of, to naukraries, 71; not abolished by Kleisthenes, 143; (*b*) Kleisthenic, 129, 131, 137.

Tyranny, 86, 124; old law against those who tried to set up, 90.

Tyrants, 86; constitution of Athens under, 122 f.; achievement of the, at Athens, 122 f., 156.

Tyrtaios, 394.

Walls, Long, demolition of, 379 ff.

War, Peloponnesian, 379; Archidamian, 260 ff.; Dekeleian-Ionian, 262, 268 ff., 280, 282 ff.

Warfare, conditions of, in pre-Solonian period, 83, 394.

Xanthippos, father of Perikles, 177, 180, 182 f., 185, 190, 194, 252, 336.

Xanthos, 328.

Xenodikai, 218 n. 5.

Xenophon, (*a*) general 441/440, 349; (*b*) the historian, on the oligarchical governments of 404 and 403, 9, 379–89; on discipline of Athenian fleet, 261; on Alkibiades' position in 407, 248; attitude of, to Theramenes, 290; on order of events during rule of the Thirty, 384–9 *passim*; interpolations in text of *Hellenika* of, 379 ff.

Xerxes, invasion of Greece by, 176, 339.

Year, conciliar (or solar), 150 and n. 1; not used to fix tenure of military posts, 348, 352.

Zeugitai, 100, 225; admitted to archonship, 102, 174, 225 and n. 2.

Zeus (*a*) Herkeios, 57, (*b*) Karios, 65, (*c*) Phratrios, 56.

PRINTED IN GREAT BRITAIN
AT THE UNIVERSITY PRESS, OXFORD
BY CHARLES BATEY, PRINTER TO THE UNIVERSITY